LIBRARY OF NEW TESTAMENT STUDIES
384

Formerly the Journal for the Study of the New Testament Supplement series

Editor
Mark Goodacre

Editorial Board
John M. G. Barclay, Craig Blomberg,
R. Alan Culpepper, James D. G. Dunn, Craig A. Evans, Stephen Fowl,
Robert Fowler, Simon J. Gathercole, John S. Kloppenborg, Michael Labahn,
Robert Wall, Steve Walton, Robert L. Webb, Catrin H. Williams

THE USE OF SCRIPTURE
IN THE MARKAN PASSION
NARRATIVE

KELLI S. O'BRIEN

t & t clark

Copyright © Kelli S. O'Brien, 2010

Published by T&T Clark International
A Continuum imprint
The Tower Building, 11 York Road, London SE1 7NX
80 Maiden Lane, Suite 704, New York, NY 10038

www.continuumbooks.com

All rights reserved. No part of this publication may be reproduced or transmitted in any form or by any means, electronic or mechanical, including photocopying, recording or any information storage or retrieval system, without permission in writing from the publishers.

Kelli S. O'Brien has asserted her right under the Copyright, Designs and Patents Act, 1988, to be identified as the Author of this work.

Nestle-Aland, Novum Testamentum Graece, 27th Revised Edition, edited by Barbara Aland, Kurt Aland, Johannes Karavidopoulos, Carlo M. Martini and Bruce M. Metzger in cooperation with the Institute for New Testament Textual Research, Münster/Westphalia, © 1993 Deutsche Bibelgesellschaft, Stuttgart. Used by permission.

British Library Cataloguing-in-Publication Data
A catalogue record for this book is available from the British Library

ISBN: 978-0-567-03379-6 (hardback)

Typeset by Free Range Book Design & Production Ltd
Printed in Great Britain by the MPG Books Group, Bodmin and King's Lynn

In loving memory of Carol Selzer O'Brien
(1932–2007)

Contents

Abbreviations	ix
Acknowledgements	xiii
Introduction	1
Scripture as Interpretive Key	1
Previous Studies	4
Focus and Goals	18
1 Methodology: Identifying an Allusion	20
Scripture and Canon	20
Defining Allusion	22
Authorial Intention	22
Identifying Allusions	28
Some Examples	41
Conclusion	46
2 Methodology: Interpretive Impact	47
The Element of Play	47
Types of Interplay	52
Attention to the Larger Context	55
Considering Exegetical Traditions	57
A Mere Wink to the Wise	58
Evaluating the Interpretation	59
Reader Recognition	60
Conclusion	66
3 Testing Proposed Allusions	67
Overview of Suggested Allusions	67
Falling Short	76
Accepted Allusions	99
Conclusion	112
4 Interpreting the Allusions	113
From Plot to Arrest	113
Trial	128
Crucifixion	141
Conclusion	154

5 Are you the Christ?	155
Are You the Christ, the Son of the Blessed? – Ps. 2.7	155
Seated at the Right Hand – Ps. 110.1	166
The Son of Man Coming with the Clouds— Dan. 7.13	172
Conclusion	189
Conclusion	191
Vindication Expected	191
Suffering to Salvation	195
The Salvation of the Community	195
Total Salvation: The Eschaton Begins	197
Summary	200
For Further Study	200
Appendix A: Textual Analysis of Quotations and Near Quotations in Mark	203
Exact or Nearly Exact Matches with LXX	205
Modified From the LXX	206
Uncertain Origin	209
Appendix B: Textual Analysis of Mark 14	215
Appendix C: Textual Analysis of Mark 15	265
Bibliography	290
Index of Ancient Sources	307
General Index	319

Abbreviations

𝔊 or 𝔊^ed	*Septuaginta: Vetus Testamentum graece auctoritate Societatis Göttingensis editum.* Göttingen: Vandenhoeck & Ruprecht, 1931–. Or where unavailable: *Septuaginta: Id est Vetus Testamentum graece iuxta LXX interpretes,* ed. Alfred Rahlfs, Stuttgart: Deutsche Bibelgesellschaft, 1979
𝔐	Masoretic Text
ό	Old Greek
θ′	Theodotian
1 Apol.	Justin, *The First Apology*
1-2 Clem.	1-2 Clement
ABD	*Anchor Bible Dictionary*, ed. D. N. Freedman, 6 vols, New York, 1992
Abod. Zar.	Avodah Zarah
ACNT	Augsburg Commentary on the New Testament
Acts Pet.	Acts of Peter
Ant.	Jewish Antiquities
Apoc. Mos.	Apocalypse of Moses
Apol.	Tertullian, *The Apology*
APOT	*The Apocrypha and Pseudepigrapha of the Old Testament*, ed. R. H. Charles, 2 vols, Oxford, 1913
Arak.	Arakhin
Ascen. Isa.	Martyrdom and Ascension of Isaiah
Autol.	Ad Autolycum
b.	Babylonian Talmud
B. Qam.	Bava Qamma
Baḥ.	Baḥodesh
Barn.	Barnabas
Ber.	Berakot
Besh.	Beshallaḥ
BETL	Bibliotheca ephemeridum theologicarum lovaniensium
BIOSCS	*Bulletin of the International Organization for Septuagint and Cognate Studies*
BR	*Biblical Research*
BZ	*Biblische Zeitschrift*
Carn.	*De carne Christi*
CBET	Contributions to Biblical Exegesis and Theology

CBQ	*Catholic Biblical Quarterly*
CGTC	Cambridge Greek Testament Commentary
Conf.	*On the Confusion of Tongues*
CTM	*Concordia Theological Monthly*
Dem.	*Demonstration of the Apostolic Preaching*
Dial.	*Dialogue with Trypho*
Did.	*Didache*
Diogn.	*Diognetus*
DJD	Discoveries in the Judaean Desert
Dreams	*On Dreams*
DSS	Dead Sea Scrolls
EKK	Evangelisch-Katholischer Kommentar zum Neuen Testament
EvQ	*Evangelical Quarterly*
ExpTim	*Expository Times*
Frg.	Fragment
Fuga	*De fuga in persecutione*
Git.	*Gittin*
Gos. Eb.	*Gospel of the Ebionites*
Gos. Pet.	*Gospel of Peter*
Haer.	*Against Heresies*
HBT	*Horizons in Biblical Theology*
Ḥag.	*Ḥagigah*
Hist. eccl.	*The Ecclesiastical History*
Ḥul.	*Ḥullin*
HNT	Handbuch zum Neuen Testament
HTKNT	Herders theologischer Kommentar zum Neuen Testament
HTR	*Harvard Theological Review*
HTS	Harvard Theological Studies
ICC	The International Critical Commentary
Instr.	*The Instructor*
Int	*Interpretation*
JBL	*Journal of Biblical Literature*
JETS	*Journal of the Evangelical Theological Society*
Jos. Asen.	*Joseph and Aseneth*
JPS	Jewish Publication Society of America
JSJ	*Journal for the Study of Judaism*
JSJSup	Supplements to the Journal for the Study of Judaism
JSNT	*Journal for the Study of the New Testament*
JSNTSup	Journal for the Study of the New Testament Supplement Series
JSPSup	Journal for the Study of the Pseudepigrapha Supplement Series
Jud.	*Adversus Iudaeos*
Ker.	*Keritot*

Ketub.	*Ketubbot*
L.A.B.	*Liber antiquitatum biblicarum*
LCL	Loeb Classical Library
Legat.	*Legatio ad Gaium*
LNTS	Library of New Testament Studies
LTQ	*Lexington Theological Quarterly*
LXX	Septuagint
Mak.	*Makkot*
Marc.	*Against Marcion*
Meg.	*Megillah*
Mek.	*Mekilta de Rabbi Ishmael*
Midr. Ps.	*Midrash Psalms or Tehillim*
Migr.	*On the Migration of Abraham*
Mo'ed Qaṭ	Mo'ed Qaṭan
MS(S)	manuscript(s)
MT	Masoretic Text
NA²⁷	*Novum Testamentum Graece*, ed. Barbara Aland et al. 27th edition, Stuttgart: Deutsche Bibelgesellschaft, 1993
NAB	New American Bible
NAC	The New American Commentary
NASB	New American Standard Bible
Ned.	*Nedarim*
Neot	*Neotestamentica*
NIV	New International Version
NovT	*Novum Testamentum*
NovTSup	Supplements to Novum Testamentum
NRSV	New Revised Standard Version
n.s.	new series
NT	New Testament
NTS	*New Testament Studies*
Odes Sol.	*Odes of Solomon*
Orat.	*Oratio ad Graecos*
OT	Old Testament
ÖTK	Ökumenischer Taschenbuchkommentar zum Neuen Testament
OTP	*The Old Testament Pseudepigrapha*, ed. J. H. Charlesworth, 2 vols, New York, 1983
PEQ	*Palestine Exploration Quarterly*
Pesaḥ.	*Pesahim*
Phld.	*To the Philadelphians*
Pis.	*Pisḥa*
Pol. *Phil.*	Polycarp, *To the Philippians*
Prax.	*Against Praxeas*
Prot.	*Protrepticus*
Ps.-Phoc.	Pseudo-Phocylides

Pss. Sol.	Psalms of Solomon
Qidd.	Qiddushin
Rab.	Rabbah
Res.	On the Resurrection of the Flesh
RevQ	Revue de Qumran
Roš. Haš.	Rosh HaShanah
Šabb.	Shabbat
Sanh.	Sanhedrin
SBL	Society of Biblical Literature
SBLDS	Society of Biblical Literature Dissertation Series
SBLMS	Society of Biblical Literature Monograph Series
Šeb.	Shevi'it
Shir.	Shirata
Sib. Or.	Sibylline Oracles
SJT	Scottish Journal of Theology
SP	Sacra Pagina
Spec.	On the Special Laws
STRev	Sewanee Theological Review
Strom.	Stromata
Sukk.	Sukkah
Syr. Men.	Sentences of the Syriac Menander
t.	Tosefta
T. Adam	Testament of Adam
Ta'an.	Ta'anit
Tanḥ.	Tanḥuma
TDNT	Theological Dictionary of the New Testament, ed. G. Kittel and G. Friedrich, trans. G. W. Bromiley, 10 vols, Grand Rapids, 1964–1976
Tg. Neof.	Targum Neofiti
Tg. Onq.	Targum Onqelos
THKNT	Theologischer Handkommentar zum Neuen Testament
trans.	translated by
VT	Vetus Testamentum
WBC	World Biblical Commentary
WUNT	Wissenschaftliche Untersuchungen zum Neuen Testament
y.	Jerusalem Talmud
Yebam.	Yebamot
Zebaḥ.	Zevaḥim
ZNW	Zeitschrift für die neutestamentliche Wissenschaft
ZTK	Zeitschrift für Theologie und Kirche

Acknowledgements

This is a much revised and enlarged version of my doctoral dissertation, done at the University of Notre Dame. No work of this magnitude is done alone, and I have many people to thank. Steve Delamarter provided invaluable assistance early on with his then unpublished index of the margin notes in *The Old Testament Pseudepigrapha*. Hindy Najman helped me with rabbinic material. John P. Meier and David Aune often showed me the errors of my ways and made this a clearer, sounder project in the process. Eugene Ulrich provided much needed assistance on the text-critical work. Richard Hays encouraged me in the project and offered considerable advice and corrections. My principal guides were Mary Rose D'Angelo and James C. VanderKam. They were ready with encouragement and had an uncanny knack for pointing me in the right direction when I was lost. I cannot imagine better advisers or sufficiently express my gratitude to them. I also have many friends to thank for their encouragement, and proof-reading, particularly in the final months of the project, now twice through. I cannot name them all, but particular mention is due to Jennifer Jacobson, Rebekah Arana, Dan Gates, Brant Pitre, Michael Anderson, Todd Hibbard, Kari Kloos, Steve O'Brien, and Michael Kolotylo. I am in your debt.

Introduction

For I handed on to you as of first importance what I in turn had received: that Christ died for our sins in accordance with the Scriptures, and that he was buried, and that he was raised on the third day in accordance with the Scriptures, and that he appeared to Cephas, then to the twelve. (1 Cor. 15.3-5)

And they crucified him, and divided his clothes among them, casting lots to decide what each should take. (Mark 15.24; Ps. 22.19)

From the earliest period, allusion to Scripture played an essential role in the telling of the passion. Scholars have long recognized the importance of Scripture for the passion, and there is a mountain of literature already on the topic. Yet important gaps and debates remain. For example, one finds significant disagreement on which allusions exist, i.e., what Scripture texts are alluded to and where, certainly a foundational issue. In addition, interpretation of allusions in the passion has been quite narrow, often confined to the christological implications of a few allusions, with the implications of the rest left unexplored. Perhaps in response to past excesses, some scholars have rejected the prominence given to Scripture allusions in scholarship and approach this area of study with a great deal of scepticism.

This study will examine the use of Scripture in the Markan passion narrative, beginning with the plot to arrest Jesus and ending with the burial (Mark 14–15), aiming to bridge some of those gaps and establish, with more precision and argument than has often been the case, just which allusions do exist and what those allusions contribute to the meaning of the narrative.

Scripture as an Interpretive Key

The Gospel of Mark presents us with the earliest extant passion narrative but until relatively recently also the most neglected. Early on, Papias described it as an account without order.[1] Nineteenth-century scholars

---

1 Eusebius, *Hist. eccl.*, 3.39.15.

ignored it as a gospel without theology. Its literary organization has been described as haphazard, with pericopes strung together at random 'like pearls on a string'. Morna Hooker questioned this evaluation:

> It will not, I hope, be regarded as a sexist remark if I suggest that only a man could have used the phrase 'like pearls on a string' to suggest a haphazard arrangement of material. Any woman would have spotted at once the flaw in the analogy: pearls need to be carefully selected and graded. And gradually it has dawned on New Testament scholars that this is precisely what the evangelists have done with their material.[2]

Pearls and pericopes are sorted to create an effect. While Mark's apparent lack of literary and theological sophistication was once valued as a guarantee of its historical reliability, scholars have slowly recognized the complexity of the narrative, a process begun with William Wrede and continuing ever since.[3] In the last 30 years or so, literary critics have sought and found connections between pericopes with literary devices such as setting, characterization, and use of symbols. The Gospel of Mark is now considered a work of considerable story-telling skill and theological insight.

The complexities of the Gospel of Mark were not missed for eighteen centuries without reason. Mark resists an easy reading. The author does not draw out connections for the reader, as do the other Synoptics, but leaves them for the reader to discover. For example, the Gospels of Matthew and Luke both clearly inform the reader that John the Baptist is Elijah (Matt. 11.14; Luke 1.17). Mark does not. Yet in Mark, too, John the Baptist is Elijah.[4] Mark indicates this with the use of Scripture. The gospel begins with a quotation of two Scripture passages. Immediately after the quotation, John the Baptist appears in the wilderness, preaching and baptizing. The juxtaposition of these two elements, the quotation and John the Baptist, is a clue to Mark's reader: consider these together.

The first passage quoted is Mal. 3.1. Mark 1.2 reads: 'See, I am sending my messenger before your face to prepare your way.'[5] In Mal. 3.23,[6] the

---

2 Morna D. Hooker, *The Message of Mark* (London: Epworth, 1983), p. 3.
3 William Wrede, *Das Messiasgeheimnis in den Evangelien zugleich ein Beitrag zum Verständnis des Markusevangeliums* (Göttingen: Vandenhoeck & Ruprecht, 1901).
4 Judith L. Wentling ('A Comparison of the Elijan Motifs in the Gospels of Matthew and Mark', *Proceedings: Eastern Great Lakes Biblical Society* 2 [1982], pp. 104–13) disagrees that John the Baptist is Elijah.
5 NRSV modified. (All English translations of the Bible are from the NRSV, unless otherwise noted.) The form of the quotation in Mark is not identical to Mal. 3.1, and some scholars believe this is a blended allusion to both Mal. 3.1 and Exod. 23.20. For a discussion, see p. 209.
6 Mal. 4.5 in some English editions. Biblical chapter and verse numbers are different in different versions. The numbers used here will be those of the Masoretic Text (MT). The

promise of Elijah so important to the gospel stories is made: 'I will send you the prophet Elijah before the great and terrible day of the LORD comes.' Elijah's task is to bring repentance; John the Baptist calls for repentance. Mark 1.6 describes John as wearing camel's hair and a leather belt around his waist, which corresponds to the description of Elijah in the Greek of 2 Kgs 1.8.[7] The description in 2 Kgs 1.8 identifies the man as Elijah: Ahaziah responds, 'It is Elijah the Tishbite.' Similarly, the allusion in Mark serves to identify John the Baptist as Elijah. Readers of Matthew and Luke know that John the Baptist is Elijah because it is made explicit. Readers of Mark identify John the Baptist as Elijah by attention to Mark's use of Scripture.

The quotation of Mal. 3.1 may have still more to tell the reader. The portion quoted in Mark 1.2 reads: 'See, I am sending my messenger to prepare the way before me.' Mal. 3.1 continues: 'and the Lord whom you seek will suddenly *come to his temple*.' As Mal. 3.2 makes clear, that will be a day of judgement. Markan scholars, particularly Donald Juel, have pointed out the importance of the temple to the Markan passion narrative.[8] Jesus comes to the temple and condemns it and its leaders (Mark 11.15-18; 11.27–12.12). He is charged with threatening the destruction of the temple at his trial and is mocked for it on the cross (Mark 14.57-58; 15.29-30). This first allusion to Scripture, itself buried in an allusion to Isaiah, points to both the beginning and the end of the gospel, both that John the Baptist is Elijah and that Jesus comes to the temple and condemns it and its priests.[9]

In Mal. 3.1, the way is prepared for God: the LORD says, 'See, I am going to send my messenger, and he will prepare the way before *me*.' Mark 1.2 states, 'See, I am sending my messenger before *your* face, who will prepare *your* way.'[10] That 'you' is Jesus. Thus, Jesus is put in the place of God. Mark follows the Malachi quotation with a quotation of Isa. 40.3: 'the voice of one crying out in the wilderness: "Prepare the way of the Lord, make His paths straight."' Isaiah speaks of the LORD, that is, God. In

---

books with the greatest differences are Psalms and Jeremiah, but differences sometimes occur in other books.

7   This allusion is faint, and the verbal correspondence may be accidental. But, as Hooker (*Message*, p. 9) notes, the faint allusion and the pattern is supported by the allusion in Mark 9.11-12 to the Elijah expectation of Mal. 3.23.

8   See Donald H. Juel, *Messiah and Temple* (SBLDS 31; Missoula: Scholars Press, 1977), passim.

9   C. H. Dodd (*According to the Scriptures* [London: Nisbet, 1952], p. 71) concludes that this is probably in the minds of the Synoptic authors, though it is not explicit. Hooker (*Message*, pp. 79–83) notes the connection, as well, but finds that Mark excluded it purposefully to avoid the connotation in Malachi 3 that the temple would be restored.

10 Both quotations NRSV modified.

Mark, the Lord is Jesus. Again, Jesus is put in the place of God.[11] Mark uses Scripture to begin to indicate what is meant when the gospel calls Jesus, in its first sentence, 'Son of God'.[12]

Just like setting and character, allusion to Scripture is a tool to help the reader discover the underlying treasure in the outwardly simple story of the Gospel of Mark. By beginning with two rich quotations, Mark immediately signals the reader to look for meaning in Scripture allusions throughout the gospel.

Previous Studies

The use of Scripture in the Markan passion narrative has already received a great deal of scholarly attention. The insights of those studies, as well as their gaps and unresolved questions, are the impetus for this one. Much of that work has focused on the historical ramifications of the allusions: did Scripture form the basis of the original passion narrative? If so, what does that say about the historical accuracy of the account? In addition, work has been done on the function or meaning of the allusions. It has been proposed that Scripture was used to communicate that Jesus' death was the will of God and for apologetic purposes. A particular area of study has been the christological implications of some allusions. Not least, the existence and location of the allusions themselves is a matter of

---

11   Cf. Rudolf Schnackenburg, *The Gospel According to St Mark* (trans. Werner Kruppa and W. J. O'Hara; 2 vols; New York: Herder and Herder, 1971), 1, p. 4; Howard C. Kee, *Community of the New Age: Studies in Mark's Gospel* (Philadelphia: Westminster, 1977), p. 129; Hooker, *Message*, p. 8; Rikki E. Watts, *Isaiah's New Exodus and Mark* (WUNT 2/88; Tübingen: Mohr Siebeck, 1997), p. 87.

Some conclude that Jesus is the 'messenger' of Isaiah and Malachi. While this is a reasonable argument, the argument that John the Baptist is the messenger is stronger. Isaiah 40.3 puts the messenger in the wilderness, where John the Baptist appears. His calling for repentance corresponds to 'preparing the way of the Lord'. His correspondence to Elijah and the messenger of Malachi 3 is further support of John the Baptist as Elijah. John the Baptist, in his preaching, arrest, and death, prepare the way for Jesus, who is put in the place of the 'Lord' in both passages.

12   While some manuscripts omit 'Son of God' and the matter is subject to debate, I consider this reading original.

Naturally, one must not jump from this use of Scripture to conclude that Mark had a developed Trinitarian theology, nor even a christology as high as that in John. Conceptions of Jewish intermediaries between God and the created world offer possible parallels, whether angels in general or more exalted figures such as Melchizedek in 11QMelch or still greater manifestations of God's power, such as the Logos in Philo's thought. Cf. Maurice Casey, 'Christology and the Legitimating Use of the Old Testament in the New Testament', in *The Old Testament in the New Testament: Essays in Honour of J. L. North* (ed. Steve Moyise; JSNTSup 189; Sheffield: Sheffield Academic, 2000), pp. 42–54.

significant disagreement. It will be helpful to begin with an overview of the scholarly conversation thus far on the use of Scripture in the Markan passion narrative.

Historical Studies

A great deal of historical-critical work done on the use of Scripture in the Markan passion narrative has focused on historical reconstruction. Many scholars have asked, for example, whether the Markan passion narrative was based on a previous passion narrative of any kind; if so, how the composition of such a pre-Markan passion narrative was affected by Scripture; and whether the use of Scripture is evidence for or against the historical accuracy of the report.[13]

At one point, a consensus had formed around Rudolf Bultmann's theory that the Markan passion narrative was based on an existing passion narrative, which had developed from the kerygma and was significantly shaped by Scripture. More recently, scholars have challenged the view that a unified pre-Markan passion narrative existed and that the passion narrative developed from the kerygma. There is no longer any single dominant view on the origins of the passion narrative or the historicity of the events it reports.[14]

Nevertheless, one aspect of the previous position continues to enjoy a consensus: most scholars agree that the passion narrative was significantly shaped by Scripture. C. H. Dodd concludes that allusions to Scripture in the passion narrative cannot be considered 'mere literary embroidery'. Rather they are 'the firm scaffolding supporting the structure'. The allusions 'must have done much to determine the forms which the narrative assumed, even, as we must suppose, in the earliest oral tradition'.[15] Donald Juel states that the passion narrative was never told

---

13 Martin Dibelius, *From Tradition to Gospel* (trans. Bertram Lee Woolf; New York: Scribner, 1965), pp. 178–217; Rudolf Bultmann, *History of the Synoptic Tradition* (trans. John Marsh; New York: Harper & Row, 1963), pp. 262–84; Werner H. Kelber, 'From Passion Narrative to Gospel', in *The Passion in Mark: Studies on Mark 14–16* (ed. Werner H. Kelber; Philadelphia: Fortress, 1976), pp. 153–80; J. D. Crossan, *The Cross That Spoke* (San Francisco: Harper & Row, 1988), passim; Helmut Koester, *Ancient Christian Gospels* (Philadelphia: Trinity, 1990), pp. 216–30.

14 See Kelber, 'From Passion Narrative to Gospel', pp. 153–80; Eta Linnemann, *Studien zur Passionsgeschichte* (Göttingen: Vandenhoeck & Ruprecht, 1970); George W. E. Nickelsburg, 'The Genre and Function of the Markan Passion Narrative', *HTR* 73 (1980), pp. 153–84; Etienne Trochmé, *The Passion as Liturgy: A Study in the Origin of the Passion Narratives in the Four Gospels* (London: SCM Press, 1983), pp. 47–92. Marion Soards ('The Question of a PreMarcan Passion Narrative', Appendix IX of *The Death of the Messiah*, by R. E. Brown [New York: Doubleday, 1994], pp. 2, 1492–524) presents an excellent overview of scholarship on the question of the pre-Markan narrative and sources.

15 C. H. Dodd, *Historical Tradition in the Fourth Gospel* (Cambridge: Cambridge University Press, 1963), p. 31.

6   *The Use of Scripture in the Markan Passion Narrative*

in a neutral fashion (as Bultmann assumed); rather, from the start, early Christians 'went to the Scriptures for language suitable to tell the story of the one whose career culminated a history of promise'.[16]

The historical reliability of the passion narrative
Dodd considered Scripture a means by which to tell the narrative. He also believed that the narrative was historically accurate on the whole, that to a great extent the Scripture passages used in the Markan passion narrative were selected because they in some fashion matched the events of history.[17] Dodd's opinion of the Markan passion narrative was similar to that of Martin Dibelius.[18] Dibelius, however, noticed that there was an increasing use of Scripture in gospels later than Mark. He noted that some events in the Matthean passion narrative were shaped to conform to Scripture; for example, Judas was given *thirty* pieces of silver in accordance with Zech. 11.12-13 (Matt. 27.9),[19] while in Mark 14.11 the amount of money is unspecified. He argued that similar processes were at work in the passion narrative of John and the *Gospel of Peter*.[20] Bultmann took the same tack on the Markan passion narrative itself. He described, for example, the mockery in Mark 15.29-32 as 'legendary', based on 'prophetic proof' from Ps. 22.8 and Lam. 2.15.[21] He concluded that the original, simple historical narrative of Jesus' death had been embellished with details that were generated from Scripture.[22] Wilhelm Bousset took note of the number of details in the Markan passion narrative that match Scripture: the division of Jesus' clothes, the mockery, and Jesus' cry from Psalm 22; the vinegar from Psalm 69; Jesus' scourging from Isa. 50.6. There is such a concentration of events matching Scripture, he concluded, that it is very unlikely that those events were historical. Instead the events were created from Scripture to supply a point in the narrative for which 'historical recollection was very defective and full of gaps'.[23]

---

16   Donald H. Juel, *Messianic Exegesis: Christological Interpretation of the Old Testament in Early Christianity* (Philadelphia: Fortress, 1988), p. 98.
17   Dodd, *Historical Tradition*, p. 49.
18   Dibelius, *Tradition*, pp. 188–89, 204.
19   Dibelius, *Tradition*, p. 188.
20   Dibelius, 'Die alttestamentlichen Motive in der Leidensgeschichte des Petrus und des Johannes Evangeliums', in *Botschaft und Geschichte: Erster Band, Zur Evangelienforschung* (Tübingen: Mohr [Siebeck], 1953), pp. 221–47.
21   Bultmann, *History of the Synoptic Tradition*, p. 273.
22   Linnemann (*Studien*, pp. 168–69) agrees with him, noting that there is no difficulty in seeing Scripture citations as a later filling out of the original narrative, which contained few details.
23   Wilhelm Bousset, *Kyrios Christos* (trans. John E. Steely; Nashville: Abingdon, 1970), pp. 113–14. Interestingly, Bousset does not exaggerate the number of details that correspond with Scripture, but discusses solid, demonstrable references. However, he fails

This position, that the sheer number of allusions to Scripture indicates that the events were generated to match Scripture, not Scripture chosen to match events, has significant scholarly support. It is held by scholars as widely different in their ideologies as Burton Mack and John Donahue. Donahue concludes that the passion narrative was generated from Scripture passages such as Isaiah 53, Zechariah, and the psalms of the suffering righteous. He writes: 'In turning to the Old Testament text as their sacred text and the source of their understanding of their salvation history, the early Christians were in effect creating a new sacred text and writing their own account of salvation history.'[24] Mack takes a harsher position. He dismisses the notion that the passion narrative could reflect Scripture and still be historically accurate, as 'the Christian myth of promise and fulfillment'.[25] Mack considers the Markan passion narrative a scribal fabrication, generated from the psalms and other passages.

Similarly, J. D. Crossan concludes the disciples knew only that Jesus had been crucified outside Jerusalem by a conjunction of Jewish and Roman authorities. The disciples then applied Scripture to this bare-bones knowledge and began to generate the passion narrative.[26] In *The Cross That Spoke*, he proposes that an earlier version of what now exists as the *Gospel of Peter*, which he calls the *Cross Gospel*, was the basis for the passion narrative in the canonical gospels. Further, he argues that nearly every detail of the *Cross Gospel* was generated from Scripture.[27] Crossan faces two significant obstacles in his argument. The first is that there is no extant manuscript of this alleged text. He reconstructs the *Cross Gospel* by excising parts (words, phrases, and sentences) of the *Gospel of Peter* which he believes cannot be explained by anything other than dependence on the canonical gospels. The remainder is the *Cross Gospel*.

---

to take into account how much of the narrative has no correspondence with Scripture. For example, the Jewish trial will prove to be a passage with many allusions, corresponding to Bousset's characterization of a point in the narrative where knowledge was defective. However, it was equally defective with respect to the trial before Pilate, and that passage contains no allusions. It is quite possible that what was said to and by Jesus on the cross was not known, and that those words are constructed from Scripture; on the other hand, it is likely that the stripping and mockery were historical, with only the details added from Scripture. After examining the use of Scripture in the passion narrative, it will be prudent to take a nuanced approach to the historicity of the narratives.

24   John R. Donahue, SJ, 'Introduction: From Passion Traditions to Passion Narrative', in Kelber, *The Passion in Mark*, p. 6.

25   Burton Mack, *A Myth of Innocence* (Philadelphia: Fortress, 1988), p. 257.

26   John Dominic Crossan, *Jesus: A Revolutionary Biography* (San Francisco: HarperSanFrancisco, 1994), pp. 145–46; *Cross That Spoke*, pp. 111, 276, 335. In Crossan's own reconstruction (*Jesus*, pp. 153–54), he concludes that Jesus' body was never buried; it was either left on the cross or thrown into a shallow grave and in either case, was eaten by animals.

27   *Cross That Spoke*, pp. 276, 335.

The second, and for this study far more significant, obstacle is that while Crossan argues that the events narrated in the *Cross Gospel* are generated from various Scripture passages, the text (either the *Cross Gospel* or the *Gospel of Peter*) frequently displays little or no verbal correspondence to those passages. Rather than arguing from the text itself, Crossan often refers to the use of those Scripture passages in other early Christian works, such as *Barnabas* or the writings of Justin or Tertullian.[28]

It must be doubted whether Crossan overcomes either obstacle. Helmut Koester takes him to task on his reconstruction of the dependence of the various sources.[29] Moreover, Crossan's appeal to other and later texts, some written more than a century later, as evidence for allusions in the *Cross Gospel* must be considered extremely dubious. Yet while his views on the original version of the *Gospel of Peter* have received little support, his argument that events were generated to match Scripture has had a more favourable reception. Despite Koester's criticism of Crossan's reconstruction of the *Cross Gospel*, he praised Crossan for contributing 'substantially to a better understanding of the passion narrative by demonstrating how it was developed through scriptural interpretation'.[30]

Indeed, significant scholarly energy is devoted to discovering which Scripture passages lay behind the construction of particular events in the passion. For example, Deborah Krause argues that the entry into Jerusalem was based on Gen. 49.11 and other Scripture passages. Mark Kiley suggests that the *Hallel* psalms (Pss. 113–118) provided texts from which to construct Jesus' prayer in Gethsemane. Christian Maurer and Lothar Ruppert conclude that Wis. 2.10-20 significantly influenced the shape of the Jewish trial in Mark, while Donahue argues that the Jewish trial is a midrash on Psalm 110. Kenneth Bailey argues that some of the events at the cross are based on Lam. 2.15-16. As these few examples show, such efforts cover events from the beginning to the end of the passion narrative.[31]

---

28 Cf. *Cross That Spoke*, pp. 131–32, 144, 251–52, 335, 386–87. Crossan often admits that verbal correspondence is slight. In a characteristic passage on the passion prophecies which Crossan sees behind the mourning in *Gos. Pet.*, he writes (*Cross That Spoke*, p. 251), 'as usual, they are hardly discernable there unless one knows their existence more clearly and explicitly from elsewhere'.

29 Koester (*Ancient Christian Gospels*, pp. 218–20) critiqued Crossan's hypothesis on the basis of its problematic reconstruction of this earlier text via 'a single late manuscript' and on its faulty recourse to a 'intracanonical tradition' on the resurrection appearance narratives. Brown (*Death*, 1, 14–17; 2, 1317–49) was also unpersuaded.

30 Koester, *Ancient Christian Gospels*, p. 220.

31 Deborah Krause, 'The One Who Comes Unbinding the Blessing of Judah: Mark 11.1-10 as a Midrash on Genesis 49.11, Zechariah 9.9, and Psalm 118.25-26', in *Early Christian Interpretation of the Scriptures of Israel: Investigations and Proposals* (ed. Craig A. Evans and James A. Sanders; JSNTSup 148; Sheffield: Sheffield Academic Press, 1997),

Introduction

The quality of these studies is, however, uneven. The evidence that the particular passages named have influenced the writing of the passion narrative is often slim indeed. That scholars have been over-eager to find allusions to Scripture in the passion narrative will be one of the key conclusions of this study. If the allusions are not so numerous as supposed, the consensus on the origin of the events of the passion narrative is misplaced, and scholars must rethink the question of passion narrative construction and historicity.

The Function and Meaning of the Allusions

Study of the function of Scripture in the passion narrative began in an attempt to understand the earliest Christian community, that is, the Christian community before the writings of the New Testament. Often such studies begin with the early creedal statement in 1 Cor. 15.3-5: 'For I handed on to you as of first importance what I in turn had received: that Christ died for our sins in accordance with the Scriptures, and that he was buried, and that he was raised on the third day in accordance with the Scriptures, and that he appeared to Cephas, then to the twelve.' The primary problem is that it is unclear precisely how the Scriptures indicate that the messiah would die for sins or rise on the third day. 'According to the Scriptures' therefore requires explanation.

Dibelius suggests that anyone with Easter faith would understand that the events of the passion must have occurred according to the will of God and that the will of God was stated in Scripture; therefore, these events *must* have been recorded in Scripture. He states that the belief that the passion and resurrection were 'according to the Scriptures' may well have been deduced before it was known in any detail. Later, specific Scriptures were found which paralleled the events of the passion. Those Scriptures were studied in connection with the passion. Informed hearers would catch the allusions in the narrative and understand their import. The allusions to Scripture in the passion narrative showed that the passion conformed to God's will.[32]

---

pp. 141–53; Mark Kiley, '"Lord, Save My Life" (Ps 116:4) as Generative Text for Jesus' Gethsemane Prayer (Mark 14:36a)', *CBQ* 48 (1986), p. 655; C. Maurer, 'Knecht Gottes und Sohn Gottes im Passionsbericht des Markusevangeliums', *ZTK* 50 (1953), p. 26; Lothar Ruppert, *Jesus als der leidende Gerechte?: Der Weg Jesu im Lichte eines alt- und zwischentestamentlichen Motivs* (Bibelstudien 59; Stüttgart: KBW, 1972), pp. 55–56; John R. Donahue, *Are You the Christ? The Trial Narrative in the Gospel of Mark* (SBLDS 10; Missoula, Mont.: SBL, 1973), pp. 173–74; Kenneth E. Bailey, 'The Fall of Jerusalem and Mark's Account of the Cross', *ExpTim* 102 (1991), p. 102–5.

32 Dibelius, *Tradition*, pp. 184–87. See also Alfred Suhl, *Die Funktion der alttestamentlichen Zitate und Anspielungen im Markusevangelium* [Gütersloh: Mohn, 1965], p. 65; Linnemann, *Studien*, pp. 47, 74–75.

In *New Testament Apologetic*, Barnabas Lindars develops these ideas further. He suggests that early Scripture interpretation occurred in three stages.

- First stage, non-apologetic application of Scripture to historical details of the passion: Scripture passages which were somehow similar to the events of the passion were used to understand its meaning.
- Second stage, apologetic use: The Scripture passages found in stage one were used in debates with non-Christian Jews.
- Third stage, subsidiary use: The original meaning of these passages was forgotten, and they were put to moral use or mined for vivid narrative details.[33]

According to Lindars, these stages were chronological in pre-New Testament history, but occur in no chronological order in the New Testament. Lindars' focus is on stage two, where Scripture is used to demonstrate that the messiah suffered according to the will of God and that Jesus suffered as the messiah.[34]

Recent scholars have agreed that the purpose of allusion in the passion narrative is to demonstrate the connection between the events and God's will, but have been less convinced regarding the emphasis on apologetic detected by Lindars and some other earlier scholars. For example, Juel states that the use of Scripture demonstrates the necessity of the events – that the events were necessary because they were predicted – but he does not agree that Scripture was used primarily for apologetic.[35] Instead, he argues that Scripture was used primarily according to what Lindars called the first stage: as a way of talking about and understanding the passion.[36] Juel concludes that the passion was always told using the language of Scripture (Scripture was not a later addition to the kerygma) and that Christian interpretation focused on images in Scripture as they interpreted Christ (not as they proved Jesus *was* the Christ).[37]

---

33 Barnabas Lindars, *New Testament Apologetic* (Philadelphia: Westminster, 1961), pp. 17–20, 22–23, 82, 134.
34 Lindars, *New Testament Apologetic*, pp. 18, 80–84.
35 Donald H. Juel, *The Gospel of Mark* (Interpreting Biblical Texts; Nashville: Abingdon, 1999), pp. 157–58; *Messianic Exegesis*, p. 60.
36 Juel, *Messianic Exegesis*, p. 14.
37 Juel, *Messianic Exegesis*, pp. 89, 98. George A. Kennedy (*Classical Rhetoric and Its Christian and Secular Tradition from Ancient to Modern Times* [Chapel Hill: University of North Carolina Press, 1980], p. 127) argues that in classical rhetoric it is the speaker's job to persuade the hearer of the truth of the message. In Christian and Jewish rhetoric, the speaker's job is merely to proclaim the message with energy. It is the hearer's job to apprehend its truth, or rather it is God's job to convince the hearer, and as with Pharaoh,

Lindars' presupposition that one can locate chronological stages in early Christian interpretation without regard to the order in which those stages surface in the New Testament allows him to begin his study of pre-New Testament exegesis with Acts and to demonstrate his points with the Gospel of John, while neglecting Mark. This approach has been less attractive to later scholars. Juel rightly points out that the majority of evidence indicates that Acts and John belong to a later stage of Christian exegesis, and proof of earlier stages of exegesis must rest on early New Testament texts.[38]

As early as 1965, Alfred Suhl questioned the idea that Mark belonged to a late stage of exegesis. Suhl wrote *Die Funktion der alttestamentlichen Zitate und Anspielungen im Markusevangelium*, to a great extent, in response to arguments that the passion narrative was constructed creatively on the basis of 'prophetic-proof' and the underlying assumption that the function of Scripture allusions in Mark is to prove a scheme of prophecy-fulfilment. Suhl writes that Matthew is palpably interested in that scheme, and Luke, though less obvious about it, is equally interested, but that Mark displays no interest at all.[39] Rather, the Markan use of Scripture proceeds from the Easter-faith 'postulate' that what happened in the passion and resurrection are in accordance with the will of God; indeed, they are acts of God. That being the case, they must be in accordance with the Word of God, Scripture. This, Suhl concludes (as did Dibelius before him), was postulated in a general sense before it was ever demonstrated through the correspondence of specific passages with the specific events of the passion. Eventually, the Christian community developed its understanding of that correspondence into the scheme of prophecy-fulfilment, buttressed with specific proof-texts. The Markan use of Scripture falls however closer to the initial postulate than to its later development. Thus, Mark rarely explicitly indicates that something happens 'in accordance with the Scriptures', and in the few cases where he does so, he does so in a generalized manner, without making allusion to the specific text fulfilled (cf. Mark 9.11-12; 14.21, 49).[40]

God may have no such intention. Thus, to the speaker, whether the hearer is persuaded is of secondary importance. If Kennedy is correct, early use of Scripture will be oriented to the meaning of events, not to apologetic. Only later, in different environments, such as the Greek church, would proofs from Scripture assume great importance.

38   Juel, *Messianic Exegesis*, pp. 14, 18–19.
39   Luke shows his interest by demonstrating the progress of salvation history (Suhl, *Funktion*, pp. 42, 167).
40   Suhl, *Funktion, passim,* esp. pp. 43–45 and 65–66. Mark 14.27 is the exception to the rule. Suhl (*Funktion*, pp. 46–47; cf. pp. 158–59), using the same general arguments, concludes that it is unlikely that the earliest community constructed a life of Jesus from diverse passages. Rather it is much more likely that it looked for passages which were similar to the stories they told each other about Jesus' death and resurrection.

Instead of emphasizing a prophecy-fulfilment pattern, Suhl concludes that Mark presents the narrative *in alttestamentlichen Farben*.[41] The function of Scripture in the gospel is to interpret the passion narrative and other events in the life of Jesus. Furthermore, Mark is less interested in interpreting the events of the passion as past history than in using them to interpret Mark's own time.[42] This aspect of Suhl's research has been widely accepted.[43]

Unfortunately, however, because Suhl is working to debunk a reigning theory on the origin of the passion narrative, and not on an interpretation of the Gospel of Mark per se, he spends only a fraction of his efforts on just how the events of the passion are interpreted by the use of Old Testament allusions.[44] Also unfortunately, despite Suhl's conclusions and their favourable reception, use of Scripture as an element affecting the interpretation of the narrative has continued to suffer neglect. Too often commentaries simply list Scripture allusions, then move on. Monographs on the meaning of Mark have been written without more than cursory attention to its use of Scripture.[45] Yet the interpretive significance of Scripture in the passion narrative has not been ignored by all and has received considerable attention from some. In the last two decades especially, such study has gained momentum.

Christology

While some early treatments focused on the use of Scripture to demonstrate that the crucifixion took place according to God's will, its function goes beyond that. Scripture was used to understand the meaning of the events, particularly to understand who Jesus was as Christ. This area has been a particular focus in past scholarship.

Dodd presented one of the first modern studies attempting to uncover a detailed interpretation of Scripture in pre-New Testament Christianity, and his work continues to be influential. Like others, Dodd suggests that the significance of the passion is indicated mainly by allusions to Scripture. He traces what he believes to be the core Scripture passages of the early

---

41   Suhl, *Funktion*, e.g., p. 47. It is a favourite phrase.
42   Suhl, *Funktion*, p. 66.
43   Note, for example, the favourable reception in Linnemann, *Studien*, and Bas M. F. van Iersel, *Mark: A Reader Response Commentary* (trans. W. H. Bisscheroux; JSNTSup 164; Sheffield: Sheffield Academic Press, 1998), pp. 60, 67.
44   He does not completely neglect the question. His remarks frequently speak to the thesis that Mark uses Old Testament texts to indicate that the Parousia is imminent. Cf. *Funktion*, pp. 66, 167–69.
45   E.g., Ernest Best, *Mark: The Gospel as Story* (Edinburgh: T&T Clark, 1983); D. Rhodes, J. Dewey and D. Michie, *Mark as Story: An Introduction to the Narrative of a Gospel* (2nd edn; Philadelphia: Fortress, 1999); Mary Ann Tolbert, *Sowing the Gospel* (Minneapolis: Fortress, 1989).

Christian community. He then interprets those core passages and their effect on early Christian understanding of the passion. One of Dodd's conclusions was that the early church understood Jesus as the Suffering Servant of Isaiah 53.[46] Dodd was by no means the first to come to such a conclusion, and for the first half of the twentieth century, it was an almost unquestioned assumption that the Suffering Servant of Isaiah was the dominant image for Jesus in the earliest church. That assumption could not remain unquestioned after Morna Hooker examined in detail the verbal correspondence between New Testament passages and the Servant passages to which they reportedly allude and found, in the vast majority of cases, very little.[47] Nevertheless, many scholars continue to hold that the Suffering Servant is an important image in the Markan passion narrative.[48]

Dodd suggests that the core Scripture passages of the early church followed the same general plot line, in which humiliation and suffering were followed by vindication and exaltation. He uses that plot line to learn more about who the early community understood Jesus to be. Dodd argues that such passages, many of them from the Psalms, show that suffering is not necessarily an indication of divine disfavour. In these passages, the righteous do suffer, but they also expect and get vindication from God. By use of such allusions, Jesus crucified is portrayed as the paradigmatic suffering righteous one.[49] Many scholars have come to similar conclusions, including Lindars, Ruppert, R. E. Brown, and Donald Senior.[50]

It is clear that Mark alludes to suffering righteous passages. Nevertheless, Juel finds fault with this interpretation of the allusions, because it does not pay sufficient attention to the royal imagery in the Markan passion narrative. It also ignores Mark's portrayal of Jesus' passion as a unique event in history. Jesus is not one of a type or even

---

46 Dodd, *According to the Scriptures*, pp. 112–13, 118–19.

47 Morna D. Hooker, *Jesus and the Servant: The Influence of the Servant Concept of Deutero-Isaiah in the New Testament* (London: SPCK, 1959), passim.

48 Otto Betz, 'Jesus and Isaiah 53', in *Jesus and the Suffering Servant: Isaiah 53 and Christian Origins* (ed. William H. Bellinger, Jr and William R. Farmer; Harrisburg, Penn.: Trinity Press International, 1998), pp. 83–87; John R. Donahue, SJ, *The Gospel of Mark* (SP 2; Collegeville, Minn.: Liturgical Press, 2002), pp. 35, 439; Douglas J. Moo, *The Old Testament in the Gospel Passion Narratives* (Sheffield: Almond, 1983), pp. 107–9; 131–32, 148, 162; Joel Marcus, *The Way of the Lord: Christological Exegesis of the Old Testament in the Gospel of Mark* (Louisville: Westminster/John Knox, 1992), pp. 193–96; Watts, *Isaiah's New Exodus*, p. 365, cf. pp. 252–57, 264–69.

49 Dodd, *Historical Tradition*, pp. 35–36.

50 Lindars, *New Testament Apologetic*, p. 100–101; Ruppert finds the portrayal only in the early Christian community (*Jesus*, pp. 48, 56); Brown, *Death*, 1, pp. 593, 634, 733–34; Donald Senior, *The Passion of Jesus in the Gospel of Mark* (Wilmington: Michael Glazier, 1984), pp. 142–44.

merely the ultimate example of a type. Jesus is the one and only. Following his teacher, Nils Dahl, Juel argues for *messianic* interpretation as the primary interpretation of the Scriptures used in the Markan passion narrative. He suggests that this messianic interpretation began with Psalm 89, which was prominent in the early church and which presents God's anointed, the messiah, suffering. That interpretation was extended to other psalms, as well, by means of royal (Davidic) attribution and catchword association. The emphasis of the Scriptures used in Mark is on Jesus as messiah and king and as a one-time, ultimate fulfilment of Scripture.[51]

Adela Yarbro Collins comes to a similar conclusion. She disagrees that the allusions to suffering righteous psalms indicate that the suffering righteous one is the primary image by which Jesus' passion is depicted. Rather Jesus suffers and dies as Son of God and Son of Man, which are both messianic. Furthermore, Mark interprets the psalms in a messianic manner. Jesus suffers as messiah, because messianic suffering is part of the divine plan in Scripture.[52]

As Collins notes, in Mark, Jesus' suffering is connected to the image of the Son of Man, and Dan. 7.13 has a prominent place in the Markan passion narrative. Albert C. Sundberg concludes that, whereas Isaiah comes only fifth in importance, Daniel receives the most emphasis in Mark.[53] Hooker considers the Son of Man of Dan. 7.13 the dominant image by which Jesus is understood. She writes that Daniel's one like a son of man is an exalted individual who suffers on behalf of the community and redeems it as its representative head. The Markan use of the image scarcely changes it.[54]

The Suffering Servant, Suffering Righteous One, Messiah, and Son of Man are the images most frequently used to understand the Markan christology in the passion narrative. A newer image for understanding Jesus and one that appears to be gaining critical ground is Jesus as a divine warrior. Joel Marcus argues that 'the way of the Lord' (from the quotation of Isa. 40.3 in Mark 1.3) is a key for the gospel as a whole. Marcus suggests that Mark understood the way of the Lord to be that of the 'conquering hero', the hero being God, with Jesus as God's earthly agent.

---

51 Juel, *Messianic Exegesis*, pp. 2, 104–17.

52 Adela Yarbro Collins, 'The Appropriation of the Psalms of Individual Lament by Mark', in *The Scriptures in the Gospels* (ed. C. M. Tuckett; Louvain: Leuven University Press, 1997), pp. 230–32; 'The Influence of Daniel on the New Testament', in *Daniel: A Commentary on the Book of Daniel* by John J. Collins (ed. Frank Moore Cross; Hermeneia; Minneapolis: Fortress, 1993), pp. 97–98.

53 Albert C. Sundberg, 'On Testimonies', *NovT* 3 (1959), p. 274. Sharyn E. Dowd ('Reading Mark Reading Isaiah', *LTQ* 30 [1995], p. 133) argues against Sundberg's assessment.

54 Hooker, 'Is the Son of Man Problem Really Insoluble?', in *Text and Interpretation: Studies in the New Testament Presented to Matthew Black* (ed. Ernest Best and R. McL. Wilson; Cambridge: Cambridge University Press, 1979), p. 166.

But Mark dramatically and ironically transforms the warrior image by making suffering and death on the cross the mode of victory.[55] Scholars propose many other christological images, as well. For example, Rikki Watts argues that Jesus is portrayed in Mark according to the image of the Exodus as it is redefined in Isaiah.[56] Géza Vermès and W. Richard Stegner argue that Jesus is understood according to the image of Isaac in the Akedah.[57] Wolfgang Roth argues that Jesus is portrayed as Elisha, commissioned by Elijah (John the Baptist) and twice as strong.[58]

Thus, there is a wide variety of opinion regarding how Markan use of Scripture speaks to christology. Some scholars argue for their own image in contradiction to others. For example, some argue that the suffering righteous one is the dominant model and conclude that the Suffering Servant was a later development, not found in Mark.[59] Some argue that Jesus is portrayed as the messiah, not as the suffering righteous one.[60] Certainly, multiple images can exist side by side, enriching one another, and need not be contradictory. Sensibly, Ernest Best concludes that no single backdrop is sufficient for the Markan portrayal of Jesus.[61]

---

55   See Marcus, *Way*, esp. pp. 12–47; summary in Marcus, 'Mark and Isaiah', in *Fortunate the Eyes That See: Essays in Honor of David Noel Freedman in Celebration of His Seventieth Birthday* (ed. Astrid B. Beck et al.; Grand Rapids: Eerdmans, 1995), p. 461. Others to use this image include Bruce A. Stevens, 'Why *Must* the Son of Man Suffer: The Divine Warrior in the Gospel of Mark', *BZ* n.s. 31 (1987), pp. 101–10; Mary J. Huie-Jolly, 'Threats Answered by Enthronement: Death/Resurrection and the Divine Warrior Myth in John 5.17-29, Psalm 2, and Daniel 7', in Evans and Sanders, *Early Christian Interpretation*, pp. 191–217; P. Duff, 'The March of the Divine Warrior and the Advent of the Greco-Roman King: Mark's Account of Jesus' Entry into Jerusalem', *JBL* 111 (1992), pp. 55–71. Not all images of the divine warrior come from Scripture. Duff's images come primarily from a Greco-Roman model.

56   Watts, *Isaiah's New Exodus*, pp. 47–51.

57   Géza Vermès, 'Redemption and Genesis XXII – The Binding of Isaac and the Sacrifice of Jesus', in *Scripture and Tradition in Judaism: Haggadic Studies* (2nd edn; Leiden: Brill, 1973), pp. 214–27; W. R. Stegner, *Narrative Theology in Early Jewish Christianity* (Louisville: Westminster/John Knox, 1989), p. 31. See Brown, 'Ap. VI: Sacrifice of Isaac', *Death*, 2, pp. 1435–44, for more on this discussion.

58   Wolfgang Roth, 'Mark, John and Their Old Testament Codes', in *John and the Synoptics* (ed. Adelbert Denaux; Louvain: Leuven University Press, 1992), pp. 458–65.

59   Cf. Evelin Albrecht, 'The Silence of Jesus in the Passion', in *Good News in History: Essays in Honor of Bo Reicke* (ed. L. Miller; Atlanta: Scholars Press, 1993), p. 35. Hooker varied this argument by claiming that Jesus is portrayed as Son of Man and that the Suffering Servant image came later (*Jesus*, passim; *The Son of Man in Mark: A Study of the Background of the Term 'Son of Man' and Its Use in St Mark's Gospel* [Montreal: McGill University Press, 1967], passim). She later revised her position, agreeing that the Suffering Servant image may be used in Paul (and thus earlier than Mark). She still does not agree that it plays a part in Mark. ('Did the Use of Isaiah 53 to Interpret His Mission Begin with Jesus?', in Bellinger and Farmer, *Jesus and the Servant*, p. 103.)

60   For example, see D. H. Juel and A. Y. Collins, noted above.

61   Ernest Best, *The Temptation and the Passion: The Markan Soteriology* (2nd edn; Cambridge: Cambridge University Press, 1990), p. lxxiv.

Another significant problem is that christological studies tend to limit themselves to the evaluation of one or two passages of Scripture and ignore the rest. They also tend to ignore other possible functions for allusions. While Hooker writes that the author of Mark was interested not so much in what Jesus did but in who he was,[62] Best concludes that the Markan community was interested not so much in who Jesus was but in what he did.[63] That is, the Markan community was interested in understanding how Jesus' life, death, and resurrection affected them. Howard Clark Kee agrees. He concludes that in Mark and related literature, the goal is to understand the realities in which the *community* operates.[64] Kee suggests that the meaning of Mark is not entirely exhausted by the cross, rather that the gospel is complex and full and that the necessities of life at the penultimate moment of history are pervasive.[65]

The same would follow for the Markan use of Scripture. Scripture is used to speak not only to christology but to other topics, as well. Note our opening example: Scripture in Mark 1.2-3 is used not only to flesh out the meaning of 'Son of God', but to identify John the Baptist as Elijah and to point to the condemnation of the temple. Here allusion to Scripture functions to interpret the narrative *as a narrative*, to define characters and to foreshadow and give meaning to events. This turns out to be one of the most common functions of allusion in general and in the Markan passion narrative in particular.

The Location of Allusions

Another major problem, really the first problem, for the study of allusions is determining which allusions exist. Scholars agree that the New Testament sometimes alludes to the Old Testament. They disagree over how often it does so.

Martin Dibelius described Scripture as the sorting principle, behind what was told and what was left out.

> Certainly much more could have been told of the process of the crucifixion, either on the basis of tradition from Simon of Cyrene, or on that of acquaintance with the usual procedure of an execution. But in spite of this, if the record was not made more ornate it was because it was limited to facts understood to be soteriological because they were in the Old Testament.

---

62 Hooker, *Message*, p. 7.
63 Best, *Temptation*, p. xiv.
64 Kee, *Community*, pp. 86–88.
65 Kee, *Community*, p. 168.

The implication here is that almost everything in the passion narrative had a parallel in Scripture, and Dibelius lists quite a number.[66] Kee asserted that there were hundreds of allusions in the Gospel of Mark.[67] Crossan and Mack argue that the entire passion narrative is constructed on the basis of Old Testament passages.[68]

A few commentators disagree. Like Suhl before him, Robert Gundry objects to such assertions and argues that many suggested allusions are not in the text.[69] Often Gundry's arguments stand on ideological ground. He is concerned to show that the Markan passion narrative is largely historical. Though Mary Ann Tolbert shows no such concern, she makes it a hermeneutical tactic to ignore 'mostly illusory allusions' in her discussions of Mark.[70]

Suhl, Gundry, and Tolbert have reason for their caution. A perusal of some commentaries on Mark and a few well-known works on the use of Scripture in the Markan passion narrative netted over 270 suggested allusions for the 120 verses in Mark 14–15, an average of more than two per verse. Moreover, every author presented a different set. Though some allusions were common to many authors, only a few were suggested by all, and many were suggested by only one or two.

Furthermore, there has been very little argument in favour of the allusions asserted. Kee simply presents a table with his conclusions regarding the allusions he sees and his assessment of whether the text came from the Greek or Hebrew – something one might consider remarkable, since in several cases the suggested allusions have no verbal correspondence with the passage in either language.[71] Commentaries almost universally list the suggested allusions without demonstrating the connections.[72]

In *Jesus and the Servant*, Morna Hooker addresses this absence of argument for a few Old Testament passages. She examines suggested allusions to the so-called 'Servant Songs' of Isaiah throughout the New Testament.[73] While other suggestions have been examined by various

---

66   Dibelius, *Tradition*, pp. 186–88.
67   Kee, *Community*, p. 45; cf. p. 189 n. 157.
68   Crossan, *Jesus*, pp. 145–46, 152; *Cross That Spoke*, pp. 405–7. Though Dibelius, Mack, and Crossan have a similar starting point, the conclusions they draw from it are quite different.
69   Suhl, *Funktion*, pp. 45–66; R. H. Gundry, *Mark: A Commentary on His Apology for the Cross* (Grand Rapids: Eerdmans, 1993).
70   Tolbert, *Sowing the Gospel*, p. 302.
71   Howard C. Kee, 'The Function of Scriptural Quotations and Allusions in Mark 11–16', in *Jesus und Paulus: Festschrift für Werner Georg Kümmel zum 70. Geburtstag* (ed. E. Earle Ellis and Erich Grässer; Göttingen: Vandenhoeck & Ruprecht, 1975), pp. 167–71.
72   Douglas Moo (*Old Testament*, passim) presents an excellent exception to this general practice. Though this author does not always agree with his conclusions, he makes a thorough and reasoned argument for every asserted allusion.
73   Hooker, *Jesus*, passim.

Focus and Goals

The goal of this study is to locate and interpret the allusions to Scripture in the Markan passion narrative, Mark 14–15. While some reasonably suggest the passion narrative begins as early as 11.1, Mark 14–15 represents the core of the passion. The study proceeds in three stages:

- First, strategies or guidelines for locating and interpreting allusions are necessary. They are discussed in Chapters 1–2.
- Next those strategies are used to locate allusions in the Markan passion narrative. The results of that examination are presented in Chapter 3.
- Finally, the allusions are interpreted in Chapters 4–5. These chapters will explore the light these allusions shed on the narrative.
- The cumulative impact of the allusions will be discussed in the Conclusion.

It is also important to note what are *not* goals of this study. Perhaps the bulk of scholarship on the use of Scripture in the Markan passion narrative, particularly through the end of the 1970s, has been devoted to historical reconstruction, both of the events surrounding the death of Jesus of Nazareth and of the narrative of that death told by the earliest Christians. At the close of a review of scholarship on the development of the passion narrative, Marion Soards writes:

> We may safely conclude that Mark uses a source [or, one might say, *sources*] in writing his PN. We know that source, however, only as incorporated in Mark. The greatest challenge that lies before us is not the separation of tradition from Marcan redaction; for, as our earlier work shows, that task may finally be an impossible one. Rather, we must investigate the rich layers of traditions that come to us in the form of the Marcan PN. This conclusion does not mean that we may simply discard any notion of editorial activity. It demands, however, that a preoccupation with the data of that editorial work not be our first concern.[74]

---

74 Soards, 'The Question', 2, pp. 1523–24. He notes that his position is similar to that of Juel, in *Messiah and Temple*. It is also similar to the approach of Joel Marcus and quite a number of other recent commentators on Mark.

Indeed, in this study, the first concern will be the interpretation of the Markan passion narrative as it now exists and the effect of Scripture on that interpretation. Though Mark undoubtedly made use of sources for at least part of his narrative, the content and shaping of those sources will not be discussed. Likewise, the study will not attempt to unravel the source or inspiration for the allusions, whether they are from narrative sources, the kerygma, Christian or Jewish liturgy, messianic testimony books, other sources, or the author himself.

Because the study focuses on what is in the text of Mark and does not address what lies behind it, it simply cannot address the historicity of the narrative. Throughout, the discussion regards the Markan narrative as such, not the historical events surrounding the crucifixion of Jesus of Nazareth. The conclusions of the study do have some implications for research on the historical Jesus and the passion.[75] Nevertheless, conclusions regarding the historical accuracy of the Markan narrative cannot be drawn according to the literary method employed in this study.

---

75 The study does address, in part, the claim that the passion narrative was constructed by means of Scripture. This is discussed briefly in the conclusion.

1. Methodology:
Identifying an Allusion

In *Echoes of Scripture in the Letters of Paul*, Richard Hays provides a simple procedure for studying allusions in a literary work:

1. Identify the allusion.
2. Identify its impact on interpretation, its meaning.[1]

That, in a nutshell, is the method of this study. Despite the simplicity of the general scheme, there are a number of subtleties to be considered and decisions to be made. This chapter discusses what an allusion is and how to establish that one exists. The next chapter deals with how to interpret an allusion. The remaining chapters carry this out for the Markan passion narrative. Chapter 3 represents step 1, identifying the allusions to Scripture in the Markan passion narrative. Chapters 4–5 represent step 2, assessing the impact of those allusions on the meaning of the narrative.

Since the study assesses allusions to Scripture, the chapter begins with a definition of Scripture. The following section defines what an allusion is, and, equally important, what an allusion is not. The third section presents guidelines for identifying an allusion and illustrates some methodological issues with examples of allusions suggested for the Markan passion narrative.

Scripture and Canon

When locating allusions to Scripture in the New Testament, an important concern is the extent of the term *Scripture*. What qualified as Scripture to New Testament authors?

New Testament scholars have on occasion favoured the shorter canon (the Rabbinical Tanak or Protestant Old Testament) as the exhaustive canon of the New Testament writers. Studies on the use of Scripture in the New Testament sometimes discuss only allusions to books in the shorter canon or

---

1 Richard Hays, *Echoes of Scripture in the Letters of Paul* (New Haven: Yale University Press, 1989), p. 19.

require much higher standards for allusions to books outside it to be considered allusions to Scripture, or to be considered allusions at all.

Such limitations are anachronistic. The canon was not yet established in the first century, particularly with regard to the Writings.[2] Scholars must allow the texts of the Second Temple period, including the New Testament, to dictate which works were considered Scripture by their authors.[3] To do so, one needs an understanding of Scripture that is distinct from a defined canon. For the purposes of this study, *Scripture* is written material which is religiously authoritative for a community. It exerts normative[4] influence on that community and shapes its world view.[5] This broad definition includes many texts not included in current canons but which are still considered authoritative, such as the Talmud or the writings of Thomas Aquinas or Calvin. Yet it is the fluidity, the very breadth of the definition that serves here. Its aim is to avoid excluding texts from consideration *a priori* merely because they are not part of a modern canon. How does one know in advance where New Testament authors drew the line between merely authoritative texts and Scripture? To avoid inappropriate exclusions, all authoritative texts will be treated equally, regardless of their status in modern canons. Because the intended audience of the Gospel of Mark is unknown, one must consider all authoritative texts for Jewish communities in the first century.[6]

---

2   See, for example, A. C. Sundberg, *The Old Testament of the Early Church* (HTS 20; Cambridge: Harvard University Press, 1964), pp. 3–48, 81, 103; Eugene Ulrich, 'The Bible in the Making: The Scriptures at Qumran', in *The Dead Sea Scrolls and the Origins of the Bible* (Grand Rapids: Eerdmans, 1999), pp. 20–22. For a discussion of canon theory, see James C. VanderKam, 'Revealed Literature in the Second Temple Period', in *From Revelation to Canon: Studies in the Hebrew Bible and Second Temple Literature* (JSJSup 62; Leiden: Brill, 2000), pp. 1–30. For a contrary view, see E. Earle Ellis, *The Old Testament in Early Christianity: Canon and Interpretation in the Light of Modern Research* (WUNT 54; Tübingen: J. C. B. Mohr [Paul Siebeck], 1991), pp. 1–50.

3   'Second Temple period' is used for the time between the building of the Second Temple until its destruction in 70 CE and a little beyond, while reactions to its destruction are still strong. This perhaps extends the normal definition of the period, but not beyond reason. The period immediately after the destruction is important to Mark (if the gospel is written shortly after 70 CE).

4   VanderKam, 'Revealed Literature', pp. 2–3.

5   Wesley A. Kort, '*Take, Read*' (University Park, Penn.: Pennsylvania State University Press, 1996), p. 6.

6   Though that body of authoritative literature will usually be called 'Scripture', it will sometimes be helpful to distinguish that set of Scripture from a different set of Scripture texts, namely, the New Testament. The terms Old Testament and Tanak will be used in such cases. (Old Testament is used only in the sense of chronologically 'older' or 'first', without the modern denigration of what is 'old' and therefore worn out and to be replaced. It should be recalled that for much of human history what was older was more venerable.)

Defining Allusion

The concepts behind allusion are not difficult to understand. However one of the problems inherent in studying allusions in biblical literature is that different scholars use the relevant terms differently. One scholar will use the term 'allusion' to refer to what another would call 'influence' or 'intertextuality' to refer to what another would call 'allusion'. For some, an 'echo' is a sort of proof-text. For others it is loaded with subtle interpretive impact. What follows will define and explain the term allusion and other terms associated with it.

Briefly put, an *allusion* is a reference made by the author to a previous work that is indicated by verbal correspondence and that has interpretive value. The detailed explanation of the concept of allusion that follows addresses three elements: authorial intention, verbal correspondence, and interpretation.

Reference is a neutral term that applies to all verbal connections between passages that are, presumably, intentional. Reference is used without consideration of the clarity of connection between the passages, that is, whether the verbal correspondence between the passages is faint or strong. Reference is also used for verbal connections to other texts without regard to their interpretive value: they may have interpretive value or be totally devoid of it. Allusion, however, must have interpretive value, that is, affect the meaning of the referring text. Thus, allusion is a sub-category of reference. That distinction does not greatly affect this study, however, because all of Mark's references appear to have interpretive value. So while allusion is a sub-category of reference, here in practice, reference appears synonymous with allusion.

Authorial Intention

Allusion concerns references to other texts, which an author intentionally included in his or her own work. This requirement distinguishes allusion from two other literary concepts: intertextuality and influence.

The term *intertextuality* was coined by Julia Kristeva to describe *all* forms of textual interrelations. Intertextuality, in this original sense, describes the large web of relationships a reader may find among any group of texts, without concern for authorial intention, historical context, literary canon and the like.[7]

---

7 See Jay Clayton and Eric Rothstein, 'Figures in the Corpus: Theories of Influence and Intertextuality', in *Influence and Intertextuality* (ed. Jay Clayton and Eric Rothstein; Madison: University of Wisconsin Press, 1991), pp. 11–29. The term has a broader definition among poststructuralists and refers to the system of semiotics, the vast array of cultural interrelations, which allow us to communicate and interpret texts and non-textual perceptions. This larger system of relations is well beyond the focus of this study, and the term is used here in its original sense of connections between literal texts.

In practice, an intertextual parallel is a juxtaposition of two texts. It is something that is seen by the reader and needs no historical basis. A modern reader may well read Genesis 2–3 with *Paradise Lost* in mind or Isaiah 53 via Handel's *Messiah*. One may interpret a thirteenth-century BCE Ugaritic work by comparing it to a thirteenth-century CE Icelandic work. Like allusions, intertextual readings can be insightful and beneficial. The larger category of intertextual readings is different from the narrower category of allusion because intertextual readings work without regard to the intention of the author or the historical relationships between the texts.

Some biblical and rabbinic scholars use the term *intertextuality* to refer to historical and intentional references to other texts.[8] That is, they use *intertextuality* to refer to what is here called *allusion*. Such usage is correct, and intentional references are within the category of intertextuality. In this study, however, the term *allusion* will be used to refer to intentional references, and *intertextuality* will be used in a narrower sense, for textual relationships that lack evidence of being intended by the author.

Influence is also a broader category than allusion. Like allusion, influence is concerned with historical relationships between texts – in this case, with the effect earlier texts have on later ones. Earlier texts *influence* later ones. An earlier text may affect the thinking or even word choice of an author. For example, the *Iliad* influenced *Paradise Lost*. Milton read the *Iliad*, his ideas were influenced by it, and he included references to it in his own poem.

Influence often shows up in allusions. However, one text may influence another without ever appearing in it as a reference. The authors of the New Testament are influenced by a broad array of Old Testament passages. Yet, in their own writings those authors create references to just a fraction of those passages. Some Old Testament passages remain an influence *behind* a New Testament book, but do not appear as allusions *in* it. For example, Seyoon Kim argues that although there are no clear allusions to 2 Sam. 7.12-16 or Zech. 3.8-9; 4.7-10; 6.12-13 in the Parable of the Vineyard in Mark 12, nevertheless, these passages are the key to its interpretation.[9] Kim considers them to have influenced the telling of the parable.

Not every Old Testament passage which can be seen to correspond to a New Testament passage necessarily *influenced* that passage. That is, there exist parallels between the Old Testament and the New Testament which have no

---

8   Cf. Hays, *Echoes*, p. 15; Daniel Boyarin, *Intertextuality and the Reading of Midrash* (Bloomington: Indiana University Press, 1990); Robert L. Brawley, *Text to Text Pours Forth Speech: Voices of Scripture in Luke–Acts* (Bloomington: Indiana University Press, 1995); Sipke Draisma (ed.), *Intertextuality in Biblical Writings: Essays in Honor of Bas van Iersel* (Kampen: Kok, 1989).
9   Seyoon Kim, 'Jesus – The Son of God, the Stone, the Son of Man, and the Servant: The Role of Zechariah in the Self-Identification of Jesus', in *Tradition and Interpretation in the New Testament: Essays in Honor of E. Earle Ellis for His 60th Birthday* (ed. Gerald F. Hawthorne and Otto Betz; Grand Rapids: Eerdmans; Tübingen: Mohr [Seibeck], 1987), p. 144.

direct historical connection; the New Testament author does not allude to the Old Testament passage, nor does the Old Testament passage shape the thinking of the New Testament author. Examples of this are found in passages sharing an unusual term or containing parallel grammatical constructions or themes, though those passages had little to no influence on a New Testament passage. For example, Mark 15.38 and Lev. 21.23 contain the word καταπέτασμα (*veil*). Leviticus 21.23 helps scholars understand the meaning of the word, but there is little evidence that the author of Mark was influenced by this passage as he wrote the passion narrative. Such similarities are no more than textual parallels.

In practice, it can be difficult to distinguish between allusions, simple intertextual parallels, and influential texts that do not appear as allusions. Nevertheless, the categories reflect real levels of connection. Some parallels are seen by and helpful to readers but were not considered by the author (intertextual parallels). Some parallels affected the thinking of the author, but that effect is not made explicit with textual connections (influence). Some parallels are included in the work as a signal to the reader (allusion).

The Difficulty of the Requirement

Literary critics define allusions to be textual connections that were intended by the author, not accidental parallels. Generally, authorial intention is determined by considering two factors: whether the author knew the passage in question and whether there is sufficient verbal correspondence between the two texts to indicate the author had that passage in mind.[10]

In addition, definitions of allusion require that the intended reader, the authorial audience, recognize the allusion and somehow use the allusion to interpret the alluding text. One definition states that an allusion is a reference that 'the writer assumes the reader will recognize'.[11] Both authorial intent and reader recognition are assumed in this definition. Another critic takes a more moderate stance, considering an allusion to be something the writer merely 'hopes' that readers will recognize, acknowledging that the effect of many allusions goes 'unnoticed by the general reader'.[12] This softer stance emphasizes authorial intention and the uneven quality of actual readers, but still requires some hope on the part of the author that readers will catch on.

These requirements, authorial intention and reader recognition, can be very difficult to prove for a particular passage, especially when dealing with ancient texts. John Hollander uses the term 'echo' primarily to escape them:

---

10   Verbal correspondence will be discussed in greater detail below.
11   Kathleen Morner, *NTC's Dictionary of Literary Terms* (Lincolnwood, Ill.: National Textbook, 1991), p. 5.
12   Martin Gray, *A Dictionary of Literary Terms* (2nd rev. edn; Harlow: Longman, 1992), pp. 17–18.

> In contrast with literary allusion [which requires authorial intention and in some fashion reader recognition], echo is a metaphor of, and for, alluding, and does not depend on conscious intention.[13]

> In contrasting poetic echo with modes of more overt allusion, I don't take up problems of actual or putative audience, or of the degree of self-awareness, of conscious design, in poetic response to the very words of an earlier text ... [Such things] matter less to me than that the revisionary power of allusive echo generates new figuration.[14]

Hollander wants to discuss the presence and significance of allusions without having to bother with the messy questions of whether the author intended such a reference or whether any previous reader ever caught it.

Scholars who study allusion in biblical literature rarely make use of such a back door. Michael Fishbane requires conscious interpretation of the referent text in his discussion of inner-biblical exegesis.[15] Benjamin Sommer requires authorial intention for allusion.[16] Hays follows Hollander in stating that intention is not necessary for what he calls echo.[17] Yet Hays' language in his discussions of echoes assumes authorial consciousness, at least to some degree. In fact, so does Hollander's language. Authorial intention, in some sense, is very basic to intuitions about the nature of allusion.

Still, who can blame Hollander for circumventing the issue? Without requirements for authorial intent and reader recognition, one may ask purely literary questions. For what readings can one make a persuasive argument from the text, now, at the present time? Does the current audience see the allusion? Does the current audience see its interpretive impact? With such requirements, one must ask historical questions. Regarding the Gospel of Mark, did the author include these allusions knowingly? What did he mean by them? Did he mean for his audience to catch them? Did he include the allusions regardless of whether they would be caught? One must also ask, did Mark understand his audience correctly? Did the original audience actually catch the allusions? Did they understand their significance? Such questions are very difficult to answer.

---

13   J. Hollander, *The Figure of Echo: A Mode of Allusion in Milton and After* (Berkeley: University of California Press, 1981), p. 64.

14   Hollander, *Figure*, p. ix.

15   Michael Fishbane, *Biblical Interpretation in Ancient Israel* (Oxford: Clarendon, 1985), pp. 13, 19.

16   Benjamin Sommer (*A Prophet Reads Scripture: Allusion in Isaiah 40–66* [Stanford: Stanford University Press, 1998], pp. 8, 15, 32) requires for allusion not only that the audience recognizes and identifies the reference but that it realizes the reference's interpretive impact.

17   Hays, *Echoes*, p. 29.

The Necessity of the Requirement

Are authorial intention and audience recognition in fact important criteria for assessing allusions? Much modern and post-modern literary theory calls into question the importance of authorial intention. Abandoning authorial intention as definitive, many modern critics consider meaning to be generated by the text itself.[18] Others consider meaning to be generated by individual readers or interpretive communities.

One does not have to be a poststructuralist to agree that ultimately the value of a work, its meaning and richness, are not determined by its author or first audience. In great literature, there may be elements of meaning which come to be there accidentally, unconsciously. They are simply there. A reader sees them. The thing works in the reading. Authors experience this phenomenon when others discuss their work and when they look at it themselves.

Neither is meaning determined by a work's first audience. Mozart and Monet were not understood until later. What critic, even the most sophisticated, understands all the allusions in *Paradise Lost*? At this moment in the scholarship of Mark, that point is extremely well taken. Mark was not fully appreciated by early audiences, and little positive was said about the author's literary abilities until the twentieth century. If current Markan scholarship has any soundness, the author used a number of literary devices which most audiences failed to grasp for almost two thousand years. The first audience does not determine meaning.

Nevertheless, most in the key interpretive communities for the Christian Bible – the church and biblical scholars – still have a place in their hermeneutic for authorial intention. Both of these interpretive communities see *continuity* with traditional or historical meaning – authorial intention and meaning for authorial audience – as an important limiting factor for their own interpretations. Both want something more than a purely literary reading (where anything goes as long as one can make a persuasive argument). Criticisms of literary readings of the gospels often reflect doubts regarding authorial intention and reader recognition. Thus, these issues must be addressed.

---

18   The plausibility of determining authorial intention is often questioned by reference to an essay called 'The Intentional Fallacy'. Unfortunately, this essay may be more often named than read. It rejects a problematic approach to literature, more prevalent in the first half of the twentieth century than today, that tended to focus on material outside the work to determine an author's intention, while leaving the work itself somewhat behind. Such critics 'prefer private evidence to public [the work itself], external to internal', or in other words letters and other biographical material to the words of the literary work (W. K. Wimsatt, Jr, and Monroe C. Beardsley, 'The Intentional Fallacy', in *The Verbal Icon* [University of Kentucky Press, 1954], p. 14). Wimsatt and Beardsley indicate that the meaning of a work, the intention of the author, as it were, is to be determined by the work itself: 'If the poet succeeded in doing it, then the poem itself shows what he was trying to do' (ibid., p. 4). One goes about it in an informed way, with the assistance of grammars and the like (ibid., p. 10), but directed mainly by the literary work. Their approach to allusion is not unlike that taken here (ibid., p. 18).

The Evidence for Authorial Intention and Reader Recognition

The general proposition that early Christian authors sometimes intentionally alluded to Scripture is beyond question. New Testament authors read Scripture and included many explicit citations of Scripture in their own writings. In addition, the New Testament contains many implicit yet clear allusions to Scripture, allusions on which virtually all scholars agree. Moreover, the frequency of sophisticated, interpretive allusions in both testaments and intertestamental literature demonstrates that allusion is an important part of the writing tradition in Judaism and in early Christianity.[19] Studies of the use of Scripture in Mark demonstrate that the author writes in this tradition.[20]

It is not enough, however, to establish a general practice. It is necessary to demonstrate the likelihood of authorial intention in each particular case. This is easy to do for quotations and for implicit references with strong verbal correspondence. The difficulty comes in cases with weak verbal correspondence. Guidelines for such cases are discussed below.

As we will see in Chapter 2, there is *prima facie* evidence that the original readers of the earliest Christian writings could have understood the allusions to Scripture within them.[21] Often that general evidence is all that is available. Sometimes, however, more can be said. If the theory of Markan priority is correct (and it is assumed in this study), Matthew and Luke are early readers of Mark, and they sometimes provide evidence that an early reader understood particular Markan allusions and their meaning. On the other hand, one might argue against a reading because it is so obscure that only a tiny fraction of the original audience could be expected to understand it.

Certainty on these points is often impossible and is never required. It is sufficient to establish for a particular allusion that authorial intention or reader recognition is probable, simply more likely than not.

Covert or Overt – or Interplay?

In English, the word *allusive* recalls the word *elusive*, and often people conclude that one of the necessary qualities of allusion is that the reference is covert, implicit. Overt, explicit references would be considered *quotations* or *citations*, distinct from allusion. But the word *allusion* comes from the Latin word *ludere*, meaning to play with, to imitate, and *alludere*, to play with, to make playful or mocking reference to. The Latin rhetorical term *allusio* means word play or punning.[22] Though not apparent to the average English speaker, the sense of word play or interaction with the referent text is dominant, not the hidden nature of the reference.

---

19 See pp. 48–52.
20 Cf. Marcus, *Way*, passim.
21 See pp. 60–65.
22 Hollander, *Figure*, pp. 63–64.

Dividing references into allusion, quotation, and citation is actually rather problematic. Is a citation a synonym for quotation, or does it have stricter limits? Does a reference have to be an exact, word-for-word match to be considered a quotation? Or is some variation acceptable, and if some, how much? And when is a reference overt? Is a word-for-word quotation overt to all audiences? That will depend on the audience's familiarity with the passage being quoted, which will vary from audience to audience. Only a word-for-word quotation with a citation formula is truly overt, and there are very few of those in Mark. On the other hand, a well-informed audience will readily catch a brief reference, without requiring explicit notification.

Echoes, covert allusions, quotations, and citations are not hard and fast divisions, but references with differing degrees of clarity. In all degrees, the author includes in the text verbal clues to point the reader to another passage. In all cases, there is a signal to the reader to interpret the text by considering the interplay between the referring and referent passages. That is, all of these references, whatever their degree of clarity, fit well in the definition of the Latin term *allusio*: word play.

Such references differ not in degree but in *kind* from other sorts of textual comparisons, such as influence, which considers the way the author was affected by a passage, even when the author does not signal to the reader to consider the interplay between the texts, or intertextuality, which takes into account only the reader's decision to consider two texts together and not whether the author saw them in that way or whether the basis for such a comparison lies in the text or the mind of the reader only.

For these reasons, the word *allusion* will be used without regard to the degree of clarity. Here, allusions are all references, whether overt or covert, that call on the reader to interpret the passage by considering the two texts together.[23]

Identifying Allusions

The first step in the study of allusions, naturally, is to locate them. One of the dangers of this type of study is to 'hear' too much, to read too many allusions into a work, to ascribe thematic parallels, even purely accidental similarities, to the status of allusion. If one goes in search of allusions – especially with all the reference tools available to modern scholars – one will find them. To help minimize that tendency, it is important to have some guidelines and limita-

---

23   See also Carmela Perri, 'On Alluding', *Poetics* 7 (1978), pp. 290, 297–98. For Perri (ibid., pp. 292, 297, 299), the covert element of allusion is not the reference itself, but the significance of that reference.

tions. Hays presents a useful and succinct procedure.[24] That procedure has been adapted and expanded here.

1. *Availability*: Was the referent passage available to the author? Because scriptural allusions are at issue, this will be easy to establish for Mark in general terms. The Jewish Scriptures were known and used by the early church, and by Mark in particular, as is known from his quotations.[25]

2. *Recurrence or clustering*: Is any particular allusion used more than once? Does the author tend to use a number of allusions from the same area of a biblical book? For example, Hays points to frequent use of passages from Isaiah 40–55 in Paul's letters.[26] If a fairly clear allusion points to a favourite passage, fainter allusions to the same passage have stronger support.

3. *Clarity*: Do the two passages have sufficient verbal correspondence? Assessing verbal correspondence is discussed at length below.

4. *Thematic Coherence*: Are the themes of the referring passage similar to the themes of the referent in its original context? The correspondence may be one of continuity or discontinuity. Themes may be used as they are understood in context, or they may be transformed and even overturned in their use in the new context. Thematic coherence and interplay are discussed in detail in Chapter 2, starting on p. 52.

5. *Distinctiveness:* Is the allusion of particular rhetorical importance in the referring text? Is the referent particularly influential to the author or his culture?

This point may be illustrated with an example. Michael Thompson presents the following pair of passages:

Some natural tears they dropp'd, but wip'd them soon;
The World was all before them, where to choose
Thir place of rest, and Providence thir guide:
They hand in hand with wand'ring steps and slow,
Through *Eden* took thir solitary way. (Milton, *Paradise Lost* XII, lines 645–49)

The earth is all before me – with a heart
Joyous, nor scared at its own liberty,
I look about, and should the guide I chuse
Be nothing better than a wandering cloud
I cannot miss my way. (Wordsworth, *The Prelude* I, lines 15–19)

---

24   Hays, *Echoes*, pp. 1–33, esp. pp. 29–33; '"Who Has Believed Our Message?" Paul's Reading of Isaiah', *SBL Seminar Papers, 1998* (2 vols; SBLSP 37; Atlanta: Scholars Press, 1998), 1, pp. 207–212.
25   See Appendix A.
26   Hays, 'Who Has Believed?', 1, pp. 215–16.

Note that only a few words are found in common (*choose, guide, way, wandering*); yet literary critics generally consider Wordsworth to allude to the end of *Paradise Lost*. The strength of the argument is the known strength of the referent passage: Milton's *Paradise Lost*, an extremely influential work. Moreover, the allusion is to the distinctive and evocative ending scene.[27]

On the other hand, Fishbane notes that different instances of a type-scene do not constitute inner-biblical exegesis unless they have lexical links. He mentions the type-scene, 'Matriarch of Israel in Danger', found in Gen. 12.10-20; 20.1-18; and 26.1-16.[28] Though some scholars see the repetition of these stories as reinterpreted tradition,[29] Fishbane warns that these stories may derive independently from a common *topos* in the oral tradition. Common rhetorical devices, like language common to a particular topic, are not secure points from which to claim allusion.[30]

Verbal Correspondence

Because allusion is concerned with historical relationships between texts, it is necessary that there be some evidence that the author intended the allusion to be seen, or at least that it is *possible* the author intended the allusion. Even a small amount of evidence may be sufficient, but *some* evidence is required. That means there must be some verbal correspondence between the two passages. If there is no verbal correspondence between the passages, the similarity should be considered a thematic parallel or shared motif. It cannot qualify as an allusion.[31]

Verbal correspondence occurs in degrees. It may be very strong, as in an exact quotation of many words. It may be a mere echo, two or three words in common, in no particular order. In such cases, as Dodd says, 'It is sometimes a delicate matter to be sure that an allusion is intended.'[32] It is important to clarify how difficult cases are to be decided and how much verbal correspondence is sufficient to indicate an allusion. Unfortunately what qualifies as sufficient is difficult to define.

One of the problems is that what is sufficient to recall a passage depends greatly on the familiarity of the audience with the referent text. Rikki Watts, an Australian scholar, presents an example of this problem. He heard a lecture at an American university in which a professor said, 'fourscore and seven years ago'. Watts was puzzled by this sudden use of archaic language, but his fellow students nodded knowingly. For Watts, the remark was cryptic.

---

27   Michael Thompson, *Clothed with Christ: The Example and Teaching of Jesus in Romans 12.1–15.13* (JSNTSup 59; Sheffield: JSOT Press, 1991), pp. 28–29.
28   Fishbane, *Biblical Interpretation*, pp. 11–12.
29   Cf. John Van Seters, *Abraham in History and Tradition* (New Haven: Yale University Press, 1975), pp. 154–66.
30   Fishbane, *Biblical Interpretation*, pp. 283–88.
31   Cf. Suhl, *Funktion*, pp. 57, 65, 158.
32   Dodd, *According to the Scriptures*, p. 31.

For his American friends, 'fourscore and seven years ago' was an explicit reference to Lincoln's Gettysburg Address and to its ideas.[33] To write, '"To be or not to be", as Shakespeare wrote in *Hamlet*', is prolix and pedantic. 'To be or not to be' is understood by a certain, fairly large audience to be a quotation of Shakespeare, without explanation. To the rabbis, a short phrase recalls an entire Scripture passage. To most beginning students of rabbinic literature, that short phrase will not have nearly the same evocative power. Some phrases are well known in one cultural environment, unknown in others. Sufficient verbal correspondence varies accordingly.

Nevertheless, there is a lower limit. 'Fourscore and seven years ago' recalls the Gettysburg Address to some audiences. 'Years' alone never does. Correspondence of just one or two common words is not sufficient to call the similarity an allusion, unless there is some other very definite evidence to support the allusion.[34] One cannot get around the problem by saying correspondence of a single common word is an echo. Again, 'years' is not an echo of the Gettysburg Address; by itself, it does not have sufficient weight to indicate an allusion, not even a faint allusion.

Distinct or rare words have much greater weight. If a word is used in only one or two passages, that single word might signal an allusion. The correspondence of such a rare word at least warrants further examination. For example, the word 'fourscore' is used so rarely now that, in an appropriate context, 'fourscore' might be an echo of the Gettysburg Address.

A string of shared words, that is, words that occur consecutively in both passages, represents stronger verbal correspondence than words shared individually.[35] 'To be or not to be' is composed entirely of common words, but the sequence of the words makes it distinct. Stegner sees lexical links to Exodus 14 in Mark 6.45-52. Yet his argument is unconvincing, because the words he mentions are extremely common, e.g., ἐπί and εἰς, θάλασσα, and verbs for telling and seeing, and the words do not occur consecutively. His argument is that a large number of the words in Mark 6.45-52 are also found in Exodus 14, but with the shared words being so common and sporadic, the link is tenuous.[36] There is very little to indicate that the similarity is anything more than accidental.

In dealing with New Testament allusions to the Old Testament, one must consider the complicating factor of translation from Hebrew or Aramaic to Greek. In such cases, a reasonably literal translation counts as verbal corres-

---

33 Watts, *Isaiah's New Exodus*, pp. 30–31.
34 Cf. Sommer, *Prophet*, p. 74.
35 Sommer, *Prophet*, p. 70.
36 W. R. Stegner, 'Jesus' Walking on Water: Mark 6.45-52', in *The Gospels and the Scriptures of Israel* (ed. Craig Evans and W. Richard Stegner; JSNTSup 104; Sheffield: Sheffield, 1994), pp. 217–21.

pondence. Consider, for example, John 19.37 and Zech. 12.10 in both the Septuagint and the Masoretic Text.

> And again another passage of scripture says, 'They will look on the one whom they have pierced.' (John 19.37)
> καὶ πάλιν ἑτέρα γραφὴ λέγει· ὄψονται εἰς ὃν ἐξεκέντησαν.

> ... so that, when they look on the one whom they have pierced ... (Zech. 12.10)
> ... καὶ ἐπιβλέψονται πρός με ἀνθ' ὧν κατωρχήσαντο ... (𝔊ed)
> ... וְהִבִּיטוּ אֵלַי אֵת אֲשֶׁר־דָּקָרוּ ... (𝔐)

The verbal correspondence between John and the LXX is slight. Yet the passage in John is a literal translation of the Hebrew, an alternative translation (whether done by the author or someone else) to that of the LXX. The degree of verbal correspondence will depend on how closely the Greek in the New Testament passage resembles the Hebrew text. A less literal but still close translation may be sufficient. A paraphrase will probably be too dissimilar.

There is no specific formula for what constitutes sufficient verbal correspondence, but correspondence must be sufficient to point to a specific text (or at least to a very small number of texts) and not merely to a group of texts or to a motif.[37] Verbal correspondence may be as strong as an exact quotation or it may be as weak as a single *distinctive* word, and still be sufficient. Verbal correspondence of a single *common* word is never sufficient. A string of three or four common words may be sufficiently distinct to point to a specific passage.

Many cases are uncertain. Different interpreters will have different ideas of what constitutes sufficient verbal correspondence. Such differences are perfectly acceptable. Guidelines will not settle every case, but rather most, and they are meant to clarify how to decide marginal cases. In those cases, it is helpful to call an allusion 'possible' or 'unlikely', depending on one's judgement, and to avoid excessive claims in either direction.

Allusive Techniques
Authors use and change the words of the referent passage in particular and deliberate ways. The words used to recall the referent sometimes signal the meaning of the allusion. These changes also complicate the task of locating allusions and deciding what is sufficient verbal correspondence. The following list describes some of the common ways authors change the words in allusions and the ways in which those changes may affect the meaning of the allusion.

---

37 Hooker (*Jesus*, p. 62) requires verbal correspondence to be so definite that it could point to only one passage. This is an unusually restrictive requirement and is not seconded by most scholars who study allusion. Instead, the requirement here, as stated above, is that the verbal correspondence points to only a small number of passages.

Ellipsis: Ellipsis is involved in most allusions.[38] The author incorporates key words from the referent, sometimes just enough to recall the passage, but leaves out most of the passage. The ellipsis may or may not create a shift in meaning.[39]

Shift: Rearranging the order of a text is common. Such rearrangements may change the meaning but not necessarily. 2 Chronicles 20.35-7 uses 1 Kings 22.49-50 and, by changing the order (1 Kings: ships lost, then a wicked alliance; 2 Chron.: a wicked alliance, then ships lost), changes the sense.[40]

Insertion: The author inserts new words into the words of the original passage, to change the sense. For example, the Chronicler inserts the name Solomon into the promise in 2 Sam. 7.12-13, to read: 'It is your son *Solomon* who shall build my house' (1 Chron. 28.6). This creates the impression that the promise was made to Solomon in particular, not to whomever would be David's heir.[41]

Paul cites the words of Deut. 30.12-14 in Rom. 10.6-8. The meaning of the passage is that the law is not too difficult for the people. But Paul inserts new words into the quotation, and utterly transforms the sense:

> But the righteousness that comes from faith says, 'Do not say in your heart, "Who will ascend into heaven?"' (that is, to bring Christ down) 'or "Who will descend into the abyss?"' (that is, to bring Christ up from the dead). But what does it say? 'The word is near you, on your lips and in your heart.'

Substituting words: An author may substitute similar words for those in the original text. The words may be similar in sound or in meaning to the original words.

For example, a subtle shifting comes in a different vocalization of the Hebrew, seen in Joseph's interpretation of pharaoh's dream, where שָׂבַע in the dream becomes שָׂבָע in the interpretation (Gen. 41.29).[42] In Gal. 4.30, Paul alludes to Gen. 21.10.

> Cast out *this* slavegirl and her son for the son of *this* slavegirl shall not inherit with *my son Isaac*. (Gen. 21.10, LXX)

> Cast out *the* slavegirl and her son, for the son of *the* slavegirl shall not inherit with *the son of the freewoman*. (Gal. 4.30)

---

38   See Hollander, *Figure*, p. 115.
39   Sometimes authors leave out quite important words from the original text and thus change its meaning in the new. For example, when Paul quotes Exod. 34.34 in 2 Cor. 3.16, he leaves out the word 'Moses', which Paul uses to effect in generalizing this passage, relating it to everyone (Hays, *Echoes*, p. 146).
40   Fishbane, *Biblical Interpretation*, pp. 401–403.
41   Fishbane, *Biblical Interpretation*, p. 466.
42   Fishbane, *Biblical Interpretation*, p. 451.

Paul changes the 'this slavegirl' to 'the slavegirl' and 'my son Isaac' to 'the son of the freewoman', though 'freewoman' is nowhere in the text. This enables him to present the passage in support of a dichotomy between the 'children of slavery' and the 'children of the promise'.[43]

Sometimes the substitution of words brings about the equation of the new context with the old. A professor mentioned a favourite theory of his which had not been received as he would have wished, saying he would not teach the theory during the course. 'I won't', he said, 'throw my pearls before the class.' The good–humoured shift in vocabulary highlighted the equation of 'class' and 'swine', in an understatement much more rhetorically successful than explicit statement. Mark does the same thing in 1.3, without the irony, when he substitutes 'his' for 'of our God' in the allusion to Isa. 40.3; he connects Jesus to God.

Text-Critical Issues

It is difficult enough to assess verbal correspondence between one piece of modern literature and another, such as deciding whether *The Prelude* contains an allusion to *Paradise Lost*. Locating allusions to Scripture in the New Testament presents an additional difficulty: modern scholars do not have the same Bible as each of the New Testament authors. It is a mistake to assume, as did Origen, that the Hebrew texts modern scholars have before them are equal to the Hebrew *Vorlagen* of the Greek translators or to think that the extant Greek manuscripts match exactly the Greek manuscripts of first-century authors. The Hebrew text was not yet finalized, and the Greek text was in an almost constant state of change from its beginning. New Testament authors worked from Greek translations of the Hebrew at some undefined, unknown point in the Septuagint's[44] complicated transmission history and from unknown branches of the Septuagintal family tree.[45]

---

43 Hays, *Echoes*, pp. 112–13, his translations, my emphasis.

44 The term *Septuagint* (LXX) is ambiguous. It can refer to the original translation only or to all Greek versions. In this study, the term is used in the latter sense, to refer to all Greek versions. It is not used, however, to refer to what are judged to be *ad hoc* or independent translations done by a New Testament author or source, translations produced merely for the sake of including the passage in another story or text. The term Old Greek will be used to refer to the original translation. The Göttingen edition of the Septuagint attempts to reconstruct the Old Greek, but no such efforts can be completely successful, and therefore the Göttingen edition of the Septuagint cannot be simply equated with the Old Greek. It will be given the shorthand note $\mathfrak{G}^{ed}$. Cf. L. Greenspoon, 'The Use and Abuse of the Term "LXX" and Related Terminology in Recent Scholarship', *BIOSCS* 20 (1987), pp. 21–29.

45 For a more in-depth discussion of the state of text-critical work on the Greek and Hebrew of the Old Testament, see Emmanuel Tov, *The Text-Critical Use of the Septuagint in Biblical Research* (2nd edn, rev. and enl.; Jerusalem Biblical Studies 3; Jerusalem: Simor, 1997); Ulrich, *The Dead Sea Scrolls*, passim.

Methodology: Identifying an Allusion

Extant LXX texts are mixed, and variants cannot be securely dated. Tov notes that any reading found either in the text or apparatus of the Göttingen edition or Rahlfs may have been part of the Old Greek.[46] He goes on to discuss the implications for text criticism of the Hebrew Bible, but this has still clearer implications for study of the New Testament. If, in principle, what is deemed to be a variant by the editors of the Göttingen edition might be part of the Old Greek, then all the more, it might be part of later LXX versions extant in the first century. Matches between a New Testament passage and a LXX variant could well be due to the presence of that reading in the New Testament author's Greek manuscript. When examining a potential allusion, one must consider LXX variants. In addition, so much manuscript evidence has been lost that, of course, many readings available to New Testament authors are no longer extant. An allusion that is not an exact match to a known LXX reading may well have been an exact match with a reading available in the first century.[47]

The variety of means by which allusions could be obtained points again to the variety of evidence that must be considered when locating an allusion. One must consider not merely LXX or MT manuscript evidence, but quotations in early church literature and other witnesses to variant forms of the text. These other witnesses are cited as variants in $\mathfrak{G}^{ed}$ and $\mathfrak{M}$, and are incorporated into what is meant by 'variants', in the discussion below.[48]

New Testament authors may have had few actual manuscripts from which to work. Authors often cited from memory. They may have made use of

---

46 Tov, *Text-Critical*, p. 51.

47 S. Jellicoe (*The Septuagint and Modern Study* [Oxford: Clarendon, 1968], p. 342) notes that the Old Greek may be preserved in a majority of early manuscripts, in a single late manuscript, or in none at all.

48 According to Dowd ('Reading Mark', p. 137, n. 13), Burton Mack suggested that to imagine a New Testament author using texts from various languages requires one to imagine the author in a library surrounded by books in various languages, studying which is the best for his purposes. The image is indeed implausible. It is not required. When Christians of different denominations worship together and say the Lord's Prayer, often all say the prayer as they know it, whatever might be written down. None of them will need to consult a library to substitute 'transgressions' for 'debts' or 'debts' for 'sins'. Changing 'deliver us from evil' to 'deliver us from the Evil One' is automatic. The example is a prayer, well known and well used, but the same applies to favourite Scripture verses. One might read a verse in the NRSV, but prefer the reading learned as a child from the RSV. In such a case, the reader need not consult the RSV to find out the exact translation. She knows it. This experience is common among Americans who read the Bible to any significant degree. If Americans, whose ability to memorize extends little beyond song lyrics and multiplication tables (and sometimes indeed not so far), simply *know* different versions of favourite passages, it seems incredible to deny such abilities to the evangelists, who belonged not only to a culture of Scripture, but to a culture of memorization, where the primary text memorized was Scripture. If a New Testament author supplies a variant that agrees with a LXX variant or with the Hebrew, that does not presume that he consulted parallel texts in a study. It presumes rather that he *knew* the text in such a form – no very great presumption.

testimony books.⁴⁹ For the purposes of this study, the exact source of the allusion (a biblical manuscript, memory, testimony book, liturgy, etc.) is unimportant.⁵⁰ The crucial point is locating the allusions to Scripture, where they exist and to what they refer.

Thus, when the allusion differs significantly from known LXX texts, the differences have a number of possible causes. Traditional interpretation or liturgical use may have intentionally changed the text.⁵¹ The author may have preferred one word over the other for his own narrative, or the author may have quoted from a slightly faulty memory. It is also possible that a New Testament author or the author's source translated from the Hebrew independently of the LXX. This possibility must at least be considered when examining allusions that significantly differ from extant LXX texts, but correspond closely to the Hebrew wording.

Markan Allusions to Scripture

The great uncertainty in the manuscript evidence complicates the process of deciding whether a possible allusion is actually an allusion. Decisions of this kind are aided by a better understanding of the way the author of Mark uses Scripture texts. Did he always use the Old Greek or did he use what are now considered variants? Did he ever translate from Hebrew or use a different Greek text than those still extant? Did he paraphrase, rearrange, or otherwise distort the text? That kind of understanding is best gained by an examination of allusions with very high verbal correspondence, that is, an examination of quotations or near quotations. There are few such allusions in the passion narrative, but there are roughly 30 in the gospel as a whole. These allusions provide a rich source of information on Mark's use of Scripture texts.

Most quotations from the Septuagint

Most of Mark's quotations match the $\mathfrak{G}^{ed}$ and are either exact quotations or modifications of the LXX to fit the context.⁵² For example, Mark 12.10-11 is an exact quotation of the LXX of Ps. 118(117).22-23:

---

49   See Martin Albl's work on the early existence of testimony collections: *'And Scripture Cannot Be Broken': The Form and Function of the Early Christian Testimonia Collections* (NovTSup 96; Leiden: Brill, 1999).
50   That a referent comes from a testimony book, for example, does not affect interpretation. The operating principle of allusion is that readers can make interpretive connections with a previous passage without having that passage in front of them. Just like a reader, an author can make interpretive connections from a list of passages or the use of Scripture in liturgy, as long as the author is familiar with the passage used.
51   Cf. Brown (*Death*, 1, p. 51) on the influence of liturgy on the Gospel of Mark, Juel (*Messianic Exegesis*, pp. 16, 56–57) on the importance of Jewish tradition.
52   Cf. Robert Horton Gundry, *The Use of the Old Testament in St Matthew's Gospel: With Special Reference to the Messianic Hope* (Leiden: Brill, 1967), p. 5.

λίθον ὃν ἀπεδοκίμασαν οἱ οἰκοδομοῦντες,
οὗτος ἐγενήθη εἰς κεφαλὴν γωνίας·
παρὰ κυρίου ἐγένετο αὕτη
καὶ ἔστιν θαυμαστὴ ἐν ὀφθαλμοῖς ἡμῶν. (Mark 12.10-11)

λίθον, ὃν ἀπεδοκίμασαν οἱ οἰκοδομοῦντες,
οὗτος ἐγενήθη εἰς κεφαλὴν γωνίας·
παρὰ κυρίου ἐγένετο αὕτη
καὶ ἔστιν θαυμαστὴ ἐν ὀφθαλμοῖς ἡμῶν. (Ps. 118[117].22-23)

In Mark 15.24, the author modifies the LXX to make the quotation fit the context:

διαμερίζονται τὰ ἱμάτια αὐτοῦ βάλλοντες κλῆρον ἐπ' αὐτά. (Mark 15.24)

διεμερίσαντο τὰ ἱμάτιά μου ἑαυτοῖς
καὶ ἐπὶ τὸν ἱματισμόν μου ἔβαλον κλῆρον. (Ps. 22[21].19)

The author follows the LXX translation, but changes the form of the verb and eliminates several words in order to adapt the passage to his narrative.

Many of Mark's differences from $\mathfrak{G}^{ed}$ are listed as variants in the apparatus. For example, the only difference between Mark 7.10 and the $\mathfrak{G}^{ed}$ of Exod. 21.17(16) is a double omission of αὐτοῦ.

ὁ κακολογῶν πατέρα ἢ μητέρα θανάτῳ τελευτάτω. (Mark 7.10)

ὁ κακολογῶν πατέρα αὐτοῦ ἢ μητέρα αὐτοῦ θανάτῳ τελευτάτω. (Exod. 21.17[16])

Those omissions are found in many LXX manuscripts. Mark could be omitting αὐτοῦ based on his Greek *Vorlage*.

Variations from the Septuagint
Though there is a distinct preference for the LXX, some of the Markan quotations display wide variations from the $\mathfrak{G}^{ed}$ and its known variants.[53]

For some of these, it is apparent that the author reworked the LXX. In four instances, Mark quotes the same verse twice, and in all four instances, the wording differs from quotation to quotation.[54] For example, Mark refers to Lev. 19.18 at 12.31, where it is quoted exactly from the LXX, and at 12.33,

---

53 Gundry (*Use of the Old Testament*, p. 28) writes: 'In strongest contrast with the almost purely Septuagintal character of the formal quotations in Mt and Mk, the allusive quotations present almost all possible permutations of text-forms, and these often within single quotations.'
54 See Lev. 19.18 in Mark 12.31 and 12.33; Deut. 6.5 in Mark 12.30 and 12.33; Ps. 110.1 in Mark 12.36 and 14.62; and Dan. 7.13 in Mark 13.26 and 14.62.

where it is in indirect discourse. Similarly, Mark 12.36 quotes Ps. 110.1 almost exactly, but in 14.62, the words are changed.

Mark almost always changes the form of the verb, as shown above in the quotation of Ps. 22.19. Word order is also often subject to change, with no equivalent variant in extant texts. For example, Mark 10.19 quotes from the Decalogue, but uses a different order:[55]

μὴ φονεύσῃς, μὴ μοιχεύσῃς, μὴ κλέψῃς, μὴ ψευδομαρτυρήσῃς, μὴ ἀποστερήσῃς, τίμα τὸν πατέρα σου καὶ τὴν μητέρα. (Mark 10.19)

τίμα τὸν πατέρα σου καὶ τὴν μητέρα ... οὐ μοιχεύσεις. οὐ κλέψεις. οὐ φονεύσεις. οὐ ψευδομαρτυρήσεις ... (Exod. 20.12-16)

Mark sometimes uses a synonym. For example, Mark 12.19b refers to Gen. 38.8

καὶ ἐξαναστήσῃ σπέρμα τῷ ἀδελφῷ αὐτοῦ. (Mark 12.19b)
καὶ ἀνάστησον σπέρμα τῷ ἀδελφῷ σου. (Gen. 38.8)

Mark has ἐξαναστήσῃ where the LXX has ἀνάστησον. The difference could have arisen from any of the causes named above.

Exact correspondence in Greek wording cannot be a criterion for deciding whether something is an allusion. Some variation in wording is an acceptable and common element in Mark's use of Scripture texts.[56]

Independent translations of the Hebrew

Some quotations stretch the limits of variation and appear not to depend on the LXX as it now exists. Some of those quotations appear to depend on the Hebrew.[57] There is considerable scholarly argument over the native language

---

55   Mark also appears to add an admonition seen in Sir. 4.1.
56   Ulrich ('Pluriformity in the Biblical Text', in *Dead Sea Scrolls*, p. 93) writes, 'the use by both Jews and Christians of diverse forms of texts in the first century shows that neither community thought that a fixed text was necessary for an authoritative book; evidently, differing forms of the text were acceptable.'
57   A word of caution is in order here. One can determine that a New Testament author was using the Greek directly. If a quotation is a very close match to the LXX in a distinctive Greek phrase, then one can be certain that the author is using a LXX text. In contrast, when the Greek wording of a New Testament passage varies significantly from the LXX but corresponds to the Hebrew, it is nearly impossible to prove that the author was translating directly from Hebrew. Any reading could come from a *different LXX text*, no longer extant, which equalled the Hebrew text now extant. For example, Ulrich ('Josephus's Biblical Text for the Books of Samuel', in *Dead Sea Scrolls*, p. 201) argues (contrary to some) that Josephus was probably never dependent on a Hebrew text against the Greek but used a 'proto-Lucianic' Greek text, some readings of which have been lost.

of Mark's author.[58] Wherever the gospel was written, it is scarcely beyond the realm of possibility that the author was Jewish. Nor can it be definitively ruled out that the author knew Aramaic. Even if the author did not know Aramaic, many of the traditions he used came from an Aramaic milieu. When these sources were translated into Greek (whether they came to the author in oral or written form), they may have provided their own translations of Scripture. In short, independent translations from Hebrew or Aramaic, either by Mark or his sources, cannot be ruled out *a priori*.

Of the quotations in Mark, there is only one case in which dependence on Hebrew is *required*: Mark 11.9 uses ὡσαννά for הוֹשִׁיעָה נָּא in Ps. 118(117).25. ὡσαννά is not a Greek word, but a transliteration of Hebrew words. Yet this example does not prove a great deal. The quote may well be a liturgical use of Scripture, which retained *hosanna* in its Hebrew form, just as *alleluia*, *amen* and *maranatha* were retained.

Other possible dependencies on the Hebrew are less compelling but may say more about Mark's use of the texts, since they are also less likely to come from a liturgical context. For example, Mark 4.32 refers to Ps. 104(103).12.

Mk: ποιεῖ κλάδους μεγάλους, ὥστε δύνασθαι ὑπὸ τὴν σκιὰν αὐτοῦ τὰ
      πετεινὰ τοῦ οὐρανοῦ κατασκηνοῦν.

𝔊: ἐπ' αὐτὰ τὰ πετεινὰ τοῦ οὐρανοῦ κατασκηνώσει,
      ἐκ μέσου τῶν πετρῶν δώσουσιν φωνήν.

𝔐: עֲלֵיהֶם עוֹף־הַשָּׁמַיִם יִשְׁכּוֹן מִבֵּין עֳפָאיִם יִתְּנוּ־קוֹל

The context of both Mark and MT put 'the birds of the air' in branches (κλάδους and עֳפָאיִם). Extant manuscripts of the LXX put them in rocks (πετρῶν). The allusion to the psalm is strengthened by the additional similarity of the branches, and it is plausible that this additional similarity is intended. This points to the use of Hebrew by Mark or his source. Nevertheless, dependence on Hebrew cannot be proven here. The similar

---

58   There is uncertainty about where the gospel was written. There is also uncertainty about the origin of the author himself. Many scholars conclude that the author was Roman or Greek and did not speak Aramaic, e.g., Achtemeier, 'Gospel of Mark', *ABD*, 4, p. 542; Donald Juel, *Mark* (ACNT; Minneapolis: Augsburg, 1990), p. 17; Brown, *Death*, 2, p. 1062. Others conclude that the author spoke Aramaic and was perhaps from Palestine or Syria, e.g., J. Marcus, 'The Jewish War and the Sitz im Leben of Mark', *JBL* 111 (1992), p. 441–62; Gerd Theissen, *The Gospels in Context: Social and Political History in the Synoptic Tradition* (trans. Linda Maloney; Minneapolis: Fortress, 1991), p. 249; Dieter Lührmann, *Das Markusevangelium* (HNT 3; Tübingen: J. C. B. Mohr [Paul Siebeck], 1987), p. 7; R. Guelich, *Mark 1–8:26* (WBC 34A; Dallas: Word Books, 1989), p. xxviii; M. Hengel, *Studies in the Gospel of Mark* (trans. John Bowden; London: SCM Press, 1985), p. 46; Kee, *Community*, p. 102. Kee (*Community*, pp. 46–47) concludes that there is little independent translation from Hebrew but allows for some. That is the conclusion here.

reference to branches in Mark and MT may be accidental, or the correspondence may have come about because Mark's Greek manuscript, unlike extant manuscripts, contained κλαδῶν, not πετρῶν.

In another important example, Mark 1.2 refers either to Mal. 3.1 or Exod. 23.20. Mal. 3.1 is more probable as the immediate reference (it in turn refers to Exod. 23.20).[59]

Mk: ἰδοὺ ἀποστέλλω τὸν ἄγγελόν μου πρὸ προσώπου σου, ὃς κατασκευάσει τὴν ὁδόν σου.

𝔊 Mal: ἰδοὺ ἐγὼ ἐξαποστέλλω τὸν ἄγγελόν μου, καὶ ἐπιβλέψεται ὁδὸν πρὸ προσώπου μου.

𝔐: הִנְנִי שֹׁלֵחַ מַלְאָכִי וּפִנָּה־דֶרֶךְ לְפָנָי

It is difficult to see how Mark could have got ὃς κατασκευάσει τὴν ὁδόν σου ('who will prepare your way') from the LXX of Mal. 3.1: καὶ ἐπιβλέψεται ὁδόν ('and he will gaze on the way'. It is still more difficult to see how Mark could have got the phrase from Exod. 23.20, in either Greek or Hebrew.) καὶ ἐπιβλέψεται ὁδόν is a literal translation of ופנה דרך (which could mean 'look on the way' but here means 'prepare the way'), though it makes no sense in Greek in this context. One would have to know the Hebrew to understand the translation. The words in Mark's allusion, ὃς κατασκευάσει τὴν ὁδόν, however, are an excellent translation of the Hebrew, catching the meaning of פנה here, and rendering the phrase in good Greek syntax. That translation was not modified from LXX translations now extant. It appears to be independently translated.

This last example is one of several references that present a smoother, less literal Greek translation than what is found in extant LXX manuscripts. Mark or his sources may be rewriting these passages into better Greek, or because the trajectory of corrections to the Old Greek was towards a more literal translation of the Hebrew, such quotations may point to earlier LXX readings which are no longer extant.

At least some of Mark's quotations come from his sources; for example, Mark 11.9 and John 12.13 refer to Ps. 118.25-26 with the same words, which probably come from a common source, possibly liturgical. When one considers the fact that Mark consulted previous tradition in composing the gospel, as well as biblical texts known to him, the wide variety in the textual character of Mark's allusions, from exact matches with known LXX texts to apparent independent translations, appears normal and understandable.

---

59 Refer to p. 209 for more information.

Methodology: Identifying an Allusion

Guidelines for evaluating possible allusions
The examination of Mark's quotations and near quotations yields the following rules of thumb for evaluating faint allusions.

1. Mark has a preference for the LXX. Most quotations come from it, either exactly or with modification to fit the new context.[60] Sometimes Mark's differences from 𝔊^{ed} correspond to LXX variants. Other differences agree with no extant variant. These may be exact quotations of LXX readings which are no longer extant or may reflect, for example, a quotation from memory.

2. Word order is often changed with no equivalent variant in extant texts.

3. Mark frequently changes the form of the verb or noun, sometimes uses synonyms, and occasionally alters syntax. Small differences in wording do not necessarily indicate that there is no allusion or that the allusion is an independent translation.

4. There are very few allusions that appear to be independent translations from Hebrew, but they do exist. When deciding on allusions, one must keep an eye on Hebrew texts, not just on Greek.

Some Examples

To illustrate some of the principles discussed in this chapter, we take up some examples of what other scholars have suggested are allusions in the passion narrative.

Son: Mark 14.61

For Mark 14.61, three passages are suggested as allusions with some frequency: Ps. 2.7; 2 Sam. 7.14; and Wis. 2.18. Psalm 2.7 is accepted as an allusion and is dealt with in Chapter 3. The other suggested allusions share only a single word, υἱός (*son*):

> I will be a father to him, and he shall be a *son* to me. (2 Sam. 7.14)
> ἐγὼ ἔσομαι αὐτῷ εἰς πατέρα, καὶ αὐτὸς ἔσται μοι εἰς υἱόν.

> For if the righteous man is God's *son*, he will help him. (Wis. 2.18)[61]
> εἰ γάρ ἐστιν ὁ δίκαιος υἱὸς θεοῦ, ἀντιλήμψεται αὐτοῦ.

The word *son* is far too common to establish an allusion on its own. Those who suggest these verses do so because these verses speak of one being the son *of God*, as does Mark 14.61. Yet this is true of other verses as well, for

---

60 Because Mark so frequently agrees with the LXX, dependence on Greek is expected, and an independent translation of the Hebrew is posited only when there are very significant differences from any known Greek translation.
61 NRSV modified.

example, Hos. 11.1, 'Out of Egypt, I called my son' (cf. Exod. 4.22).[62] These verses stand as thematic parallels to Mark 14.61 and other passages in Mark which speak of Jesus as Son of God, but are not allusions in Mark 14.61.

Passover and Unleavened Bread: Half a Dozen Possibilities

This example is significant not so much because many scholars suggest that it exists, on the contrary, but because it illustrates the methodological problems associated with many suggested allusions.

There is significant verbal correspondence between Mark 14.1:

> It was two *days* (ἡμέρας) before *the Passover and* [the festival of] *Unleavened Bread* (τὸ πάσχα καὶ τὰ ἄζυμα).

and 2 Chron. 35.17:

> The people of Israel who were present kept *the passover* (τὸ φασεχ) at that time, and *the festival of unleavened bread* (τὴν ἑορτὴν τῶν ἀζύμων) seven *days* (ἡμέρας).

While ἑορτή (*feast*) does not appear in Mark 14.1, it does appear in 14.2, thus increasing verbal correspondence somewhat. Note that the word for *Passover* is different in Mark (τὸ πάσχα) and 2 Chron. 35.17 (τὸ φασεχ). The parallel text of 1 Esd. 1.17 is preferable, because it uses πάσχα, as does Mark.

> And the people of Israel who were present at that time kept *the passover* (τὸ πασχα) and *the festival of unleavened bread* (τὴν ἑορτὴν τῶν ἀζύμων) seven *days* (ἡμέρας).

Interestingly, no one suggested 1 *Esd.* 1.17 as an allusion for this verse, even though verbal correspondence is slightly better. There is a bias for the Jewish/Protestant canon in the Scripture allusions scholars tend to suggest.

However, any of the following are also possible explanations for the difference between Mark 14.1 and 2 Chron. 35.17: the Markan text corresponds with Hebrew; the author's knowledge of a LXX variant for the spelling of Passover in 2 Chron. 35.17; or simply the author's substitution of a word for Passover that was more normative in the Markan community.[63] That is, the verbal correspondence between Mark 14.1 and 2 Chron. 35.17 and 1 *Esd.* 1.17 should be considered roughly equivalent.

The main verbal correspondence is in naming Passover and the feast of Unleavened Bread. These words appear in the same sentence in the Old

---

62 See Frank J. Matera, *The Kingship of Jesus: Composition and Theology in Mark 15* (SBLDS 66; Chico: Scholars Press, 1982), pp. 140–41, on sonship in the Old Testament.

63 πάσχα is more common in the Old Testament, and φασεχ does not appear in the New Testament.

Methodology: Identifying an Allusion 43

Testament less often than one might expect: in 2 Chron. 35.17 and its parallels *1 Esd.* 1.17 and Ezek. 45.21, where verbal correspondence to Mark 14.1 is still greater:

Mark 14.1: It was two *days* (ἡμέρας) before *the Passover* (τὸ πάσχα) and [the festival of] *Unleavened Bread* (τὰ ἄζυμα).

Ezek. 45.21: In the first month, on the fourteenth day of the month, you shall celebrate *the festival of the passover* (τὸ πασχα ἑορτή), and for seven *days* (ἡμέρας) *unleavened bread* (ἄζυμα) shall be eaten.

Ezekiel 45.21 was not suggested as an allusion, which is interesting, since it has more thematic connections with the Markan passion narrative than does 2 Chronicles 35. Ezekiel 45 describes the glorious restoration of Israel, which whatever its precise meaning when it was written, would have been interpreted eschatologically by the time Mark was written. In contrast, 2 Chronicles 35 has little apparent thematic correspondence with the Markan passion narrative, nor does it have any prominence in the early Jewish and Christian tradition. It appears only in Josephus, *Ant.* 10.4.5, in a straightforward retelling of the 2 Chronicles 35 narrative.

Thus we have significant verbal correspondence with three verses, almost equal, but arguably best for Ezek. 45.21. Ezekiel 45.21 also provides the best thematic correspondence. However the correspondence is mainly in the names of the feasts (since ἡμέρας is so common, it adds little), and may well be accidental. It is important to consider how often the words occur together in the New Testament. Again, the answer is not terribly often. It occurs in Mark 14.1 and its parallel in Luke 22.1, as well as in Mark 14.12 and its parallels in Matt. 26.17 and Luke 22.7, a total of five times.

That the phrase also occurs at Mark 14.12 is significant. The allusion to 2 Chron. 35.17 was suggested only for Mark 14.1. The verbal correspondence for Mark 14.12 is similar to that for Mark 14.1 with 2 Chron. 35.17 (ἡμέρα/ἡμέρας; τῶν ἀζύμων; τὸ πάσχα/τὸ φασεχ) or *1 Esd.* 1.17 (ἡμέρα/ἡμέρας; τῶν ἀζύμων; τὸ πάσχα), but greater with Ezek. 45.21.

Mark 14.12: *On the first day* (τῇ πρώτῃ ἡμέρᾳ) of *Unleavened Bread* (τῶν ἀζύμων), when *the Passover lamb* (τὸ πάσχα) is sacrificed, his disciples said to him, 'Where do you want us to go and make the preparations for you to *eat* (φάγῃς) *the Passover* (τὸ πάσχα)?'

Ezek. 45.21: *In the first* (τῷ πρώτῳ) month, on the fourteenth day of the month, you shall celebrate the festival of *the passover* (τὸ πάσχα), and for seven *days* (ἡμέρας) *unleavened bread* (ἄζυμα) shall be *eaten* (ἔδεσθε).

In all cases, the correspondence of ἑορτή (which was found in Mark 14.2) is lost with Mark 14.12. Otherwise, for 2 Chron. 35.17 and *1 Esd.* 1.17, the correspondence is essentially equivalent in both Mark 14.1-2 and Mark 14.12. On the other hand, there are two additional, though common, words corresponding between Mark 14.12 and Ezek. 45.21: τῇ πρώτῃ/τῷ πρώτῳ and φάγῃς/ἔδεσθε (from ἐσθίω). Objectively one must say that Mark 14.12 has at least as strong a possibility for an allusion to Ezek. 45.21 as Mark 14.1 does to 2 Chron. 35.17; yet it was not suggested. This is significant, if only to teach one caution regarding scholars' assessments of New Testament allusions to Old Testament passages. They are less systematic than one would wish.

The fact that there is similar verbal correspondence in two verses in Mark 14, mainly consisting of naming the festival of Passover and Unleavened Bread, to 2 Chron. 35.17; *1 Esd.* 1.17; and Ezek. 45.21 (where the correspondence in Mark 14.12 is somewhat greater) increases the likelihood that the correspondence is accidental. An important factor to consider is whether Mark's early editors saw a correspondence between these passages. In the parallels to Mark 14.1, 12, Matthew and Luke do not edit towards any of the three Old Testament verses and in some cases edit away from them. There is no evidence that Matthew or Luke saw a correspondence between any of these passages.

Thus, we have verbal correspondence that may be accidental between Mark 14.1 and 14.12 and 2 Chron. 35.17; *1 Esd.* 1.17; and Ezek. 45.21. There is similar verbal correspondence in two Markan verses to these passages. Mark's early editors did not see the correspondence. Taken together, the evidence points away from an allusion, towards accidental correspondence.

In assessing the suggestion that there is an allusion to 2 Chron. 35.17 at Mark 14.1, some digging was necessary. It was important to see how meaningful the verbal correspondence was, whether the words in common were unique or part of biblical idiom. There were three passages with roughly equivalent verbal correspondence. Perhaps more significantly, there was an additional passage in Mark which had similar verbal correspondence to the suggested passage and to the parallel passage at *1 Esdras*, but which had still greater verbal correspondence to a third passage. Of all six possible combinations, the Mark 14.12 – Ezek. 45.21 connection was the strongest. Yet it was not suggested; a combination with less correspondence was. Thematically, the Ezekiel passage is also a better match, since it has eschatological connotations that seem to be missing in the 2 Chronicles passage. Footwork was necessary properly to assess the suggestion and the potential parallels. Indeed, it was the fact that there were six possible parallels that made the correspondence seem accidental.

Anointing: Mark 14.3 and Cant. 1.12-13
The anointing in Mark 14.3:

> While [Jesus] was at Bethany in the house of Simon the leper, *as he sat at the table* (κατακειμένου αὐτοῦ), a woman came with an alabaster jar of very costly *ointment*

of nard (μύρου νάρδου), and she broke open the jar and poured the ointment on his head.

has verbal parallels to Cant. 1.12-13:

While the king was *on his couch* (ἐν ἀνακλίσει/במסבו), my *nard* (νάρδος/נרד) gave forth its *fragrance* (ὀσμήν/ריחו). My beloved is to me a bag of *myrrh* (στακτῆς/מר) that lies between my breasts.

There is significant verbal correspondence here. νάρδος is rare, occurring only here and Cant. 4.13-14. The correspondence with the Hebrew is better, with additional correspondence between μύρου and מר (also rare) and similarities between κατακειμένου and במסבו.

John 12.2-3 contains a similar scene:

There they gave a dinner for him. Martha served, and Lazarus was one of those *at the table* (ἀνακειμένων) with him. Mary took a pound of costly *perfume* made of pure *nard* (μύρου νάρδου), anointed Jesus' feet, and wiped them with her hair. The house was filled with *the fragrance of the perfume* (τῆς ὀσμῆς τοῦ μύρου).

The verbal correspondence is similar, again mainly with the Hebrew, with the additional word for *fragrance* in common. The setting is similar for Mark, John, and Canticles – reclining – though different wording is used. In addition, the allusion to the king in Canticles is a thematic connection to both gospel scenes. Though Jesus interprets the act of anointing as for burial (Mark 14.8), it seems likely that the anointing also carries the meaning of messianic anointing, and messiah is taken in a royal sense in both Mark and John, something emphasized in both passion narratives.

Other thematic correspondence is difficult to assess. That John might use a love scene from Canticles to colour a scene in his narrative is not that difficult to imagine. John seems to use such colourful imagery elsewhere.[64] Mark seems less likely to do so. Clearly, the scenes come from a common tradition. Is there an allusion to Cant. 1.12-13 in that tradition, spilling over into Mark's account? Or did John see the potential in the traditional material and edge in that direction by adding a reference to the fragrance filling the house?

The early tradition on the Canticles passage is slight. There are no other allusions to it in the New Testament, no allusions at all in the church fathers. The rabbis use it with regard to Israel and Mount Sinai – that is, regarding

---

64 See, e.g., L. Eslinger, 'The Wooing of the Woman at the Well', in *The Gospel of John as Literature: An Anthology of Twentieth-Century Perspectives* (ed. Mark W. G. Stibbe; Leiden: Brill, 1993), pp. 165–82.

the making (and breaking) of the covenant.[65] While this would be a suitable thematic use, it is unclear that such a tradition existed in the first century.

Thus, we have here significant verbal correspondence, but problems with thematic correspondence, where there is a connection in the royal theme, but seemingly not in the love theme in Mark. The Canticles verse has no prominence in the Christian and pre-rabbinic tradition. While there is at least a reasonable possibility that Cant. 1.12-13 is used in the parallel version of the anointing story in John, there is no indication that Matthew or Luke saw an allusion to Cant. 1.12-13 in Mark. Matthew edits the scene (26.6-7) but not toward the verse. Luke's anointing scene (7.36-38) is substantially different and is the least like Cant. 1.12-13 of all the stories. That the verse has so little currency in the tradition, either in pre-rabbinic exegesis or in connection with the anointing story itself, and that there are problems with thematic correspondence weighs against the acceptance of an allusion in Mark. While an allusion is possible, it is not probable. Canticles 1.12-13 is not accepted as an allusion.

Conclusion

- An allusion is a reference to another passage which is indicated by verbal correspondence. The verbal correspondence may be as strong as a quotation or as faint as an echo, or anywhere between. If there is no verbal correspondence, there is no allusion. Parallels with insufficient verbal correspondence may represent passages that influenced the author or intertextual parallels that exerted no direct influence.
- An allusion also contains thematic interplay with the referent passage. This will be discussed in Chapter 2.
- An allusion must be conceivable as intended by the author and recognizable by competent, informed readers in the authorial audience (that is the community originally addressed by the author). This will be difficult to establish in many cases. Room must be made for the lack of extant evidence and the judgement of the interpreter.

---

65   Mek. Bah. 3.102; b. Šabb. 88b; b. Git. 36b, Song of Songs Rab. 1.12.

2. METHODOLOGY:
INTERPRETIVE IMPACT

Locating the allusions is the first step in evaluating allusions. The second step is to assess the effect those allusions have on the meaning of the referring text. Does the reference affect the meaning of the text or is it merely a literate form of name-dropping, a display of literary knowledge? Even mere display may affect interpretation of a text. Readers, recognizing the acumen on display, may change in some fashion their interpretation of the work. But much greater significance is possible for a literary allusion.

The Element of Play

Hollander calls this greater power of significance 'transumption' or 'metalepsis'.[1] The idea is that there is a resonance between the two texts which produces a 'new figuration', a deeper sense of significance that moves the interpretation of the referring text to a new level.[2] The term metalepsis comes from μεταλαμβάνω, meaning *to receive, share, partake in, eat*. Figuratively, it also means *to take words in another sense, to interpret*, and for patristic authors, *to transfer to the spiritual from the literal level*.[3] Metalepsis, as a literary concept, goes beyond merely incorporating passages from authoritative predecessors in order to assume their authority – though this sort of reference is common.[4] μεταλαμβάνω is used for sharing a meal, and in metalepsis, there is a sharing, a mutual participation in meaning between the evoked text and evoking text. There is a receiving that implies absorption, digestion, then interpretation. This sharing of meaning comes from a resonance of contexts, a

---

1   Hollander, *Figure*, pp. 133–49.
2   Cf. Hays, *Echoes*, pp. 24–26.
3   See H. G. Liddell and R. Scott, 'μεταλαμβάνω', *A Greek-English Lexicon* (9th edn; Oxford: Clarendon, 1968), p. 1113; G. W. H. Lampe, 'μεταλαμβάνω', *A Patristic Greek Lexicon* (Oxford: Clarendon, 1961), pp. 852–53.
4   Hollander, *Figure*, p. 118.

dialectical relationship between the shared words or image in the old setting and in the new.[5]

One of the problems modern biblical scholars have had with New Testament allusions to Scripture is that the interpretation of the referent passage so often does violence to the sense of that passage in its original, historical context. Historical-critical scholarship has often seen the use of Scripture in the New Testament as proof-texting in the service of apologetic, principally seeing it as an attempt at proof from prophecy that Jesus was the messiah. For such an enterprise, persuasive exegesis of the passage is necessary to convince and, at least for many, that persuasive exegesis is lacking. From this line of thinking, New Testament allusions often seem less than satisfactory. But this is probably not the best way to go about it. Allusions rarely intend to define the meaning of the referent passages in their original contexts. In the poem quoted on p. 29, Wordsworth does not intend to define the meaning of the Milton passage. Rather he uses the passage as a trope, as a figure of speech, to say much in a short space. With this allusion, he evokes the sense of possibility and hope in Milton's ending. In Milton, the hope is tied to a Christian sense of providence, but Wordsworth loosens the tie: 'should the guide I chuse / Be nothing better than a wandering cloud.' If understanding the allusion in Wordsworth required one to understand the Milton passage differently, according to Wordsworth's world view, the power of the allusion would be lost. That power comes from the interaction of the referent and referring text, and in this particular case from their difference, *not* in their sameness. The same dynamic obtains in New Testament allusions. Hays notes that Paul's allusions function as tropes, not proofs.[6] Sommer makes the same point for allusion in Deutero-Isaiah.[7] Allusion does not say what the previous text *said*. It uses, *plays* with, what was said in order to say something new and possibly very different. Hollander speaks of new figuration.[8] Harold Bloom calls it the strong misreading the strong.[9]

Long Tradition of Allusion
The use of Scripture in the early church in general and Mark in particular belongs to a long tradition of Scripture allusion and interpretation in Judaism. Michael Fishbane's monumental work, *Biblical Interpretation in Ancient*

---

5   The sense of interplay, of touching on and playing with a referent passage, is inherent in the Latin roots of the word *allusion*. See p. 27.
6   Hays, *Echoes*, p. 24.
7   After catching an allusion, the reader may understand the previous text differently, but this is not necessitated by the allusion (Sommer, *Prophet*, p. 173).
8   Hollander, *Figure*, p. ix.
9   Harold Bloom, *The Anxiety of Influence: A Theory of Poetry* (New York: Oxford University Press, 1973), p. 30.

Israel, argues that allusion to Scripture begins in the Tanak itself. Fishbane shows that use of authoritative texts (Scripture) is an ancient element of the Jewish tradition and that such use represents a conscious hermeneutic. The quality, breadth, and number of his examples support his claim that these allusions are not accidental, mere random similarity of language, but products of human ingenuity. Their cumulative effect is to establish that authors of the Tanak read, interpreted, and reused existing scriptural texts.[10]

Fishbane also argues for more than interpretive re-use. He argues for sophisticated interplay between the texts in some cases. The difference may be illustrated with his examples from Chronicles and the prophets. Fishbane understands Chronicles to have been written as an interpretive re-use of Samuel and Kings; it does not allude to but *replaces* those works in the mind of the author. In contrast, Fishbane considers many other Tanak passages to play with the meaning of the original text, so that the new can be seen *in conjunction with* the old. He cites examples from the prophets (e.g., Mic. 7.15, Jer. 16.14-15, and Isa. 43.16-21) which use the tradition of the Exodus to describe a new exodus and return. In such cases, the '*traditum* does not serve as the backdrop and foil for a discontinuous *traditio*, but is rather the screen upon which national hope and renewal is contextualized, even imagined'.[11]

Fishbane's conclusions support the extensive research on the use of Scripture in the New Testament. The work of Dodd, Lindars, Juel, Marcus, Watts and others has already been mentioned. Many more scholars investigate the topic, such as E. Earle Ellis on Paul, Krister Stendahl and Robert Gundry on Matthew, Lars Harman on Mark, and Jon Paulien on Revelation.[12] Similar to many of these scholars, Hays demonstrates that Scripture references are often more than mere window-dressing or proof-texting; they interact with the referent passages. The meaning of the New Testament passage is drawn out, clarified or heightened, by the meaning of the Old Testament passage. Examples of the way this is done are presented later in the chapter.[13]

Furthermore, such playful, interpretive use of texts does not end in the first century. Daniel Boyarin and James Kugel make similar arguments for rabbinic use of Scripture.[14] Scholars such as Fishbane, Kugel, Hays, and Boyarin,

---

10   Fishbane, *Biblical Interpretation*, passim.
11   Fishbane, *Biblical Interpretation*, pp. 412–13.
12   E. Earle Ellis, *Paul's Use of the Old Testament* (Edinburgh: Oliver and Boyd, 1957); Krister Stendahl, *The School of St Matthew, And Its Use of the Old Testament* (Ramsey, NJ: Sigler, 1991); Gundry, *Use of the Old Testament*; Lars Hartman, *Prophecy Interpreted: The Formation of Some Jewish Apocalyptic Texts and of the Eschatological Discourse Mark 13 par.* (Lund: Gleerup, 1966); Jon Paulien, *Decoding Revelation's Trumpets: Literary Allusions and Interpretation of Revelation 8:7-12* (Berrien Springs, Mich.: Andrews University Press, 1987).
13   See pp. 52–58.
14   Boyarin, *Intertextuality*; James L. Kugel, *In Potiphar's House* (San Francisco: HarperSanFrancisco, 1990), pp. 247–70.

among many others, have demonstrated that references to Scripture in the Tanak, New Testament and rabbinic literature are often more than simple proof-texts. Such allusions interpret authoritative texts and interact with them to create new (and, as it happened, authoritative) texts.

Hays points out that Paul's use of Scripture may be in continuity with the sense of the passage in the Old Testament or deliberate discontinuity with it. He suggests, for example, that in the echo of Job 13.16 in Phil. 1.19, 'this will turn out for my deliverance' (τοῦτό μοι ἀποβήσεται εἰς σωτηρίαν), Paul places himself in continuity with the figure of Job as a righteous sufferer undergoing trial. Even so, Paul is in discontinuity with the Job passage in that Paul looks to God solely as his defender, whereas Job sees God, in part, as his antagonist. Hays argues that these aspects of meaning are tacitly incorporated into Philippians by Paul's use of the Old Testament passage.[15]

Robert Brawley suggests that in Acts 4.25 Luke plays with the meaning of Psalm 2. Luke transfers the meaning of λαοί from 'the Gentiles' in the psalm, to the 'Jewish people' in Acts 4.27.[16] While this is a violation of sense according to historical-critical exegesis, it is a perfectly ordinary use of allusion; irony and reversal were part of allusive writing for centuries before Luke.[17] As with Wordsworth and Milton, the punch to Luke's use of Psalm 2 is just this ironic twist. The Jews, Luke suggests, are acting just as the Gentiles did, and this points all the more strongly to what Luke saw as a covenantal violation in the crucifixion of Jesus.[18] Luke's use of Psalm 2 is not 'exegesis' or 'eisegesis' – it is strong misreading, appropriation of sense.

New Testament authors do not play by historical-critical rules. What is perhaps more disturbing, is that they often seem to play by no rules at all. Hays concludes that, in contrast with Philo, Paul is not concerned with methodological control.[19] Fishbane reminds the interpreter steeped in rabbinic traditions of exegesis that there are no stated rules in inner-biblical exegesis.[20]

Nevertheless, these misreadings of the text do not occur in a vacuum. Rather they occur in a specific historical context, underwritten by specific historical points of view. What first-century readers thought about Scripture affected how the text could be meaningfully appropriated. Allusion to texts will be, in some fashion, in 'continuity' with tradition – if one keeps in mind that continuity does not equal rigidity. Patricia Tull Willey puts it this way:

---

15 Hays, *Echoes*, pp. 21–22.
16 Brawley, *Text to Text*, pp. 6–10.
17 See Fishbane, *Biblical Interpretation*, pp. 332–34; Richard Garner, *From Homer to Tragedy: The Art of Allusion in Greek Poetry* (London: Routledge, 1990), pp. 180–83.
18 Brawley, *Text-to-Text*, pp. 7–8.
19 Hays, *Echoes*, p. 160.
20 Fishbane, 'Inner Biblical Exegesis: Types and Strategies of interpretation in Ancient Israel', in *Midrash and Literature* (ed. S. Budick and G. Hartmann; New Haven: Yale University Press, 1986), p. 34.

Not just anything can be said: new interpretations tend to be circumscribed by what the tradition, interpreted according to the community's exegetical norms, will yield ... The self-recognition of interpreters as heirs to a distinct tradition means that their creative freedom is limited to living 'within the ideologies of the theological *traditum* and its literary fund'.[21]

One of the most important ways such readings of Scripture are in continuity with tradition is in the underlying point of view that God's mind on any current concern is to be found in Scripture, reinterpreted for the present moment. This is decidedly the Jewish view of Scripture in the Second Temple period. But this view begins much earlier, according to Fishbane, who calls the texts of Scripture the 'imaginative matrix' for understanding and communication in ancient Israel.[22] The faithful responded to crises with creative reinterpretation and transformation of authoritative texts.[23] For example, when reality does not match the current understanding of a prophetic text, the text is reinterpreted – as in Daniel's reinterpretation of Jeremiah's 70 years to mean 70 weeks of years (Jer. 25.11; Dan. 9.24-27). This reinterpretation extends the divine voice in the text to one's own time. Even a less traumatic difficulty can spur such reinterpretation. For example, the idea of vicarious punishment for sin, found in the attribute formulas of God ('visiting the iniquity of the parents upon the children and the children's children, to the third and the fourth generation', Exod. 34.7) is no longer acceptable in later periods. So the tradition is reinterpreted, in Jer. 31.29-30, Ezekiel 18, and elsewhere.[24]

This type of reinterpretation comes from the view that Scripture is 'written for our instruction', as Paul said (Rom. 15.4; cf. Rom. 4.23-24; 1 Cor. 9.10), that it points to the present ('See, now is the acceptable time; see, now is the day of salvation!' 2 Cor. 6.2).[25] That view was held by the people of Qumran.[26] The words of Scripture are to help the faithful interpret their world. But such interpretation is done neither according to the literal sense of the words nor without regard to what is written; rather the interpreter reveals the mysteries that lie hidden within the text. Hays calls Paul's hermeneutic one of poetics and 'spirit-experience', where Paul discovers the latent, metaphoric

---

21   Patricia Tull Willey, *Remember the Former Things: The Recollection of Texts in Second Isaiah* (SBLDS 161; Atlanta: Scholars Press, 1997), p. 70; quoting Fishbane, *Biblical Interpretation*, p. 435.
22   Fishbane, *Biblical Interpretation*, p. 435.
23   Cf. Fishbane, 'Inner Biblical Exegesis', p. 34; *Biblical Interpretation*, pp. 18, 408.
24   Fishbane, *Biblical Interpretation*, pp. 521–23, 336–38, 410.
25   Hays, *Echoes*, pp. 165–68, 171.
26   See, for example, 1QpHab xi 3-8, where the words of the prophet refer to the persecution of the Teacher of Righteousness by the Wicked Priest.

sense of the text in the freedom and inspiration of the Holy Spirit.[27] Fishbane writes frequently that exegesis is revelation.[28]

Types of Interplay

Allusions play with the meaning of the evoked text. They use the text in a figurative way. It is helpful to note in advance some of the ways meaning can be transformed in the process. The following list is not meant to be exhaustive or systematic but heuristic.[29]

Straight reading: This type of allusion incorporates the meaning of the referent into the text with little transformation. The words mean generally the same thing in both contexts. The benefit of the allusion is that it brings a developed sense to the new text. Shared words are not just words, but a figure, a concept. Isaiah 52.1-8 alludes to Nah. 2.1-3, with the figure of the herald on the mountains, announcing good news. Though the vanquished enemy changes to Babylon from the Assyrians, little else of substance is changed.[30]

Extension and transcendence: The author extends the scope of the ordinary sense of the passage. For example, oracles in Scripture relating to a specific individual or small group are applied to the whole nation of Israel.[31] In Lev. 21.5-6, there is a law against priests cutting themselves while they are in mourning because they are holy to God. Deuteronomy views the whole nation of Israel as holy to God, and therefore extends the injunction to the whole nation: no Israelite may cut himself in mourning (Deut. 14.1-2).[32] Likewise, Deutero-Isaiah extends to the nation as a whole promises made to David – e.g., Isa. 61.1-11 and Ps. 132.9-18.[33]

Transcendence is extension to a greater degree, where the sense in the new context goes well beyond the sense of the original. Hollander refers to the trope of a spear like a mast from Homer, which Milton transcends with: 'His spear, to equal which the tallest Pine / Hewn on Norwegian hills, to be the Mast / of some great Ammiral, were but a wand' (*Paradise Lost* 1.292–94).[34] Deutero-Isaiah uses an oracle from Jeremiah, which referred literally to the nation of Israel gathering and to literal blind people among the returnees, and

---

27 Hays, *Echoes*, pp. 108, 186.
28 See, for example, Fishbane, 'Inner Biblical Exegesis', pp. 20, 35; *Biblical Interpretation*, p. 277.
29 Bloom (*Anxiety of Influence*, pp. 14–16) contains an important list. Moo (*Old Testament*, pp. 25–56) has a thorough discussion of interpretive techniques in Judaism.
30 Sommer, *Prophet*, pp. 82–83.
31 Fishbane, *Biblical Interpretation*, pp. 469–70.
32 Fishbane, 'Inner Biblical Exegesis', p. 31.
33 Sommer, *Prophet*, pp. 112–13.
34 Hollander, *Figure*, pp. 117–120.

transcending Jeremiah's sense, speaks of the nations gathering and the figuratively blind, those who do not understand (Isa. 43.5-9; Jer. 31.1-8).[35]

Shift: A simple shift in the context or speaker may effect a shift in meaning. Fishbane presents examples of laws transformed into exhortations, narratives recast as oracles, and words of God transformed into prayers.[36] New Testament allusions frequently reverse the latter, recasting prayers into words of God, psalms into oracles (e.g., John 19.23-24).

Analogy/typology:[37] This is the use of a story or image as a model for understanding the present situation. This also is common in inner-biblical exegesis. For example, the Book of Joshua uses the Exodus as a model for the conquest: the parting of Jordan reflects the parting of Red Sea (Josh. 3–4; Exod. 14–15).[38] Images from the wilderness period are used in many of the prophets, for example, Hos. 2.16-17; Mic. 7.15; Isa. 43.16-21; and Jer. 16.14-15.[39] Isaiah 65.17 uses creation as a prototype for future redemption. 'For I am about to create new heavens and a new earth.'[40]

Dissimile and reversal: In dissimile, the allusion is used in explicit contrast to the referent text. For example, Paul tells the Corinthians that he is *not* like Moses (2 Cor. 3.13). One of the interesting elements of dissimile is that it not only draws contrasts, but it implicitly asserts similarities. Paul is not like Moses in that he is not veiled and conceals nothing, but perhaps he is like Moses in the grandeur of the revelation he has received.[41]

In reversal, the same dynamic is at work but not explicitly. Jeremiah 31.29-30 rejects the idea that the Lord punishes children for the sins of the parents in a reversal of the divine attribute formula found in Exod. 34.7.[42] Isaiah 19.19-25 deliberately uses the language of Exod. 3.7-9; 8.16-24 to declare that the Egyptians, the enemies of God in Exodus, will be redeemed.[43] In Gal. 4.25, Paul reverses the symbolic import of Mount Sinai and the law when he associates them not with Sarah, but with Hagar. He does this through a deliberate reworking of categories: the slave woman points to the slavery of the law.[44]

---

35   Sommer, *Prophet*, p. 46.
36   Fishbane, *Biblical Interpretation*, p. 425.
37   The term is used here in the sense intended by Fishbane, who notes that it does *not* include its developed sense, particularly in the later Christian community (*Biblical Interpretation*, pp. 350–52).
38   Fishbane, *Biblical Interpretation*, pp. 358–59.
39   Fishbane, *Biblical Interpretation*, 361-68. See also S. Talmon, 'The "Desert Motif" in the Bible and in Qumran Literature', in *Biblical Motifs: Origins and Transformations* (ed. A. Altmann; Cambridge, Mass.: Harvard University Press, 1966), pp. 31–63.
40   Fishbane, *Biblical Interpretation*, p. 354.
41   Hays, *Echoes*, pp. 141–43.
42   Fishbane, *Biblical Interpretation*, p. 337.
43   Fishbane, *Biblical Interpretation*, pp. 367–68.
44   Hays, *Echoes*, p. 115.

Irony: 'A figure of speech in which the actual intent is expressed in words that carry the opposite meaning.'[45] In irony, the author challenges the reader to figure out what he means, without his directly saying so. The reader is to unravel the incongruity or discrepancy.[46] Malachi 1.6–2.9 puts the priestly blessing (Num. 6.23-27) to ironic use, as he asserts that a human governor would not be pleased with the poor state of offerings given to the Lord. 'Will he be gracious to you? ... Beseech the countenance of God.'[47] Acts 4.25 uses 'people' of Ps. 2.1 ironically, as we saw above, to refer to Jews instead of Gentiles.

Linking texts: An allusion can link passages into a web which has a significance not found in the texts on their own. Fishbane notes as an example of this the psalm titles, which link the psalms to previously unrelated texts (often through linguistic affinities) and which significantly affect the meaning of the psalms.[48]

Hays argues that in Romans 4, Paul links Gen. 15.5-6; Ps. 32.1-21; and Gen. 17.5. The effect of the combination is to present Abraham as the forefather of Gentile Christians by faith, supporting Paul's claim that faith 'transcends the boundaries of Jewish ethnic descent and Torah observance'.[49] In 2 Cor. 3.1-3, Paul rejects the need for letters of recommendation, saying the Corinthians are letters 'written on our hearts'. In this passage, Hays argues, Paul links Jeremiah's theme of the new covenant written on hearts in Jer. 31.33 with God as covenant writer in Exod. 31.18 and with opposition of stone and flesh in Ezek. 36.26. Hays notes that these texts were later linked in the Palestinian lectionary, and may have already been linked in Paul's time. In 1 Corinthians 3, the effect of the linking is 'to set up an implicit dissonance in 2 Cor. 3:1-3 between the Mosaic covenant and the new covenant'.[50]

Reading through tradition: This type of allusion uses the reference according to its interpretation in the community's tradition. Hays presents an example of this in the reference to Gen. 21.1-10 in Gal. 4.21-31. In Gal. 4.29, with 'the child who was born according to the flesh persecuted the child who was born according to the Spirit', Paul may be relying on a tradition, seen in later rabbinic literature, that Ishmael persecuted Isaac. Though Ishmael's persecution of Isaac is not in Genesis, it is a traditional explanation for what seems to be harsh treatment from a matriarch. Paul does not invent this interpretation; he makes use of it.[51] This practice is widespread in the New

---

45 W. Harmon and C. H. Holman, *A Handbook to Literature* (7th edn; Upper Saddle River, NJ: Prentice Hall, 1996), pp. 277–78.
46 Wayne C. Booth, *A Rhetoric of Irony* (Chicago: University of Chicago Press, 1974) pp. 1–31, esp. 6–7.
47 Fishbane, *Biblical Interpretation*, pp. 332–34, his translation.
48 Fishbane, *Biblical Interpretation*, p. 404.
49 Hays, *Echoes*, pp. 54–57.
50 Hays, *Echoes*, pp. 128–29.
51 Hays, *Echoes*, p. 117.

Testament,[52] and we will return to deal with it at greater length later in the chapter.

Attention to the Larger Context

Allusion, by its nature, incorporates more of the sense of the referent text than just the words quoted. The question in interpretation is how much of the surrounding text is incorporated into an allusion.[53] New Testament scholars debate this. Dodd's discovery of a similar plot line in early Christian allusions led him to the conclusion that for the core texts of early Christian exegesis, Christians interpreted by analogy and with respect for the original context and meaning of the passages.[54] Allusions to particular words often recalled the sense of a larger passage and took into account more than the bare words quoted.[55] Dodd has received a strong following on this point, and sometimes it is assumed that an allusion includes the larger context if the 'plot' of the Old Testament passage is seen to correspond to the 'plot' of the New Testament passage. This is seen frequently in interpretations of allusions to Psalm 22 in the Markan passion narrative. A number of scholars conclude that the whole psalm is meant, including the thanksgiving portion at the end of the psalm (to which Mark does not allude), because the exaltation at the end of the psalm corresponds to the exaltation at the end of Mark.[56]

Dodd and others have been taken to task on this position. For example, Sundberg objects that a New Testament allusion to an Old Testament passage rarely takes into account the larger context.[57] Though in *New Testament Apologetic* Lindars agrees with Dodd, elsewhere he states that taking the larger context into account can distort the meaning of a New Testament passage.[58]

---

52 Many examples can be found in J. L. Kugel, *Traditions of the Bible: A Guide to the Bible As It Was at the Start of the Common Era* (Cambridge, Mass.: Harvard University Press, 1998); Martin McNamara, *The New Testament and the Palestinian Targum to the Pentateuch* (Rome: Pontifical Biblical Institute, 1966).

53 Cf. Garner, *From Homer to Tragedy*, pp. 184–85.

54 Dodd, *According to the Scriptures*, pp. 109, 126–33; *The Old Testament in the New* (Philadelphia: Fortress, 1965), p. 19. Ruppert (*Jesus*, pp. 50–52) comes to a similar conclusion when he states that the suffering and vindication theme of the suffering righteous one is reflected in the allusions to the suffering righteous passages in Mark.

55 Dodd, *According to the Scriptures*, pp. 126–27.

56 See pp. 151–54.

57 Sundberg, 'On Testimonies', pp. 275–76.

58 Lindars, *New Testament Apologetic*, pp. 16–17; 'The Place of the Old Testament in the Formation of New Testament Theology', *NTS* 23 (1977), p. 65. Cf. Suhl, *Funktion*, p. 47. For other scholars on this issue, see Marcus, *Way*, p. 21, nn. 34–35.

Despite the initial impression, Lindars' positions are not contradictory. Dodd does not claim that all references to Scripture take into account the larger context. Sundberg does not claim that references to Scripture never do so. The question is one of degree: how frequently and to what extent does this occur?

Lindars correctly notes that taking more of a passage into account than the author intended can distort the meaning of a passage. That fact might lead an interpreter to play it safe and always discount the context of a referent when interpreting a passage containing an allusion. Yet, as Hays argues, the opposite is also true: ignoring the larger context can distort the meaning of the New Testament passage. He points to the debate over justification in Rom. 1.17, 'The one who is righteous will live by faith.' Though there has been considerable debate over the exact nature of justification, most often Paul's use of Hab. 2.4 has been considered merely a proof-text, without regard to its sense in Habakkuk. Yet, in context, the statement stands as God's answer to the prophet's complaint against God's apparent indifference to injustice: 'Your eyes are too pure to behold evil, and you cannot look on wrongdoing; why do you look on the treacherous, and are silent when the wicked swallow those more righteous than they?' (Hab. 1.13). Paul refers to this passage in a letter which is concerned primarily with theodicy, that is, with God's faithfulness to Israel.[59] Though Western Christianity has traditionally understood Paul's concern to be individual salvation, it has been able to maintain that reading 'only by strenuously suppressing the voice of scripture in Paul's letters'.[60]

Worse still, when attention to context is neglected, the New Testament's use of Scripture can be considered mere window-dressing, a rhetorical trope without substance. This can lead to a faulty understanding of the place of the Old Testament in Christianity and a low estimate of the Old Testament itself. As scholarship affirms the importance of the Jewish Scriptures to Christianity, it is necessary to consider the interaction between the contexts in New Testament references to Old Testament passages.

The dual dangers of taking into account too much or too little of the context and meaning of the Old Testament passage point to the need for a reasoned approach by which to determine how much of the context is recalled in each allusion. Hays argues that scriptural allusions incorporate the context surrounding the referent passage, but does not assume that an allusion automatically evokes the full context. Rather, he examines the context of the referring passage for correspondences and differences in theme, language, and sense, with the referent passage. The extent of the allusion is decided by the extent of the interplay.[61] By deciding the extent of the interplay on a case-by-

---

59   Hays, *Echoes*, pp. 39, 53.
60   Hays, *Echoes*, p. 159.
61   For example, with the allusion in Phil. 1.19, Paul summons the image not merely of Job 13.16 but of many other elements in that particular speech in Job (*Echoes*, pp. 21–23).

case basis, Hays avoids the extremes of assuming that the allusion is made without regard to its context and of assuming that it incorporates all of the surrounding material. No single perspective is imposed on every allusion. The extent of the connections between the passages determines how much of the referent passage is included in the allusion.

That is the method used here. In doing so, the tendencies of particular authors will surface. Paul (and as we will see, Mark) tends to use surrounding context in Scripture references. Matthew does so less consistently.[62] For authors who do use context consistently, one may maintain some minimum expectations, for example, that the interplay extends not merely to the corresponding words but to the full verse of the referent, even to the verses immediately surrounding the referent. For example, while it is too much to assume that an allusion to the beginning of Psalm 22 includes the whole psalm in its extent, for such authors it is safe to assume that an allusion to Ps. 22.2 includes Ps. 22.3 in its extent. The more one includes of the referent's context, the greater the need for evidence that the interplay extends so far.

Considering Exegetical Traditions

Matthew Black argued that early Christian exegesis is deeply rooted in Jewish exegesis. Christian exegesis did not occur in a vacuum, but rather was influenced by the culture and religion out of which Christianity grew.[63] Though this position has long been widely accepted, scholars have not always attended to it in practice. Black himself did not neglect it and did much to further understanding of early Jewish exegesis and its effect on Christian exegesis. Hooker understood the use of Daniel in Mark with reference to other uses of the Son of Man image.[64] Juel and Marcus have written excellent monographs on Mark's use of Scripture with generous attention to early Jewish exegesis.[65] Craig A. Evans has used Jewish exegesis to understand the historical Jesus, but his comments often help to illuminate the meaning of passages in Mark. Evans claims, for example, that some parables cannot be understood apart from Scripture in its first-century interpretation.[66]

---

62 E.g., Matt. 2.15 refers to Hos. 11.1, apparently without reference to its context. Church fathers often seem to use references to Scripture with little to no reference to their contexts.

63 Matthew Black, 'The Theological Appropriation of the Old Testament by the New Testament', *SJT* 39 (1986), pp. 1–17. Cf. Lindars, 'Place of the Old Testament', p. 61; A. Collins, 'Appropriation', in Tuckett, *Scriptures*, p. 240; Christopher Bryan, 'As it is Written: Notes on the Essentially Oral Characteristics of Mark's Appeal to Scripture', *STRev.* 36 (1992), pp. 89–90; Moo, *Old Testament*, pp. 5–78.

64 Hooker, *Son of Man*.

65 Juel, *Messianic Exegesis*; Marcus, *Way*.

66 Craig A. Evans, 'On the Isaianic Background of the Sower Parable', *CBQ* 47 (1985), p. 464; cf. 'Jesus and the Dead Sea Scrolls from Qumran Cave 4', in *Eschatology, Messianism, and the Dead Sea Scrolls* (ed. C. A. Evans and Peter Flint; Grand Rapids: Eerdmans, 1997), pp. 97–99.

The insights gained from these studies indicate that attention to the meaning of Scripture allusions in Mark benefits from attention to the interpretation of those passages in Second Temple Judaism. Some evidence of early exegetical traditions remains in the works of Philo and Josephus, in the Old Testament apocrypha and pseudepigrapha, and in the Dead Sea scrolls. In addition, early Christian and rabbinic literature contains evidence of early exegetical traditions that may have been available in the first century.

These last two sources of information are especially problematic, however. Early Christian material contains traditions available to Mark (or to his sources) but, in addition, contains much material developed after the gospel was written. Even the earliest rabbinic literature was written nearly a century and a half after the gospel. As it happens, the Mishnah and *Mekilta* (compiled in the third century) contain very few parallels to the specific passages at issue in this study, and much is found in the Babylonian Talmud, which was composed in the sixth century and continued to be redacted after that.[67] These works contain early traditions; they clearly also contain a great deal of interpretation that post-dates the gospel, sometimes by centuries. Such texts should be used more for the purpose of supporting or clarifying a tradition already indicated by earlier materials than for the generation of new interpretations on their own.

In addition, material that was written before or contemporary to the Gospel of Mark was not necessarily known to the author. Philo pre-dates Mark, but there is very little evidence that the author was acquainted with his writings or interpretive method. It is also unlikely that the author was acquainted with the Qumran community or its writings. These and other works reflect exegetical traditions that may be dated earlier than the gospel and with which it is theoretically possible the author was acquainted. However, there is no guarantee that these traditions exerted any influence on the gospel. Therefore one must proceed with caution. When interpreting allusions, the exegetical traditions on each verse are examined and compared with the Gospel of Mark. When clues in the Markan narrative appear to correspond with a specific tradition, it may be used. If not, while it is not impossible that the author had such a tradition in mind, it is more prudent to set such a tradition aside for the interpretation of the narrative.

A Mere Wink to the Wise

It is important to note that not all references are metaleptic. Sometimes a reference is mere similarity of language, simple parroting. Robert Alter

---

67   H. L. Strack and G. Stemberger, *Introduction to the Talmud and Midrash* (trans. Markus Bockmuel; Edinburgh: T&T Clark, 1991), pp. 138–39, 255, 192–97.

describes this covert sharing of literary knowledge as a 'wink to the wise', 'the high fun of literature'.[68] Such references are often interesting, but they are not interpretive.

As Sommer points out, determining whether a reference is metaleptic depends greatly on the critic. He refers to an example presented by Ziva Ben-Porat of a cheese advertisement using the phrase, 'This is the smell that launched a thousand barbecues.' Ben-Porat concludes that the interplay between the referent text (the face that launched a thousand ships) and the referring text has interpretive impact for the discerning reader. The deepened meaning is, 'Buy this popular cheese because it is a special product for special (intelligent) people.' Sommer considers such an interpretive revision unlikely. The reference is interesting, a wink to the wise, but not interpretive.[69] On the other hand, references can be understood too shallowly. Hays pointed to many scriptural allusions in Paul that had been largely ignored, and consequently scholars had little comprehension of their significance.[70] Yet that significance remained under the surface, waiting to be found. Ultimately, disputes over a claim that a reference is metaleptic are decided by the persuasiveness of the reading presented.

Evaluating the Interpretation

It is difficult, if not impossible, to be certain of the exact type and extent of interplay intended by the author for particular allusions. The very nature of allusion leaves it to the reader to draw from the possible interplay of texts what appears to be a satisfactory and faithful interpretation.[71] Still, not all interpretations are of equal merit. When considering the interpretation of an allusion, it is important to evaluate it from several angles. Hays proposes the following:[72]

- *Historical plausibility*: Is it plausible that a first-century author would use a passage in the manner proposed?[73] Does it correspond to what is known about first-century biblical interpretation and traditions on the sense of the referent passage?
- *History of interpretation*: Was the reference seen by previous interpreters in the history of the church? Was it interpreted in a similar

---

68   Robert Alter, *The Pleasures of Reading in an Ideological Age* (New York: Simon and Schuster, 1989), p. 124.
69   Sommer, *Prophet*, p. 16.
70   Cf. Hays, *Echoes*, pp. 6–12, 35–83, 159.
71   Cf. Garner, *From Homer to Tragedy*, p. 186.
72   Hays, *Echoes*, pp. 30–32.
73   See Hays, *Echoes*, p. 18.

manner? Early readers of Mark exist in the Gospels of Matthew and Luke and may provide evidence that an allusion was recognized. Hays writes a caution on this point: not finding a parallel interpretation in the tradition does not invalidate an interpretation. With the passing of very few years, the key issues facing early Christians changed. What were issues for Paul were not necessarily issues for Mark. What were issues for Mark were not necessarily issues for Matthew and Luke. Later readers in different circumstances put different questions to the texts, and so they may have missed what was originally the focus.

- *Satisfaction*: Does the reading proposed make good sense of the new work? Does it help one understand the meaning of the section under study or of the work as a whole? Has the study brought to light interpretations previously overlooked? This is Hays' most subjective guideline, in an already subjective project. Yet, this subjectivity is the reality of interpretation, and the equally subjective satisfaction of a penetrating reading is its reward.

Reader Recognition

One of the concerns about literary readings of the Bible is that they sometimes seem overly subtle. This is certainly a potential problem for the interpretation of allusion. Are we pasting modern literary practices onto ancient works created according to very different rules? How realistic is it to imagine that New Testament authors used allusions in the way described or that first-century readers would have had the tools to see it, if they did?

As we have seen in preceding sections, allusion is not a modern literary device, but has a long history, a history that extends to both Testaments. Allusion is in fact a biblical literary device, used with great sophistication.

The more difficult question is that of reader recognition. How often could first-century readers have been expected to catch the intricate and nuanced interactions of allusive texts presented by modern scholars?[74] It might be said that the same complaint could be lodged against a great number of scholarly conclusions in other areas, as well, but such a response would not negate the problem.

Hays', Sommer's, and others' arguments about the meaning of the text suffer if the texts' intended readers read them with little to no sophistication. Sommer makes that point explicitly. According to his definition, unless the historical audience of Isaiah recognized, identified, and realized the interpretive impact of a reference, that reference cannot be called an allusion.[75]

---

74 Cf. Brown, *Death*, 1, p. 10; Best, *Temptation*, p. lxiii.
75 Sommer, *Prophet*, pp. 12, 15–16.

Unfortunately, despite his emphasis on the necessity of reader recognition and historical study, he never makes an argument for reader recognition actually occurring in Deutero-Isaiah's ancient audiences. Like Sommer, Hays does not address the practice of reading for Paul's audiences. Ironically, though he makes little argument for Paul's audience having caught allusions, he makes a fairly good case that Paul includes an allusion that was almost impossible for his audience to catch. Hays points out that Paul's statement, 'the Rock was Christ' (1 Cor. 10.4), is indecipherable to a Greek audience that does not know the Hebrew form of Deuteronomy 32. Though the Hebrew form of the text uses 'rock' (צוּר) as a metaphor for God at several points (vv. 4, 15, 18, 30-31), the LXX translates according to the metaphorical, not literal, sense and uses θεός instead. Judging from the extant LXX texts, the reader of Greek alone cannot catch the allusion. Yet the allusion is there, supported by an allusion to Deut. 32.21 at 1 Cor. 10.22 and the general use of wilderness imagery in the chapter.[76]

Reader recognition comes up in a discussion of whether Chronicles was written as a replacement for Samuel–Kings or was allusive, with interpretive interplay between the books. Fishbane concludes the former, T. Willi the latter. Willi argues that the only way Chronicles could be understood was in light of Samuel–Kings and that this was indeed the way ancient readers understood it. Fishbane disagrees: 'There is, first of all, no evidence to justify the view that ancient Israelite readers knew such historical sources as Samuel–Kings, or that the Chronicler expected or intended a synoptic-comparative reading of his work in relation to them.'[77] He continues with arguments from the presentation and style of Chronicles but, like Willi, his concern is with the reader: is it probable that the ancient reader dealt with Chronicles, Samuel and Kings – whole books – synoptic-style?

These two examples show that reader recognition is a concern not only for those sceptical of a sophisticated approach to allusion in Scripture, but for the very scholars who use it. Still, though it is easier to assess the practices of first-century authors than first-century readers (which is saying something), reading in the early period is not entirely inscrutable, and one can draw from what is known a faint sketch of what first-century readers might be expected to catch.

First, it is appropriate to note that the issue is not black and white. It is equally unreasonable to assert either that no first-century reader would have been able to understand a subtle use of allusion or that every first-century reader was sharp and insightful. Readers differ now. They differed then. Again, it is equally unreasonable to assert that early readers would have caught every allusion in a New Testament work or that every allusion would

---

76 Hays, *Echoes*, p. 94; cf. pp. 91–94.
77 Fishbane, *Biblical Interpretation*, p. 382.

have passed by unnoticed. The question here again is one of degree. Patricia Tull Willey notes that there are always 'real problems of slippage between the allusions a writer may intend and the allusions a reader may recognize'. Whether the reader catches the allusion depends on the reader's own assessment of the text and 'repertoire of texts and memories'. If the author is far removed from the culture or knowledge base of the reader, it is likely that allusions will be missed.[78]

The endeavour is not helped by a very strong early reading of Mark. As mentioned previously, Mark was damned with faint praise by Papias and suffered considerable neglect by the church fathers. Fortunately, however, two early and talented readings of Mark survived in the Gospels of Matthew and Luke.[79] Authors of both gospels recognized allusions to Scripture in Mark. Matthew, in particular, clarifies some of those allusions by rendering them closer to the original passage or by making them explicit. For example, Mark 13.14 mentions the 'desolating sacrilege' (τὸ βδέλυγμα τῆς ἐρημώσεως), probably an implicit reference to Dan. 12.11. The parallel in Matt. 24.15 reads, 'when you see the desolating sacrilege standing in the holy place, *as was spoken of by the prophet Daniel.*'

The Introduction to this study noted that Mark 1.2-3 contains allusions to Mal. 3.1 and Isa. 40.3, and that the allusions are used to identify John the Baptist as Elijah. Luke wrote a very different opening to his gospel, which nevertheless leaves large clues regarding his reading of Mark. Consider the following portion of Zechariah's speech:

And you, child, will be called the prophet of the Most High;
for you will go *before the Lord to prepare his ways*. (Luke 1.76)

Here Luke uses the Isa. 40.3 portion of the Markan quotation in a speech about John the Baptist. Luke seems also to catch the reference to Mal. 3.1; he alludes to a later passage from that chapter in Gabriel's speech, also regarding John the Baptist:

With the spirit and power of Elijah he will go before him, *to turn the hearts of parents to their children* and the disobedient to the wisdom of the righteous, to make ready a people prepared for the Lord. (Luke 1.17, alluding to Mal. 3.23).

Such examples are easily multiplied. But Matthew and Luke are only two readers, two exceptional readers. Was such sophisticated reading widespread? That is a more difficult question to answer. One can begin by asking the question Fishbane poses: did the readers know the material alluded to? One might ask further, did they know it well enough to catch subtle allusions? To

---

78 Willey, *Remember*, pp. 78–79.
79 That is, assuming that the theory of Markan priority is correct.

assume that readers caught allusions, one must assume a rather high degree of cultural literacy. Robert Alter writes that this is 'something of a problem for [modern] contemporaries, who often come to literary texts from a background of loose canons, little reading, and languid memory', but it is 'an easy assumption in traditional societies with fixed literary canons and a high capacity for verbatim retention of texts'.[80] Joseph Fitzmyer backs up Alter's claim, suggesting that some Jews memorized Scripture word for word.[81]

There is also some evidence that early Christians studied Scripture diligently, e.g., in the references to such knowledge by the Apostolic Fathers:[82]

> For you have understanding, you have a good understanding of the sacred Scriptures, beloved, and you have studied the oracles of God. (1 Clem. 53.1)[83]

> Now I imagine that you are not ignorant that the living 'Church is the body of Christ'. For the scripture says, 'God made man male and female'; the male is Christ, the female is the church. And moreover the books and the Apostles declare that the Church belongs not to the present, but has existed from the beginning. (2 Clem. 14.2)

> For I am confident that you are well versed in the Scriptures, and from you nothing is hid ... (Polycarp, Phil. 12.1)

Knowledge of Scripture is presupposed in Ignatius' statement to the Philadelphians:

> For I heard some men saying, 'if I find it not in the charters (τοῖς ἀρχείοις) in the Gospel I do not believe.' (Ignatius, Phld. 8.2)

Scripture study is also presupposed in a similar statement in Rom. 15.4:

> For whatever was written in former days was written for our instruction, so that by steadfastness and by the encouragement of the Scriptures we might have hope.

Study of Scripture is also presupposed in the writings of the second-century apologists. For example, Justin, Tatian, and Theophilus say that they became Christians through Scripture study, and Justin recommends Scripture study broadly to non-Christians.[84] While it is difficult to know just how widespread

---

80   Alter, *Pleasures*, p. 119.
81   Joseph Fitzmyer, 'Judaic Studies and the Gospels: The Seminar', in *The Relationships Among the Gospels: An Interdisciplinary Dialogue* (ed. William O. Walker, Jr; San Antonio: Trinity University Press, 1978), p. 246.
82   On this issue, see also Harry Y. Gamble, *Books and Readers in the Early Church: A History of Early Christian Texts* (New Haven: Yale University Press, 1995), pp. 8–10, 212–13.
83   All quotations of the Apostolic Fathers are from Kirsopp Lake, trans., *Apostolic Fathers*, (LCL; 2 vols; Cambridge: Harvard University Press, 1912–13).
84   Justin, *Dial.* 7-8; Tatian, *Orat.* 29; Theophilus, *Autol.* 1.14. Cf. Justin, *1 Apol.* 44.

such extensive knowledge of Scripture was (for example, it seems unlikely that the ordinary labourer would be able to devote the time necessary to know the texts in the impressive manner of the rabbis), it is clear that such knowledge existed within both Jewish and Gentile Christian communities.

It appears that the ancients often read in community, not alone, as modern readers tend to do. New Testament documents seem to have been read aloud to a group and explained by the reader or another teacher.[85] Paul's letters were delivered by messengers who were acquainted with Paul's thought.[86] Consider the conversation between Philip and the Ethiopian eunuch in Acts 8.27-35. Philip asks, 'Do you understand what you are reading?' The eunuch answers, 'How can I, unless someone guides me?' In *The Shepherd of Hermas* 2.4, Grapte is to exhort the widows and orphans from a copy of the revelation. Current scholarship tends to see the gospels as written for a particular community from within that community. If that is accurate, such communities had still greater access to the thoughts of the author.

That texts were read in community and expounded alleviates some of the difficulty of establishing recognition for the allusions. One need not think of each member of the original audience reading Mark at her own desk and catching and relishing sophisticated literary allusions to Scripture. Instead, one might think of an original community that was *taught* to see the allusions. Dibelius suggested that early Christians studied certain Scripture passages 'in connection with the Passion story'. Because previous study connected the narrative with the passages to which it alludes, the informed listener would catch the allusions.[87]

Greek rhetorical handbooks present another interesting bit of evidence in favour of reader recognition in the Greco-Roman world. Demetrius states that it is an insult to the reader to draw everything out; the reader should be left with a significant role in the production of meaning:

> [N]ot everything should be given lengthy treatment with full details but some points should be left for our hearer to grasp and infer for himself. If he infers what you have omitted, he no longer just listens to you but acts as your witness, one too who is predisposed in your favor since he feels he has been intelligent and you are the person who has given him this opportunity to exercise his intelligence. In fact, to tell your hearer everything as if he were a fool is to reveal that you think him one. (Demetrius, *On Style* 222)[88]

---

85   Cf. Gamble, *Books and Readers*, pp. 204–7. This was made necessary by the low rates of literacy in the ancient world. Gamble (*Books*, pp. 10, 231) estimates a literacy rate among Christians of no more than 10–20 per cent. He (*Books*, pp. 7, 19) notes that among Jews, literacy rates were higher, but still not up to modern, Western standards.

86   Cf. 1 Thess. 5.27; Rom. 16.1; Phil. 2.28; and Gamble, *Books*, p. 206.

87   Dibelius, *Tradition*, pp. 185–87; also Dodd, *Historical Tradition*, p. 40.

88   D. C. Innes, trans., in *Ancient Literary Criticism: The Principal Texts in New Translations* (ed. D. A. Russell and M. Winterbottom; Oxford: Clarendon, 1972).

Methodology: Interpretive Impact

Demetrius is not speaking of allusions specifically, but he points to a general principle that is relevant to the topic: allowing the hearer to draw out the meaning of a work increases its impact.

> In some cases brevity, especially aposiopesis, creates grandeur, since some things are more impressive if they are not openly expressed but merely implied. (Demetrius, *On Style* 103)

Fishbane, too, notes that involving the reader in the text, and providing some surprises, gives a work 'rhetorical punch'.[89]

Hays points to this aspect of reading in his discussions of some Pauline allusions. For example, regarding the implications of an allusion to Job 13.16 in Phil. 1.19, Hays states that Paul's figurative language 'invites the reader to participate in an imaginative act necessary to comprehend the portrayal of Paul's condition offered here'.[90] He makes a similar point in a discussion of Paul's use in 2 Cor. 8.15 of the manna tradition from Exod. 16.18:

> Paul can use the manna story to good effect in depicting the Corinthians' material "abundance" (2 Cor. 8:14) as a superfluous store that could and should be made available to supply "the wants of the saints." (Cf. the warning in Deut. 8:11-20 about the dangers of complacency that can accompany material prosperity.) Thus, his application of the story taps and draws out hermeneutic potential that is already fairly oozing out of the Exodus narrative – or, more precisely, Paul taps Exodus 16 and then walks away, leaving the reader to draw out the sap. If we as readers demand our significations drawn, processed, and canned for sale, we will miss the sweetness here.[91]

Reading is a cooperative process between author and reader. Ancients as well as moderns understood that appreciation of a work is significantly increased when the reader is given room to discover elements of meaning below the surface.

In practice, some readers would have been more attuned to allusions than others. Some allusions may have been recognized only on the second or later reading; some allusions may have gone unrecognized until they became the object of scholarly scrutiny. Yet evidence regarding early readers of Mark and early reading practices present *prima facie* evidence that some members of the original audience of Mark would have been able to recognize at least some of its allusions to Scripture.

---

89 Fishbane, *Biblical Interpretation*, pp. 427–28.
90 Hays, *Echoes*, p. 23.
91 Hays, *Echoes*, p. 90.

Conclusion

- Allusions are often metaleptic. That is, the allusion interacts with the referent, playing with its meaning, and that interaction affects and deepens the meaning of the referring text.
- The extent of the interplay with the surrounding text of the referent will be determined for each case, though one may assume for some authors that at least the immediate context (the verse or two surrounding the referent text) is meant. The interplay operates according to the interpretive standards of the author's time and culture.
- Literary allusion is not a modern phenomenon and is found extensively in ancient texts, including in both Testaments. Correspondingly, we find evidence of ancient readers who recognized allusions and their meaning. Some readers would have been better prepared than others for this endeavour, but this difficulty would have been alleviated by the communal reading of texts.

3. Testing Proposed Allusions

Having established literary guidelines for determining what allusions are and how to locate them, it is time to examine the possible allusions in the Markan passion narrative. The chapter is divided into three parts. The first presents an overview of the results. The second discusses some of the important suggestions that failed to meet the criteria. The third argues in favour of the allusions that met the criteria.

Overview of Suggested Allusions

As a step towards locating the allusions in the Markan passion narrative, suggestions were gathered from a number of commentaries, monographs, and articles.[1] For the roughly 120 verses belonging to the Markan passion narrative, almost 270 references were suggested in those works.[2] The following tables list those suggestions. One of the difficulties in sorting out the suggestions is that scholars have not always been precise in their terminology with regard to allusions and thematic parallels. While an effort was made to eliminate them, the tables below may contain some passages that were

---

1   James A. Brooks, *Mark* (NAC 23; Nashville: Broadman, 1991); Adela Y. Collins, *Mark: A Commentary* (ed. Harold Attridge; Hermeneia; Minneapolis: Fortress, 2007); C. E. B. Cranfield, *The Gospel According to Saint Mark: An Introduction and Commentary* (CGTC; Cambridge: Cambridge University Press, 1959); J. Duncan M. Derrett, *The Making of Mark: The Scriptural Bases of the Earliest Gospel* (2 vols; Shipston-on-Stour, Engl.: Drinkwater, 1985); Donahue, *Mark*; Joachim Gnilka, *Das Evangelium nach Markus* (EKK; 2 vols; Zürich: Benziger, 1978–79); Walter Grundmann, *Das Evangelium nach Markus* (THKNT 2; 7th revised edn; Berlin: Evangelische Verlagsanstalt, 1977); Gundry, *Mark*; Ernst Haenchen, *Der Weg Jesu: Eine Erklärung des Markus-Evangeliums und der kanonischen Parallelen* (Berlin: Alfred Töpelmann, 1966); van Iersel, *Mark*; Juel, *Mark*; Kee, 'Function'; Lindars, *New Testament Apologetic*; Lührmann, *Das Markusevangelium*; Moo, *Old Testament*; Rudolf Pesch, *Das Markusevangelium* (HTKNT; 2 vols; Freiburg: Herder, 1976–77); John Reumann, 'Psalm 22 at the Cross: Lament and Thanksgiving for Jesus Christ', *Int* 28 (1974), pp. 39–58; Walter Schmithals, *Das Evangelium nach Markus* (ÖTK; 2 vols; rev. edn; Gütersloh: Gütersloher Verlagshaus Mohn, 1986); Schnackenburg, *St Mark*; Eduard Schweizer, *The Good News According to Mark* (Richmond: John Knox, 1970); Vincent Taylor, *The Gospel According to St Mark* (London: Macmillan, 1966).
2   Kee (*Community*, p. 45; cf. p. 189 n. 157) claims that there are hundreds of allusions in the Gospel of Mark.

considered only to be parallels of some kind, not allusions. The tables are not meant to be the definitive word on any particular scholar or exhaustive of the proposed allusions for the Markan passion narrative. Rather they are representative of the kinds of suggestions made.

The suggestions are sorted into three columns, according to the degree of verbal correspondence between the Markan verse and the suggested passage. Those with no significant words corresponding are shown in col. 3. Those corresponding in only a single common word are shown in col. 2, along with the corresponding word.[3] All suggestions that have verbal correspondence greater than a single common word, for example, two common words or a single unusual word, are listed in col. 1. Suggestions in col. 1 are listed roughly in order of the strength of the correspondence. Suggestions that have been accepted as allusions are shown in bold type. The texts for suggested allusions are examined in detail in Appendices B–C.

Suggested allusions to Mark 14–15
An asterisk (*) indicates that there are no suggestions for this verse.

Markan v.	1. Correspondence Greater than One Common Word	2. Correspondence of a Single Common Word	3. No Significant Words Corresponding
14.1	**Hos. 6.2** 2 Chron. 35.17 Ps. 37.32 Ps. 10.7-9	Ps. 52.4 (δόλος) Ps. 35.20 (δόλος) Prov. 12.6-7 (δόλιος)	
14.2*			
14.3	Cant. 1.12-13	Exod. 30.25, 34 (μύρον) Num. 12.10 (λεπροῦ/λεπρῶσα)	
14.4-6*			
14.7	Deut. 15.11		
14.8		Isa. 53.9 (ἐποίησεν; ἐνταφιασμόν/ταφῆς)[3]	Ps. 41.2, 6, 8, 10
14.9*			

---

3 If the passages present the same form of the word, that form is shown. If not, the corresponding word is shown in lexical form. Verbal correspondence of a root, not of an actual word, is usually rather weak and thus may be listed in this column even when the words used are not particularly common or when there is more than one common word cor-responding (cf. Mark 14.8/Isa. 53.9). The same may be true for correspondence between Greek and Hebrew (cf. Mark 14.56/Ps. 109.2-5).

Testing Proposed Allusions

Markan v.	1. Correspondence Greater than One Common Word	2. Correspondence of a Single Common Word	3. No Significant Words Corresponding
14.10	Isa. 53.6, 12	Dan. 6 (ἀπῆλθεν or קריבו)	Ps. 41.10 Ps. 55.13-16 Ps. 109.4-5, 8
14.11	Zech. 11.12-13		
14.12	Exod. 12.1-6, 14-20 Deut. 16.2	Lam. 2.21 (ἡμέρᾳ)	Isa. 53.7
14.12-16	1 Sam. 10.1-10		
14.14	Jer. 14.8		
14.15-17*			
14.18	Ps. 41.10		
14.19*			
14.20	Ruth 2.14		Ps. 41.10
14.21		Isa. 53.12 (παραδίδωμι)	
14.22*			
14.23	Ps. 75.9 Ps. 116.13	Lam. 4.21 (ποτήριον)	
14.24	**Exod. 24.8** Zech. 9.11 Isa. 53.12 Gen. 15.10, 17-18	Jer. 31.31 (διαθήκη)	Lam. 5.9
14.25	Isa. 65.13	Isa. 25.6 (πίνω) Isa. 62.9 (πίνω)	
14.26*			
14.27	**Zech. 13.7** 2 Chron. 18.16 Num. 27.17 Jdt. 11.19 Ezek. 34.5	1 Kgs 22.17 (ποιμήν) Ps. 119.165 (σκανδαλισθήσεσθε/σκάνδαλον)	
14.28		Zech. 13.8-9 (προάξω/הבאתי)	
14.29*			

Markan v.	1. Correspondence Greater than One Common Word	2. Correspondence of a Single Common Word	3. No Significant Words Corresponding
14.30	Isa. 31.7		
14.31*			
14.32-42	Ps. 119.145-50		
14.33	Sir. 30.9	Ps. 31.10 (ἀδημονεῖν/צר)	Ps. 22.15 Ps. 39.13 Ps. 42.12 Ps. 62.3 Ps. 116.11 Isa. 53.12
14.34	**Ps. 42.6,12; 43.5** Jon. 4.8-9 Sir. 37.2 Ps. 6.4 Isa. 53.12 Ps. 31.10-11, 23 Ps. 69.1-5	Ps. 22.16 (θανάτου) Ps. 116.3 (θανάτου)	Ps. 22.20
14.35*			
14.36	Job 42.2 Zech. 8.6 Jer. 25.15, 17, 28 Ps. 75.9 Isa. 51.17, 22 Ezek. 23.31-34 Jer. 49.12	Gen.18.14 (δυνατά/μὴ ἀδυνατεῖ) Jer. 51.7 (ποτήριον) Ps. 116.13 (ποτήριον) Ps. 22.15-16 (πάντα) Ps. 31.23 (λέγω)	Ps. 43.1-5 Wis. 2.13, 16, 18
14.37			Ps. 31.13 Ps. 69.11
14.38	Ps. 51.13-14		Dan. 12.10
14.39*			
14.40		Gen. 44.16 (εὗρεν)	
14.41	Isa. 53.6, 12	Ps. 116.6-10 (ἀναπαύεσθε/ἀνάπαυσιν) Deut. 1.6 (λέγω; ἀπέχει/רב לכם) Deut. 2.3 (λέγω; ἀπέχει/רב לכם)	
14.42-43*			
14.44		Lam. 1.14, 19 (δίδωμι)	

Testing Proposed Allusions

Markan v.	1. Correspondence Greater than One Common Word	2. Correspondence of a Single Common Word	3. No Significant Words Corresponding
14.45		Prov. 27.6 (κατεφίλησεν/φιλήματα)	Ps. 41.10
14.46*			
14.47	Ezek. 23.24-31 Ezek. 21.8-10	Gen. 49.5-7 (μάχαιραν/מכרה) Lam. 1.18, 19 (ἀρχιερέως/יערeῖς)	
14.48	1 Sam. 17.45 2 Sam. 12.10	Isa. 53.12 (λῃστήν/פשעים)	
14.49			Isa. 53.7, 12 Zech. 13.7
14.50		1 Sam. 17.51 (ἔφυγον)	Zech. 13.7
14.51-52	Gen. 39.12 Amos 2.16 Isa. 31.8-9	Isa. 3.4 (νεανίσκος) Lam. 2.21 (νεανίσκος)	Lam. 1.19
14.53			Ps. 31.14
14.54	Ps. 38.12 Isa. 44.10-20	Isa. 50.11 (φῶς)	
14.55	**Ps. 37.32**	Ps. 54.5 (ζητέω)	Lam. 1.15
14.56	**Exod. 20.16//** **Deut. 5.20** Dan. Sus. 61 Ps. 27.12	Ps. 109.2-5 (ἐψευδομαρτύρουν/שקר)	Deut. 5.6 Ps. 31.14
14.56-59	Ps. 35.11-12		
14.58	Dan. 2.34, 45 Hos. 6.2 *Tg. Isa.* 53.5		
14.59-60*			
14.61	**Isa. 36.21** **Ps. 2.7**	Ps. 38.11-18 (ἐσιώπα/אלם) Ps. 39.10 (ἐσιώπα/אלם) Isa. 53.7 (ἐσιώπα/אלם) 2 Sam. 7.14 (υἱός) Wis. 2.10-20 (υἱός) Ps. 86.14-17 (υἱός) Ps. 89.26-27 (σὺ εἶ/εἶ σύ)	Ps. 22.16 Ps. 27.12-13 Ps. 35.11-12 Ps. 37.12-14 Ps. 37.32-33 Ps. 63.10 Ps. 70.2-4 Ps. 109.2-4, 16 Isa. 53.12

72 The Use of Scripture in the Markan Passion Narrative

Markan v.	1. Correspondence Greater than One Common Word	2. Correspondence of a Single Common Word	3. No Significant Words Corresponding
14.62	**Dan. 7.13** **Ps. 110.1** Exod. 3.14	Zech. 12.6 (ἐκ δεξιῶν) Zech. 12.10 (ὁράω)	
14.63*			
14.64	Dan. Sus. 53 Jer. 26.11 Lev. 24.16	Wis. 2.20 (θάνατος)	
14.65	**Isa. 50.6** Mic. 4.14 1 Kgs 22.24-25	Isa. 53.3-5 (τὸ πρόσωπον)	Isa. 3.4 Isa. 11.1-4 Isa. 50.10 Lam. 5.8
14.66-72		Ps. 39.12 (ἄνθρωπον)	Ps. 31.12 Ps. 88.9, 19
14.72			2 Sam. 19.5 Isa. 50.11
15.1	Judg. 15.9-13	Ps. 27.12 (παραδίδωμι) Ps. 74.19 (παραδίδωμι) Ps. 119.121 (παραδίδωμι) Isa. 53.6, 12 (παραδίδωμι)	Judg. 13.25
15.2		Ps. 119.46 (βασιλεύς) Zech. 9.9 (βασιλεύς)	
15.2-5			Ps. 37.12 Ps. 109.3
15.4-5			Ps. 38.13-14 Isa. 53.7
15.5		Isa. 52.15 (θαυμάζω)	Ps. 38.12-14 Ps. 109.4 Isa. 53.7, 9
15.6			Isa. 53.12
15.7		Isa. 53.9 (ποιέω)	Lam. 3.58
15.8-12*			
15.13		Ps. 22.6 (κράζω)	Isa. 53.3
15.14		Ps. 38.20-21 (κακός) Ps. 109.5 (κακός)	

Testing Proposed Allusions

Markan v.	1. Correspondence Greater than One Common Word	2. Correspondence of a Single Common Word	3. No Significant Words Corresponding
		Isa. 53.9 (ποιέω)	
15.15		Isa. 53.5-6, 12 (παραδίδωμι)	Isa. 58.6 Isa. 59.3 Isa. 63.3 Zech. 9.11-12
15.16*			
15.17	Zech. 3.1-5	Zech. 6.11 (στέφανος) Lam. 5.16, 18 (στέφανος) Exod. 3.22 (περιτιθέασιν/שׂם)	Tg. Isa. 55.13
15.18*			
15.19	Isa. 50.6	Isa. 53.4-5 (ἔτυπτον/מכה) Mic. 4.14 (ἔτυπτον/יכּ')	
15.20a			Ps. 22.6 Isa. 53.3
15.20b		Lev. 24.14 (ἐξάγω) Num. 15.35-36 (ἐξάγω)	
15.21-22*			
15.23	Prov. 31.6-7	Ps. 69.22 (δίδωμι)	
15.24	**Ps. 22.19**		Ps. 22.16 Lam. 1.14 Lam. 5.12-13
15.25-26*			
15.27			Ps. 22.7 Isa. 53.12
15.29-30	**Ps. 22.8-9** Lam. 2.15 Jer. 18.16 Ps. 109.25	Lam. 1.12 (παραπορευόμενοι)	Isa. 53.12 Wis. 2.17-18
15.31	Isa. 46.1-2	Ps. 22.9 (σῴζω)	Ps. 89.50-51
15.32	Zeph. 3.15	Ps. 42.11 (ὀνειδίζω αὐτόν/με) Ps. 69.10 (ὀνειδίζω αὐτόν/σε) Ps. 31.12 (ὠνείδιζον/ὄνειδος) Wis. 2.17-18 (ἴδωμεν)	Ps. 22.13-14, 17

74 The Use of Scripture in the Markan Passion Narrative

Markan v.	1. Correspondence Greater than One Common Word	2. Correspondence of a Single Common Word	3. No Significant Words Corresponding
15.33	**Amos 8.9-10** Exod. 10.21-23 Isa. 60.2 Isa. 13.9-10 Jer. 4.27-28	Isa. 50.2-3 (σκότος)	Isa. 34.4 Jer. 15.6-9
15.34	**Ps. 22.2** Gen. 27.34	Joel 4.16 (φωνή) Ps. 42.10-11 (εἰς/διὰ τί)	
15.35*			
15.36	**Ps. 69.22** Wis. 2.17		Ps. 69.2 Lam. 3.15, 19
15.37		Ps. 31.23 (φωνή)	Num. 33.38 Ps. 68.20 Lam. 1.19 Lam. 5.13
15.38	Exod. 26.31-33 Lev. 21.23		Isa. 25.7-8 Lam. 2.17
15.39		Isa. 52.13 (ἰδού)	Ps. 22.29
15.40	Ps. 38.12		
15.41-42*			
15.43	1 Sam. 1.1		Isa. 53.9, 12
15.44-45*			
15.46	1 Sam. 14.33 Lam. 3.53	1 Sam. 7.12 (λίθον)	Isa. 53.9
15.47*			

Analysis

Many (though not all) of the suggestions in col. 1 have significant verbal correspondence. Deciding whether those passages are allusions or non-allusive parallels of some kind can be a matter of judgement. The suggestions in the second and third columns correspond in only a single common word (such as 'son' or 'stone') or in no significant words whatsoever. Almost two-thirds of the suggestions fall into these two columns.[4] That is, most suggestions are motivated by factors other than verbal correspondence.

Sometimes the motivating factor is a theological conviction with a basis outside the Gospel of Mark. Notice that Isa. 52.13–53.12 appears very often in cols 2–3, 25 times. It occurs only four times in the first column (once more for the *Isaiah Targum*). None are judged here to be allusions; only Mark 14.24 is a moderate, though not strong, candidate. Though verbal correspondence is weak, many scholars consider this passage the foundation (or one of two or three bases) of Mark's interpretation of Jesus' passion.[5] Isaiah 53 has long been seen by the church as best fitting Jesus Christ, and that is, as Morna Hooker notes, a perfectly good spiritual insight of the church.[6] That does not mean that the author of the Gospel of Mark must have interpreted Jesus in this manner. Similarly, other passages used by other early Christian authors are suggested as allusions in Mark, though little or nothing in Markan wording indicates such an allusion. It is important to judge the allusions in Mark from the text of Mark first, and only if there is sufficient verbal correspondence should one appeal to other early Christian texts.

Of course, not all the suggestions in cols 2–3 are sparked entirely by factors external to Mark. Some suggestions are motivated by other genuine allusions elsewhere in the Markan narrative. For example, the suggestion of an allusion to Ps. 37.12-14 in Mark 14.61 could be sparked by an allusion to Psalm 37 in Mark 14.55. Many of the suggestions to Psalm 22 in cols 2–3 are inspired by the three allusions to that psalm in the crucifixion scene.

Some of the suggested allusions share an unusual word without other connections between the passages. For example, the place name Αρμαθαιμ occurs in 1 Sam. 1.1 and Mark 15.43. Other suggestions reflect thematic parallels; for example the several parallels for Mark 14.61 containing the word υἱός are passages in the Old Testament where someone is described as a 'son' of God.

Surprisingly often, the above allusions were suggested without any justification. Pesch does more than most when he asserts that in Mark 14.55, Ps. 37.32 '*ist gewiss im Blick*' and moves on.[7] This study supports Pesch's

---

4   99 in col. 1 (37 per cent), 84 in col. 2 (31 per cent), and 85 in col. 3 (32 per cent).
5   See discussion of the Suffering Servant, starting on p. 76. These scholars include, among others, Lindars, *New Testament Apologetic*; Moo, *Old Testament*; Senior, *Passion of Jesus*; Watts, *Isaiah's New Exodus*.
6   Hooker, *Jesus*, p. 163.
7   Pesch, *Markusevangelium*, 2, p. 431.

conclusion. Yet declaring a passage 'certainly in view' is hardly sufficient to establish the case. The connections between the passages should be demonstrated, not assumed. This chapter will take up that task for accepted allusions.

Falling Short

Before moving on to that task, it is first necessary to discuss in greater detail some of the suggestions that have been eliminated. Some of them have received significant scholarly support, many of those relating to the Suffering Servant or to passages regarding the suffering righteous. In addition, the section treats Perrin's suggestion that Mark 14.62 is based on Zech. 12.10 and two suggested allusions to Susanna, which have not received much scholarly attention, but which are worthy of note nevertheless.

The Suffering Servant

The Suffering Servant depicted in Isa. 52.13–53.12 as a model for understanding Jesus' suffering and death is one of the commonest and most venerable Christian interpretations of Scripture. As early as *1 Clement*, Isaiah 53 was quoted with regard to the meaning of Jesus' passion.[8] There is some evidence of such an interpretation in Rom. 4.25, and thus the interpretation may have begun with Paul.[9]

Some scholars insist that this interpretation begins, not with Paul, but with Jesus, and it continues in the gospels.[10] Debate on the topic has sometimes been impassioned. William Bellinger, Jr, and William Farmer, in their introduction to *Jesus and the Suffering Servant: Isaiah 53 and Christian Origins*, state the theological concerns behind that passion:

> We can phrase the question even more precisely: 'Did Jesus interpret God's will for Israel, and therefore for himself and for his disciples, in terms of the suffering Servant of Isaiah 52:13-53:12?'
>
> Before proceeding, the reader has a right to know what is at stake in how this question is answered. What is at stake is how members of the body of Christ understand the essence of their faith. The essence of the Christian faith (without which Christianity is indistinguishable from the faith of those who worship the God of Abraham, Isaac, and Jacob yet do not know themselves to be Christians) is a ready

---

8   *1 Clem.* 16; cf. *Barn.* 4.1-2; 5.2; Justin, *Dial.* 111.
9   Hooker ('Did the Use', in Bellinger and Farmer, *Jesus and the Servant*, p. 103), famous for her critique of the idea that the Servant was a central interpretation of the passion in early New Testament books, agreed that the correspondence between Rom. 4.25 and Isa. 53.11-12 meets her strict requirements for an allusion. See also the uses of Isaiah 53 in Matt. 8.17; Luke 22.37; John 12.38; Acts 8.32-33; 1 Pet. 2.22, 24-25.
10   For instance, Dodd, *According to the Scriptures*, pp. 91–96, 109–10; Moo, *Old Testament*, p. 168; Otto Betz, 'Jesus and Isaiah 53', in Bellinger and Farmer, *Jesus and the Servant*, pp. 83–87.

assent to the affirmation that 'Christ died for our sins' (Gal. 1:14). ... This raises the question whether it would have been possible for Jesus to have acted so unnaturally as to have died for the unjust without reference to Isaiah's teaching about the righteous Servant of the Lord, who poured out his soul to death and bore the sins of many (Isa. 53:11-12).[11]

They admit that it is *possible* that Jesus' death could have been redemptive if Jesus saw his death in another way: 'At least it is possible in the sense that one can hardly assert the contrary – that it is *impossible*.' The inevitable limitations of knowledge make such a concession necessary. But it is clear that the authors think this unlikely, and they state that history does not deal in mere possibilities, but in probabilities.[12]

Bellinger and Farmer are convinced that the foundation of Christianity rests on whether Jesus understood himself to be the Servant of the Lord as depicted in Isaiah 53. That being the case, the only thing left to do is to prove it true. Often a very slim body of evidence appears sufficient to the task. In fact, the very slimness of that evidence is used as further evidence for the conclusion. The very obscurity of an alleged allusion is considered indicative of its centrality – the allusion and interpretation are so fundamentally accepted as to be assumed by author and audience alike. In contrast, clear allusions are taken to indicate marginal interpretations, novel ideas that had to be spelled out by the author.[13] After all, if Jesus taught his disciples that he suffered as the Servant of the Lord and that teaching was widespread, New Testament authors needed only passing and vague allusions to it, and their audiences would understand them. Consequently, very slight verbal correspondence is taken as proof of an allusion to a well-known passage.

This is a rather extraordinary way for historical-critical scholarship to proceed. That some modern scholars are unable to see how Jesus' death could otherwise be meaningfully interpreted does not necessitate that Jesus and the New Testament authors were equally constrained.[14] It is *possible* that

---

11 Bellinger and Farmer, 'Introduction', in *Jesus and the Servant*, pp. 1–2.
12 Bellinger and Farmer, 'Introduction', pp. 2–3.
13 Dodd (*According to the Scriptures*, pp. 18–23, 127) writes that what was part of traditional, early Christian interpretation is assumed in Pauline letters and some other New Testament passages. Dodd generally avoids using this procedure, however, to locate allusions. Instead, he examines the repeated use of particular passages in fairly clear (or at least debatable) allusions. Dodd's procedure is well suited to his goal. It is less reasonable to take his initial observation – that traditional interpretation is assumed in the Pauline letters, Acts, and elsewhere – as support for the existence of allusions when there is very little verbal correspondence. This procedure is used particularly often to justify alleged allusions to Isaiah 53. See for example Lindars, *New Testament Apologetic*, pp. 78–79; Moo, *Old Testament*, pp. 169–70.
14 It is not clear that all modern scholars feel this limitation. Many see Jesus' death according to other patterns. For example, Kee (*Community*, pp. 107, 135) and Hooker (*Not Ashamed of the Gospel: New Testament Interpretations of the Death of Christ* [Grand Rapids:

passing and vague allusions point to the clear, certain, and central interpretation of Jesus' death. But Bellinger and Farmer are right: history deals not in possibilities, but probabilities. The study will proceed from the otherwise unexceptionable notion that what is central is also clear.[15] That Jesus' death has been profitably seen in light of Isaiah 53 does not mean that this is the only profitable way to see it and does not necessitate that the author of Mark saw it so. The text of Mark will have precedence over the texts of other authors, even authors as venerable as Justin Martyr or Paul. Since this work does not deal with the historical Jesus, but rather the Jesus of Mark, how Jesus interpreted his suffering, if such a thing can even be determined, will not come into play. Mark is to be judged first and foremost by Mark.

With these presuppositions in mind, what follows considers in detail the suggested allusions to Isaiah 53 in the Gospel of Mark.

Jesus handed over
It has been suggested that the παραδίδωμι of Mark 15.1 refers to Isa. 53.6 or 53.12.[16] The texts are as follows:

> As soon as it was morning, the chief priests held a consultation with the elders and scribes and the whole council. They bound Jesus, led him away, and *handed him over* to Pilate. (Mark 15.1)
> Καὶ εὐθὺς πρωὶ συμβούλιον ποιήσαντες οἱ ἀρχιερεῖς μετὰ τῶν πρεσβυτέρων καὶ γραμματέων καὶ ὅλον τὸ συνέδριον, δήσαντες τὸν Ἰησοῦν ἀπήνεγκαν καὶ <u>παρέδωκαν</u> Πιλάτῳ.

Eerdmans, 1994], pp. 55–56), who see little of Isaiah 53 in Mark, see Jesus' death according to the pattern of Exodus, God's paradigmatic act of redemption in the Old Testament. Watts (*Isaiah's New Exodus*, pp. 47–52, 264–69) sees both Isaiah 53 and the Exodus as interpreted by Isaiah as the pattern for Mark. Hengel (*Studies*, pp. 56–57) and others see Jesus according to the Moses-Elijah pattern. Dale C. Allison (*The End of the Ages Has Come: An Early Interpretation of the Passion and Resurrection of Jesus* [Philadelphia: Fortress, 1985], pp. 26–39) and others interpret Jesus' death and resurrection according to an eschatological pattern. Neither is it clear that Second Temple Judaism felt the limitation. 4 Macc. 6.29-30 (cf. 17.21-22) speaks of the martyrs' blood as propitiation for the nation. *The Rule of the Community* speaks of the faithful acts of the community in a similar manner (1QS ix 3-6). In neither of these texts is atonement tied to Isaiah 53.

15   Juel (*Messianic Exegesis*, pp. 60, 95) points to the emphasis some scholars place on reading Isaiah 53 in the gospel passion narratives as an excellent example of back-reading later interpretations into previous ones. Juel recommends beginning with what is clearest and only then moving towards what is obscure. That he feels he must make an argument for this demonstrates the pervasiveness of the problem.

16   See, for example, A. Collins, *Mark*, p. 712; Gnilka, *Markus*, 2, p. 299.

Testing Proposed Allusions

All we like sheep have gone astray; we have all turned to our own way, and the Lord has *laid on him* the iniquity of us all. (Isa. 53.6)
πάντες ὡς πρόβατα ἐπλανήθημεν, ἄνθρωπος τῇ ὁδῷ αὐτοῦ ἐπλανήθη· καὶ κύριος <u>παρέδωκεν</u> αὐτὸν ταῖς ἁμαρτίαις ἡμῶν.

Therefore I will allot him a portion with the great, and he shall divide the spoil with the strong, for whom his soul *was handed over* to death. Among the transgressors he was numbered; and he bore the sins of many, and because of their sins he was *handed over*. (Isa. 53.12)[17]
διὰ τοῦτο αὐτὸς κληρονομήσει πολλοὺς καὶ τῶν ἰσχυρῶν μεριεῖ σκῦλα, ἀνθ' ὧν <u>παρεδόθη</u> εἰς θάνατον ἡ ψυχὴ αὐτοῦ, καὶ ἐν τοῖς ἀνόμοις ἐλογίσθη· καὶ αὐτὸς ἁμαρτίας πολλῶν ἀνήνεγκε καὶ διὰ τὰς ἁμαρτίας αὐτῶν <u>παρεδόθη</u>.

They correspond in a single significant Greek word: παραδίδωμι. There is no further correspondence with the Hebrew.

Mark uses the word παραδίδωμι 20 times. Eighteen of those occurrences are used directly or indirectly in connection with the passion, and only twice with no such connotation (4.29 and 7.13). It is reasonable to argue that in Mark παραδίδωμι is a technical term referring to the passion.

It is much more difficult to argue that in Mark παραδίδωμι refers clearly and uniquely to Isaiah 53, out of the over 250 occurrences of the word in the LXX. Some scholars would overcome that statistical improbability by noting that παραδίδωμι occurs not once but three times in Isaiah 53 (once in v. 6, twice in v. 12).[18] If that line of reasoning were accepted for Isaiah 53, it would have to be equally applicable to other potential referents. For example, Derrett suggests that Mark 15.1 is a 'glancing allusion' to Judg. 15.9-13.[19] Those two passages share the word δέω (*bind*). δέω is less common than παραδίδωμι, occurring only about a fourth as often. Moreover, it occurs in Judges 15–16 *fourteen* times, almost one tenth of the total occurrences in the LXX. (For Isaiah 53 to match this frequency, it would also have to use the word παραδίδωμι at least twelve times.) In fact, παραδίδωμι itself occurs three times in Judges 15, equalling the number of occurrences in Isaiah 53, and it occurs twice more in Judges 16. When one considers the frequency with which a shared word is used, Judges 15 has a much greater claim than Isaiah 53 to be the referent of an allusion in Mark 15.1. Yet almost none of the commentators insisting on an allusion to Isa. 53.6, 12 acknowledge correspondence between Judg. 15.9-13 and Mark 15.1. Only Derrett even mentions it. The argument from frequency of use does not seem to be evenly applied. In truth,

---

17 NRSV modified toward the LXX.
18 See for example Moo (*Old Testament*, p. 96), who argues that Jesus alluded to Isaiah 53 via the Aramaic מסר, which occurs four times in the Targum of Isaiah 53, and that παραδίδωμι is the word chosen to capture this allusion.
19 Derrett, *The Making of Mark*, 2, p. 260.

counting the frequency of use of a relatively uncommon word can be helpful in determining whether an allusion exists. But when the case involves extremely common words, such as παραδίδωμι, it is less helpful.

Yet one might still argue that the technical use of παραδίδωμι for the passion points to *something* and that, since application of Isaiah 53 to the passion may have occurred before Mark (in Rom. 4.25), one reasonable conclusion is that it points to Isaiah 53. That clearly is possible, but it is argued here that this is neither a necessary nor even probable conclusion. Norman Perrin surveys the use of παραδίδωμι to refer to the passion throughout the New Testament and concludes that it became a characteristic or technical term for the passion before it had any theological application, certainly before it became associated with Isaiah 53.[20] That is, the use of the term παραδίδωμι as a technical term for the passion pre-dates the use of Isa. 53.6, 12 and has no necessary connections with it.

Verbal correspondence between Mark 15.1 and Isa. 53.6 or 12 is too slight to indicate an allusion on its own. As shall be seen, there is no other evidence in Mark sufficient to bolster such a claim.

Jesus' silence
During the trial before the Sanhedrin, Jesus does not answer the false witnesses or the high priest when he is asked about them:

But he was *silent* and did not answer. (Mark 14.61)
ὁ δὲ ἐσιώπα καὶ οὐκ ἀπεκρίνατο οὐδέν.

This is often said to allude to Isa. 53.7:[21]

He was oppressed, and he was afflicted, yet he did not open his mouth; like a lamb that is led to the slaughter, and like a sheep that before its shearers is *silent*, so he did not open his mouth.

---

20 Norman Perrin, 'The Use of (παρα)διδόναι in Connection with the Passion of Jesus in the New Testament', in *Der Ruf Jesu und die Antwort der Gemeinde: Festschrift für Joachim Jeremias* (ed. E. Lohse et al.; Göttingen: Vandenhoeck & Ruprecht, 1970), pp. 208–9. He further argues (ibid., pp. 209–12) that other Scripture passages were applied to the term, in service of apologetic, before Isaiah 53; and that application of Isaiah 53 to the passion represents a later, soteriological stage. It must be noted that Perrin concludes that Mark uses δίδωμι in Mark 10.45 in connection with Isaiah 53, that is, in that later soteriological stage. But the point essential to this argument remains: (παρα)δίδωμι alone does not necessarily point to Isaiah 53. Further clues from the text are needed to make that connection.

21 For example, see Linnemann, *Studien*, p. 131; Lührmann, *Markusevangelium*, p. 249; Moo, *Old Testament*, p. 148; Pesch, *Markusevangelium*, 2, p. 436; Schweizer, *Good News*, p. 330; Senior, *Passion of Jesus*, p. 94. Linnemann (*Studien*, pp. 55–56) also asserts the parallel for the Roman trial. Gundry (*Mark*, p. 908) notes that Isa. 53.7 corresponds to the event, but that Mark does not use it.

καὶ αὐτὸς διὰ τὸ κεκακῶσθαι οὐκ ἀνοίγει τὸ στόμα· ὡς πρόβατον ἐπὶ σφαγὴν ἤχθη καὶ ὡς ἀμνὸς ἐναντίον τοῦ κείροντος αὐτὸν ἄφωνος οὕτως οὐκ ἀνοίγει τὸ στόμα αὐτοῦ.

נִגַּשׂ וְהוּא נַעֲנֶה וְלֹא יִפְתַּח־פִּיו
כַּשֶּׂה לַטֶּבַח יוּבָל וּכְרָחֵל לִפְנֵי גֹזְזֶיהָ נֶאֱלָמָה
וְלֹא יִפְתַּח פִּיו:

Again the passages correspond in a single word, *silence* (Mark σιωπάω and MT אלם). That the LXX does not translate אלם in Isa. 53.7 with σιωπάω is not really a problem; the LXX translates אלם that way elsewhere. The word is perfectly apt, and it is possible that Mark translated the passage himself or used a variant translation that is no longer extant. The real problem is that the two passages share only a single word and that word, while not common, is not nearly rare enough to indicate an allusion. Mark uses σιωπάω in four other passages (3.4; 4.39; 9.34; 10.48), but for none of these is the suggestion of an allusion to Isa. 53.7 made. Verbal correspondence is weak; this is not an allusion.[22]

'Let the Scriptures be fulfilled'
During the arrest scene, Jesus says:

> 'Have you come out with swords and clubs to arrest me as though I were a *bandit*? Day after day I was with you in the temple teaching, and you did not arrest me. But let the scriptures be fulfilled.' (Mark 14.48-49)
> καὶ ἀποκριθεὶς ὁ Ἰησοῦς εἶπεν αὐτοῖς· ὡς ἐπὶ <u>λῃστὴν</u> ἐξήλθατε μετὰ μαχαιρῶν καὶ ξύλων συλλαβεῖν με; καθ' ἡμέραν ἤμην πρὸς ὑμᾶς ἐν τῷ ἱερῷ διδάσκων καὶ οὐκ ἐκρατήσατέ με· ἀλλ' ἵνα πληρωθῶσιν αἱ γραφαί.

This is seen in conjunction with Isa. 53.12:

> Therefore I will allot him a portion with the great, and he shall divide the spoil with the strong; because he poured out himself to death, and was numbered with the *transgressors*; yet he bore the sin of many, and made intercession for the *transgressors*. (LXX, 'was given over because of their sins'.)

---

22 Unquestionably, Isa. 53.7 appears often in early church literature as an interpretation of Jesus' silence, but it does not do so universally. Justin interprets the silence as a fulfilment of Isa. 50.4 in *Dial.* 102. *Odes Sol.* 31.10 and *Sib. Or.* 8.290-94 interpret the silence theologically without discernable recourse to any passage of Scripture. (See Crossan's discussion in *Cross That Spoke*, pp. 174–87.) Crossan (ibid., pp. 185–86) suggests that Mark seems to show no interest in Isa. 53.7 or any Scripture passage when narrating Jesus' silence, but that Mark may instead be interested in showing the community the right way to respond to interrogations.

διὰ τοῦτο αὐτὸς κληρονομήσει πολλοὺς καὶ τῶν ἰσχυρῶν μεριεῖ σκῦλα, ἀνθ᾽ ὧν παρεδόθη εἰς θάνατον ἡ ψυχὴ αὐτοῦ, καὶ ἐν τοῖς ἀνόμοις ἐλογίσθη· καὶ αὐτὸς ἁμαρτίας πολλῶν ἀνήνεγκε καὶ διὰ τὰς ἁμαρτίας αὐτῶν παρεδόθη.

לָכֵן אֲחַלֶּק־לוֹ בָרַבִּים וְאֶת־עֲצוּמִים יְחַלֵּק שָׁלָל
תַּחַת אֲשֶׁר הֶעֱרָה לַמָּוֶת נַפְשׁוֹ וְאֶת־פֹּשְׁעִים נִמְנָה
וְהוּא חֵטְא־רַבִּים נָשָׂא וְלַפֹּשְׁעִים יַפְגִּיעַ׃

Maurer proposes that Mark 14.48 goes directly to the Hebrew for ληστήν, as opposed to the LXX ἀνόμοις.[23] Yet it would appear that ἀνόμοις is at least as good a rendering of פשע (*rebels, transgressors*) as ληστής. While it is true that later ληστής is used for some of those who revolted against Rome, and thus were rebels, it is uncertain that Mark used the term in that sense rather than in the common sense of *bandit* (as it is rendered in the NRSV, for example). Even if it were so meant, it is unclear that a political rebel is meant by פשע. It seems generally to mean transgressor, one who sins, often against God, but also against a neighbour. Again, even if פשע were to mean political rebel, it seems unlikely that the correspondence of פשע and ληστήν here would be enough to draw the reader to this passage – פשע is not sufficiently rare, with about 50 occurrences of the verb.

Mark 14.49 is important here not for its verbal correspondence, but for its call to 'let the Scriptures be fulfilled'. What exactly is meant by this is unclear. Does it mean a particular passage or Scripture in general?[24] Without a strong allusion to Isaiah 53, it is unlikely that is what is meant.

---

23 Maurer, 'Knecht', p. 8.
24 There are a number of possibilities. Some see this as relating directly to Isa. 53.12, e.g., Sharyn Dowd, *Reading Mark: A Literary and Theological Commentary on the Second Gospel* (Macon, Ga.: Smyth & Helwys, 2000), p. 153; Ezra P. Gould, *Critical and Exegetical Commentary on the Gospel According to St Mark* (ICC; Edinburgh: T&T Clark, 1982), p. 275; Ben Witherington, III, *Gospel of Mark: A Socio-Rhetorical Commentary* (Grand Rapids: Eerdmans, 2001), p. 382. Some see it as referring simply to Scripture in general: e.g., Eduard Schweizer, *Good News*, pp. 318–19; van Iersel, *Mark*, p. 440. Psalm 41.10 may be in view, since that passage may be evoked in Mark 14.18 in connection with the betrayal which is now unfolding. (Cf. C. F. D. Moule, *The Gospel According to Mark* [London: Cambridge University Press, 1965], p. 119.) Verbal correspondence there is weak, however, and seems insufficient for an allusion. Still the evidence of the Jewish as well as Christian tradition bolsters its case, and one cannot be certain. See below, p. 91. Zechariah 13.7, the only explicit Scripture citation in the passion narrative, cited just a short while before (Mark 14.27) may be in view. (See David E. Garland, *Mark* [The NIV Application Commentary; Grand Rapids: Zondervan, 1996], p. 546.) The actions that allusion treats are also just now taking place.

Cup of my blood

The best possibility for verbal correspondence between Isaiah 53 and the Markan passion narrative is the word over the cup in Mark 14.24.[25]

> This is my blood of the covenant, which is *poured out* for many.
> τοῦτό ἐστιν τὸ αἷμά μου τῆς διαθήκης τὸ <u>ἐκχυννόμενον</u> ὑπὲρ <u>πολλῶν</u>.

ἐκχυννόμενον is said to recall Isa. 53.12:

> Therefore I will allot him a portion with the great, and he shall divide the spoil with the strong; because he *poured out* himself to death, and was numbered with the transgressors; yet he bore the sin of many, and made intercession for the transgressors.
> διὰ τοῦτο αὐτὸς κληρονομήσει <u>πολλοὺς</u> καὶ τῶν ἰσχυρῶν μεριεῖ σκῦλα, ἀνθ' ὧν παρεδόθη εἰς θάνατον ἡ ψυχὴ αὐτοῦ, καὶ ἐν τοῖς ἀνόμοις ἐλογίσθη· καὶ αὐτὸς ἁμαρτίας <u>πολλῶν</u> ἀνήνεγκε καὶ διὰ τὰς ἁμαρτίας αὐτῶν παρεδόθη.
> לָכֵן אֲחַלֶּק־לוֹ <u>בָרַבִּים</u> וְאֶת־עֲצוּמִים יְחַלֵּק שָׁלָל
> תַּחַת אֲשֶׁר <u>הֶעֱרָה</u> לַמָּוֶת נַפְשׁוֹ וְאֶת־פֹּשְׁעִים נִמְנָה
> וְהוּא חֵטְא־<u>רַבִּים</u> נָשָׂא וְלַפֹּשְׁעִים יַפְגִּיעַ׃

Douglas Moo writes:

> ἐκχύννω does not appear in the LXX of Is. 53 ... However, ἐκχυννόμενον is a literal translation of Heb. הֶעֱרָה (Is. 53:12) and in conjunction with πολλῶν (πολλοί twice in Is. 53:12) is best understood as a conscious allusion to this OT verse.[26]

Or, one could say, ἐκχυννόμενον translates הֶעֱרָה (*poured out*), and πολλῶν translates רַבִּים (*many*, which occurs twice). πολύς and רַב are so common that they contribute little to verbal correspondence. The contribution would be greater if in Isa. 53.12 (as in Mark 14.24) רַבִּים were connected to הֶעֱרָה, but it is not; they occur in separate clauses. עָרָה however, is considerably less common, occurring only fifteen times and still less frequently with this meaning. The verb ἐκχύννω is still rarer, occurring in the LXX only in a single variant; the noun form ἔκχυσις occurs elsewhere just three times to translate שֶׁפֶךְ (*pour out*: Lev. 4.12; 1 Kgs 18.28; Sir. 27.15). ἐκχύννω is uncommon in the New Testament as well, occurring eleven times, three of them in this

---

25 Mark 15.28 is clearly a quotation of Isa. 53.12. However, this is not often used in arguments for the presence of the Fourth Servant Song in the Markan passion narrative, because it is widely regarded as a later interpolation. For an argument in favour of its authenticity, see Peter Robert Rodgers, 'Mark 15.28', *EvQ* 61 (1989), pp. 81–84.
26 Moo, *Old Testament*, pp. 130–31.

saying (Mark 14.24; Matt. 26.28; Luke 22.20; though not in 1 Cor. 11.25). In Mark, it is used only here. The infrequency with which these words occur increases the degree of verbal correspondence. Yet when verbal correspondence comes through translation, it is weakened.

Is the verbal correspondence sufficient? Does ἐκχύννω, with πολλοί, have the force to recall Isa. 53.12? Since the significant word here is ἐκχύννω, one could begin to answer that question by examining the connotations of the word in its other New Testament uses. In Luke 5.37, it is used for spilling wine, in Acts 10.45 for the pouring out of the Holy Spirit, and in Rom. 5.5 for the pouring out of God's love. It is used most frequently however with regard to shedding blood. In Matt. 23.35//Luke 11.50, it is used for the death of the prophets and in Acts 22.20 for Stephen's death. None of these uses points specifically to Isa. 53.12. More significant, perhaps, is the use in Acts 1.18, in which ἐκχύννω describes the disembowelment of Judas. In Jude 11, it is used for people who abandon themselves to 'Balaam's error'. These uses show clearly that ἐκχύννω did not have any particular associations with the *pour out* of Isa. 53.12. It seems unlikely that the addition of the word *many* (πολλοί) would be sufficient to direct the reader to that verse. Luke does not appear to see the reference (22.20). It is unclear whether Matthew did. Matthew 26.28 adds 'for the forgiveness of sin' to the passage, which corresponds thematically with Isa. 53.12, connecting the Servant with atonement. On the other hand, Matthew could add a reference to forgiveness of sin without recourse to Isa. 53.12, as happens often in the New Testament, and aside from the word 'sin' itself, Matthew does not edit toward the wording of Isa. 53.12. An allusion to Isa. 53.12 is far from certain in Matt. 26.28. That Mark 14.24 contains such an allusion is unlikely.

A ransom for many
Perhaps the best suggestion for an allusion to Isaiah 53 in the Gospel of Mark as a whole concerns the ransom saying:

> For the Son of Man came not to be served but to serve, and *to give his life* as a ransom for many. (Mark 10.45)
> καὶ γὰρ ὁ υἱὸς τοῦ ἀνθρώπου οὐκ ἦλθεν διακονηθῆναι ἀλλὰ διακονῆσαι καὶ <u>δοῦναι τὴν ψυχὴν αὐτοῦ</u> λύτρον ἀντὶ πολλῶν.

'Give his life as a ransom for many' is said to be an allusion to Isa. 53.10. Scholars who support the allusion consider it a translation from Hebrew.

> Yet it was the will of the LORD to crush him with pain. When *you make his life a guilt-offering*, he shall see his offspring, and shall prolong his days; through him the will of the LORD shall prosper. (Isa. 53.10)[27]

---

27 NRSV modified.

וַיהוָה חָפֵץ דַּכְּאוֹ הֶחֱלִי אִם־תָּשִׂים אָשָׁם נַפְשׁוֹ
יִרְאֶה זֶרַע יַאֲרִיךְ יָמִים וְחֵפֶץ יְהוָה בְּיָדוֹ יִצְלָח:

Verbal correspondence between these passages is debated. All agree that the words *give* or *make* (δοῦναι/תָּשִׂים) and *his life* or *soul* (τὴν ψυχὴν αὐτοῦ/נַפְשׁוֹ) correspond.[28] The rest of the verbal correspondence is not as clear. In addition, part of the strength of the parallel is its thematic correspondence, but that is not as strong as at first appears. The issues will be taken up in order.

Isaiah 53.10 does not have words corresponding to the Markan *for many* (ἀντὶ πολλῶν). Some argue that because *many* occurs in succeeding verses (53.11-12), *for many* also contributes to verbal correspondence.[29] Perhaps they are correct. However, it can contribute very little. Though the word *many* occurs in two subsequent verses, it is separated from the phrase in question by a number of independent clauses in Hebrew (four and six). In addition, the word for *many* is extremely common; רַב occurs in this sense 429 times in the MT. The correspondence of an extremely common word that occurs not particularly close to the phrase in question can increase verbal correspondence only slightly.

Moo suggests that λύτρον (*ransom* or *redemption*)[30] in Mark is a translation of the Hebrew word אָשָׁם (*guilt-offering*).[31] Yet there is no instance of λυτρόω or its cognates translating אָשָׁם in the LXX, and no instance of אָשָׁם in Isa. 53.10 being translated with λυτρόω or its cognates in any early Christian quotation of Isa. 53.10.[32] It is unlikely that λύτρον in Mark 10.45 is the single exception to the rule.

Thus, verbal correspondence is weak. The corresponding words for *give* and *his soul* are very common, and *many* contributes little to the cumulative correspondence. Verbal correspondence between the passages is insufficient to indicate an allusion.[33]

---

28   The word translated as 'his soul' also means 'life' (the same ambiguity exists in Greek).
29   E.g., Moo, *Old Testament*, p. 125.
30   Cf. Liddell and Scott, 'λύτρον', p. 1067.
31   Moo, *Old Testament*, pp. 122–25.
32   It is not hard to extend the meaning of the word λύτρον–*ransom* to mean rescue not only from slavery or bandits, etc., but also from the power of sin (also ἀπολύτρωσις, cf. 1 Peter 1.18-19; Tit. 2.14; Rom. 3.24; Eph. 1.7; for patristic use, see Lampe, 'λύτρον', p. 815). That is not to say it is equivalent in meaning to *guilt-offering* or *sacrifice*, etc. It is not, and there is no evidence of it ever being used to translate אָשָׁם. See Hooker, *Jesus*, pp. 76–78; C. K. Barrett, 'The Background of Mark 10.45', in *New Testament Essays: Studies in Memory of Thomas Walter Manson* (ed. A. J. B. Higgins; Manchester: Manchester University Press, 1959), pp. 5–7.
33   Vincent Taylor (*Jesus and His Sacrifice* [London: MacMillan & Co, 1959], pp. 101–2) recognizes the difficulty and suggests that λύτρον comes from Isa. 49.7-8. Nevertheless he states that there is 'little doubt that the ideas which lie behind the saying are those of Isa. liii'.

Still, one might argue that Isa. 53.10 is a rare passage in the Old Testament where a person is said to give his life for others, perhaps the only such passage.[34] Thus, even though the verbal correspondence between the passages is not strong, it is bolstered by an important thematic parallel. There is some difficulty here as well. In English versions, אם תשים אשם נפשו is often translated as: 'if he gives his life as a guilt-offering'.[35] However, the Hebrew text does not support this translation. There are two possibilities here. The verb form תשים can be read as second masculine singular, so that the phrase reads: 'if *you give his soul* (as) a guilt-offering'.[36] The verb can also be read as third feminine singular; in that case 'his soul' becomes the subject (not the object), and the translation runs: 'if *his soul gives* a guilt offering'. Though the verb form is ambiguous, it *cannot* be read as a third masculine singular, and the phrase cannot properly be translated 'if *he gives his life* as a guilt-offering'. The LXX translates using second person plural and separates 'give' and 'soul' into two clauses: 'if you (pl.) give concerning sin, your (pl.) soul will see (your) offspring live long' (ἐὰν δῶτε περὶ ἁμαρτίας, ἡ ψυχὴ ὑμῶν ὄψεται σπέρμα μακρόβιον). That is, in neither Hebrew nor Greek does this verse speak of a person giving his own life as an offering. Thus, the thematic correspondence is only apparent, created by an English translation which does not follow the original.[37]

Neither verbal nor thematic correspondence is sufficient to establish that Mark 10.45 refers to Isa. 53.10. If one were nevertheless to insist that Mark 10.45 is an echo of Isa. 53.10, that would not help to make other suggested allusions to Isaiah 53 stand. A suggested allusion with slight verbal correspondence will be bolstered by another allusion with clear verbal correspondence elsewhere in the narrative. The deficiency of one allusion cannot be remedied with yet another faint, uncertain allusion.

Other allusions to Deutero-Isaiah
Mark certainly alludes to other passages from Deutero-Isaiah elsewhere, for example, Mark 1.3 cites Isa. 40.3. It alludes to Isa. 50.6, the so-called 'Third Servant Song', at 14.65. Allusions to passages such as Isa. 40.3 and 50.6 cannot support an allusion to Isaiah 53, however. Allusions to parts of Deutero-Isaiah do not imply the entire work, and certainly do not point away from the specific text alluded to and towards Isaiah 53 instead, as is

---

34   It would not be the only such passage. Moses offers his life in solidarity with the people of Israel in Exod. 32.32.
35   The RSV, NAB, NASB, and the JPS *Tanakh* translate this way.
36   The NRSV translates in a similar way, 'when you make his life an offering for sin'. The NIV translates the phrase with 'though the Lord makes his life a guilt offering'. This is not a literal translation but probably accurately captures the sense.
37   The Hebrew of Isa. 53.12 does state, 'he poured out his soul to death'. The LXX translates this as 'his soul was handed over to death', the divine passive, understanding the subject of 'he poured out' to be God.

sometimes claimed. There is too much distance between the referent passages, the closest being Isa. 50.6, to include Isaiah 53 in the larger context of the referent – the context of an allusion does not stretch that far. Yet one might counter that the four Servant Songs of Isaiah are a unit. Might an allusion to one of these songs bolster the case for an allusion to another? It would, *if* these songs were considered a unit by the first-century reader. There is, however, no evidence that was the case.[38] Because these texts were not seen as a unit, then an allusion to one is not an allusion to all. Readers seeing in Mark 14.65 an allusion to Isa. 50.6 would have no reason to connect that passage with Isa. 53.10. Thus, other allusions to Deutero-Isaiah do not help establish allusions to Isaiah 53. Those suggestions must stand on their own merits.

Conclusion
Though the preceding has examined the best of the suggested allusions, it found no clear or certain allusion to Isaiah 52.13–53.12 in Mark. Though Jesus is given many titles and epithets in this gospel, no word for servant is ever applied to Jesus.[39] The Servant of the Lord is not the pattern by which the Gospel of Mark portrays Jesus' passion.

The Suffering Righteous One
Another group of passages is often considered to have decisive influence on the passion narrative, and allusions are suggested even though the passages have little or no verbal correspondence. This group of passages describes the suffering of an innocent person, called 'the suffering just one' or 'suffering righteous one'. It includes the psalms of lament, Wis. 2.10-20 and 5.1-7, and many other texts.[40]

These passages present a promising field for allusions. There is significant overlap in theme between the passion narrative and passages about the suffering righteous one: the person who suffers is innocent, the suffering is brought on by treacherous and often powerful enemies, and danger of death is common. Moreover, it is beyond question that some of these passages influence the gospels. For example, all four gospel passion narratives allude to Psalms 22 and 69.

Nevertheless, important matters remain unresolved regarding both the extent and meaning of the allusions. This section focuses on the extent of the

---

38 Hooker, *Jesus*, pp. 156–58.
39 In the Parable of the Vineyard, which in Mark is a sort of allegory, Jesus is even contrasted with the servants. The owner sends the *servants* (the prophets, etc.), and then sends his *son* (Jesus). Certainly, Jesus is portrayed as one who serves (Mark 10.45), but no word for servant is ever applied to him as an epithet. In other words, service is something Jesus *does*. He *is* the Son of God and the Christ.
40 Exactly which texts are included in this group varies from scholar to scholar. This issue will be taken up later in the section.

88   *The Use of Scripture in the Markan Passion Narrative*

allusions, but some of the conclusions drawn here will affect the meaning of the passages that are used – a subject discussed in Chapters 4–5.

Silence as a characteristic of the suffering righteous
Some scholars extrapolate from the secure allusions to suffering righteous passages to conclude that other items in the passion narrative that parallel other suffering righteous passages are *allusions* to those passages. Pesch's commentary on the passion is filled with claims regarding such allusions. Gnilka concludes that the portrayal of the Jewish trial is substantially influenced by the psalms of the suffering righteous one.[41] In particular, several scholars propose that Jesus' silence in the Jewish trial (Mark 14.61) refers to the silence of the suffering righteous one of Ps. 38.14-16 or 39.10.[42] Yet there is only scant verbal correspondence between these passages. Indeed, exactly the same correspondence obtains between 14.61 and Isa. 53.7: σιωπάω and אלם. Again, verbal correspondence is insufficient to indicate an allusion.

Still, Mark contains other clear allusions to suffering righteous passages. So, despite the tenuous verbal correspondence, the proposed correspondence could hold if there were something to connect these passages in the minds of the original audience. That is, the suggested allusions regarding silence could hold if the suffering righteous one were a conventional literary figure or traditional motif, and silence were a stereotypical feature of that motif. The larger question, whether the suffering righteous one is a traditional motif, will be addressed below. Here it is sufficient to ask whether silence is characteristic of the suffering righteous one.

Certainly, the psalmist of Ps. 38.14-16 and 39.10 is silent. Yet, though the suggestion regarding Ps. 39.10 is apt, it is odd that Ps. 38.14 should be used to characterize the suffering righteous one. Note Ps. 38.4-6:

> There is no soundness in my flesh because of your [God's] indignation; there is no health in my bones because of my sin. For my iniquities have gone over my head; they weigh like a burden too heavy for me. My wounds grow foul and fester because of my foolishness.

These are hardly the marks of the suffering righteous one. The psalm does not fit the model and cannot be used to support the idea that the suffering righteous one is stereotypically silent.

---

41   Gnilka, *Markus*, 2, p. 278; also see his suggested allusions, for example, 2, pp. 279–84.
42   See Gnilka, *Markus*, 2, p. 281; Pesch, *Markusevangelium*, 2, p. 436; Lührmann, *Markusevangelium*, p. 249; Albrecht, 'Silence', p. 35. Often the silence is said to indicate Jesus' obedience as the suffering righteous one; cf. Robert H. Smith, 'Darkness at Noon: Mark's Passion Narrative', *CTM* 44 (1973), p. 333.

Examples of the silence of the suffering righteous one are actually rather limited. Examples of the vocal sufferer, on the other hand, are plentiful. The sufferer in the psalms quoted in Mark is not silent. Consider Ps. 22.2-3:

> Why are you so far from helping me, from the words of my groaning? O my God, I cry by day, but you do not answer; and by night, but find no rest.

Consider Ps. 69.4:

> I am weary with my crying; my throat is parched.

The suffering righteous one of these passages cries out continually. The martyrs of 2 Maccabees 6–7 speak not only for deliverance but also to condemn those who persecute them. (The psalmist in Psalm 69 has no shortage of words to the same effect. See vv. 23-29.) In the most extensive suffering righteous text in the canon, Job is not silent and is abused by his friends for his vociferous self-defence. Many more examples could be added (cf. Daniel 3, Susanna; *4 Maccabees*; and Esther). Silence is not particularly distinctive of suffering righteous passages.

It hardly needs mentioning that silence is found in many passages having little to do with the suffering righteous one. The idols are silent in Hab. 2.18. Daniel is silent when the angelic messenger speaks to him (Dan. 10.15). The people on the wall in Isa. 36.21 are silent. Even God is said to be silent from time to time, for example, in Pss. 83.2 and 109.1. Silence is not characteristic of suffering righteous passages, and it is not limited to such passages. There is little verbal correspondence between the Markan passages and the suggested referents. The claim that Jesus' silence in the two trials refers to the silence of the suffering righteous one is unwarranted by the evidence.

Any element of the passion narrative that is said to refer to a suffering righteous passage is subject to the same examination. That element must be either characteristic of or limited to the portrait of the suffering righteous one. If not, there can be little justification for positing an allusion without significant verbal correspondence.

The Jewish trial and Wisdom 2

Consider a suggestion with more extensive implications. Maurer, followed by Ruppert, sees significant thematic links between the Jewish trial in Mark and the themes of Wis. 2.10-20.[43] The most important of these is the focus of the Jewish trial: as the enemies of the righteous one in Wisdom 2 plan to kill him because he claims to be a child of God (Wis. 2.13, cf. 16, 18), so also the enemies of Jesus plan to kill him because of his claim to be Son of the Blessed.

---

43   Maurer, 'Knecht', p. 26; Ruppert, *Jesus*, pp. 53–56.

Ruppert concludes that Wisdom 2 had decisive influence on the pre-Markan passion narrative.[44] His position is quite difficult to support. It is not certain even that there was a pre-Markan passion narrative or, if it existed, that it contained a Jewish trial. If it did contain a Jewish trial, it is unclear what material it contained and what Mark added. Did the pre-Markan passion narrative operate on the basis of the temple charge or on the basis of a messianic question and answer or both?[45] With all of these factors unknown, it is impossible to compare the Jewish trial in its pre-Markan form to Wisdom 2 to find verbal correspondence. In fact, Ruppert never addresses verbal correspondence. Yet without it, all that remains is a similarity of theme, and similarity of theme does not guarantee that a passage was used by an ancient author.[46] The pre-Markan passion narrative, if it existed, may have been influenced by Wisdom 2. It may not have been. It is impossible to know.

Maurer concludes that Wisdom 2 had decisive influence on the shape of the Markan trial as it stands.[47] Maurer's certainty is based entirely on similarity of theme. He never attempts to show verbal correspondence. Indeed, there is very little to show. Mark 14.61 corresponds with Wis. 2.18 in the word υἱός (*son*); Mark 14.64 corresponds with Wis. 2.20 in the word θάνατος (*death*).[48] There is very little verbal evidence that the author of Mark either saw the Jewish trial in light of Wis. 2.10-20 or intended his audience to do so.[49]

The same set of issues exists for the correspondence between Wis. 2.10-20 and the mockery at the cross, and the same answer holds. Only at Mark 15.36 does verbal correspondence exceed a single common word. There it extends to two words shared with Wis. 2.17: ἴδωμεν εἰ (*let us see if*). The words are very common, and again this is not sufficient verbal correspondence to indicate an allusion.[50]

Thematic correspondence is not sufficient to indicate an allusion. Verbal correspondence is slight. While we cannot know whether the author thought

---

44 Ruppert, *Jesus*, pp. 55–56.
45 On the uncertain state of research on the pre-Markan passion narrative, see Soards, 'PreMarcan', in Brown, *Death*, 2, pp.1492–524. See Donahue ('Passion Traditions', in Kelber, *The Passion in Mark*, pp. 14–16) for an argument against the existence of a pre-Markan passion narrative.
46 Note that Maurer ('Knecht', p. 24) uses Wis. 2, 5 to prove that the Suffering Servant of Isaiah 53 is the dominant motif, while Ruppert (*Jesus*, p. 14) uses it to show that the suffering righteous is the dominant motif, apart from Isaiah 53. Arguments based only on similarity of theme will vary widely.
47 Maurer, 'Knecht', p. 26. Donahue (*Mark*, pp. 35, 389, 440) concludes that Wisdom 2 motifs shape other elements of the passion narrative, including the plot to arrest Jesus and the Roman trial.
48 See pp. 257–58, 262.
49 Cf. Suhl, *Funktion*, pp. 59–60.
50 This represents the strongest verbal correspondence for all the suggested allusions to Wis. 2.10-20.

of Wisdom 2 while writing, we can confidently conclude that there are no clear allusions to Wis. 2.10-20 in the Markan passion narrative.

The one eating with me and Psalm 41.10

Another suffering righteous passage has stronger credentials. Many scholars suggest that Mark 14.18:

> And when they had taken their places and were eating, Jesus said, 'Truly I tell you, one of you will betray me, *one who is eating* with *me*.'
> καὶ ἀνακειμένων αὐτῶν καὶ ἐσθιόντων ὁ Ἰησοῦς εἶπεν· ἀμὴν λέγω ὑμῖν ὅτι εἷς ἐξ ὑμῶν παραδώσει με <u>ὁ ἐσθίων</u> μετ' <u>ἐμοῦ</u>.

is an allusion to Ps. 41.10:

> Even my bosom friend in whom I trusted,
> *who ate* of *my* bread, has lifted the heel against me.
> καὶ γὰρ ὁ ἄνθρωπος τῆς εἰρήνης μου, ἐφ' ὃν ἤλπισα,
> <u>ὁ ἐσθίων</u> ἄρτους <u>μου</u>, ἐμεγάλυνεν ἐπ' ἐμὲ πτερνισμόν·

The verbal correspondence is not strong, consisting of only very common words (ὁ ἐσθίων [*the one eating*], ἐμοῦ/μου [*me/my*]), though verbal correspondence is strengthened in that the words are nearly consecutive. The passage has some volume in the Jewish tradition, where it is used in almost exactly the same fashion.[51] John 13.18 uses it as a fulfilment citation.

Nevertheless, Matthew and Luke both edit away from the passage (Matt. 26.23; Luke 22.21). Mark does not highlight the passage, which would have been easy to do. Simply adding ἄρτους (*bread*) to Mark 14.18 would have strengthened verbal correspondence, in a very natural way. In Mark 14.20, Jesus repeats his statement that one close to him would betray him, but does not use words from the psalm, but rather 'one who is dipping with me in the bowl'.[52] While Ps. 41.10 is used in John, that seems not to be the case in Mark.

The suffering righteous one as a conventional figure

Earlier it was suggested that clear allusions to suffering righteous passages would help point to other suffering righteous passages if there were something to hold those passages together in the minds of the original audience, that is, if the suffering righteous one were a conventional literary figure or traditional motif. It would be such a figure or motif if portraits of the suffering righteous one somehow corresponded to a typical pattern (beyond describing an innocent person who suffers).

An example from English literature may help to demonstrate what a conventional literary figure is. Petrarchan sonnets describe a lady who rebuffs

---

51 Cf. 1QH xiii 23-24; *b. Sanh.* 107.
52 Author's translation.

the poet's advances and who has a distinct set of characteristics, such as golden hair, brilliant eyes, and an icy heart.

> A youthful lady under a green laurel
> I saw, whiter and colder than snow
> ... There have never been such lovely eyes,
> either in our age or in the first years;
> they melt me as the sun does the snow:
> whence there comes forth a river of tears
> that Love leads to the foot of the harsh laurel
> that has branches of diamond and golden locks.[53]

The Petrarchan Lady, called Laura, becomes a figure, a trope. When one of her traits is mentioned, the reader can assume them all. Laura is such a stereotypical figure that other poets can make allusive plays on the motif. Perhaps the most famous example of this is the following sonnet by Shakespeare:

> My mistress' eyes are nothing like the sun;
> Coral is far more red than her lips' red;
> If snow be white, why then her breasts are dun;
> If hairs be wires, black wires grow on her head;
> I have seen roses damasked, red and white,
> But no such roses see I in her cheeks;
> And in some perfumes is there more delight
> Than in the breath that from my mistress reeks.
> I love to hear her speak, yet well I know
> That music hath a far more pleasing sound;
> I grant I never saw a goddess go;
> My mistress when she walks treads on the ground.
>   And yet, by heaven, I think my love as rare
>   As any she belied with false compare.[54]

The beloved of this sonnet is the opposite of Petrarch's Laura, and this reversal is what gives the sonnet its punch.

If the suffering righteous one were a conventional figure, then Mark's clear allusions to some suffering righteous passages would evoke everything belonging to the figure of the suffering righteous one, just as a brief allusion to one or two characteristics of the Petrarch's Laura recalls them all. Mark could play with the meaning of the figure and such interplay would affect the meaning of the Markan passion narrative. Thus, one must ask whether the suffering righteous one was a conventional figure.

---

53   Poem 30 in Robert M. Durling, trans., *Petrarch's Lyric Poems: The* Rime sparse *and Other Lyrics* (Cambridge, Mass.: Harvard University Press, 1976).
54   Sonnet 130 in Katherine Duncan-Jones, *Shakespeare's Sonnets* (Thomas Nelson, 1997).

Detlev Dormeyer and George Nickelsburg discuss suffering righteous passages in different variations and answer in the affirmative. Nickelsburg compares the Joseph narratives in Genesis, stories from Daniel, *Ahiqar*, and others, and suggests that these stories were told in similar ways and contained a number of stereotypical elements, such as a provocation, a decision by the martyr to be faithful, a prayer for deliverance, rescue at the brink of death, and vindication.[55] He concludes that the Markan passion narrative is composed according to the conventions of this motif.

Dormeyer concludes that there are two motifs here, the suffering righteous one and the martyr. Both the righteous one and the martyr are accused and threatened. The righteous one complains to God about the injustice and prays for deliverance, but is silent before his accusers. There is no formal trial, and he is rescued from death. The martyr speaks in front of his accusers, does not complain about the execution, refuses solace, and dies with honour.[56]

The description of the martyr fits well with the texts. The stereotypical elements occur in the stories of 2 and 4 Maccabees, for example, and many later Christian martyr stories. There is more difficulty with the characterization of the suffering righteous one. In Susanna, there is a formal trial, Susanna is not silent before her accusers (Sus. 22-23, 42-43), and she is rescued. She fits neither of Dormeyer's types. The division fails as well with the ordeal of Shadrach, Meshach, and Abednego (Daniel 3), among other examples.

While the list of stereotypical elements for the suffering righteous one fails, Dormeyer's division into two motifs, the righteous one who does not die and the martyr who does, is helpful. It also points to the problem: no single set of characteristics fits all suffering righteous passages. The Old Testament is filled with descriptions of righteous people suffering. One need go no further than Genesis 4, the murder of Abel, to find the first example of innocent suffering. Joseph, though righteous, suffers. Abraham himself suffers, having to wander as an exile from his homeland and subject to the distresses that such exile imposes. It is precisely his obedience that causes him to suffer. Job, pointedly innocent, suffers dramatically. Daniel describes the trials of devout Jews under foreign rule. Ruppert presents a broad array of examples of suffering righteous passages in intertestamental literature.[57] For example, 2 Maccabees describes the sufferings of devout Jews under Antiochus IV. When one takes into consideration the broader range of literature, the 'figure' loses all distinction. The innocent sufferers of Scripture and intertestamental literature have no single set of characteristics. They live and suffer in different ways. They respond to suffering in different ways. Their suffering ends in different ways. No stereotypical figure or motif of a suffering righteous one appears.

---

55 Nickelsburg, 'Genre', pp. 157–61.

56 Detlev Dormeyer, *Die Passion Jesu als Verhaltensmodell: Literarische und theologische Analyse der Traditions- und Redaktionsgeschichte der Markuspassion* (Munster: Aschendorff, 1974), pp. 43–49, 248–53.

57 See Ruppert's survey of the literature in *Jesus*, pp. 17–26.

This problem might be addressed by defining which texts belong to the group of suffering righteous passages and which are excluded. Yet precisely which texts belong is a consistent problem in treatments of the suffering righteous one. Ruppert admires Schweizer's treatment of the suffering righteous one as an important influence on the Markan passion narrative, but he criticizes it as eclectic, noting that it is not clear which psalms of the suffering righteous Schweizer considers to have influenced Mark.[58] The same problem applies to many treatments of the suffering righteous one, including Ruppert's. For example, Ruppert calls Wis. 2.10-20 the classic example of the suffering righteous one, but he distinguishes between the suffering righteous one and the Suffering Servant of Isaiah 53.[59] Why is Wis. 2.10-20 included but the Suffering Servant excluded? On what basis would one make such distinctions? Would a first-century reader have made the same distinctions? Would the figure created by such a set of texts have been recognizable to a first-century reader as a distinct figure with a particular set of stereotypical characteristics?

In treatments of the suffering righteous one, it is unclear which texts are included and which are not and why some texts should be distinguished from others which also describe a righteous person who suffers. Without a defined set of texts, the literature is too large and diverse to support claims of a particular set of stereotypical characteristics. That is, the breadth of the literature shows that the suffering righteous one is *not* a conventional figure. There is no distinct set of characteristics (such as silence, the presence or absence of a trial, a prayer by the righteous one) that fits all or most passages on the topic. Thus, the Markan allusions to particular passages cannot be used to imply the characteristics found in other suffering righteous passages.

Is Jesus the suffering righteous one in Mark?
For the sake of argument, let's suppose that the suffering righteous one were a literary figure or motif to which Jesus could be compared or which Jesus could fulfil as the *quintessential* suffering righteous one.[60] Would that change matters for the Markan passion narrative? The answer is still no.

Ruppert rightly notes that for Jesus' passion to be depicted according to the model of the suffering righteous one, Jesus absolutely *must* be called 'righteous'.[61] That is not the case in Mark. As Ruppert himself admits, the author of Mark is concerned to show that Jesus suffers, not as the suffering righteous one, but as the Christ and the Son of God.[62]

---

58 See Ruppert, *Jesus*, pp. 14–16.
59 Ruppert, *Jesus*, p. 14.
60 See Ruppert, *Jesus*, p. 45.
61 Ruppert, *Jesus*, pp. 46–47.
62 In fact, Ruppert (*Jesus*, pp. 47, 55–57) states that the portrayal of Jesus' passion according to the suffering righteous one is obscured in all the Synoptics, even Matthew and Luke,

The suffering righteous one as a theology
Though the suffering righteous one is not a conventional figure, Ruppert's extensive examples do point to some less expansive conclusions. He shows that the suffering of the righteous was considered a scandal in the early literature, but by the Second Temple period, the suffering of the righteous brings certainty of salvation (*Heilsgewissheit*).[63] Ruppert shows there was a significant trend in Second Temple Judaism rejecting the assumption that suffering indicates guilt and divine punishment.[64] The theology and anthropology of Second Temple Judaism recognized that innocent people do suffer. The authors envisioned for such people a future exaltation that would more than compensate for present suffering. The stories all conclude with the same assumptions: that God will vindicate the righteous who suffer, either in this life or the next. So, although the suffering righteous one is not a stereotypical figure, the suffering of the righteous *is* a *topos*, a common topic, of intertestamental literature, and there are distinct ideas associated with the topic.

This insight into the thought of Second Temple Judaism is helpful when one considers the passion narrative. For example, it argues against the notion that Jesus' suffering automatically indicated guilt to outsiders and that apologetic was a priority for every passion narrative.[65] There were pre-existing, flourishing theological categories in which the suffering of an innocent person could be understood and his innocence assumed. These texts also present background for the exaltation that comes after the suffering and that is expected for both Jesus and the Christian community. Since some of these texts mention atonement or redemption, they should also play a part in scholars' attempts to understand early Christian understandings of how Jesus' death had redemptive significance. The theology of these texts can help modern Christians understand Jesus' passion. It probably helped early Christians to understand it.[66]

---

who do use the word 'righteous' to describe Jesus. For Ruppert, this model operates only in the very early Christian community, and influences the pre-Markan passion narrative, not its canonical developments. Cf. A. Collins, 'Appropriation', in Tuckett, *Scriptures*, pp. 230–32.

63 Ruppert, *Jesus*, p. 28 (calling this a 'dogma'). It is sometimes said that here Ruppert claims that the righteous one *must* suffer, but there is nothing in his language to indicate that. That claim is made by others, however, including Gérard Rossé, *The Cry of Jesus on the Cross: A Biblical and Theological Study* (trans. Stephen Wentworth Arndt; New York: Paulist, 1987), p. 55; cf. Matera, *Kingship*, p. 132.

64 Perhaps that ought to be expected of a developed theology, but human nature seems particularly prone to associating suffering with divine punishment. Deuteronomy makes a point of this. So do Job's friends. So do the disciples in John 9.2 when they ask who sinned to cause a man to be born blind. So do the people of Malta in Acts 28.4 who conclude that Paul, bitten by a viper, must be a murderer. This tendency is not merely ancient.

65 Cf. D. E. Nineham, *The Gospel of St Mark* (Middlesex: Penguin, 1963), p. 366.

66 Cf. Ruppert, *Jesus*, p. 48.

Conclusion

Mark refers to some psalms that describe the suffering of an innocent person, 'psalms of the suffering righteous one'. Because the literature is so broad and diverse, there is no single set of characteristics which fit all or most suffering righteous passages. Therefore one should not use the allusions in the Markan passion narrative to some suffering righteous passages to argue that Mark means the reader to think of others too. Allusions to suffering righteous passages are determined in the same way as other allusions: with verbal corres-pondence for each.

It is also unwarranted to claim that the suffering righteous one is the dominant description or portrayal of Jesus in the Markan passion narrative. In Mark, the central images for Jesus are those that are named: Christ, Son of God, and Son of Man. However, the topic of righteous people suffering appears frequently in the Second Temple period. Treatments of the topic show that Second Temple Judaism did not, as is sometimes supposed, automatically consider suffering to be a sign of divine disfavour. There was at least a substantial element in Judaism that considered the suffering of righteous people to be an inevitable part of life in the world as it existed. However, there was widespread expectation that God would not allow such perversions of justice to go on forever. If God did not intervene to save some people in their moment of trial, then the salvation and vindication would occur in the next life. In either case, God was certain to vindicate and exalt those who suffered for their obedience.

Within that general ideological framework, the suffering of righteous people could be depicted in many ways. To understand how righteous suffering is depicted in the Gospel of Mark, one must attend not to all passages on the topic but to those passages to which the gospel specifically alludes.

Mark 14.62 and Zechariah 12.10

Norman Perrin considers it significant that Mark's clearest uses of Dan. 7.13 (Mark 13.26 and 14.62) are both preceded by ὄψομαι (the future tense of ὁράω, *to see*), even though the word does not occur in the LXX of Dan. 7.13. Perrin argues that the word comes from Zech. 12.10 and that Zech. 12.10 significantly influences the meaning of Mark 14.62. At first glance, this appears rather implausible, since ὄψομαι does not occur in the LXX of Zech. 12.10 either. It does occur, however, in quotations of Zech. 12.10 in John 19.37 and Rev. 1.7.

> And again another passage of scripture says, '*They will look on the one whom they have pierced* (ὄψονται εἰς ὃν ἐξεκέντησαν).' (John 19.37)

> Look! He is coming with the clouds; every eye *will see* (ὄψεται) him, even those who *pierced* (ἐξεκέντησαν) him; and all the tribes of the earth *will mourn for him* (κόψονται ἐπ' αὐτόν). So it is to be. Amen. (Rev. 1.7)[67]

---

67 NRSV modified. 'All the tribes of the earth' alludes to Zech. 12.12.

And I will pour out a spirit of compassion and supplication on the house of David and the inhabitants of Jerusalem, so that, when *they look on the one whom they have pierced, they shall mourn for him* (ἐπιβλέψονται πρός με ἀνθ' ὧν κατωρχήσαντο, καὶ κόψονται ἐπ' αὐτόν), as one mourns for an only child, and weep bitterly over him, as one weeps over a firstborn. (Zech. 12.10)

Revelation and John agree in ὄψομαι and ἐκκεντέω (*to pierce*) against most LXX manuscripts,[68] in a good translation of the Hebrew.

What makes the fact that both of these New Testament texts begin their quotation of Zech. 12.10 with ὄψομαι more interesting is the additional fact that Rev. 1.7 combines Zech. 12.10-14 with Dan. 7.13, the verse found in Mark 14.62. Perrin argues that Mark combines two early Christian traditions on Dan. 7.13. One of those traditions pairs Dan. 7.13 with Ps. 110.1, as is clearly the case in Mark 14.62. The other tradition pairs Dan. 7.13 with Zech. 12.10, as is shown in the Rev. 1.7 passage above. The first pairing, with Ps. 110.1, Perrin argues, refers to Jesus' ascension. The second, with Zech. 12.10, refers to the Parousia. Mark 14.62 combines the two pairs, Dan. 7.13 and Ps. 110.1 (ascension) with Dan. 7.13 and Zech. 12.10 (Parousia).[69] Perrin's position has won significant support, though it is not without detractors.[70]

Perrin's thesis is that Mark 14.62 is 'the end product of a Christian pesher tradition'. This may or may not be an accurate reconstruction of the history of this verse. The matter at hand, however, is not with the sources *behind* Mark but the allusions *in* it. One of the requirements of an allusion is that it is distinct, that it is capable of being caught by an able reader. Suppose that the author of Mark or his source had two traditions at his disposal and combined them. The resulting combination retains of Zech. 12.10 only the single and very common word ὄψομαι. It is unlikely that anyone who did not already expect to find Zech. 12.10 in this quotation would have been able to find it there based on that one common word. Perrin's best defence against this commonsense detraction is that Matthew appeared to see it. Matthew 24.30, parallel to Mark 13.26, adds Zech. 12.10-14 to the quotation of Dan. 7.13 in a manner almost identical to the combination of Dan. 7.13 and Zech. 12.10-14 in Rev. 1.7.[71] Note however that Matthew does not add Zech. 12.10-14 to his parallel to Mark 14.62, the verse in question. Rather than insisting that the word ὄψομαι had the power to evoke the recollection of

---

68 ἐκκεντέω is found in some LXX manuscripts.

69 Norman Perrin, 'Mark XIV. 62: The End Product of a Christian Pesher Tradition?' *NTS* 12 (1966), pp. 153, 155. Cf. Lindars, *New Testament Apologetic*, p. 123.

70 Pesch, *Markusevangelium*, 2, p. 438; Gnilka, *Markus*, 2, p. 282. Maurice Casey (*Son of Man: The Interpretation and Influence of Daniel 7* [London: SPCK, 1979], pp. 180–82) makes a solid argument against the position that the original Christian interpretation of Dan. 7.13 was necessarily with regard to the ascension. For more on these arguments, see p. 187, n. 134.

71 Cf. Lindars, *New Testament Apologetic*, p. 123.

Zech. 12.10 and that Matt. 24.30 attests to this power, it is easier to imagine that Matthew, seeing the quotation of Dan. 7.13 standing alone in Mark 13.26, added to it the allusion to Zechariah 12, in accordance with tradition and in accordance with his tendency to add more Scripture allusions.[72] When he saw Dan. 7.13 combined with Psalm 110 in Mark 14.62, he added nothing more to it; it was already complete. Luke did not appear to see Zech. 12.10 in either Mark 13.26 or 14.62. Even if ὄψομαι in Mark 13.26 and 14.62 had come from Zech. 12.10, the connection is almost completely obscured in Mark. It is not an allusion.

Susanna

Allusions were suggested for two verses of the Susanna chapter of Daniel: Mark 14.56 alluding to Sus. 61 and Mark 14.64 to Sus. 53. The verbal correspondence in both of these suggestions was quite good. Both pairs share rare words, one a combination of rare words:

All of them *condemned* him as *deserving death*. (Mark 14.64)
οἱ δὲ πάντες κατέκριναν αὐτὸν ἔνοχον εἶναι θανάτου.

You are entrusted to hear and to judge, to pronounce the sentence of *death*. And you *condemn* the innocent, but the *guilty* you acquit. (Sus. 53)[73]
(ο´) πιστευθεὶς ἀκούειν καὶ κρίνειν κρίσεις θάνατον ἐπιφερούσας καὶ τὸν μὲν ἀθῷον κατέκρινας, τοὺς δὲ ἐνόχους ἠφίεις ...

Both contain κατακρίνω, ἔνοχος, and θάνατος. θάνατος is common, but the others are rare. ἔνοχος occurs about 20 times. κατακρίνω occurs (depending on the way one counts) roughly five times.[74] They occur together in the LXX only in the ο´ text of Sus. 53. Yet this study concludes this is not an allusion.

The words used in a clause in Mark 14.64 are not only not in a string in Sus. 53, they are used in three different clauses: the judges pronounce a sentence of *death*, *condemn* the innocent, and acquit the *guilty*. That ἔνοχος occurs with ἀφίημι (*acquit*), not with κατακρίνω (*condemn*), is contrary to its sense in Mark, disturbs the parallel, and increases the probability that the correspondence is accidental.[75]

Though ἔνοχος is quite rare in the LXX, it not so rare in the New Testament. It occurs ten times, including four times in Matthew's Sermon on the Mount and one other time in Mark (at 3.29, where the leaders from Jerusalem are said to be guilty of an eternal sin). κατακρίνω also is not as rare

---

72   This is particularly true of references to Zechariah, cf. Matt. 21.5-7; 27.9.
73   Author's translation of the ο´ text. The θ´ text has lower verbal correspondence.
74   It occurs only twice outside of this chapter (Est. 2.1 and Wis. 4.16).
75   Alluding to a passage in a way that is contrary to its sense is something that occurs regularly in general, but is not common in Mark.

in the New Testament, occurring about fifteen times in many different contexts, with no clear link to Susanna. κατακρίνω and ἔνοχος are completely natural and obvious word choices in Mark 14.64, which makes it more likely that verbal correspondence is accidental. Compare the verbal correspondence here to the allusion to Isa. 50.6 in Mark 14.65, where the corresponding words are also not in sequence, but they are rarer and used in a specialized sense in the New Testament.[76] Though Mark 14.64 and Sus. 53 have good verbal and thematic correspondence, this seems to be a parallel rather than an allusion.

Regarding the other suggestion, both Mark 14.56 and Sus. 61 contain the word ψευδομαρτυρέω. In the LXX, that word appears only in Sus. 61 and in the Decalogue (Exod. 20.16 and Deut. 5.20). Mark 14.56 shows no signs of referring to a combination of texts; one must decide between the two possibilities. The verbal correspondence to the Decalogue is slightly better, but the more telling evidence in that direction is that Mark 10.19 clearly quotes several of the commandments in the Decalogue. When a clear quotation exists elsewhere in the narrative, that passage must have preference. Mark 14.56 is an allusion to the Decalogue, not to Sus. 61.

Still it is interesting that there should be *two* excellent possible allusions to Susanna. Mark contains other allusions to Daniel and uses the LXX; the author may well have known the story of Susanna. The theme of the story is compatible with the trial scene. It is entirely possible that these two excellent *possible* allusions are in fact *actual* allusions. These are instances of marginal cases. Sensible and clear criteria take one only so far. The goal of using specific criteria to evaluate potential allusions is not to determine every case with certainty, but to make most cases clear. The art of reading remains for the rest.

Accepted Allusions

The following passages were accepted as allusions:

- Mark 14.1 and Hos. 6.2
- Mark 14.24 and Exod. 24.8
- Mark 14.27 and Zech. 13.7*
- Mark 14.34 and Ps. 42.6, 12; 43.5
- Mark 14.55 and Ps. 37.32
- Mark 14.56-57 and Exod. 20.16//Deut. 5.20
- Mark 14.61 and Isa. 36.21; Ps. 2.7
- Mark 14.62 and Ps. 110.1; Dan. 7.13*
- Mark 14.65 and Isa. 50.6

76   See p. 108.

- Mark 15.24 and Ps. 22.19*
- Mark 15.29-30 and Ps. 22.8-9
- Mark 15.33 and Amos 8.9-10
- Mark 15.34 and Ps. 22.2*
- Mark 15.36 and Ps. 69.22

Those marked with an asterisk are quotations or near quotations, accepted by all. The texts for these passages are compared in Appendices A–C, and that material is not repeated here. The remaining allusions are not as clear. For example, Isa. 50.6 has been disputed, and Isa. 36.21 appears not to have been suggested previously. This section discusses the verbal correspondence between those passages.[77] Thematic correspondence will be taken up in Chapters 4–5.

Mark 14.1 and Hosea 6.2
Time references are important to the Markan passion narrative. Indeed, the narrative begins with one:

> The Passover and the festival of Unleavened Bread were to occur *after two days*.[78]
> ⁵Ἦν δὲ τὸ πάσχα καὶ τὰ ἄζυμα μετὰ δύο ἡμέρας.

'After two days' is said to allude to Hos. 6.2:

> *After two days* he will revive us; on the third day he will raise us up, that we may live before him.
> ὑγιάσει ἡμᾶς μετὰ δύο ἡμέρας· ἐν τῇ ἡμέρᾳ τῇ τρίτῃ ἀναστησόμεθα καὶ ζησόμεθα ἐνώπιον αὐτοῦ

While the words are common, the phrase occurs only in Hos. 6.2, Mark 14.1, and the parallel in Matt. 26.2.[79] Nevertheless, the phrase is so unremarkable in and of itself, one must ask whether anyone might have noticed the correspondence. It appears that Mark's first editors did not. The phrase still stands in the Matthean parallel at 26.2; yet while Matthew edits the passage from Mark considerably, he does not edit towards the verse in Hosea. Luke omits the phrase entirely in 22.1.

---

77   See also Appendices B–C.
78   Author's translation.
79   'Two days' alone is common enough, occurring in Exod. 16.29; Num. 9.22; 11.19; 2 Sam. 1.1; Est. 9.27; Tob. 5.6. John 4.40 also has 'two days', while John 4.43 is a close parallel to the phrase in Mark 14.1: μετὰ δὲ τὰς δύο ἡμέρας. Both occur in the story of the Samaritan woman. John 11.6 also has 'two days' in a puzzling sentence in the story of the resurrection of Lazarus. The context makes an allusion to Hos. 6.2 possible there.

Testing Proposed Allusions

Still it may not be that simple to dismiss the reference. Hosea 6.2 appears to be used in the passion predictions (Mark 8.31; 9.31; 10.34). All three have the same phrasing relative to Hos. 6.2. Mark 10.34 will serve as an example:

> they will mock him, and spit upon him, and flog him, and kill him; and *after three days he will rise again* (μετὰ τρεῖς ἡμέρας ἀναστήσεται).[80]

Again, Hos. 6.2:

> After two days he will revive us; *on the third day he will raise us up* (ἐν τῇ ἡμέρᾳ τῇ τρίτῃ ἀναστησόμεθα), that we may live before him.

Though an allusion to Hos. 6.2 at Mark 10.34 is not widely accepted, the verbal correspondence between them is good. Some LXX manuscripts have εν τη τριτη ημερα rather than ἐν τῇ ἡμέρᾳ τῇ τρίτῃ, with word order corresponding to that of Mark. There are two major differences. One is the preposition: μετά rather than ἐν and the use of 'three days', instead of 'the third day'. It is at least conceivable that the Markan text is an alternative translation of the Hebrew: ביום השלישי. Though there seems to be a real difference in meaning here ('after three days', rather than 'on the third day'), I hesitate to reject the reference over this difference, particularly because Mark's phrasing is rather odd, since there is no reason after the fact to state the time in such a way that the resurrection occurs differently in the gospel (on the third day, that is, on Sunday) than as predicted in that very gospel (after three days, leading one to expect his resurrection on Monday or later). One does wonder how carefully the literal difference of meaning between these two phrases was noted at the time. In Matt. 27.63-64, 'after three days' (μετὰ τρεῖς ἡμέρας) and 'until the third day' (ἕως τῆς τρίτης ἡμέρας) stand together as equivalents (cf. Matt. 12.40 and 16.21).[81] Hosea 6.2 is the only passage containing the words 'three days' and 'raise' (ἀνίστημι). Despite the difference of preposition, the verbal correspondence of the passion predictions in Mark to Hos. 6.2 is strong.

There are quite a few possible allusions to Hos. 6.2 elsewhere in the New Testament, as well. There are references to Jesus (or 'the Son of Man' or 'the messiah', or even metaphorically, 'the temple') being raised on the third day.[82] A variety of phrasing is used in these passages, but clearly the formulation of

---

80 Mark 9.31 has exactly the same phrasing. Mark 8.31 uses a different form of the verb (ἀναστῆναι).

81 Harvey K. McArthur ("'On the Third Day'" *NTS* 18 [1971], p. 85) argues that for the rabbis 'on the third day' and 'after three days' are functional equivalents, even if not exactly the same thing. Cf. Gerhard Delling, 'ἡμέρα', *TDNT* 2, pp. 949–50. Such an equivalence would make the difference between Mark's formulation and that of Hos. 6.2 inconsequential. In terms of pure verbal correspondence, it is inconsequential, since in allusions the forms of words often change.

82 Matt. 16.21; 17.23; 20.19; 27.63-64; Luke 9.22; 18.33; 24.7, 46; John 2.19-20; Acts 10.40; 1 Cor. 15.4.

'rise' with 'the third day' is traditional. The question is whether that tradition points to Hos. 6.2. Two passages are particularly telling. In Luke 18.33, the author edits Mark 10.34 towards Hos. 6.2, with an almost exact correspondence to the LXX:

Luke 18.33: τῇ ἡμέρᾳ τῇ τρίτῃ ἀναστήσεται

Hos. 6.2: ἐν τῇ ἡμέρᾳ τῇ τρίτῃ ἀναστησόμεθα

1 Corinthians 15.4 uses different phrasing: ἐγήγερται τῇ ἡμέρᾳ τῇ τρίτῃ. The verb used is different than that of the LXX, but this is a literal translation of the Hebrew (קום). Paul follows this traditional formulation with 'according to the Scriptures' (κατὰ τὰς γραφάς). The connection to Hos. 6.2 is also strong in John 2.19-22. John 2.19 has 'Destroy this temple, and in three days I will raise it up (καὶ ἐν τρισὶν ἡμέραις ἐγερῶ αὐτόν)', again, with verbal correspondence to the Hebrew. John 2.20 is similarly worded. This saying is tied explicitly to Jesus' resurrection and to Scripture in the following verses, especially 2.22: 'After he was raised from the dead, his disciples remembered that he had said this; and they believed the scripture and the word that Jesus had spoken.' Connection to the Scriptures is present also in Luke 24.46, here using ἀναστῆναι. Thus, in 1 Cor. 15.4, John 2.19-22, and Luke 24.46, 'rise on the third day' is connected with Scripture. The only Old Testament passage to contain such a phrase is Hos. 6.2.

These passages present a variety of wording. The verb in 1 Cor. 15.4, ἐγείρω, is used in many of the 'third day' passages listed above: Matt. 16.21; 17.23; 20.19; 27.63-64; Luke 9.22; John 2.19-20. The first five of these passages are parallels to the Markan passion predictions but change the Markan verb to ἐγείρω, which seems to be the more traditional formulation, again, possibly an independent translation of Hos. 6.2. Luke 18.33; 24.7, 46; and Acts 10.40 use ἀνίστημι, as in the Markan passion predictions and the LXX of Hos. 6.2. The exact wording of 'the third day' varies among the passages. In most, the words are either τῇ ἡμέρᾳ τῇ τρίτῃ or τῇ τρίτῃ ἡμέρᾳ. The Markan passion predictions and John 2.19-20 have unique phrasing (μετὰ τρεῖς ἡμέρας and ἐν τρισὶν ἡμέραις, respectively). So, while the phrasing varies among the passages, they remain fairly similar to each other. Several of the passages present strong cases for an allusion, including 1 Cor. 15.4, Luke 18.33, and John 2.19-22.

Verbal correspondence is supported by important thematic correspondence. Also critical is the prominence of Hos. 6.2 in the early Jewish tradition and the similarity of Jewish and Christian interpretation. In several uses of Hos. 6.2 in Jewish texts, the reference is to the 'two days' portion of the clause. This increases somewhat the volume of 'two days' in the verse. If some of these are early traditions, it increases the possibility that Mark might have expected someone to associate the 'after two days' reference in 14.1 with Hos. 6.2.[83]

---

83 See pp. 114–15 for a survey of these uses.

In light of the total evidence, it seems likely that all or most of these New Testament passages refer to Hos. 6.2 in connection with Jesus' resurrection. The likelihood of an allusion to Hos. 6.2 in the Markan passion predictions is high.

That brings us back to Mark 14.1, and the correspondence of μετὰ δύο ἡμέρας with Hos. 6.2. The phrase is in and of itself unremarkable, but it may stand out because of the interpretive traditions regarding the verse, and, more certainly, because Hos. 6.2 is present in other passages in Mark and is prominent in the New Testament tradition.[84] In view of the total evidence, an allusion to Hos. 6.2 at Mark 14.1 is reasonable, even likely.

Mark 14.24 and Exodus 24.8
In Mark 14.24, Jesus

> *said* to them, 'This is my *blood of the covenant*, poured out for many.'
> <u>καὶ εἶπεν</u> αὐτοῖς· τοῦτό ἐστιν <u>τὸ αἷμά</u> μου <u>τῆς διαθήκης</u> τὸ ἐκχυννόμενον ὑπὲρ πολλῶν.

The concept of initiating a covenant with blood reminds many readers of the Sinai covenant, Exod. 24.8 in particular:

> Moses *took* the blood and dashed it on the people, *and said*, 'See *the blood of the covenant* that the Lord has made with you in accordance with all these words.'
> λαβὼν δὲ Μωυσῆς τὸ αἷμα κατεσκέδασεν τοῦ λαοῦ <u>καὶ εἶπεν</u> Ἰδοὺ <u>τὸ αἷμα τῆς διαθήκης</u>, ἧς διέθετο κύριος πρὸς ὑμᾶς περὶ πάντων τῶν λόγων τούτων.

Although the words are common, the key words, τὸ αἷμα τῆς διαθήκης (*the blood of the covenant*), occur mainly in sequence, and the phrase is not common. Only one other passage, Zech. 9.11, contains a similar phrase. Verbal correspondence and other evidence make Exod. 24.8 a stronger candidate than Zech. 9.11.[85]

As would be expected, Exodus 24 has some prominence in the Jewish tradition, though there are no mentions of this particular verse in the pre-Christian Jewish materials. While Matthew and Luke do not edit toward the verse, it is clearly used in Hebrews.[86] Thus, we have significant verbal correspondence to a passage with significant volume in the tradition. An allusion to Exod. 24.8 at Mark 14.24 is likely.

---

84   It may be worth noting here that the New Testament refers to Hosea rather frequently. Quotations are found in Matt. 2.15; 9.13; 12.7; Luke 23.30; Rom. 9.25-27; 1 Cor. 15.55; 1 Pet. 2.10; and Rev. 6.16. Further New Testament passages contain other, fainter allusions. Hosea as a whole has some prominence in the early Christian tradition.
85   See pp. 227–28 for further discussion.
86   See pp. 118–19 for further information.

Mark 14.34 and Psalms 42.6, 12; 43.5
Jesus' expression of distress in Gethsemane seems to refer to Pss. 42.6, 12; 43.5:

> My *soul is troubled*, even to death. (Mark 14.34)[87]
> καὶ λέγει αὐτοῖς· περίλυπός ἐστιν ἡ ψυχή μου ἕως θανάτου·

> Why *are* you *troubled*, O [my] *soul*, and why are you disquieted within me?[88]
> ἵνα τί περίλυπος εἶ, ψυχή, καὶ ἵνα τί συνταράσσεις με;

Verbal correspondence consists of περίλυπος (*troubled*), εἰμί (*to be*), and ψυχή (*soul*) in sequence and is significant. περίλυπος is rare. It occurs only eight times in the LXX, three of them in these psalm verses. It is used four times in the New Testament, two of them in this saying (here and Matt. 26.38). However, the two remaining uses are not strictly analogous. Luke uses it with regard to the rich ruler walking away troubled (Luke 18.23). More problematic is Mark 6.26, where it is used of Herod being troubled regarding his oaths, which bind him to putting John the Baptist to death. It is unlikely that Mark intends an allusion to Ps. 42.6, etc., in both the Herod and Gethsemane passages. Thus, the rarity of περίλυπος alone is insufficient to direct the reader to these psalm passages. However, the correspondence does not rest on this word alone, since in Mark 14.34 there is the additional correspondence of the verb *to be* and *soul*, all in sequence. Verbal correspondence is sufficient to call this a probable allusion.

Mark 14.55 and Psalm 37.32
Mark 14.55 seems to echo Ps. 37.32:

> Now the chief priests and the whole Council were *seeking* testimony against Jesus *to put him to death*; but they found none. (Mark 14.55)[89]
> Οἱ δὲ ἀρχιερεῖς καὶ ὅλον τὸ συνέδριον ἐζήτουν κατὰ τοῦ Ἰησοῦ μαρτυρίαν εἰς τὸ θανατῶσαι αὐτόν, καὶ οὐχ ηὕρισκον·

> The wicked watch for the righteous, and *seek to put him to death*. (Ps. 37.32)[90]
> κατανοεῖ ὁ ἁμαρτωλὸς τὸν δίκαιον καὶ ζητεῖ τοῦ θανατῶσαι αὐτόν

The passages in Mark and the psalm have similar wording, sharing the words ζητέω; τὸ θανατῶσαι αὐτόν. All of the shared words are common, and ζητέω is separated from the rest of the string in the Markan verse. This

---

87 NRSV modified.
88 NRSV modified. The psalm verses are nearly identical. Psalm 42.6 is used as an example.
89 NRSV modified.
90 NRSV modified.

separation does not disqualify the suggestion; separating words was common practice in ancient (and modern) allusions.[91]

Since, in Mark, changes in wording tend not to alter the sense of the referent, it is significant that the interruption does not do so, but merely supplies the means by which the Sanhedrin sought to put Jesus to death. Verbal correspondence is weak enough that the possibility of accidental correspondence is real, and it is impossible to be certain an allusion was intended. Yet there is enough verbal similarity to be sure that the possibility is located in the text and is not solely in the perspective of the reader. The degree of correspondence, though merely moderate, warrants further consideration. A look at the sense of the psalm and its use in Second Temple Judaism further confirms the allusion. That part of the study is discussed in Chapter 4.

Mark 14.56-57 and Exodus 20.16//Deuteronomy 5.20
Mark 14.56-57 speaks of false witnesses using wording which clearly refers to the Decalogue:

> For many *bore false testimony against* him, and their testimony did not agree. Some stood up and *bore false testimony against* him, saying …[92]
> πολλοὶ γὰρ ἐψευδομαρτύρουν κατ' αὐτοῦ, καὶ ἴσαι αἱ μαρτυρίαι οὐκ ἦσαν. καί τινες ἀναστάντες ἐψευδομαρτύρουν κατ' αὐτοῦ λέγοντες ….

Exodus 20.16 and Deut. 5.20 are equally suitable as referents. Exodus 20.16 reads:

> You shall not *bear false witness against* your neighbor.
> οὐ ψευδομαρτυρήσεις κατὰ τοῦ πλησίον σου μαρτυρίαν ψευδῆ.

The passages share the words ψευδομαρτυρέω κατά. ψευδομαρτυρέω is rare, occurring in the LXX only in these verses and in Sus. 61. Thus verbal correspondence to one of these passages is very strong. Deciding between them is not difficult. While Mark has no clear allusions to Susanna,[93] Mark 10.19 quotes several commandments from the Decalogue, including the commandment against false witness. Mark 14.56-57 refers to Exod. 20.16//Deut. 5.20.

Mark 14.61 and Isaiah 36.21
Jesus' silence in the trial is the subject of a great deal of speculation. Previously suggested allusions for this passage have lacked significant verbal correspondence. It is quite possible that it refers to no Scripture passage at all. There is,

---

91 See p. 33.
92 NRSV modified.
93 See pp. 98–99.

however, one possibility for Scripture allusion that, to my knowledge, has not before been suggested. Mark 14.61 reads:

[Jesus] *was silent and did not answer* anything.[94]
ὁ δὲ <u>ἐσιώπα καὶ οὐκ ἀπεκρίνατο</u> οὐδέν.

Isaiah 36.21 reads:

They *were silent and no one answered* a word.[95]
καὶ <u>ἐσιώπησαν, καὶ οὐδεὶς ἀπεκρίθη</u> αὐτῷ λόγον.

The two passages share the sequence σιωπάω καὶ οὐκ/οὐδεὶς ἀποκρίνομαι. The words occur consecutively, and only the form of the words is changed. All of the words are common in both the LXX and New Testament, except for σιωπάω (*to be silent*), which is not common in the LXX, occurring 37 times. Nor is it particularly common in the New Testament, occurring ten times. The two verbs σιωπάω and ἀποκρίνομαι (*to answer*) occur together in the LXX only twice, here and in Sir. 20.6. Verbal correspondence between Mark and Sir. 20.6 is weaker, and Sir. 20.6 contains a proverb that does not connect thematically with the Markan context. Those facts point to a fairly strong verbal correspondence with Isa. 36.21.

However, there is also some evidence dictating caution. The distinctiveness of the verbal correspondence with Isa. 36.21 comes from the combination of verbs σιωπάω (the subject is silent) and ἀποκρίνομαι (the subject does not answer). Yet repetition is a regular feature of Markan style.[96] And, though σιωπάω is not common in either the LXX or the New Testament in general, it is rather common in Mark, which uses it five times (3.4; 4.39; 9.34; 10.48; 14.61). These two facts increase the possibility that the verbal correspondence is accidental.

Nevertheless, the verbal correspondence between Mark 14.61 and Isa. 36.21 is much stronger than that of other suggested allusions for the passage. Although there is a reasonable possibility that it is accidental, verbal correspondence is sufficient to warrant further study. That study, taken up in Chapter 4, supports the allusion.

Mark 14.61 and Psalm 2.7
One of Mark's most common epithets for Jesus is 'Son of God' (or variations thereof).[97] The high priest's question in Mark 14.61 is one such passage:

---

94   NRSV modified.
95   NRSV modified.
96   See F. Neirynck, *Duality in Mark: Contributions to the Study of the Markan Redaction* (rev. edn with supplementary notes; BETL 31; Louvain: Leuven University Press, 1988), pp. 71–72, 94.
97   For example, Jesus is called son of God at Mark 1.11 and 9.7, by a voice from heaven; 1.1, by the narrator; 15.39, by the centurion; and 5.7, by demons.

Are you the Christ, *the Son* of the Blessed?⁹⁸
σὺ εἶ ὁ χριστὸς ὁ υἱὸς τοῦ εὐλογητοῦ;

That appears to be an allusion to Ps. 2.7:

I will tell of the decree of the Lord:
He said to me, '*You are my son*; today I have begotten you.
διαγγέλλων τὸ πρόσταγμα κυρίου
Κύριος εἶπεν πρός με Υἱός μου εἶ σύ,
ἐγὼ σήμερον γεγέννηκά σε.

The words shared are extremely common. Moreover, the sequence is broken and the flavour changed. Rather than God declaring the subject God's son, as in Ps. 2.7, the high priest is asking Jesus if he is God's son. However, Mark 14.61 also shares the word χριστός (*Christ* or *anointed*) with Ps. 2.2, a few verses earlier, which adds some verbal correspondence and considerable thematic correspondence.

Still, on its own, verbal correspondence between Mark 14.61 and Ps. 2.7 is insufficient for an allusion.

But in this case, as in some others, the allusion does not stand on its own. In the baptismal scene, a voice from heaven tells Jesus (Mark 1.11):

You are my Son (σὺ εἶ ὁ υἱός μου), the Beloved; with you I am well pleased.

This is likely an allusion to Ps. 2.7. The two verses share σὺ εἶ/εἶ σύ; υἱός μου, again very common words, but that the words occur as a sequence, even though the order is shifted, strengthens the correspondence.⁹⁹

The verbal correspondence of Mark 1.11 and 14.61 to Ps. 2.7 is similar, except that Mark 14.61 lacks μου, and the sequence is broken. However, the sequence is broken with ὁ χριστός, which actually strengthens the connection with the psalm.

Since an allusion to Ps. 2.7 is likely in Mark 1.11, the requirement for verbal correspondence at Mark 14.61 is lowered. In addition, the psalm has some importance in the tradition. This is a probable allusion.

---

98   NRSV modified.
99   James W. Watts ('Psalm 2 in the Context of Biblical Theology', *HBT* 12 [1990], p. 81) notes that the Western text has a clearer reference to Psalm 2. The baptismal voice is also explicitly connected with Psalm 2 in other early Christian literature, e.g., *Gos. Eb.* and Justin, *Dial.* 88.8.
   A number of other suggestions are made for this passage, including Gen. 22.2; Exod. 4.22-23; and Isa. 42.1. (See Marcus, *Way*, pp. 49–55, for a discussion of the evidence.) In brief, Ps. 2.7 (possibly combined with Isa. 42.1) is preferred because of its greater verbal correspondence and the significant use of this psalm in the New Testament.

Mark 14.65 and Isaiah 50.6
In Mark 14.65, Jesus is beaten after the trial:

> Some began to *spit* on him, to cover his *face*, and to beat him, saying to him, 'Prophesy!' The guards also took him over and *struck* him.[100]
> Καὶ ἤρξαντό τινες <u>ἐμπτύειν</u> αὐτῷ καὶ περικαλύπτειν αὐτοῦ <u>τὸ πρόσωπον</u> καὶ κολαφίζειν αὐτὸν καὶ λέγειν αὐτῷ· προφήτευσον, καὶ οἱ ὑπηρέται <u>ῥαπίσμασιν</u> αὐτὸν ἔλαβον.

Isaiah 50.6 reads:

> I gave my back to blows, and my cheeks to *strikes*; I did not turn my *face* from the insult of *spitting*.[101]
> τὸν νῶτόν μου δέδωκα εἰς μάστιγας, τὰς δὲ σιαγόνας μου εἰς <u>ῥαπίσματα</u>, τὸ δὲ <u>πρόσωπόν</u> μου οὐκ ἀπέστρεψα ἀπὸ αἰσχύνης <u>ἐμπτυσμάτων</u>·

The corresponding words are ἐμπτύειν/ἐμπτυσμάτων (*spit*[*ting*]), τὸ πρόσωπον (*face*), and ῥάπισμα (*strike*). ἐμπτύω and ῥάπισμα are the most telling. ἐμπτύω and its noun form, ἔμπτυσμα, occur only three times in the LXX. ῥάπισμα and its verb form, ῥαπίζω, are also rare, occurring only four times. In the LXX, these two words occur together only in Isa. 50.6. The words are equally rare in the New Testament. ἐμπτύω occurs six times, either in a passion prediction or a passion narrative.[102] ῥάπισμα occurs only five times, four of them in the passion narratives,[103] and the fifth in Matt. 5.39, which also appears to be an allusion to Isa. 50.6. The weak point of verbal correspondence is that the words correspond individually; there is no string.[104] Nevertheless, these words are so rare and used in such a specialized sense in the New Testament, that the verbal correspondence is more than sufficient for an allusion.

Mark 15.29-30 and Psalm 22.8-9
The mockery at the cross in Mark 15.29-30 is reminiscent of Psalm 22. The Markan passage reads:

> Those who passed by derided him, *shaking their heads* and saying, 'Aha! You who would destroy the temple and build it in three days, *save yourself*, and come down from the cross!'

---

100 NRSV modified.
101 Author's translation from the LXX.
102 Matt. 26.67; 27.30; Mark 10.34; 14.65; 15.19; Luke 18.32.
103 Matt. 26.67; Mark 14.65; John 18.22; 19.3.
104 Hooker (*Jesus*, pp. 90–91) finds against the allusion on that basis, so also Suhl (*Funktion*, p. 59).

Καὶ οἱ παραπορευόμενοι ἐβλασφήμουν αὐτὸν <u>κινοῦντες τὰς κεφαλὰς</u> αὐτῶν καὶ λέγοντες· οὐὰ ὁ καταλύων τὸν ναὸν καὶ οἰκοδομῶν ἐν τρισὶν ἡμέραις, <u>σῶσον σεαυτὸν</u> καταβὰς ἀπὸ τοῦ σταυροῦ.

Psalm 22.8-9 reads:

'All who see me mock at me; they make mouths at me, they *shake their heads*; 'Commit your cause to the LORD; let him deliver – let him *save him* in whom he delights!'[105]
πάντες οἱ θεωροῦντές με ἐξεμυκτήρισάν με,
ἐλάλησαν ἐν χείλεσιν, <u>ἐκίνησαν κεφαλήν</u>
Ἤλπισεν ἐπὶ κύριον, ῥυσάσθω αὐτόν·
<u>σωσάτω αὐτόν</u>, ὅτι θέλει αὐτόν.

The passages share the words: κινέω [τὰς] κεφαλάς/κεφαλήν (*to shake one's head*); σῴζω σεαυτόν/αὐτόν (*save yourself/him*). Though the phrase κινέω κεφαλήν occurs regularly in the LXX, verbal correspondence is strengthened by the correspondence of the taunt, 'save yourself/him', in both passages. Moreover, Mark 15 has two strong references to Psalm 22: Mark 15.24, the casting of lots, nearly quotes Ps. 22.19; and Mark 15.34, the cry of dereliction, quotes Ps. 22.2. Thus, Mark 15.29-30 is surrounded by strong allusions to the psalm, and Ps. 22.8-9, the verses suggested here, are likewise surrounded by other referents. Verbal correspondence is moderate, but because the reader's attention is so securely drawn to Psalm 22 in this section of Mark that correspondence is sufficient.[106]

That conclusion is supported by the evidence of two early readers. At 27.39-40, Matthew retains the parallel and adds a near quotation later in the scene (Matt. 27.43).[107] Luke 23.35 is revised toward the psalm:

And the people stood by, *watching*; but the leaders *mocked* him, saying 'He saved others; *let him save himself* if he is the Messiah of God, his chosen one!' [108]
Καὶ εἱστήκει ὁ λαὸς <u>θεωρῶν</u>. <u>ἐξεμυκτήριζον</u> δὲ καὶ οἱ ἄρχοντες λέγοντες·
ἄλλους ἔσωσεν, <u>σωσάτω ἑαυτόν</u>, εἰ οὗτός ἐστιν ὁ χριστὸς τοῦ θεοῦ ὁ ἐκλεκτός.

---

105 NRSV modified.
106 Linnemann (*Studien*, p. 153) notes the correspondence between Ps. 22.9 and the taunt of Mark 15.30-31, but considers the catchword σῴζω insufficient on its own to securely establish the allusion. She is certainly correct in her caution. The totality of the evidence is the basis here for the conclusion that this is an allusion.
107 NA[27] suggests Ps. 22.8 as a parallel to Matt. 27.29, but those two passages have very little verbal correspondence. Matthew 27.29 is closer to Zech. 6.11.
108 NRSV modified.

Luke revises the beginning of the parallel, changing Mark's οἱ παραπορευόμενοι (*the passersby*) to ὁ λαὸς θεωρῶν (*the crowd watching*), where θεωρῶν corresponds to οἱ θεωροῦντες of Ps. 22.8. More significantly, he changes ἐμπαίζοντες (*mocking*) of Mark 15.31 to ἐξεμυκτήριζον, which corresponds with ἐξεμυκτήρισαν of Ps. 22.8. ἐκμυκτηρίζω is rare, occurring only four times in the LXX and twice in the New Testament, both in Luke (16.14 and here). Luke also revises the language of the taunt to make it just a bit closer to the language of Ps. 22.9, changing Mark's σῶσον to σωσάτω, matching the verb form in the psalm. The Lukan parallel distinctly corresponds to Ps. 22.8-9. It appears that both Matthew and Luke recognized an allusion to Ps. 22.8-9 in Mark 15.29-30.

Mark 15.33 and Amos 8.9-10

The suggestion of a reference to Amos 8.9-10 in Mark 15.33 passes the requirements for an allusion. Yet the strength of the correspondence is not as great as one might have guessed from the number of its advocates.

First consider the verbal correspondence of Mark 15.33 to the Greek of Amos 8.9-10:

> And when it was the sixth hour, *darkness came* over *the* whole *land* until the ninth hour. (Mark 15.33)[109]
> Καὶ γενομένης ὥρας ἕκτης <u>σκότος ἐγένετο ἐφ'</u> ὅλην <u>τὴν γῆν</u> ἕως ὥρας ἐνάτης.

> And on that day, says the Lord GOD, the sun will go down at noon, and daylight *will become dark on the earth.* I will turn your feasts into mourning, and all your songs into lamentation; I will bring sackcloth on all loins, and baldness on every head; I will make it like the mourning for an only son, and the end of it like a bitter day. (Amos 8.9-10)[110]
> καὶ ἔσται ἐν ἐκείνῃ τῇ ἡμέρᾳ, λέγει κύριος, καὶ δύσεται ὁ ἥλιος μεσημβρίας, καὶ <u>συσκοτάσει ἐπὶ τῆς γῆς</u> ἐν ἡμέρᾳ τὸ φῶς· καὶ μεταστρέψω τὰς ἑορτὰς ὑμῶν εἰς πένθος καὶ πάσας τὰς ᾠδὰς ὑμῶν εἰς θρῆνον καὶ ἀναβιβῶ ἐπὶ πᾶσαν ὀσφὺν σάκκον καὶ ἐπὶ πᾶσαν κεφαλὴν φαλάκρωμα καὶ θήσομαι αὐτὸν ὡς πένθος ἀγαπητοῦ καὶ τοὺς μετ' αὐτοῦ ὡς ἡμέραν ὀδύνης.

Verbal correspondence in Greek is only moderate; the two passages share the words σκότος/συσκοτάσει and γῆς. συσκοτάζω (*become very dark*) is rare, occurring only eleven times in the LXX, but σκότος (*darkness*) is fairly common, occurring 30 times in the New Testament. In addition, correspondence is weakened by the inexact correspondence of noun and verb.

---

109 NRSV modified.
110 NRSV modified.

Correspondence is bolstered, however, by several additional connections. μεσημβρία (*noon*) of Amos 8.9 has the same meaning as ὥρα ἕκτη (*sixth hour*) of Mark 15.33. Amos 8.10 refers to ἑορτή (*feast*); the passion occurs during the ἑορτή (Mark 14.2; 15.6). Amos 8.10 also uses the word ἀγαπητός (*beloved*), which is relatively uncommon, occurring 23 times in the LXX. ἀγαπητός is very common in the New Testament, a particular favourite of Paul's for addressing the members of Christ, but it is not common in Mark, where it is used three times, always referring to Jesus: applied by the heavenly voice to Jesus (Mark 1.11 and 9.7), and in the Parable of the Vineyard describing the beloved son of the vineyard owner, who, at least in Mark, represents Jesus (Mark 12.6).

Now consider the correspondence with the Hebrew of Amos 8.9-10, which is better.[111] The Markan words σκότος ἐγένετο ἐφ᾽ ὅλην τὴν γῆν represent a fairly literal translation of the latter portion of Amos 8.9: והחשכתי לארץ. The correspondence in sense between *feast* in Amos 8.10 remains. The sense of ἀγαπητός also remains. יחיד with the meaning of *only child* is always translated by ἀγαπητός or in the case of Prov. 4.3, by ἀγαπώμενος.[112]

The total evidence for correspondence makes it likely that Mark 15.33 is an allusion to Amos 8.9-10.

Mark 15.36 and Psalm 69.22
In Mark 15.36, someone offers Jesus vinegary wine:

> And someone ran, filled a sponge with *vinegary wine*, put it on a stick, and *gave it to him to drink*, saying, 'Wait, let us see whether Elijah will come to take him down.'[113]
> δραμὼν δέ τις [καὶ] γεμίσας σπόγγον <u>ὄξους</u> περιθεὶς καλάμῳ <u>ἐπότιζεν αὐτὸν</u> λέγων· ἄφετε ἴδωμεν εἰ ἔρχεται Ἡλίας καθελεῖν αὐτόν.

This is an allusion to Ps. 69.22:

> They gave me poison for food, and for my thirst they *gave me vinegar to drink*.
> καὶ ἔδωκαν εἰς τὸ βρῶμά μου χολὴν
> καὶ εἰς τὴν δίψαν μου <u>ἐπότισάν με ὄξος</u>.

The passages share the words: ὄξος (*vinegary wine*) and ποτίζω αὐτόν/με (*gave him/me to drink*). ὄξος is rare, occurring only four times in the LXX and six in the New Testament, all of the latter with regard to this incident.[114]

---

111 See p. 281 for the complete Hebrew text.
112 Cf. Gen. 22.2, 12, 16; Judg. 11.34; Prov. 4.3; Jer. 6.26; Amos 8.10; Zech. 12.10.
113 NRSV modified.
114 Matt. 27.48; Mark 15.36; Luke 23.36; and three times in John 19.29-30.

Word order is changed, but that is common in Mark's use of texts. Verbal correspondence is fairly strong.[115] This is a probable allusion.

Conclusion

Scholars have suggested a large number of allusions for the Markan passion narrative. Almost two-thirds of the suggestions had either no verbal correspondence or correspondence of a single common word. None of these can be considered an allusion, even though some of these suggestions have significant scholarly support, such as the suggestion that Mark alludes to Isa. 52.13–53.12 at various points in the narrative or that the silence in the trial refers to the suffering righteous one.

Sixteen suggestions were accepted as having sufficient verbal and thematic correspondence to signal an allusion. It is now time to turn to the task of determining how those allusions affect the meaning of the Markan passion narrative.

---

115 For a contrary opinion, see Suhl, *Funktion*, pp. 61–62.

4. Interpreting the Allusions

Chapter 3 examined the suggested allusions for the Markan passion narrative to determine which allusions are most likely to be present. This chapter and the next will analyse each of the confirmed allusions to determine their contribution to the meaning of the narrative, considering thematic correspondence and the interplay between the referring and referent passages. This chapter examines most of the allusions in Mark 14–15, in the following sections:

- From Plot to Arrest – Mark 14.1-52
- The Trial Narrative – Mark 14.53–15.15
- The Crucifixion and Burial – Mark 15.16-47

Because the allusions in the high priest's question and Jesus' answer (Mark 14.61-62) have more complex histories, they require more discussion and are treated separately in Chapter 5.

Analysis of each allusion is accompanied by a survey of other uses of the referent passage in early Judaism and Christianity. The goal of the survey is to locate possible interpretive traditions for the passage and to determine whether any assist in the interpretation of Mark.[1] There is no reliable method for sorting out which traditions were not only in existence before the gospel was written but were known to the author, not only known but influential. Direct connections between the gospel and these other uses cannot be assumed. Instead they are considered in light of the Gospel of Mark, and judgements are made concerning their possible relevance and helpfulness for understanding the allusion in Mark.[2]

From Plot to Arrest

After two days – Mark 14.1 and Hosea 6.2
Opening the Markan passion narrative proper is the seemingly unremarkable phrase, 'it was *two days before* (μετὰ δύο ἡμέρας) the Passover', containing

---

1   Because the surveys have the purpose of helping to interpret Mark, they are not necessarily complete. Unrelated uses, e.g., a particular halakic application, are omitted.
2   See pp. 57–58.

a probable, though faint, allusion to Hos. 6.2: 'After two days (μετὰ δύο ἡμέρας) he will revive us; on the third day he will raise us up, that we may live before him.'

Early Jewish interpretation
Hosea 6.2 is used regularly in Jewish literature regarding resurrection. For example, *3 Enoch* 28.10 quotes Hos. 6.2 with respect to judgement after death.[3] In the first two days, one's character is assessed. On the third day, the Watchers 'sanctify the body and the soul with lashes of fire, as it is written, "on the third day he will raise us and we shall live in his presence"'. The blows to the body and soul make one fit for the presence of God and eternal life. The mention of the body indicates that resurrection is meant here.

In rabbinic literature Hos. 6.2 is used regarding resurrection in some very different contexts:

- *Sifre Haazinu* 329[4] states that Hos. 6.2, 'after two days He will revive us', is one of four assurances of the resurrection to Israel.
- *Y. Ber.* 5.2 and *y. Ta'an.* 1.1[5] explain that the prayer for rain and resurrection are connected because Hos. 6.2 refers to resurrection, while Hos. 6.3 refers to rain.
- In *y. Sanh.* 11.6, the rabbis discuss whether a sign is necessary to verify a prophecy. One says yes, citing the example of Hezekiah asking for a sign that he would be healed and enter the temple 'on the third day' (2 Kgs 20.8). Another discounts that example by connecting its 'on the third day' with that of Hos. 6.2, and saying, based on the latter, 'That is a special case, because at issue was the resurrection of the dead.'[6]
- The Talmud (*b. Roš. Haš.* 31a; *b. Sanh.* 97a) indicates that in the course of the Eschaton, the world will be desolate 2,000 years, corresponding to the two days of Hos. 6.2, after which the resurrection will occur.
- The Targum replaces the days of Hos. 6.2 with what they were understood to represent: 'He will give us life *in the days of consolations that will come; on the day of the resurrection of the dead* he will raise us up and we shall live before him.'[7]

---

3   P. Alexander (*OTP* 1, p. 229) concludes that *3 Enoch* 'contains some very old traditions', but probably received its final redaction in the fifth or sixth centuries. He also provides the translation.

4   Redaction of *Sifre Deuteronomy* is put in the late third century (Strack and Stemberger, *Introduction*, p. 273).

5   Strack and Stemberger (*Introduction*, p. 171) conclude the Jerusalem Talmud was redacted in the early fifth century.

6   Translations of the Jerusalem Talmud by Jacob Neusner, *The Talmud of the Land of Israel* (35 vols; Chicago: University of Chicago Press, 1982–94).

7   Targum translations from Martin McNamara et al. (eds), *The Aramaic Bible: The Targums* (21 vols; Collegeville: Liturgical Press, 1987–).

While none of these references stem from the first century or earlier, the interpretation is widespread and represented in some fairly early texts (e.g., *Sifre*). Since Hos. 6.2 becomes closely associated with Jesus' resurrection in Christian thought, it seems more likely that early Christian interpretation was influenced by existing Jewish tradition than that Jewish interpreters would unanimously take up this particular thought from Christianity. If that assumption is correct, these later Jewish texts would be reflecting a tradition that went back at least to the first century.

Other early Christian uses
Early Christian texts apply Hos. 6.2 to Jesus' resurrection. All of the gospels appear to allude to the passage in passion predictions and similar sayings. One of the closest in wording is Luke 18.33. Similarly, Hos. 6.2 seems to be indicated in John 2.19-22, where Jesus speaks of raising the temple in three days, referring to his death and resurrection, as is made explicit in 2.21-22. This saying, as well as 1 Cor. 15.4 and Luke 24.46, explicitly tie rising on the third day to Scripture and quite plausibly to Hos. 6.2.[8] Tertullian also interprets the verse as referring to resurrection (*Jud.* 13.23; *Marc.* 4.43.1).

Markan use
The Markan passion predictions appear to allude to Hos. 6.2.[9] The first will serve as an example:

> Then he began to teach them that the Son of Man must undergo great suffering, and be rejected by the elders, the chief priests, and the scribes, and be killed, and *after three days rise* again. (μετὰ τρεῖς ἡμέρας ἀναστῆναι; Mark 8.31)

> After two days he will revive us; *on the third day he will raise us up* (ἐν τῇ ἡμέρᾳ τῇ τρίτῃ ἀναστησόμεθα), that we may live before him. (Hos. 6.2)

As in later Jewish and Christian uses of the text, Hos. 6.2 is used regarding resurrection, here Jesus' resurrection, and may have additional significance as well. Hosea 6.1 states that while God is the one who strikes down, God also is the one to heal:

> Come, let us return to the LORD; for it is he who has torn, and he will heal us; he has struck down, and he will bind us up.

Divine agency in Hos. 6.1 connects with the δεῖ (it is necessary) of the passion predictions: the passion is necessary because God has willed it, and God will bring it about. (This is similar to Zech. 13.7, quoted in Mark 14.27, where

---

8 See p. 102.
9 See p. 101.

God strikes the shepherd and the sheep are scattered.) The allusion to Hos. 6.2 affirms that God is behind the events of the passion and that God will bring restoration, 'as sure as the dawn' (Hos. 6.3).

Mark 14.1 opens the passion narrative proper:

> It was *two days before* the Passover and the festival of Unleavened Bread. The chief priests and the scribes were looking for a way to arrest Jesus by stealth and kill him.

Several elements of this passage link to the passion predictions, including the reference to arresting and killing Jesus and the common use of Hos. 6.2. The allusion reminds readers of what they learned about the passion from those predictions, most clearly, that the suffering of the passion is God's plan and that God will assuredly raise Jesus up.

As mentioned above, the Markan uses of Zech. 13.7 and Hos. 6.1 are related.[10] These passages speak of a restored relationship with God, which is emphasized in the allusion to Zech. 13.7[11] and important also in the allusion to Hos. 6.2. One of their common themes concerns recognizing the Lord:

> They will call on my name, and I will answer them. I will say, 'They are my people'; and they will say, 'The LORD is our God.' (Zech. 13.9)

> Come, let us return to the LORD ... Let us know, let us press on to know the LORD; his appearing is as sure as the dawn; he will come to us like the showers, like the spring rains that water the earth. (Hos. 6.1, 3)

Elsewhere in Markan allusions, Jesus is put in the place of the Lord, even explicitly called 'Lord' in Mark 11.3.[12] Here the Lord of Hos. 6.3 may also be understood as Jesus (in a polyvalent sense, not exclusive of God). If so, the allusion has something to say about how one responds to Jesus. While the chief priests and scribes refuse to 'press on to know the Lord', the woman at Bethany uses her wealth to recognize and honour him. She will be honoured in return (Mark 14.1-9).

Hosea 6.3 affirms that the Lord's 'appearing is as sure as the dawn'. If the Lord is Jesus here, then Jesus' appearing is as sure as the dawn. This appearance may correspond to his resurrection or, again in a polyvalent sense, to the Parousia. Mark 14.1 is the transition between the 'little apocalypse' of Mark 13, where Jesus explains what will happen in the Eschaton, and the passion narrative, where Jesus experiences that Eschaton in part.[13]

---

10 Zechariah 13.7 and Hos. 6.1 also share the (admittedly common) keyword 'strike' (πατάσσω).
11 See pp. 123–24.
12 See pp. 3–4.
13 Many of the elements of Mark 13 are repeated in Mark 14–15, such as arrests, trials,

Mark 13.26-27 affirms that the Son of Man will appear, with great power and glory, and the chosen will be gathered. Hosea 6.1-3 is parallel: the Lord will appear and heal. Read this way, the resurrection of Hos. 6.2 would apply not only to Jesus but also to his followers in the general resurrection of the Eschaton, similar to the way the passage is used in Jewish literature. The allusion to Hos. 6.2 in this transition between 'little apocalypse' and passion narrative seems to indicate that it matters a great deal whether one responds to Jesus as do the leaders or the woman at Bethany.

Blood of the Covenant – Mark 14.24 and Exodus 24.8
Jesus' word over the cup, 'This is my *blood of the covenant* (τὸ αἷμά μου τῆς διαθήκης), which is poured out for many', appears to allude to Exod. 24.8, 'Moses took the blood and dashed it on the people, and said, "See the *blood of the covenant* (τὸ αἷμα τῆς διαθήκης) that the Lord has made with you in accordance with all these words."'

Early Jewish interpretation
There is surprisingly little direct comment on Exod. 24.8 in early Jewish literature, though the Sinai event itself, including the larger context of Exodus 24, is central to Jewish thought.[14] Theophany is one of the elements often noted in early Jewish use of the chapter.[15] This stems directly from the text. Before the initiation of the covenant, the people hear God like a trumpet and see God in fire, storm, and earthquake (Exod. 19.16-19). After the covenant is initiated, the elders go up the mountain and see God (Exod. 24.11).

John Hilber argues that Exodus 24 is also seen in its very earliest interpretations as a type of the eschatological banquet, an interpretation stemming from Exod. 24.11 where the elders eat and drink in the presence of God. Isaiah 24.23 invokes the scene, speaking of God manifesting his glory to the elders at the final judgement. Isaiah 25.6-10 seems also to allude to it when it describes a sacrificial feast on God's mountain, celebrating the Eschaton and the swallowing up of death.[16]

---

and executions, references to the Son of Man coming, whether one 'keeps awake', etc. In Jesus' passion, the Eschaton comes, though only in part. For example, the sun and stars are not totally destroyed (13.24-25), only darkened for three hours (15.33). Jesus' passion is portrayed as a foretaste of what is to come. See also below on Amos 8.9.

14   Cf., e.g., 4Q158 frg. 4 and 4Q356 frg. 15; Josephus, *Ant.* 3.5.

15   See Philo, *Migr.* 168; *Conf.* 96; *Dreams* 62, 222; Aristobulus frg. 2.13; *Jubilees* 1.28; 4 *Ezra* 9.29-31. In the (later) Targums, the theophany is less direct; for example, the elders see 'the Glory of the *Shekinah* of the Lord', rather than God per se. Still, the added words, necessary to make the encounter less direct seem actually to emphasize it, simply by taking longer to describe it, especially with the repeated mention of the Glory of the *Shekinah* of the Lord in vv. 11, 13, 16, and 17.

16   John W. Hilber, 'Theology of Worship in Exodus 24', *JETS* 39 (1996), p. 187.

118   *The Use of Scripture in the Markan Passion Narrative*

At its most basic level, Exod. 24.8 describes the initiation of the covenant. It is when Moses sprinkles them with the blood that Israel becomes bound to the Law (*Mek. Baḥ.* 3.24-26).[17] The passage is used to discern what rites are necessary for the initiation of a proselyte (*b. Yebam.* 46b, *b. Ker.* 9a; cf. *Mek. Baḥ.* 3.28-32), and the act of sprinkling blood here is associated with circumcision (*t. Ned.* 2.5; *y. Ned.* 3.9).[18] That is, the rabbis move from the initiation of the wilderness generation to initiation in their own day. *Targum Onqelos* and *Pseudo-Jonathan* understand the sprinkling to bring atonement.

Other early Christian uses
Variations of the phrase 'blood of the covenant' occur seven times in the New Testament, four of them in Last Supper pericopes. Matthew edits his parallel (26.28) in important ways, but not toward the wording of Exod. 24.8. Luke 22.20 seems to be edited toward the tradition found in 1 Cor. 11.25, which with varied wording refers to 'the new covenant in my blood'; neither of these passages has any particular connection to Exod. 24.8.[19] So neither of Mark's first editors appears to emphasize an allusion to Exod. 24.8, nor does the Pauline version in 1 Cor. 11.25.

On the other hand, the phrase 'blood of the covenant' is prominent in Hebrews, where it is tied explicitly to Exod. 24.8 by a quotation in Heb. 9.20. The making of the first covenant is a type of the new covenant, both made with the shedding of blood (9.15-22). Variations of 'the blood of the covenant' occur twice thereafter, in 10.29, referring to the covenant in Christ and continuing the connection to Exod. 24.8, and in 13.20.[20] The larger context is concerned with the inauguration of a new covenant (Heb. 8.6, 13; 9.15-22; 10.9) and purification from sin (9.13-14, 22–10.22). Sin is forgiven, and the people are enjoined to avoid future sin (8.10-12; 10.16, 23–13.21). All three concepts are drawn together in 9.18-22, where Exod. 24.8 is quoted. Later, the author states that those who have received the blood of the (new) covenant have been sanctified by it, and that should they engage in wilful sin, there will be no forgiveness for them (10.26-31). The closing benediction connects the blood of the covenant with God's work of completing the faithful in all goodness, so that they might accomplish God's will (13.20-21). The focus on

---

17   The *Mekilta* was redacted in the late third century (Strack and Stemberger, *Introduction*, p. 255).
18   The Tosefta was redacted mainly in late third or early fourth century (Strack and Stemberger, *Introduction*, p. 157).
19   See p. 229 for further discussion of the suggested allusion to Jer. 31.31.
20   Some commentators also see a reference to the Eucharist in Heb. 10.29, which would, of course, further tie it to the passage in Mark 14.24. Harold W. Attridge (*The Epistle to the Hebrews* [ed. Helmut Koester; Hermeneia; Philadelphia: Fortress, 1989], pp. 257–58) and Alan C. Mitchell (*Hebrews* [SP 13; Collegeville: Liturgical Press, 2007], p. 189) warn that a connection to the Eucharist, if it is there at all, is certainly not emphasized. The connection between these passages in Hebrews and Mark are simply by way of Exod. 24.8.

inauguration of the covenant, purification from sin, and the consequent obligation to fulfil the commands of God corresponds to the interpretation of Exod. 24.8 in the Jewish material.

Also like the Jewish material, Hebrews takes note of the theophany at Sinai. Hebrews 12.18-21 reminds the reader of the terrifying aspect of the mountain during the initiation of the first covenant. Then it says, the faithful 'have come to Mount Zion and to the city of the living God ... and to God the judge of all, and to the spirits of the righteous made perfect, and to Jesus, the mediator of a new covenant, and to the sprinkled blood that speaks a better word than the blood of Abel' (12.22-24). Coming into the presence of God and Jesus is connected here to 'the sprinkled blood'. Hebrews 10.19 is similar, in that 'we have confidence to enter the sanctuary by the blood of Jesus'.

Atonement plays a key role in the interpretation of Exod. 24.8 in Hebrews, as later in the Targums. So it is possible that Matthew's addition to the Markan cup word, 'this is my blood of the covenant, which is poured out for many *for the forgiveness of sins*' (26.28), indicates that he saw the reference to Exod. 24.8 and was making its connection to atonement explicit.

Markan use

Mark seems to use Exodus 24 first in the transfiguration. Bruce Chilton argues that Exodus 24 is the pattern on which the transfiguration story is based. In Mark, he sees connections in the mountain (Exod. 24.13; Mark 9.2), the time frame of six days (Exod. 24.16; Mark 9.2), the voice of God in the cloud (Exod. 24.16; Mark 9.7), and seeing the glory of God as reflected in Jesus' clothes (Exod. 24.10; Mark 9.3). Peter's reference to booths (Mark 9.5) also connects to the wilderness experience and thus indirectly to the Sinai covenant.[21] The presence of Moses obviously evokes this episode, but so does that of Elijah, who goes to Horeb, the 'mountain of God', and experiences his own theophany, though in an ironic manner (1 Kgs 19.8-12). One might add that Exodus 24 is an occasion when Joshua, or 'Jesus' in the language of the LXX, plays a role, ascending the mountain with Moses (Exod. 24.13). It is perhaps also relevant that when Jesus and the three descend the mountain, there is a crowd surrounding the epileptic boy whom the disciples could not heal, and Jesus responds to the event by saying, 'You faithless generation, how much longer must I be among you?' (Mark 9.19). This evokes the scene of Moses descending the mountain only to find the people in sin, revelry, and chaos. In response, God at first refuses to go on with the people (Exod. 32.15–33.3). Though the verbal parallels are not terribly strong, a series of

---

21 Bruce Chilton, 'The Transfiguration: Dominical Assurance and Apostolic Vision', *NTS* 27 (1980), pp. 120–22.

specific markers tie the texts together, and the conclusion that the transfiguration is based on Exodus 24 is a reasonable one.[22]

While much about the transfiguration is less than obvious, some aspects are quite clear: it has epiphanic and eschatological implications and is connected with Jesus' death and resurrection. Jesus' garments, an unearthly white (Mark 9.3), recall those of God and his angels in *1 Enoch* 14.21; 71.1. The mountain itself, particularly when coupled with the descent of a cloud with a voice emanating from it, evoke a sense of the presence of God. Moses and Elijah both speak with God in their Sinai/Horeb experiences. Here they speak with Jesus. The three disciples seem to play the role of the elders who see God in Exodus 24.11. In Mark, the vision is of Jesus. Moses and Elijah listened to God. The disciples are to listen to Jesus (Mark 9.7).[23]

Similar to the allusion to Exodus 24 in Isaiah 24–25, the transfiguration has an eschatological tenor. Before this episode, Jesus tells his disciples, 'Truly I tell you, there are some standing here who will not taste death until they see that the kingdom of God has come with power' (Mark 9.1). Following this episode, Jesus speaks of Elijah's coming, which must happen first, and of his own death and resurrection (9.9-13). Indeed, his death and resurrection frame the transfiguration narrative, since they are tied to his role as messiah in the preceding episode (8.29-31).

Like the transfiguration, the Last Supper is tied to Jesus' death and resurrection, when Jesus speaks to his disciples of his betrayal and death (14.17-25). It is likewise tied to the eschatological banquet, when Jesus says: 'Truly I tell you, I will never again drink of the fruit of the vine until that day when I drink it new in the kingdom of God' (14.25). The allusion to Exodus 24 reinforces this. The banquet of Exod. 24.11 is theophanic; the elders eat and drink and see God. The eschatological banquet will be held in the presence of heavenly beings (cf. Isa. 25.6-10; 1QSa ii 3-22). In Mark, the concept is likely to be that of epiphany, an experience of Christ, as in the transfiguration. The connections between Mark's transfiguration, Last Supper, and Exodus 24 are perhaps evidence that Mark considered the Supper to be epiphanic in some fashion, evoking the presence of the risen Lord in the later community.[24]

---

22   Some will protest that the same sort of correspondence exists for passion narrative and Isaiah 53, a conclusion which I reject. The difference is that in the transfiguration, one sees a half dozen markers in as many verses. In the entire Markan passion narrative, one sees at most two or three markers for Isaiah 53.

23   In the Gospel of Mark, Jesus is presented in both narrative symbol and use of allusion as *somehow* heavenly, *somehow* divine. What exactly that means is unclear. Judaism provides a number of 'levels' of divine beings as models, so there are multiple possibilities for what Mark might plausibly have had in mind. See p. 4, n. 12.

24   This seems to be the case for Paul and Corinth (1 Cor. 10.20-21). See Günther Bornkamm, *Early Christian Experience* (New York: Harper & Row, 1969), pp. 145–46.

Interpreting the Allusions 121

That later community comes into existence only because, in the view of early Christians, the Last Supper inaugurated a (new) covenant in Christ. Mark 14.24 certainly uses Exod. 24.8 in that sense, as do Hebrews and, *mutatis mutandis*, the rabbis regarding the initiation of new people into the original covenant. For Mark, those who partake of the Eucharist belong to this covenant, just as those who were sprinkled by Moses belonged to the Sinai covenant.

There are reliable parallels in Mark for almost all of the themes in the Jewish and Christian traditions on Exodus 24 mentioned above. The remaining theme is atonement. Is this present in Mark? It may be present in Matthew, if Matthew added wording about forgiveness of sin to make that element explicit in the allusion to Exodus 24. Whether atonement plays a role in the Markan allusion is unclear. There is nothing in either Markan use of Exodus 24 to highlight the theme of purification from sin. Still, the prominence of this theme in the use of this passage in Hebrews may indicate that such an understanding lies below the surface in Mark. Forgiveness of sin is something that the Son of Man brings (Mark 2.5-12, 15-17), and it may be implied in the use of Exodus 24 in the Last Supper scene, as well.

Striking the Shepherd, Scattering the Sheep – Mark 14.27 and Zechariah 13.7
There is only one explicit quotation of Scripture in the passion narrative:

> And Jesus said to them, 'You will all become deserters; for it is written, "*I will strike the shepherd, and the sheep will be scattered* (πατάξω τὸν ποιμένα, καὶ τὰ πρόβατα διασκορπισθήσονται)."' (Mark 14.27)

> Awake, O sword, against my shepherd,
> against the man who is my associate,' says the LORD of hosts.
> *Strike the shepherd, that the sheep may be scattered* (πατάξατε τοὺς ποιμένας καὶ ἐκσπάσατε [or διασκορπισθησονται] τὰ πρόβατα);
> I will turn my hand against the little ones. (Zech. 13.7)[25]

Early Jewish interpretation
Zechariah 11 and 13.7-9 both treat a shepherd theme. It is uncertain whether these passages were originally united or independent. It is unclear even whether the shepherd of Zech. 13.7-9 was originally intended to be seen as good or bad: the shepherd is struck in an act of judgement, but is called God's associate (v. 7). The judgement is devastating, but it ends in restoration (v. 9), and the preceding text speaks of a great mourning which cleanses the land (Zech. 12.10–13.6).[26] How might these ambiguities in Zechariah 13 have been

---

25 Discussion of verbal correspondence is found on pp. 206 and 230.
26 Stephen L. Cook ('The Metamorphosis of a Shepherd: The Tradition History of Zechariah 11:17 + 13:7-9', *CBQ* 55 [1993], pp. 460–62) argues that in its current context, Zech.

interpreted in Mark's time? Unfortunately, in contrast to the clarity of the reference in Mark, Zech. 13.7 itself does not have much volume in the tradition, and what is there does not have any clear tendency.

Zechariah 13.7 is quoted in the *Damascus Document* (CD^B xix 7-9), where it is interpreted as a prophecy of punishment for those who do not follow the law. They will be killed by the sword when the messiah comes, in contrast to those who revere God, 'the poor of the flock' (Zech. 11.7), who will be saved.[27] Here the shepherd of Zech. 13.7 and his flock are clearly understood to be wicked (contrary to those of Zechariah 11). Similarly, in the Targum, the shepherd and flock of Zech. 13.7 appear to be understood in a negative light; they are transformed into the king and the princes who are the king's (not God's) associates.

A different approach is taken in the *Avot of Rabbi Nathan*.[28] Zechariah 13.7 is quoted regarding one of two rabbis who are executed. The implication is that both rabbis are good, but perhaps having some lack, some moment of arrogance or failure. In version B, R. Ishmael says that they deserve to be executed. Even so, the passage is not interpreted as the striking of truly bad shepherds, but as a lament over genuinely good, if imperfect, ones.

Other early Christian uses

Christian uses of the verse do not clarify matters dramatically. Luke omits the quotation, and Matt. 26.31 uses it in the same manner as Mark, discussed below. In the church fathers, it is used as a proof-text for the scattering of Christians, either the disciples (Irenaeus, *Dem.* 76) or Christians generally throughout the world (Justin, *Dial.* 53.5-6). It is also used, as in the *Damascus Document*, for judgement: in *Barn.* 5.12, to condemn Israel for the crucifixion of Jesus; by Tertullian (*Fuga* 11.2) to upbraid clergy who flee during persecution.

More generally, Zechariah 12–14 seems to be a source of eschatological thought in the New Testament,[29] and judgement is a major theme in this

---

13.7-9 describes a good shepherd, though that was probably not its original meaning. James D. Nogalski ('Zechariah 13.7-9 as a Transition Text: An Appreciation and Re-evaluation of the Work of Rex Mason', in *Bringing Out the Treasure: Inner Biblical Allusion in Zechariah 9–14* [ed. Mark Boda and Michael Floyd; London: Sheffield Academic Press, 2003], p. 297) disagrees.

27   Author's translation.

28   Strack and Stemberger (*Introduction*, p. 227) indicate that *Avot of Rabbi Nathan* originates in the third century and is edited through the seventh to ninth centuries. Version B is earlier and less modified in later centuries than A. Zech. 13.7 is quoted in version A in ch. 38, in B in ch. 41.

29   For example, Zech. 14.7 may be the source of the idea that only the Father knows the time of the Eschaton (Mark 13.32; Matt. 24.36) and the image of the new Jerusalem without night (Rev. 21.25). Zech. 14.5 contains elements similar to those in Mark 13.14, 27 and 1 Thess. 3.13.

section. Zechariah 13.8 speaks of the destruction of two thirds of the people, an idea incorporated into the use of Zech. 13.7 as judgement in the *Damascus Document* and *Barnabas*. Revelation 1.7 uses Zech. 12.10-14, 'they will look on me, the one they pierced' and the mourning that follows, to describe the eschatological judgement. Matthew 24.30 uses Zech. 12.10 in a similar fashion.[30] Yet Matt. 24.31 describes the gathering of the elect, also picking up on the restoration of Zech. 13.1.[31]

Markan use
While the shepherd of Zech. 13.7 can be read in either a positive or negative light, in Mark, the shepherd struck is clearly Jesus and thus pre-eminently good. Jesus is the agent of God, fittingly called God's 'associate' (Zech. 13.7).

While Zech. 13.7-9 begins with severe judgement – two thirds of the people are struck down – it ends with purification and reconciliation between God and the remnant:

> And I will put this third into the fire, refine them as one refines silver, and test them as gold is tested. They will call on my name, and I will answer them. I will say, 'They are my people'; and they will say, 'The LORD is our God.' (Zech. 13.9)

The implication is that striking the shepherd brings about the purification of the sheep, the people of God. The judgement and restoration encapsulated in this passage make it ripe for the eschatological use it is put to in the *Damascus Document* and the New Testament.

In Mark, however, Zech. 13.7 is used as a fulfilment quotation less for the striking of the shepherd than for the scattering of the sheep, the disciples:[32] 'And Jesus said to them, "You will all become deserters; for it is written, 'I will strike the shepherd, and the sheep will be scattered.'"' Jesus continues the shepherd and flock metaphor, 'But after I am raised up, I will go before you to Galilee' (Mark 14.27-28), which implies that the scattered flock will be gathered together again. This scattering and regathering of the disciples corresponds to the purification and reconciliation of Zech. 13.7-9. Though

---

The latter portions of Zechariah have some prominence in the New Testament. Matthew, as is well known, makes much of Zechariah, e.g., using Zech. 11.12-13 for the thirty pieces of silver paid to Judas (Matt. 26.15; 27.9). Zech. 9.9 is nearly quoted in Matt. 21.5 and paraphrased in John 12.15 for the entry into Jerusalem. (Mark 11.2-7 does not seem to use it.)

30   John 19.37 also quotes Zech. 12.10, as a fulfilment citation at the crucifixion. That three New Testament authors use it suggests that it may have been a testimonium.

31   Both Mark 13 and 1 Thess. 3.13 also employ images found in Zech. 14.5 with regard to the gathering of the elect at the Eschaton.

32   Regarding Jesus' death, the quotation emphasizes God as the one who strikes down. That is, the passion is God's plan and action.

severely tested, the remnant will be united with God. While the judgement aspect of Zechariah 12–14 is highlighted in the tradition, and, as we will see, this theme is prominent in other allusions in the Markan passion narrative, it is not highlighted here. Mark's context puts the focus on restoration.

Excursus: Explicit citation

Mark 14.27 is the only passage in the passion narrative which begins with a citation formula, 'for it is written', followed by a near quotation. It is appropriate to ask: how significant is this and what does it signify?

In determining how significant it is, it is important not to isolate the passion narrative too much from the rest of Mark. It turns out that Mark uses explicit citations relatively often in the gospel as a whole. There are a number of citation formulas:

- 'It is written', used here in Mark 14.27, is also found in Mark 1.2; 7.6; and 11.17, followed by an Old Testament quotation. Twice, the formula 'it is written' is used without an accompanying reference, and it is uncertain what passage is in mind or even whether a particular passage is meant. Both instances are related to the passion: Mark 9.12-13, the Son of Man and Elijah are treated as it is written of them, and Mark 14.21, 'the Son of Man goes as it is written of him'.
- Mark 12.10 refers to 'Scripture' and follows with a quotation. The marker 'Scriptures' is used without an accompanying text in Mark 14.49 ('let the Scriptures be fulfilled'), again concerning the passion.[33]
- Some passages are cited as Scripture with 'Moses' (1.44; 7.10; 10.3-4; 12.19; 12.26), 'commandment' (10.19; 12.28-31), or 'lawful' (2.24-26).[34]
- Mark 12.36 uses the marker, 'David himself, by the Holy Spirit, declared', before a psalm quotation.
- Some quotations or near quotations are not preceded by any citation formula: 4.12; 11.9-10; 13.25-26; 14.62; 15.34.

Nearly all of these passages are cited in speech, by Jesus or others. The only ones occurring in narration are the initial quotations in Mark 1.2-3. Many of the speeches are adversative, more or less (which is not unusual for Mark as a whole), and Scripture is used to take a position in a more emphatic or authoritative manner. Many of these passages deal with law, not messianic exegesis. Although most of the explicit citations or near quotations occur in speech, narration throughout Mark also contains allusions to Scripture. These

---

33 Mark 12.24 also uses 'Scriptures' but the text is not identified or quoted until 12.26, with the marker, 'Moses'.

34 Sometimes 'lawful' is also used to identify appropriate behaviour, not necessarily a particular Scripture passage (Mark 3.4; 6.18; 10.2; 12.14).

allusions tend to be less distinct, blended into the narrative (e.g., the allusion to Isa. 63.19 [64.1] in Mark 1.10), which is similar to what we find in the passion narrative.

Returning to Mark 14.27 then, we see that this fits the normal pattern for explicit citation in the gospel as a whole. It is likely that this saying is accompanied by an explicit citation because it is dealing with a subject of some embarrassment to the early church: the defection of the disciples. Jesus backs up his controversial assertion (which the disciples predictably contradict) with the authority of Scripture, as he often does. In the process, Jesus' character is lifted up (this did not happen to him without his foreknowledge), and the disciples are let just a bit off the hook (their defection was preordained). The end result is that they will be gathered together again, which was also preordained. This is a fairly neat use of just a few sentences. Allusion to Scripture enables the author of Mark to pack a great deal of meaning into very few words – which is, in fact, the normal use of allusion in literature of all kinds, in all eras.

Scholars very frequently attribute use of Scripture in the passion narrative to messianic apologetic or exegesis, independent of actual events, and events are thought to be constructed to match those messianic passages. Yet the explicit citation of Zech. 13.7 is used regarding an event – the flight of the disciples – which is easy to imagine having happened in actual fact, most unlikely to have been invented by the early church, and whose historicity is not much challenged. The event clearly was not invented to conform to a messianic proof-text. Indeed, though the passage is used in connection with the Eschaton, no use of this Zechariah passage independent of Mark contains any messianic exegesis. This is true of most passages alluded to in the Markan passion narrative. Consequently, most passages used in the Markan passion narrative must have been picked for reasons other than their power to prove or explain messianic claims about Jesus. In this case, Zech. 13.7 was picked for its power to explain and interpret the disciples' failure. Interpreters must be alert to the many possible functions of allusions in the narrative.

My Soul is Grieved – Mark 14.34 and Psalms 42.6, 12; 43.5
To express Jesus' deep anguish before his suffering, Mark alludes to the psalms:

> And [Jesus] said to them, '*I am deeply grieved* (περίλυπός ἐστιν ἡ ψυχή), even to death; remain here, and keep awake.' (Mark 14.34)

> Why are you *cast down*, O *my soul* (περίλυπός εἶ, ψυχή),
>   and why are you disquieted within me?
> Hope in God; for I shall again praise him,
>   my help and my God.

Here the allusion is to a refrain in what are now divided into two psalms that were probably originally a single unit. The passage alluded to is nearly identical in Pss. 42.6, 12; 43.5.

Early Jewish interpretation

Use of this passage is not common in early Jewish literature. It plays a significant role, however, in 1QH xvi [viii] 31-32, which uses the same words as those in Mark 14.34 and weaves in other images from the psalm, as well: 'Breakers rush against me, and *my soul* within me *has weakened* (=*is downcast*) right to destruction.'[35] The reference to breakers corresponds to Ps. 42.8, 'all your breakers and swells have washed over me'.[36] The *Hodayot* passage is a clear allusion to Ps. 42.6-8.

The hymn itself is composed of two loosely related sections. The section alluding to Psalm 42 is a lament in which the speaker describes overwhelming distress, a distress that can only be expressed in terms of death:

> For my sore breaks out in bitter pains
>   and in an incurable sickness impossible to stay;
> [my heart laments] within me
>   as in those who go down to Hell (Sheol).
> My spirit is imprisoned with the dead
>   for [my life] has reached the Pit;
> My soul languishes [within me]
>   day and night without rest. (1QH xvi 27-30) [37]

In important ways, the hymn follows the sense of the psalm. While the psalmist cries out for God's judgement ('Vindicate me, O God, and plead my cause', Ps. 43.1), the speaker of the hymn describes his distress as God's judgement, not ultimately that of his enemies, and God's judgement is truth and kindness (1QH xvii 9-10, cf. God's *ḥesed* in Ps. 42.9). As the psalmist encourages himself in the refrain to trust in God, to wait for deliverance, so also the speaker of the hymn trusts in God's salvation. 'Thy rebuke shall become my joy and gladness, and my scourges shall turn to [eternal] healing and everlasting [peace]' (1QH xvii 24-25).[38]

Other early Christian uses

The psalm passage has been called a testimonium, with the suggestion that it is used in Heb. 5.7-8 and multiple passages in John.[39] The evidence for these allusions is weak. The best is perhaps John 12.27, but even there the verbal

---

35 Author's emphasis and insertion. Translation by Florentino García Martínez and Eibert J. C. Tigchelaar, *The Dead Sea Scrolls Study Edition* (2 vols; Leiden: Brill, 1997), 1, p. 183.

36 Author's translation.

37 Author's insertion. Unless otherwise noted, translations of the Dead Sea Scrolls are by Géza Vermès, *The Complete Dead Sea Scrolls in English* (New York: Penguin Books, 2004).

38 In *Midr. Ps.* 42.5, the speaker of the psalm is taken to be righteous Israel, which suffers at the hands of the nations and waits for God's redemption. The text laments the waiting, seeming so cruel, but trusts that salvation will indeed come.

39 Johannes Beutler, 'Psalm 42/43 im Johannesevangelium', *NTS* 25 (1978), pp. 37–38.

correspondence to Ps. 6.4-5 is stronger than that to Psalms 42–43. The verbal correspondence of Heb. 5.7-8 is in the single word 'tears', which is certainly found elsewhere, e.g., in Ps. 6.7, 9.[40] The parallel saying to Mark 14.34 in Matt. 26.38 is unchanged. Luke omits the saying, perhaps finding it unsuitable, and transfers λύπη (*grief*) from Jesus to the disciples (22.45).[41] The lack of verbal correspondence between most of these passages and Psalms 42–43 tells against the use of these psalms as a testimonium. The allusion is found only in Mark and in a parallel, not enhanced use in Matthew.

Markan use
Strikingly, Mark 14.34 uses the psalm passage in the same manner as the *Hodayot*: to express suffering so deep it can only be described as death. In the *Hodayot*, the allusion follows a description of the psalmist as one dead. In Mark, the allusion is followed by a reference to death: 'And [Jesus] said to them, "I am deeply grieved, even to death; remain here, and keep awake."' This similarity may be derived from Ps. 42.11: 'As with a deadly wound in my body, my adversaries taunt me.' The possibility is strengthened in that this verse immediately precedes a verse containing the refrain to which Mark and the *Hodayot* allude.

There are a number of elements that tie the allusion in Mark particularly closely to the refrain in Ps. 42.12. The nearby verses, 42.10–43.2, are similar to elements to come in the trial and crucifixion narratives. Psalms 42.10 and 43.2 ask, 'why have you forgotten me?' and 'why have you cast me off?' anticipating the cry of dereliction in Mark 15.34.[42] Psalm 42.11 refers to the mockery of enemies, as do Mark 15.17-20, 29-32. Psalm 43.1 evokes the image of a trial scene and calls on God to plead the psalmist's case, to vindicate him, calling his adversaries deceitful (δόλιος).[43] This links to the trial scene, where the allusions to Scripture often have trial themes. δόλιος also corresponds to the noun used regarding the plot of Jesus' enemies, 'they sought to arrest him by stealth (δόλος)', in Mark 14.1, a verse that points

---

40 Edwin D. Freed, 'Psalm 42/43 in John's Gospel', *NTS* 29 (1983), pp. 65–66 and passim.

41 Luke changes the saying to the more emotionally controlled, 'Pray that you may not come into the time of trial' (Luke 22.40), deriving the new statement from Jesus' comments to the three disciples later in the Markan pericope. This is similar to the change Luke made in the crucifixion scene, where he omitted the Markan cry of dereliction and replaced it with the calm 'Father, into your hands I commend my spirit' (Luke 23.46). There too, the replacement statement was inspired by the Markan pericope: Luke exchanged a quote of one psalm verse (Ps. 22.2) for another (Ps. 31.6).

42 Different Greek words are used in each instance.

43 The hymn in *Hodayot*, which alludes to this psalm, also refers to God pleading the speaker's cause (1QH xvii 23). This, however, is almost a column removed from the allusion to Ps. 42.6-7 in 1QH xvi 32 and may be nothing more than a stock metaphor, not a renewed allusion to the psalm.

forward both to the arrest and to Mark 14.55, the opening of the trial scene. That is, a number of the elements of the verses surrounding Ps. 42.12 resonate with the events of the passion narrative. Still, it may be too constricting to narrow the context of the allusion to a few verses; other verses of Psalms 42–43 also resonate with the Markan narrative. For example, Ps. 42.5 speaks of leading the festive throng to the temple with shouts of joy, which is similar to the entrance into Jerusalem in Mark 11.1-11. An allusion to the refrain may well be an allusion to the whole of both psalms.

Psalms 42–43 attribute to God the disturbing events which the psalmist is experiencing, either to God's absence (42.3-4, 10) or more directly to God's action, as in 42.8, where God's breakers wash over the psalmist. At the same time, these psalms look to God for vindication, as in 43.1, where God is asked to plead the psalmist's case, or in 43.3, where God is asked to send truth and light to guide the psalmist back to God's presence on God's holy mountain. Indeed, the refrain which expresses such distress concludes with the expectation that God will indeed come to the rescue:

> Why are you cast down, O my soul,
>   and why are you disquieted within me?
> Hope in God; for I shall again praise him,
>   my help and my God. (Pss. 42.6, 12; 43.5)

The allusion evokes not only the pain and distress that Jesus suffers, but once again, the sense in Mark that God's hand is behind the events of the passion and that God's ultimate plan is vindication and salvation.

Trial

Seeking to Put Jesus to Death – Mark 14.55 and Psalm 37.32

As we will see in the next section, Philo deplores the act of bearing false witness because it corrupts otherwise just judges, but in Mark the judges are *not* otherwise just. This is made clear long before the trial, notably in 14.1, where those who judge Jesus were seeking a way to seize him by stealth and kill him. At the trial, the false witness will be given because the leaders *seek* it (Mark 14.55):

> Now the chief priests and the whole Council were *seeking* (ἐζήτουν) testimony against Jesus *to put him to death* (τὸ θανατῶσαι αὐτόν).[44]

This line, which echoes Mark 14.1, may also echo Ps. 37.32:

---

44 NRSV modified.

The wicked watch for the righteous, and *seek to put him to death* (ζητεῖ τοῦ θανατῶσαι αὐτόν).⁴⁵

Early Jewish interpretation
There are only a few allusions to Psalm 37 in early Jewish literature.⁴⁶ But 4Q171, a commentary on certain psalms, contains a thoroughgoing interpretation.⁴⁷ This scroll understands the person described as 'the righteous one' to be the Teacher of Righteousness, who will not be condemned when the wicked one, that is the Wicked Priest, comes after him. While the Teacher of Righteousness escapes the clutches of the Wicked Priest, the Wicked Priest is condemned. In the interpretation, the Teacher of Righteousness is delivered because of Ps. 37.33; the Wicked Priest's demise is expected as a judgement based on Ps. 37.34:

> The LORD will not abandon [the righteous one] into his hand, or let him be condemned when he is brought to trial. Wait for the LORD, and keep to his way, and he will exalt you to inherit the land; you will look on the destruction of the wicked. (Ps. 37.33-34)⁴⁸

Interpreting Ps. 37.14-15 and 23-24, the scroll states that the Priest (who is identified with the Teacher of Righteousness in 4Q171 iii 15) and the men of his council will be saved from the plots of the wicked (ii 18-20). God will not allow the schemes of the Wicked Priest to succeed, because he will not abandon the Teacher of Righteousness and allow him to be condemned when he is tried (iv 6-12). That is, God will vindicate the Teacher and the community in their distress. In doing so, God will judge the temple leadership. Interpreting Ps. 37.32-33, the scroll says the 'Wicked [Priest]' will be delivered 'into the hand of the violent of the nations, that they may execute upon him [judgement]' (iv 8-10).

The interpretation of the psalm is also connected to the establishment of a new community. In response to Ps. 37.23-24, which states that God will establish the steps of God's follower and will support him, it says that God chose the Teacher of Righteousness to build a congregation (iii 15-16).

As is common in Qumran materials, there is an eschatological tenor to the interpretation. In response to Ps. 37.10-11, the scroll states that the wicked will be blotted out in 40 years (ii 8; cf. iii 7-8, 11-12), and 'all who possess

---

45 NRSV modified.
46 The Talmud states that 'the wicked' seeking to kill the righteous is the Evil Impulse, but God will help the righteous prevail against it (*b. Sukk.* 52b; *b. Qidd.* 30b).
47 See J. M. Allegro, 'A Newly Discovered Fragment of a Commentary on Psalm XXXVII', *PEQ* 86 (1954), pp. 69–75.
48 NRSV modified. In the LXX, the Hebrew word for *abandon* is translated as ἐγκαταλείπω; the same word is used in Mark 15.34.

the earth shall delight and prosper on exquisite food' (ii 9-12). The penitents will live for a thousand generations and receive all the glory of Adam (iii 1-2, cf. 10-12). Many fragmentary lines also tend clearly in this direction. The judgement of all the wicked and the salvation and glory of the righteous community is the focus of the interpretation.

Other early Christian uses
There is little indication that Matthew saw this allusion in Mark; he edits away from the psalm in his parallel passage. Luke contains no parallel passage. There are no clear uses of this passage elsewhere in the New Testament, nor any quotation of any verse in the psalm. Likewise, there are no allusions to Ps. 37.32 in early church literature. Though several authors quote other verses of Psalm 37, none do so regarding the passion or in a way relevant to the current topic (e.g., *1 Clem.* 14.3-5 uses Ps. 37.9, 35-38 to encourage Christians to be kind to one another). The New Testament does seem to contain fainter references to several other verses of the psalm. One of the clearest of these occurs in Acts. The context is Stephen's trial, in which Luke applies to Stephen a number of motifs applied to Jesus in the Markan passion narrative.[49] In Acts 7.54, those who heard Stephen's defence 'became enraged and *gnashed their teeth at him* (ἔβρυχον τοὺς ὀδόντας ἐπ' αὐτόν)'. In moments they will stone him. The wording of Acts 7.54 corresponds to that of Ps. 37.12, 'The wicked plot against the righteous, and *gnash their teeth at them* (βρύξει ἐπ' αὐτὸν τοὺς ὀδόντας αὐτοῦ).' This verse is very similar in meaning to Ps. 37.32, the verse echoed in Mark 14.55.[50] Thus, between Mark and Acts there is some similarity both in the verses used and the function of the verse in the narrative. Though the evidence is not conclusive, it is possible that Luke recognized the allusion to Ps. 37.32 in Mark 14.55 and moved it to his account of the trial, condemnation, and vindication of Stephen.

Markan use
There is no evidence that the author of Mark or his original audience had contact with the Qumran community. Nevertheless, they have a good deal in common. They both condemn the temple leadership and either expect God's intervention regarding it or interpret recent events in that fashion. Both the original audience of Mark and the Qumran community had a charismatic founder who had serious difficulties with the Jerusalem leadership and whose purpose it was to form a new community, which, unlike the temple leadership, would follow God's will. Both communities had an eschatological outlook and expected that the near future would bring the ultimate judgement and the end

---

49 Cf. Brown, *Death*, 2, p. 978.
50 Psalm 37.12 is followed by the assessment of God, 'but the LORD laughs at the wicked, for he sees that their day is coming' (Ps. 37.13), as is the verse echoed in Mark 14.55.

to all unjust suffering. Both used what scholars often refer to as 'actualizing exegesis', that is, interpreting Scripture to refer to the experience of their own community or group.

Considering these similarities, it would not be surprising if the two groups shared, indirectly, some interpretive traditions. The Gospel of Mark, in particular the passion narrative, takes up a number of themes that play a role in the interpretation of Psalm 37 in 4Q171. These include concern for the leader in his time of trial and for the well-being of the group in its own trials, the stealth of the temple leadership and its condemnation, the creation of a new community, and eschatological judgement and reward.

Building a new community: In 4Q171, interpretation of Psalm 37 indicates that the Teacher of Righteousness will establish a congregation. In Mark 14.56-59, Jesus is accused of saying that he would destroy the temple made with hands and in three days build a temple without hands, and this accusation is obviously important to the thrust of the narrative, particularly since it is repeated at Mark 15.29.[51] Many commentators agree that though it is called false testimony, the temple accusation is somehow ironically true, and that the temple built without hands refers to the new community, the Christian community, which will come into being after the resurrection.[52]

The trials of the leader and community: Obviously the Markan passion narrative is concerned with the trials of its leader. In numerous passages, Mark also describes the trials that members of the authorial audience will undergo (4.16-17; 10.28-30, 39; 13.9-23; cf. 2.20; 6.11; 8.34-38). It has a more sombre view of the period of trial than does 4Q171. Though the scroll admits that the community will endure a season of penance (ii 10), the emphasis there is on God's protection and deliverance from the calamities laid at their door. In Mark, the emphasis is reversed. The gospel frequently refers to persecution and trials. Only infrequently does it comfort those who will endure them. For example, at 10.29-30, it promises that those who leave houses and family will receive the same a hundredfold in this life, along with the persecutions. Mark 13.11 states that the Holy Spirit will give words of defence to those who are brought to trial – though it does not go so far as to promise that they will not be condemned. Indeed it promises that they will be betrayed by their nearest relatives and killed (13.12-13). But those who persevere will receive their reward.

---

51 See Juel, *Messiah and Temple*, p. 55.
52 See the argument in Juel, *Messiah and Temple*, pp. 159–209; for Donahue (*Are You the Christ?*, pp. 137–39, 185) the new community begins proleptically in Jesus' lifetime, but is established only at the Parousia. Cf. Best, *Temptation*, p. 99; Senior, *Passion of Jesus*, pp. 92, 156. Note that this is not the only possible interpretation of the new temple; it may refer to Jesus' body, as it does in John 2.19-22. Linnemann (*Studien*, pp. 123–26) argues that although such an interpretation is appropriate elsewhere in the New Testament, it is not justifiable for Mark.

Temple leadership: 4Q171 emphasizes the judgement of the Wicked Priest. Likewise, a central theme in the Markan passion narrative is the destruction of the temple and of the temple leadership.[53] The allusion to Ps. 37.32 indicates a threat to Jesus' enemies, since succeeding verses speak of 'the destruction of the wicked'. Though one's foes seem as strong as cedars, they will be 'no more' (Ps. 37.34-36). Other uses of Scripture in the passion narrative work the same way, for example, the allusion to Ps. 110.1 in Jesus' answer to the high priest.[54]

Eschatological outlook: Much of Mark, particularly chapter 13, is thoroughly eschatological. The chosen ones will face devastating trials, but in the end they will be gathered together by the Son of Man in glory (13.27). The words used to promise the moment of glory in Mark 13, words from Dan. 7.13 regarding the Son of Man coming with the clouds, are reiterated in the trial, in Jesus' answer to the high priest. Many of the promised signs of the end of the age occur in part in Jesus' passion, for example the sun is darkened at the cross (13.24; 15.33).[55]

What is one to make of all of these similarities between Mark and 4Q171? It would be dangerous to conclude too much on the basis of an uncertain allusion and an interpretation of that passage in 4Q171, which the evangelist had probably never seen. Nevertheless, some possibilities present themselves. One is that these two groups share a common tradition on the interpretation of the psalm. Another is that they interpreted the psalm independently, though in a similar fashion. Most of the interpretive themes in 4Q171 flow naturally and easily from the psalm itself. The single thread that takes one by surprise is the establishment of a new community as an interpretation of Ps. 37.23-24, and that common thread may be total coincidence, since in Mark reference to the new community comes in the general context of the psalm allusion but is not directly tied to it. All other themes, though 'actualized', come from the literal sense of the psalm that in the last analysis God rewards the righteous and punishes the wicked. That the Qumran community would view this psalm as eschatological comes as no surprise, and it was by no means unique in that exegetical tendency. Thus, general similarity in the interpretation of this psalm by Mark and the Qumran community does not require direct contact and should not occasion too much surprise. The meaning of the allusion in Mark most likely includes eschatological rewards for Jesus and those who follow him, as well as punishments for those who oppose him (the temple leadership).

---

53   See Juel, *Messiah and Temple*, passim.
54   See pp. 171-2.
55   See p. 116, n. 13.

In the passion narrative, naturally enough, the immediate focus is not on the trials of the authorial audience, but on Jesus' own suffering. Jesus endures not merely a figurative testing, but a literal trial. The key question that remains is how the psalm is interpreted with regard to Jesus' fate at that trial. The literal meaning of Psalm 37, and its interpretation by the people of Qumran, is that God will not allow the righteous to be condemned when he is tried. Nor will God abandon the righteous. Yet Jesus *is* condemned to death, and at 15.34 Jesus cries out that God has abandoned him.

Despite these difficulties, one possibility for the function of Psalm 37 in the Markan passion narrative is that the psalm is taken literally. Note that Jesus is *not* condemned based on the testimony the leaders seek. Even though the leaders *plant* witnesses, the testimony still does not agree. Jesus is not condemned by the schemes of the leaders. With this interpretation, the use of the psalm demonstrates that the leaders' plan to find false witnesses does not work because *God* will not let it work. It demonstrates that God *can* save Jesus, and allows him to be put to death only on Jesus' terms. The plotting of the wicked does not condemn Jesus; rather a cooperation of Jesus' will with God's brings about the sentence. This meaning would be similar to that of John 10.18: 'No one takes [my life] from me, but I lay it down of my own accord.'

Another possibility is that the psalm is taken in a spiritualized sense, rather in the manner of Mark 8.35: 'those who lose their life for my sake, and for the sake of the gospel, will save it.' Though Jesus is condemned at trial and abandoned on the cross, this happens to his ultimate glory. By these means, he receives dominion and is seated at the right hand of Power, to reign until he comes again to punish the wicked and gather the chosen. So what seems like loss and abandonment is in fact part of the process of exaltation. If this is meant, it represents an ironic reversal of the psalm. God allows the righteous to be condemned, but only so that the righteous can be vindicated in an extraordinary fashion at the resurrection. God abandons the righteous, but only to embrace him more fully in the heavenly court.

False Witnesses – Mark 14.56-57 and Exodus 20.16

The Jewish leaders condemn Jesus based on his answer to the high priest.[56] However, the trial begins with false witnesses. The wording 'they *bore false witness against* (ἐψευδομαρτύρουν κατά) him' is a clear allusion to the ninth commandment: 'you shall not *bear false witness against* (ψευδομαρτυρήσεις κατά) your neighbour' (Exod. 20.16).

---

56 See pp. 184–90, esp. p. 186, n. 132.

Early Jewish interpretation

References to the Ten Commandments are common in Jewish literature. Passages advise their readers to avoid false witness[57] and warn about what will happen to them if they commit it.[58] Many halakic materials determine legal penalties for false witness and what crimes are to be punished under this particular commandment.[59] The *Mekilta* explains that Joseph kept all the commandments, including the commandment against false witness.[60]

Some Jewish texts describe the particularly heinous nature of the crime. The Tosefta indicates that all who transgress the commandments in the Decalogue having to do with person-to-person sin (honouring parents, murder, adultery, etc.), do so only because they have already denied the One who gave the commandments (*t. Šeb.* 3.6). Philo writes that witnesses are necessary only when other proof is lacking and the accused would otherwise be acquitted. The judges who unknowingly condemn someone on the basis of false witness are thus made to record unjust and illegal votes. Philo declares this a deliberate sin and those who commit it impious (*Decal.* 138-41).

Other early Christian uses

Matthew 26.59-60 retains the allusion in its passion narrative parallel, with the same sense as the Markan passage.[61] Mark also uses this commandment in the story of the rich man, and Matthew and Luke retain it in their parallels, with the same sense (Mark 10.19; Matt. 19.18; Luke 18.20).

Despite the differences between Jews and Christians on the law, early Christian sources treat the Decalogue with great respect and in a way not unlike Jewish sources. The *Didache* lists this commandment and others as concrete examples of the commandment to 'Love your neighbor as yourself' (*Did.* 1.2, 2.3; cf. Tertullian, *Marc.* 4.16.17; Mark 12.30-31). Clement of Alexandria considers the Ten Commandments to be the way of righteousness (*Instr.* 3.12) and the laws of heaven (*Prot.* 10). Keeping them leads to salvation. All sources indicate the Ten Commandments are foundational to a godly life.

---

57   Ps.-Phoc. 12-13; *Syr. Men.* 144; *Tg. Onq.* ad loc.
58   *L.A.B.* 11.12; *Tg. Neof.* ad loc.
59   Cf. *m. Mak.*1.3; *t. Mak.* 1.5; *y. Ketub.* 3.1; *y. Sanh.* 11.6; *y. Mak.* 1.1; *b. Sanh.* 10a.
60   Joseph would never have borne false witness because he did not publicly accuse his brothers. If he did not bear witness against them truthfully, he would never have done so falsely (*Mek. Besh.* 1.142).
61   Luke has no parallel in the passion narrative, but portrays a parallel scene in Stephen's trial in Acts 6–7. As in the passion narratives of Matthew and Mark, the false testimony does not bring about a conviction. Rather the defendant's (in this case, Stephen's) own words bring about this condemnation. The possible allusion to Exod. 20.16 occurs in Acts 6.13, but here the verbal similarity is lower, because the key word, the rare verb ψευδομαρτυρέω, is here an ordinary noun phrase, μάρτυρας ψευδεῖς.

Markan use

In Mark 10.17-22, the rich man asks what he must do to inherit eternal life. Jesus answers: 'You know the commandments, "You shall not murder; You shall not commit adultery; You shall not steal; You shall not bear false witness; You shall not defraud; Honor your father and mother."' Here Mark clearly quotes the Decalogue, listing many of the person-to-person sins. When the rich man answers that he has kept the commandments since his youth, Jesus says that there is something further: the rich man should sell what he has and give it to the poor. The passage indicates that the commandments are essential and basic, the first level of a proper response to God.[62]

In the trial scene, the allusion to the commandment against false witness to describe the behaviour of Jesus' opponents points out how fundamentally opposed to the reign of God they are. They fall far short of the rich man, who though seemingly unable to sell all and follow Jesus, is able to avoid this sin. Philo's opinion is that bearing false witness is gravely impious. The Tosefta concludes that those who would commit false witness have denied God. As Mark 14.56-57 points to violation of the Ten Commandments, it points to the profound guilt of those who commit the act.

Silence – Mark 14.61 and Isaiah 36.21

When the false witnesses speak, Jesus 'is *silent* and does not answer'. This silence is often tied to Isa. 53.7, where the Servant is 'like a sheep that before its shearers is *silent*'. The verbal correspondence between these verses is marginal and insufficient. It is equally scant for other suggested allusions.[63]

There is another possible allusion here. Mark 14.61 reads:

[Jesus] *was silent and did not answer* (ἐσιώπα καὶ οὐκ ἀπεκρίνατο) anything.

Isaiah 36.21 reads:

They *were silent and no one answered* (ἐσιώπησαν, καὶ οὐδεὶς ἀπεκρίθη) a word.[64]

The context in Isaiah is Sennacherib's siege of Jerusalem. His agent, Rabshekah, blasphemes God (ὀνειδίζω, Isa. 37.4, 6), saying that the God of Israel is incapable of saving Jerusalem from the Assyrians and is just as helpless as the gods of the other nations (Isa. 36.18-20). At the close of Rabshekah's blasphemous speech, the people of Jerusalem refuse to answer him: 'They were silent and no one answered a word.' The outcome of it all

---

62 Cf. Suhl, *Funktion*, p. 96.
63 See pp. 80–81, 88–89, and 256–57.
64 Author's translations. For more on verbal correspondence, see pp. 105–6, 256.

is that God, through the prophet Isaiah, condemns the Assyrian blasphemy and promises to save Jerusalem. Shortly thereafter, 185,000 Assyrians are killed by the angel of the Lord (Isa. 37.36).

Early Jewish interpretation
The entire story of Isaiah 36–37 is picked up frequently in early Jewish literature (Sir. 48.17-25; Jdt. 6.2-3; 1 Macc. 7.41; 2 Macc. 8.19; 15.22-24; *T. Adam* 4.6; Josephus, *Ant.* 10.1.2-4.).[65] One of these, 1 Macc. 7.41, highlights the Isaian themes of mockery, blaspheming God, and threats to Jerusalem and the temple. When the priests and elders greet Nicanor as he arrives at Mount Zion:

> He mocked them and derided them and defiled them and spoke arrogantly, and in anger he swore this oath, 'Unless Judas and his army are delivered into my hands this time, then if I return safely I will burn up this house [the temple].' And he went out in great anger. At this the priests went in and stood before the altar and the temple; they wept and said,
>
> 'You chose this house to be called by your name, and to be for your people a house of prayer and supplication. Take vengeance on this man and on his army, and let them fall by the sword; remember their blasphemies (δυσφημιῶν), and let them live no longer.'
>
> ... Then Judas prayed and said, 'When the messengers from the king spoke blasphemy (ἐδυσφήμησαν), your angel went out and struck down one hundred eighty-five thousand of the Assyrians. So also crush this army before us today; let the rest learn that Nicanor has spoken wickedly against the sanctuary, and judge him according to this wickedness.'
>
> So the armies met in battle ... The army of Nicanor was crushed, and he himself was the first to fall in the battle. (1 Macc. 7.34-38, 40-43)

The story of Nicanor and the Maccabeans in 1 Maccabees is carefully structured to parallel the story in Kings/Isaiah. Here, as in every case where the story is used, the emphasis is on the punishment the Assyrians (and others) receive for their impudence.

---

65 The emphasis on this story begins early. It is contained in Kings and Chronicles, as well as Isaiah. This multiplicity is not entirely surprising; Isaiah contains all the material on Hezekiah which is also contained in Kings; the story suits the purposes of Chronicles. Nevertheless, the fact that it was included three times in authoritative Scripture (or for those who did not accept the authority of Chronicles, the fact that it was included twice in the Prophets) may have given the story additional significance to Second Temple interpreters. In the end, the relative emphasis given to this passage in Second Temple Judaism may simply be due to its compelling nature. It is a good story and presents a useful lesson.

Other early Christian uses

In contrast to the frequent use of this story in Jewish literature, there is a dearth of references in early Christian literature. There are no indications that an allusion here was caught by Matthew or Luke. Matthew edits away from the verse; Luke has no parallel. Matthew 27.43, in the mockery at the cross, may allude to Isa. 36.7, 20, but the verbal correspondence is slight. There are no certain uses of Isaiah 36 in the New Testament. Likewise, Isaiah 36 is generally ignored in early church literature.[66]

Markan use

Like the reference in 1 Maccabees 7, the Markan account picks up not only words but also themes from Isaiah 36: blasphemy and mockery, threats to the temple, and whether those who rely on God will be saved. Blasphemy is of particular importance in the relationship between Jesus and the leaders of Jerusalem in Mark. Jesus is not convicted on the basis of false witness; when he confesses his identity, however, the leaders convict him of blasphemy. It is possible that Mark intends the reader to view this conviction in light of the previous references to the leaders planting false witnesses. A common meaning for the term βλασφημέω (*blaspheme*) is *slander*, and ψευδομαρτυρέω (*bear false witness*) is to a degree a synonym. The leaders planted false witnesses in order to slander Jesus; now they convict Jesus of slander. Already in Mark 3.28-29, the leaders of Jerusalem are indicted for blasphemy against the Holy Spirit. They are therefore said to be 'guilty of an eternal sin'.

The verbal and thematic correspondence points to an allusion. If the allusion is there, it indicates a major reversal. Jesus' refusal to answer to the high priest regarding the false witness – the blasphemy – against him, is similar to the people's refusal to answer the blasphemy of Rabshekah. This allusion and a later allusion in the mocking at the cross put the leaders of Jerusalem in the place not of Hezekiah who goes to the temple to plead for help from God, but of the Assyrians who blaspheme God and say that God is unable to save (cf. Mark 15.31-32).[67] It points to the temple leaders as arrogant and blasphemous.

---

66 Clement of Alexandria (*Strom.* 5.14) does use it, but in rather unexpected fashion. He combines elements from multiple verses of Rabshekah's speech and uses his combination as proof that the Gentiles know God, but the combined quotation is contrary to the sense of the original passage.

67 It is ironic that the temple leaders, and not the Romans, are characterized as the Assyrians, one of the great enemies in the Old Testament. This reversal is similar to the reversal of roles found in 4Q171, where the 'wicked' of Psalm 37 is said to refer to the high priest. Watts (*Isaiah's New Exodus*, pp. 107, 164) suggests that in Mark the real enemy is not the foreign invaders but Israel's leaders and Satan. Still, the Romans are not exonerated. Jesus' silence in the Roman trial echoes his silence in the Jewish trial and carries a similar meaning.

There is a strong tendency in the early Jewish literature to emphasize the punishment accorded to the Assyrians. The same tendency can be expected in Mark, pointing again to the guilt of the Jerusalem leaders and their eventual punishment. The punishment of the Assyrians also means deliverance for the people of Jerusalem. Thus, an allusion to this passage would, once again, reiterate that God does vindicate God's chosen ones, and God will certainly deliver Jesus.

It is nearly impossible to conclude that Mark 14.61 is an allusion to Isa. 36.21 if the focus is entirely on christology. How could Jesus be compared to the ordinary men on the wall, ordered by their king to silence? Such insignificance seems inappropriate to the Son of Man who is to come with the clouds. But if one looks beyond christology, to the broader question of how the passion narrative works as a narrative, then one finds a tight web of thematic parallels: mockery and blasphemy, threats to the temple (and with it, Jerusalem), punishment for those who mock God (in Mark, by mocking God's agent, Jesus), and God's vindication of those who act in obedience to God.

The verbal correspondence, the web of thematic parallels, and the prominence of this story in the early Jewish literature add up to a surprisingly solid case for the allusion. The allusion would point, as do others, to the guilt of the Jerusalem leadership and their eventual punishment, as well as to the vindication of those who are faithful to God.

The Jewish Mockery – Mark 14.65 and Isaiah 50.6
The mockery and abuse Jesus receives at the Jewish trial allude to Isa. 50.6:

> Some began to *spit* (ἐμπτύειν) on him, to cover his *face* (τὸ πρόσωπον), and to beat him, saying to him, 'Prophesy!' The guards also took him over and *struck* him (ῥαπίσμασιν). (Mark 14.65)[68]

> I gave my back to blows, and my cheeks to *strikes* (ῥαπίσματα); I did not turn my *face* (τὸ πρόσωπον) from the insult of *spitting* (ἐμπτυσμάτων). (Isa. 50.6)[69]

Early Jewish interpretation
Interpretation of this verse receives little assistance from the Jewish tradition. There are no clear allusions to Isa. 50.6 in Second Temple Judaism and nothing helpful in the early rabbinic literature.[70]

---

68 NRSV modified.
69 Author's translation of the LXX. Though there are only three words in common here, the allusion is fairly strong because two of those words are rare. See p. 108.
70 The only early rabbinic text which quotes Isa. 50.6 uses it to explain that a person is liable not only for injuries done to another but for injuries done to oneself and attributes self-harm to the evil impulse and lack of self-control (*t. B. Qam.* 9.31).

Interpreting the Allusions

Other early Christian uses

Luke edits away from the allusion to Isa. 50.6 in his parallel (22.63-65). Matthew, however, retains the allusion in his Jewish trial and adds it to the Roman trial (26.67; 27.30).[71] In addition, Matthew uses the language of Isa. 50.6 in the Sermon on the Mount (Matt. 5.39): 'But I say to you, Do not resist an evil-doer. But if anyone *strikes* (ῥαπίζει) you on the right *cheek* (σιαγόνα), *turn* (στρέψον) the other also.'

Isaiah 50.6 is mentioned frequently in early church literature and applied to Jesus' suffering. For example, *Barn.* 5.13–6.7 uses Isa. 50.6-9 to show that Jesus' sufferings were necessary.[72] Irenaeus uses Isa. 50.6 and other passages to indicate that Christ suffered all things and that this suffering was foreseen (*Dem.* 68; *Haer.* 4.33.12; cf. Tertullian, *Res.* 20.5). *Sibylline Oracles* 8.290 and *Gos. Pet.* 3.9 use the language of Isa. 50.6 to recount the passion, to tell how he was whipped, and in *Gos. Pet.*, also spat on – that is, Isa. 50.6 applies to Jesus' suffering mockery and abuse.[73]

Some authors use Isa. 50.6 to interpret the relationship between Jesus and God during the passion. In *Dem.* 34, Irenaeus uses Isa. 50.6 to point out the obedience of Christ, using it to show that through obedience regarding the tree, he undid Adam's disobedience regarding the tree. Justin (*1 Apol.* 38) follows the quotation of Isa. 50.6 with Isa. 50.7, 'the Lord God helps me', and interprets Isa. 50.6-7 to indicate that God helps Jesus in his suffering.

Markan use

Mark may allude to Isa. 50.6 in the third passion prediction:

> See, we are going up to Jerusalem, and the Son of Man will be handed over to the chief priests and the scribes, and they will condemn him to death; then they will hand him over to the Gentiles; they will mock him, and *spit* (ἐμπτύσουσιν) upon him, and *flog* (μαστιγώσουσιν) him, and kill him; and after three days he will rise again. (Mark 10.33-34)

The allusion to Isa. 50.6 occurs in v. 34, with the verbs for *spit* and *flog*. Jesus says that these things will be done by the Gentiles, and the Romans do them

---

71 *Contra* Suhl, *Funktion*, pp. 58–59. Suhl notes that Matt. 26.67 does not make *explicit* use of the passage and asks why, if Matthew understood the allusion to be there, did he not make greater use of it, as he has of other passages in Isaiah? This objection implies that Matthew is required to make a prophetic fulfilment out of every allusion in the passion narrative. This is too stringent. Matthew's prophecy-fulfilment pattern does not require absolute adherence, and Matthew, as well as Mark, may sometimes opt for 'Schilderung in alttestamentlichen Farben', e.g., Matt. 24.30 and 25.31-34, alluding to Dan. 7.13-14.

72 Isaiah 50.6-9 is also used, among other passages, to condemn Jews for opposing Jesus (*Barn.* 5.11–6.7).

73 Cf. Crossan, *Cross That Spoke*, pp. 135–37, 141–42.

all in chapter 15. Yet when the Romans do spit and flog, Mark makes no allusion to Isa. 50.6. The verb for flog is changed (φραγελλόω, 15.15), and this is separated by four verses from the spitting (ἐμπτύω, 15.19), which by itself is insufficient to recall the allusion to Isaiah.[74]

Instead of picking up on this potential for an allusion in the Roman trial and mockery, Mark transfers it to the Jewish trial and mockery. Like the passion prediction, the abuse occurs after the Jewish leaders condemn Jesus; unlike the prediction, it occurs before they hand him over to the Gentiles.

The words of Isa. 50.6 emphasize humiliation and abuse. The context, Isa. 50.4-9, describes the obedience and trust of the speaker in the midst of that humiliation.

> The Lord GOD has opened my ear, and I was not rebellious, I did not turn backward. I gave my back to those who struck me, and my cheeks to those who pulled out the beard; I did not hide my face from insult and spitting. (Isa. 50.5-6)

The speaker listens to God and carries out God's will, even to his detriment. The reason he is able to do so is that he has total confidence that God will ultimately vindicate him:

> The Lord GOD helps me; therefore I have not been disgraced; therefore I have set my face like flint, and I know that I shall not be put to shame; he who vindicates me is near. (Isa. 50.7-8)

The speaker is undaunted by his adversaries:

> Who will contend with me? Let us stand up together. Who are my adversaries? Let them confront me. It is the Lord GOD who helps me; who will declare me guilty? All of them will wear out like a garment; the moth will eat them up. (Isa. 50.8-9)

The speaker describes his situation in language appropriate to a trial. 'Near is the one who declares me just (ὁ δικαιώσας). Who is the one would pass sentence against (ὁ κρινόμενος) me?' (Isa. 50.8).

Mark applies the verse in a trial setting. Like the speaker of Isa. 50.6, Jesus endures the trial and the beating and humiliation because of his obedience to God.[75] That this is so is emphasized in Jesus' prayers in Gethsemane, 'yet not what I want, but what you want' (Mark 14.36). Jesus endures these things in full expectation that God will ultimately vindicate him; God will declare him innocent and come to his aid. There is, in the allusion, a hint about the

---

74 Cf. p. 273.
75 This use of the passage stands in anticipatory counterpoint to the Tosefta tradition that to submit voluntarily to such treatment is to do an injustice to oneself. Jesus does this not in a perverse spirit of self-hatred, but out of obedience to God's will.

Interpreting the Allusions

ultimate destruction of the members of the council, his adversaries – they shall all wear out like a garment – though the hint is not strong. Similar to other uses of Isa. 50.6 in early Christian literature, the allusion here emphasizes Jesus' suffering and with it the cause of his humiliation – his obedience to the will of God, a will which he knows because he is a pupil of God (Isa. 50.4). Use of the passage also indicates the certainty of God's assistance.[76]

Crucifixion

The crucifixion scene is dominated by allusions to Psalm 22. This section will begin with the allusions outside of the psalm and end with those to it.

Darkness – Mark 15.33 and Amos 8.9
Nearly all commentators consider Mark 15.33 an allusion to Amos 8.9:

> At the sixth hour [noon], *darkness came over* (σκότος ἐγένετο ἐφ') *the* whole *land* (τὴν γῆν) until the ninth hour. (Mark 15.33)[77]

> On that day, says the Lord GOD, I will make the sun go down at noon, and *darken the land* (συσκοτάσει ἐπὶ τῆς γῆς/והחשכתי לארץ) in broad daylight. (Amos 8.9)[78]

The verbal correspondence is less than overwhelming but real, with additional correspondence to Amos 8.10. The correspondence of sense is very strong: at noon the land will be darkened. As we will see, the correspondence of themes is likewise strong.

Early Jewish interpretation
Amos 8.9 appears only a few times in early Jewish literature. *1 Enoch* 80.4 and *4 Ezra* 5.4 (as well as other apocalyptic texts) describe the derangement of celestial order, but neither appears to allude to this verse in particular.

---

76 Suhl (*Funktion*, pp. 58–59) rejects Mark 14.65 as an allusion to Isa. 50.6. In part, his reason is that the sense of the passage in Isa. 50.6 must be twisted to make it conform to the sense of its use in Mark. There are two objections to this line of reasoning. The first is that, as Suhl readily admits (*Funktion*, p. 47), the earliest community was quite willing to use texts in a manner that did violence to their original sense. This, therefore, cannot be an objection. The other is that, even so, the violence reputed to be done here is trivial. Suhl writes: 'zu einer antithetischen Parallelität oder ähnlichem Zuflucht nehmen müsste, z.B. wenn Lohmeyer meint: "… mein Antlitz habe ich *nicht* verborgen (*daher* περικαλύπτειν) …"' The degree of literal correspondence to which this objection submits the passages far exceeds that necessary to posit an allusion. Jesus submits to maltreatment, which includes spitting and striking, in obedience to God, just as does the prophet. It is of no consequence whether someone covers his face.
77 NRSV modified.
78 NRSV modified.

1 Maccabees 1.39 alludes to it when the collector of tribute and his people occupy Jerusalem and desecrate the temple. Tobit 2.6 explicitly quotes it, with regard to the situation of the Jews in the story and Tobit's own feast turned to mourning. The Talmud quotes it with regard to two deaths: R. Eleazar compares the day of R. Pedath's death to the day in Amos 8.9-10; R. Johanon says the passage describes the day of Josiah's death (*b. Mo'ed Qat.* 25b).[79] The common element in the tradition is an emphasis on mourning.[80]

Other early Christian uses
The darkness receives more attention in early Christian literature than does Amos 8.9 per se. Matthew and Luke do not edit either away from or towards the passage. It is difficult to know whether they saw an allusion. If there, the allusion would indicate the darkness as an eschatological sign. It is interesting that Luke moved the tearing of the veil (also often seen as an eschatological sign), juxtaposing it to the darkness (Luke 23.44-45).[81] Whether Luke saw an allusion or not, he appears to have understood the darkness in an eschatological sense. In a parallel passage, the darkness is mentioned three times in the *Gospel of Peter*; the first mention (5.15) incorporates an allusion to Amos 8.9, and that darkness, as in the Jewish tradition, is connected with mourning by the people.[82]

Tertullian sometimes refers to the darkness at the cross, without referring to Amos 8.9 (cf. *Res.* 22; *Apol.* 21.19). In other cases the allusion to Amos 8.9 is clear. In *Marc.* 4.42, Tertullian quotes a number of passages to indicate that the details of the passion were foretold in Scripture; Amos 8.9 foretold the darkness (cf. Irenaeus, *Haer.* 4.33.12). In *Jud.* 10.17, he relates the feast of Amos 8.10 to the feast of Passover, during which Jesus was crucified and to the mourning of the Jews regarding it (cf. Luke 23.48).[83]

---

79   Amos 8.10 appears more often. Early halakic materials use Amos 8.10 to help determine rules for mourning (*y. Mo'ed Qat.* 3.5; *b. Ber.* 16b; *b. Sukk.* 25b; *b. Mo'ed Qat.* 15b, 20a, 21a; *b. Zebah.* 100b).
80   Rodger David Aus (*Samuel, Saul, and Jesus: Three Early Palestinian Jewish Christian Gospel Haggadoth* [Atlanta: Scholars Press, 1994], pp. 134–47) traces connections between prodigies at death, Josiah, Amos 8, and Zechariah 12 in Jewish tradition.
81   On the tearing of the veil as an eschatological sign, cf. Allison, *End of the Ages*, pp. 31–32; Brown, *Death*, 2, p. 1145.
82   Crossan (*Cross That Spoke*, pp. 198, 220, 232–33) returns frequently to the theme of darkness in the *Gospel of Peter*, and concludes that the three mentions of darkness depend on three separate Scripture passages: Amos 8.9-10; Isa. 59.10; and Zech. 14.7.
83   See Crossan, *Cross That Spoke*, pp. 252–53, who considers Tertullian to combine two traditions on mourning regarding the passion: the people lament because they have wrongly crucified a just man or because the crucifixion causes the destruction of Jerusalem, and only then they lament.

Markan use
The similarity of elements and of themes between Mark 15.33 and Amos 8.9-10 is unmistakable. In both, the darkness over the land comes at noon. Jesus is crucified during the Feast of Passover; in Amos 8.10, God turns their feasts into mourning, like the mourning for an only son. In the LXX יחיד (*only son*) is translated with ἀγαπητός, a word the heavenly voice uses to describe Jesus at the baptism and the Transfiguration (1.11, 9.7).

Several different interpretations have been offered for the darkness in Mark. It has been seen as a portent to mark the death of a great man, as God's judgement, as a sign of cosmic significance, and as a sign of the end.[84] The allusion to Amos confirms the darkness as an eschatological sign. In Amos the darkness at noon will come 'on that day', a day of God's judgement. Though not the original sense of the passage, in the first century such verses were taken to refer to the eschatological Day of the Lord, the day of final judgement.

In apocalyptic texts of the period, unnatural darkness is commonly an eschatological sign (e.g., *1 Enoch* 80.4 and Rev. 6.12-13; 8.12). This is so in Mark 13.24, just before the gathering of the chosen: 'the sun will be darkened, and the moon will not give its light.' There Mark quotes Isa. 13.10. Like Amos 8.9, Isa. 13.10 belongs to a passage about God's judgement.[85]

At Mark 15.29-32, the leaders, the chief priests and the scribes, along with others, mock Jesus at the cross. This is followed immediately by the darkness. The juxtaposition may suggest that these two statements be read together, that God's judgement falls on those who mock Jesus.[86] But Jesus has been mocked twice previously in the passion narrative, and darkness did not result. It is perhaps more likely that the darkness is tied to what follows: Jesus' cry and his death, that is, Jesus' suffering on the cross. Dale Allison argues persuasively that in Mark, Jesus' death on the cross ushers in the eschatological period.[87] But the eschatological period is ushered in only partially. The darkness of Mark 13.24 is permanent and final. The darkness of the crucifixion scene lasts three hours. The darkness and the tearing of the veil (cf. Mark 13.2) could be considered something of an eschatological pledge, a foretaste of what is to

---

84   Allison (*End of the Ages*, pp. 27–29) presents a summary of the positions. The portent marking the death of a great man is often seen as Hellenistic (cf. Virgil, *Georgics*, 1.466-67; Plutarch, *Romulus* 27.6), but is not necessarily. *2 Enoch* 67 marks Enoch's death with darkness (cf. *Adam and Eve* 46; *Apoc. Mos.* 36). The Talmud attributes to a rabbi the opinion that Amos 8.9-10 describes the events on the day of Josiah's death (see above).

T. A. Burkill ('St Mark's Philosophy of the Passion', *NovT* 2 [1958], p. 266) regards the darkness as an eschatological event which testifies to Jesus' divine status.

85   In Amos, the judgement is of Israel; in Isaiah the judgement is of Babylon.

86   Cf. Brown, *Death*, 2, p. 1035.

87   Allison (*End of the Ages*, pp. 26–39) notes, among other things, the parallels in the passion narrative to the eschatological events predicted in Mark 13, for example, fleeing, darkness, and the rending of the temple veil as a symbolic destruction.

come when the Son of Man comes with the clouds. The allusion to Amos 8.9 points to the judgement that will occur at that time. The traditions surrounding this day (including Mark 13, where the Son of Man's coming is tied to the Day of the Lord) indicate that such a day would also be one of deliverance for some.[88]

The tradition on Amos 8.9 emphasizes mourning. Amos 8.10 refers to 'the mourning of an only son', an ἀγαπητός (יחיד). An allusion to Amos 8.9 would point once again to Jesus as ἀγαπητός, son, beloved. The Christian tradition sometimes envisions the darkness as part of the wrath of God inflicted on Jesus on the cross, part of the process of substitutionary atonement.[89] Though the cross is portrayed as God's will throughout Mark, the allusion to Amos 8.9 suggests that, rather than being a sign of God's judgement, the darkness is, in part, God's expression of mourning for God's beloved Son. It is because of Jesus' great significance that his death ushers in the eschatological period.

Vinegary Wine – Mark 15.36 and Psalm 69.22
After Jesus' cry of dereliction, a bystander offers *him vinegary wine* (ὄξους) *to drink* (ἐπότιζεν αὐτόν). This is a secure allusion to Ps. 69.22, 'for my thirst they gave me *vinegar to drink* (ἐπότισάν με ὄξος)'.

Early Jewish interpretation
There is little about Ps. 69.22 in the Jewish materials. There is a single rabbinic citation, in which it is used as an exclamation in an episode with a *min* (*b. Ḥul.* 87a). It is also used in the *Hodayot*, which contains a clear allusion to the passage:

> And they, teachers of lies and seers of falsehood,
>   have schemed against me a devilish scheme,
> to exchange the Law engraved on my heart by Thee
>   for the smooth things (which they speak) to Thy people.
> And they withhold from the thirsty the drink of Knowledge,
>   and *assuage their thirst with vinegar* (ולצמאם ישקום חומץ;
>   cf. Ps. 69.22 ולצמאי ישקוני חמץ),
> that they may gaze on their straying,
>   on their folly concerning their feast-days,
>   on their fall into their snares. (1QH xii [iv] 9-12)[90]

---

88 Smith ('Darkness at Noon', p. 334) sees in the darkness judgement on the old order and the dawn of the new order.
89 Cf. Best, *Temptation*, pp. 153, 156.
90 First insertion, Vermès'; second mine. See E. L. Sukenik, *The Dead Sea Scrolls of the Hebrew University* (Jerusalem: Magnes Press, Hebrew University, 1955), columns 1–18 frgs. 1–66, plates 35–58; É. Puech, 'Un hymne essénien en partie retrouvé et les Béatitudes: 1QH V 12-VI 18 (=col. XIII-XIV 7) et 4QBéat.', *RevQ* 13 (1988), pp. 59–88, plate III.

Interpreting the Allusions   145

This is placed in a context where the speaker in the hymn is despised and all his friends are driven far from him (xii 9). But the teachers of lies and seers of falsehood will not succeed in their schemes, because God's purpose shall be accomplished (xii 12-13). The false teachers will be destroyed, those who please God will stand (xii 20-22), and though despised, the speaker in the hymn will also stand (xii 22-23).

Other early Christian uses
Psalm 69 makes frequent appearances in the New Testament. It is used in all parallels to this Markan verse (Matt. 27.48; Luke 23.36; John 19.29). In John, Jesus says 'I thirst', in order to fulfil Scripture; then the vinegary wine is offered. In Luke, the vinegary wine retains the same general meaning as in Mark (see below), but is moved together with the rest of the mockery on the cross. Matthew expands the reference by turning Mark's initial offer of wine mixed with myrrh (Mark 15.23) into an allusion to the psalm, by having them offer wine *mixed with gall* (Matt. 27.34).

There are also a number of other allusions to Psalm 69 elsewhere in the New Testament. John 2.17 quotes Ps. 69.10, 'zeal for your house will consume me'; the quotation of the psalm ties Jesus' action in the temple to his crucifixion. Romans 15.3 quotes it apparently with reference to the mockery of the passion narrative: 'For Christ did not please himself; but, as it is written, "The insults of those who insult you have fallen on me"' (Ps. 69.10).[91] Clearly, this psalm, just like Psalm 22, is tied to the crucifixion very early in the Christian tradition.

That emphasis continues in early church literature. *Gospel of Peter* 5.16 and Irenaeus, *Dem.* 82, use Ps. 69.22 to narrate the vinegary wine episode.[92] Psalm 69.22 is frequently included in lists of passion prophecies (e.g., *Barn.* 7.3; Irenaeus, *Haer.* 3.19.2; Tertullian, *Jud.* 10.4, 13.10; *Res.* 20.5). The offer of the vinegary wine is interpreted as mockery or abuse (*Sib. Or.* 6.24-25, 8.303). A number of texts use the passage as part of anti-Jewish rhetoric, recounting abuses perpetrated by Jews (*Gos. Pet.* 5.16-17; *Sib. Or.* 1.367).

The *Odes of Solomon* use Ps. 69.24 in a fashion more closely related to the use of Psalm 69 in 1QH xii 9-12. Though Christian, the *Odes* are thoroughly 'Jewish in tone and perspective'.[93] *Odes Sol.* 5.5 uses Ps. 69.24 as part of the prayer of a righteous person who is suffering and expects vindication.

---

91   Psalm 69 is quoted in two other places as well. Romans 11.9-10 quotes Ps. 69.23-24, stating that God hardened some of the Jews. Acts 1.20 quotes Ps. 69.26 regarding the replacement of Judas: 'let his homestead be desolate.'
92   Crossan (*Cross That Spoke*, pp. 210–11) concludes that the purpose of the wine in the *Gospel of Peter* is similar to that in Matt. 27.34: it is a poison. In the *Gospel of Peter* it is necessary to kill Jesus immediately because of the strange darkness and the need to bury him before sunset (cf. Deut. 21.22-23; *Cross That Spoke*, pp. 200–1).
93   J. H. Charlesworth, who dates them to 100 CE, *OTP*, 2, pp. 725–27.

Markan use
In the explicit narrative, it is unclear whether the offer of the vinegary wine in Mark 15.36 is an act of compassion or another element in the ongoing mockery of Jesus. It is tied to the comment, 'let us see whether Elijah will come to take him down'. On the surface of things, that is a hopeful comment, the sort of thing a sympathizer might say. It is followed shortly thereafter by what a great number of commentators consider the only fully Christian confession of the gospel, the centurion's, 'Truly this man was God's Son!' Such factors could indicate the offer of vinegary wine is a turning point in the narrative, where action ceases being entirely hostile and people act in ways that are generous and good (the centurion, the women at a distance, Joseph of Arimathea, and Pilate releasing the body to be buried).

Because of the allusion, however, that interpretation is unlikely.[94] Psalm 69 is a psalm about mockery. ὀνειδίζω (to mock) and its cognates occur six times, in vv. 8, 10, 11, 20 and 21. Mark uses ὀνειδίζω only once, four verses previously, to describe those who mocked Jesus on the cross at 15.32. By placing the vinegary wine segment with the mockery at the cross, Luke demonstrates that he understood it too as mockery (Luke 23.36). Paul uses Ps. 69.10 with respect to insults and mockery (Rom. 15.3). 1QH xii 8, 22 uses it regarding a speaker who is despised, ridiculed, and mocked.

Psalm 69 brings out the pathos of the mockery and humiliation Jesus undergoes. At 69.21, the MT says 'mockery has shattered my heart, and it is incurable'; the LXX has 'my soul expects mockery and suffering'.[95] The psalmist looks for sympathy and comfort from others, but instead they give him poison for food and vinegar to drink. The use of this image in Mark intensifies his depiction of Jesus' sufferings. The image does not have this effect in John, because of the way John distances Jesus from suffering. Jesus says, 'I thirst', to fulfil the Scriptures and there is no mockery in the scene. Jesus remains always in control, impassive. It is not so in Mark, where Jesus is mocked by many and his only words from the cross are a wrenching lament to God.

In the psalm, the enemies of the psalmist are ἐναντίον God (69.20); ἐναντίον (or the Hebrew נגד) can mean simply *facing* or it can take on the connotation of *hostile to, opposed to*, and this latter sense is the implication of the psalm. The psalmist's enemies are not merely *his* enemies; they are also, or even primarily, *God's* enemies: 'It is zeal for your house that has consumed me; the insults of those who insult you have fallen on me' (Ps. 69.10). In the psalm, the image of giving vinegar to drink is immediately followed by the psalmist's imprecations against those who do so. With intensity and at length,

---

94   Brown (*Death*, 2, pp. 1063–64) and K. Brower ('Elijah and the Markan Passion Narrative', *JSNT* 18 [1983], p. 91) note the ambiguity and the effect of the psalm.
95   Author's translations.

he calls for vengeance (69.23-29). In 1QH, the speaker calls for judgement on those who treat him so and clearly expects such judgement to come (xii 18-20). Jesus does not speak these words, nor does he curse anyone in Mark. But again the Scripture imagery emphasizes judgement for those who crucify Jesus.

Again, corresponding to the psalmist's expectations that his enemies will be punished are his expectations of his own salvation (69.14-19, 31-37). These expectations are clearly expressed, but they are placed far enough away from the image Mark uses that it may be stretching matters too far to say they are drawn into Mark's meaning. Nevertheless, the possibility is there, and it would be consistent with the significance of other allusions in the passion narrative.

The allusion to Psalm 69 does not offer a particularly christological insight, but rather provides an image that assesses a specific narrative action, the giving of sour wine, as well as the general plot of the passion narrative, and evaluates the behaviour of players in the drama.

Three Allusions to Psalm 22

There are two, probably three, allusions to Psalm 22 in the Markan passion narrative. The first comes at Mark 15.24:

> [They] *divided his clothes* (διαμερίζονται τὰ ἱμάτια αὐτοῦ) among them, *casting lots* (βάλλοντες κλῆρον) to decide what each should take.

This is clearly an allusion to Ps. 22.19:

> They *divide my clothes* (διεμερίσαντο τὰ ἱμάτιά μου) among themselves, and for my clothing *they cast lots* (ἔβαλον κλῆρον).[96]

Mark 15.34, the translation of Jesus' 'cry of dereliction',

> *My God, my God, why have you forsaken me?* (ὁ θεός μου ὁ θεός μου, εἰς τί ἐγκατέλιπές με;)

nearly quotes Ps. 22.2:

> *God, my god* (ὁ θεὸς ὁ θεός μου), hear me, *why have you forsaken me?* (ἵνα τί ἐγκατέλιπές με;)[97]

Sandwiched between these two very clear allusions, is the mockery at Mark 15.29-30:

---

96   For a discussion of verbal correspondence, see pp. 275–76.
97   Author's translation from the LXX. For a discussion of verbal correspondence, see pp. 213–14 and 283.

Those who passed by derided him, *shaking their heads* (κινοῦντες τὰς κεφαλάς) and saying, 'Aha! You who would destroy the temple and build it in three days, *save yourself* (σῶσον σεαυτόν), and come down from the cross!'

This contains possible echoes of Ps. 22.7-9:

> [I am the] reproach[98] of humanity and contempt[99] of crowds. All who see me scoff at me; they make mouths at me, *they shake their heads* (ἐκίνησαν κεφαλήν); 'He hoped in the Lord; let him rescue him – let him *save him* (σωσάτω αὐτόν) because he wants him!'[100]

Early Jewish interpretation

Joseph and Aseneth seems to allude to Psalm 22 in Aseneth's prayer. There are echoes of Ps. 22.22 in 'You, Lord, rescue me from his hands, and from his mouth deliver me, lest he carry me off like a lion ...' (*Jos. Asen.* 12.11[10]).[101] 'My mouth has become dry as a drum ... and my lips as a potsherd' recalls Ps. 22.16 (*Jos. Asen.* 13.9[8]). Aseneth's prayer is filled with biblical language, referring to many different psalms and other books. Though Psalm 22 is not singled out, it is considered one of the texts appropriate to describe Aseneth's great humiliation, her anguish, and her prayer to God, her only help.

Psalm 22 *is* singled out to describe Esther's prayer approaching the king in rabbinic material. The rabbis use verses from Psalm 22 to describe various moments of this encounter.

> *And stood in the inner court of the king's house.* [Est. 5.2] R. Levi said: When [Esther] reached the chamber of the idols, the Divine Presence left her. She said, *My God, my God, why hast thou forsaken me?* Dost thou perchance punish the inadvertent offence like the presumptuous one, or one done under compulsion like one done willingly? Or is it because I called him 'dog', as it says, *Deliver my soul from the sword, mine only one from the power of the dog?* [Ps. 22.21] She straightaway retracted and called him lion, as it says, *Save me from the lion's mouth.* [Ps. 22.22]

---

98 ὄνειδος.
99 This rare noun, ἐξουδένημα, is related to the relatively rare verb for contempt, ἐξουδενέω, used to discuss the future sufferings and contemptible treatment of the Son of Man in Mark 9.12.
100 Modified towards the LXX. 'Because he wants him' (ὅτι θέλει αὐτόν) translates כִּי חָפֵץ בּוֹ, 'if he delights in him'. כִּי was often translated by ὅτι, even when כִּי did not mean *that* and, as here, it was used to introduce a condition and meant *if*. It is possible that readers of the LXX understood that ὅτι could be used to introduce a condition in translation Greek. If so, they may have read, 'let him save him *if* he wants him!' (εἰ, meaning *if*, is a variant translation for כִּי in LXX mss).
101 Translation by C. Burchard, who dates it from 100 BCE to 135 CE (*OTP* 2, p. 187).

And it was so, when the king saw Esther the queen. R. Joḥanan said: Three ministering angels were appointed to help her at that moment ... (*b. Meg.* 15b; cf. *b. Yoma* 29a)[102]

In the *Mekilta*, the rabbis assert that to call on *El* is to call on the divine attribute of mercy (as opposed to calling on *Elohim*, invoking the divine attribute of justice). They support this claim by citing Ps. 22.2, 'My God, My God (*Eli, Eli*), why have you forsaken me?' without further comment. They cite two more verses containing *El*, Num. 12.13 and Ps. 118.27, as further proof.[103] The latter two passages do obviously concern mercy; the Numbers passage calls on God to heal Miriam from leprosy, and Psalm 118 rings with the refrain, 'his steadfast love (חסדו) endures forever'. While Ps. 22.2 seems not so obviously to fit the pattern, to the Tannaim, it was so clear that Ps. 22.2, 'My God, My God (*Eli, Eli*), why have you forsaken me?', proves that to call on *El* is to call on the attribute of mercy that no explanation was required.[104]

Other early Christian uses
Psalm 22 is used frequently in the New Testament. All three of Mark's allusions to Psalm 22 have parallels in other gospel passion narratives.

- All gospels contain an allusion to Ps. 22.19 (Matt. 27.35; Luke 23.34; John 19.23-24). John cites it explicitly as a fulfilment of Scripture.

---

102 Translations of the Talmud from I. Epstein (ed.), *The Babylonian Talmud* (London: Soncino, 1961).
103 *Mek. Shir.* 3.76; cf. J. N. Epstein and Ezra Zion Melamed (eds), *Mekhilta de Rabi Shimʿon ben Yoḥai* (Jerusalem: 1979), p. 80.
104 There are no clear interpretations of Psalm 22 at Qumran. Heinz-Josef Fabry ('Die Wirkungsgeschichte des Psalms 22', in *Beiträge zur Psalmenforschung: Psalm 2 und 22* [ed. J. Schreiner; Würzburg: Echter, 1988], p. 298), followed by Marcus (*Way*, p. 179), asserts that 4QPs^f is constructed as an interpretation of Psalm 22, where other materials are included as an extension of that psalm. This claim is unwarranted. Fabry considers the contents of the extant fragments to be the contents of the full scroll and to constitute the Essene interpretation of Psalm 22. For example, Fabry argues that Psalms 107 and 109 are used to interpret Psalm 22. Marcus indicates that the scroll begins with Psalm 22. The total extent of the scroll's contents is not known, however, and Peter Flint (*Qumran Cave 4: XI Psalms to Chronicles* [ed. Ulrich et al.; DJD XVI; Oxford: Clarendon, 2000], p. 95) assumes that Psalm 108 would have gone between Psalms 107 and 109. There are no extant edges to Psalm 22, and it is not at all clear that psalm represents the beginning of the scroll – in fact, that seems unlikely. In other words, since the material is very fragmentary, and one must assume that other materials were included in the scroll, one cannot conclude anything from material which happens to be absent from extant fragments. Fabry considers the inclusion of three apocryphal psalms in 4QPs^f important. But their presence and their designation as apocryphal is significant only if one assumes that psalters at Qumran ought to match contemporary psalters, and they clearly do not. 4QPs^f was a songbook, a psalter, of which a few fragments remain. Psalm 22 cannot be said to play any greater role in it than any other of its contents. Fabry ('Wirkungsgeschichte', pp. 299-302) also suggests a number of allusions in the *Hodayot* to Psalm 22. Verbal correspondence for most is slight; the best of these is 1QH x (v) 31 to Ps. 22.16. None are clear enough to use as a comparative tradition.

- Matthew retains and Luke revises toward Ps. 22.8-9 in the mockery scene.[105] There is no parallel in John.
- Only Matthew retains the cry of dereliction from Mark; he clearly recognizes it as a verse from the psalm, changing the cry from Aramaic to Hebrew (Matt. 27.46). Scholars have generally agreed that Luke found the cry too stark or startling; he exchanged it for another psalm verse, 'Father, into your hands I commit my spirit.' (Luke 23.46; Ps. 31.6) John has no corresponding cry.
- Hebrews is the only New Testament book to quote the thanksgiving portion of the psalm. Hebrews 2.12 quotes Ps. 22.23, 'I will proclaim your name to my brothers and sisters, in the midst of the congregation I will praise you.'

Psalm 22 also appears frequently in early church literature on the passion, for example:

- The *Gospel of Peter* uses Psalm 22 in a manner similar to the canonical gospels, to narrate the dividing of garments (4.12) and Jesus' death cry (5.19).[106]
- The psalm is very frequently included in lists of texts which foretell the passion (Justin, *1 Apol.* 38; Irenaeus, *Haer.* 4.33.12; Tertullian, *Marc.* 4.42.4; *Jud.* 10.4; *Res.* 20.5). Tertullian declares that Psalm 22 contains the entire passion of Christ (*Marc.* 3.19.5; *Jud.* 10.13). Justin concludes that Psalm 22 foretells not only the details of the passion, but other details of Jesus' life (*Dial.* 97-106). Irenaeus uses the words of Psalm 22 to narrate the passion (*Dem.* 80). *Barnabas* 6.6 uses Ps. 22.19 to condemn Jews for opposing Jesus and indicate that Jesus' sufferings were necessary.
- Clement (*1 Clem.* 16.15-17) uses the psalm in a section about Jesus' passion and its meaning, which in his view is to bear the sins of many by suffering. He interprets the passage to indicate Christ's humiliation, though his emphasis is on the appropriate Christian response. *Odes of Solomon* 31.9 likewise interprets Psalm 22 as indicating Jesus' humiliation in enduring the mockery, pain, and injustice of the crucifixion; he did so to save and instruct his followers.

Markan use
Psalm 22 is central to the crucifixion scene. Unfortunately, scholarly attention to its meaning is often cursory,[107] though not always, and scholars have presented a number of views on its interpretation.

---

105 See pp. 109–10.
106 Cf. Crossan, *Cross That Spoke*, pp. 192, 221–23.
107 Cf. Juel's (*Messianic Exegesis*, pp. 114–16) brief treatment of the meaning of the psalm, though his project is to interpret the significance of Scripture in Mark. Often scholarly attention

One prominent approach to the meaning of the psalm in the Markan passion narrative is to group it with other psalms of lament used in the narrative, such as Psalm 37 or 69, and then to argue that Jesus is seen as the suffering righteous one. Dodd was one of the first to urge this reading. He suggested that the 'plot' of the suffering righteous one – that a righteous person is threatened and humiliated and subsequently exalted – was one of the models for understanding Jesus' passion.[108]

Donald Juel and Adela Collins argue against this kind of reading. Juel notes that this 'plot' is too general to be applicable in the first century.[109] Collins notes that Jesus is not described as the suffering righteous one.[110] Both argue instead that Psalm 22 and other psalms of lament in the passion narrative portray Jesus as the messiah. Juel argues for Psalm 22 as messianic by means of its royal attribution; it was thought to have been written by David. Its cry was David's cry, and it was 'part of a tradition that narrated the death of the King of the Jews'.[111] In his view, such a reading originated by means of Psalm 89, a psalm which describes the messiah suffering. This psalm was connected to Psalm 22 and others by means of catch-word association, as well as royal attribution.[112] Collins states that messianic interpretation of Psalm 22 may not have been a Christian innovation. She notes a similar interpretation by a Jewish group in the third century CE, and she believes this interpretation to be uninfluenced by Christianity.[113] Joel Marcus perhaps presents the best (and simplest) argument for the messianic interpretation of Psalm 22 among Christians when he notes that allusions to the psalm (Mark 15.24, 29, 34) are interspersed with references to Jesus as king (Mark 15.18, 26, 32).[114] One might expect a first-century reader to take note of the psalm's royal attribution; however, it may be too much to expect the readers of Mark to have jumped from Psalm 22 to Psalm 89, as Juel's theory requires, when Psalm 89 is not used in the Markan passion narrative.[115] Collins may be correct that the third-century Jewish group was uninfluenced by Christian interpretation, but such matters are difficult to know. Many scholars are more impressed by

---

to the psalm is directed at historical, rather than interpretive, questions. Scholars ask, for example, whether Jesus could have uttered the cry, and if he did, what was his state of mind and how much of the psalm could he have uttered while being crucified. Cf. Brown, *Death*, 2, pp. 1046, 1085–88.

108 Dodd, *According to the Scriptures*, pp. 96–103. Cf. Ruppert, *Jesus*, pp. 46-48; Rossé, *Cry*, p. 55; Marcus, *Way*, pp. 177–79.
109 Juel, *Messianic Exegesis*, pp. 21–22.
110 A. Collins, 'Appropriation', in Tuckett, *Scriptures*, pp. 230–32.
111 Juel, *Messianic Exegesis*, p. 116; cf. Juel, 'The Origin of Mark's Christology', in *The Messiah: Developments in Earliest Judaism and Christianity* (ed. James H. Charlesworth et al.; Minneapolis: Fortress, 1992), p. 458. See also Matera, *Kingship*, pp. 134–35.
112 Juel, *Messianic Exegesis*, pp. 104–110.
113 A. Collins, 'Appropriation', in Tuckett, *Scriptures*, pp. 231–34, 237–39.
114 Marcus, *Way*, pp. 181–82.
115 As Juel notes (*Messianic Exegesis*, p. 104).

the lack of evidence for such a reading in earlier sources. Still, Marcus presents a possible messianic reading based on the text of Mark and the psalm themselves.[116] Allusions to Psalm 22 may well identify Jesus as messiah.

Yet they do so in an extraordinary way, because the psalm is not used to describe Jesus' glorification, as are Ps. 2.7, Dan. 7.13, and Ps. 110.1 (see Chapter 5). Psalm 22 is used to describe Jesus' humiliation and suffering: first his public stripping, then public mockery, and finally the climax of suffering with Jesus' cry of dereliction, 'My God, my God, why have you forsaken me?'

This cry has been a focal point of scholarly discussion. Some say it indicates despair on Jesus' part.[117] Others deny that any alienation is indicated here or that Jesus (either in history or in Mark) felt abandonment.[118] More frequent is the observation that this is a prayer which indicates that Jesus expects vindication from God.

The arguments for the latter position have often been weak. As mentioned above, Dodd argues that the plot of the passion and resurrection narratives matches the plot of the psalm, which begins with suffering and ends with thanksgiving. In this he is followed by a number of scholars.[119] However, the assumption that because the resurrection would correspond to the end of the psalm, therefore the end of the psalm is in view is problematic. Mark never alludes to the end of Psalm 22, in either the passion or resurrection narratives, and one simply cannot assume that the end of the psalm is meant.[120] Does the absence of an allusion to the thanksgiving portion of the psalm require one to understand the allusion solely as a description of desperation?

Two Hebrew Bible scholars, Claus Westermann and Patrick Miller, have taken an interest in the meaning of Psalm 22 for the Markan passion narrative.[121] Westermann describes the character of psalms of lament (such

---

116 Juel and Collins, too, at bottom, base their readings on the Markan text: Psalm 22 is tied to Jesus' death as king.

117 Best (*Temptation*, p. lxvi) interprets the cry as an indication of God's judgement on Jesus, as he dies for the sins of others. On this position, see Brown, *Death*, 2, pp. 1045–47. Otto Piper ('God's Good News: The Passion Story According to Mark', *Int* 9 [1955], pp. 180–81) concludes that the entire psalm is not meant in Mark, but that neither is Jesus in despair. Rather Jesus finds comfort in 'God's revealed word', not human wisdom. Likewise, Burkill ('St Mark's Philosophy', pp. 262–63) suggests that the cry does not indicate despair but fulfilment of God's will.

118 Cf. Brown, *Death*, 2, pp. 1047–51.

119 For a discussion of scholarly positions on whether the whole psalm is meant or only a portion, see Matera, *Kingship*, pp. 133–35. Marcus (*Way*, p. 182) is one of the scholars who continue to argue that Mark includes the whole psalm.

120 *Contra* Daniel Guichard, 'La reprise du Psaume 22 dans le récit de la mort de Jésus (Marc 15, 21-41)', *Foi et vie* 87 (1988), pp. 62–64; F. Danker, 'The Literary Unity of Mark 14.1-25', *JBL* 85 (1966), p. 471.

121 Claus Westermann, 'The Role of Lament in the Theology of the Old Testament,' in *Praise and Lament in the Psalms* (Atlanta: John Knox, 1981), pp. 259–280; Patrick Miller, *Interpreting the Psalms* (Philadelphia: Fortress, 1986), pp. 101–111.

as Psalm 22) and concludes that a description of one's sufferings is always followed by petition, by a request that God would change the situation. He writes: 'There is not a single Psalm of lament that stops with lamentation. Lamentation has no meaning in and of itself ... What the lament is concerned with is not a description of one's own sufferings or with self-pity, but *with the removal of the suffering itself*.'[122] One 'can say that the lament as such is a movement toward God'.[123]

In Psalm 22, one finds this movement towards God already in the fifth verse: 'In you our ancestors trusted; they trusted, and you delivered them.' The sixth verse is like it: 'To you they cried and were saved; in you they trusted, and were not put to shame.'[124] Thus even without the argument that the entire psalm is invoked by the correspondence of plots, the point still holds. Psalm 22.5-6 shows that this is not a psalm of despair. The first words of the psalm describe the plight of the psalmist, that he no longer experiences God's protection or presence. Immediately after expressing his plight, the psalmist expresses his reliance on God and his understanding of God as one who delivers those who cry out to him in their suffering. As John Reumann puts it, 'the lament not only questions God's goodness in current experience but also lays claim to him, thus setting up a tension which persists throughout'.[125]

The prayer of Aseneth (alluding to Psalm 22) and the prayer of Esther (composed of Psalm 22) clearly indicate hopeful expectation of deliverance, though neither alludes to the end of the psalm and its thanksgiving. The *Mekilta* shows that just the first line of Psalm 22 invokes the divine attribute of mercy. This very verse is emblematic of calling on God's mercy and compassion. It seems likely that to Jewish readers of the first century, 'My God, my God, why have you forsaken me?' would have seemed to call on God's mercy and benevolent action. Jesus' cry was at once vivid complaint and expectant petition.[126]

---

122 Westermann, *Praise and Lament*, p. 266, my emphasis. Note that Psalm 88 is no exception to this rule. It has no thanksgiving, but it is filled with petition.
123 Westermann, *Praise and Lament*, p. 273.
124 Miller, *Interpreting*, p. 102; cf. Matera, *Kingship*, p. 132.
125 Reumann, 'Psalm 22', p. 44. Similarly, Miller, *Interpreting*, pp. 101–2.
126 Markan scholarship has considered the use of Psalm 22 in an either/or fashion. Either Mark meant the whole psalm or he did not. Whitney Shiner ('The Ambiguous Pronouncement of the Centurion and the Shrouding of Meaning in Mark', *JSNT* 78 [2000], pp. 16–17) rightly points out that this is a false dichotomy. The Markan passion narrative is filled with irony and operates throughout on two levels of meaning. On the level of literal narrative, Jesus speaks out the beginning of the psalm, but the passion narrative does not include the thanksgiving in the final portion of the psalm. Indeed, it could not; when Jesus speaks it, he expects divine aid, but his agony is not yet over. Yet the Markan community read the passion narrative knowing its final outcome, the resurrection. While Mark does not allude to the end of the psalm, the prominence of Psalm 22 in the gospel passion narratives makes it very likely that the community would have used the psalm in its worship and study. Thus, it is entirely possible that on the second level of

That the Markan Jesus does not cry out in despair does not mean, as Gérard Rossé cautions, that Jesus experiences no abandonment and that the words are stripped of their significance.[127] The allusions to Psalm 22 portray Jesus in the midst of ultimate suffering. Everything has been stripped from him, not merely his clothes. He suffers physically. He is abandoned by his friends. He suffers mockery, nakedness, and shame. Now he suffers the loss even of God's presence. And he, in that moment of intense human suffering, cries out to God – and the psalm points out that this cry is just what his Israelite ancestors did in their distress, and God heard them and saved them.

In the use of Psalm 22, Mark paints a picture of utter desolation. He describes a Jesus who does not ride high to victory, as he does in John, but goes through depths of suffering before the victory. Also through the use of this psalm and, as we will see, other aspects of the Markan text, the Markan Jesus identifies himself paradigmatically with the people and with their suffering, particularly the suffering of separation from God.[128] Jesus' identification with the people in suffering is not merely suffering *with* but suffering *for* and on the behalf of the people. The purpose of Jesus' suffering is to effect the end of suffering.[129]

Conclusion

As the preceding examination shows, the allusions in the Markan passion narrative help to interpret the narrative.[130] The allusions treated in this chapter portray Jesus' suffering. They also indicate his obedience and an expectation of God's vindication and judgement on his enemies. These elements are set in an eschatological context. The following chapter continues analysing the meaning of the allusions, taking up those in Mark 14.61-62.

---

meaning, the level at which the community knows something else to be true than what the literal words say, the community understood the entire psalm to have been fulfilled at the conclusion of Jesus' passion-resurrection experience. While to do so is to go beyond the text, it is to go where the text points, and though it is possible that this is not the intended reading, it is a sound reading. Similarly, Reumann, 'Psalm 22', p. 54; Matera, *Kingship*, p. 133.

127   Rossé, *Cry*, pp. 108–9.
128   Cf. Rossé, *Cry*, p. 112.
129   Miller, *Interpreting*, p. 109. For a similar viewpoint from a more theological perspective, see J. L. Mays, 'Prayer and Christology: Psalm 22 as Perspective on the Passion', *Theology Today* 42 (1985), pp. 322–31.
130   Cf. Suhl, *Funktion*, pp. 66, 167; van Iersel, *Mark*, p. 67.

5. ARE YOU THE CHRIST?

Mark 14.61-62 presents a rich set of allusions to Ps. 2.7, Dan. 7.13, and Ps. 110.1. These allusions are some of the most directly christological in the Markan passion narrative and are tightly connected to one another.

Are You the Christ, the Son of the Blessed? – Psalm 2.7

The high priest's question, '*Are you the Christ, the Son* of the Blessed (σὺ εἶ ὁ χριστὸς ὁ υἱὸς τοῦ εὐλογητοῦ)?'[1] contains a faint allusion to Ps. 2.7, '*You are my Son*; today I have begotten you (υἱός μου εἶ σύ; with χριστός corresponding to Ps. 2.2).'

Early Jewish Interpretation
Psalm 2 in general has high volume in early Judaism, though not necessarily v. 7. Probably the clearest early use is in *Florilegium* (4Q174), where Ps. 2.1 is quoted. The document is an extended interpretation of 2 Sam. 7.10-14, the Nathan oracle, and contrasts the destruction brought by the nations on Israel with the eternal peace that will come to the just in the last days. The interpretation understands the oracle to promise the messiah, though the term 'son' is not used as a messianic designation, rather 'Branch of David', based on Isa. 11.1 (4Q174 i 11).[2] Despite this reference to the messiah and the presence of 'anointed' in Ps. 2.2, 4Q174 applies Ps. 2.1 not to the messiah, but to 'the elect of Israel', those who 'practise the whole Law' (i 19; ii 2), focusing on the opposition between the righteous and the wicked. The document as a whole portrays the nations as destructive and counter to the peace of Israel. God will deliver Israel from them in the last days, by raising up the Branch of David, and the faithful will enjoy the peace.[3]

---

1 NRSV modified.
2 This is the norm. Dennis C. Duling ('Promises to David', *NTS* 20 [1973], pp. 55–69) argues that the messiah is commonly described in Jewish texts with metaphorical language based on Isaiah 11 and other traditions linked to the promise to David in 2 Samuel 7. The use of 'son' is uncommon (see ibid., esp. pp. 68–69). On the branch metaphor, see ibid., pp. 58–59.
3 There is an interesting combination of passages in this text: 2 Samuel 7 and Psalms 1 and 2. Psalms 1 and 2 are sometimes taken to be a single psalm in the early literature (cf. *b. Ber.*

There is considerable question about whether the *Rule of the Congregation* alludes to Psalm 2. The first difficulty is whether 1QSa ii 11-12 should be restored with יוליד (*begets*) or יוליך (*leads* or *brings*). While not certain, it appears that יוליד (*begets*) is to be preferred.[4] Supposing that to be the case, the text would read:

> When [God] begets the messiah, [the priest] will come with them at the head of the congregation …[5]

The unusual conjunction of begetting (Ps. 2.7) and messiah (Ps. 2.2) here could well point to Psalm 2. However, that is not certain either.[6] Still, it is reasonable to conclude both that this reading of the manuscript is the correct one and that the passage either alludes to Psalm 2 or, at the very least, is a parallel text for understanding its interpretation at the time. Psalm 2.7 is then applied to the messiah, in this case, the messiah of Aaron who is contrasted with the messiah of Israel, the royal messiah (ii 14). It is unfortunately not at all clear what begetting the messiah, perhaps by God, means.[7] Perhaps the most likely

---

9b-10a; a variant of Acts 13.33). 2 Samuel 7 and Psalm 2 are combined elsewhere (in *Psalms of Solomon* 17 and Hebrews 1.5, see below). However, the combination may not be particularly significant here, since each is separated by a long *vacat* in the MS (Annette Steudel, 'Psalm 2 im antiken Judentum', in *Gottessohn und Menschensohn: exegetische Studien zu zwei Paradigmen biblischer Intertextualität* [ed. Dieter Sänger; Neukirchen-Vluyn: Neukirchener Verlag, 2004], p. 196).

    4   D. Barthélemy and J. T. Milik, *Qumran Cave 1* (DJD I; Oxford: Clarendon, 1955), p. 117; John J. Collins, *The Scepter and the Star: The Messiahs of the Dead Sea Scrolls and Other Ancient Literature* (New York: Doubleday, 1995), pp. 164–65; Vermès, *Complete Dead Sea Scrolls*, p. 161. Robert Gordis ('The "Begotten" Messiah in the Qumran Scrolls', *VT* 7 [1957], pp. 191–94) argues for the *yolid* reading from a philological point of view. For alternative readings, see Lawrence Schiffman, *The Eschatological Community of the Dead Sea Scrolls* (SBLMS 38; Atlanta: Scholars Press, 1989), p. 54 n. 6.

    5   Author's translation, from the Barthélemy and Milik transcription (see above note). 'The priest' proposed in the lacuna may be identical with the messiah. Note that *God* is missing from the text. There is a lacuna in the manuscript immediately following the verb, the typical position for the subject. It is usually restored with God (אל), which would fit either of the proposed readings. See Barthélemy and Milik, *Qumran Cave 1*, p. 118.

    6   The allusion is accepted, for example, by Craig A. Evans ('Jesus and the Messianic Texts', in *Jesus and His Contemporaries: Comparative Studies* [Leiden: Brill, 1995], p. 96). Others have their doubts. See Paul Mailberger, 'Das Verständnis von Psalm 2 in der Septuaginta, im Targum, in Qumran, im frühen Judentum und im Neuen Testament', in Schreiner, *Beiträge*, pp. 101–5; Steudel, 'Psalm', in Sänger, *Gottessohn*, pp. 191–92. These latter point out that if there is no reference to Psalm 2 in 1QSa, there is no application of this passage to the messiah at Qumran.

    7   Note that description of the messiah using texts with a father–son relationship is not unique to 1QSa, even at Qumran. As noted above, *Florilegium* attributes the father–son passage of the Nathan oracle to the messiah. J. Collins (*The Scepter and the Star*, p. 165) notes another fragmentary text, 4Q369, seeming to make a similar connection: 'in eternal light, and you made him for you a first-bo[rn] son […] like him, to (be) a prince and ruler in all /your/ inhabited world

possibility is that it simply means, 'when God brings the messiah into history'.[8] Needless to say, with so much uncertain in this reading, one cannot put much weight on this text. However, as we will see, it does not stand alone in the Jewish tradition in the use of Psalm 2 for the messiah. What would be unusual here would be the attribution of the passage to a priestly messiah.

The *Psalms of Solomon*, a text with connections with Qumran literature,[9] clearly alludes to Psalm 2, and in a fashion similar to that of *Florilegium*.[10] *Psalms of Solomon* 17 condemns the sinful Maccabees and their followers, saying that God brought Pompey on them in judgement, and then condemns the Romans as being still worse.[11] In answer to the ubiquity of sin in the land, the text looks forward to eschatological judgement and restoration, in the form of a Davidic messiah (e.g., 17.18-22), described in terms reflecting 2 Samuel 7 and Isaiah 11 (17.4-5, 22-29, 35-37). The messiah is to 'smash the arrogance of sinners like a potter's jar; to shatter all their substance with an iron rod' (17.23-24; Ps. 2.9), so that the Gentiles and all sinners will be expelled (17.27-28). The condemnation of the Gentiles is not unrelenting. They will not be destroyed, but the nations will serve under the messiah's yoke (17.30, perhaps reflecting Ps. 2.3). They will come to Jerusalem with gifts, to give glory to the son of David and to God (*Pss. Sol.* 17.30-31).

The language used to describe the messiah is exalted. The nations will glorify not only God, but the messiah, who is described as 'the Lord Messiah' (17.32).[12] In several places, it is difficult to tell whether the text speaks of God or the messiah (e.g., 17.31). The attributes of the messiah are those of God. God is Lord and King, as is the messiah (17.32, 46). The messiah judges with righteousness, as does God (2.32-35; 17.26-29). The similarity of God and the anointed is found in Psalm 2, where God is the implied king, sitting (enthroned) in heaven,

[...]' (trans. García Martínez, 2, p. 731). The context seems to indicate the Nathan oracle is in mind, perhaps with reference to Exod. 4.22. While 'son' is not a title for the messiah, biblical passages using such terms are applied to the messiah. The wording of 4Q369, 'you made him for you a first-born son', would indicate that no metaphysical relationship is indicated. The relationship is adoptive.

8   Evans, 'Jesus and the Messianic Texts', in *Jesus and His Contemporaries*, pp. 97–98.
9   R. B. Wright, *OTP* 2, pp. 642, 648–49. He dates the work *c*. 70–45 BCE (*OTP* 2, p. 641) and provides the translations below.
10 Both use 2 Samuel and Isaiah 11 to interpret the messiah. Both refer to Israel as the son (see *Pss. Sol.* 18.4, though there 'the son' does not seem to come from Ps. 2.7). Both focus on the ravages of the Gentiles and look forward to their expulsion in the Eschaton. On the similarities of *Pss. Sol.* 2 and Hebrews, see Gert J. Steyn, 'Psalm 2 in Hebrews', *Neot* 37 (2003), pp. 266–68.
11 Similar judgements are expressed in *Pss. Sol.* 2 and 8, the other psalms with historical referents. There are considerable similarities between these judgements and those found in the literature at Qumran. *Pss. Sol.* 17.16-18 seems even to refer to that community.
12 The text is often emended here to 'the Lord's messiah', but Wright (*OTP* 2, p. 667) points out that the MSS are uniform in this reading. This designation is also found in *Midr. Ps.* 2.3, 9. This line in *Pss. Sol.* 17.32, 'their king shall be the Lord Messiah', may echo Ps. 2.2 (Lord and messiah) and 2.6 (king) or reflect the ideas found there.

who installs his king on Zion, whose power reflects the power of God (Ps. 2.4, 6, 9). In Psalm 2, as in *Pss. Sol.* 17, it can be difficult to tell whether the passage speaks of God or of God's anointed (cf. Ps. 2.12 – whose wrath is kindled?).

Psalms of Solomon 18 continues these ideas and also seems to echo Psalm 2. Mention of 'the appointed day when his Messiah will reign' (18.5) may reflect Ps. 2.2, 6-7, and 'the rod of discipline of the Lord Messiah' (18.7) may reflect Ps. 2.2, 9.[13] These references, while faint, are strengthened by the stronger allusions in *Pss. Sol.* 17. Here the focus is on the blessings enjoyed by Israel in the messianic generation. The phrase 'firstborn son, an only child' (18.4), is applied not to the messiah, but to Israel.[14]

Psalms of Solomon 2 alludes to Psalm 2 and speaks of the judgement of Pompey for his arrogance in plundering Jerusalem. The 'officials of the earth' are warned about the judgement of the Lord, who destroys those who do not acknowledge him, while those with understanding fear the Lord and receive God's mercy (*Pss. Sol.* 2.31-35; Ps. 2.2, 10-12). Here the text speaks of God, not the messiah. While judgement has already taken place in the case of Pompey, others are warned about future judgements and instructed to take refuge in God.

Other Old Testament pseudepigrapha seem to allude to Psalm 2. *Sibylline Oracles* 3.663-65, in a traditional (Jewish) passage,[15] speaks of 'the kings of the peoples' who will gather to attack the land of Israel and the temple, reflecting Ps. 2.1-2. This action will bring their judgement (3.664), which will be an eschatological judgement (3.669-700).[16] In *1 Enoch* 48.8, 10, 'the kings of the earth' and landowners are condemned because 'they have denied the Lord of the Spirits and his Messiah' (Ps. 2.2).[17] Again an eschatological judgement is implied. The allusion is used in connection with the messiah, here described in terms of the Son of Man vision of Daniel 7 (46.1-5; 47.3).[18] In *4 Ezra*, 'an innumerable multitude [of nations, cf. 13.33] shall be gathered together, as you

---

13   The rod of discipline may reflect Isa. 11.4, which seems to be alluded to with the phrase 'word of his mouth' in *Pss. Sol.* 17.24, 35. *Pss. Sol.* 18.7 continues with language reflecting Isa. 11.2. Since both Psalm 2 and Isaiah 11 are used in *Pss. Sol.* 17-18, it may not be important to distinguish them. In fact, the common 'rod' may be one factor connecting the two passages in the minds of those who use both.

14   Here the 'son' terms do not reflect Psalm 2, but other passages, such as Exod. 4.22 and perhaps Gen. 22.2.

15   John J. Collins, *OTP* 1, p. 354. He dates the section to 163–45 BCE (*OTP* 1, p. 355) and provides the translations below.

16   *Sib. Or.* 8.248 alludes to Ps. 2.9 in a distinctly Christian section.

17   Translations by Michael A. Knibb, with Edward Ullendorff, *The Ethiopic Book of Enoch: A New Edition in the Light of the Aramaic Dead Sea Fragments* (2 vols; Oxford: Clarendon, 1978). For dates, see p. 173.

18   *1 Enoch* 46.5 may perhaps be considered an echo of Ps. 2.1-3, 10-12. The context and interpretation are the same as in the clearer allusion in *1 Enoch* 48. See Aquila H. I. Lee, *From Messiah to Preexistent Son: Jesus' Self-Consciousness and Early Christian Exegesis of Messianic Psalms* (Tübingen: Mohr Siebeck, 2005), p. 246.

saw, desiring to come and conquer him. But he will stand on the top of Mount Zion ... And he, my Son, will reprove the assembled nations', and destroy them (*4 Ezra* 13.31-39; Ps. 2.1-2, 6-7).[19] Once again, Psalm 2 is applied to a messianic figure described in terms of Daniel 7 (13.1-3) and bringing eschatological judgement.

Rabbinic literature refers often to Psalm 2, with various concerns. One theme predominates, however, and that is God's response to Gentiles who oppose Israel. Most often Ps. 2.1-2 is taken to refer to Gog and Magog and eschatological war.[20] However, the psalm can be used in a discussion of any enemy of Israel, such as Pharaoh, Sennacherib, even Esau.[21] Sometimes the Gentiles' opposition is not war but opposition to Torah. In the messianic age, Gentiles say they want to keep the law but are not sincere. They either show contempt for one simple command, or after a short period of keeping the law, they join up with Gog and Magog for the eschatological battle.[22] The focus of these texts is Gentile malice, and they are condemned.[23]

Against whom do the Gentiles contend? Psalm 2 describes the nations' opponents as not only God, but also God's anointed, God's son (Ps. 2.2, 7), who is often understood to be Israel,[24] since passages such as Exod. 4.22 call Israel God's son. The anointed son is also understood to be the messiah. While Aaron makes the list as an anointed one, the Davidic messiah is the one generally spoken of.[25]

Interestingly, *Midr. Ps.* 2.9 interprets Ps. 2.7 while providing extended quotations of Ps. 110.1 and Dan. 7.13-14, exactly the combination of passages in Mark 14.61-62.[26] In *Midr. Ps.* 2.9, these verses are used to argue, somewhat opaquely, that the son is Israel. In Mark, they are used differently.

---

19 While the accuracy of 'son' in various passages in *4 Ezra* has been questioned, John J. Collins ('The Son of God Text from Qumran', in *From Jesus to John: Essays on Jesus and New Testament Christology in Honour of Marinus de Jonge* [ed. M. C. de Boer; Sheffield: Sheffield Academic, 1993], pp. 76–77) indicates that at least in *4 Ezra* 13, they should be considered accurate. Translations of *4 Ezra* by B. M. Metzger, who dates it to the end of the first century CE (*OTP*, 1, p. 520).

20 *Tanh.* 2.25; *Lev. Rab. Emor* 27.11; *b. Ber.* 7b and 10a; *b. Avod. Zar.* 3b; *Midr. Ps.* 2.4 and 118.12. *Mek. Shir.* 7.64-65 implies this.

21 *Mek. Shir.* 7.64-65; *Midr. Ps.* 2.1-4.

22 This is a common interpretation of Ps. 2.3, 'let us burst their bonds asunder' (*Tanh.* 5.9; *b. Abod. Zar.* 3a-b; *Midr. Ps.* 2.5, where another option is that they want to stop the Israelites from keeping the law).

23 *Midr. Ps.* 2.7, 17 contrasts God's mercy to Israel with God's wrath on the nations.

24 *Mek. Shir.* 7.64-65; *Tanh.* 3.12; *Lev. Rab. Emor* 27.11; *Midr. Ps.* 2 throughout, but esp. 9 and 17.

25 *B. Sukk.* 52a; *Midr. Ps.* 2.3, 9-10; implied in *b. Ber.* 7b, 10a and *b. Abod. Zar.* 3b. For Aaron, see *Midr. Ps.* 2.3.

26 While there are some additions of 'local and temporary coloring', 'the overwhelming body of material in the *Midrash Psalms* or *Tehillim* goes back to the Talmudic period' (William Braude, *The Midrash on Psalms* [New Haven: Yale University Press, 1959], p. xi).

The LXX and Targum have significant differences from the MT, some of which highlight the wisdom theme present in the MT to a lesser degree. For example, both begin v. 12 with 'grasp instruction', rather than 'kiss the son' (a common English translation of a difficult Hebrew phrase). Another important difference in the LXX is found in v. 9, which has 'you will *shepherd* them with a rod of iron, crush them like ceramic vessels'.[27] The MT has 'you will *break* them with a rod of iron', which is a more sensible parallel to 'crush them'. In Christian sources, Ps. 2.9 is often understood to read 'rule them with a rod of iron'. This is based on the LXX's use of 'shepherd' and the use of shepherding as a metaphor for kingship in Scripture.[28]

The LXX ends v. 2 with a *diapsalma*, a musical notation, which creates a pause between vv. 2 and 3. Werner Kahl notes that this makes it possible to interpret the speakers of v. 3, 'let us rebel', as the Lord and his anointed, rather than the rulers of the earth. This resolves some of the strangeness of the psalm. After all, when was Israel ever such an empire that the nations of the earth ever had to unite to cast off its fetters? Yet Israel was again and again subject to the rule of the nations and had to be freed.[29] New Testament authors do seem to presume that the subjects of Ps. 2.1-2 are those who oppose the work of God from positions of power and that those on God's side are powerless without God's help. Jewish authors use all enemies of Israel as fitting examples of what is meant by the nations in Ps. 2.1-2, that is, anyone who seeks to do Israel harm, including the powerful (Pharaoh and Pompey) and the ineffectual (Esau).

Psalm 2 is used in early Jewish literature in disparate contexts with varied interpretation but with at least one common thread: the texts tend to paint a deeply negative portrait of the nations, who conspire to oppose God. They are condemned for their arrogance, often destroyed for the sake of Israel.

Other Early Christian Uses
Psalm 2, verse 7 especially, is used frequently in the New Testament.[30] Many New Testament allusions demonstrate similarities of interpretation with those of early Jewish literature. For example, Revelation uses Ps. 2.2 to describe the

---

Interestingly, Psalms 2 and 110 are linked in Heb. 5.5-6, as well.

27 Author's translation.

28 A number of patristic passages use Psalm 2 to establish that Jesus must be the Christ, because the Gentiles believe (Justin, *Dial.* 122.6; Irenaeus, *Dem.* 49; Tertullian, *Jud.* 12.1; 14.12; *Marc.* 3.20.3). Psalm 2.9 is taken to mean that the Christ will rule over the Gentiles because the Gentiles submit themselves to him by faith (cf. Ps. 2.10-12). This is in stark contrast to the usual interpretation of Ps. 2.9 in the Jewish tradition and the New Testament.

29 Kahl, 'Psalm 2 und das Neue Testament', in Sänger, *Gottessohn*, p. 240.

30 Many allusions have been suggested for Psalm 2 in the New Testament, with greater and lesser probability. The following discussion presents those that are relatively clear, along with the less clear but commonly named suggested allusion at Rom. 1.3-4.

final eschatological battle (Rev. 11.15; 17.18; 19.19), similar to the eschatological interpretation found in *Psalms of Solomon* or *Florilegium*, and particularly close to the rabbinic reference to the battle of Gog and Magog. Revelation uses Ps. 2.8-9, in variations of the phrase 'rod of iron', to indicate that in this battle, the decisive winners will be those on God's side (Rev. 2.26-27; 12.5; 19.15). In contrast, Heb. 1.2 alludes to Ps. 2.8 in a manner rather friendlier than the norm.[31] Here the inheritance of the Son appears to be entirely positive, describing the Son's greatness.

References to the conspiring rulers do not always indicate the nations in the final battle, but sometimes much more limited enemies. Acts 4.25 uses Ps. 2.1 to describe the enemies of Jesus and his followers – here the leaders of Jerusalem. This is similar to many uses in Jewish literature in which the conspiring rulers are anyone who would do Israel harm (e.g., Pompey in *Pss. Sol.* 2 or Pharaoh in *Mek. Shir.* 7.64-65). Nor is it unique for Luke to use Ps. 2.1 to describe Jewish leaders. *Florilegium* (i 8, 19; ii 1-2) uses it for those who persecute the Qumran community, including Jewish leaders.

In the New Testament, not surprisingly, most references to Psalm 2 indicate, explicitly or implicitly, that the anointed one and son is Jesus, the messiah, understood in the Davidic or royal sense. For example, Rev. 19.15 pairs Ps. 2.9 with Isa. 11.4 for Jesus, indicating the Davidic messiah. This is particularly clear in Acts 13.33, where Jesus and Ps. 2.7 are connected explicitly with the promises to David (Acts 13.22-23, 32-34). However, there are exceptions to the general rule. For example, Heb. 5.5 uses Ps. 2.7 in its argument that Jesus is the great high priest.[32] Both Acts 4.25-31 and Rev. 2.26-27 apply Psalm 2 to the church. While this may seem strange – the psalm is about the king – it is traditional. In early Jewish use, the psalm is applied to Israel or at Qumran, to the chosen of Israel.[33]

---

31 While the wording of Heb. 1.2 only faintly indicates Ps. 2.8, it is followed by a quotation of the psalm. Hebrews 1.1-4 serves as an introduction to the catena of quotations that follow, including Psalms 2 and 110, both subjects of this chapter. Often in the early Jewish material and the New Testament, Ps. 2.8 is paired with v. 9 and used to describe the destruction of the enemies of God. This is not universally the case however. In *b. Sukk.* 52 and *Midr. Ps.* 2.10, a gentler interpretation is given, in which the messiah asks for his life or the life of Israel.

32 It is interesting that Hebrews 5 and potentially 1QSa ii 11-12 use an apparently royal psalm to describe a priestly figure. This may have several causes. One of them, at least for Hebrews, is the connection of Psalms 2 and 110 (see pp. 160–61, n. 26); another is that God sets his king on *Zion*, his holy hill (Ps. 2.6), the location of the temple. Groups interested in the priesthood (undoubtedly including Qumran and the author of Hebrews) may well interpret this figure as an anointed priest, and eschatologically, as *the* anointed priest.

33 See above, e.g., 4Q174 i 18-19; *Midr. Ps.* 2.9. Duling ('Promises', 72) points out an interesting parallel use of 2 Samuel 7 in 2 Cor. 6.18, where the promises made explicitly to David for his son are transformed into promises to the whole church – 'I will be your [plural] father, and you shall be my sons and daughters, says the Lord Almighty' – while Paul goes on to speak of 'us', that is, the people, receiving the Davidic promises, promises which were also taken in a messianic sense by Paul and most likely by those to whom Paul is writing. The two interpretations stand together, apparently without tension.

It becomes apparent that while Psalm 2 is not interpreted in an entirely uniform manner, the early Jewish and Christian material shares several lines of interpretive tradition. The psalm is applied not only to the Davidic messiah, but potentially to the priestly messiah, and certainly to the people of God (Israel, the chosen of Israel, or the church). It is interpreted eschatologically, as an ultimate battle, but not necessarily so, with the interpretation of those who put Jesus to death as the conspiring rulers, corresponding to the non-eschatological interpretation of *Pss. Sol.* 2 and some rabbinic material. The thread tying most of these interpretations together is that the psalm portends judgement of the gathered enemies, whoever they may be.

Psalm 2 is also used in some obscure contexts. Acts 13.33 is one of the clearest references to Scripture in the entire New Testament, with not only a verbatim quotation of Ps. 2.7, but a reference to 'the second psalm'.[34] But what does the quotation establish? When one goes beyond the basic level of meaning – that Jesus is the Davidic messiah – much is unclear. The context is ambiguous. Paul says:

> And we bring you the good news that what God promised to our ancestors he has fulfilled for us, their children, by raising Jesus; as also it is written in the second psalm, 'You are my Son; today I have begotten you.' (Acts 13.32-33)

Does Ps. 2.7 establish that God fulfilled the promises or raised Jesus? What does 'raising' mean here: bringing onto the scene of history or resurrecting? It might appear that the psalm establishes that God fulfilled the promise of the Davidic messiah through Jesus and that 'raising' means bringing on to the scene of history. However, in the verses preceding and following this one 'raise' is used with 'from the dead', obviously meaning 'resurrect'. Would Luke use the same verb in one sense in v. 30, in a different sense in v. 33, and again in the first sense in vv. 34 and 37? The improbability of that supposition leads many to conclude that Acts 13.33 uses Psalm 2 regarding Jesus' resurrection.[35] But what is the connection of Psalm 2 to resurrection? Mailberger suggests the connection is traditional, citing such a use in *Midr. Ps.* 2.11.[36] Yet a closer look at that passage indicates that Ps. 2.9 is used there to argue *against* resurrection by a Jew who has lost his faith: we are like clay pots that, once broken, cannot be put together again. R. Jose responds with Gen. 2.7, saying that we are glass vessels which can be reshaped by the breath of God, as a glassblower blows into heated glass. In another interpretation, R. Isaac says that sinners can repent *before* death, like the potter's vessel of Ps. 2.9, which

---

34   Some MSS have 'first psalm'. In some texts, Psalm 1 and 2 were seen as a single unit. See p. 155, n. 3.
35   For a summary of the debate, see Lee, *From Messiah*, pp. 251–55. Many uses of Psalm 2 in the New Testament, not just here in Acts 13.33, are often understood to refer to Jesus' resurrection.
36   Mailberger, 'Verständnis', in Schreiner, *Beiträge*, p. 113.

is not yet fired and can be reshaped. The arguments of both rabbis use fire as a metaphor for death, but neither uses Ps. 2.9 for resurrection.

Aquila Lee proposes that for Christians the connection to resurrection comes through Ps. 2.6, 'I have installed my king on Zion, my holy hill'.[37] The earliest church saw Jesus' resurrection and ascension to the right hand of God as his coronation, his 'installation' as king. While Ps. 2.6 is not alluded to in the New Testament, Lee argues that it stands behind Christian interpretation of the psalm. Allusions to Ps. 110.1 serve instead of Ps. 2.6 to communicate the idea.[38] While the absence of allusions to Ps. 2.6 is significant, Lee's solution is still a reasonable one. The context of referent passages is usually a part of the New Testament's allusive use of Scripture – the question is generally only how much of the context to include. That verse 6 is implied in some allusions to verse 7 is not a stretch.

Another solution may be that proposed by Dennis Duling for the 'promises to David' tradition as a whole (though he does not suggest it for Psalm 2 in particular), a tradition that includes Nathan's oracle and quite a few related texts in the Old Testament and later literature. A surprising number of these texts speak of 'raising up' (ἀνίστημι) David's descendant (e.g., 2 Sam. 7.12; Jer. 23.5; *Pss. Sol.* 17.21), meaning, bringing the Son of David onto the scene of history. The same term is commonly used for Jesus' resurrection. The Christian imagination could easily transfer the meaning of 'raising up' the Son of David from its original sense into this new sense of resurrection. Duling suggests that this may have been 'the earliest point of entry of the promise tradition into early Christianity'.[39]

The tradition of the promises to David forms something of a whole, and Psalm 2 is part of that tradition. This is seen in a number of ways, including the typical combinations of passages from the tradition found in the later literature. For example, Psalm 2 is combined with 2 Samuel 7 or Isaiah 11 or both in *Pss. Sol.* 17, *Florilegium*, *4 Ezra* 13, Hebrews 1, and Rev. 19.15. The term 'raising up' seems to have become associated with the Son of David figure, not merely with Old Testament passages from the tradition which use the word, since we see 'raising up' used for the figure in later literature.[40] Because 'raising up' and Psalm 2 are part of the tradition, raising up could be associated with Psalm 2, even though it does not use the term. Since 'raising' David's son would have had double meaning in Christian circles, the difficulty in determining just how Luke is using ἀναστήσας in Acts 13.33 may simply be due to a word play: God 'fulfilled the promises to our ancestors' by 'raising up'

---

37 NRSV modified.
38 Lee, *From Messiah*, pp. 256–58.
39 Duling, 'Promises', pp. 71–77, esp. p. 77.
40 The figure coming out of the promises to David tradition (unlike the suffering righteous one, see pp. 91–94) does seem to be a conventional literary figure. For more information on the promises tradition, see Duling, 'Promises', passim.

Jesus in both senses of that term. This makes sense both of the ambiguity of Acts 13.33 – it is intentional – and the repeated use of Psalm 2 in the New Testament to refer to Jesus' resurrection and exaltation.[41]

Romans 1.3-4 is often taken to allude to Ps. 2.7. Verbal correspondence is modest, somewhat stronger with the Hebrew than the Greek, but bolstered by thematic correspondence: Jesus is declared Son of God, which is connected to the obedience of the nations in v. 5 (Ps. 2.6-12). While an allusion to 2 Sam. 7.12 is clearer, Rom. 1.3-4 may well echo Ps. 2.6-7. The exact meaning of this passage is debated. For the present purpose, it is sufficient to say that in the echo of Psalm 2, Jesus' resurrection is connected with some kind of divine status (whatever that might be precisely): he is 'declared to be Son of God … Jesus Christ our Lord'. This is a significant departure from Jewish tradition on the use of Psalm 2 but is not alone in the New Testament. Hebrews 1.2-5 uses Psalm 2 to show that the Son is greater than the angels, the one through whom God created the worlds, who sustains all things, who is 'the exact imprint of God's very being'.[42] Psalm 2 is also used by the church fathers to indicate Jesus' great, even exalted status (*Gos. Eb.*; Justin, *Dial.* 88.8; Tertullian, *Prax.* 7.2; 11.3; Clement of Alexandria, *Instr.* 1.6).[43]

Markan Use

Mark alludes to Ps. 2.7 in several passages. One of the clearest is in the baptismal scene, where a heavenly voice tells Jesus (Mark 1.11):

You are my Son (σὺ εἶ ὁ υἱός μου), the Beloved; with you I am well pleased.

I will tell of the decree of the LORD: He said to me, '*You are my son* (υἱός μου εἶ σύ); today I have begotten you.' (Ps. 2.7)[44]

'With you I am well pleased' probably alludes to Isa. 42.1, while the rending of the heavens (Mark 1.10) alludes to Isa. 63.19 (64.1).[45] Both of these passages speak of the coming of the Holy Spirit and of justice. Isaiah 63 in particular has a strong flavour of eschatological judgement, while Isaiah 42 speaks more gently of restoration, particularly for the nations. Like Mark 1.2-3,[46] the baptismal scene is eschatological, with both the condemnation of the

---

41 This approach avoids the weakness of Lee's solution, that the verse that provides the link between exaltation in the psalm and resurrection in the New Testament is never actually used in the New Testament (nor often in Jewish literature).
42 There is debate about the exact christology in both Romans 1 and Hebrews 1. Lee (*From Messiah*, pp. 264–69 and 272–77) provides a summary.
43 *Diogn.* 11.5 uses Ps. 2.7 in a series of passages on Jesus' exalted nature, but it is not clear how the psalm itself is interpreted.
44 See pp. 106–7.
45 Marcus, *Way*, pp. 49–55.
46 See pp. 2–4.

wicked and the restoration of the just highlighted in the passages alluded to.[47] In this context, one might note the strong tendency of the tradition to use Psalm 2 to speak of judgement of the wicked, particularly of the nations, similar to Isaiah 63.

Also like Mark 1.2-3, the allusions address Jesus' identity. One might assume that the allusion to Psalm 2 must indicate Jesus' royal identity, since it speaks of the installation of a king, but as we have seen, this is not necessarily so, since Psalm 2 is often interpreted to refer to Israel as a whole. The baptismal scene, with its allusion to Psalm 2, is followed by Jesus' temptation in the wilderness, which recapitulates Israel's experience. That means we cannot completely rule out the possibility that Jesus as God's son via Psalm 2 indicates that Jesus is representative of Israel. Nor should these possibilities be too strictly separated. Israel is God's son, as is the king. The king represents Israel. Both are tied intimately together, and both are included in the interpretive tradition on Psalm 2. Still, the use of Psalm 2 in early Christianity heavily favours the Davidic, messianic interpretation for Jesus himself. Certainly, the scene highlights Jesus' extraordinary status. The heavens are torn open, and a heavenly voice speaks to Jesus, calling him beloved son and declaring his praise, as God's Spirit descends on him. The scene has the appearance of an 'installation', where Jesus is 'anointed' for his eschatological task (Ps. 2.2, 6). To use the words of the Davidic tradition, he has been 'raised up'.

The phrasing of the heavenly voice in the transfiguration (Mark 9.7) is further removed from Ps. 2.7, too much to be an echo, but the scene is a clear parallel to the baptism and helps interpret it. The scene is set up as a foretaste of the eschatological Reign (Mark 9.1) and is bracketed by references to Jesus' death and resurrection (Mark 8.31; 9.9). Jesus' exalted status is highlighted. His clothes take on a divine whiteness (cf. Dan. 7.9; Rev. 20.11; *1 Enoch* 14.20-21). He, unlike Moses and Elijah, is God's son. Similar to *Pss. Sol.* 17 and Hebrews 1, the use of Psalm 2 imagery in the baptism and transfiguration seems to highlight Jesus' exalted status in an eschatological context.[48]

The Parable of the Vineyard also echoes the baptismal voice, with its 'beloved son', and Ps. 2.8, with its reference to the son as 'heir' (Mark 12.6-7). The parable emphasizes how much greater the son is than the servants who went before. It also incorporates the theme of opposition, so central to Psalm 2.[49] Like the opponents of Psalm 2, the tenants conspire against the son, and they are to be destroyed (Mark 12.7-9; Ps. 2.1-5, 9).

---

47   Interestingly, like the allusion to Mal. 3.1, the allusion to Isa. 63.19 is adjacent to a verse which speaks of the destruction of the temple; Isa. 63.18 condemns those who destroyed it.
48   See also pp. 119–20.
49   Marcus, *Way*, p. 71.

Finally, the high priest's question, 'Are you the Anointed, the Son of the Blessed?'[50] echoes Psalm 2, precisely where it identifies its subject as the anointed, God's son (Ps. 2.2, 7). Jesus' identity and consequence are the main concern of the trial narrative. The use of Psalm 2, along with Jesus' answer, to be discussed below, points to his highly exalted status. Jesus' answer points to a second installation, another 'raising up', where he will be 'seated at the right hand of the Power'. This recalls Ps. 2.6, where God says, 'I have set my king on Zion, my holy hill.' In this context, 'my [God's] holy hill', may be understood in a heavenly sense. There the anointed Son will rule over all: 'I will make the nations your heritage, and the ends of the earth your possession' (Ps. 2.8). In this scene, Jesus' exaltation is revealed to his enemies, as it had been revealed to his disciples at the transfiguration.

This passage is tied to the Parable of the Vineyard and its theme of opposition, where the leaders, the 'tenants', gather and conspire to kill the son, the anointed (Mark 14.1, 53, 55; Ps. 2.1-2). They can expect their destruction, seen both in the parable and in the psalm, 'you shall break them with a rod of iron, and dash them in pieces like a potter's vessel' (Ps. 2.9), where the meaning is decidedly like that seen in early Judaism and Revelation: eschatological judgement.

Seated at the Right Hand – Psalm 110.1

Mark 14.62 alludes to Ps. 110.1:

> 'you will see the Son of Man *seated at the right hand* (ἐκ δεξιῶν καθήμενον) of the Power, and coming with the clouds of heaven. (Mark 14.62)

> The Lord says to my lord, '*Sit at my right hand* (κάθου ἐκ δεξιῶν μου) until I make your enemies your footstool.' (Ps. 110.1)[51]

Mark 14.62 inserts the phrase from Ps. 110.1 into the allusion to Dan. 7.13 (discussed later in the chapter) and following the allusion to Ps. 2.7. A glance at Psalm 2, Psalm 110, and Daniel 7 shows how easily they could be combined. Psalm 2.6 speaks of installing the king on Zion, God's holy hill. Daniel 7 speaks of thrones and can be understood to mean that the one like a son of man will sit on one with the Ancient of Days (7.9, 13-14).[52] This combines naturally with Ps. 110.1, where the Lord, that is, God, requests that 'my lord' sit at God's right hand. In Ps. 2.8-9, the anointed son crushes the nations and possesses the ends of the earth. In Dan. 7.10-13, the son of man

---

50   NRSV modified.
51   Discussion of verbal correspondence is found on pp. 213 and 259.
52   J. Collins, *Daniel*, p. 301.

figure appears immediately after the court sits in judgement and does away with the king-beasts. Psalm 110.5-6 declares that God, at 'your' right hand, will shatter the kings and judge the nations. All three passages speak of a kingdom of surpassing power. Daniel 7 and Psalm 110 speak of this kingdom lasting for eternity (Dan. 7.14; Ps. 110.4-6).

Early Jewish Interpretation
While this study unearthed no indisputable references to it in Second Temple literature, Psalm 110 does appear to *influence* at least one extant text: 11QMelch (11Q13). Psalm 110 contains one of the two Old Testament references to Melchizedek (the other being Gen. 14.17-24). During the late Second Temple period, Melchizedek is mentioned in the *Genesis Apocryphon* and 11QMelch and by Philo and Josephus.[53] Hebrews also refers to Melchizedek and alludes to Psalm 110.[54] Because Mark does not mention Melchizedek, traditions on him are relevant only in so far as they are interpretations of Psalm 110. The texts of Philo, Josephus, and the *Genesis Apocryphon* are not relevant to Mark, because they refer only to Genesis 14, not Psalm 110. Hebrews does clearly refer to Psalm 110 and provides important comparative material, to be discussed later. Matters are not so clear cut in 11QMelch.

As Joseph Fitzmyer points out, the extant fragments of 11QMelch do not refer to Psalm 110, though they refer to many other Scripture passages.[55] Despite Fitzmyer's doubts, many commentators remain convinced that the picture of Melchizedek drawn in that document reflects interpretations developed from Psalm 110. They are persuaded by a number of similar themes between Psalm 110 and 11QMelch. It can be reasonably stated that though 11QMelch does not clearly refer to Psalm 110, it is more likely than not that 11QMelch reflects a tradition based on Psalm 110.[56]

---

53   Philo, *Leg. All.* 3.79-82; *Congr.* 99; Josephus, *Ant.* 1.10.2; 1QapGen[ar] xxii 14-26; 11QMelch passim. The Melchizedek episode falls in a lacuna in *Jubilees*, at 13.25. It is likely that the episode was mentioned because the narrative picks up again with a discussion of tithes.

54   Hebrews 5.6-10; 6.19–7.28. (Though this section deals with Second Temple Judaism, Hebrews is included here for the sake of comparison.)

55   Joseph A. Fitzmyer, 'Further Light on Melchizedek From Qumran Cave 11', in *Essays on the Semitic Background of the New Testament* (Grand Rapids: Eerdmans, 1997), pp. 253–54: repr. from *JBL* 86 (1967). Fred Horton (*The Melchizedek Tradition: A Critical Examination of the Sources, to the Fifth Century A.D. and in the Epistle to the Hebrews* [Cambridge: Cambridge University Press, 1976], pp. 79–80) shares his reserve.

56   Cf. Kugel, *Traditions*, pp. 279–81; Marcus, *Way*, p. 133; P. Kobelski, *Melchizedek and Melchireša* (Washington, DC: CBA, 1981), pp. 53–55. David M. Hay (*Glory at the Right Hand: Psalm 110 in Early Christianity* [Nashville: Abingdon, 1973], pp. 27, 138) takes the *via media*; he recognizes that a Jewish reader of 11QMelch would naturally associate that text with Genesis 14 and Psalm 110, but also states that it is possible the author did not make that association.

The characterization of Melchizedek in 11QMelch as a member of the divine court can be seen to come from Psalm 110. In the psalm, God speaks to someone called 'my lord'. If 'my lord' is taken to refer to Melchizedek,[57] then in v. 1, Melchizedek is invited to sit at God's right hand. According to Second Temple exegetical understanding, sitting at God's right hand is appropriate only to heavenly beings.[58] In 11QMelch, Melchizedek is a heavenly being, part of the heavenly court,[59] and can be considered an angel.[60]

Melchizedek's execution of divine justice may also be seen as a reflection on the psalm. Psalm 110.6 states, 'he will execute judgement among the nations' and 'shatter the heads over the wide earth'. The psalm probably refers to God here, but the subject is implicit and as often happens, changes throughout the psalm. Thus, it is possible to interpret the subject as 'my lord' or Melchizedek. Kugel sees this verse, in addition to Melchizedek's name (which means *king of justice*), as the source of the 11QMelch statement that Melchizedek will execute God's justice:[61] 'Melchizedek will avenge the vengeance of the judgements of God ... and he will drag [them from the hand of] Belial and from the hand of all the sp[irits of] his [lot]' (ii 13). In 11QMelch, Melchizedek's justice is eschatological, coming at the end of days (ii 4).[62] He effects not only judgement on Belial and his lot, but reward for the righteous, as well (ii 4-6, 9). The extant text begins with quotations of Lev. 25.13, Deut. 15.2, and perhaps Isa. 61.1, all of which deal with the jubilee. 11QMelch describes the ultimate jubilee, in which 'all the Sons of [Light] and the men of the lot of Mel[chi]zedek will be atoned for ... For this is the moment of the Year of Grace for Melchizedek' (ii 8-9).

Rabbinic treatments of Psalm 110 reflect similar themes.[63] Most relevant for our purposes is the quotation of Ps. 110.1-5 in the *Mekilta*. The psalm is used in a context of justice and punishment, in this case regarding God's self-vindication: 'Thou hast shown Thyself exceedingly great against those that rose up against Thee'; for example, God destroyed Pharaoh, Sisera, Sennacherib,

---

57   Kugel (*Traditions*, p. 279) states that such a view was indeed held, caused by an ambiguity in Ps. 110.4. This verse could be read, 'You are a priest forever by my order [or 'on my account'], O *Melchizedek*' (Kugel's insertion, my emphasis).

58   Cf. Kugel, *Traditions*, p. 279.

59   That is the implication of 11QMelch ii 9-11. See, for example, Horton, *Melchizedek Tradition*, pp. 71–77, M. de Jonge and A. S. van der Woude, '11Q Melchizedek and the New Testament', *NTS* 12 (1966), p. 304.

60   Kugel, *Traditions*, p. 279.

61   Kugel, *Traditions*, p. 280. Cf. Kobelski, *Melchizedek*, p. 54.

62   Horton, *Melchizedek Tradition*, p. 77. Kugel (*Traditions*, p. 279) states that Melchizedek executes justice 'in the great day of reckoning'.

63   The Talmud interprets the psalm as a description of the transference of the priesthood from Melchizedek to Abraham (*b. Ned.* 32b), and an explanation of Abraham's unexpected victory (*b. Sanh.* 108b). These interpretations do not appear to connect with Mark's use of the text. Kobelski (*Melchizedek*, p. 53) notes that later rabbinic material applies it to David and the messiah.

etc. (*Mek. Shir.* 6.38-50).[64] The implication is that here, just as in 11QMelch, justice and vengeance on God's enemies is central to the understanding of Psalm 110.

Other Early Christian Uses

Psalm 110 appears frequently among New Testament allusions to Scripture. The following sketches the major lines of thought there.

There is an emphasis on heavenly status and the Parousia. This is true of Mark, as we will see; Matthew and Luke use Psalm 110 in a manner similar to that of Mark (Matt. 22.44; 26.64; Luke 20.42-43; 22.69). Also in a roughly similar fashion, 1 Cor. 15.25 uses it to explain that Jesus' heavenly reign will endure until the last enemy is overcome (there the last enemy is death, v. 26). Acts 2.34-35 uses Ps. 110.1 regarding Jesus' ascension. Hebrews uses Ps. 110.1 to show Jesus' superiority to the angels, as one enthroned in the heavens (Heb. 1.13), and Ps. 110.4 to establish Jesus' function as heavenly priest (Heb. 5.6; 7.17, 21).[65]

Uses are similar in other early Christian texts. Psalm 110 is used to demonstrate Jesus' exalted status. *1 Clement* 36.5 uses Ps. 110.1 in a catena similar to that of Hebrews 1. *Barnabas* 12.10-11 uses Ps. 110.1 to prove that Jesus is not just Son of Man but also Son of God; Christ is not David's son but God's son. Psalm 110 is frequently used as a proof that Jesus is Lord, and thus divine (cf. Justin, *Dial.* 56; 127; Irenaeus, *Haer.* 2.28.7; 3.6.1; 3.16.3; *Dem.* 48; Tertullian, *Prax.* 13.3).

It is also used to discuss the Eschaton. *Martyrdom and Ascension of Isaiah* 10.7-16 begins and ends with allusions to Ps. 110.1. In between, it interpolates a command from God to 'my lord Christ' to descend to earth so that there may be judgement, and then ascend once again to heaven and sit at God's right hand.[66] The glory, divinity, and rule of Christ are emphasized. Tertullian

---

64   Translation by Jacob Z. Lauterbach, *Mekilta de-Rabbi Ishmael* (2 vols; Philadelphia: JPS, 1933, 2004).

65   See Hay, *Glory*, p. 144. He suggests (pp. 151, n. 94; 132–33, n. 15) there may be an underlying tradition linking Jesus' heavenly enthronement to his priesthood. He sees this reflected in Heb. 10.12-13; Rev. 1.13, where '"one like a son of man" wears priestly costume' (his assessment here may go beyond the evidence; see D. E. Aune, *Revelation* [WBC 52; 3 vols, Dallas: Word Books, 1997], 1, pp. 93–94); and Mark 14.58-62, where mention of the temple not built with hands immediately precedes the description of the heavenly enthronement. It may also lie behind Stephen's criticism of the earthly temple (Acts 7.47-50).

This is an interesting observation, and the source of the connection between the heavenly court and the priestly role is not hard to find. Mark 14.62, one of the passages Hay notes, quotes Ps. 110.1 about the heavenly court, and Ps. 110.4 designates the subject of the psalm as 'a priest forever'. This observation may provide a further insight into the interpretation of Psalm 110 in the Christian, and possibly pre-Markan, tradition. The second evangelist however makes no use of such an interpretation, and one cannot include it in an interpretation of the gospel.

66   M. A. Knibb (*OTP* 2, p. 150) dates this section to approximately the second century CE and provides the translation.

considers Psalm 110 fulfilled in the future, at the Parousia. *Adversus Iudaeos* 14.5 uses it as one of many proofs that there are two advents of Christ, one in humility and one in glory, where Ps. 110.1 proves that Christ will come again in glory. Like 1 Cor. 15.25, *Res.* 22.9 notes that Christ's enemies are not yet fully subjected, and that the general resurrection will occur in the future.[67]

Like Tertullian, Irenaeus considers the passage fulfilled in the future (*Dem.* 85). Yet he also considers the passage to have been fulfilled already, when Christ rose from the dead (*Haer.* 3.10.5; 4.33.11). Justin declares it fulfilled in part when Jesus ascended to heaven (*Dial.* 32; 36; *1 Apol.* 45). That is, it is used with respect to resurrection and ascension.

Markan Use

Mark uses Ps. 110.1 in both 12.36 and 14.62. In Mark 12.36, Ps. 110.1 appears by itself as a nearly exact quotation from the LXX, in a controversy over the identity or nature of the messiah.

> While Jesus was teaching in the temple, he said, 'How can the scribes say that the Messiah is the son of David? David himself, by the Holy Spirit, declared,
> "*The Lord said to my Lord, 'Sit at my right hand,*
> *until I put your enemies under your feet.'*"
> David himself calls him Lord; so how can he be his son?' And the large crowd was listening to him with delight.

The passage implies that the scribes misunderstand who the messiah is, without saying exactly how. Some understand this passage to be a repudiation of the 'Son of David' title. This seems unlikely since 'Son of David' is used without correction in Mark 10.47-48, where it is placed on the lips of Bartimaeus who is portrayed as an ideal disciple, following Jesus 'on the way' (10.52). An alternative understanding of Mark 12.35-37 is that Ps. 110.1 is used to indicate that the messiah is not merely David's son, but something greater, one who has more than human status. This would be in line with other early Jewish and Christian interpretations of the psalm, seen above, which emphasize heavenly status.

Psalm 110.1 is used in early Christian literature for Jesus' resurrection and ascension, and some hold that it *must* refer to the ascension (sitting at God's right hand) and cannot refer to the Parousia. That would present a conflict for Mark 14.62. Because the use of Dan. 7.13 there refers to the Parousia, the elements in Mark 14.62 – Psalm 110 (ascension) and Dan. 7.13 (Parousia) – would be in tension.[68] The discussion sometimes rests at the literal level: how

---

67 Tertullian also uses Ps. 110.1 frequently in discussions of the Trinity (cf. *Marc.* 4.41.4; 5.17.6; *Prax.* 4.2; 11.7; 30.5).

68 See p. 187, n. 134, on whether the combination of Dan. 7.13 and Ps. 110.1 refers to the ascension or the Parousia.

can the Son of Man *sit* (Ps. 110.1) and *come* (Dan. 7.13) at once?[69] Donahue disagrees that ascension and Parousia must be in tension, noting that the two elements are combined elsewhere. For example, 1 Cor. 15.25 uses Ps. 110.1 to refer to Christ's reign until the end. Christ ascends to heaven and there reigns until he comes again.[70]

Despite the image of sitting at God's right hand, the reign implied in Psalm 110 is not one of quiet waiting but of active subjugation of enemies, of judgement and complete victory:

> The LORD sends out from Zion your mighty sceptre.
> Rule in the midst of your foes.
> Your people will offer themselves willingly
> on the day you lead your forces in holy splendor. (Ps. 110.2-3)[71]

Such elements correspond not to the ascension but to the Parousia. That again is the implied interpretation of Psalm 110 in 11QMelch. The statement in Ps. 110.1 that the subject should sit at God's right hand until God makes his enemies a footstool for his feet can imply an end-time, and 'you will be a priest forever' (v. 4) denotes an eternal state. Psalm 110.1, 5-6 describe the punishment of the wicked:

> The Lord is at your right hand; he will shatter kings on the day of his wrath.
> He will execute judgement among the nations, filling them with corpses;
> he will shatter heads over the wide earth. (vv. 5-6)

In Mark and 11QMelch, as elsewhere, such thoroughgoing punishment of the wicked points to the final judgement. It is thus logical that the psalm should be taken in an eschatological sense in Mark and 11QMelch.[72]

Hebrews uses Psalm 110 to describe Christ's priestly and specifically *atoning* power, and 11QMelch makes much of the atonement that Melchizedek effects. It is possible that such a sense is latent in Mark, but if so, it is entirely latent. Only a knowledge of such traditions would bring out that sense.

---

69 Sometimes the discussion considers the order of the allusions, that Psalm 110 (ascension) must come before Daniel 7 (Parousia). For a summary of the discussion, see Hooker, *Son of Man*, p. 169; Craig A. Evans, 'In What Sense "Blasphemy"?', *SBL Seminar Papers, 1991* (ed. Eugene H. Lovering, Jr; SBLSP 30, Atlanta: Scholars Press, 1991), p. 220.

70 Donahue, *Are You the Christ?*, pp. 161–62, 174–75. Maurice Casey (*Son of Man*, p. 182) agrees, suggesting that the sense of ascension in the use of Psalm 110 complements the 'coming' sense of Daniel very well.

71 NRSV modified. Note the similarity to crushing foes with an iron sceptre in Ps. 2.9.

72 It is not argued here that Psalm 110 in Mark 14.62 in no way connotes the ascension. Ascension and Parousia are not, in the world of allusion, mutually exclusive. Symbolic language is elastic.

Simple knowledge of the psalm would not be enough; although the psalm designates 'my lord' as a priest forever, it does not mention atonement (or any reward for the righteous).

Instead, Psalm 110 emphasizes judgement, punishment, and subjugation of enemies. References to victory over enemies are found in Ps. 110.1-2, perhaps v. 3, and vv. 5-6 – nearly every verse. This emphasis on judgement and the destruction of enemies is retained in the interpretation of Ps. 110 in the *Mekilta* and the implied interpretation in 11QMelch. Some commentators see Mark 14.62 as a positive statement, emphasizing the vindication of the righteous (principally Jesus himself), and that may well be so, especially through the use of Dan. 7.13. Yet the inclusion of Psalm 110 indicates that the ὄψεσθε, 'you will see', spoken to the council is ominous. What follows are words of threat and judgement. Though they judge Jesus now, the members of the council will be judged when they see the Son of Man returning in full glory.[73]

Yet despite the emphasis on judgement in the psalm, one should not miss the still clearer emphasis on glory and royal power.[74] Though Jesus has powerful political foes now, the use of Ps. 110.1 implies that he will reign despite them.[75] Indeed, v. 2 implies that he will reign over them: 'The Lord sends out from Zion your mighty sceptre. Rule [κατακυρίευε] in the midst of your foes.' The compound κατακυριεύω denotes complete dominance. Sitting at the right hand, especially in combination with the anointed Son of Psalm 2 and the son of man figure from Dan. 7.13, emphasizes Jesus' heavenly status and power. The reign of the anointed Son will be thorough and eternal.

The Son of Man Coming with the Clouds— Daniel 7.13

Along with the allusion to Ps. 110.1, Mark 14.62 also clearly alludes to Dan. 7.13:

You will see *the Son of Man* (τὸν υἱὸν τοῦ ἀνθρώπου) seated at the right hand of the Power and *coming with the clouds of heaven* (ἐρχόμενον μετὰ τῶν νεφελῶν τοῦ οὐρανου; Mark 14.62)

I saw one like *a son of man coming with the clouds of heaven* (μετὰ τῶν νεφελῶν τοῦ οὐρανοῦ ὡς υἱὸς ἀνθρώπου ἐρχόμενος; Dan. 7.13).[76]

---

73   See below, pp. 181–82, 187–88, on this issue. Donahue (*Are You the Christ?*, pp. 174–75) argues that Psalm 110 indicates that Jesus reigns and operates in judgement at the Parousia.
74   Matera, *Kingship*, pp. 111–13. Note that Mark 12.36 attributes Ps. 110.1 to David and considers it addressed to the messiah.
75   Cf. de Jonge, 'Jesus, Son of David and Son of God', in Draisma, *Intertextuality in Biblical Writings*, p. 99.
76   NRSV modified. See pp. 208–9 and 259 for more information on verbal correspondence.

Thus ends the clarity of the issue. Great quantities of ink have been spilled over various aspects of the seemingly simple phrase 'son of man'. It is therefore necessary briefly to discuss the secondary literature on the meaning of 'son of man' in the first century as it relates to the meaning of the Son of Man in Mark 14.62. Fortunately, despite much debate regarding the origin and original meaning of the phrase 'son of man', there is consensus on most of the issues that concern interpretation of Mark 14.62.[77] Or perhaps it is wiser to say, a great deal of interpretation can be accomplished by focusing on the matters on which most agree. Scholars steadfastly divided over the origin of the phrase agree, for example, that in the gospels it refers to Jesus and is used christologically.[78] And while there remains significant debate about the meaning of the phrase 'son of man' when there is no reference to Dan. 7.13, there is much greater agreement when a reference is clear, as in Mark 14.62. The present aim is to exploit such areas of agreement in order better to understand the meaning of the allusion to Dan. 7.13 in Mark 14.62. Thus, the following discussion of the phrase son of man is conducted entirely regarding its meaning relative to Daniel 7.

Early Jewish Interpretation
The following discussion will begin with the treatment of Dan. 7.13-14 in Second Temple literature, then move to the early rabbinic material. Finally, it will assess whether there is a common understanding of the son of man figure in Daniel 7.

Second Temple Judaism
The *Similitudes of Enoch* and *4 Ezra* clearly allude to the vision of Daniel 7.[79] The *Similitudes* are generally dated between 100 BCE and 70 CE.[80] *4 Ezra* is

---

77 Because much of the Son of Man debate concerns the historical Jesus, it may be worthwhile here to reiterate that this study treats Jesus only as portrayed in the Gospel of Mark. It does not deal with the historical Jesus, the authenticity of sayings attributed to him, or the original meaning of authentic sayings.

78 Cf. H. E. Tödt, *The Son of Man in the Synoptic Tradition* (trans. Dorothea M. Barton; Philadelphia: Westminster, 1965), pp. 37–39; Regnar Leivestad, 'Exit the Apocalyptic Son of Man', *NTS* 18 (1972), pp. 247, 262–63; D. Hare, *The Son of Man Tradition* (Minneapolis: Fortress, 1990), p. 183; Maurice Casey, *The Solution to the 'Son of Man' Problem* (ed. Mark Goodacre; LNTS 343; London: T&T Clark, 2007), pp. 118, 242, 266–67, 272–73.

79 See especially *1 Enoch* 46.1; 47.3; *4 Ezra* 13.1-3.

80 J. T. Milik suggested that the existence at Qumran of fragments from all portions of *1 Enoch* except for the *Similitudes* indicates a late date for that portion ('Problèmes de la littérature Hénochique à la lumière des fragments Araméens de Qumrân', *HTR* 64 [1971], pp. 377–78). Milik's suggestions have been widely rejected, and scholars generally date the *Similitudes* before the fall of Jerusalem. Cf. Michael Knibb, 'The Date of the Parables of Enoch: A Critical Review', *NTS* 25 (1979), pp. 345–59; John J. Collins, 'The Son of Man in First-Century Judaism', *NTS* 38 (1992), p. 452; Casey, *Son of Man*, p. 99. Lindars (*Jesus, Son of Man: A Fresh Examination of the Son of Man Sayings in the Gospels in the Light of Recent Research* [Grand Rapids:

generally dated to the late first century CE.[81] Though it is likely that the *Similitudes* were written before Mark and Mark before *4 Ezra*, there was not necessarily any direct literary influence between these texts. Rather *Similitudes* and *4 Ezra* attest to ideas current in the cultural context out of which the author of Mark wrote.[82]

Scholars disagree on the exact content of the phrase 'son of man' in the *Similitudes* or *4 Ezra*, and with regard to the *Similitudes*, whether the son of man is Enoch.[83] Nevertheless, all agree that the *Similitudes* and *4 Ezra* allude to the vision described in Daniel 7 and that the phrase 'son of man' recalls the figure 'resembling a son of man' in Dan. 7.13. Though in Daniel 7 that figure is a symbol for the collective 'people of the holy ones of the Most High' (Dan. 7.27),[84] in the *Similitudes* and *4 Ezra*, it becomes an individual, a character.[85]

The *Similitudes* describe a single figure with a combination of epithets or tropes: the Righteous One, the Anointed, the Chosen One, and 'that Son of Man'.[86] The Son of Man figure is identified with the messiah and functions

---

Eerdmans, 1983], p. 158) dates the *Similitudes* to the end of first century, at the same time as *4 Ezra*, *2 Baruch*, and Revelation. Hare (*Son of Man*, p. 13) notes that the exact date of the *Similitudes* is not important for comparison with the gospels, because he considers the gospels and *Similitudes* independent.

81   Metzger, *OTP*, 1, p. 520.

82   E. Isaac (*OTP*, 1, p. 10) finds it likely that *1 Enoch* influenced most of the New Testament writers. While Mark is not in the list of examples presented, it seems unlikely that Mark would be specifically excluded. Nevertheless, direct influence is not necessary here, simply a common tradition reflected in different texts.

83   See below.

84   Author's translation.

85   J. Collins ('Son of Man', p. 451; *Daniel*, p. 305) sees the Daniel 7 figure somewhat differently. He identifies the one like the son of man there as a heavenly individual, not merely as a collective symbol, 'probably the archangel Michael', who is of the mythic-realistic type. Thomas Slater ('One Like a Son of Man in First-Century CE Judaism', *NTS* 41 [1995], pp. 183–84, 188–90) makes a helpful distinction. Just as the other figures in Daniel 7 are said to be *like* a lion, *like* a bear, etc., but are not bears, lions, etc., they are symbolic of something else; so also the figure in 7.13 is not said to *be* a son of man but rather *like* a son of man, and is thus a symbol for something else. 'Son of man' per se means 'human being', but the dream uses the phrase comparatively to describe a figure that is not human. Slater agrees with Collins that it probably refers to an angelic figure. Cf. Dan. 8.15; 10.16, 18 where angelic figures are described as appearing like human beings.

Regarding *1 Enoch*, see James C. VanderKam, 'Righteous One, Messiah, Chosen One, and Son of Man in *1 Enoch* 37–71', in Charlesworth, *Messiah*, p. 190.

86   Though the *Similitudes* are composite and the picture itself is made up of separate elements, it is generally agreed that in the final piece, the composite refers to a single figure. See, for example, VanderKam, 'Righteous One', in Charlesworth, *Messiah*, pp. 185–86; G. Oegema, *The Anointed and His People: Messianic Expectations From the Maccabees to Bar Kochba* (JSPSup 27; Sheffield: Sheffield Academic Press, 1998), pp. 141–44.

in the Eschaton (45.4-5; 48.10; 51.1-5). He is a judge (49.4; 55.4; 61.8). He destroys sinners and the enemies of God (46.4-6), but has mercy on the righteous (50.3).

The Son of Man figure has a supernatural, heavenly character. He is enthroned in the heavenly court (45.3-4; 51.3; 55.4; 61.8) and his glory lasts forever (49.2). *1 Enoch* 48.6 says, 'And because of this he [the Son of Man] was chosen and hidden before him [the Lord of Spirits] before the world was created, and for ever' (cf. 62.7). Thus, the Son of Man figure is pre-existent in some sense.

Yet Enoch, a human being, is identified as 'son of man' in 71.14. A number of scholars use that identification to interpret the exalted figure. For example, Maurice Casey, Norman Perrin, and James C. VanderKam interpret pre-existence in a way that would be consistent with human existence. VanderKam, agreeing with T. W. Manson, suggests that pre-existence may mean only that the figure was 'a project in the mind of God'.[87] Perrin states that in apocalyptic thought, pre-existence refers to things that exist as prototypes in heaven; thus Enoch sees a prototype of himself in a vision.[88] Casey disagrees, stating that the *Similitudes* do mean that the Son of Man was a pre-mundane being, genuinely hidden. But, he suggests, Enoch is no different from other righteous people, who in the *Similitudes* were also pre-existent.[89]

A number of commentators have been unconvinced by attempts to reconcile the exalted Son of Man figure with the human being Enoch. Some have attempted to deal with the problem by emending the text or dismissing 70–71 as a late addition, inconsistent with the rest of the work.[90] John Collins argues that although Enoch is called son of man in 71.14, the statement in 70.1 that Enoch's name ascended to the Son of Man 'makes a clear distinction between Enoch and the Son of Man, which cannot be avoided'. He adds that this distinction 'seems to be presupposed throughout the *Similitudes*, where Enoch sees the Son of Man without any suggestion that he is seeing himself'.[91] Collins is equally unconvinced that the Son of Man's pre-existence could be less than genuine existence and interprets *1 Enoch* 48.3 as meaning that 'the

---

87   Cf. *1 Enoch* 39.11. VanderKam, 'Righteous One', in Charlesworth, *Messiah*, pp. 181–82. Casey, 'The Use of the Term "Son of Man" in the *Similitudes* of Enoch', *JSJ* 7 (1976), pp. 13, 28; *Solution*, p. 101.

88   Norman Perrin, *Rediscovering the Teaching of Jesus* (New York: Harper & Row, 1967), p. 168.

89   Casey, 'Use of the Term', p. 13; cf. *1 Enoch* 39.11.

90   R. H. Charles (*APOT*, 2, p. 237) emended the text. For a discussion of suggestions that 70–71 are a later addition, see VanderKam, 'Righteous One', in Charlesworth, *Messiah*, pp. 177–79. Collins ('Son of Man', p. 455) tried this approach in an earlier study, but he admits that the approach, even if it were correct, would not resolve the problem. It merely moves the origin of the difficulty from the original author to the final redactor.

91   Collins ('Son of Man', p. 454) responds to VanderKam's argument that the identification is consistent. Casey (*Solution*, p. 110) indicates that Enoch is seeing 'himself as he would be after his translation'.

Son of Man was created before the sun and the stars'. Collins suggests that Enoch is not *identified* with the exalted Son of Man, whom he saw in a vision, and that the Son of Man is not the supernatural double for the individual Enoch. Rather throughout the *Similitudes*, the Son of Man is placed in close relationship with the community of righteous. The Chosen One is closely connected to the chosen ones, the Righteous One to the righteous ones. The Son of Man is the heavenly saviour and the counterpart to all the righteous on earth. When he is no longer hidden, but manifested, then the righteous on earth, who are now oppressed, will share in his glory. Enoch is called son of man because, 'In so far as Enoch is pre-eminent among righteous human beings he has a unique affinity with the heavenly Son of Man.' Enoch, like all righteous human beings, shares in the destiny of the Righteous One, the Son of Man. So far from being a mere 'human one', even the extraordinary human Enoch, the Son of Man sits on the throne of God (51.3) and is the recipient of worship (48.5). Collins insists that the Son of Man is no less than the pre-existent, exalted, heavenly messiah.[92]

The exact identity of the Son of Man and his relationship with Enoch remains unresolved. Still, without such resolution, commentators paint a fairly consistent picture of the Son of Man in the *Similitudes*. The Son of Man is the heavenly counterpart to the righteous ones and chosen ones on earth, is the eschatological judge, defeats the wicked and the kings of the earth and inaugurates the creation of a new earth (45.4-5), is somehow pre-existent, and is a rightful recipient of worship. This Son of Man is a heavenly individual of very exalted status.[93]

4 Ezra 11-13 is also dependent on Daniel 7. This is made explicit at 12.11-12, where the angel indicates that Ezra will now receive an interpretation of the vision superior to the one Daniel received. In *4 Ezra*, the Son of Man figure is different from the figure in the *Similitudes*, but is also similar in important ways. The figure participates in judgement, destroying the nations by means of the law (13.38, cf. 13.49) and delivering the righteous of Israel (13.39-50). He is identified with the messiah and as God's son.[94] He is also somehow pre-

---

92   Collins, 'Son of Man', pp. 454–59. Interestingly, Casey (*Solution*, pp. 102–10), who argues stridently against some of Collins' conclusions, agrees that Enoch (in his translated state) is heavenly, exalted, and an object of worship.

93   Hare (*Son of Man*, p. 15) argues against an absolute heavenly identity for the figure. He points out that the figure 'receives' glory, supernatural wisdom, etc., but does not possess them by his nature. By nature he possesses only righteousness, which is appropriate for human beings. This could be seen as hair-splitting. Why is wisdom not a trait appropriate to human beings, but righteousness is? Certainly, observation indicates difficulties with both characteristics. Hare (*Son of Man*, pp. 13–14) is on firmer ground when he asserts that the words 'son of man' do not, by themselves, add anything to the understanding of the figure in the *Similitudes*; the traits given to the figure are given to it through the context, not the phrase.

94   In *4 Ezra* 12.31-32, the figure is the lion, but this figure is the same one as the Son of Man. Collins ('Son of Man', pp. 462–64) argues that the Son of Man figure is identified with messianic Scriptures, such as Psalm 2 and Isaiah 11. He is also called 'my son' in the Latin and Syriac versions (13.37, 52), and is identified with the messiah, who may be called 'my son', in 7.28.

existent and hidden ('this is he whom the Most High has been keeping for many ages', 13.26), whom no one can see until the proper time (13.52). He is portrayed in the language of theophany (e.g., coming from the sea in a storm and melting all like wax, 13.1-4, or with fire issuing from his mouth, 13.10).[95]

Rabbinic Literature
Daniel 7.13 is quoted twice in the Talmud. *B. Pesaḥ.* 119a refers to the Ancient of Days concealing things, where what is concealed is Torah. *B. Sanhedrin* juxtaposes the verse with Zech. 9.9, in a series of statements about the messiah:

> R. Joshua opposed two verses: it is written, And behold, one like the son of man came with the clouds of heaven; whilst [elsewhere] it is written, [behold, thy king cometh unto thee ...] lowly, and riding upon an ass! (*b. Sanh.* 98a)

The verses are seen to be in contradiction because both the 'one like the son of man' of Dan. 7.13 and 'thy king' of Zech. 9.9 are the messiah. The contradiction is resolved by saying that if the people are worthy, the messiah will come on the clouds; if not, on an ass. The key issue here is that for the rabbis the figure of 'one like a son of man' is the messiah.[96]

Also relevant is the discussion about two thrones in Dan. 7.9. R. Akiba states that one is set for David. He is rebuked by R. Jose the Galilean for profaning the Divine Presence (*b. Ḥag.* 14a; *b. Sanh.* 38b). Caragounis considers it likely that R. Jose found Akiba's statement profane because R. Jose was thinking of an earthly messiah; R. Akiba did not see it so because he was thinking of a heavenly messiah. In any case, Akiba associates the thrones set in Dan. 7.9 with the messiah.[97]

A Shared Tradition
One unresolved issue of current debate on the son of man significantly affects interpretation of the Markan passion narrative: was there a 'Son of Man concept' of any kind, or was there a shared interpretation of Daniel 7? In the

---

95   Collins, 'Son of Man', p. 464. Hare (*Son of Man*, p. 10) argues against seeing Dan. 7.13 as theophanic and provides examples of human beings travelling through heaven on clouds. He does not, however, provide counterexamples for the full combination of heavenly imagery presented by Collins, e.g., the sea and the melting away of obstacles. Hare (*Son of Man*, pp. 11–15, 31, 208) does concede that the figure is endowed with supernatural powers, but points out that such supernatural powers were given to the Davidic messiah. He also agrees that this is a messianic interpretation of Daniel 7.
96   Cf. Hare, *Son of Man*, pp. 19–20.
97   See Chrys C. Caragounis, *The Son of Man: Vision and Interpretation* (WUNT 38; Tübingen: J. C. B. Mohr [Siebeck], 1986), pp. 133–34. He says (ibid., p. 131) that wherever Dan. 7.13-14 is mentioned in rabbinic literature, it is connected with the messiah.

middle of the twentieth century, scholars agreed that in first-century Judaism there had been a unified and widespread expectation of a saviour entitled 'Son of Man', and that Daniel 7, the *Similitudes,* and *4 Ezra* were all expressions of that expectation. This perspective was promoted, in varying forms, by scholars such as R. Bultmann, H. E. Tödt, R. H. Fuller, and F. H. Borsch. That position has rightly been abandoned for a number of reasons, including especially that there is no evidence of a Son of Man concept in Judaism prior to Daniel and that the *Similitudes* and *4 Ezra* are dependent on Daniel for their son of man figure.[98] The solid defeat of this early Son of Man concept has led some New Testament scholars to the view that there are no notable connotations to the 'one like a son of man' in any work, that in the *Similitudes, 4 Ezra,* and the New Testament, just as in Daniel, 'son of man' means merely 'human being' or something equally indefinite and solidly terrestrial.[99]

Collins argues that, in some cases, this is to retreat too far. It was right to discard the old understanding of the Son of Man concept. Still the *Similitudes* and *4 Ezra* provide substantial evidence for a consistent interpretation of Daniel 7 and *its* one like a son of man – an interpretation which goes well beyond terms such as 'human being' or 'that man'. In both works, the figure is conceived as an individual (not as, in Daniel, a collective symbol), is identified with the messiah, is pre-existent in some fashion and hidden by God, appropriates imagery traditionally used for God, and plays an active role in the destruction of the wicked and the reward of the righteous. Collins argues that these shared characteristics reflect a shared interpretation of Daniel 7, and whether they amount to a first-century 'Son of Man concept' is merely 'a matter of definition'.[100]

---

98   See John R. Donahue, 'Recent Studies on the Origin of "Son of Man" in the Gospels', *CBQ* 48 (1986), pp. 485–86; Perrin, *Rediscovering,* pp. 165–66.

99   Cf. Géza Vermès, 'Appendix E: The Use of בר נשא/בר אנשא in Jewish Aramaic', in Matthew Black, *An Aramaic Approach to the Gospels and Acts* (Oxford: Clarendon, 1967), pp. 320–27; Lindars, *Jesus, Son of Man,* pp. 11-16; Casey, 'Use of the Term', p. 11; Hare, *Son of Man,* passim.

100   Collins, 'Son of Man', pp. 465–66. Casey (*Solution,* pp. 82–115) argues against the idea that any sort of concept is attached to 'son of man' before the gospels. In terms of the phrase 'son of man' itself, he is correct. However, Casey does not deal with the son of man figures in *1 Enoch* and *4 Ezra* as *interpretations* of Daniel 7. 'Son of man' as a phrase may well mean just what Casey argues. There is no 'Son of Man concept', per se; rather there is a common interpretation of the figure in Daniel 7. (As an aside, the meaning of the phrase per se is not beyond question. Paul Owen and David Shepherd ['Speaking Up for Qumran, Dalman and the Son of Man: Was *Bar Enasha* a Common Term for "Man" in the Time of Jesus?' *JSNT* 81 (2001), pp. 81–122] present an interesting and significant argument against the common understanding of the phrase 'son of man' in the period. They conclude that the phrase is not common at the time, and that it is never used in the way Casey and others suggest, as a generic phrase with a self-referential element.)

Collins' view finds some support in the writings of Norman Perrin. Perrin wrote extensively to debunk the theory of the old Son of Man concept,[101] but did not consider all uses of 'son of man' to mean merely 'human being' in the first century. Rather, recognizing some of the similarities between the *Similitudes* and *4 Ezra* and some New Testament passages, he spoke of 'varied use of "Son of man imagery" in Jewish apocalyptic and midrashic literature'. Daniel uses a figure based in mythology to provide comfort to those who suffer in the Maccabean period and to assure them that 'their suffering will not go unrewarded'. The sense of Daniel 7 and the mythology behind it points toward the glory and power that would come to those who persevered. That the figure is like a son of man 'is probably a pure accident'; its human appearance is merely a contrast to the beasts. Daniel 7 becomes the source for other apocalyptic writings, and that scene is creatively interpreted by a number of authors in whose work the son of man figure is anything but an ordinary mortal. Perrin proposes that the authors of the New Testament are among the exegetes of Daniel 7 who make much of its son of man image.[102]

Yet uses of that image are not entirely the same, and on that basis, Perrin argued that interpretation of Daniel 7 was done completely independently, that the *Similitudes*, *4 Ezra*, and the New Testament reflect independent interpretations of the son of man figure.[103] Perrin wrote when the older Son of Man concept still enjoyed favour, and, in his efforts to debunk that theory, he overemphasized the differences between the portraits in the *Similitudes* and *4 Ezra*. His approach suffers because it does not adequately explain the similarities. Why is the Son of Man figure independently associated with the messiah in *Similitudes*, *4 Ezra*, the New Testament, and the Talmud? Perrin is confident that the son of man coming from heaven to earth with the clouds is a Christian innovation, but he does not explain how the same idea was either also independently produced in the Talmud or borrowed by the rabbis from Christian messianic exegesis.[104] The similarities among the traditions make the theory articulated by Collins more persuasive. There was a coherent interpretive tradition on Daniel 7. It included understanding its son of man figure as a heavenly being, the messiah, agent of the Eschaton, and judge. The *Similitudes*, *4 Ezra*, the New Testament, and the Talmud shared this tradition.[105] Particular authors modified or expanded the tradition to suit their requirements.

---

101 See especially Perrin's collection of essays, *A Modern Pilgrimage in New Testament Christology* (Philadelphia: Fortress, 1974).
102 Perrin, *Rediscovering*, pp. 166–67, 172–73.
103 Perrin, *Rediscovering*, pp. 172–73.
104 Cf. Perrin, *Rediscovering*, pp. 171–75.
105 Cf. Slater, 'One Like', p. 196; Lindars, *Jesus, Son of Man*, p. 159; W. Horbury, 'The Messianic Associations of the "Son of Man"', *JTS* n.s. 36 (1985), pp. 34–55; Black, 'Theological', p. 16; Caragounis, *The Son of Man*, p. 136.

Other Early Christian Uses

There are numerous references to Dan. 7.13 in the New Testament. Some are rather faint, others quite clear. Matthew retains the allusions in both Mark 13.26 and 14.62 (Matt. 24.30, revised towards Dan. 7.13; Matt. 26.64; cf. Matt. 25.31). Luke 21.27 retains the clear allusion to Dan. 7.13 in Mark 13.26.[106] The allusions function in Matthew and Luke as they do in Mark (see below).

The Book of Revelation refers to the exalted Jesus as 'like a Son of Man' (1.13; 14.14). Revelation 1.7 and 14.14 clearly allude to Dan. 7.13 regarding the eschatological judgement. In Rev. 14.14-20, the Son of Man and an angel have sickles in their hands and 'harvest' the earth.[107] Revelation 1.7 combines Dan. 7.13 with Zech. 12.10 to present in an image of worldwide mourning, thus conveying the judgement element of the Parousia. The preceding verses refer to the Christian community's rewards, including being made a kingdom (Rev. 1.5-6). Revelation 1.6 ends with 'to him be glory and dominion forever and ever'. The idea of glory and dominion forever corresponds to Dan. 7.14, where the one like a son of man is given dominion, glory, and a kingdom forever, and the people of every nation will serve him. On their own, the words used in Rev. 1.6 do not sufficiently correspond to those of Dan. 7.14 to be considered an allusion. However, they immediately precede a clear reference to Dan. 7.13; so it is fair to say that Rev. 1.6-7 alludes to Dan. 7.13-14. It does so in a reference to the Parousia which includes both the judgement of the earth and the rewards of the chosen community.

The images of Daniel 7 are continued in Rev. 1.13-14. There the Son of Man figure has hair like wool and a fiery presence, images used in Dan. 7.9 for God.[108] John falls down as if dead at the very sight, as in a theophany (Rev. 1.17). Clearly here again, the Son of Man is a heavenly figure of highly exalted status.

Not surprisingly, Daniel 7 is used frequently in early Christian literature outside the New Testament, again in the senses we have already seen in the Jewish tradition. The Son of Man in Dan. 7.13 is identified with the messiah in Justin (*Dial.* 31).[109] Regarding the Eschaton, *Barn.* 4.4-5 uses Daniel 7 to persuade Christians to live virtuously, mindful of the last days. *1 Clement* 34.5-7 uses Dan. 7.10 to show that Christians are to be obedient and ready to serve, observing that when they do so, they will share in the rewards which God has promised. Both Irenaeus and Tertullian expect the Son of Man to return as judge (*Haer.* 3.19.2; *Marc.* 4.10.12).

---

106 In the parallel to Mark 14.62, Luke edits away from the passage (Luke 22.69; Hare, *Son of Man*, p. 74).

107 While the angel clearly harvests for wrath (cf. 14.16), the action of the Son of Man is ambiguous and could refer to judgement or the gathering of the elect. See Aune, *Revelation*, 2, pp. 844-45.

108 Revelation 1.13-15 also seems to play with the images of the divine messenger in Dan. 10.5-7.

109 Hare, *Son of Man*, p. 33.

Discussions of the Son of Man of Dan. 7.13 deal not only with the Parousia, but with the Son of Man's exalted status. Justin (*Dial.* 14; *1 Apol.* 51), Irenaeus (*Haer.* 3.19.2; 4.33.1), and Tertullian (*Jud.* 14.4, *Marc.* 3.7; 4.10, 39) understand Daniel 7 to refer to Christ's second coming and the glory Christ will then manifest. In *Dial.* 79, Justin concludes that the Son of Man's dominion and glory are so complete that even the angels must serve him. *Acts of Peter* 24.5 lists Dan. 7.13 among the prophecies which foretold the divine nature of Christ (cf. Irenaeus, *Haer.* 4.20.11; Tertullian, *Marc.* 4.41). Justin Martyr interprets Dan. 7.13 as a proof of Christ's human and divine nature (*Dial.* 76; cf. Tertullian, *Carn.* 15).

Christian interpreters have clear continuity with Jewish interpretation of Daniel 7, interpreting the Son of Man figure as the messiah, who plays an active role in the Eschaton, including its judgement and rewards, and a heavenly figure, who takes on the attributes of God.

Markan Use

As we will see, Mark also partakes in the interpretive tradition on Daniel 7. While Mark 14.62 is the clearest, the gospel contains other allusions to Dan. 7.13. We will look briefly first at these other uses and their implications, then at the use of Dan. 7.13 in Jesus' answer to the high priest in Mark 14.62.

Mark 13.26-27 alludes to Dan. 7.13-14 in a passage about the Parousia:

> Then they will see the *Son of Man coming in clouds* (υἱὸν [τοῦ] ἀνθρώπου ἐρχόμενον ἐν νεφέλαις) with great power and glory. Then he will send out his angels to gather his elect from the four winds, from the ends of the earth to the ends of heaven.

Verbal correspondence with Dan. 7.13 is good. In addition, 'power and glory' sum up what is given to the one like a son of man in Dan. 7.14; 'angels' may also refer to 'the holy ones' of Dan. 7.18. The allusion to Dan. 7.13 immediately follows an allusion to Isa. 13.10 and 34.4 in Mark 13.24-25. Both Isaian passages speak of God's wrath and the devastation to come on the Day of the Lord. Thus, the combination of allusions to Isaiah and Daniel in Mark 13.24-27 communicate the double events of the Parousia: judgement and wrath on the nations and reward to those who are chosen.

In a fainter allusion, Mark 8.38–9.1 plays with the images of Dan. 7.13-14.[110] Mark 8.38 speaks of the Son of Man coming with the glory of his Father and with the angels. Mark 9.1 refers to the coming of the Reign of God with power. Luke did not edit either towards or away from the passage; so it is difficult to know if he saw the connection. Matthew apparently did. He

---

110 Lindars, *Jesus, Son of Man*, p. 107; Marcus, *Way*, p. 165.

revised his parallel (Matt. 16.27-28) toward Dan. 7.13-14, especially at v. 28, where he changed Mark's 'see that the kingdom of God has come with power' to 'see the Son of Man coming in his kingdom'. Tying the kingdom directly to the Son of Man points more clearly to Dan. 7.14.

The general sense of Mark 8.38 is clear, that those who are now ashamed of Jesus will be held accountable for it in the final judgement. Less clear is who will be the judge: the Son of Man or the Father? Mark says of those who are ashamed of Jesus and his words, 'of them the Son of Man will also be ashamed when he comes in the glory of his Father'. Does this mean that the Son of Man testifies against them to the Father who judges?[111] Or does it mean that when the Son of Man comes, he will judge them himself?[112] If the Father judges, the text remains fairly close to Daniel 7, where the son of man receives power and glory, but nothing is said of him participating directly in the heavenly judgement; rather he comes after God has sat in judgement on the beasts.[113] If the Son of Man judges in Mark 8.38, then the passage shares in the tradition of the Son of Man as judge, as seen in the *Similitudes* and implied in *4 Ezra*. Because Mark 8.38 speaks only of the action of the Son, with no action by the Father (who is mentioned only in that the Son 'comes in the glory of his Father'), the passage tends toward the interpretation of Son of Man as judge, the interpretive tradition seen in the *Similitudes*.[114]

C. K. Barrett argued that the much-disputed Mark 10.45, 'the Son of man came not to be served but to serve, and to give his life a ransom for many', alludes to Dan. 7.13.[115] Barrett has not received much following here, but he did find support at least in his student Morna Hooker and in Ernest Best.[116] Mark 10.45 is by no means a clear allusion to Dan. 7.13, but Barrett made several good arguments in its favour. First is the simple use of the phrase 'Son of Man', which does not necessarily allude to Dan. 7.13 in Mark, but it is a solid hint in that direction. That hint is helped a bit by the fact that here, as in Dan. 7.13, the Son of Man *comes* (ἔρχομαι). Barrett also argues for allusive interplay between the passages. Daniel 7.14 explicitly states that all

---

111 For the view that the Son of Man acts as advocate or prosecutor, not judge, see Hooker, 'Is the Son of Man', pp. 161–64.

112 For the view that the Son of Man acts as judge, see Black, 'The Messianism of the Parables of Enoch: Their Date and Contributions to Christological Origins', in Charlesworth, *Messiah*, p. 164; Lindars, *Jesus, Son of Man*, p. 107; Hooker, *Son of Man*, p. 171 (her earlier position); Donahue, *Are You the Christ?*, p. 175; Piper, 'God's Good News', p. 179; Kee, *Community*, pp. 134–35.

113 Matera, *Kingship*, p. 109.

114 In a related use of Daniel 7, Matt. 25.31-46 makes explicit that the Son of Man acts as judge. Since in these texts the Son of Man figure is interpreted in conjunction with royal messianic ideas, this should not be surprising. One of the functions of kings is to judge.

115 At the time, many scholars understood Mark 10.45 to refer to Isaiah 53. Though this opinion is today less widespread, it is still held by some.

116 Hooker, *Son of Man*, p. 141; Best, *Temptation*, pp. 142–43.

peoples, nations, and languages would *serve* the Son of Man, saying, in effect, that the Son of Man came *not to serve, but to be served* by the many. Mark 10.45 says the opposite. The οὐκ–ἀλλά of Mark 10.45 indicates a metaleptic reversal.[117]

Against the allusion, it can be argued the verb for *serve* is different in Mark 10.45 (διακονέω) and Dan. 7.14 (δουλεύω in θ´; λατρεύω in ο´). The trouble is, those arguing against Barrett's conclusion are often doing so in favour of an allusion to Isa. 53.10-12, and Isa. 53.10-12 uses the same verb for *serve* as Dan. 7.13-14 θ´; δουλεύω.[118] Some impressive acumen has been marshalled to support the correspondence of this pair of verbs for *serve* between Mark 10.45 and Isa. 53.10-12.[119] This evidence would establish in equal measure the correspondence of the same pair of verbs in Mark 10.45 and Dan. 7.14.

The verbal correspondence of Mark 10.45 with Isa. 53.10-12 was examined in Chapter 3 and found insufficient for an allusion, and Mark yields no clear allusions to Isaiah 53 to bolster the case.[120] The verbal correspondence of Mark 10.45 to Dan. 7.13-14 is also weak, and standing alone, it cannot be established as an allusion. However, it does not stand alone. There are two clear allusions to Dan. 7.13-14 in Mark 13.26 and 14.62, as well as a probable allusion in Mark 8.38-9.1. That Mark 10.45 is an allusion to Dan. 7.13-14 is a reasonable conclusion, considering the total evidence.

Mark 10.45 is important because it is one of a very few verses in Mark to indicate the purpose or effectiveness of Jesus' death. Because this saying is often seen as an allusion to Isaiah 53, it is often interpreted as if it read, 'The *Servant* came ... to give his life a ransom for many.' Yet the verse says that the *Son of Man* gives his life as a ransom. As such, it points to the death of the Son of Man specifically as redemptive, effective for salvation of the many. If this verse alludes to Dan. 7.13-14, it hints that the answer to how the death of the Son of Man could be effective is to be found in Daniel 7.[121] We will return to this later in the study.

---

117 Barrett, 'The Background', p. 8. He goes on to say that the contrast, where 'the truth is expressed first negatively, then positively', argues against an allusion to Isa. 53.12. It would be 'more than a little precious to insist that the Servant did not come to be served'. The contrast implied by the construction would be retained in saying such a thing of the Son of Man. Barrett is right that οὐκ–ἀλλά indicates a contrast but wrong in saying that it argues against the allusion to Isa. 53.12. The contrast required by the construction is perfectly preserved by, 'The Servant came not (οὐκ) to be served but (ἀλλά) to serve.' Barrett implies not only that the construction indicates a contrast, but that it indicates something of a surprise. This is simply not necessary.

118 Hare is the exception. He makes this argument (*Son of Man*, pp. 203–4), and does not do so in favour of an allusion to Isaiah 53.

119 See e.g., Watts, *Isaiah's New Exodus*, pp. 271–74.

120 See pp. 76–87.

121 Cf. Hooker, *Son of Man*, pp. 141–44.

In Mark 14.62, the allusion to Dan. 7.13 touches on Jesus' identity, the events to follow his death, and even the manner in which Jesus' death is redemptive. Those three elements are in fact interrelated, and each must be examined.[122]

In *1 Enoch*, the son of man figure of Daniel 7 is united with the figures of the Chosen One, the Judge, and the messiah. In *4 Ezra*, the son of man figure is associated with the messiah.[123] Likewise, in Mark 14.61-62 the Son of Man is united with other roles. Donahue has noted the conglomeration of christological titles in 14.61-62.[124] In a few short words, Jesus claims to be the messiah, Son of the Blessed, and the Son of Man figure of Dan. 7.13.

Some have argued against Son of Man as a christological title, in part because it seems not to have been used as a messianic title in pre-Christian Judaism.[125] Nevertheless, the interpretative tradition consistently identifies the figure of the one like a son of man in Daniel 7 with the messiah. It does so in the *Similitudes*, *4 Ezra*, and the rabbinic material. When the high priest asks Jesus if he is the Christ, and he answers, 'I am; and you will see the Son of Man …', Mark, too, unequivocally identifies the Son of Man with the messiah. This connection is likewise made in Mark 8.29-31, where immediately after Peter's confession that Jesus is the Christ, Jesus speaks of the Son of Man suffering.[126]

---

122 A. Collins (*Mark*, pp. 58–72) provides a summary of the Son of Man and linked traditions and their relationship to Mark.

123 See pp. 174–77.

124 Donahue, *Are you the Christ?*, p. 139. Hare (*Son of Man*, p. 208) makes a substantial argument that 'Son of Man' is not a *title* in Mark and states directly his opposition to Donahue on this issue. However, Hare's difficulties could be removed by rephrasing: there is a conglomeration of christological *concepts*, messiah, Son of the Blessed, and messianic *interpretation* of Daniel 7. Cf. Hare, *Son of Man*, pp. 20, 205; Leivestad, 'Exit', pp. 247, 264.

125 Against pre-Christian use of Son of Man as a title, see Casey, 'Use of the Term', p. 14; Lindars, *Jesus, Son of Man*, pp. 9–10; Hare, *Son of Man*, passim. Casey (*Solution*, pp. 266–67) agrees that it has become a christological title in Mark. For the view that it was a christological title previously, see Horbury, 'Messianic Associations', p. 53.

126 Another concern about Son of Man having christological content is the difficulty that would pose for the 'messianic secret' in Mark. This is not so much a concern at 14.62, because here Jesus is claiming to be the messiah openly in the context of his trial and death. The concern is directed to Jesus' earlier use of the title, especially in Mark 2.10, 28. It must be remembered, first, that the messianic secret is an interpretive principle, something scholars have found helpful for understanding Mark, but not a firm standard to which the gospel is bound. Indeed, the messianic secret is quite messy. Though Jesus tells demons to be quiet about him, he tells them so after they have already said who he is (e.g., 1.24-25). Though he tells people to be silent, as often as not, they speak freely about him (e.g., 1.44-45). In the Son of Man sayings of Mark 2.10 and 2.28, Jesus speaks about his identity, obscurely, but in a way that undoubtedly claims

Messianic expectations in the first century were somewhat diverse. The title messiah was therefore somewhat ambiguous and required definition. This is accomplished both by the context and by the connections with Daniel 7 and its interpretive tradition. Matera points out that Daniel 7 stresses royal authority.[127] Daniel 7.14 grants to the son of man figure 'dominion and glory and kingship ... His dominion is an everlasting dominion that shall not pass away, and his kingship is one that shall never be destroyed.' The interpretation of the vision states that the kingdoms of the beasts will be abolished and 'the kingship and dominion and the greatness of the kingdoms under the whole heaven shall be given to the people of the holy ones of the Most High; their kingdom shall be an everlasting kingdom, and all dominions shall serve and obey them' (Dan. 7.26-27). Jesus is identified as the Son of Man and the messiah, and both are distinctly royal images. Jesus, as glorified Son of Man, will reign. His reign will not be like others'. His will be superbly glorious and everlasting. Mark uses the Son of Man of Daniel 7 to help give content to the title messiah, to indicate just what sort of messiah Jesus was.[128]

Like Son of Man, Son of God had not been a title prior to the New Testament, and it needed to be defined to be understood.[129] Mark 14.61-62 connects the Danielic Son of Man with Son of God and thus helps to give Son of God content.[130] Daniel's one like a son of man reigns like no human king.

---

authority. In saying that the Son of Man has authority to forgive sins, Jesus claims an authority that belongs to God. This leads to the charge of blasphemy in 2.7 (just like the Son of Man saying in 14.62). In 2.28, Jesus connects the Son of Man to David. No response to this saying is presented, but both are part of a series of actions which lead to Jesus' enemies conspiring to destroy him (Mark 3.6). Whatever the precise limits of these sayings in Mark 2, Jesus' claims there are not innocuous, any more than any other of his actions in the gospel. While these sayings seem not to allude to Daniel 7, and thus do not directly participate in its interpretive traditions, the contexts of the Mark 2 Son of Man sayings point to aspects of Jesus' identity that will be stated more openly and connected with other Son of Man sayings later in the gospel: the reference to David in Mark 2.25 faintly connects the Son of Man to the messiah (cf. the connection of Son of Man with the messiah in 8.29-31; 14.61-62); the claim that the Son of Man has authority to forgive sins, something which belongs to God alone, connects the Son of Man to what is divine (cf. the connection of Son of Man with Son of God in 14.61-62). In the Son of Man passages in Mark 2, Jesus makes claims that his hearers do not fully understand, but the reader, knowing who Jesus is from the start, will see the connections, both to David and to God.

127   Matera, *Kingship*, pp. 109–10.

128   Juel (*Messiah and Temple*, pp. 49–52) argues that the term *christ* has specifically Davidic or royal connotations in Mark and that 'Jesus is King' is the main thrust of the Markan passion narrative.

129   See, for example, Norman Perrin, 'The High Priest's Question and Jesus' Answer (Mark 14:61-62)', in Kelber, *The Passion in Mark*, pp. 86–88; Fitzmyer, 'The Background of "Son of God" as a Title for Jesus', in *The Dead Sea Scrolls and Christian Origins* (Studies in the Dead Sea Scrolls and Related Literature; Grand Rapids: Eerdmans, 2000), pp. 63–72.

130   For the identification of Son of God and Son of Man, see Matera, *Kingship*, pp. 107, 119. Juel ('The Origin of Mark's Christology', in Charlesworth, *Messiah*, pp. 455–56) argues the Son of God is royal.

The Son of Man figures in the *Similitudes* and *4 Ezra* are exalted beyond human limitations. They are heavenly beings.[131] They sit in the heavenly court. They are, in some sense, pre-existent and hidden by God until the appropriate time. In Mark, the treatment of the Son of Man is similar. Jesus at first attempts to remain hidden, but when his hour has come, tells the high priest that he will come on the clouds of heaven, that he will return as an exalted, heavenly being.[132]

The three figures of Mark 14.61-62 – the messiah, the Son of God, and the Son of Man – are one. That figure is royal, heavenly, and exalted. If Mark was influenced by that aspect of the tradition, that figure is also somehow pre-existent, either in the will of God or in actual being. Perhaps that is the implication of Mark 10.45, when Jesus says 'the Son of Man *came* to serve', and sayings like it, such as, 'I *have come* to call not the righteous but sinners' (2.17). Certainly, here 'come' implies purpose (as does being 'sent' by the vineyard owner in the Parable of the Vineyard, 12.2, 4-6). It may also imply timing, the arrival of something expected, perhaps long-expected, as it does in Jesus' opening call, 'The time is fulfilled, and the kingdom of God has come near; repent, and believe in the good news' (1.15). Mark 14.62 also uses *come* to imply the arrival of something expected, in this case the arrival of the Son of Man from the heavens: 'you will see the Son of Man ... coming with the clouds of heaven.' With the inclusion of pre-existence in the tradition on the son of man figure and with the 'coming' of the Son of Man in Mark 10.45 and 14.62, it is possible that the author of Mark conceived of the Son of Man as somehow pre-existent.[133]

---

131   If Enoch is identified with the Son of Man, that is so only after his translation to heaven.

132   Because of this answer, Jesus is convicted of blasphemy and sent to Pilate to be crucified. The problem of the charge is well known. Jesus is not guilty of blasphemy according to the definition in the Mishnah, and it does not appear that making a claim to be the messiah was considered blasphemous in the period. Thus, on what possible basis could Jesus be guilty of blasphemy?

Hooker (*Son of Man*, p. 173) points out that in Mark 2.7 the scribes accuse Jesus of blasphemy because he forgives the sin of the paralytic, 'Why does this fellow speak in this way? It is blasphemy! Who can forgive sins but God alone?' That is, Jesus is accused of blasphemy because he arrogates to himself what was considered solely a divine right. Hooker argues that to do so dishonours God and is thus a blasphemous offence. She suggests that, with the allusions of 14.62, Jesus there again appropriates the prerogatives of God and that this is what triggers the charge of blasphemy by the high priest. (See also Juel, *Messiah and Temple*, pp. 102–5; Evans, 'In What Sense', pp. 221–22.)

Although Lindars (*Jesus Son of Man*, pp. 111–12) protests against this sort of reasoning, the argument has merit. In the Markan narrative, whatever the exact reasoning behind the charge, it is clear that Jesus' statement causes it. Certainly, in this reading of the meaning of the allusion, Jesus is making claims to divine status.

133   The arrival of something expected applies not only to Jesus, but also to the Elijah figure: 'Elijah is indeed coming first to restore all things ... Elijah has come ...' (9.12-13) Such pre-existence may well be in the sense of 'a project in the mind of God'. (See p. 175.) One thing is clear: if it is there, pre-existence is not emphasized in Mark, as it is in John.

Are You the Christ?

The allusion to Daniel 7 in Mark 14.62 and other passages does not simply point to the status or nature of this figure. The allusion points to his function as well. The Son of Man ushers in the Reign. In Dan. 7.13-14, when the one like the son of man is presented to the Ancient of Days, he is given everlasting dominion and glory and his enemies are subjected to him. In the interpretation, the angel tells Daniel that this symbolizes the people of God receiving dominion and glory and that their enemies are crushed (Dan. 7.26-27).

Similarly, in the *Similitudes* and *4 Ezra*, the Son of Man figure executes the final judgement and the reward of the righteous. In answer to the high priest's question, Jesus tells the high priest and others, 'you will see the Son of Man ... coming with the clouds of heaven.' There is general agreement that here Dan. 7.13 is used to refer to the coming of the Son of Man at the Parousia.[134]

---

134 T. F. Glasson, followed by J. A. T. Robinson, argues that because Dan. 7.13 referred to one like a son of man coming *to* the Ancient of Days, not coming from heaven to earth; therefore early in the Christian exegetical tradition, Dan. 7.13 must have referred to the ascension, not the Parousia. Casey (*Son of Man*, p. 179) reviews the arguments for this position.

Perrin agrees with Glasson's assessment. Perrin (*Rediscovering*, pp. 175–85) also states that combinations of Dan. 7.13 and Ps. 110.1 must have referred to the ascension, not the Parousia; however, that is clearly not the case here in Mark 14.62. Perrin believes that the ὄψεσθε at the beginning of the verse comes from Zech. 12.10. (See pp. 96–98.) He argues that the combination of Zech. 12.10 with Dan. 7.13 always referred to the Parousia, because Zechariah 12 describes the Day of the Lord, and thus the Parousia. Perrin concludes that the word ὄψεσθε in Mark 14.62 indicates that the author combined the two previous combinations: Dan. 7.13 and Ps. 110.1 (which referred to Jesus' ascension) with Dan. 7.13 and Zech. 12.10 (which referred to Jesus' Parousia). The meaning of the second combination overpowers the first, and thus the combination refers to the Parousia, not to the ascension as expected.

There are problems with Perrin's argument. He says that there are two independent examples of the combination of Ps. 110.1 and Dan. 7.13 and both refer to the ascension. Perrin's examples are Acts 7.56 and Mark 14.62.

It is not entirely clear that Acts 7.56 contains either Dan. 7.13 or Ps. 110.1, but that may be conceded for the sake of argument. Just before Stephen dies, he says, 'I see the heavens opened and the Son of Man standing at the right hand of God.' Perrin himself describes this as an individual *Parousia* for Stephen (*Rediscovering*, p. 177). How then could this verse be used as evidence that the combination of Ps. 110.1 and Dan. 7.13 refers to the ascension? Perrin does not explain.

Regarding Mark 14.62, Perrin quotes only a portion: '... the Son of man sitting at the right hand of Power'. Then he says that without the rest of the verse and 'you will see' at the beginning, 'there would be no hint of a Parousia' (*Rediscovering*, p. 177). Yet the portion Perrin quotes alludes to Ps. 110.1 and contains little of Dan. 7.13, only 'Son of Man'. Perrin's evidence does not support the conclusion that here Dan. 7.13 refers to the ascension. The most that could be said from it is that Ps. 110.1 alone, without Dan. 7.13, can refer to the ascension, and this is generally acknowledged.

Both of Perrin's examples fail. There is no evidence that the combination of Dan. 7.13 with Ps. 110.1 ever referred to the ascension.

Furthermore, Casey (*Son of Man*, pp. 180–82) argues against the starting point of the position. He rightly notes that despite the consensus of modern scholars that the Son of Man is going *towards* God in Dan. 7.13, there is no example of the verse being interpreted that way in

There is less agreement on the tenor of Jesus' statement. Does it imply that they will see Jesus vindicated, and along with him, the elect?[135] Or does it have a threatening sense, and refer to the judgement of those convicting Jesus?[136]

In Mark 13.26, the allusion to Dan. 7.13 refers solely to the gathering and vindication of the elect. That argues in favour of the former position, that the tenor of Mark 14.62 is a promise of vindication for the community. So does the sense of Daniel 7, where the interpretation of the vision states that 'the people of the holy ones of the Most High', after being persecuted by the fourth kingdom, receive dominion and greatness (vv. 23-27); that is, the people of God are rewarded for their faithfulness, and after suffering oppression, they are vindicated. This sense is picked up in *4 Ezra* and the *Similitudes*, as well, with the Son of Man figure playing a role in the reward of the righteous. The direct sense of Mark 14.62 is that Jesus will be vindicated in the sight of those who now condemn him. Recalling Mark 13.26 and Dan. 7.23-27, it is likely that the allusion in Mark 14.62 is meant to imply the vindication of the elect, as well.

Yet there is no need to consider the vindication of Jesus and the community to be in opposition to judgement of Jesus' enemies.[137] Daniel 7.26 declares that the vindication comes after the heavenly 'court shall sit in judgement' and take away the dominion of the fourth beast. Daniel 7 speaks as much of judgement and the destruction of enemies as it does of the Reign of God being given to the people of God. That element of judgement was not lost on the tradition. *4 Ezra* speaks of the son of man figure destroying the wicked, and the *Similitudes* emphasizes the son of man figure as judge. The Son of Man as judge may be the meaning of Mark 8.38, as well. It is likely that in Mark 14.62 Jesus is making a veiled threat to those who oppose him, telling them that though they judge him now, they will see him return as judge. This would be consistent with the use of Psalms 2 and 110, also alluded to here, where victory over enemies is a major element. Implicit in the allusion to Dan. 7.13 is both the promise of vindication for Jesus and the Christian community and a threat to those who oppose Jesus.

Second Temple or early rabbinic literature. The New Testament presents no exceptions. Casey finds it interesting that Perrin admits this, but retains his theory nevertheless (cf. Perrin, *Rediscovering*, pp. 176–77). Casey remarks, Perrin's 'hypothesis that [this interpretation of Dan. 7.13] existed at an early stage encourages him to use very low standards of proof'.

Mark 14.62 refers to the Parousia, and its allusion to Dan. 7.13 does not indicate otherwise.

135 So Perrin, 'The High Priest's Question', in Kelber, *The Passion in Mark*, pp. 91–92; Gundry, *Mark*, pp. 886–87; A. Collins, 'The Influence of Daniel on the New Testament', in J. Collins, *Daniel*, p. 98; Juel, *Messiah and Temple*, p. 95.

136 Haenchen, *Weg Jesu*, p. 512; Lindars, *New Testament Apologetic*, p. 49; de Jonge, 'Jesus', in Draisma, *Intertextuality in Biblical Writings*, p. 99; Bas van Iersel, '"Son of God" in the New Testament', in *Jesus, Son of God?* (ed. Edward Schillebeeckx and Johannes-Baptist Metz; New York: Seabury, 1982), p. 42.

137 Cf. Donahue, *Are you the Christ?*, p. 164; Senior, *Passion of Jesus*, p. 100; Brown, *Death*, 1, pp. 494–95, 515.

In Mark, the Son of Man ushers in the Eschaton, subjugating his enemies and rewarding the elect (cf. Mark 13.26-27). But how does this happen? In Daniel, the one like a son of man is a symbol for the people of God; that is, the one like the son of man is completely identified with the people. In the *Similitudes* and *4 Ezra*, the Son of Man functions as a 'representative head'; what happens to the Son of Man affects the righteous.[138] In these cases, what happens to the Son of Man also happens to the people. In Daniel 7 the presentation of the one like the son of man to the Ancient of Days is connected with the defeat of the kingdoms of the beasts and brings everlasting dominion and glory to the people of God. Similarly, in Mark the death of the Son of Man brings defeat to his enemies and the Reign of God to the elect.

In Daniel, the *Similitudes*, and *4 Ezra*, the son of man figure does not suffer.[139] Yet in Mark, Jesus suffers precisely *as* the Son of Man (Mark 8.31; 9.31; 10.33-34; 14.62). Although the Son of Man suffering is not part of the general interpretive tradition on Daniel 7, it is not difficult to imagine a Christian interpreter making this innovation. The saints suffer in Dan. 7.21, 23, and the one like a son of man symbolizes them. It is but a small step for a Christian interpreter to see the Son of Man suffering as well, and by that suffering, effecting the Reign.[140]

The allusion to Dan. 7.13 helps to demonstrate the meaning and function of Jesus' death in Mark. When Jesus suffers as the Son of Man, he suffers as representative head.[141] By means of suffering, Jesus, the Son of Man, will be glorified and not just Jesus, but all the saints who will be gathered together and exalted with him.

Conclusion

In Mark 14.61-62, the allusions to Psalm 2, Daniel 7, and Psalm 110 paint a consistent picture. Jesus is about to be exalted as a heavenly king and his reign will be everlasting. That reign will mean the judgement and subju-

---

138 J. Collins, 'Son of Man', p. 459; Kee, *Community*, pp. 131. The notion of 'representative head' is a recurrent theme in Jewish thought. For example, what the king does affects the whole nation. (Cf. Black, 'Theological', pp. 16–17.)

139 This point is generally accepted at present. That was not so previously. See Kee, *Community*, pp. 135–36, for a brief review of the subject.

140 Hooker (*Son of Man*, pp. 27–28, 142; 'Is the Son', p. 166) concludes that suffering is essential to the conception of the Son of Man in Daniel 7, and that the Son of Man, is identified with the people before as well as after the glorification. Cf. Jane Schaberg, 'Daniel 7, 12 and the New Testament Passion-Resurrection Predictions', *NTS* 31 (1985), pp. 216–17.

141 Cf. Dodd, *According to the Scriptures*, pp. 117–19; Kee, *Community*, p. 131. Responding to Casey's argument that in *1 Enoch* son of man means exalted 'man', Hooker ('Is the Son', pp. 166–67) concludes that Jesus used the phrase to mean 'man', but also to mean that he was the human representative of the community, embodying the Danielic idea of suffering and vindication.

gation of his enemies. Jesus suffers for the community, as the representative of the elect. In his exaltation, Jesus will likewise make available to them the Reign of God. This is to be brought to completion at the Parousia.

Conclusion

In the previous chapters, we examined methodological questions surrounding the study of allusions in the New Testament and systematically analyzed the suggested allusions in Mark 14–15. While most of the suggested allusions had very little verbal correspondence, the following were found to have significant verbal and thematic correspondence.

- Mark 14.1 and Hos. 6.2
- Mark 14.24 and Exod. 24.8
- Mark 14.27 and Zech. 13.7
- Mark 14.34 and Ps. 42.6, 12; 43.5
- Mark 14.55 and Ps. 37.32
- Mark 14.56-57 and Exod. 20.16//Deut. 5.20
- Mark 14.61 and Isa. 36.21; Ps. 2.7
- Mark 14.62 and Ps. 110.1; Dan. 7.13
- Mark 14.65 and Isa. 50.6
- Mark 15.24 and Ps. 22.19
- Mark 15.29-30 and Ps. 22.8-9
- Mark 15.33 and Amos 8.9-10
- Mark 15.34 and Ps. 22.2
- Mark 15.36 and Ps. 69.22

After the allusions were identified, each was examined individually for its impact on meaning. It is time now to consider the allusions' cumulative impact on the meaning of the passion narrative as a whole.

Vindication Expected

Some scholars have seen in the Markan passion narrative an emphasis on Jesus' innocence.[1] This study did not confirm that emphasis. In fact, it found that Mark – in contrast to Luke – evinces no concern to convince the reader

---

1 Cf. Nineham, *Gospel*, p. 366.

of Jesus' innocence. This should not be entirely surprising. The Gospel of Mark appears to be written for Christians, and Christians were fully convinced of Jesus' innocence. Furthermore, it would not be difficult to defend Jesus' innocence to outsiders. The theological viewpoints of Second Temple Judaism present ready-made categories into which to put Jesus' death. Many Second Temple works present cases of innocent people condemned to death by authorities, both Gentile and Jewish. Literature about the undeserved suffering of prophets and martyrs is just one of many types of works from the period acknowledging that righteous people suffer. There is no evidence in the explicit Markan narrative or in its allusions to Scripture which suggests an anxiety to defend Jesus' innocence. That innocence is assumed throughout.[2]

Enemies Condemned

Instead Markan allusions to Scripture point to a contrary emphasis: that the Jerusalem leaders are guilty. It is important to emphasize that Jewish *leaders* are characterized here. The nation as a whole is not condemned in Mark.

This emphasis on the guilt of the leadership is entirely in line with Mark's emphasis both on the destruction of the temple and the unworthiness of its leaders in chapters 11–12. Many now consider what has been called 'the cleansing of the temple' in Mark 11 a symbolic act signifying the temple's destruction. Chapter 12 begins with the Parable of the Vineyard. George Brooke and Craig Evans have shown that the Scriptures used in this parable, Isa. 5.1-7 and Ps. 118.22-23, were both interpreted to refer to the temple during the first century. The parable concludes with the owner of the vineyard coming to '*destroy* the tenants', and Mark 12.12 declares that the chief priests, scribes, and elders 'realized that [Jesus] had told this parable against them'. The temple, its destruction, and the rejection of its leadership form an important focus for the preliminaries of the passion narrative.[3]

Likewise, in the trial scene in particular but in the crucifixion scene as well, allusions to Scripture point to the condemnation and destruction of Jesus' enemies. Using Exod. 20.16 (Mark 14.56-57) to portray the witnesses as false emphasizes the heinousness of their behaviour and how contrary it is to the behaviour necessary to enter the Reign of God. That use is particularly apparent in the emphasis on the subjection of enemies in Psalms 2 and 110

---

2   See Kelli S. O'Brien, 'Innocence and Guilt: Apologetic, Martyr Stories, and Allusion in the Markan Trial Narratives', in *The Trial and Death of Jesus: Essays on the Passion Narrative in Mark* (ed. G. C. M. van Oyen and Tom Shepherd; CBET 45; Leuven: Peeters, 2006), pp. 205–28. Cf. Best, *Temptation*, p. xlvii.

3   On the action in the temple, see especially Juel, *Messiah and Temple*, pp. 130–31, 212–13; E. P. Sanders, *Jesus and Judaism* (Philadelphia: Fortress, 1985), pp. 61–76. On the Parable of the Vineyard, see Brooke, '4Q500 and the Use of Scripture in the Parable of the Vineyard', *Dead Sea Discoveries* 2 (1995), pp. 268–94; Evans, 'On the Vineyard Parables of Isaiah 5 and Mark 12', *BZ* 28 (1984), pp. 82–86.

(Mark 14.61-62). Psalm 37.32 (Mark 14.55) points no less to the destruction of the psalmist's enemies, and Isa. 36.21 (Mark 14.61) focuses entirely on that subject. That sense occurs as well in Dan. 7.13 (Mark 14.62), Amos 8.9-10 (Mark 15.33), and Ps. 69.22 (Mark 15.36).

The Markan narrative, both explicitly and in its allusions to Scripture, consistently condemns the leaders of Jerusalem for their rejection of Jesus and, as implied in the Parable of the Vineyard, their rejection of all God's agents. They face judgement and destruction, which Mark knows either to have come already or to be coming imminently, at the conclusion of the First Jewish Revolt.

Jesus Exalted

The condemnation and destruction of Jesus' enemies is only one half of the vindication equation. The other, perhaps more important half is that Jesus himself will be exalted. Jesus' ultimate status as an agent of God, and perhaps even in some sense as a divine being himself, is another focus of the explicit narrative. The larger narrative leaves no doubt as to Jesus' power to heal and to bind 'the strong man' and plunder his goods (3.27). He has unique authority, both to teach and to forgive sins (1.22, 27; 2.5-12).

Expectation of Jesus' vindication is expressed almost as often as expectation of his betrayal and death. Every passion prediction ends with a prediction of the resurrection (8.31; 9.31; 10.33-34). At the Last Supper, Jesus predicts that the disciples will betray him; immediately afterwards, he speaks of being raised (14.28). He will no longer drink of the fruit of the vine, until he drinks it in the Reign of God (14.25). The announcement of his resurrection in 16.6-7 comes not as a surprise or an appendix, but as a necessary fulfilment of the narrative's promises.

Several allusions to Scripture point out that God will come to Jesus' aid, for example, those to Isa. 50.6 and Psalms 22 and 42-43. As seen in Ps. 37.32, God will not abandon his righteous one into the hands of his enemies. God's aid and ultimate vindication is the confident expectation of many allusions. The allusion to Hos. 6.2 points specifically to resurrection.

Yet resurrection, which any righteous person might experience, is not the end of the matter. For Jesus something greater is expected. The narrative points to Jesus as somehow greater than ordinary people. Jesus is repeatedly called Son of God, even from the first clause of the gospel (1.1; cf. 3.11; 5.7).[4] That 'Son of God' means more than 'holy person' is made clear in the Parable of the Vineyard (12.1-12). The owner of the vineyard repeatedly sends his slaves; then he sends his *son*. This move is expressed as an escalation, and the owner expects the tenants to respond differently to the authority of the son; their abuse of that authority, unlike their abuse of the slaves, cannot be tolerated. At least in the Markan version of this parable, the slaves represent

---

4   'Son of God' in 1.1 is accepted here as original.

the prophets and the son represents Jesus; thus, the gospel makes a clear distinction between the status of the prophets and that of Jesus. Jesus walks on water, speaks with Moses and Elijah, and is spoken to and about by a heavenly voice (6.48; 9.4-7; 1.11).

It is often taken for granted that Mark contains a low christology. Yet many scholars view the gospel differently. Juel is one of them; he notes that the scholarly schema which posits that early christologies must be 'low' and only late christologies 'high' does not tally with the data. For example, Acts contains low christology, and Phil. 2.5-11 and 1 Cor. 8.6 contain high christology.[5] There is nothing to prevent Mark from having a high christology. Bas van Iersel suggests that the Markan Jesus is closer to God than all people, though not equal to God.[6] Kee notes that Jesus is called 'Lord' at Mark 1.3, 2.28, and 11.3.[7] Hooker notes that only God 'tramples the waves of the sea' (Job 9.8); yet Jesus walks on water.[8] Burkill takes frequent note of Jesus' glory and exalted status in Mark.[9]

Allusions to Scripture emphasize Jesus' exalted status. Psalm 110 speaks of an unending kingdom and a seat at God's right hand. Psalm 2.7 speaks of the son's appointment by God, and Mark's use, along with traditions on the passage, speaks of one whose status is just less than God's. Traditions on Dan. 7.13 point to the eschatological judge, the agent who not only initiates the destruction of his enemies and the eternal kingdom, but who also sits on a heavenly throne, ruling with God.

---

5   Juel, *Messianic Exegesis*, pp. 23–24. James D. G. Dunn (*The Theology of Paul the Apostle* [Grand Rapids: Eerdmans, 1998], pp. 281–88) argues that in Philippians 2 Paul is conceiving of Jesus as the New Adam, without reference to Jesus' pre-existence. That works well for Phil 2.6, but it is hard to see how it works for 2.7-8 (or 1 Cor. 8.6). Only a pre-existent being can act or make decisions before being born. Dunn's major objection to the more obvious reading of these texts, that they imply Jesus' pre-existence, is that such a thing would be anathema to Paul, a monotheistic Jew. However, he acknowledges that early Christians took current Jewish beliefs about various divine beings associated with God (as manifestations of God's power or as God's agents) and associated them with Jesus, such as the Logos and Wisdom. There are similarities between Jesus and the heavenly Melchizedek of 11QMelch and the likewise heavenly Son of Man of in *1 Enoch*. See pp. 167–88. That such beings were not considered fully equal to God is probable. Still, equating Jesus with pre-existent, divine beings with roles in the divine plan from creation to the Eschaton can hardly be considered low christology.

6   Van Iersel, 'Son of God', pp. 42–43.

7   Kee, *Community*, pp. 128–29. Cf. Robert A. Guelich, '"The Beginning of the Gospel": Mark 1.1-15', *BR* 27 (1982), p. 9; Piper, 'God's Good News', p. 170.

8   Hooker, *Message*, p. 44.

9   Burkill, 'St Mark's Philosophy', pp. 252–53, 264, 266.

Suffering to Salvation

Jesus' exaltation comes in an unexpected way. Jesus does not ascend to the throne in a smooth sweep of acclaim, moving from glory to glory. He does not usher in the beginning of his reign by crushing his enemies with the 'mighty sceptre' pictured in Psalm 110. There is no triumphant conquest. Instead there is suffering.[10]

In the passion, Jesus endures persecution and suffering. The scene in Gethsemane portrays a man who chooses to do what God has commanded, as well as pointing to the horror of that command. Though the Gospel of Mark does not revel in bloody descriptions,[11] it does emphasize Jesus' suffering. The betrayals, the injustice, the mockery and humiliations all contribute to the picture.[12] Allusions to the psalms of lament (Pss. 22.2, 8-9, 19; 37.32; 42.12; 69.22), which dominate the crucifixion scene but are present throughout, display Jesus in intense suffering.[13] Jesus' cry of dereliction demonstrates his experience of the deepest sort of human suffering.

Yet that suffering anticipates salvation. The psalms of lament all reach out to God for an end to suffering. Psalm 22 appeals to God as saviour, not only at the end, but from v. 4 on. Psalm 22.6 declares, 'to you [our ancestors] cried, and were saved'. Several scholars consider Psalm 22, which so poignantly describes Jesus' sufferings, as a psalm identifying him as messiah, king. References to Jesus' suffering are tied to references of Jesus' exaltation. It is through suffering that Jesus' Reign begins.[14]

The Salvation of the Community

It is clear that Mark portrays Jesus' suffering in anticipation not only of his own salvation, but of the community as well. The allusion to Exod. 24.8 in the Last Supper scene points to the formation of a new community in the

---

10   Several scholars draw attention to this, especially regarding 'divine warrior' imagery. Cf. pp. 14–15. Burkill ('St Mark's Philosophy', pp. 245, 263) notes that suffering and glory are intimately related, and the relationship is more than that between means and an end. Hooker (*Message*, p. 103) notes that, in Mark, the real and bitter agony of the cross was the way to glory, whereas in other gospels, particularly in John, the messiness of the way is cleaned up.

11   In contrast to 2 Maccabees 7, *4 Maccabees*, and Philo, *Legat.* 18-20.

12   Dodd (*Old Testament in the New*, pp. 25–26) sees the same tendency in the darkness of Amos 8.9. He notes that in the Old Testament, darkness is a symbol to demonstrate the horror of the Day of the Lord and concludes the same meaning carries through to New Testament passion narratives, where the darkness points out the horror of the crucifixion. Cf. Brown, *Death*, 2, p. 1035.

13   Cf. Brower, 'Elijah', pp. 91, 93.

14   Cf. p. 189.

covenant of Jesus' blood. The quotation of Zech. 13.7 is used to speak of the gathering of this community, after the devastation has passed. Hos. 6.2 may be used to speak of the resurrection of the community, not only of Jesus.

Jesus suffers on behalf of the many, 'as a ransom for many' (Mark 10.45; 14.24). The gospel is never explicit about how this can be so. Those who favour allusions to Isaiah 53 propose a model of sacrificial atonement, one of the models used in the Pauline epistles and Hebrews. However, even if Mark 10.45 were alluding to Isaiah 53, his use of λύτρον takes a potentially cultic term, אשם, and translates it with a word having no cultic association in the New Testament.[15] If sacrificial atonement and the cultic model do not operate to make Jesus' death a ransom for many, what does?

Jesus the Representative Head

Jesus' answer to the high priest may provide the answer. The high priest's question itself is part of that answer, reflecting Ps. 2.7, which the tradition understood to reflect both the messiah and the people, sometimes in interpretations which stood side by side. Daniel 7, alluded to in Jesus' answer, depicts the restoration of order after the devastation of the four beast-kings. When the one like a Son of Man is presented before the Ancient of Days, he inherits power and dominion, and his kingdom will have no end (Dan. 7.14). Daniel 7 links the fate of the Son of Man figure to that of the people of God. The people of God suffer under the four kingdoms. When the Son of Man figure is presented to God and inherits the eternal reign, the people inherit it. In Daniel, the Son of Man figure is a symbol for the people (cf. Dan. 7.27); what happens to him happens to them.

In Second Temple Judaism, the Danielic Son of Man figure is not merely a symbol for the people, but an individual being who *represents* the people.[16] For example, in the *Similitudes*, the Son of man is 'the heavenly counterpart to the righteous on earth. While they are oppressed and lowly, he is enthroned and exalted. When he is manifested at the eschatological judgement, they will be exalted too.'[17] What happens to the Son of Man figure happens to his counterparts on earth.[18]

A Christian interpreter might have interpreted this correspondence in the other direction as well. What happens to the Son of Man happens to the

---

15   See p. 85.
16   Black, 'Messianism', in Charlesworth, *Messiah*, p. 160. This view is similar to that of Stevens, 'Why', pp. 108–9.
17   J. Collins, 'Son of Man', p. 459.
18   Cf. Marinus de Jonge, 'Jesus' Death for Others and the Death of the Maccabean Martyrs', in *Text and Testimony: Essays on New Testament and Apocryphal Literature in Honour of A. F. J. Klijn* (ed. T. Baarda et al.; Kampen: Kok, 1988), p. 145.

community. What happens to the community happens to him. Because the people suffer, the Son of Man suffers. Because the Son of Man is exalted, the people are exalted.

The context of Dan. 7.13 is the hinge on which the Son of Man giving his life turns. Jesus, as Danielic Son of Man, is the representative head, the agent through which the ultimate Reign of God will come to the saints. Jesus ransoms the many by suffering as their representative.[19]

Total Salvation: The Eschaton Begins

This view fits with a motif of eschatological thought.[20] Suffering precedes the Eschaton and is a sign of its coming. The Son of Man's suffering initiates the new age, and it redeems by propelling the community into the new age.[21] That this suffering is effective is demonstrated during the crucifixion scene. In chapter 13 Jesus tells the disciples that just before the Son of Man appears in the clouds, there will be signs in the heavens: 'the sun will be darkened, and the moon will not give its light' (13.24). During the final hours of Jesus' crucifixion, at midday, the whole land becomes dark (15.33). The first eschatological sign appears. A second happens immediately after Jesus' death: the temple veil is torn from top to bottom. Jesus' passion has cosmic significance. With it comes a pledge of the eschatological Reign of God.[22] The eschatological theme is reflected in most of the allusions. Some, like Hos. 6.2 and Amos 8.9-10, are used for eschatological phenomena. Some, like Ps. 2.7, Ps.

---

19   Cf. Hooker, 'Son of Man', p. 166. She follows T. W. Manson (*The Teaching of Jesus: Studies of its Form and Content* [Cambridge: Cambridge University Press, 1967], pp. 227, 231–33, 267–68), who wrote about the Son of Man's death as communal, not by representation, but through Jesus' teaching that the disciples follow him to the cross and in suffering. Initially, at the passion of Jesus, the communal aspect is unfulfilled; Jesus suffers alone. But after, and because of Jesus' passion, others such as Paul follow him in suffering.

Dodd (*According to the Scriptures*, pp. 19–20, cf. 96–97) concludes that Jesus is representative head of all humanity via Scripture in Heb. 2.5-13. Lindars (*New Testament Apologetic*, p. 93) concludes that Psalm 22 demonstrates that Jesus suffers as representative head.

Crossan (*Cross That Spoke*, pp. 331–36) comes to a similar conclusion based on the universalizing of the court tale, the genre in which he concludes the *Cross Gospel* is written.

20   Eschatological thought has an important place in the Gospel of Mark. See Joel Marcus, *Mark 1-8: A New Translation with Introduction and Commentary* (AB 27; New York: Doubleday, 2000), p. 71; Kee, *Community*, p. 66; Allison, *End of the Ages*, pp. 26–39.

21   Smith, 'Darkness at Noon', pp. 333–34; Allison, *End of the Ages*, p. 38. Stevens, 'Why', pp. 108–9. Marcus (*Way*, p. 177) concludes that in the Second Temple period, many Jews understood the suffering righteous psalms eschatologically; they were expressions of the eschatological pattern of suffering-exaltation. Cf. Lindars, *New Testament Apologetic*, p. 77; Matera, *Kingship*, p. 135.

22   Kee, *Community*, p. 76. Marcus (*Mark 1-8*, p. 72), A. Collins ('"Remove This Cup": Suffering and Healing in the Gospel of Mark', in *Suffering and Healing in Our Day* [ed. Francis A. Eigo, OSA; Proceedings of the Theology Institute of Villanova University; Villanova, Penn.:

110.1, and Dan. 7.13, speak of eschatological judgement, and Jesus' place in that judgement. Exod. 24.8 and Zech. 13.7 speak of the new community's experience of eschatological blessing and perhaps the interim experience of epiphany, its knowledge of the risen, exalted Christ.

More than Forgiveness

When Isaiah 53 is considered to be the main text underlying the passion narrative, interpretation tends to focus on the passion as atonement, as a means to forgiveness of sin.[23] In Mark, this emphasis on atonement and forgiveness of sins is misplaced – and too narrow.

Clearly, Mark *is* concerned with forgiveness of sin. John the Baptist proclaims a baptism of repentance for the forgiveness of sins (1.4). Jesus begins his public ministry calling people to '*repent* and believe in the good news' (1.15). Jesus also forgives the sins of the paralytic let down through the roof (2.5). Forgiveness of sin does play a role in Mark, but not the central role.

Mark offers few explicit interpretations of the passion. One important text in this regard is Mark 14.24: 'this is my blood of the covenant, which is poured out for many.' Note that Mark does not say, 'poured out for many *for the forgiveness of sins*'. The phrase 'forgiveness of sins' occurs in Matt. 26.28 and should not be used to limit the interpretation of Mark. In Mark, the blood is simply 'poured out for many'.

Rather than emphasizing forgiveness of sin, Mark 1–8 emphasizes the larger range of human suffering and its relief.[24] One of Jesus' first acts after announcing that the Reign of God has come near is to enter a synagogue and cast out a demon (1.23-27). His next act is to heal Simon's mother-in-law of a fever and the sick people brought to the door (1.29-34). These acts help to define what the Reign of God is. Jesus spends an enormous amount of time in this gospel relieving human suffering. The Markan Jesus reproaches the Pharisees because they are so concerned with their traditions, that they fail to

---

Villanova University Press, 1990], p. 53), and Allison (*End of the Ages*, pp. 36–38) conclude that in Mark salvation means liberation from hostile cosmic powers. In contrast, Best (*Temptation*, pp. lvii, lxxi, 43) argues that Jesus does *not* die to win a victory over cosmic powers, but to atone for sin.

23   Cf. Dodd, *According to the Scriptures*, pp. 123–25, *Old Testament in the New*, p. 12; Lindars, *New Testament Apologetic*, pp. 77–82. Hengel (*Studies*, p. 37) and Best (*Temptation*, pp. lvii, 148–50, 190–91) do not see Isaiah 53 in Mark but still emphasizes forgiveness of sins. Dodd himself points out that in the early period there was more than one understanding of the significance of the passion. 'The Jerusalem *kerygma* [as given in Acts] does not assert that Christ died *for our sins*' (*The Apostolic Preaching and Its Developments* [New York: Harper & Row, 1964], p. 25).

24   Edwin K Broadhead (*Prophet, Son, Messiah: Narrative Form and Function in Mark 14-16* [JSNTSup 97; Sheffield: JSOT Press, 1994], pp. 272–73, 294) concludes, in contrast to Weeden, that Mark 14–16 is not a 'correction' of 1–13, but an enlargement of it – there is no conceptual division between the two. To adequately understand the soteriological implications of Jesus, one must study not just the passion, but the ministry as well.

have compassion on a sick man (3.4) and interfere with a grown child's support of aging parents (7.9-13). In contrast to their hardness of heart (3.5), Jesus hears and answers all who come to him for help. As Adela Collins notes, the Reign of God 'includes compassion for those suffering physical, emotional, mental and spiritual distress'. It is not just a matter of individual souls or social dynamics, but it comprehends all of human experience. 'The cross is God's answer to Job.'[25]

Yet Jesus tells his followers to be willing to suffer and that they must be ready to pick up their own crosses (8.34-38; 13.9-13). How is this consistent? One of the strategies in the Gospel of Mark is progressive elucidation.[26] In its simplest form, this is seen in phrases such as 'this day, this very night, before the cock crows twice' (14.30), where each successive element is more specific than the last.[27] In a more complex fashion, the word *save* (σώζω) is the subject of progressive elucidation. Early in the story it retains its secular sense: save, rescue, heal (e.g., 3.4, 5.23). The woman with the flow of blood believes that if she touches Jesus' clothing, she will be saved (5.28). When she does so, her flow of blood stops; then, after speaking with her, Jesus tells her that her faith has made her well. The meaning of σώζω is further refined with those 'who lose their life for my sake, and for the sake of the gospel, will save it' (8.35). In the little apocalypse, the one who endures to the end will be saved (13.13). As Donahue notes, before Mark 8.27 the focus is on the present reality of the Reign of God. Afterwards there is a radical orientation to its future coming.[28] With this shift comes a redefinition of the meaning of salvation. In the beginning of the gospel people suffer and are saved from their suffering. In the end, people are said to suffer and by enduring that suffering they are saved and enjoy eternal life. Enduring persecution is required of those who follow Jesus, but though they lose their lives, their lives will be saved. The Gospel of Mark presents a complex view of suffering and salvation. Jesus relieves human suffering and saves people, but he also commands his followers to endure suffering, so that they can be saved. In the end, his ultimate act of salvation on behalf of many is his own suffering.

---

25   A. Collins, 'Remove This Cup', pp. 43, 54. See also Kee, *Community*, p. 121. Best (*Mark*, pp. 56–62) notes the connection in Mark between healing and saving. Jesus cares for his people, both in physical and spiritual ways. Hooker (*Message*, pp. 41, 80) writes that healing demonstrates the coming of the Reign. Both Best and Hooker conclude that salvation includes forgiveness of sin and rescue from other evils. Best (*Mark*, pp. 65, 74, 91–92) emphasizes that Jesus continues to heal and care for the church after the resurrection.
26   Cf. Neirynck, *Duality*, pp. 45–53, 71–72; V. K. Robbins, *Jesus the Teacher: A Socio-Rhetorical Interpretation of Mark* (Philadelphia: Fortress, 1984), p. 22.
27   Neirynck, *Duality*, p. 46.
28   Donahue, *Are you the Christ?*, pp. 166–67.

Summary

The genuine allusions contribute to the meaning of, or to put it more simply, interpret the Markan passion narrative. These allusions appear to interact with nearby verses in the referents. They do so according to the methods and standards of Jewish exegesis in the first century. The verses contribute to the portrayal of Jesus' identity. They show that after Jesus' suffering, he will be glorified. They depict Jesus on the verge of an exalted, heavenly kingship. At the Parousia, he will act as judge over those who now judge him. In the same capacity, Jesus will also reward those loyal to him.

Scripture allusions also contribute to the portrayal of Jesus' enemies. They indicate not only that those enemies will be punished, but the seriousness of their treatment of God's chosen agent.

The seriousness of Jesus' suffering is heightened by means of Scripture allusions, drawing out the mockery, humiliation, and pain he endures. Yet the same Scripture passages also highlight the hope and value attached to that suffering. They also depict reliance on God's faithfulness and redemption for those who trust in him. They show Jesus as representative head, who in dying for others, brings salvation near and enables the saints to inherit the Reign of God.

For Further Study

Several questions present themselves as a result of this study. The findings with regard to the passion narrative were profitable enough to justify further research on a larger section, including all of the final week, beginning with the triumphal entry and incorporating Mark 13. That study would locate and assess the allusions in those sections and consider how the larger section of material corrected or supported the findings above. In addition, though much research has been done on the use of Scripture in Mark 1 and 11–16, much less has been done on Mark 2–10. Because the author of Mark appears to use Scripture as a way to communicate with his reader, fruitful work could be done there.

The analysis of this study on suggested allusions casts some doubt on the theory that the passion narrative originated on the basis of scriptural interpretation or that Scripture was the sorting principal that determined what would be told and what would be left out. Almost two thirds of the allusions suggested for the passion narrative had very weak verbal correspondence or none at all. Most of the established allusions occur in two short sections of narrative: seven occur in the Jewish trial, from 14.55-65; five others occur in the crucifixion proper, 15.24-36. The remainder are, one each, in the time reference opening the passion narrative (14.1), the Last Supper (14.24), the prediction of the disciples' flight (14.27), and the prayer in Gethsemane (14.34). Most scenes contained no allusions. That is, there were no allusions in the anointing, Judas' betrayal and the arrest (though they are said to be in fulfilment of the Scriptures), the disciples' flight and Peter's denial (though the prediction of these events is tied to Zechariah), the trial before Pilate, Pilate's interaction with the crowd, the Roman mockery, and the burial. Instead of 270 allusions in almost every one of the 120 verses of the passion narrative, 16 allusions were found in 16 verses. While it is possible to find parallels to every event in the passion narrative, it is likely that scholarly ingenuity, if applied to the task, could find Scripture parallels to every sentence in the gospel. Mere assertions of parallels do not prove that the author considered those passages when writing. They certainly do not prove that the author based his narrative on those passages. This study indicates that scholars may have been too hasty to conclude that the entire passion narrative was composed by means of Scripture.[29] The question might be revisited with profit.

This study raises another, perhaps more important, question. Does the Gospel of Mark understand Jesus to have succeeded in effecting the end to suffering?

The very simplest answer is yes, the gospel portrays the effort to have succeeded, because Jesus, whose words have absolute authority, said that it would. He promised that his life would be given as a ransom for many. The brief, confined eschatological signs of the three-hour darkness and the tearing of the veil demonstrate that the promised Eschaton has somehow begun, even if in part. Mark portrays a Jesus who gave his life, not only as an answer to human culpability, but as an answer to the entire range of injustice, suffering, and evil of human experience. Jesus came and died to initiate the Eschaton, to judge the unjust and conquer demonic forces, and to bring the Reign of God in all its fullness to those who are chosen. Mark portrays Jesus' ministry as bringing that Reign near and his crucifixion as a pledge on the coming end and new beginning.

That would make sense to the author of Mark. There is good reason to believe that, though it was delayed, the author of Mark still expected the Parousia to come quickly.[30] If Jesus' ministry and death initiated the coming Reign, and that Reign were to come in full within a generation or two, then Mark's scheme is powerful. Nearly two thousand years later, such a scheme presents a problem for the church.[31] How can it be said that Jesus' death effected an end to human suffering? In the face of stark realities, it is much

---

29 Suhl (*Funktion*, pp. 45–66) made a similar argument, over 35 years ago. Unfortunately, those who continued to claim that the passion narrative was created based on Scripture have all too often ignored his challenge.

30 Suhl (*Funktion*, pp. 25, 54–55), for example, concludes that Mark expects the end to come within a generation (cf. Kee, *Community*, p. 67). But scholarly opinion is not uniform on the subject. Best (*Mark*, pp. 42–43) is among those who argue that Mark expected a longer delay.

31 Theodore J. Weeden (*Mark – Traditions in Conflict* [Philadelphia: Fortress, 1971], pp. 159–60) believes the tension already exists in Mark.

easier simply to say that his death atoned for human sin, that it justified believers before God. But those stark realities were just as real for the author of Mark, and despite them the church has never abandoned the idea that Christ's death and resurrection somehow touched all human suffering. Indeed, the Eastern Orthodox church has always viewed the passion, and the whole life of Jesus, as redemptive of the entire creation, not only of human culpability.

Such questions are raised by the conclusions of this study, but they cannot be answered here. To do so is to take up the struggle of the church with the problem of pain. Nevertheless, the church does well not to lose sight of Mark's vision of the effect of Jesus' death and resurrection. It goes beyond forgiveness of sin, and touches all aspects of the human experience.

Appendix A
Textual Analysis of Quotations and Near Quotations in Mark

This appendix presents the results of analysis of the quotations and near quotations (as judged by the editors of NA^{27})[1] in Mark and their relationship to extant Greek and Hebrew texts of the OT. These data are the basis for the guidelines on the Markan handling of texts, presented in Chapter 1.

The analysis compared Mark's quotation, word by word, to the Göttingen edition (or Rahlfs, if the Göttingen is not available for the book in question). Where there are differences, the apparatus is checked for LXX variants which match Mark's wording. If Mark's quotation does not appear sufficiently close to the LXX, including variants, its similarity to the Hebrew is considered.

Texts are presented in three categories:

- Exact or nearly exact quotations from the LXX: these quotations clearly match extant LXX readings, though some of these quotations do change the wording slightly to fit the context.
- Quotations significantly modified from the LXX: these quotations largely match extant LXX readings in important respects, but have been more substantially modified to fit the new literary context.
- Uncertain origin: these quotations do not match extant LXX readings, and the source of the quotation is difficult to identify. These quotations may come from LXX readings that are no longer extant, reflect word changes caused by Christian interpretation or liturgical use, represent a quote from memory or a paraphrase of the original, or reflect an independent translation from Hebrew. In many cases, one cannot be certain which of these possibilities obtains.

The groupings in the table below are heuristic, not definitive. The categories do not represent hard and fast divisions, but differences of degree. The first two categories represent clear uses of the LXX, with various degrees of modification. The third category contains references which differ more significantly from known LXX MSS and are thus of uncertain origin. For various reasons, other

---

1 Some of these 'quotations' are not terribly close to either the Greek or Hebrew (such as Mark 12.19 and Deut. 25.5-6).

researchers would have made different decisions about the categories in which particular references belong. Despite this uncertainty, the categories provide a preliminary grouping from which data can be more easily analyzed. Within the three categories, quotations are shown in Markan order.

Results in Markan verse order

Markan verse	Exact or Nearly Exact Match with LXX	Modified from LXX	Uncertain Origin
1.2			Mal. 3.1 (independent)
1.3		Isa. 40.3	
4.12		Isa. 6.9-10	
4.32			Ps. 104.12 (independent)
6.34			Num. 27.17 (independent)
7.6-7	Isa. 29.13		
7.10	Deut. 5.16; Exod. 21.17		
8.18			Jer. 5.21 (independent)
9.11			Mal. 3.23 (summary)
9.48	Isa. 66.24		
10.6	Gen. 1.27		
10.7-8	Gen. 2.24		
10.19		Exod. 20.12-16 with Sir. 4.1	
11.9			Ps. 118.25-26 (independent)
11.10			Ps. 148.1 (?)
11.17	Isa. 56.7	Jer. 7.11	
12.10-11	Ps. 118.22-23		
12.19			Deut. 25.5 (summary)
12.19b			Gen. 38.8 (?)
12.26			Exod. 3.6 (LXX)
12.29-30	Deut. 6.4-5		
12.31	Lev. 19.18		
12.32	Deut. 6.4; 4.35		
12.33		Lev. 19.18	Deut. 6.5 (paraphrase)
12.36	Ps. 110.1		
13.14		Dan. 12.11	
13.24		Isa. 13.10	
13.25			Isa. 34.4 (independent)
13.26			Dan. 7.13-14 (?)
14.27	Zech. 13.7		
14.34		Ps. 42.6	
14.62		Dan. 7.13	Ps. 110.1 (paraphrase)
15.24		Ps. 22.19	
15.34			Ps. 22.2 (?)

Appendix A: Textual Analysis of Quotations

Exact or Nearly Exact Matches with LXX

Mark 7.6-7/Isa. 29.13 – All differences are found in LXX variants. Mark may have quoted exactly from his Greek MS.

Mark 7.10/Deut. 5.16 – This is an exact match with the LXX. The words are simple, and this could be an independent translation, but on Ockham's razor, it is LXX.

Mark 7.10/Exod. 21.17(16) – The only difference is found in a LXX variant. Mark may have quoted exactly from his Greek MS.

Mark 9.48/Isa. 66.24 – Mark omits γάρ to fit the context. The different form of τελευτάω is found in a LXX (and Markan) variant. Mark is quoting from his Greek MS

Mark 10.6/Gen. 1.27 – The Markan quotation is an exact match with the LXX.

Mark 10.7-8/Gen. 2.24 – Some Markan MSS contain μητερα αυτου, agreeing with the MT (and some LXX MSS) against most LXX MSS; however, most omit αυτου, agreeing with most LXX MSS against MT. Most Markan MSS contain καὶ προσκολληθήσεται πρὸς τὴν γυναῖκα αὐτοῦ; some do not. This phrase could be a later insertion to fill out the quotation and the sense. In either case, the quotation is taken from the LXX.

Mark 11.17/Isa. 56.7 – Mark omits γάρ to fit the context. Otherwise, this is an exact match with the LXX.

Mark 12.10-11/Ps. 118(117).22-23 – The Markan quotation is an exact match with the LXX.

Mark 12.29-30/Deut. 6.4-5 – The major difference between Mark and most LXX MSS is that the latter include three elements (διάνοια, ψυχή, and δύναμις), as do the MT and some Markan MSS, but most Markan MSS include four (καρδία, ψυχή, διάνοια, ἰσχύς). Nevertheless, Mark is not unique in this; other LXX MSS do contain four elements, though a different four. Extant LXX MSS contain a great number of variants at this point. The confusion in the LXX MSS renders Mark's differences from $\mathfrak{G}^{ed}$ insignificant. In all probability, Mark is quoting the Greek of the passage, as he knows (or remembers) it. Compare Mark 12.33a below.

Mark 12.31/Lev. 19.18 – The Markan quotation is an exact match with the LXX. Compare Mark 12.33b below.

Mark 12.32/Deut. 6.4 – This is a repetition and abbreviation of Mark 12.29, see above, and is an exact match with the LXX.

Mark 12.32/Deut. 4.35 – Mark could be quoting from either Deut. 4.35 or Isa. 45.21. The passage differs from Deut. 4.35 in having ἄλλος rather than ἔτι but αλλος is found in some variants of Deut. 4.35. Because this passage in Mark follows a reference to Deut. 6.4 (see above), for simplicity, Deut. 4.35 is preferred here over an allusion to Isa. 45.21. This is probably an exact quotation of Deut. 4.35.

Mark 12.36/Ps. 110(109).1 – Mark differs from Ps. 110 in the omission of a ὁ and more significantly in having ὑποκάτω instead of the LXX's ὑποπόδιον. The change may be due to Mark's LXX text or some other cause. However, most of the quotation matches the LXX exactly, which is its source.[2]

Mark 14.27/Zech. 13.7 – Though there are several differences between Mark and 𝔊^ed (πατάξω for πατάξατε; τὸν ποιμένα for τοὺς ποιμένας; διασκορπισθήσονται for ἐκσπάσατε; and τὰ πρόβατα διασκορπισθήσονται for ἐκσπάσατε τὰ πρόβατα, a difference in order), all of the differences exist as variants in LXX MSS; none is unique to Mark. The differences could reflect Mark's LXX text or be changes to fit the new context or even be an independent translation of the Hebrew. A preference for the simplest option favours a quotation from the LXX.

Modified from the LXX

Mark 1.3/Isa. 40.3 – Mark changes τοῦ θεοῦ ἡμῶν to αὐτοῦ. The change is a modification to apply the first part of the passage to Jesus. This passage is part of a combined quotation, containing Mal. 3.1 and possibly Exod. 23.20 as well. The remainder of the quotation is discussed below.

Mark 4.12/Isa. 6.9-10 – The Markan text uses the following portions of the LXX text:

Ἀκοῇ ἀκούσετε καὶ οὐ μὴ συνῆτε καὶ βλέποντες βλέψετε καὶ οὐ μὴ ἴδητε· ...
μήποτε ... ἐπιστρέψωσι καὶ ἰάσομαι αὐτούς.

There are a number of significant differences between Mark and the portions of the LXX text it uses, including the order and forms of the verbs ἀκούω and βλέπω and changing the final verb from ἰάσομαι to ἀφεθῇ. In every case, the MT agrees with the LXX against Mark. Mark changed the metaphorical verb 'heal' to bring out the sense of the metaphor, 'be forgiven'. This is a sense given to רפא in a number of texts and may be a traditional interpretation of this text. Note that all other words use the same roots as those found in the LXX. Mark has modified the LXX passage to fit his context.

Mark 10.19/Exod. 20.12-16; Sir. 4.1 – There are several differences between Mark and 𝔊^ed. An additional commandment, corresponding to Sir. 4.1, is included.[3] The apodictic commandments from Exodus are placed in the (more natural) imperative form. The text of Sirach is already in this form (and is an exact match).

---

2   Perrin (*Pilgrimage*, p. 22) concludes that this quotation a conflation between Ps. 110.1 and Ps. 8.6. Yet the difference between the quotation and Ps. 110.1 is in a single significant word. Text forms were not fixed, and quotations are frequently not exact. Perrin's conclusion is unwarranted.
3   Some Markan MSS omit μὴ ἀποστερήσῃς.

Appendix A: Textual Analysis of Quotations

The most significant difference is in the order of the commandments. The commandments appear in several different orders in the primary literature. Mark differs from all (except pars. Matt. 19.18-19 and Luke 18.20) in placing the commandment to honour father and mother at the end. All sources agree in placing the commandment against bearing false witness following the commandments against murder, adultery, and stealing. There is significant variation, however, on the order of the latter three. Mark agrees with MT and Matt. 19.18 in ordering them: do not murder, do not commit adultery, and do not steal. Certain Markan MSS reverse the order of the commandments against adultery and murder, and these MSS agree with the order found in Philo, *Decal.* 10; some LXX MSS; Luke 18.20; Rom. 13.9; and Jas. 2.11. In determining which order is original to Mark, Gundry asks whether Mark is the source of the order in Matthew or Luke. In part because the Matthean order agrees with the MT, Gundry concludes that Mark is the source of the order in Luke, and that the original text of Mark read μὴ μοιχεύσῃς, μὴ φονεύσῃς.[4] However, that Luke agrees in order with several other independent texts indicates that the Lukan order was a common variation, and Mark need not be its source. On the other hand, Matthew agrees in order with the MT, and thus the Markan order need not be the source of the Matthean order either. One cannot conclude from the parallels which order was original to Mark.

The problem, put simply, is this: Mark differs in the order of the commandments within its own MS tradition. Both of the Markan MS traditions differ in order from $\mathfrak{G}^{ed}$. Some of those MSS agree in order with Matthew and, in part, with the MT. Others of the Markan MSS agree in order with Luke, Romans, James, Philo, and some LXX MSS. It is difficult to determine which order was original with Mark.

All of the Greek texts noted above use the same roots for the commandments, and all of them show influence by the LXX in other quotations. Aside from the question of order, it would appear that all of them are influenced by the LXX in the translation of the Decalogue. The simplest reconstruction of the matter is that there were several variations in the order of the commandments in circulation at this period. Mark is reproducing the commandments as translated in the LXX, but in a different order, which was either familiar or useful to him. It is quite likely that Mark (or his sources) did not need to consult an actual MS for this quotation and that he (or they) cited from memory. If the original Markan order was μὴ φονεύσῃς, μὴ μοιχεύσῃς (agreeing with the MT against $\mathfrak{G}^{ed}$ in order, but with $\mathfrak{G}^{ed}$ in word choice), citation from memory would make the mixture of MT and $\mathfrak{G}^{ed}$ elements easy to understand. If the original Markan order was μὴ μοιχεύσῃς, μὴ φονεύσῃς, it agrees with LXX MSS in both order and word choice.[5] In either case, the quotation in Mark is a modification of the LXX.

---

4   Gundry, *Use of the Old Testament*, p. 17.
5   The difference lies only in the degree of influence of the MT order.

Note: Deut. 5.16-20 is an equivalent referent for this quotation.

Mark 11.17/Jer. 7.11 – Mark adds πεποιήκατε and changes an implied command (LXX, or question, MT) to an indicative declaration. The differences between Mark and LXX are significant. There are, however, more important similarities. Mark uses second person plural forms, as do both MT and LXX (later in the verse). The telling agreement is in σπήλαιον ληστῶν. This is connected to ὁ οἶκός μου, which is stated in the LXX and is the antecedent for αὐτόν in Mark (see ὁ οἶκός μου in the previous clause). Note the difference in the Hebrew: הבית הזה. This passage is modified from the LXX.

Mark 12.33b/Lev. 19.18 – This verse rephrases, in indirect discourse, Jesus' words in 12.31, which match the LXX exactly.

Mark 13.14/Dan. 12.11 – Only the phrase τὸ βδέλυγμα τῆς ἐρημώσεως is taken from the LXX. While most θ´ MSS omit the articles τό and τῆς, some θ´ and most ο´ MSS include them. Whether or not they were original, this quotation could be from either LXX tradition.

Note that the phrase also occurs in 1 Macc. 1.54. Sharon Pace argues that in the time of the Maccabees, this was a common phrase and that the use of this phrase in 1 Maccabees does not necessitate dependence on Daniel.[6] During the first century CE, however, the phrase was less common and is more likely to be a literary allusion. Because of other allusions to Daniel, this allusion is more likely to come from Dan. 12.11 than from 1 Macc. 1.54 or another source.[7] Gundry notes the additional similarity of theme and language between Mark 13.14, ὁ ἀναγινώσκων νοείτω, and LXX θ´ 12.10, καί οἱ νοήμονες συνήσουσι, is further indication that the passage in view is Dan. 12.11.[8]

Mark 13.24/Isa. 13.10 – There are significant differences from the LXX. Mark may have simplified σκοτισθήσεται τοῦ ἡλίου ἀνατέλλοντος to ὁ ἥλιος σκοτισθήσεται. Mark's φέγγος is found in some LXX MS. The quotation appears to be adapted from the LXX.[9]

Mark 14.34/Ps. 42(41).6 – Mark adapts the LXX to his context.

Mark 14.62/Dan. 7.13 – Here Mark's μετὰ τῶν νεφελῶν τοῦ οὐρανοῦ agrees with θ´ (Mark 13.26 differs).[10] The difference between ἐρχόμενος (θ´)

---

6   Sharon Pace, 'Stratigraphy of the Text of Daniel', *BIOSCS* 17 (1984), p. 24.
7   Cf. also Dan. 9.27 and 11.31. Some Markan MSS name Daniel as the source for this passage, but they are probably not original.
8   Gundry, *Use of the Old Testament*, p. 49.
9   Gundry (*Use of the Old Testament*, p. 51) decides differently. Based on the differences between the texts of Mark and LXX, he concludes that Mark represents an independent rendering of the Hebrew.
10 Gundry (*Use of the Old Testament*, p. 60) notes that Justin (*Dial.* 31; 1 *Apol.* 51) quotes Dan. 7.13 with different prepositions: μετά and ἐπάνω. Note that Mark is similar to θ´, not to ο´. This and other OT similarities to θ´ has led to a theory of a proto-Theodotianic text (or *kaige*-Theodotian), as early as Henry B. Swete, *An Introduction to the Old Testament in Greek* (rev. by R. R. Ottley; New York: Ktav, 1968), p. 403. See also Ulrich, *The Dead Sea Scrolls*, pp. 212–23, 231; R. E. Brown et al., 'Texts and Versions', pp. 1092–93, sects 70–74, in *The New Jerome Biblical Commentary* (ed. R. E. Brown et al.; Englewood Cliffs, NJ: Prentice hall, 1990).

and ἐρχόμενον (Mark) is merely to account for the use in a different sentence. Thus the only significant differences are the use of articles with υἱὸς ἀνθρώπου and its use as a straightforward subject (without ὡς), which is a theological change in Mark. This appears to be a modification of the LXX to fit the new context.[11]

Mark 15.24/Ps. 22(21).19 – Mark closely follows the LXX, but modifies it to fit the new context. Nothing indicates an independent translation.

Uncertain Origin

Mark 1.2/Mal. 3.1; Exod. 23.20 – This quotation could be from either Mal. 3.1, Exod. 23.20, or a combination of the two. (Note that Mal. 3.1 refers to the Exodus narrative, in an instance of inner-biblical exegesis.)

The Markan passage begins with almost exactly the same words as the LXX of Exod. 23.20 (ἰδοὺ ἀποστέλλω τὸν ἄγγελόν μου πρὸ προσώπου σου), the only difference being the omission of ἐγώ after ἰδού. Mark's second clause, however, bears little resemblance to that passage in either the LXX (ἵνα φυλάξῃ σε ἐν τῇ ὁδῷ) or MT, beyond the reference to a road.

The major difference between Mark 1.2 and Mal. 3.1 is Mark's ὃς κατασκευάσει rather than καὶ ἐπιβλέψεται, which is a literal but meaningless translation of ופנה, read as a Qal, rather than Piel.[12] Mark's ὃς κατασκευάσει is a much smoother, more accurate translation of the sense of the Hebrew. The smooth Greek transition ὃς subordinates the second verbal clause to the first and makes this a single sentence. This structure gives the translator some freedom in placing the final clause, πρὸ προσώπου σου (though order is very often changed in Mark's quotations and no particular justification is required here). This quotation is quite plausibly an independent translation of Mal. 3.1.

Mark 4.32/Ps. 104(103).12 – Mark's τὰ πετεινὰ τοῦ οὐρανοῦ κατασκηνοῦν parallels the LXX's τὰ πετεινὰ τοῦ οὐρανοῦ κατασκηνώσει. This phrase is put in the context of birds *in branches*, κλάδοι, parallel to the birds singing from branches in the MT, עפאים (*foliage, branches*). Extant MSS of the LXX however follow this phrase with the birds singing from the midst of rocks, ἐκ μέσου τῶν πετρῶν. The common use of *branches* in Mark and the MT points to the use of a LXX text, no longer extant, which refers to branches or perhaps to an independent translation from Hebrew.[13]

---

11 For more on whether ὄψεσθε reflects Zech. 12.10, see pp. 96–98.
12 For a discussion of the LXX of this passage and Mark's treatment of it, see Watts, *Isaiah's New Exodus*, pp. 61–63. Marcus ('Mark 9, 11-13: "As It Has Been Written"', ZNW 80 [1989], pp. 44–46) concludes this is a conflation.
13 Gundry (*Use of the Old Testament*, p. 35), following Lohmeyer, considers this a composite allusion to Ezek. 17.23 and Dan. 4.9, 18 and notes Ps. 104.12 only as a point of comparison.

Mark 6.34/Num. 27.17 – Mark has μὴ ἔχοντα ποιμένα instead of οἷς οὐκ ἔστιν ποιμήν. This difference may represent merely a change to fit the allusion more smoothly into the narrative. On the other hand, it presents a different verb and grammatical structure. Because the corresponding words are obvious choices for translation, they are not weighty arguments for dependence on the LXX. This could be either an adaptation of the LXX or an independent translation.

Mark 8.18/Jer. 5.21 – There are differences in form between Mark and the LXX for the entire quotation, excluding οὐ, ὦτα, and οὐκ, and the Markan passage has a different sentence structure. Still, the change from third to second person in the finite verbs is easily explained by the change in context. The words that are shared, though in different form (e.g., ὀφθαλμούς and ὀφθαλμοί), are exceedingly common and literal translations of the Hebrew, and consequently they indicate nothing about the origin of the quotation. Because of the structure (note: the same as that of 6.34, that is ἔχω for –ל), this may well be an independent translation.

Mark 9.11/Mal. 3.23 – This passage is not a quotation, though it is cited as such in NA[27]. It is an assessment of the meaning of the passage. Nothing is indicated about Mark's text.

Mark 11.9/Ps. 118(117).25-26 – The Markan ὡσαννά is a transliteration of הושיעה נא. ὡσαννά does not occur in the LXX. In fact, it is used nowhere else in the NT either, except the parallels in Matt. 21.9 and, interestingly, John 12.13 which is an exact match with Mark 11.9. Luke (19.38) replaced it with the Greek words εὐλογημένος and, in the subsequent quotation, εἰρήνη.

The exact parallel in John points to the possibility that Mark and John shared a tradition that presented the psalm in this fashion. Though there is a minority position that John was dependent on the Synoptics, few believe John to be dependent on Mark (and here Mark equals John but is different from Matthew and Luke). This presents the further possibility that the quotations in Mark that appear to have come from the Hebrew may have been translated by one of Mark's sources.

Mark 11.10/Ps. 148.1/Job 16.19 – The Markan ἐν τοῖς ὑψίστοις is an exact match with LXX Ps. 148.1. ὡσαννά and the larger context of the Markan passage bring out the idea of salvation, which is not in the psalm. This idea is present in Job 16.19, as suggested by NA[27], in συνίστωρ μου ἐν ὑψίστοις, but it is not a strong enough verbal connection to account for the ὡσαννά in Mark.

Another possibility is that Mark is using ὡσαννά (inspired by its use in the previous verse) in a very unliteral fashion, parallel to the French *Salud!* ὡσαννὰ ἐν τοῖς ὑψίστοις may mean nothing more than 'Praise the Heavens', or something similar. In that case, ὡσαννά would be functioning as a liturgical exclamation, like *alleluia* or *amen*. This idea is supported by the fact that Mark does not translate it (nor do Matthew or John), as he does other Semitic words.

Mark 12.19/Deut. 25.5 – This is a summary of the sense of the law, not a quotation. All the elements in Mark are contained in both the LXX and MT. Many of the words used in Mark are different than those used in the LXX, for example καὶ μὴ ἀφῇ τέκνον instead of σπέρμα δὲ μὴ ᾖ αὐτῷ. Since this is not a strict quotation, that does not indicate much about Mark's text. He could have summed up the sense of the passage in his own words, referring to the passage in either Greek or Hebrew.

Mark 12.19b/Gen. 38.8 – Mark 12.19b may refer to Gen. 38.8, as well as or instead of Deut. 25.5 (described above). While the first half of the clause sets up the situation and has nothing in common beside τὴν γυναῖκα, the latter portions, following Mark's καί and the second καί in Gen. 38.8, are quite similar, the differences being Mark's ἐξαναστήσῃ instead of ἀνάστησον and αὐτοῦ for σου (adapting to the new context). That is, there is a string of six consecutive equal or equivalent words. Still, most are simple words in the order of the Hebrew and do not tell for or against independent translation. The Markan ἐξαναστήσῃ, corresponding to הקם (with a change in verb form to fit the context), seems easier to explain as an independent translation than as a modification of the Greek for the sake of the context, but there is no compelling reason to do so, particularly since the text may well be a paraphrase of Deut. 25.5.

Mark 12.26/Exod. 3.6 – The LXX is a direct and simple translation of the Hebrew. Mark's text is different and could easily reflect an independent translation of Hebrew. The only indication in Mark of dependence on LXX is in the spelling of the names, which could come from knowledge of the LXX without dependence on this particular verse.

Yet the differences between Mark and $\mathfrak{G}^{ed}$ are not that significant: the omission of εἰμί and the possible addition of articles that are also included in various LXX MSS. Because Mark agrees with the MT in omitting the verb *to be*, one might conclude that this is an independent translation. Yet as Gundry notes, this omission in Mark agrees with Acts 7.32, and it may reflect a LXX variant no longer extant. Gundry suggests as another possibility that the omission of εἰμί is part of the larger omission of θεὸς τοῦ πατρός σου.[14]

It is possible that this quotation reflects an independent translation of Hebrew. It may equally well represent a modification of the LXX.

Mark 12.33a/Deut. 6.5 – This is a paraphrase of a passage that was quoted a few verses earlier, in Mark 12.30. In that passage, the text is a fairly literal quote from the LXX. Note that there the issue was that Mark included four elements (heart, soul, mind, and strength), against both the MT and LXX. Here Mark has only three, as do the MT and most LXX MSS.

The three elements Mark includes differ from most LXX MSS. The second element here, σύνεσις, is not found in any extant LXX MS nor in the list in

---

14   Gundry, *Use of the Old Testament*, pp. 20-21.

Mark 12.30, though it is equivalent in meaning to διάνοια, the third element in Mark 12.30.

If the previous passage did not exist, one might be tempted to call this an independent translation. Because the previous quote of the passage is so clearly from LXX, it seems unlikely that this quotation represents an independent translation. Mark may feel even freer than usual to paraphrase here. After all, his readers know the passage now; he can do as he likes with it. Mark has rephrased it in his own words.

Mark 13.25/Isa. 34.4 – The LXX and Mark agree in using πίπτω, *fall*, for 'the stars', where the MT uses נבל, *wither*. One might conclude that Mark absolutely *must* be dependent on the LXX here. But this example demonstrates the reason for caution. 1QIsa^a differs significantly from MT in the first half of the passage, including in the phrase וכול צבא השמים יפולו: 'all the hosts of heaven will *fall*'. That is, there is a Hebrew attestation of the verb *fall*, and Mark is not necessarily dependent on the LXX.

The LXX appears to be translating a text that is similar to the MT but which had (or the scribe read) נפל where the MT has נבל, in the second half of the verse. Some LXX MSS have τακησονται αι δυναμεις των ουρανων, agreeing with the MT, but most omit it, agreeing with 1QIsa^a. The differences and agreements in all three (LXX, 1QIsa^a, and MT) attest to some confusion in the text here. If Mark's quotation were a translation from Hebrew, it would be a translation of a text with elements from both text types – as is the LXX. Mark could be a paraphrase of a fuller LXX text. It could also be an independent translation of a mixed text, combining elements in 1QIsa^a and the MT, something as likely as not, considering the differences in the MT, 1QIsa^a, and the LXX (itself having significant variants).[15]

Mark 13.26/Dan. 7.13-14 – The allusion is analysed in two parts. The first part, τὸν υἱὸν τοῦ ἀνθρώπου ἐρχόμενον ἐν νεφέλαις, resembles Dan. 7.13 (θ΄). The second, μετὰ δυνάμεως πολλῆς καὶ δόξης, evokes 7.14.

Part 1: Mark's sentence structure is shifted, so υἱὸς ἀνθρώπου is the object, and the order of the elements reversed, so that υἱὸς ἀνθρώπου is mentioned before the clouds. Mark omits both ὡς before son of man and τοῦ οὐρανοῦ after clouds and uses ἐν instead of the μετά or ἐπί of all LXX MSS. All differences could be considered stylistic (or theological) changes, with the possible exception of the use of ἐν for μετά. The use of ἐν is insufficient alone to argue for independent translation. On the other hand, none of the similarities proves dependence on the LXX. The words are common and could easily be arrived at independently.

Part 2: There is only one verbal similarity to either of the LXX texts: δόξης corresponds to δόξα in ο΄. If Mark is dependent on the LXX here, this is a

---

15   Cf. the analysis in Jozef Verheyden, 'Describing the Parousia: The Cosmic Phenomena in Mk 13,24-25', in Tuckett, *Scriptures*, pp. 534–40.

complete rewriting, going beyond the degree of change seen even in the summary of Mark 12.19.

A comparison to the Aramaic, however, presents a slightly different picture. δυνάμεως πολλῆς καὶ δόξης is a reasonable translation of שלטן ויקר, with πολλῆς as an adjective giving the full force of שלטן or economically representing the force of the entire verse, which is that this figure is given great power. There is no consensus on the native language of the author of Mark or of his sources. Knowledge of Aramaic cannot be ruled out.[16]

This allusion to Daniel may indicate independent translation; however, it does not compel such a conclusion. The allusion to Dan. 7.13 in Mark 14.62, discussed previously, appears to be a modification of the LXX. As seen in previous comparisons, Mark contains several double allusions to the same passage in which one allusion was fairly close to the LXX and the other a paraphrase. The same pattern could well be in place here: Mark is dependent on the LXX and shows that in 14.62, while in 13.26 he is paraphrasing. Another possibility is that in both cases Mark is translating from the Aramaic, choosing ἐν here and μετά in 14.62 to translate עם. A third possibility is that one of these quotes comes from Mark's source (or that both come from different sources), and that one source quotes the text one way and Mark (or another source) quotes the text differently.[17] The question remains open.

Mark 14.62/Ps. 110(109).1 – Ps. 110.1 appears as an almost exact quote from the LXX in Mark 12.36. The form of this allusion, however, differs considerably from the LXX, which is a fairly literal translation of the Hebrew. The changed form comes from the sentence structure in the new context. In Psalm 110, the right hand is God's, and Mark indicates this with the unusual epithet δυνάμεως.[18] Because of the exact quotation earlier in the narrative, this appears to be a paraphrase of the LXX.

Mark 15.34/Ps. 22(21).2 – The source of this quotation is uncertain. Some of the words it shares with the LXX, such as ὁ θεός μου, are obvious choices and do not indicate dependence. Yet it also shares the main verb, ἐγκατέλιπες, with the LXX, and there are a number of translation options for this verb. On the other hand, Mark agrees with the MT against the LXX

---

16 See pp. 38–40.
17 A look at Table 3, above, shows that Mark quotes four passages twice. Two of those passages are quoted twice in the same pericope (Lev. 19.18 and Deut. 6.4-5, all in the space of three Markan verses, 12.31-33). Only this passage (Dan. 7.13) and Ps. 110.1 are quoted in different pericopes and have the possibility of different sources.
18 Lindars (*Jesus Son of Man*, p. 110) proposes that the use of δυνάμεως to refer to God may be derived from the quotation of Dan. 7.13 in Mark 13.26. Gundry (*Use of the Old Testament*, p. 60) cites it as a Semitic periphrasis of the divine name.
Note that some Markan MSS have καθημενον εκ δεξιων, rendering the phrase a bit closer to the LXX. However, this variant may be a scribal correction toward the LXX, Matt. 26.64, or Luke 22.69.

in two differences; both Mark and MT have 'my God, my God', where the LXX has 'God, my God'; the LXX includes the petition πρόσχες μοι, omitted in both MT and Mark.

The quotation is first presented in Mark in a Semitic language. There is some discussion of whether the Semitic is Hebrew or Aramaic, while the verb appears to be Aramaic.[19] Mark may have written *lema* or *lama* (there is a variant here, NA[27] prefers *lema*), but even if he had written *lama*, some allowance must be made for dialect and the inexact science of transliterating a language without written vowels. The case for Aramaic appears stronger.[20]

Several possibilities present themselves for the origin of the Greek quotation. It may come originally from a LXX MS more like the MT. It may be a translation of the Aramaic cry, with recourse to the LXX for its choice of verb. It may be a translation of the cry without regard to the Greek of Psalm 22. This last option is the least likely. Because Mark 15.24 quotes Ps. 22.19 with only slight modifications to the LXX, it is probable that the author knew the LXX translation of Ps. 22.2. Therefore some recourse to the LXX of Ps. 22.2 is likely here. Whether the entire quote depends on a LXX MS no longer extant or melds a translation of the Aramaic with the LXX translation is unclear.

---

19   See Gundry, *Use of the Old Testament*, pp. 64–66, on the Markan variants here.
20   Cf. Brown, *Death*, 2, pp. 1051–56. Note that Brown does not mention the textual variant of *lema, lama*, though the evidence for *lema* is significant.

Appendix B
Textual Analysis of Mark 14

Reading the Comparisons

Below and in Appendix C the suggested references for Mark 14–15 are examined in detail. Texts with verbal correspondence are displayed together, the NA[27] text of Mark first, then the Göttingen edition of the LXX (when available, otherwise the text of Rahlfs is given). If at least part of the verbal correspondence is with the Hebrew, then the MT is given. After the texts, words in common to the two passages are listed. This is followed by an analysis and a conclusion about the likelihood that the suggestion is an actual reference. A table summarizing the results of this analysis is included in Chapter 3.

Only verses with significant words in common are shown. If a large passage is suggested, but only a portion of that passage has corresponding words, only that portion will be shown. Passages with no significant words in common are noted, but the passages are not shown.

Variants have been checked for all suggestions with the Göttingen edition of the Septuagint, or if that is unavailable for a particular book, with Rahlfs. Variants are shown only if they have material impact on verbal correspondence. For example, a reference is suggested between Mark 14.10 and Ps. 55.13-16. A Markan MS has ηλθεν, which also occurs in the psalm, but this would not significantly improve verbal correspondence, because the word is extremely common and would not be part of a string. Therefore the variant is not shown.

The following rules govern the lists of corresponding words:

- For the purpose of determining verbal correspondence, articles, conjunctions, prepositions, pronouns, and εἰμί are ignored unless they fall in a string of words in common. One does not connect two passages because they both contain the word καί or αὐτός.
- If words correspond in Greek and Hebrew, they are generally shown only in Greek. If words correspond in Hebrew but not Greek, they are shown in Hebrew.
- Words are given in the lexical form, if the form differs between the texts. That is generally the case and does not argue against verbal correspondence. If the words are in the same form, the correspondence is greater; so that will be indicated by listing the words in the form in

which they occur. Sometimes it is helpful to show the forms in both texts or to demonstrate that different words correspond. In such cases the words from each text are separated by a slash, with the words from Mark shown first. For example, ἐψευδομαρτύρουν/μάρτυρες indicates that the Markan text contains ἐψευδομαρτύρουν and the OT passage contains μάρτυρες.
- If words are in a string they are shown without punctuation, for example, ἀπὸ μακρόθεν. If words match but not in a string, they are separated by a semi-colon, for example, δόλος; ἀπκοτείνω.

Mark 14.1

Hos. 6.2

Mk: Ἦν δὲ τὸ πάσχα καὶ τὰ ἄζυμα <u>μετὰ δύο ἡμέρας</u>. καὶ ἐζήτουν οἱ ἀρχιερεῖς καὶ οἱ γραμματεῖς πῶς αὐτὸν ἐν δόλῳ κρατήσαντες ἀποκτείνωσιν·

𝔊: ὑγιάσει ἡμᾶς <u>μετὰ δύο ἡμέρας</u>· ἐν τῇ ἡμέρᾳ τῇ τρίτῃ ἀναστησόμεθα καὶ ζησόμεθα ἐνώπιον αὐτοῦ

Corresponding words: μετὰ δύο ἡμέρας.

This phrase exists only here in the OT. Verbal correspondence is significant. Mark also seems to allude to Hos. 6.2 in the passion predictions in Mark 8.31; 9.31; and 10.34. This is a probable allusion. See pp. 100–3 for further discussion.

2 Chron. 35.17

Mk: Ἦν δὲ <u>τὸ πάσχα</u> καὶ <u>τὰ ἄζυμα</u> μετὰ δύο <u>ἡμέρας</u>. καὶ ἐζήτουν οἱ ἀρχιερεῖς καὶ οἱ γραμματεῖς πῶς αὐτὸν ἐν δόλῳ κρατήσαντες ἀποκτείνωσιν·

𝔊: καὶ ἐποίησαν οἱ υἱοὶ Ισραηλ οἱ εὑρεθέντες <u>τὸ φασεχ</u> ἐν τῷ καιρῷ ἐκείνῳ καὶ τὴν ἑορτὴν <u>τῶν ἀζύμων</u> ἑπτὰ <u>ἡμέρας</u>.

Corresponding words: τὸ πάσχα/τὸ φασεχ; τὰ ἄζυμα/τῶν ἀζύμων; ἡμέρας; [ἑορτή with Mark 14.2].

There are significant words in common, and they do not occur together often, even though they are words that belong together in the description of the feast of Passover and Unleavened Bread. Yet thematically, 2 Chron. 35.17 describes the renewal of these feasts under Josiah, and there is little connection to the themes of the Markan passion narrative. The verbal correspondence seems accidental. See pp. 42–44 for further discussion.

Ps. 37(36).32

Mk: Ἦν δὲ τὸ πάσχα καὶ τὰ ἄζυμα μετὰ δύο ἡμέρας. καὶ <u>ἐζήτουν</u> οἱ ἀρχιερεῖς καὶ οἱ γραμματεῖς πῶς αὐτὸν ἐν δόλῳ κρατήσαντες

```
            ἀποκτείνωσιν·
𝔊:          κατανοεῖ ὁ ἁμαρτωλὸς τὸν δίκαιον
            καὶ ζητεῖ τοῦ θανατῶσαι αὐτόν
𝔐:                                              צוֹפֶה רָשָׁע לַצַּדִּיק וּמְבַקֵּשׁ לַהֲמִיתוֹ׃
```

Corresponding words: ζητέω/וּמְבַקֵּשׁ; ἀποκτείνωσιν/לַהֲמִיתוֹ.

There is a reference to Ps. 37.32 in Mark 14.55, and that passage alludes to Mark 14.1. The verbal correspondence between Mark 14.1 and Ps. 37.32 is not as strong. Still the meaning of Mark 14.1 is tied to Mark 14.55 because of the verbal correspondence of those two verses in Mark itself, and thus the meaning of Mark 14.1 is affected by the reference to Ps. 37.32 in 14.55. For more information, see pp. 104–5.

'Stealth'

Mark 14.1b states that the Jerusalem leaders wanted to seize Jesus *by stealth*, ἐν δόλῳ. A number of passages are suggested as references for this half verse. δόλος is neither common nor rare, with approximately 30 instances in the LXX, δόλιος with about 25, together, 12 times in the New Testament (in Mark, here and at 7.22). There is nothing in the verbal correspondence to tie the word in Mark to one particular OT passage and thus create a reference. Even the stronger correspondence of δόλῳ/δόλου and ἀποκτείνω with Ps. 10.7-9 is insufficient to indicate a reference, because ἀποκτείνω is very common. δόλος has greater emphasis in Ps. 52.4 because it occurs twice in the psalm, but still there seems to be no particular attention to it. Neither of these passages was prominent in the tradition, with no apparent references to Ps. 52.4 in the early Jewish or Christian tradition and only a single reference to Ps. 10.7 in Rom. 3.14. There is not sufficient evidence to indicate a reference in Mark 14.1 to any of these passages.

Often the correspondence of stealth in Mark 14.1 and these passages is used to indicate that Jesus is the suffering righteous one, beset by cunning enemies. The trouble is that stealth is just too common a theme to narrow it to one particular literary figure, and there is no cohesive suffering righteous figure to which Jesus could correspond.[1] A stronger conclusion is simply that a common way of describing unjust enemies includes stealth. Stealth is a trope, not an allusion.

Mk: Ἦν δὲ τὸ πάσχα καὶ τὰ ἄζυμα μετὰ δύο ἡμέρας. καὶ ἐζήτουν οἱ ἀρχιερεῖς καὶ οἱ γραμματεῖς πῶς αὐτὸν ἐν <u>δόλῳ</u> κρατήσαντες ἀποκτείνωσιν·

---

1   See pp. 91–94.

Ps. 10.7-9 (9.28-30)
𝔊: ²⁸ οὗ ἀρᾶς τὸ στόμα αὐτοῦ γέμει καὶ πικρίας καὶ <u>δόλου</u>, ...
²⁹ ἐγκάθηται ἐνέδρᾳ μετὰ πλουσίων
ἐν ἀποκρύφοις <u>ἀποκτεῖναι</u> ἀθῷον, ...

Corresponding words are with vv. 28-29: δόλος; ἀποκτείνω

Ps. 52(51).4
𝔊: ἀδικίαν ἐλογίσατο ἡ γλῶσσά σου·
ὡσεὶ ξυρὸν ἠκονημένον ἐποίησας <u>δόλον</u>

Corresponding word: δόλος; [δόλιος with Ps. 52.6].

Ps. 35(34).20
𝔊: ὅτι ἐμοὶ μὲν εἰρηνικὰ ἐλάλουν
καὶ ἐπ' ὀργὴν <u>δόλους</u> διελογίζοντο

Corresponding word: δόλος.

Prov. 12.6-7
𝔊: λόγοι ἀσεβῶν <u>δόλιοι</u>,
στόμα δὲ ὀρθῶν ῥύσεται αὐτούς.
Corresponding word is with Prov. 12.6: δόλῳ/δόλιοι.

Mark 14.2

There are no suggested references.

Mark 14.3

Cant. 1.12-13
Mk: Καὶ ὄντος αὐτοῦ ἐν Βηθανίᾳ ἐν τῇ οἰκίᾳ Σίμωνος τοῦ λεπροῦ, <u>κατακειμένου αὐτοῦ</u> ἦλθεν γυνὴ ἔχουσα ἀλάβαστρον <u>μύρου νάρδου</u> πιστικῆς πολυτελοῦς, συντρίψασα τὴν ἀλάβαστρον κατέχεεν αὐτοῦ τῆς κεφαλῆς.
𝔊: ¹² Ἕως οὗ ὁ βασιλεὺς ἐν ἀνακλίσει αὐτοῦ,
<u>νάρδος</u> μου ἔδωκεν ὀσμὴν αὐτοῦ.
¹³ ἀπόδεσμος τῆς στακτῆς ἀδελφιδός μου ἐμοί,
ἀνὰ μέσον τῶν μαστῶν μου αὐλισθήσεται·
𝔐: ¹² עַד־שֶׁהַמֶּלֶךְ בִּמְסִבּוֹ <u>נִרְדִּי נָתַן</u> רֵיחוֹ׃
¹³ צְרוֹר הַמֹּר דּוֹדִי לִי בֵּין שָׁדַי יָלִין׃

Corresponding words: κατακειμένου αὐτοῦ/במסבו; μύρον/מר; νάρδος/נרד.

There is significant verbal correspondence here, but the passage is not accepted as a reference. For a discussion, see pp. 44-46.

Exod. 30.25, 34
Verbal correspondence exists for only v. 25.
Mk: Καὶ ὄντος αὐτοῦ ἐν Βηθανίᾳ ἐν τῇ οἰκίᾳ Σίμωνος τοῦ λεπροῦ, κατακειμένου αὐτοῦ ἦλθεν γυνὴ ἔχουσα ἀλάβαστρον <u>μύρου</u> νάρδου πιστικῆς πολυτελοῦς, συντρίψασα τὴν ἀλάβαστρον κατέχεεν αὐτοῦ τῆς κεφαλῆς.
𝔊: ²⁵ καὶ ποιήσεις αὐτὸ ἔλαιον χρῖσμα ἅγιον, <u>μύρον</u> μυρεψικὸν τέχνῃ μυρεψοῦ· ἔλαιον χρῖσμα ἅγιον ἔσται.

Corresponding word: μύρον.

μύρον is not common. However, this verse is about the mix for sacred anointing oil. This is an accidental parallel.

Num. 12.10
Mk: Καὶ ὄντος αὐτοῦ ἐν Βηθανίᾳ ἐν τῇ οἰκίᾳ Σίμωνος τοῦ <u>λεπροῦ</u>, κατακειμένου αὐτοῦ ἦλθεν γυνὴ ἔχουσα ἀλάβαστρον μύρου νάρδου πιστικῆς πολυτελοῦς, συντρίψασα τὴν ἀλάβαστρον κατέχεεν αὐτοῦ τῆς κεφαλῆς.
𝔊: καὶ ἡ νεφέλη ἀπέστη ἀπὸ τῆς σκηνῆς, καὶ ἰδοὺ Μαριὰμ <u>λεπρῶσα</u> ὡσεὶ χιών· καὶ ἐπέβλεψεν Ἀαρὼν πρὸς Μαριάμ, καὶ ἰδοὺ <u>λεπρῶσα</u>.

Corresponding word: λεπροῦ/λεπρῶσα.

Interestingly, the scholar who suggested this stated that the words in common were both leprosy and Miriam/Mary, but there is no Mary in the Markan pericope, where the woman is anonymous. (She is named in John.) This is not a reference.

Mark 14.4-6

There are no suggested references.

Mark 14.7

Deut. 15.11
Mk: πάντοτε γὰρ τοὺς <u>πτωχοὺς</u> ἔχετε <u>μεθ'</u> ἑαυτῶν καὶ ὅταν θέλητε δύνασθε αὐτοῖς εὖ <u>ποιῆσαι</u>, ἐμὲ δὲ οὐ πάντοτε ἔχετε.

𝔊: οὐ γὰρ μὴ ἐκλίπῃ ἐνδεὴς ἀπὸ τῆς γῆς· διὰ τοῦτο ἐγώ σοι ἐντέλλομαι <u>ποιεῖν</u> τὸ ῥῆμα τοῦτο λέγων Ἀνοίγων ἀνοίξεις τὰς χεῖράς σου τῷ ἀδελφῷ σου τῷ πένητι καὶ τῷ ἐπιδεομένῳ τῷ ἐπὶ τῆς γῆς σου.

𝔐: כִּי לֹא־יֶחְדַּל אֶבְיוֹן מִקֶּרֶב הָאָרֶץ עַל־כֵּן אָנֹכִי מְצַוְּךָ לֵאמֹר פָּתֹחַ תִּפְתַּח אֶת־יָדְךָ לְאָחִיךָ לַעֲנִיֶּךָ וּלְאֶבְיֹנְךָ בְּאַרְצֶךָ׃

Corresponding words: πτωχούς/אביון; μεθ'/מקרב; ποιέω.

The corresponding words are very common. This is a thematic parallel, but the verbal correspondence is not sufficient to indicate a reference.

Mark 14.8

Isa. 53.9
Mk: ὃ ἔσχεν <u>ἐποίησεν</u>· προέλαβεν μυρίσαι τὸ σῶμά μου εἰς τὸν <u>ἐνταφιασμόν</u>.
𝔊: καὶ δώσω τοὺς πονηροὺς ἀντὶ τῆς <u>ταφῆς</u> αὐτοῦ καὶ τοὺς πλουσίους ἀντὶ τοῦ θανάτου αὐτοῦ· ὅτι ἀνομίαν οὐκ <u>ἐποίησεν</u>, οὐδὲ εὑρέθη δόλος ἐν τῷ στόματι αὐτοῦ.

Corresponding words: ἐποίησεν; ἐνταφιασμόν/ταφῆς.

ποιέω is very common. ἐνταφιασμός (*burial*) occurs only twice in NT, here in Mark and in the parallel in John 12.7, and never in the LXX. ταφή/τάφος is neither especially common nor rare, occurring about 80 times in the LXX. There is nothing in this passage in Mark to point to one ταφή passage over another, and there is no clear reference to any passage from Isaiah 53 in Mark. This is not a reference.

Ps. 41(40).2, 6, 8, 10
There are no significant words in common. This is not a reference.

Mark 14.9

There are no suggested references.

Mark 14.10

Isa. 53.6, 12
Mk: Καὶ Ἰούδας Ἰσκαριὼθ ὁ εἷς τῶν δώδεκα ἀπῆλθεν πρὸς τοὺς ἀρχιερεῖς ἵνα αὐτὸν <u>παραδοῖ αὐτοῖς</u>.
𝔊: ⁶πάντες ὡς πρόβατα ἐπλανήθημεν, ἄνθρωπος τῇ ὁδῷ αὐτοῦ

ἐπλανήθη· καὶ κύριος <u>παρέδωκεν αὐτὸν</u> ταῖς ἁμαρτίαις ἡμῶν.
¹² διὰ τοῦτο αὐτὸς κληρονομήσει πολλοὺς καὶ τῶν ἰσχυρῶν
μεριεῖ σκῦλα, ἀνθ᾽ ὧν <u>παρεδόθη</u> εἰς θάνατον ἡ ψυχὴ αὐτοῦ, καὶ ἐν
τοῖς ἀνόμοις ἐλογίσθη· καὶ αὐτὸς ἁμαρτίας πολλῶν ἀνήνεγκε
καὶ διὰ τὰς ἁμαρτίας <u>αὐτῶν παρεδόθη</u>.

Corresponding words: παραδίδωμι αὐτός.

The two words come in succession in all verses. However, αὐτός is so common, it adds little to verbal correspondence. Since παραδίδωμι is not at all rare, occurring more than 250 times, verbal correspondence is not sufficient for a reference. See pp. 76–87 for further discussion.

Daniel 6

The text proposed as a reference is too long to print here. There is very little verbal correspondence: ἀπῆλθεν corresponds with ἀπῆλθεν (Dan. 6.19 θ´) and קריבו (Dan. 6.13). Clearly this is not a reference. This is a thematic parallel to the passion narrative, where Daniel's enemies, jealous of his success, hand him over to destruction. The foreign ruler makes an attempt to rescue him but is not successful. Ultimately Daniel and Jesus are vindicated. Nevertheless, it is difficult to see in this passage a parallel to Judas, one of Jesus' disciples, betraying him to those jealous enemies, as is the case in Mark 14.10.

Others

Pss. 41(40).10; 55(54).13-16; 109(108).4-5, 8: There are no significant words in common. There is no reference to these passages.

Mark 14.11

Zech. 11.12-13

Mk: οἱ δὲ ἀκούσαντες ἐχάρησαν καὶ ἐπηγγείλαντο αὐτῷ <u>ἀργύριον</u>
<u>δοῦναι</u>. καὶ ἐζήτει πῶς αὐτὸν εὐκαίρως παραδοῖ.

𝔊: ¹² καὶ ἐρῶ πρὸς αὐτούς Εἰ καλὸν ἐνώπιον ὑμῶν ἐστι, <u>δότε</u> τὸν
μισθόν μου ἢ ἀπείπασθε· καὶ ἔστησαν τὸν μισθόν μου τριάκοντα
<u>ἀργυροῦς</u>. ¹³ καὶ εἶπε κύριος πρός με Κάθες αὐτοὺς εἰς τὸ
χωνευτήριον, καὶ σκέψομαι εἰ δόκιμόν ἐστιν, ὃν τρόπον
ἐδοκιμάσθην ὑπὲρ αὐτῶν. καὶ ἔλαβον τοὺς τριάκοντα <u>ἀργυροῦς</u>
καὶ ἐνέβαλον αὐτοὺς εἰς τὸν οἶκον κυρίου εἰς τὸ χωνευτήριον.

Corresponding words: ἀργύριον/ἀργυροῦς; δίδωμι.

Both δίδωμι and ἀργύριον are extremely common. ἀργύρεος is relatively common. This seems to be a reference in Matt. 26.15, but not in Mark.

Mark 14.12

Exod. 12.1-6, 14-20
Only verses with substantial verbal correspondence are shown.
Mk: Καὶ τῇ <u>πρώτῃ ἡμέρᾳ</u> τῶν <u>ἀζύμων</u>, ὅτε τὸ <u>πάσχα</u> ἔθυον, λέγουσιν αὐτῷ οἱ μαθηταὶ αὐτοῦ· ποῦ θέλεις ἀπελθόντες ἑτοιμάσωμεν ἵνα <u>φάγῃς</u> τὸ <u>πάσχα</u>;
𝔊: ¹⁵ἑπτὰ <u>ἡμέρας ἄζυμα ἔδεσθε</u>, ἀπὸ δὲ τῆς <u>ἡμέρας</u> τῆς <u>πρώτης</u> ἀφανιεῖτε ζύμην ἐκ τῶν οἰκιῶν ὑμῶν· πᾶς, ὃς ἂν <u>φάγῃ</u> ζύμην, ἐξολεθρευθήσεται ἡ ψυχὴ ἐκείνη ἐξ Ἰσραήλ, ἀπὸ τῆς <u>ἡμέρας</u> τῆς <u>πρώτης</u> ἕως τῆς <u>ἡμέρας</u> τῆς ἑβδόμης.
¹⁸ἐναρχομένου τῇ τεσσαρεσκαιδεκάτῃ <u>ἡμέρᾳ</u> τοῦ μηνὸς τοῦ <u>πρώτου</u> ἀφ' ἑσπέρας <u>ἔδεσθε ἄζυμα</u> ἕως <u>ἡμέρας</u> μιᾶς καὶ εἰκάδος τοῦ μηνὸς ἕως ἑσπέρας.

Corresponding words: πρῶτος (vv. 2; 15, 16, 18); ἡμέρα (vv. 14-19; v. 6 in Hebrew); ἄζυμος (vv. 15, 18, 20); πάσχα (v. 11, though not suggested); λέγω (vv. 1, 3); ἐσθίω (vv. 15, 18-20).

Exodus 12.1-6, 14-20 was suggested as a reference for Mark 14.12, which is a rather large section to suggest for an allusion. While many words of Mark 14.12 correspond to words in Exod. 12.1-6, 14-20, they are mainly very common words: *first, day, unleavened, Passover, speak,* and *eat*. None are in a string, and they are distributed over many verses. The verbal correspondence is more concentrated in vv. 15 and 18, shown above. Still, there is no string of corresponding words.

Exodus 12.15-16 has great prominence in the Jewish tradition, but mainly in halakah about keeping the Passover and what is permitted on feast days or the Sabbath.[2] Interestingly, this passage is also used by Tertullian (*Marc.* 4.12.10) to discuss work on the Sabbath, as well. Such issues are certainly within the interests of the Gospel of Mark, but not within the focus of the passion narrative, per se.

Mark 14.12 has roughly equal verbal correspondence with several other texts, including Ezek. 45.21.[3] The verbal correspondence is accidental, having to do with these particular words being associated with these holidays. Exodus 12.1-20 is a background text for any passage dealing with Passover and the feast of Unleavened Bread, not a reference.

Deut. 16.2
Mk: Καὶ τῇ πρώτῃ ἡμέρᾳ τῶν ἀζύμων, ὅτε <u>τὸ πάσχα ἔθυον</u>, λέγουσιν αὐτῷ οἱ μαθηταὶ αὐτοῦ· ... ἵνα φάγῃς τὸ πάσχα;

---

2 References occur at, e.g., Philo, *Spec.* 2.150-161; *Mek. Pis.* 10.4; *Sifre Re'eh* 134; *b. Pesaḥ.* 4b.
3 See pp. 42–44.

𝔊 : καὶ <u>θύσεις τὸ πάσχα</u> κυρίῳ τῷ θεῷ σου πρόβατα καὶ βόας ἐν τῷ τόπῳ, ᾧ ἂν ἐκλέξηται κύριος ὁ θεός σου αὐτὸν ἐπικληθῆναι τὸ ὄνομα αὐτοῦ ἐκεῖ.

Corresponding words: τὸ πάσχα; θύω.

Verbal correspondence is supported slightly by the correspondence in Deut. 16.3 of ἡμέρα, ἄζυμος, and φαγεῖν, again the words we tend to see associated with descriptions of these holidays.

This is a significant thematic parallel. The passage in Deuteronomy instructs Israel to eat the Passover in the place the Lord chooses. This, of course, is what the passage is about in Mark. (Jesus as 'Lord' would have to be taken from the similar 'you will find' pericope of the colt, cf. Mark 11.3). Nevertheless, if a reference were intended Mark could easily have made the verbal correspondence stronger. In particular, he could have used κύριος (*Lord*), as he did in the first 'you will find' story or the word ἐκλέγω for *choose*, etc. This is a thematic parallel, not a reference.

Lam. 2.21
Mk: Καὶ τῇ πρώτῃ <u>ἡμέρᾳ</u> τῶν ἀζύμων ...
𝔊 : Ἐκοιμήθησαν εἰς γῆν ἐξόδων παιδάριον καὶ πρεσβύτης· παρθένοι μου καὶ νεανίσκοι μου ἔπεσαν ἐν ῥομφαίᾳ· ἀπέκτεινας ἐν <u>ἡμέρᾳ</u> ὀργῆς σου, ἐμαγείρευσας, οὐκ ἐφείσω.

Corresponding word: ἡμέρα.
ἡμέρα is extremely common. This is not a reference.

Isa. 53.7
There are no significant words in common. This is not a reference.

Mark 14.12-16

1 Sam. 10.1-10
Most verbal correspondence occurs in 1 Sam. 10.5 and Mark 14.13.

Mk: ¹³ καὶ ἀποστέλλει δύο τῶν μαθητῶν αὐτοῦ καὶ <u>λέγει</u> αὐτοῖς· ὑπάγετε <u>εἰς τὴν πόλιν, καὶ ἀπαντήσει</u> ὑμῖν ἄνθρωπος κεράμιον ὕδατος βαστάζων· ἀκολουθήσατε αὐτῷ
𝔊 : ⁵ καὶ μετὰ ταῦτα <u>εἰσελεύσῃ</u> εἰς τὸν βουνὸν τοῦ θεοῦ, οὗ ἐστιν <u>ἐκεῖ</u> τὸ ἀνάστημα τῶν ἀλλοφύλων, ἐκεῖ Νασιβ ὁ ἀλλόφυλος· καὶ ἔσται ὡς ἂν <u>εἰσέλθητε ἐκεῖ εἰς τὴν πόλιν, καὶ ἀπαντήσεις</u> χορῷ προφητῶν καταβαινόντων ἐκ τῆς Βαμα, καὶ ἔμπροσθεν αὐτῶν νάβλα καὶ τύμπανον καὶ αὐλὸς καὶ κινύρα, καὶ αὐτοὶ προφητεύοντες·

Corresponding words: ἡμέρα (Mark 14.12; 1 Sam. 10.8, 9); ἔθυον/θυσίας (Mark 14.12; 1 Sam. 10.8); λέγω (Mark 14.12-14, 16; 1 Sam. 10.2); ἀπέρχομαι (Mark 14.12; 1 Sam. 10.2, 3, 9); εἰς τὴν πόλιν καὶ ἀπαντάω (Mark 14.13; 1 Sam. 10.5; εἰς τὴν πόλιν also with Mark 14.16); εἰσέρχομαι (Mark 14.14; 1 Sam. 10.5); μέγας (Mark 14.15; 1 Sam. 10.2); ἐκεῖ (Mark 14.15; 1 Sam. 10.3, 5); ἔρχομαι (Mark 14.16; 1 Sam. 10.8-10); εὑρίσκω (Mark 14.16; 1 Sam. 10.2-3, 7).

There are many corresponding words, most of them quite common, though ἀπαντάω is not particularly so, occurring about 50 times in the LXX, and it is part of a string: εἰς τὴν πόλιν καὶ ἀπαντάω. So there is genuine verbal correspondence between Mark 14.13 and 1 Sam. 10.5, shown above.

The passage has very little prominence in the tradition, and one must ask whether this verbal correspondence is both intended and sufficient for a reader to think of it. A great deal more verbal correspondence would have been possible. For example, why not have the man carry a wine skin instead of ceramic jar? Why not use the same verb for carry? Why not use the words of 1 Sam. 10.9, regarding the fulfilment of the prophecy? It is possible that 1 Sam. 10.1-10 influenced the Markan account; a reference is also possible but does not seem probable.

Mark 14.14

Jer. 14.8
Mk: καὶ ὅπου ἐὰν εἰσέλθῃ εἴπατε τῷ οἰκοδεσπότῃ ὅτι ὁ διδάσκαλος λέγει· ποῦ ἐστιν τὸ <u>κατάλυμά</u> μου ὅπου τὸ πάσχα μετὰ τῶν μαθητῶν μου φάγω;
𝔊 : ὑπομονὴ Ισραηλ, κύριε, καὶ σῴζεις ἐν καιρῷ κακῶν· ἵνα τί ἐγενήθης ὡσεὶ πάροικος ἐπὶ τῆς γῆς καὶ ὡς αὐτόχθων ἐκκλίνων εἰς <u>κατάλυμα</u>;

Corresponding word: κατάλυμα.

κατάλυμα is relatively rare, occurring about 13 times in the LXX. However, it has no association with any concept. It is simply a room, used for any purpose; there is no reason to think of it as a special word, pointing to a particular verse or even concept. Jeremiah 14.8 is not a particularly good thematic fit. A reference here is unlikely.

Mark 14.15-17

For Mark 14.15-16, see 'Mark 14.12-16' above. For Mark 14.17, there are no suggested references.

Mark 14.18

Ps. 41(40).10
Mk: καὶ ἀνακειμένων αὐτῶν καὶ ἐσθιόντων ὁ Ἰησοῦς εἶπεν· ἀμὴν λέγω ὑμῖν ὅτι εἷς ἐξ ὑμῶν παραδώσει με <u>ὁ ἐσθίων</u> μετ᾽ <u>ἐμοῦ</u>.
𝔊 : καὶ γὰρ ὁ ἄνθρωπος τῆς εἰρήνης μου, ἐφ᾽ ὃν ἤλπισα, <u>ὁ ἐσθίων</u> ἄρτους <u>μου</u>, ἐμεγάλυνεν ἐπ᾽ ἐμὲ πτερνισμόν·

Corresponding words: ὁ ἐσθίων [μετ᾽/ἄρτους] (ἐ)μου.
  The verbal correspondence is not particularly strong. However, the verse gets some attention in the tradition, and thus could be more easily spotted by the reader. Still, if Mark had intended this as a reference, it would have been easy to strengthen verbal correspondence. This is probably not an allusion. See p. 91 for more discussion.

Mark 14.19

There are no suggested references.

Mark 14.20

Ruth 2.14
Mk: ὁ δὲ <u>εἶπεν αὐτοῖς</u>· εἷς τῶν δώδεκα, ὁ <u>ἐμβαπτόμενος</u> μετ᾽ ἐμοῦ εἰς τὸ τρύβλιον.
𝔊 : καὶ <u>εἶπεν αὐτῇ</u> Βόος Ἤδη ὥρα τοῦ φαγεῖν πρόσελθε ὧδε καὶ φάγεσαι τῶν ἄρτων καὶ <u>βάψεις</u> τὸν ψωμόν σου ἐν τῷ ὄξει. καὶ ἐκάθισεν Ῥοὺθ ἐκ πλαγίων τῶν θεριζόντων, καὶ ἐβούνισεν αὐτῇ Βόος ἄλφιτον, καὶ ἔφαγεν καὶ ἐνεπλήσθη καὶ κατέλιπεν.
𝔐 : וַיֹּאמֶר לָה בֹעַז לְעֵת הָאֹכֶל גֹּשִׁי הֲלֹם וְאָכַלְתְּ מִן־הַלֶּחֶם וְטָבַלְתְּ פִּתֵּךְ בַּחֹמֶץ ...

Corresponding words: εἶπεν αὐτός; ἐμβαπτόμενος/βάψεις/טבל.
  Verbal correspondence is not strong, consisting of the common phrase 'he said to them/her' and 'dip'. The words are not an exact match in Greek, and more verbal correspondence could have been achieved with 'dip in the vinegar' or something similar. In addition, there is little thematic correspondence between Boaz prompting Ruth to dip in the vinegar and Jesus identifying his betrayer as someone who dips in the dish with him. A reference here is unlikely.

Ps. 41(40).10
There are no significant words in common. This is not a reference.

Mark 14.21

Isa. 53.12
Mk: ὅτι ὁ μὲν υἱὸς τοῦ ἀνθρώπου ὑπάγει καθὼς γέγραπται περὶ αὐτοῦ, οὐαὶ δὲ τῷ ἀνθρώπῳ ἐκείνῳ δι' οὗ ὁ υἱὸς τοῦ ἀνθρώπου <u>παραδίδοται</u>· καλὸν αὐτῷ εἰ οὐκ ἐγεννήθη ὁ ἄνθρωπος ἐκεῖνος.

𝔊 : διὰ τοῦτο αὐτὸς κληρονομήσει πολλοὺς καὶ τῶν ἰσχυρῶν μεριεῖ σκῦλα, ἀνθ' ὧν <u>παρεδόθη</u> εἰς θάνατον ἡ ψυχὴ αὐτοῦ, καὶ ἐν τοῖς ἀνόμοις ἐλογίσθη· καὶ αὐτὸς ἁμαρτίας πολλῶν ἀνήνεγκε καὶ διὰ τὰς ἁμαρτίας αὐτῶν <u>παρεδόθη</u>.

Corresponding word: παραδίδωμι.

παραδίδωμι occurs over 250 times and is too common to draw the reader to this verse. See pp. 76–87 for further discussion. This is not a reference.

Mark 14.22

There are no suggested references.

Mark 14.23

Ps. 75(74).9
Mk: καὶ <u>λαβὼν</u> <u>ποτήριον</u> εὐχαριστήσας ἔδωκεν αὐτοῖς, καὶ <u>ἔπιον</u> ἐξ αὐτοῦ <u>πάντες</u>.

𝔊 : ὅτι <u>ποτήριον</u> ἐν χειρὶ κυρίου
οἴνου ἀκράτου πλῆρες κεράσματος,
καὶ ἔκλινεν ἐκ τούτου εἰς τοῦτο,
πλὴν ὁ τρυγίας αὐτοῦ οὐκ ἐξεκενώθη,
<u>πίονται</u> <u>πάντες</u> οἱ ἁμαρτωλοὶ τῆς γῆς.

Corresponding words: ποτήριον; πίνω; πάντες.

The corresponding words are not in succession. While πίνω and πᾶς are very common, ποτήριον is not particularly so, occurring about 35 times in the LXX, still not rare enough to point to a single verse. The passages have a very different theme: Mark speaks of drinking the cup of the Eucharist which, whatever it meant precisely, was positive. Psalm 75.9 speaks of drinking to the dregs the cup of God's wrath. A reference is not likely here.

Ps. 116.13 (115.4)
Mk: καὶ <u>λαβὼν</u> <u>ποτήριον</u> εὐχαριστήσας ἔδωκεν αὐτοῖς, καὶ ἔπιον ἐξ αὐτοῦ πάντες.

𝔊 : <u>ποτήριον</u> σωτηρίου <u>λήμψομαι</u>
καὶ τὸ ὄνομα κυρίου ἐπικαλέσομαι.

Corresponding words: λαμβάνω; ποτήριον.

λαμβάνω is very common; ποτήριον is less common but not rare. The words are not in sequence. This is not a reference.

Lam. 4.21
Mk: καὶ λαβὼν <u>ποτήριον</u> εὐχαριστήσας ἔδωκεν αὐτοῖς, καὶ ἔπιον ἐξ αὐτοῦ πάντες.
𝔊 : Χαῖρε καὶ εὐφραίνου, θύγατερ Ἰδουμαίας ἡ κατοικοῦσα ἐπὶ τῆς γῆς· καί γε ἐπὶ σὲ διελεύσεται <u>ποτήριον</u> κυρίου, μεθυσθήσῃ καὶ ἀποχεεῖς.

Corresponding word: ποτήριον.

ποτήριον occurs about 35 times in the LXX and is not rare enough to point to a single verse. This is not a reference.

Mark 14.24

Exod. 24.8
Mk: <u>καὶ εἶπεν</u> αὐτοῖς· τοῦτό ἐστιν <u>τὸ αἷμά</u> μου <u>τῆς διαθήκης</u> τὸ ἐκχυννόμενον ὑπὲρ πολλῶν.
𝔊 : λαβὼν δὲ Μωυσῆς τὸ αἷμα κατεσκέδασεν τοῦ λαοῦ <u>καὶ εἶπεν</u> Ἰδοὺ <u>τὸ αἷμα τῆς διαθήκης</u>, ἧς διέθετο κύριος πρὸς ὑμᾶς περὶ πάντων τῶν λόγων τούτων.

Corresponding words: καὶ εἶπεν; τὸ αἷμα [μου] τῆς διαθήκης. The use of λαβών in Mark 14.23 and Exod. 24.8 adds slightly to verbal correspondence.

The corresponding words are common, but the string 'blood of the covenant' is significant. This is probably a reference. See p. 103 for further discussion.

Zech. 9.11
Mk: καὶ εἶπεν αὐτοῖς· τοῦτό ἐστιν τὸ <u>αἷμά</u> μου τῆς <u>διαθήκης</u> τὸ ἐκχυννόμενον ὑπὲρ πολλῶν.
𝔊 : καὶ σὺ ἐν <u>αἵματι διαθήκης</u> ἐξαπέστειλας δεσμίους σου ἐκ λάκκου οὐκ ἔχοντος ὕδωρ.
𝔐 : גַּם־אַתְּ בְּדַם־<u>בְּרִיתֵךְ</u> שִׁלַּחְתִּי אֲסִירַיִךְ מִבּוֹר אֵין מַיִם בּוֹ׃

Corresponding words: αἷμα [μου τῆς] διαθήκης.

Verbal correspondence exists in two words which are nearly sequential. The Hebrew has 'the blood of *your* covenant' (בריתך), rather than 'of *my* covenant' as it is sometimes translated in English (e.g., the NRSV, NASB, and NIV). The Greek says 'blood of [a] covenant'.

Neither of Mark's first editors appear to have seen Zech. 9.11. Matthew 26.28 is not edited towards it, which is significant, since Matthew has a clear affinity for Zechariah.⁴ Neither Luke 22.20 nor 1 Cor. 11.25 are closer to Zech. 9.11. There is not much use of Zech. 9.11 in either Christian or Jewish tradition. Exodus 24.8 is to be preferred.

Isa. 53.12
Mk: καὶ εἶπεν αὐτοῖς· τοῦτό ἐστιν τὸ αἷμά μου τῆς διαθήκης τὸ <u>ἐκχυννόμενον</u> ὑπὲρ <u>πολλῶν</u>.
𝔊: διὰ τοῦτο αὐτὸς κληρονομήσει <u>πολλοὺς</u> καὶ τῶν ἰσχυρῶν μεριεῖ σκῦλα, ἀνθ᾽ ὧν παρεδόθη εἰς θάνατον ἡ ψυχὴ αὐτοῦ, καὶ ἐν τοῖς ἀνόμοις ἐλογίσθη· καὶ αὐτὸς ἁμαρτίας <u>πολλῶν</u> ἀνήνεγκε καὶ διὰ τὰς ἁμαρτίας αὐτῶν παρεδόθη.
𝔐: לָכֵן אֲחַלֶּק־לוֹ בָרַבִּים וְאֶת־עֲצוּמִים יְחַלֵּק שָׁלָל
תַּחַת אֲשֶׁר הֶ<u>עֱרָה</u> לַמָּוֶת נַפְשׁוֹ וְאֶת־פֹּשְׁעִים נִמְנָה
וְהוּא חֵטְא־<u>רַבִּים</u> נָשָׂא וְלַפֹּשְׁעִים יַפְגִּיעַ:

Corresponding words: ἐκχυννόμενον/הֶעֱרָה; πολύς.

Some Markan MSS have εις αφεσιν αμαρτιων at the end of the verse. This would provide an additional match with ἁμαρτίας in Isa. 53.11 and 12 (where there are two occurrences). However, this plus in Mark is mostly likely not original, but a result of harmonizing with the parallel verse in Matt. 26.28.⁵ See pp. 76–87 for further discussion of suggested references to Isaiah 53. This is not a reference.

Gen. 15.10, 17-18
Verbal correspondence exists only with v. 18

Mk: καὶ <u>εἶπεν</u> αὐτοῖς· τοῦτό ἐστιν τὸ αἷμά μου τῆς <u>διαθήκης</u> τὸ ἐκχυννόμενον ὑπὲρ πολλῶν.
𝔊: ¹⁸ἐν τῇ ἡμέρᾳ ἐκείνῃ διέθετο κύριος τῷ Ἀβραμ <u>διαθήκην</u> <u>λέγων</u> Τῷ σπέρματί σου δώσω τὴν γῆν ταύτην ἀπὸ τοῦ ποταμοῦ Αἰγύπτου ἕως τοῦ ποταμοῦ τοῦ μεγάλου, ποταμοῦ Εὐφράτου

Corresponding words: λέγω; διαθήκη.

The corresponding words are very common and not in sequence. This is not a reference.

---

4 See p. 98, n. 72 and pp. 122–23, n. 29.
5 It does not even warrant mention in Bruce M. Metzger, *A Textual Commentary on the Greek New Testament: A Companion Volume to the United Bible Societies' Greek New Testament (fourth revised edition)* (2nd edn; Stuttgart: Deutsche Bibelgesellschaft, 1994), p. 95.

Jer. 31(38).31
Mk: καὶ εἶπεν αὐτοῖς· τοῦτό ἐστιν τὸ αἷμά μου τῆς <u>διαθήκης</u> τὸ ἐκχυννόμενον ὑπὲρ πολλῶν.
𝕲 : Ἰδοὺ ἡμέραι ἔρχονται, φησὶ κύριος, καὶ διαθήσομαι τῷ οἴκῳ Ισραηλ καὶ τῷ οἴκῳ Ιουδα <u>διαθήκην</u> καινήν

Corresponding word: διαθήκη.

Many Markan MSS have της καινης διαθηκης. However, this is not considered original.[6] Without the variant, the verbal correspondence is very weak, the single corresponding word being very common.

Matthew 26.28 is not edited toward this verse. The tradition found in Luke and 1 Corinthians are closer, with 'new covenant in my blood' (Luke 22.20: ἡ καινὴ διαθήκη ἐν τῷ αἵματί μου; 1 Cor. 11.25: ἡ καινὴ διαθήκη ἐστὶν ἐν τῷ ἐμῷ αἵματι), corresponding to 'new covenant' (διαθήκην καινήν) in Jer. 31.31.

While the Jewish tradition on Jer. 31.31 is weak, the Christian tradition is rather strong. Hebrews 8.8-12 quotes Jer. 31.31, saying that a new covenant was necessary. Justin, Irenaeus, and Tertullian use the text to indicate the creation of a new covenant for Christians, differing from the Sinai covenant.[7] This use of Jer. 31.31 supports the influence, at least, of Jer. 31.31 on the Christian tradition, which may be reflected in the 'new covenant' wording found in 1 Cor. 11.25 and Luke 22.20. It is possible, though far from certain, that Jer. 31.31 exerted an influence on the tradition of the cup word per se and thus on Mark 14.24. However, there is no reference to Jer. 31.31 in Mark.

Lam. 5.9
There are no significant words in common. This is not a reference.

Mark 14.25

Isa. 65.13
Mk: ἀμὴν <u>λέγω</u> ὑμῖν ὅτι οὐκέτι οὐ μὴ <u>πίω</u> ἐκ τοῦ γενήματος τῆς ἀμπέλου ἕως τῆς ἡμέρας ἐκείνης ὅταν αὐτὸ <u>πίνω</u> καινὸν ἐν τῇ βασιλείᾳ τοῦ θεοῦ.
𝕲 : Διὰ τοῦτο τάδε <u>λέγει</u> κύριος Ἰδοὺ οἱ δουλεύοντές μοι φάγονται, ὑμεῖς δὲ πεινάσετε· ἰδοὺ οἱ δουλεύοντές μοι <u>πίονται</u>, ὑμεῖς δὲ διψήσετε· ἰδοὺ οἱ δουλεύοντές μοι εὐφρανθήσονται, ὑμεῖς δὲ αἰσχυνθήσεσθε·

---

6   See Metzger, *Textual Commentary*, p. 95.
7   E.g., *Dial.* 11.3; *Dem.* 90; *Marc.* 4.1.6.

Corresponding words: λέγω; πίνω.
The corresponding words are common and not in sequence. This is not a reference.

Isa. 25.6
Mk: ἀμὴν λέγω ὑμῖν ὅτι οὐκέτι οὐ μὴ <u>πίω</u> ἐκ τοῦ γενήματος τῆς ἀμπέλου ἕως τῆς ἡμέρας ἐκείνης ὅταν αὐτὸ <u>πίνω</u> καινὸν ἐν τῇ βασιλείᾳ τοῦ θεοῦ.
𝔊 : καὶ ποιήσει κύριος σαβαωθ πᾶσι τοῖς ἔθνεσιν ἐπὶ τὸ ὄρος τοῦτο. <u>πίονται</u> εὐφροσύνην, <u>πίονται</u> οἶνον

Corresponding word: πίνω.
This is an interesting parallel regarding the eschatological banquet for all peoples, but πίνω is too common for a reference.

Isa. 62.9
Mk: ἀμὴν λέγω ὑμῖν ὅτι οὐκέτι οὐ μὴ <u>πίω</u> ἐκ τοῦ γενήματος τῆς ἀμπέλου ἕως τῆς ἡμέρας ἐκείνης ὅταν αὐτὸ <u>πίνω</u> καινὸν ἐν τῇ βασιλείᾳ τοῦ θεοῦ.
𝔊 : ἀλλ' ἢ οἱ συνάγοντες φάγονται αὐτὰ καὶ αἰνέσουσι κύριον, καὶ οἱ συνάγοντες <u>πίονται</u> αὐτὰ ἐν ταῖς ἐπαύλεσι ταῖς ἁγίαις μου.

Corresponding word: πίνω.
πίνω is very common. This is not a reference.

Mark 14.26

There are no suggested references.

Mark 14.27

Zech. 13.7
Mk: καὶ λέγει αὐτοῖς ὁ Ἰησοῦς ὅτι πάντες σκανδαλισθήσεσθε, ὅτι γέγραπται·
<u>πατάξω τὸν ποιμένα, καὶ τὰ πρόβατα</u> διασκορπισθήσονται.
𝔊 : ...<u>πατάξατε τοὺς ποιμένας</u> καὶ ἐκσπάσατε <u>τὰ πρόβατα</u> ...

Corresponding words: πατάσσω ὁ ποιμήν καὶ ... τὰ πρόβατα [διασκορπισθήσονται].
The differences between the Mark's text and 𝔊^{ed} are found in LXX variants or in the MT, including the most significant difference, διασκορπισθησονται. Mark 14.27 is an explicit quotation of Zech. 13.7. See p. 206.

2 Chron. 18.16

Mk: καὶ <u>λέγει</u> αὐτοῖς ὁ Ἰησοῦς ὅτι πάντες σκανδαλισθήσεσθε, ὅτι γέγραπται·
πατάξω τὸν <u>ποιμένα</u>, καὶ τὰ <u>πρόβατα</u> διασκορπισθήσονται.

𝔊: καὶ <u>εἶπεν</u> Εἶδον τὸν Ισραηλ διεσπαρμένους ἐν τοῖς ὄρεσιν ὡς <u>πρόβατα</u> οἷς οὐκ ἔστιν <u>ποιμήν</u>, καὶ <u>εἶπεν</u> κύριος Οὐκ ἔχουσιν ἡγούμενον, ἀναστρεφέτωσαν ἕκαστος εἰς τὸν οἶκον αὐτοῦ ἐν εἰρήνῃ.

Corresponding words: λεγώ; ποιμήν; πρόβατα.
See discussion of Mark 14.27 and Num. 27.17 below.

Num. 27.17

Mk: καὶ λέγει αὐτοῖς ὁ Ἰησοῦς ὅτι πάντες σκανδαλισθήσεσθε, ὅτι γέγραπται·
πατάξω τὸν <u>ποιμένα</u>, καὶ τὰ <u>πρόβατα</u> διασκορπισθήσονται.

𝔊: ὅστις ἐξελεύσεται πρὸ προσώπου αὐτῶν καὶ ὅστις εἰσελεύσεται πρὸ προσώπου αὐτῶν, καὶ ὅστις ἐξάξει αὐτοὺς καὶ ὅστις εἰσάξει αὐτούς, καὶ οὐκ ἔσται ἡ συναγωγὴ κυρίου ὡσεὶ <u>πρόβατα</u>, οἷς οὐκ ἔστιν <u>ποιμήν</u>.

Corresponding words: ποιμήν; πρόβατα.
This is not a reference here, because the correspondence to Zech. 13.7 is so thorough, and there is nothing to point to a reference to Num. 27.17 in addition. Interestingly, however, Mark 6.34 is an exact translation of the MT of Num. 27.17. There are also thematic links. In Num. 27.17-18, Moses prays for a leader so that the people are not like sheep without a shepherd, and God responds by appointing Joshua. Still, one must note that the metaphor of sheep without a shepherd also occurs in 1 Kgs 22.17//2 Chron. 18.16; Ezek. 34.5; and Jdt. 11.19. So a reference at Mark 6.34 to Num. 27.17 (or any of these other passages) is not certain.

Jdt. 11.19

Mk: καὶ λέγει αὐτοῖς ὁ Ἰησοῦς ὅτι πάντες σκανδαλισθήσεσθε, ὅτι γέγραπται·
πατάξω τὸν <u>ποιμένα</u>, καὶ τὰ <u>πρόβατα</u> διασκορπισθήσονται.

𝔊: καὶ ἄξω σε διὰ μέσου τῆς Ἰουδαίας ἕως τοῦ ἐλθεῖν ἀπέναντι Ἰερουσαλὴμ καὶ θήσω τὸν δίφρον σου ἐν μέσῳ αὐτῆς, καὶ ἄξεις αὐτοὺς ὡς <u>πρόβατα</u>, οἷς οὐκ ἔστιν <u>ποιμήν</u>, καὶ οὐ γρύξει κύων τῇ γλώσσῃ αὐτοῦ ἀπέναντί σου· ὅτι ταῦτα ἐλαλήθη μοι κατὰ πρόγνωσίν μου καὶ ἀπηγγέλη μοι, καὶ ἀπεστάλην ἀπαγγεῖλαί σοι.

Corresponding words: ποιμήν; πρόβατα.
This is not a reference. See discussion of Mark 14.27 and Num. 27.17 above.

Ezek. 34.5
Mk: καὶ λέγει αὐτοῖς ὁ Ἰησοῦς ὅτι πάντες σκανδαλισθήσεσθε, ὅτι γέγραπται·
πατάξω τὸν <u>ποιμένα</u>, καὶ τὰ <u>πρόβατα</u> διασκορπισθήσονται.
𝕲: καὶ διεσπάρη τὰ <u>πρόβατά</u> μου διὰ τὸ μὴ εἶναι <u>ποιμένας</u> καὶ ἐγενήθη εἰς κατάβρωμα πᾶσι τοῖς θηρίοις τοῦ ἀγροῦ·

Corresponding words: ποιμήν, πρόβατα.
This is not a reference. See discussion of Mark 14.27 and Num. 27.17 above.

1 Kgs 22.17
Mk: καὶ λέγει αὐτοῖς ὁ Ἰησοῦς ὅτι πάντες σκανδαλισθήσεσθε, ὅτι γέγραπται·
πατάξω τὸν <u>ποιμένα</u>, καὶ τὰ πρόβατα διασκορπισθήσονται.
𝕲: καὶ εἶπεν Μιχαιας Οὐχ οὕτως· ἑώρακα πάντα τὸν Ισραηλ διεσπαρμένον ἐν τοῖς ὄρεσιν ὡς ποίμνιον, ᾧ οὐκ ἔστιν <u>ποιμήν</u>, καὶ εἶπεν κύριος Οὐ κύριος τούτοις, ἀναστρεφέτω ἕκαστος εἰς τὸν οἶκον αὐτοῦ ἐν εἰρήνῃ.

Corresponding word: ποιμήν.
This is not a reference. See discussion of Mark 14.27 and Num. 27.17 above.

Ps. 119(118).165
Mk: καὶ λέγει αὐτοῖς ὁ Ἰησοῦς ὅτι πάντες <u>σκανδαλισθήσεσθε</u>, ὅτι γέγραπται·
πατάξω τὸν ποιμένα, καὶ τὰ πρόβατα διασκορπισθήσονται.
𝕲: εἰρήνη πολλὴ τοῖς ἀγαπῶσιν τὸν νόμον σου,
καὶ οὐκ ἔστιν αὐτοῖς <u>σκάνδαλον</u>.

Corresponding words: σκανδαλισθήσεσθε/σκάνδαλον.
These words are uncommon in the LXX, but σκανδαλίζω is not rare in the NT. It occurs about 30 times, eight of those in Mark. Verbal correspondence is not sufficient for a reference.

Mark 14.28

Zech. 13.8-9
Verbal correspondence exists only with v. 9:

Mk: ἀλλὰ μετὰ τὸ ἐγερθῆναι με <u>προάξω</u> ὑμᾶς εἰς τὴν Γαλιλαίαν.
𝕲: ⁹ καὶ διάξω τὸ τρίτον διὰ πυρὸς καὶ πυρώσω αὐτούς, ὡς πυροῦται τὸ ἀργύριον, καὶ δοκιμῶ αὐτούς, ὡς δοκιμάζεται τὸ χρυσίον· αὐτὸς ἐπικαλέσεται τὸ ὄνομά μου, καὶ ἐγὼ ἐπακούσομαι αὐτῷ καὶ ἐρῶ Λαός μου οὗτός ἐστι, καὶ αὐτὸς ἐρεῖ Κύριος ὁ θεός μου.

𝔐: ⁹ וְהֵבֵאתִ֞י אֶת־הַשְּׁלִשִׁ֣ית בָּאֵ֗שׁ וּצְרַפְתִּים֙ כִּצְרֹ֣ף אֶת־הַכֶּ֔סֶף
וּבְחַנְתִּ֖ים כִּבְחֹ֣ן אֶת־הַזָּהָ֑ב
ה֤וּא יִקְרָ֣א בִשְׁמִ֔י וַאֲנִ֖י אֶעֱנֶ֣ה אֹת֑וֹ
אָמַ֙רְתִּי֙ עַמִּ֣י ה֔וּא וְה֥וּא יֹאמַ֖ר יְהוָ֥ה אֱלֹהָֽי׃

Corresponding words: προάξω/הבאתי.

προάγω is not rare in the NT, occurring about 20 times, five times in Mark (6.45; 10.32; 11.9; 14.28; 16.7). בוא occurs over 2,500 times. This is not a reference.

Mark 14.29

There are no suggested references.

Mark 14.30

Isa. 31.7
Mk: καὶ λέγει αὐτῷ ὁ Ἰησοῦς· ἀμὴν λέγω σοι ὅτι σὺ <u>σήμερον</u> ταύτῃ τῇ νυκτὶ πρὶν ἢ δὶς ἀλέκτορα φωνῆσαι τρίς με <u>ἀπαρνήσῃ</u>.
𝔊: ὅτι <u>τῇ ἡμέρᾳ ἐκείνῃ</u> <u>ἀπαρνήσονται</u> οἱ ἄνθρωποι τὰ χειροποίητα αὐτῶν τὰ ἀργυρᾶ καὶ τὰ χρυσᾶ, ἃ ἐποίησαν αἱ χεῖρες αὐτῶν.

Corresponding words: σήμερον/τῇ ἡμέρᾳ ἐκείνῃ; ἀπαρνέομαι.

Verbal correspondence is significant. Though there is not exact verbal correspondence for 'that day' and 'today', it is not impossible that Mark made that change in transposing the passage to its new context. The significant correspondence, however, comes with the verb ἀπαρνέομαι, which is rare. It is used only once in the LXX, here at Isa. 31.7. It is used twelve times in the NT. In Mark 14.30-31, 72 (and pars.), it is used for Peter's denial of Jesus; and in Mark 8.34 (and pars.), it is used for a warning to those who would deny the Son of Man.

Nevertheless, one must ask whether a reader would associate this verse with this word and this passage in Mark. Neither Matthew nor Luke edits towards the verse. Isaiah 31.7 is almost totally ignored in the early Jewish and Christian tradition.[8] Thematically, it appears unsuitable. What are denied in Isa. 31.7 are idols, that which must be denied. In Mark, Peter will deny Jesus, to whom he should be loyal. This is accidental correspondence.

---

8   There is only a single mention of it, in *Sib. Or.* 3.605, where it is used in a literal manner.

Mark 14.31

There are no suggested references.

Mark 14.32-42

Ps. 119 (118).145-50
Only the sections with verbal correspondence are shown.

Mk: ⁴⁰καὶ πάλιν ἐλθὼν εὗρεν αὐτοὺς καθεύδοντας, ἦσαν γὰρ αὐτῶν <u>οἱ ὀφθαλμοὶ</u> καταβαρυνόμενοι, καὶ οὐκ ᾔδεισαν τί ἀποκριθῶσιν αὐτῷ. ...⁴² ἐγείρεσθε ἄγωμεν· ἰδοὺ ὁ παραδιδούς με <u>ἤγγικεν</u>.
𝔊: ¹⁴⁸προέφθασαν <u>οἱ ὀφθαλμοί</u> μου πρὸς ὄρθρον ...
¹⁵⁰<u>προσήγγισαν</u> οἱ καταδιώκοντές με ἀνομίᾳ ...

Corresponding words: οἱ ὀφθαλμοί (Mark 14.40; Ps. 118.148); ἤγγικεν/ προσήγγισαν (Mark 14.42; Ps. 118.150).

Considering the length of the passages named, there is very little verbal correspondence. Mark could certainly have styled this closer to the psalm. This is not a reference.

Mark 14.33

Sir. 30.9
Mk: καὶ παραλαμβάνει τὸν Πέτρον καὶ [τὸν] Ἰάκωβον καὶ [τὸν] Ἰωάννην μετ' αὐτοῦ καὶ ἤρξατο <u>ἐκθαμβεῖσθαι</u> καὶ ἀδημονεῖν
𝔊: τιθήνησον τέκνον, καὶ <u>ἐκθαμβήσει</u> σε· σύμπαιξον αὐτῷ, καὶ λυπήσει σε.

Corresponding word: ἐκθαμβέω.

The corresponding word is rare. It occurs in the LXX only here, in the NT only in Mark. However, it occurs four times in Mark: here, twice for the alarm of the women at the tomb (16.5-6), and once for the crowd at the base of the mountain after the transfiguration (9.15). There is nothing about Mark 14.33 that points to Sir. 30.9 any more than the other Markan passages. Thematically, they are dissimilar. Sirach 30.9 is about raising your children strictly or they will 'terrorize' you. This is a rare word but the correspondence is accidental.

Ps. 31(30).10
Mk: καὶ παραλαμβάνει τὸν Πέτρον καὶ [τὸν] Ἰάκωβον καὶ [τὸν] Ἰωάννην μετ' αὐτοῦ καὶ ἤρξατο ἐκθαμβεῖσθαι καὶ <u>ἀδημονεῖν</u>

𝔊 : ἐλέησόν με, κύριε, ὅτι θλίβομαι·
ἐταράχθη ἐν θυμῷ ὁ ὀφθαλμός μου,
ἡ ψυχή μου καὶ ἡ γαστήρ μου.
𝔐 : חָנֵּנִי יְהוָה כִּי צַר־לִי עָשְׁשָׁה בְכַעַס עֵינִי נַפְשִׁי וּבִטְנִי׃

Corresponding word: ἀδημονεῖν/צר.

The corresponding words are uncommon: ἀδημονεῖν occurs three times in the NT, only here in Mark; it occurs only in late variants in the LXX. צר is relatively rare, occurring less than thirty times. Nevertheless, there is nothing particular connecting these two words or pointing to this verse in particular. There is not enough correspondence for a reference.

Others
Pss. 22(21).15; 39(38).13; 42(41).12; 62(61).3; 116.11 (115.2); Isa. 53.12: There are no significant words in common. Some Markan MSS have λυπεισθαι, which is similar to περίλυπος of Ps. 42.12. However, this would not constitute sufficient verbal correspondence for a reference (though there is a probable reference at Mark 14.34).[9] None of these passages are references.

Mark 14.34

Ps. 42(41).6, 12; 43(42).5
Verbal correspondence is the same for all verses. Psalm 42.6 is shown:

Mk: καὶ λέγει αὐτοῖς· <u>περίλυπός ἐστιν ἡ ψυχή</u> μου ἕως θανάτου· ...
𝔊 : ἵνα τί <u>περίλυπος εἶ, ψυχή</u>, καὶ ἵνα τί συνταράσσεις με;

Corresponding words: περίλυπος εἰμί [ἡ] ψυχή

περίλυπος is uncommon, and the words occur in sequence. This is relatively strong verbal correspondence. See p. 104 for discussion. This is a probable reference.

Jon. 4.8-9
Mk: καὶ λέγει αὐτοῖς· <u>περίλυπός</u> ἐστιν <u>ἡ ψυχή</u> μου <u>ἕως θανάτου</u>· ...
𝔊 : ⁸... καὶ ὠλιγοψύχησε καὶ ἀπελέγετο <u>τὴν ψυχὴν</u> αὐτοῦ καὶ εἶπε Καλὸν ἀποθανεῖν με ἢ ζῆν. ⁹ καὶ εἶπεν ὁ θεὸς πρὸς Ιωναν Εἰ σφόδρα <u>λελύπησαι</u> σὺ ἐπὶ τῇ κολοκύνθῃ; καὶ εἶπε Σφόδρα <u>λελύπημαι</u> ἐγὼ <u>ἕως θανάτου</u>.

---

9   Some note that Symmachus has αδημονειν in Pss. 62(61).3; 116.11 (115.2). This variant does not appear in the current Göttingen edition of Psalms, because it was attempting only to describe the earliest material. Symmachus' variants are left out because they do not represent probable early material. Thus, neither do they materially affect verbal correspondence with Mark.

Corresponding words: περίλυπος/λυπέω; ἡ ψυχή; ἕως θανάτου.

Verbal correspondence here is genuine. περίλυπος occurs only four times in the NT; with λυπέω occurring about 60 times in the LXX. Still the correspondence for Ps. 42.6, etc., is better, because the words occur in sequence. This is probably not a reference.

Sir. 37.2
Mk: καὶ λέγει αὐτοῖς· <u>περίλυπός</u> ἐστιν ἡ ψυχή μου <u>ἕως θανάτου</u>· ...
𝔊 : οὐχὶ <u>λύπη</u> ἐγγιεῖ <u>ἕως θανάτου</u>
ἑταῖρος καὶ φίλος τρεπόμενος εἰς ἔχθραν;

Corresponding words: περίλυπος/λύπη; ἕως θανάτου.

This is a nice thematic parallel, where the sorrow comes from a friend turning into an enemy. However, the verbal correspondence of Ps. 42.6. is stronger and is to be preferred.

Ps. 6.4
Mk: καὶ λέγει αὐτοῖς· <u>περίλυπός</u> ἐστιν <u>ἡ ψυχή μου</u> ἕως θανάτου· ...
𝔊 : καὶ <u>ἡ ψυχή μου</u> ἐταράχθη σφόδρα·
καὶ σύ, κύριε, ἕως πότε;
𝔐 : וְנַפְשִׁי נִבְהֲלָה מְאֹד וְאַתָּ יְהוָה עַד־מָתָי׃

Corresponding words: περίλυπος/נבהל; ἡ ψυχή μου.

The verbal correspondence for Ps. 42.6 is stronger. This is probably not a reference.

Isa. 53.12
Mk: καὶ λέγει αὐτοῖς· περίλυπός ἐστιν <u>ἡ ψυχή μου</u> <u>ἕως θανάτου</u>· ...
𝔊 : διὰ τοῦτο αὐτὸς κληρονομήσει πολλοὺς καὶ τῶν ἰσχυρῶν μεριεῖ σκῦλα, ἀνθ᾽ ὧν παρεδόθη εἰς <u>θάνατον</u> <u>ἡ ψυχὴ αὐτοῦ</u>, καὶ ἐν τοῖς ἀνόμοις ἐλογίσθη·

Corresponding words: ἡ ψυχή μου/αὐτοῦ; θάνατος.

The corresponding words are very common. Even the strings ἡ ψυχὴ αὐτοῦ and ἡ ψυχή μου are common. There is, of course, some thematic correspondence here. The verbal correspondence, however, is insufficient for a reference.

Ps. 31(30).10, 11, 23
Only verses with verbal correspondence are shown:

Mk: καὶ <u>λέγει</u> αὐτοῖς· <u>περίλυπός</u> ἐστιν <u>ἡ ψυχή μου</u> ἕως θανάτου· ...
𝔊 : ¹⁰ ἐλέησόν με, κύριε, ὅτι θλίβομαι·
ἐταράχθη ἐν θυμῷ ὁ ὀφθαλμός μου,
<u>ἡ ψυχή μου</u> καὶ ἡ γαστήρ μου.

²³ ἐγὼ δὲ <u>εἶπα</u> ἐν τῇ ἐκστάσει μου
Ἀπέρριμμαι ἄρα ἀπὸ προσώπου τῶν ὀφθαλμῶν σου.
διὰ τοῦτο εἰσήκουσας τῆς φωνῆς τῆς δεήσεώς μου
ἐν τῷ κεκραγέναι με πρὸς σέ.

𝔐 : ¹⁰ חָנֵּנִי יְהוָה כִּי צַר־לִי עָשְׁשָׁה בְכַעַס עֵינִי <u>נַפְשִׁי</u> וּבִטְנִי
¹¹ כִּי כָלוּ בְיָגוֹן חַיַּי וּשְׁנוֹתַי בַּאֲנָחָה
כָּשַׁל בַּעֲוֺנִי כֹחִי וַעֲצָמַי עָשֵׁשׁוּ׃
²³ וַאֲנִי אָמַרְתִּי בְחָפְזִי נִגְרַזְתִּי מִנֶּגֶד עֵינֶיךָ
אָכֵן שָׁמַעְתָּ קוֹל תַּחֲנוּנַי בְּשַׁוְּעִי אֵלֶיךָ׃

Corresponding words: λέγω; περίλυπος/כעס (v. 10; or יגון, v. 11); ἡ ψυχή μου.

The verbal correspondence for Ps. 42.6 is stronger. This is probably not a reference.

Ps. 69(68).1-5

Only v. 2 has verbal correspondence with Mark 14.34.
Mk: καὶ λέγει αὐτοῖς· περίλυπός ἐστιν <u>ἡ ψυχή μου ἕως</u> θανάτου· ...
𝔊 : ² Σῶσόν με, ὁ θεός, ὅτι εἰσῆλθοσαν ὕδατα <u>ἕως ψυχῆς μου</u>.

Corresponding words: ἡ ψυχή μου ἕως/ἕως ψυχῆς μου.

The corresponding words are quite common, including the sequence ψυχή μου, and is not sufficient for a reference. While Psalm 69 is used in Mark 15.36, there is no reference to it here.

Ps. 22(21).16

Mk: καὶ λέγει αὐτοῖς· περίλυπός ἐστιν ἡ ψυχή μου ἕως <u>θανάτου</u>· ...
𝔊 : ἐξηράνθη ὡς ὄστρακον ἡ ἰσχύς μου,
καὶ ἡ γλῶσσά μου κεκόλληται τῷ λάρυγγί μου,
καὶ εἰς χοῦν <u>θανάτου</u> κατήγαγές με.

Corresponding word: θανάτου.

Obviously this is an important psalm for the passion narrative, but there is not sufficient verbal correspondence for a reference here.

Ps. 116(114).3

Mk: καὶ λέγει αὐτοῖς· περίλυπός ἐστιν ἡ ψυχή μου ἕως <u>θανάτου</u>· ...
𝔊 : περιέσχον με ὠδῖνες <u>θανάτου</u>,
κίνδυνοι ᾅδου εὕροσάν με·
θλῖψιν καὶ ὀδύνην εὗρον.

Corresponding word: θανάτου.
θάνατος is very common. This is not a reference.

238   *The Use of Scripture in the Markan Passion Narrative*

Ps. 22(21).20
There are no significant words in common. This is not a reference.

Mark 14.35

There are no suggested references.

Mark 14.36

Job 42.2
Mk: καὶ ἔλεγεν· αββα ὁ πατήρ, <u>πάντα δυνατά σοι</u>· παρένεγκε τὸ
    ποτήριον τοῦτο ἀπ' ἐμοῦ· ἀλλ' οὐ τί ἐγὼ θέλω ἀλλὰ τί σύ.
𝕲 : Οἶδα ὅτι <u>πάντα δύνασαι</u>,
    ἀδυνατεῖ δέ <u>σοι</u> οὐθέν.

Corresponding words: πάντα δυνατά/δύνασαι; σοι.

Verbal correspondence is reasonably good. Though common, the words are used the same way, two in sequence. Note that the sentence structure differs, the Job passage using the verbal phrase 'you can do all things' in both Greek and Hebrew, the Mark passage using a noun phrase 'everything is possible for you'. Ordinarily one must make allowances for changes in structure; however, when verbal correspondence is slight and quite possibly accidental, it is something to take into account. Mark 10.27 uses similar phrasing: 'For mortals it is impossible, but not for God; for God all things are possible (πάντα δυνατὰ παρὰ τῷ θεῷ).'

Mark's early editors do not seem to have seen references. Neither Matthew nor Luke edits towards the Job passage in the rich man parallel. In the passion narrative parallel, both eliminate the key phrase, 'all things are possible for you'. In addition, there is little mention of Job 42.2 in either the early Jewish or Christian tradition. The sum of the evidence leads to the conclusion that Mark 10.27 and 14.36 are simply affirming the power of God, not making a particular reference to the same affirmation in Job 42.2. This is most likely accidental correspondence, not a reference.

Zech. 8.6
Mk: καὶ <u>ἔλεγεν</u>· αββα ὁ πατήρ, πάντα <u>δυνατά</u> σοι· παρένεγκε τὸ
    ποτήριον τοῦτο ἀπ' ἐμοῦ· ἀλλ' οὐ τί ἐγὼ θέλω ἀλλὰ τί σύ.
𝕲 : τάδε <u>λέγει</u> κύριος παντοκράτωρ Διότι εἰ <u>ἀδυνατήσει</u> ἐνώπιον
    τῶν καταλοίπων τοῦ λαοῦ τούτου ἐν ταῖς ἡμέραις ἐκείναις …

Corresponding words: λέγω; δυνατά/ἀδυνατήσει.
The corresponding words are common. This is not a reference.

Gen. 18.14
Mk: καὶ ἔλεγεν· αββα ὁ πατήρ, πάντα <u>δυνατά</u> σοι· παρένεγκε τὸ ποτήριον τοῦτο ἀπ᾽ ἐμοῦ· ἀλλ᾽ οὐ τί ἐγὼ θέλω ἀλλὰ τί σύ.
𝔊: <u>μὴ ἀδυνατεῖ</u> παρὰ τοῦ θεοῦ ῥῆμα; εἰς τὸν καιρὸν τοῦτον ἀναστρέψω πρὸς σὲ εἰς ὥρας, καὶ ἔσται τῇ Σάρρᾳ υἱός.

Corresponding words: δυνατά/μὴ ἀδυνατεῖ.
The corresponding words are common, and the phrasing is opposite: 'nothing is impossible for God' and 'everything is possible for you [God]'. Clearly the concept is the same, but verbal correspondence is not sufficient for a reference.

'Cup'

A number of verses are suggested with verbal correspondence to the 'cup' of Mark 14.36. Many of them could be considered good thematic parallels or as background for the cup concept here in Mark. However, ποτήριον occurs about 35 times in the LXX and is a biblical idiom. The various suggestions have roughly equivalent verbal correspondence, most having λέγω and τὸ ποτήριον in common. There is nothing in Mark 14.36 to refer the reader to any verse in particular.

A note on the idiom: In the psalms, *cup* often means something positive, for example, 'The LORD is my chosen portion and my cup' (Ps. 16.5); 'my cup overflows' (Ps. 23.5); 'the cup of salvation' (Ps. 116.13). If one considers these parallels, then the cup Jesus drinks leads, one might suppose, to salvation. There is a strong tendency, however, for cup to mean experiencing something negative, often God's wrath. If one considers those parallels, as is more often the case, the cup Jesus drinks is the cup of God's wrath. It is interesting though that there is a set of language for this idiom, including words like wine, wrath, hand, drink, etc., and Mark does not use that additional language, only the word 'cup'. Thus the cup in Mark 14.36 is not necessarily the cup of wrath. Indeed, Jesus asks James and John if they are willing to drink the cup he drinks, and one does not normally assume that cup means wrath (Mark 10.38). Nevertheless, that cup, like the one Jesus drinks, is still something difficult. As is often the case in the OT, the connotation of *cup* is a negative, difficult experience.

Mk: καὶ <u>ἔλεγεν</u>· αββα ὁ πατήρ, <u>πάντα</u> δυνατά σοι· παρένεγκε <u>τὸ ποτήριον</u> τοῦτο ἀπ᾽ ἐμοῦ· ἀλλ᾽ οὐ τί ἐγὼ θέλω ἀλλὰ τί σύ.

Words in common for most verses (with some verses having fewer): λέγω; πᾶς; τὸ ποτήριον.

Jer. 25(32).15, 17, 28
𝔊: [15]Οὕτως <u>εἶπε</u> κύριος ὁ θεὸς Ισραηλ Λάβε <u>τὸ ποτήριον</u> τοῦ οἴνου τοῦ ἀκράτου τούτου ἐκ χειρός μου καὶ ποτιεῖς <u>πάντα</u> τὰ ἔθνη,

πρὸς ἃ ἐγὼ ἀποστέλλω σε πρὸς αὐτούς,
¹⁷καὶ ἔλαβον τὸ ποτήριον ἐκ χειρὸς κυρίου καὶ ἐπότισα τὰ ἔθνη,
πρὸς ἃ ἀπέστειλέ με κύριος πρὸς αὐτά,
²⁸καὶ ἔσται ὅταν μὴ βούλωνται δέξασθαι τὸ ποτήριον ἐκ τῆς
χειρός σου ὥστε πιεῖν, καὶ ἐρεῖς Οὕτως εἶπε κύριος Πιόντες
πίεσθε·

Ps. 75(74).9
𝔊 : ὅτι ποτήριον ἐν χειρὶ κυρίου
οἴνου ἀκράτου πλῆρες κεράσματος,
καὶ ἔκλινεν ἐκ τούτου εἰς τοῦτο,
πλὴν ὁ τρυγίας αὐτοῦ οὐκ ἐξεκενώθη,
πίονται πάντες οἱ ἁμαρτωλοὶ τῆς γῆς.

Isa. 51.17, 22
𝔊 : ¹⁷Ἐξεγείρου ἐξεγείρου ἀνάστηθι, Ιερουσαλημ ἡ πιοῦσα τὸ
ποτήριον τοῦ θυμοῦ ἐκ χειρὸς κυρίου· τὸ ποτήριον γὰρ τῆς
πτώσεως, τὸ κόνδυ τοῦ θυμοῦ ἐξέπιες καὶ ἐξεκένωσας.
²²οὕτως λέγει κύριος ὁ θεὸς ὁ κρίνων τὸν λαὸν αὐτοῦ Ἰδοὺ
εἴληφα ἐκ τῆς χειρός σου τὸ ποτήριον τῆς πτώσεως, τὸ κόνδυ
τοῦ θυμοῦ, καὶ οὐ προσθήσῃ ἔτι πιεῖν αὐτό·

Ezek. 23.31-34
𝔊 : ³¹ἐν τῇ ὁδῷ τῆς ἀδελφῆς σου ἐπορεύθης, καὶ δώσω τὸ ποτήριον
αὐτῆς εἰς χεῖράς σου. ³²τάδε λέγει κύριος Τὸ ποτήριον τῆς
ἀδελφῆς σου πίεσαι τὸ βαθὺ καὶ τὸ πλατὺ τὸ πλεονάζον τοῦ
συντελέσαι μέθην ³³καὶ ἐκλύσεως πλησθήσῃ· τὸ ποτήριον
ἀφανισμοῦ, ποτήριον ἀδελφῆς σου Σαμαρείας, ³⁴καὶ πίεσαι
αὐτό· καὶ τὰς ἑορτὰς καὶ τὰς νουμηνίας αὐτῆς ἀποστρέψω·
διότι ἐγὼ λελάληκα, λέγει κύριος.

Jer. 49.12 (29.13)
𝔊 : ὅτι τάδε λέγει κύριος Οἷς οὐκ ἦν νόμος πιεῖν τὸ ποτήριον, ἔπιον·
καὶ σὺ ἀθῳωμένη οὐ μὴ ἀθῳωθῇς.

Jer. 51(28).7
𝔊 : ποτήριον χρυσοῦν Βαβυλὼν ἐν χειρὶ κυρίου μεθύσκον πᾶσαν τὴν
γῆν· ἀπὸ τοῦ οἴνου αὐτῆς ἐπίοσαν ἔθνη, διὰ τοῦτο ἐσαλεύθησαν.

Ps. 116.13 (115.4)
𝔊 : ποτήριον σωτηρίου λήμψομαι
καὶ τὸ ὄνομα κυρίου ἐπικαλέσομαι.

Ps. 22(21).15-16
There is verbal correspondence only with v. 15.

Mk: καὶ ἔλεγεν· αββα ὁ πατήρ, <u>πάντα</u> δυνατά σοι· παρένεγκε τὸ
  ποτήριον τοῦτο ἀπ' ἐμοῦ· ἀλλ' οὐ τί ἐγὼ θέλω ἀλλὰ τί σύ.
𝔊 : ¹⁵ὡσεὶ ὕδωρ ἐξεχύθην,
  καὶ διεσκορπίσθη <u>πάντα</u> τὰ ὀστᾶ μου,
  ἐγενήθη ἡ καρδία μου ὡσεὶ κηρὸς τηκόμενος
  ἐν μέσῳ τῆς κοιλίας μου·

Corresponding word: πάντα.
  πᾶς is extremely common. This is not a reference.

Ps. 31(30).23
Mk: καὶ <u>ἔλεγεν</u>· αββα ὁ πατήρ, πάντα δυνατά σοι· παρένεγκε τὸ
  ποτήριον τοῦτο ἀπ' ἐμοῦ· ἀλλ' οὐ τί ἐγὼ θέλω ἀλλὰ τί σύ.
𝔊 : ἐγὼ δὲ <u>εἶπα</u> ἐν τῇ ἐκστάσει μου
  Ἀπέρριμμαι ἄρα ἀπὸ προσώπου τῶν ὀφθαλμῶν σου.
  διὰ τοῦτο εἰσήκουσας τῆς φωνῆς τῆς δεήσεώς μου
  ἐν τῷ κεκραγέναι με πρὸς σέ.

Corresponding word: λέγω.
  λέγω is extremely common. This is not a reference.

Others
Psalm 43(42).1-5; Wis. 2.13, 16, 18: There are no significant words in common. There is no reference to these passages here (though Ps. 43.5 may be used in Mark 14.34).

Mark 14.37

Psalms 31(30).13; 69(68).11: There are no significant words in common. There is no reference to these passages.

Mark 14.38

Ps. 51(50).13-14
Correspondence is with v. 14:

Mk: γρηγορεῖτε καὶ προσεύχεσθε, ἵνα μὴ ἔλθητε εἰς πειρασμόν· τὸ μὲν
  <u>πνεῦμα πρόθυμον</u> ἡ δὲ σὰρξ ἀσθενής.
𝔊 : ¹⁴ἀπόδος μοι τὴν ἀγαλλίασιν τοῦ σωτηρίου σου
  καὶ πνεύματι ἡγεμονικῷ στήρισόν με.
𝔐 : ¹⁴ הָשִׁיבָה לִּי שְׂשׂוֹן יִשְׁעֶךָ וְרוּחַ נְדִיבָה תִסְמְכֵנִי׃

Corresponding words: πνεῦμα πρόθυμον/רוח נדיבה.

The word נדיב occurs less than 50 times, not common but not rare enough to draw attention to itself on its own. Indeed little attention is paid to it. Luke omits the passage in Mark; Matthew does not edit it. The verse gets sparse mention in the tradition, this particular phrase still less. Because the phrase has so little volume, the verbal correspondence is not sufficient for a reference.

Dan. 12.10
There are no significant words in common. This is not a reference.

Mark 14.39

There are no suggested references.

Mark 14.40

Gen. 44.16
Mk: καὶ πάλιν ἐλθὼν <u>εὗρεν</u> αὐτοὺς καθεύδοντας, ἦσαν γὰρ αὐτῶν οἱ ὀφθαλμοὶ καταβαρυνόμενοι, καὶ οὐκ ᾔδεισαν τί ἀποκριθῶσιν αὐτῷ.
𝔊: εἶπεν δὲ Ἰούδας Τί ἀντεροῦμεν τῷ κυρίῳ ἢ τί λαλήσωμεν ἢ τί δικαιωθῶμεν; ὁ δὲ θεὸς <u>εὗρεν</u> τὴν ἀδικίαν τῶν παίδων σου ...

Corresponding word: εὗρεν.
εὑρίσκω is quite common. This is not a reference.

Mark 14.41

Isa. 53.6, 12
Mk: καὶ ἔρχεται τὸ τρίτον καὶ λέγει αὐτοῖς· καθεύδετε τὸ λοιπὸν καὶ ἀναπαύεσθε· ἀπέχει· ἦλθεν ἡ ὥρα, ἰδοὺ <u>παραδίδοται</u> ὁ υἱὸς τοῦ <u>ἀνθρώπου</u> εἰς τὰς χεῖρας τῶν <u>ἁμαρτωλῶν</u>.
𝔊: ⁶πάντες ὡς πρόβατα ἐπλανήθημεν, <u>ἄνθρωπος</u> τῇ ὁδῷ αὐτοῦ ἐπλανήθη· καὶ κύριος <u>παρέδωκεν</u> αὐτὸν ταῖς <u>ἁμαρτίαις</u> ἡμῶν. ¹²διὰ τοῦτο αὐτὸς κληρονομήσει πολλοὺς καὶ τῶν ἰσχυρῶν μεριεῖ σκῦλα, ἀνθ' ὧν <u>παρεδόθη</u> εἰς θάνατον ἡ ψυχὴ αὐτοῦ, καὶ ἐν τοῖς ἀνόμοις ἐλογίσθη· καὶ αὐτὸς <u>ἁμαρτίας</u> πολλῶν ἀνήνεγκε καὶ διὰ τὰς <u>ἁμαρτίας</u> αὐτῶν <u>παρεδόθη</u>.

Corresponding words: παραδίδωμι (Isa. 53.6, 12); ἄνθρωπος (Isa. 53.6); ἁμαρτωλῶν/ἁμαρτίας (Isa. 53.6, 12).
 The corresponding words are very common and not in sequence. This is not a reference.

Ps. 116.6-10 (114.6–115.1)
Verbal correspondence exists only with Ps. 116.7.

Mk: καὶ ἔρχεται τὸ τρίτον καὶ λέγει αὐτοῖς· καθεύδετε τὸ λοιπὸν καὶ <u>ἀναπαύεσθε</u>· ἀπέχει· ἦλθεν ἡ ὥρα, ἰδοὺ παραδίδοται ὁ υἱὸς τοῦ ἀνθρώπου εἰς τὰς χεῖρας τῶν ἁμαρτωλῶν.

𝔊: ⁷ ἐπίστρεψον, ἡ ψυχή μου, εἰς τὴν <u>ἀνάπαυσίν</u> σου, ὅτι κύριος εὐηργέτησέν σε

Corresponding words: ἀναπαύεσθε/ἀνάπαυσιν.

The words are not rare, ἀναπαύω occurring about twelve times in the New Testament (in Mark at 6.31 and here), ἀνάπαυσις occurring about 60 times in the LXX. This is not a reference.

Deut. 1.6; 2.3

Mk: καὶ ἔρχεται τὸ τρίτον καὶ <u>λέγει</u> αὐτοῖς· καθεύδετε τὸ λοιπὸν καὶ ἀναπαύεσθε· <u>ἀπέχει</u>· ἦλθεν ἡ ὥρα, ἰδοὺ παραδίδοται ὁ υἱὸς τοῦ ἀνθρώπου εἰς τὰς χεῖρας τῶν ἁμαρτωλῶν.

𝔊: ¹·⁶ Κύριος ὁ θεὸς ἡμῶν ἐλάλησεν ἡμῖν ἐν Χωρὴβ <u>λέγων</u> Ἱκανούσθω ὑμῖν κατοικεῖν ἐν τῷ ὄρει τούτῳ·
²·³ Ἱκανούσθω ὑμῖν κυκλοῦν τὸ ὄρος τοῦτο, ἐπιστράφητε οὖν ἐπὶ βορρᾶν·

𝔐: ¹·⁶ יְהוָה אֱלֹהֵינוּ דִּבֶּר אֵלֵינוּ בְּחֹרֵב לֵאמֹר <u>רַב־לָכֶם</u> שֶׁבֶת בָּהָר הַזֶּה:
²·³ <u>רַב־לָכֶם</u> סֹב אֶת־הָהָר הַזֶּה פְּנוּ לָכֶם צָפֹנָה:

Corresponding words: λέγω; possibly ἀπέχει/רב לכם.

The only significant verbal correspondence is the proposed correspondence between ἀπέχει/רב לכם, meaning 'enough'. The LXX does not use ἀπέχει to translate רב לכם here. In most cases, it is translated with ἱκανούσθω.[10] There is no reason to expect the reader to jump from ἀπέχει to רב לכם, or even from רב לכם to Deut. 1.6 or 2.3. This is not a reference.

Mark 14.42-43

There are no suggested references.

Mark 14.44

Lam. 1.14, 19
There is verbal correspondence only with v. 14.

---

10   See Num. 16.7; Deut. 1.6; 2.3; 1 Kgs 12.28; Ezek. 44.6; 45.9. Numbers 16.3 translates the phrase with ἐχέτω.

Mk: <u>δεδώκει</u> δὲ ὁ παραδιδοὺς αὐτὸν σύσσημον αὐτοῖς λέγων· ὃν ἂν φιλήσω αὐτός ἐστιν, κρατήσατε αὐτὸν καὶ ἀπάγετε ἀσφαλῶς.
𝔊: ¹⁴... ἀνέβησαν ἐπὶ τὸν τράχηλόν μου· ἠσθένησεν ἡ ἰσχύς μου, ὅτι <u>ἔδωκε</u> κύριος ἐν χερσί μου, οὐ δυνήσομαι στῆναι.

Corresponding word: δίδωμι.
The corresponding word is extremely common. This is not a reference.

Mark 14.45

Prov. 27.6
Mk: καὶ ἐλθὼν εὐθὺς προσελθὼν αὐτῷ λέγει· ῥαββί, καὶ <u>κατεφίλησεν</u> αὐτόν·
𝔊: ἀξιοπιστότερά ἐστιν τραύματα φίλου
 ἢ ἑκούσια <u>φιλήματα</u> ἐχθροῦ.

Corresponding words: κατεφίλησεν/φιλήματα.
The verbal correspondence is too vague for a reference, though it is a nice thematic parallel.

Ps. 41(40).10
There are no significant words in common. This is not a reference.

Mark 14.46

There are no suggested references.

Mark 14.47

Ezek. 23.24-31
Verbal correspondence is with Ezek. 23.25.

Mk: εἷς δέ [τις] τῶν παρεστηκότων σπασάμενος τὴν <u>μάχαιραν</u> ἔπαισεν τὸν δοῦλον τοῦ ἀρχιερέως καὶ <u>ἀφεῖλεν</u> αὐτοῦ τὸ <u>ὠτάριον</u>.
𝔊: ²⁵... καὶ δώσω τὸν ζῆλόν μου ἐν σοί, καὶ ποιήσουσι μετὰ σοῦ ἐν ὀργῇ θυμοῦ· μυκτῆρά σου καὶ <u>ὦτά</u> σου <u>ἀφελοῦσι</u> καὶ τοὺς καταλοίπους σου ἐν ῥομφαίᾳ καταβαλοῦσιν. αὐτοὶ υἱούς σου καὶ θυγατέρας σου λήμψονται, καὶ τοὺς καταλοίπους σου πῦρ καταφάγεται.

Appendix B: Textual Analysis of Mark 14

𝔐 : ²⁵... וְאָזְנַיִךְ יָסִירוּ וְאַחֲרִיתֵךְ בַּחֶרֶב תִּפּוֹל הֵמָּה בָנַיִךְ
וּבְנוֹתַיִךְ יִקָּחוּ וְאַחֲרִיתֵךְ תֵּאָכֵל בָּאֵשׁ:

Corresponding words: μάχαιραν/חרב; ἀφαιρέω; ὠτάριον/ὦτα/אזניך יסירו.

ἀφαιρέω is quite common. οὖς is also common both in the LXX and the NT, though ὠτίον is rarer, with about sixteen occurrences in the LXX, three in the NT (Matt. 26.51; Luke 22.51; John 18.26). ὠτάριον does not occur in the LXX. It occurs twice in the NT (Mark 14.47; John 18.10). Verbal correspondence is shaky in the Greek, perhaps stronger with the Hebrew. There is no clear use of Ezek. 23.24-31 in any parallel text.

The thematic correspondence is in the cutting off of an ear. While this is a genuine correlation, it seems insufficient. The context in Ezekiel is the brutal wrath of God and destruction of cities. This is not a good match to the scene in Mark, especially with Jesus' comment implying that they don't need to come against him with weapons. In terms of wording, Mark could certainly have made this clearer by keeping the word order of Ezek. 23.24-31or sticking more closely to the forms used there. This is probably not a reference.

Ezek. 21.8-10
Verbal correspondence is similar in all verses. Verse 8 is used as the best example.

Mk: εἷς δέ [τις] τῶν παρεστηκότων <u>σπασάμενος τὴν μάχαιραν</u> ἔπαισεν τὸν δοῦλον τοῦ ἀρχιερέως καὶ ἀφεῖλεν αὐτοῦ τὸ ὠτάριον.

𝔊 : ⁸ καὶ ἐρεῖς πρὸς τὴν γῆν τοῦ Ισραηλ Ἰδοὺ ἐγὼ πρὸς σὲ καὶ ἐκσπάσω τὸ ἐγχειρίδιόν μου ἐκ τοῦ κολεοῦ αὐτοῦ καὶ ἐξολεθρεύσω ἐκ σοῦ ἄδικον καὶ ἄνομον·

𝔐 : ⁸ וְאָמַרְתָּ לְאַדְמַת יִשְׂרָאֵל כֹּה אָמַר יְהוָה הִנְנִי אֵלַיִךְ
<u>וְהוֹצֵאתִי חַרְבִּי</u> מִתַּעְרָהּ וְהִכְרַתִּי מִמֵּךְ צַדִּיק וְרָשָׁע:

Corresponding words: σπασάμενος τὴν μάχαιραν/חרב הוצאתי.

In v. 8, some MSS have σπασω; other late versions have την μαχαιραν.

The corresponding words are common. Though they are in sequence, the sequence or the equivalent (the exact words are not relevant, since the correspondence is between Greek and Hebrew) is relatively common. It is found here at Ezek. 21.8, 9, 10, and, for example, at Ezek. 5.2; 12; 12.14; Exod. 15.9; Lev. 26.33; Judg. 8.20; 9.54; 1 Sam. 17.51; 2 Sam. 24.9; Ps. 37.14.

Ezekiel 21 is about God's wrath against Israel. The thematic match is not strong. Neither Matthew nor Luke edit towards the passage. This is not a reference.

Gen. 49.5-7
Verbal correspondence is with v. 5.

Mk: εἷς δέ [τις] τῶν παρεστηκότων σπασάμενος τὴν μάχαιραν
ἔπαισεν τὸν δοῦλον τοῦ ἀρχιερέως καὶ ἀφεῖλεν αὐτοῦ τὸ
ὠτάριον.
𝔊: ⁵ Συμεων καὶ Λευί ἀδελφοί·
συνετέλεσαν ἀδικίαν ἐξ αἱρέσεως αὐτῶν.
𝔐: ⁵ שִׁמְעוֹן וְלֵוִי אַחִים כְּלֵי חָמָס מְכֵרֹתֵיהֶם:

Corresponding words: μάχαιραν/מכרה.
 Words for sword are very common. This is not a reference.

Lam. 1.18, 19
Verbal correspondence is with v. 19.

Mk: εἷς δέ [τις] τῶν παρεστηκότων σπασάμενος τὴν μάχαιραν
ἔπαισεν τὸν δοῦλον τοῦ <u>ἀρχιερέως</u> καὶ ἀφεῖλεν αὐτοῦ τὸ
ὠτάριον.
𝔊: ¹⁹ Ἐκάλεσα τοὺς ἐραστάς μου, αὐτοὶ δὲ παρελογίσαντό με·
οἱ <u>ἱερεῖς</u> μου καὶ οἱ πρεσβύτεροί μου ἐν τῇ πόλει ἐξέλιπον,
ὅτι ἐζήτησαν βρῶσιν αὑτοῖς, ἵνα ἐπιστρέψωσι ψυχὰς αὐτῶν,
καὶ οὐχ εὗρον.

Corresponding words: ἀρχιερέως/ἱερεῖς.
 The corresponding word is very common. This is not a reference.

Mark 14.48

1 Sam. 17.45
Mk: καὶ ἀποκριθεὶς ὁ Ἰησοῦς <u>εἶπεν</u> αὐτοῖς· ὡς ἐπὶ λῃστὴν <u>ἐξήλθατε</u>
μετὰ <u>μαχαιρῶν</u> καὶ ξύλων συλλαβεῖν με;
𝔊: καὶ <u>εἶπεν</u> Δαυιδ πρὸς τὸν ἀλλόφυλον Σὺ <u>ἔρχῃ</u> πρός με ἐν ῥομφαίᾳ
καὶ ἐν δόρατι καὶ ἐν ἀσπίδι ...
𝔐: ... וַיֹּאמֶר דָּוִד אֶל־הַפְּלִשְׁתִּי אַתָּה בָּא אֵלַי בְּחֶרֶב וּבַחֲנִית וּבְכִידוֹן

Corresponding words: εἶπεν; ἐξήλθατε/ἔρχῃ; μαχαιρῶν/חרב.
 The corresponding words are common. There is not sufficient verbal correspondence for a reference.

2 Sam. 12.10
Mk: καὶ ἀποκριθεὶς ὁ Ἰησοῦς εἶπεν αὐτοῖς· ὡς ἐπὶ λῃστὴν ἐξήλθατε

μετὰ <u>μαχαιρῶν</u> καὶ ξύλων <u>συλλαβεῖν</u> με;
𝔊 : καὶ νῦν οὐκ ἀποστήσεται ῥομφαία ἐκ τοῦ οἴκου σου ἕως αἰῶνος
ἀνθ' ὧν ὅτι ἐξουδένωσάς με καὶ <u>ἔλαβες</u> τὴν γυναῖκα τοῦ Ουριου
τοῦ Χετταίου τοῦ εἶναί σοι εἰς γυναῖκα.
𝔐 : וְעַתָּה לֹא־תָסוּר חֶרֶב מִבֵּיתְךָ עַד־עוֹלָם עֵקֶב כִּי בְזִתָנִי <u>וַתִּקַּח</u>
אֶת־אֵשֶׁת אוּרִיָּה הַחִתִּי לִהְיוֹת לְךָ לְאִשָּׁה:

Corresponding words: μαχαιρῶν/חרב; συλλαβεῖν/ἔλαβες.
The corresponding words are common. Verbal correspondence is not sufficient for a reference.

Isa. 53.12

Mk: καὶ ἀποκριθεὶς ὁ Ἰησοῦς εἶπεν αὐτοῖς· ὡς ἐπὶ <u>λῃστὴν</u> ἐξήλθατε
μετὰ μαχαιρῶν καὶ ξύλων συλλαβεῖν με;
𝔊 : διὰ τοῦτο αὐτὸς κληρονομήσει πολλοὺς καὶ τῶν ἰσχυρῶν μεριεῖ
σκῦλα, ἀνθ' ὧν παρεδόθη εἰς θάνατον ἡ ψυχὴ αὐτοῦ, καὶ ἐν τοῖς
ἀνόμοις ἐλογίσθη· καὶ αὐτὸς ἁμαρτίας πολλῶν ἀνήνεγκε καὶ διὰ
τὰς ἁμαρτίας αὐτῶν παρεδόθη.
𝔐 : לָכֵן אֲחַלֶּק־לוֹ בָרַבִּים וְאֶת־עֲצוּמִים יְחַלֵּק שָׁלָל
תַּחַת אֲשֶׁר הֶעֱרָה לַמָּוֶת נַפְשׁוֹ וְאֶת־<u>פֹּשְׁעִים</u> נִמְנָה
וְהוּא חֵטְא־רַבִּים נָשָׂא וְלַפֹּשְׁעִים יַפְגִּיעַ:

Corresponding words: λῃστήν/פשעים.
This is not a reference. For discussion, see pp. 81–82.

Mark 14.49

Isaiah 53.7; Zech. 13.7: There are no significant words in common. There is no allusion to these passages here. For possible referents for 'let the Scriptures be fulfilled', see p. 82, n. 24.

Mark 14.50

1 Sam. 17.51

Mk: Καὶ ἀφέντες αὐτὸν <u>ἔφυγον</u> πάντες.
𝔊 : καὶ ἔδραμεν Δαυιδ καὶ ἐπέστη ἐπ' αὐτὸν καὶ ἔλαβεν τὴν ῥομφαίαν
αὐτοῦ καὶ ἐθανάτωσεν αὐτὸν καὶ ἀφεῖλεν τὴν κεφαλὴν αὐτοῦ. καὶ
εἶδον οἱ ἀλλόφυλοι ὅτι τέθνηκεν ὁ δυνατὸς αὐτῶν, καὶ <u>ἔφυγον</u>.

Corresponding word: ἔφυγον.
φεύγω is very common in the LXX. This is not a reference.

Zech. 13.7

There are no significant words in common. This is not a reference, but the reader may be meant to see it as the fulfilment of Jesus' prediction in 14.27, where Zech. 13.7 is quoted.

Mark 14.51-52

Gen. 39.12

Mk: ⁵¹ καὶ νεανίσκος τις συνηκολούθει αὐτῷ περιβεβλημένος σινδόνα ἐπὶ γυμνοῦ, καὶ κρατοῦσιν αὐτόν· ⁵² ὁ δὲ καταλιπὼν τὴν σινδόνα γυμνὸς ἔφυγεν.

𝔊: καὶ ἐπεσπάσατο αὐτὸν τῶν ἱματίων λέγουσα Κοιμήθητι μετ' ἐμοῦ. καὶ καταλιπὼν τὰ ἱμάτια ἐν ταῖς χερσὶν αὐτῆς ἔφυγεν καὶ ἐξῆλθεν ἔξω.

𝔐: וַתִּתְפְּשֵׂהוּ בְּבִגְדוֹ לֵאמֹר שִׁכְבָה עִמִּי וַיַּעֲזֹב בִּגְדוֹ בְּיָדָהּ וַיָּנָס וַיֵּצֵא הַחוּצָה׃

Corresponding words: καὶ κρατοῦσιν αὐτόν/תתפשהו; καταλιπὼν τὴν σινδόνα/בגדו יעזב; ἔφυγεν/וינס.

Verbal correspondence is real, with generally common words almost in sequence. (The only rare word is σινδών, but its importance is mitigated in that it corresponds with a common word in Hebrew, בגד, and the words do not correspond exactly in meaning.[11]) Thematic correspondence is more problematic. Potiphar's wife grabs Joseph's garment, and he flees to save his integrity.[12] The young man who flees in Mark loses his integrity. This could be a reversal used to demonstrate how bad that flight is. More likely, however, is that this is an accidental correspondence of common words, due to a somewhat parallel act in very different stories.

Amos 2.16

Mk: ⁵¹ καὶ νεανίσκος τις συνηκολούθει αὐτῷ περιβεβλημένος σινδόνα ἐπὶ γυμνοῦ, καὶ κρατοῦσιν αὐτόν· ⁵² ὁ δὲ καταλιπὼν τὴν σινδόνα γυμνὸς ἔφυγεν.

𝔊: καὶ εὑρήσει τὴν καρδίαν αὐτοῦ ἐν δυναστείαις, ὁ γυμνὸς διώξεται ἐν ἐκείνῃ τῇ ἡμέρᾳ, λέγει κύριος.

---

11 Nowhere in the LXX is σινδών used for בגד, though their meanings overlap.

12 This scene has some prominence in the rabbinic tradition, where the interpretations generally deal with the issue of Joseph's integrity. Often they emphasize it (Joseph only remained in the house when all the other men were away because he needed to work on the books). Or they draw out the potential temptation for Joseph, seen as a young man, who nevertheless overcomes temptation and flees – which is really another way to emphasize Joseph's integrity in the end. See e.g., *Mek. Besh.* 4.63 and the Targums vs. *b. Soṭah* 36b. Kugel (*Traditions*, p.455) treats the scene.

Appendix B: Textual Analysis of Mark 14

𝔐: וְאַמִּיץ לִבּוֹ בַּגִּבּוֹרִים עָרוֹם יָנוּס בַּיּוֹם־הַהוּא נְאֻם־יְהוָה׃

Corresponding words: γυμνὸς ἔφυγεν/ערום ינוס.

Some LXX MSS have γυμνος φευξεται.

Verbal correspondence is moderate, with this the only instance of the phrase 'flee naked' in the OT. The correspondence is also with the Greek, since there is a (late) LXX variant that matches Mark very closely. Despite the important verbal correspondence, it is doubtful whether this should be considered a reference. Amos 2.16 has no prominence in the Jewish or Christian tradition. So it seems unlikely that the reader would think of Amos 2.16 with simply the words 'flee naked'. In addition, while one expects metaleptic reversals, one wonders at substituting a barely clothed boy leaving his wrap behind and fleeing for 'the mighty' fleeing naked in Amos 2.16. That is the sort of comparison that parodies, and irony not parody is the norm in the passion narrative. This is more likely to be accidental verbal correspondence.

Isa. 31.8-9

Mk: ⁵¹ καὶ <u>νεανίσκος</u> τις συνηκολούθει αὐτῷ περιβεβλημένος σινδόνα ἐπὶ γυμνοῦ, καὶ κρατοῦσιν αὐτόν· ⁵² ὁ δὲ καταλιπὼν τὴν σινδόνα γυμνὸς <u>ἔφυγεν</u>.

𝔊: ⁸ καὶ πεσεῖται Ασσουρ· οὐ μάχαιρα ἀνδρὸς οὐδὲ μάχαιρα ἀνθρώπου καταφάγεται αὐτόν, καὶ <u>φεύξεται</u> οὐκ ἀπὸ προσώπου μαχαίρας· οἱ δὲ <u>νεανίσκοι</u> ἔσονται εἰς ἥττημα, ⁹ πέτρα γὰρ περιλημφθήσονται ὡς χάρακι καὶ ἡττηθήσονται, ὁ δὲ <u>φεύγων</u> ἁλώσεται.

Corresponding words: νεανίσκος; φεύγω.

The corresponding words are common in the LXX and not in sequence. This is not a reference.

Isa. 3.4

Mk: ⁵¹ καὶ <u>νεανίσκος</u> τις συνηκολούθει αὐτῷ περιβεβλημένος σινδόνα ἐπὶ γυμνοῦ ...

𝔊: καὶ ἐπιστήσω <u>νεανίσκους</u> ἄρχοντας αὐτῶν, καὶ ἐμπαῖκται κυριεύσουσιν αὐτῶν.

Corresponding word: νεανίσκος.

νεανίσκος is common in the LXX. This is not a reference.

Lam. 2.21

Mk: ⁵¹ καὶ <u>νεανίσκος</u> τις συνηκολούθει αὐτῷ περιβεβλημένος σινδόνα ἐπὶ γυμνοῦ ...

𝔊: Ἐκοιμήθησαν εἰς γῆν ἐξόδων παιδάριον καὶ πρεσβύτης· παρθένοι μου καὶ <u>νεανίσκοι</u> μου ἔπεσαν ἐν ῥομφαίᾳ·

ἀπέκτεινας ἐν ἡμέρᾳ ὀργῆς σου, ἐμαγείρευσας, οὐκ ἐφείσω.

Corresponding word: νεανίσκος.
νεανίσκος is common in the LXX. This is not a reference.

Lam. 1.19
There are no significant words in common. This is not a reference.

Mark 14.53

Psalm 31(30).14: There are no significant words in common. This is not a reference.

Mark 14.54

Ps. 38(37).12
Mk: καὶ ὁ Πέτρος <u>ἀπὸ μακρόθεν</u> ἠκολούθησεν αὐτῷ ἕως ἔσω εἰς τὴν αὐλὴν τοῦ ἀρχιερέως καὶ ἦν συγκαθήμενος μετὰ τῶν ὑπηρετῶν καὶ θερμαινόμενος πρὸς τὸ φῶς.
𝔊 : οἱ φίλοι μου καὶ οἱ πλησίον μου ἐξ ἐναντίας μου ἤγγισαν καὶ ἔστησαν, καὶ οἱ ἔγγιστά μου <u>ἀπὸ μακρόθεν</u> ἔστησαν·

Corresponding words: ἀπὸ μακρόθεν.

ἀπὸ μακρόθεν is infrequent in the LXX. However, it is frequent in Mark, occurring five times (Mark 5.6; 8.3; 11.13; 14.54; 15.40). For the first three uses of ἀπὸ μακρόθεν no one suggests a reference to Psalm 38. Yet the verbal correspondence to Psalm 38 is no greater in either Mark 14.54 or 15.40. The author of Mark could easily have strengthened the verbal correspondence in these verses, if he wished. He could have used φίλος, ἐγγύς, or πλησίος to refer to the characters. He could have the women 'stand' far away, while they watch in 15.40. That the author declined to make these changes tells against a reference.

There are no clear uses of Psalm 38 in Mark. Matthew does not edit toward the psalm in his parallels. Luke edits away from the psalm in 22.54 by deleting ἀπό and edits toward the psalm in 23.49, by changing θεωρέω to ἵστημι. Thus there is the possible use in Luke 23.49, but there are no clear uses of Ps. 38.12 in the NT or in other early Jewish literature.

The psalm passage has no particular prominence and the phrase ἀπὸ μακρόθεν has no particular prominence in Mark. The evidence does not support Mark 14.54 or 15.40 as a reference to Ps. 38.12.

Isa. 44.10-20
Only verses with verbal correspondence are shown:

Appendix B: Textual Analysis of Mark 14

Mk: καὶ ὁ Πέτρος ἀπὸ μακρόθεν ἠκολούθησεν αὐτῷ ἕως ἔσω εἰς τὴν αὐλὴν τοῦ ἀρχιερέως καὶ ἦν συγκαθήμενος μετὰ τῶν ὑπηρετῶν καὶ <u>θερμαινόμενος</u> πρὸς τὸ φῶς.

𝔊: ¹⁵ ἵνα ᾖ ἀνθρώποις εἰς καῦσιν· καὶ λαβὼν ἀπ' αὐτοῦ <u>ἐθερμάνθη</u>, καὶ καύσαντες ἔπεψαν ἄρτους ἐπ' αὐτῶν· τὸ δὲ λοιπὸν εἰργάσαντο εἰς θεούς, καὶ προσκυνοῦσιν αὐτούς. ¹⁶ οὗ τὸ ἥμισυ αὐτοῦ κατέκαυσαν ἐν πυρί· καὶ ἐπ' αὐτοῦ κρέας ὀπτήσας ἔφαγεν καὶ ἐνεπλήσθη· καὶ <u>θερμανθεὶς</u> εἶπεν Ἡδύ μοι ὅτι <u>ἐθερμάνθην</u> καὶ εἶδον πῦρ.

Corresponding word: θερμαίνω.

θερμαίνω is rare, occurring only thirteen times in the LXX, three of them in this section. The word is also relatively rare in the NT. Mark uses it twice with regard to Peter's denial (14.54, 67). John uses it three times, again all in Peter's denial (18.18, 25). The only other NT use is Jas. 2.16, 'Be warm and well fed'. Both Matthew and Luke edit away from the parallel. The parallel would be inappropriate for their portrayal of Peter; so their editing does not tell either way.

Psalm 39(38).4 and Wis. 16.27 also contain θερμαίνω and πῦρ, like Isa. 44.15-16 and unlike Mark 14.54. No verse contains θερμαίνω and φῶς. Thus the 'gap', the distinctive word in the Markan passage, φῶς instead of πῦρ, is unmatched. The idea of warming oneself by the fire is natural and does not call attention to itself as a reference. The theme of the Isaian text seems inappropriate. It describes an idol maker making an idol with one part of a log and warming himself with another. Peter's denial is greatly significant, but is it equivalent to making an idol? Though the corresponding word is rare, the naturalness of the word for the context and the disjunction in theme between the two passages tells against a reference.

Isa. 50.11

Mk: καὶ ὁ Πέτρος ἀπὸ μακρόθεν ἠκολούθησεν αὐτῷ ἕως ἔσω εἰς τὴν αὐλὴν τοῦ ἀρχιερέως καὶ ἦν συγκαθήμενος μετὰ τῶν ὑπηρετῶν καὶ θερμαινόμενος πρὸς τὸ <u>φῶς</u>.

𝔊: ἰδοὺ πάντες ὑμεῖς πῦρ καίετε καὶ κατισχύετε φλόγα· πορεύεσθε τῷ <u>φωτὶ</u> τοῦ πυρὸς ὑμῶν καὶ τῇ φλογί, ᾗ ἐξεκαύσατε· δι' ἐμὲ ἐγένετο ταῦτα ὑμῖν, ἐν λύπῃ κοιμηθήσεσθε.

Corresponding word: φῶς.

φῶς is a common word, occurring over 150 times in the LXX. No reference can depend on it alone. This is not a reference.

Mark 14.55

Ps. 37(36).32
Mk: Οἱ δὲ ἀρχιερεῖς καὶ ὅλον τὸ συνέδριον ἐζήτουν κατὰ τοῦ Ἰησοῦ
μαρτυρίαν εἰς τὸ θανατῶσαι αὐτόν, καὶ οὐχ ηὕρισκον·
𝔊 : κατανοεῖ ὁ ἁμαρτωλὸς τὸν δίκαιον
καὶ ζητεῖ τοῦ θανατῶσαι αὐτόν

Corresponding words: ζητέω; τὸ θανατῶσαι αὐτόν.
Verbal correspondence is of common words, but they are nearly in sequence. It is strong enough for a reference. See pp. 104–5 for a discussion.

Ps. 54(53).5
Mk: Οἱ δὲ ἀρχιερεῖς καὶ ὅλον τὸ συνέδριον ἐζήτουν κατὰ τοῦ Ἰησοῦ
μαρτυρίαν εἰς τὸ θανατῶσαι αὐτόν, καὶ οὐχ ηὕρισκον·
𝔊 : ὅτι ἀλλότριοι ἐπανέστησαν ἐπ' ἐμέ,
καὶ κραταιοὶ ἐζήτησαν τὴν ψυχήν μου· ...

Corresponding word: ζητέω.
ζητέω is a very common word, occurring about 300 times in the LXX. This is not a reference.

Lam. 1.15
There are no significant words in common. This is not a reference.

Mark 14.56

Exod. 20.16//Deut. 5.20
Exodus 20.16 is shown:

Mk: πολλοὶ γὰρ ἐψευδομαρτύρουν κατ' αὐτοῦ, καὶ ἴσαι αἱ μαρτυρίαι οὐκ ἦσαν.
𝔊 : οὐ ψευδομαρτυρήσεις κατὰ τοῦ πλησίον σου μαρτυρίαν ψευδῆ.

Corresponding words: ψευδομαρτυρέω κατά.
ψευδομαρτυρέω is rare, occurring only three times, in Exod. 20.16//Deut. 5.20 and Dan. Sus. 61. Verbal correspondence is strong. Mark quotes this verse at 10.19. This is a reference. See p. 105 for further discussion.

Dan. Sus. 61
Mk: πολλοὶ γὰρ ἐψευδομαρτύρουν κατ' αὐτοῦ, καὶ ἴσαι αἱ μαρτυρίαι οὐκ ἦσαν.
𝔊 : (θ') καὶ ἀνέστησαν ἐπὶ τοὺς δύο πρεσβυτέρους, ὅτι συνέστησεν αὐτοὺς Δανιηλ ἐκ τοῦ στόματος αὐτῶν ψευδομάρτυρας ὄντας,

Appendix B: Textual Analysis of Mark 14

καὶ ἐποίησαν αὐτοῖς ὃν τρόπον ἐπονηρεύσαντο τῷ πλησίον

Corresponding words: ψευδομαρτυρέω; [ἀνίστημι Mark 14.57].

Because ψευδομαρτυρέω is quite rare, verbal correspondence is strong. Thematic correspondence is also strong. Nevertheless, Mark quotes Exod. 20.16 at Mark 10.19, and there is no clear quotation in Mark of Susanna. There is nothing to indicate a reference to both passages. So Exod. 20.16 is to be preferred.

Ps. 27(26).12
Mk: πολλοὶ γὰρ ἐψευδομαρτύρουν κατ' αὐτοῦ, καὶ ἴσαι αἱ μαρτυρίαι οὐκ ἦσαν.
𝔊: μὴ παραδῷς με εἰς ψυχὰς θλιβόντων με,
ὅτι ἐπανέστησάν μοι μάρτυρες ἄδικοι,
καὶ ἐψεύσατο ἡ ἀδικία ἑαυτῇ.

Corresponding words: ἐψευδομαρτύρουν/μάρτυρες; ἐψεύσατο.

ψευδομαρτυρέω corresponds roughly with μάρτυρες, ἐψεύσατο. The correspondence with Exod. 20.16 is much stronger, however, and is to be preferred.

Ps. 109(108).2-5
Verbal correspondence is with v. 2:

Mk: πολλοὶ γὰρ ἐψευδομαρτύρουν κατ' αὐτοῦ, καὶ ἴσαι αἱ μαρτυρίαι οὐκ ἦσαν.
𝔊: ² ὅτι στόμα ἁμαρτωλοῦ καὶ στόμα δολίου ἐπ' ἐμὲ ἠνοίχθη, ἐλάλησαν κατ' ἐμοῦ γλώσσῃ δολίᾳ
𝔐: ² כִּי פִי רָשָׁע וּפִי־מִרְמָה עָלַי פָּתָחוּ דִּבְּרוּ אִתִּי לְשׁוֹן שָׁקֶר

Corresponding words: ἐψευδομαρτύρουν/שָׁקֶר.

שָׁקֶר corresponds roughly to ἐψευδομαρτύρουν, but is common (occurring roughly 120 times). Verbal correspondence is insufficient for a reference.

Others
Deuteronomy 5.6; Ps. 31(30).14: There are no significant words in common. There is no reference to these passages.

Mark 14.56-59

Ps. 35(34).11-12
Only verses with verbal correspondence are shown.

Mk: ⁵⁶ πολλοὶ γὰρ ἐψευδομαρτύρουν κατ' αὐτοῦ, καὶ ἴσαι αἱ

μαρτυρίαι οὐκ ἦσαν. ⁵⁷ καί τινες ἀναστάντες ἐψευδομαρτύρουν κατ' αὐτοῦ λέγοντες ... ⁵⁹ καὶ οὐδὲ οὕτως ἴση ἦν ἡ μαρτυρία αὐτῶν.

𝔊: ¹¹ ἀναστάντες μάρτυρες ἄδικοι ἃ οὐκ ἐγίνωσκον ἠρώτων με·

Corresponding words: μαρτυρία(ι)/μάρτυρες; ἀναστάντες.

The root to which μαρτυρία and μάρτυς belong is common, occurring over 250 times in the LXX. ἀνίστημι is also common, occurring over 350 times. The idea of witnesses standing up against a person recurs in the psalms. This may be a thematic parallel. Verbal correspondence is too slight, however, to indicate a reference.

Mark 14.58

Dan. 2.34, 45
Verbal correspondence is similar for both verses. Verse 45 is shown:

Mk: ὅτι ἡμεῖς ἠκούσαμεν αὐτοῦ λέγοντος ὅτι ἐγὼ <u>καταλύσω</u> τὸν ναὸν τοῦτον τὸν χειροποίητον καὶ διὰ τριῶν <u>ἡμερῶν</u> ἄλλον <u>ἀχειροποίητον</u> οἰκοδομήσω.

𝔊: ⁴⁵ (θ') ὃν τρόπον εἶδες ὅτι ἀπὸ ὄρους ἐτμήθη λίθος <u>ἄνευ χειρῶν</u> καὶ ἐλέπτυνε τὸ ὄστρακον, τὸν σίδηρον, τὸν χαλκὸν, τὸν ἄργυρον, τὸν χρυσόν. ὁ θεὸς ὁ μέγας ἐγνώρισε τῷ βασιλεῖ ἃ δεῖ γενέσθαι μετὰ ταῦτα, καὶ ἀληθινὸν τὸ ἐνύπνιον, καὶ πιστὴ ἡ σύγκρισις αὐτοῦ.

𝔐: ⁴⁵ כָּל־קֳבֵל דִּי־חֲזַיְתָ דִּי מִטּוּרָא אִתְגְּזֶרֶת אֶבֶן דִּי־לָא בִידַיִן
וְהַדֶּקֶת פַּרְזְלָא נְחָשָׁא חַסְפָּא כַּסְפָּא וְדַהֲבָא אֱלָהּ רַב הוֹדַע
לְמַלְכָּא מָה דִּי לֶהֱוֵא אַחֲרֵי דְנָה וְיַצִּיב חֶלְמָא וּמְהֵימַן פִּשְׁרֵהּ׃

Corresponding words: καταλύσω/הדקת; ἀχειροποίητον/ἄνευ χειρῶν/ לָא בִידַיִן.

Verbal correspondence is significant. It is possible that the passage in Mark is a translation of the Aramaic of Dan. 2.45. Such a reference would involve changing the position of the words so that the metaphor is mixed; the thing (made) without hands no longer does the crushing, but is now a thing which is made after something else is crushed. This transformation of sense by rearranging the words is possible for a reference in the Second Temple period. It is uncommon in Markan practice, however. Though the word order is often changed, there is no clear instance in Mark where word order is changed to revise the sense of the referent passage. Though a reference here is possible, it does not appear probable.

Hos. 6.2
Mk: ὅτι ἡμεῖς ἠκούσαμεν αὐτοῦ λέγοντος ὅτι ἐγὼ καταλύσω τὸν ναὸν

τοῦτον τὸν χειροποίητον καὶ διὰ <u>τριῶν ἡμερῶν</u> ἄλλον ἀχειροποίητον οἰκοδομήσω.

𝔊: ὑγιάσει ἡμᾶς μετὰ δύο ἡμέρας· ἐν τῇ <u>ἡμέρᾳ τῇ τρίτῃ</u> ἀναστησόμεθα καὶ ζησόμεθα ἐνώπιον αὐτοῦ

Corresponding words: τριῶν/τρίτῃ ἡμέρα.

The suggestion that 'three days' in Mark 14.58 is a reference to Hos. 6.2 stems from the probable allusions to Hos. 6.2 in the passion predictions (see p. 101). Indeed, Mark 14.1, with its reference to 'two days', is considered a reasonably likely allusion based on the connection to Hos. 6.2 established in the passion predictions, and this case would seem analogous. However there the phrase 'two days' is unique, whereas 'three days' occurs repeatedly in the OT.[13] Verbal correspondence here is not sufficient for an allusion. It is more likely that 'three days' in Mark 14.58 refers instead to 'three days' in the passion predictions. While one could thus argue that Mark 14.58 contains an indirect reference to Hos. 6.2, through the allusion to the passion predictions, it is preferable to consider allusions only in a direct sense. There is insufficient correspondence for an allusion to Hos. 6.2 in Mark 14.58.

Tg. Isa. 53.5

Mk: ὅτι ἡμεῖς ἠκούσαμεν αὐτοῦ λέγοντος ὅτι ἐγὼ καταλύσω τὸν <u>ναὸν</u> τοῦτον τὸν χειροποίητον καὶ διὰ τριῶν ἡμερῶν ἄλλον ἀχειροποίητον <u>οἰκοδομήσω</u>.

Tg: והוא יבני בית מקדשא דאיתחל בחובנא אתמסר בעויתנא
ובאל פניה שלמיה יסגי עלנא ובדנתנהי לפתגמוהי
חובנא ישתבקון לנא:

Corresponding words: ναόν/בית מקדשא; οἰκοδομήσω/יבני.

The Targum of Isaiah interprets the passage to mean that the messiah will build a new temple, which corresponds somewhat to the sense of the passage in Mark. It is possible that this interpretation of Isa. 53.5 existed in the first century. It is unlikely that the words in Mark would have been recognized as having verbal correspondence with a particular expression of this interpretation. This is a thematic parallel, not a reference.

Mark 14.59-60

There are no suggested references.

---

13   It occurs about 40 times, for example, at Josh 1.11; 2.16; 1 Sam. 30.12; Jon. 2.1; 3.3 (which also contains ἀνίστημι, as in the passion predictions, but with a different meaning); 2 Chron. 20.25; Ezra 8.32. Cf. George M. Landes, 'The "Three Days and Three Nights" Motif in Jonah 2.1', *JBL* 86 (1967), pp. 446–47. 'Third day' is also very common, occurring an additional 30 times.

Mark 14.61

Isa. 36.21
Mk: ὁ δὲ <u>ἐσιώπα καὶ οὐκ ἀπεκρίνατο</u> οὐδέν ...
𝔊 : καὶ <u>ἐσιώπησαν, καὶ οὐδεὶς ἀπεκρίθη</u> αὐτῷ λόγον διὰ τὸ προστάξαι τὸν βασιλέα μηδένα ἀποκριθῆναι.

Corresponding words: σιωπάω καὶ οὐκ/οὐδεὶς ἀποκρίνομαι.

This is the author's suggestion and is the only reference under examination that has not been suggested by others. The two verbs σιωπάω and ἀποκρίνομαι occur together in the LXX only twice, here and Sir. 20.6. Verbal correspondence between Mark and Sir. 20.6 is weaker, and the passage contains a proverb that does not connect thematically with the Markan context. Verbal correspondence between Mark 14.61 and Isa. 36.21 is well within Mark's margin for Scripture allusion and is sufficient to warrant further study. That study, taken up in Chapter 4, supports the allusion. Verbal correspondence is discussed in greater detail on pp. 105–6.

Ps. 2.7
Mk: ... πάλιν ὁ ἀρχιερεὺς ἐπηρώτα αὐτὸν καὶ λέγει αὐτῷ· <u>σὺ εἶ</u> ὁ χριστὸς ὁ <u>υἱὸς</u> τοῦ εὐλογητοῦ;
𝔊 : διαγγέλλων τὸ πρόσταγμα κυρίου
Κύριος εἶπεν πρός με <u>Υἱός</u> μου <u>εἶ σύ</u>,
ἐγὼ σήμερον γεγέννηκά σε·

Corresponding words: σὺ εἶ/εἶ σύ; υἱός; [χριστός with Ps. 2.2].

Verbal correspondence is moderate. Mark probably refers to Ps. 2.7 at 1.11, where verbal correspondence can be considered greater, because the words occur in sequence. Mark 14.61 recalls Mark 1.11 and provides an additional link to the content of Ps. 2.7 with the inclusion of χριστός. This is probably an allusion. See pp. 106–7 for more discussion.

Ps. 38(37).11-18
Verbal correspondence exists only for v. 14:

Mk: ὁ δὲ <u>ἐσιώπα</u> καὶ οὐκ ἀπεκρίνατο οὐδέν ...
𝔊 : ¹⁴ ἐγὼ δὲ ὡσεὶ κωφὸς οὐκ ἤκουον
καὶ ὡσεὶ ἄλαλος οὐκ ἀνοίγων τὸ στόμα αὐτοῦ
𝔐 : ¹⁴ וַאֲנִי כְחֵרֵשׁ לֹא אֶשְׁמָע וּכְ<u>אִלֵּם</u> לֹא יִפְתַּח־פִּיו׃

Corresponding word: ἐσιώπα/אלם.

The issues of verbal correspondence here are the same as those for Mark 14.61 and Isa. 53.7. See below.

Ps. 39(38).10
Mk: ὁ δὲ <u>ἐσιώπα</u> καὶ οὐκ ἀπεκρίνατο οὐδέν ...
𝔊 : ἐκωφώθην καὶ οὐκ ἤνοιξα τὸ στόμα μου, ὅτι σὺ εἶ ὁ ποιήσας με.
𝔐 : נֶאֱלַמְתִּי לֹא אֶפְתַּח־פִּי כִּי אַתָּה עָשִׂיתָ׃

Corresponding word: ἐσιώπα/נאלמתי.
The issues of verbal correspondence here are the same as those for Mark 14.61 and Isa. 53.7. See below.

Isa. 53.7
Mk: ὁ δὲ <u>ἐσιώπα</u> καὶ οὐκ ἀπεκρίνατο οὐδέν ...
𝔊 : καὶ αὐτὸς διὰ τὸ κεκακῶσθαι οὐκ ἀνοίγει τὸ στόμα· ὡς πρόβατον ἐπὶ σφαγὴν ἤχθη καὶ ὡς ἀμνὸς ἐναντίον τοῦ κείροντος αὐτὸν ἄφωνος οὕτως οὐκ ἀνοίγει τὸ στόμα αὐτοῦ.
𝔐 : נִגַּשׂ וְהוּא נַעֲנֶה וְלֹא יִפְתַּח־פִּיו
כַּשֶּׂה לַטֶּבַח יוּבָל וּכְרָחֵל לִפְנֵי גֹזְזֶיהָ נֶאֱלָמָה
וְלֹא יִפְתַּח פִּיו׃

Corresponding words: ἐσιώπα/נאלמה.
אלם is relatively rare, occurring only nine times as a verb and six times as an adjective, and is elsewhere translated by σιωπάω, which occurs in Mark 14.61. σιωπάω is somewhat uncommon in the LXX, but it is used to translate eight different Hebrew roots and does not point automatically to אלם, in either the LXX or the NT. In fact, Mark uses σιωπάω in 3.4, 4.39, 9.34, and 10.48, as well as in 14.61. For no other Markan use of the verb do scholars insist on a reference to Isa. 53.7; the assertion of correspondence here stems from a theological position that originates outside the passage. The verbal correspondence between Mark 14.61 and Isa. 53.7 is too slight to indicate a reference.

2 Sam. 7.14
Mk: ... πάλιν ὁ ἀρχιερεὺς ἐπηρώτα αὐτὸν καὶ λέγει αὐτῷ· σὺ εἶ ὁ χριστὸς ὁ <u>υἱὸς</u> τοῦ εὐλογητοῦ;
𝔊 : ἐγὼ ἔσομαι αὐτῷ εἰς πατέρα, καὶ αὐτὸς ἔσται μοι εἰς <u>υἱόν</u>· καὶ ἐὰν ἔλθῃ ἡ ἀδικία αὐτοῦ, καὶ ἐλέγξω αὐτὸν ἐν ῥάβδῳ ἀνδρῶν καὶ ἐν ἀφαῖς <u>υἱῶν</u> ἀνθρώπων·

Corresponding word: υἱός.
This may be a thematic parallel. It goes without saying that υἱός is an extremely common word (occurring thousands of times in the LXX). Verbal correspondence is too slight to indicate a reference.

Wis. 2.10-20
Verbal correspondence exists only with v. 18:

Mk: ... πάλιν ὁ ἀρχιερεὺς ἐπηρώτα αὐτὸν καὶ λέγει αὐτῷ· σὺ εἶ ὁ
χριστὸς ὁ <u>υἱὸς</u> τοῦ εὐλογητοῦ;
𝔊 : ¹⁸εἰ γάρ ἐστιν ὁ δίκαιος <u>υἱὸς</u> θεοῦ, ἀντιλήμψεται αὐτοῦ
καὶ ῥύσεται αὐτὸν ἐκ χειρὸς ἀνθεστηκότων.

Corresponding word: υἱός.

Here again is a reference to a υἱός θεοῦ, and a possible thematic parallel, but the verbal correspondence is too slight to indicate a reference.

Ps. 86(85).14-17
Verbal correspondence exists only with v. 16:

Mk: ... πάλιν ὁ ἀρχιερεὺς ἐπηρώτα αὐτὸν καὶ λέγει αὐτῷ· σὺ εἶ ὁ
χριστὸς ὁ <u>υἱὸς</u> τοῦ εὐλογητοῦ;
𝔊 : ¹⁶ἐπίβλεψον ἐπ' ἐμὲ καὶ ἐλέησόν με,
δὸς τὸ κράτος σου τῷ παιδί σου
καὶ σῶσον τὸν <u>υἱὸν</u> τῆς παιδίσκης σου.

Corresponding word: υἱός.

In this case, the 'son' is of 'your handmaiden', τῆς παιδίσκης σου, not of God. The evidence is insufficient to support a reference.

Ps. 89(88).26-27
Verbal correspondence is with Ps. 89.27:

Mk: ... πάλιν ὁ ἀρχιερεὺς ἐπηρώτα αὐτὸν καὶ λέγει αὐτῷ· <u>σὺ εἶ</u> ὁ
χριστὸς ὁ υἱὸς τοῦ εὐλογητοῦ;
𝔊 : ²⁷αὐτὸς ἐπικαλέσεταί με Πατήρ μου <u>εἶ σύ</u>,
θεός μου καὶ ἀντιλήμπτωρ τῆς σωτηρίας μου·

Corresponding words: σὺ εἶ/εἶ σύ.

This may be a thematic parallel. The verbal correspondence however is too slight to indicate a reference.

Others
Psalms 22(21).16; 27(26).12-13; 35(34).11-12; 37(36).12-14, 32-33; 63(62).10; 70(69).2-4; 109(108).2-4, 16; Isa. 53.12: There are no significant words in common. Some LXX MSS of Ps. 35(34).11-12 have επηρωτων, which is neither common nor rare in the LXX, occurring about 80 times. The word means merely 'to ask' and alone would be insufficient to indicate a reference. There is no reference to these passages.

Mark 14.62

Dan. 7.13
Verbal correspondence is best with θ´:

Mk: ... ὄψεσθε τὸν <u>υἱὸν τοῦ ἀνθρώπου</u> ... καὶ <u>ἐρχόμενον μετὰ τῶν νεφελῶν τοῦ οὐρανοῦ</u>
𝔊: (θ´) ἐθεώρουν ἐν ὁράματι τῆς νυκτὸς καὶ ἰδοὺ <u>μετὰ τῶν νεφελῶν τοῦ οὐρανοῦ</u> ὡς <u>υἱὸς ἀνθρώπου ἐρχόμενος</u> ...

Corresponding words: υἱὸς [τοῦ] ἀνθρώπου; ἔρχομαι; μετὰ τῶν νεφελῶν τοῦ οὐρανοῦ.
This is a near quotation. For differences from the LXX, see pp. 209–10. This is a reference.

Ps. 110(109).1
Mk: ...<u>ἐκ δεξιῶν καθήμενον</u> τῆς δυνάμεως ...
𝔊: <u>Κάθου ἐκ δεξιῶν</u> μου

Corresponding words: ἐκ δεξιῶν; κάθημαι.
Mark 14.62 is a paraphrase of the LXX, which is quoted exactly in Mark 12.36. Details of the correspondence are discussed in Appendix A. This is a reference.

Exod. 3.14
Mk: ὁ δὲ Ἰησοῦς <u>εἶπεν</u>· <u>ἐγώ εἰμι</u>, καὶ ὄψεσθε <u>τὸν υἱὸν</u> τοῦ ἀνθρώπου ἐκ δεξιῶν καθήμενον τῆς δυνάμεως καὶ ἐρχόμενον μετὰ τῶν νεφελῶν τοῦ οὐρανοῦ.
𝔊: καὶ <u>εἶπεν</u> ὁ θεὸς πρὸς Μωυσῆν <u>Ἐγώ εἰμι</u> ὁ ὤν· καὶ <u>εἶπεν</u> Οὕτως ἐρεῖς <u>τοῖς υἱοῖς</u> Ισραηλ Ὁ ὢν ἀπέσταλκέν με πρὸς ὑμᾶς.

Corresponding words: εἶπεν; ἐγώ εἰμι; ὁ υἱός.
Some Markan MSS have του θεου after δυνάμεως, corresponding with ὁ θεός of Exod. 3.14.
The words are very common, but the phrase ἐγώ εἰμι is distinct. It is used as a divine name both in Exod. 3.14 and in Deutero-Isaiah (cf. Isa. 43.10, 25; 45.18; 51.12; 52.6). ἐγώ εἰμι generally has the more ordinary meaning 'it is I' or 'I am the one'. Though the words come to be used for the divine name in Christian tradition, it is unclear whether the phrase alone would have had that connotation when Mark was written. (The distinctiveness of the phrase in Isaiah is helped considerably by context.) In addition, as Gundry notes, the answer ἐγώ εἰμι matches perfectly with the question σύ εἰ, which argues against this as a divine claim.[14] A reference is possible but not probable.

---

14 Gundry, *Mark*, p. 910.

Zech. 12.6
Mk: ὁ δὲ Ἰησοῦς εἶπεν· ἐγώ εἰμι, καὶ ὄψεσθε τὸν υἱὸν τοῦ ἀνθρώπου <u>ἐκ δεξιῶν</u> καθήμενον τῆς δυνάμεως καὶ ἐρχόμενον μετὰ τῶν νεφελῶν τοῦ οὐρανοῦ.
𝔊 : ἐν τῇ ἡμέρᾳ ἐκείνῃ θήσομαι τοὺς χιλιάρχους Ιουδα ὡς δαλὸν πυρὸς ἐν ξύλοις καὶ ὡς λαμπάδα πυρὸς ἐν καλάμῃ, καὶ καταφάγονται <u>ἐκ δεξιῶν</u> καὶ ἐξ εὐωνύμων πάντας τοὺς λαοὺς κυκλόθεν, καὶ κατοικήσει Ιερουσαλημ ἔτι καθ' ἑαυτήν.

Corresponding words: ἐκ δεξιῶν.
Verbal correspondence is weak. δεξιός occurs about 200 times in the LXX, frequently with ἐκ. The evidence for a reference to Ps. 110.1 is stronger. Nothing suggests a combined quotation. This is not a reference.

Zech. 12.10
Mk: ὁ δὲ Ἰησοῦς εἶπεν· ἐγώ εἰμι, καὶ ὄψεσθε τὸν υἱὸν τοῦ ἀνθρώπου ἐκ δεξιῶν καθήμενον τῆς δυνάμεως καὶ ἐρχόμενον μετὰ τῶν νεφελῶν τοῦ οὐρανοῦ.
𝔊 : καὶ ἐκχεῶ ἐπὶ τὸν οἶκον Δαυιδ καὶ ἐπὶ τοὺς κατοικοῦντας Ιερουσαλημ πνεῦμα χάριτος καὶ οἰκτιρμοῦ, καὶ ἐπιβλέψονται πρός με ἀνθ' ὧν κατωρχήσαντο, καὶ κόψονται ἐπ' αὐτὸν κοπετὸν ὡς ἐπ' ἀγαπητὸν καὶ ὀδυνηθήσονται ὀδύνην ὡς ἐπὶ πρωτοτόκῳ.

There are no significant words in common in 𝔊^{ed}, though θ', John 19.37, and Rev. 1.7 have ὄψονται for Zech. 12.10. Despite the very weak verbal correspondence, Norman Perrin makes a significant argument for a parallel. However, even if one grants Perrin's argument that Mark 14.62 reflects a Christian pesher tradition which combines Dan. 7.13 and Zech. 12.10, that tradition remains *behind* the text of Mark, and the reference to Zech. 12.10 is almost completely obscured in Mark 14.62. The only remaining word, ὄψεσθε, is very common: ὁράω occurs over 400 times in the LXX. Thus, verbal correspondence is too weak to indicate a reference. (See pp. 96–98 for further discussion.)

Mark 14.63

There are no suggested references.

Mark 14.64

Dan. Sus. 53
Verbal correspondence is best for ο':

Appendix B: Textual Analysis of Mark 14

Mk: ἠκούσατε τῆς βλασφημίας· τί ὑμῖν φαίνεται; οἱ δὲ πάντες <u>κατέκριναν</u> αὐτὸν <u>ἔνοχον</u> εἶναι <u>θανάτου</u>.

𝔊: (οʹ) πιστευθεὶς ἀκούειν καὶ κρίνειν κρίσεις <u>θάνατον</u> ἐπιφερούσας καὶ τὸν μὲν ἀθῷον <u>κατέκρινας</u>, τοὺς δὲ <u>ἐνόχους</u> ἠφίεις, τοῦ κυρίου λέγοντος Ἀθῷον καὶ δίκαιον οὐκ ἀποκτενεῖς·

Corresponding words for οʹ: κατακρίνω; ἔνοχος; θάνατος

Verbal correspondence with the οʹ text is quite good: κατακρίνω and ἔνοχος are rare in the LXX, occurring together only here. Though there is no clear reference to this verse in the NT, Matt. 27.24 and Acts 20.26 contain near quotations of Dan. Sus. 46.

Yet the reference is rejected. The corresponding words are not only not in a string, they are used in three different clauses. ἔνοχος and κατακρίνω are not particularly rare in the NT and are natural and obvious word choices here. Whether the verbal correspondence is deliberate or accidental is a matter of judgement. In the opinion of the author, the total evidence tells against this as a reference. For further discussion see pp. 98–99.

Jer. 26(33).11

Mk: <u>ἠκούσατε</u> τῆς βλασφημίας· τί ὑμῖν φαίνεται; οἱ δὲ <u>πάντες</u> <u>κατέκριναν</u> αὐτὸν ἔνοχον εἶναι <u>θανάτου</u>.

𝔊: καὶ εἶπαν οἱ ἱερεῖς καὶ οἱ ψευδοπροφῆται πρὸς τοὺς ἄρχοντας καὶ <u>παντὶ</u> τῷ λαῷ <u>Κρίσις</u> <u>θανάτου</u> τῷ ἀνθρώπῳ τούτῳ, ὅτι ἐπροφήτευσε κατὰ τῆς πόλεως ταύτης, καθὼς <u>ἠκούσατε</u> ἐν τοῖς ὠσὶν ὑμῶν.

Corresponding words: ἀκούω; πᾶς; κατέκριναν/κρίσις; θανάτου.

This passage in Jeremiah presents a strong thematic parallel to Mark 14.64. The corresponding words, however, are common and do not occur in a string. That makes it unlikely that a reader would be able to catch the allusion without other help, that is, without a clear reference to this passage or its context elsewhere in Mark. There is no such clear reference, either in Mark or in the rest of the NT. Though this is a reasonable suggestion, the verbal correspondence is more likely than not a coincidence.

Lev. 24.16

Mk: ἠκούσατε τῆς <u>βλασφημίας</u>· τί ὑμῖν φαίνεται; οἱ δὲ πάντες κατέκριναν αὐτὸν ἔνοχον εἶναι <u>θανάτου</u>.

𝔊: ὀνομάζων δὲ τὸ ὄνομα κυρίου <u>θανάτῳ</u> θανατούσθω· λίθοις λιθοβολείτω αὐτὸν πᾶσα συναγωγὴ Ἰσραήλ· ἐάν τε προσήλυτος ἐάν τε αὐτόχθων, ἐν τῷ ὀνομάσαι αὐτὸν τὸ ὄνομα κυρίου τελευτάτω.

𝔐: וְנֹקֵב שֵׁם־יְהוָה מוֹת יוּמָת רָגוֹם יִרְגְּמוּ־בוֹ כָּל־הָעֵדָה כַּגֵּר
כָּאֶזְרָח בְּנָקְבוֹ־שֵׁם יוּמָת׃

Corresponding words: βλασφημίας/נקב; θάνατος.
The corresponding words are very common. Verbal correspondence is too slight to indicate a reference.

Wis. 2.20
Mk: ἠκούσατε τῆς βλασφημίας· τί ὑμῖν φαίνεται; οἱ δὲ πάντες κατέκριναν αὐτὸν ἔνοχον εἶναι <u>θανάτου</u>.
𝔊 : <u>θανάτῳ</u> ἀσχήμονι καταδικάσωμεν αὐτόν, ἔσται γὰρ αὐτοῦ ἐπισκοπὴ ἐκ λόγων αὐτοῦ.

Corresponding word: θάνατος.
The corresponding word is very common. Verbal correspondence is too slight to indicate a reference.

Mark 14.65

Isa. 50.6
Mk: Καὶ ἤρξαντό τινες <u>ἐμπτύειν</u> αὐτῷ καὶ περικαλύπτειν αὐτοῦ <u>τὸ πρόσωπον</u> καὶ κολαφίζειν αὐτὸν καὶ λέγειν αὐτῷ· προφήτευσον, καὶ οἱ ὑπηρέται <u>ῥαπίσμασιν</u> αὐτὸν ἔλαβον.
𝔊 : τὸν νῶτόν μου δέδωκα εἰς μάστιγας, τὰς δὲ σιαγόνας μου εἰς <u>ῥαπίσματα</u>, <u>τὸ</u> δὲ <u>πρόσωπόν</u> μου οὐκ ἀπέστρεψα ἀπὸ αἰσχύνης <u>ἐμπτυσμάτων</u>·

Corresponding words: ἐμπτύειν/ἐμπτυσμάτων; τὸ πρόσωπον; ῥάπισμα.
ἐμπτύω (and its noun form, ἔμπτυσμα) and ῥάπισμα are rare in both the LXX and the NT. In the LXX, they occur together only here. The verbal correspondence is very strong. This is a reference. For further discussion, see p. 108.

Mic. 4.14 (5.1)
Mk: Καὶ ἤρξαντό τινες ἐμπτύειν αὐτῷ καὶ περικαλύπτειν αὐτοῦ <u>τὸ πρόσωπον</u> καὶ <u>κολαφίζειν</u> αὐτὸν καὶ λέγειν αὐτῷ· προφήτευσον, καὶ οἱ ὑπηρέται ῥαπίσμασιν αὐτὸν ἔλαβον.
𝔊 : νῦν ἐμφραχθήσεται θυγάτηρ ἐμφραγμῷ, συνοχὴν ἔταξεν ἐφ' ἡμᾶς, ἐν ῥάβδῳ πατάξουσιν ἐπὶ σιαγόνα τὰς φυλὰς τοῦ Ισραηλ.
𝔐 : עַתָּה תִּתְגֹּדְדִי בַת־גְּדוּד מָצוֹר שָׂם עָלֵינוּ
בַּשֵּׁבֶט יַכּוּ עַל־הַלְּחִי אֵת שֹׁפֵט יִשְׂרָאֵל׃

Corresponding words: τὸ πρόσωπον/הלחי; κολαφίζειν/יכו
πρόσωπον (*face*) is a near equivalent of הלחי (*cheek* or *jawbone*). The words are common and not in sequence. Verbal correspondence with Isa. 50.6 is to be preferred.

1 Kgs 22.24-25
Verbal correspondence is with v. 24:

Mk: Καὶ ἤρξαντό τινες ἐμπτύειν αὐτῷ καὶ περικαλύπτειν αὐτοῦ <u>τὸ πρόσωπον</u> καὶ <u>κολαφίζειν</u> αὐτὸν καὶ λέγειν αὐτῷ· προφήτευσον, καὶ οἱ ὑπηρέται ῥαπίσμασιν αὐτὸν ἔλαβον.

𝕲 : ²⁴ καὶ προσῆλθεν Σεδεκιου υἱὸς Χανανα καὶ ἐπάταξεν τὸν Μιχαιαν ἐπὶ τὴν σιαγόνα καὶ εἶπεν Ποῖον πνεῦμα κυρίου τὸ λαλῆσαν ἐν σοί;

𝔐 : ²⁴ וַיִּגַּשׁ צִדְקִיָּהוּ בֶן־כְּנַעֲנָה וַיַּכֶּה אֶת־מִיכָיְהוּ עַל־<u>הַלֶּחִי</u> וַיֹּאמֶר אֵי־זֶה עָבַר רוּחַ־יְהוָה מֵאִתִּי לְדַבֵּר אוֹתָךְ׃

Corresponding words: τὸ πρόσωπον/הַלֶּחִי; κολαφίζειν/יכה

Verbal correspondence is the same as that for Mic. 4.14. See above. Though this is an interesting thematic parallel, verbal correspondence is not sufficient to indicate a reference.

Isa. 53.3-5
Verbal correspondence exists only with v. 3.

Mk: Καὶ ἤρξαντό τινες ἐμπτύειν αὐτῷ καὶ περικαλύπτειν αὐτοῦ <u>τὸ πρόσωπον</u> καὶ κολαφίζειν αὐτὸν καὶ λέγειν αὐτῷ· προφήτευσον, καὶ οἱ ὑπηρέται ῥαπίσμασιν αὐτὸν ἔλαβον.

𝕲 : ³ ἀλλὰ τὸ εἶδος αὐτοῦ ἄτιμον ἐκλεῖπον παρὰ πάντας ἀνθρώπους, ἄνθρωπος ἐν πληγῇ ὢν καὶ εἰδὼς φέρειν μαλακίαν, ὅτι ἀπέστραπται <u>τὸ πρόσωπον</u> αὐτοῦ, ἠτιμάσθη καὶ οὐκ ἐλογίσθη.

Corresponding word: τὸ πρόσωπον.

Verbal correspondence is too slight to indicate a reference.

Others
Isaiah 3.4; 11.1-4; 50.10; Lam. 5.8: There are no significant words in common. There is no reference to these passages.

Mark 14.66-72

There are no suggested references for individual verses in Mark 14.66-71. There are a number of suggestions for Mark 14.66-72 collectively.

Ps. 39(38).12
Verbal correspondence exists only with Mark 14.71:

Mk: ⁷¹ ὁ δὲ ἤρξατο ἀναθεματίζειν καὶ ὀμνύναι ὅτι οὐκ οἶδα τὸν

ἄνθρωπον τοῦτον ὃν λέγετε.
𝔊 : ἐν ἐλεγμοῖς ὑπὲρ ἀνομίας ἐπαίδευσας ἄνθρωπον,
καὶ ἐξέτηξας ὡς ἀράχνην τὴν ψυχὴν αὐτοῦ·
πλὴν μάτην ταράσσεται πᾶς ἄνθρωπος. διάψαλμα.

Corresponding word: ἄνθρωπον.
Verbal correspondence is extremely weak and cannot support a reference.

Others
Psalms 31(30).12; 88(87).9, 19: There are no significant words in common. There is no reference to these passages.

Mark 14.72

2 Samuel 19.5; Isa. 50.11: There are no significant words in common. There is no reference to these passages

Appendix C
Textual Analysis of Mark 15

Mark 15.1

Judg. 15.9-13
Verbal correspondence is the same for both the A and B versions; only verses with verbal correspondence are shown, in the A version.

Mk: Καὶ εὐθὺς πρωῒ συμβούλιον ποιήσαντες οἱ ἀρχιερεῖς μετὰ τῶν πρεσβυτέρων καὶ γραμματέων καὶ ὅλον τὸ συνέδριον, <u>δήσαντες</u> τὸν Ἰησοῦν ἀπήνεγκαν καὶ <u>παρέδωκαν</u> Πιλάτῳ.

𝔊: A ¹⁰καὶ εἶπαν αὐτοῖς πᾶς ἀνὴρ Ιουδα῀Ινα τί ἀνέβητε ἐφ᾽ ἡμᾶς; καὶ εἶπαν οἱ ἀλλόφυλοι <u>Δῆσαι</u> τὸν Σαμψων καὶ ποιῆσαι αὐτῷ ὃν τρόπον ἐποίησεν ἡμῖν. ... ¹²καὶ εἶπαν αὐτῷ Τοῦ <u>δῆσαί</u> σε κατέβημεν καὶ <u>παραδοῦναί</u> σε εἰς χεῖρας ἀλλοφύλων. καὶ εἶπεν αὐτοῖς Σαμψων Ὀμόσατέ μοι μὴ ἀποκτεῖναί με ὑμεῖς καὶ <u>παράδοτέ</u> με αὐτοῖς, μήποτε ἀπαντήσητε ὑμεῖς ἐν ἐμοί. ¹³καὶ ὤμοσαν αὐτῷ λέγοντες Οὐχί, ἀλλὰ δεσμῷ <u>δήσομέν</u> σε καὶ <u>παραδώσομέν</u> σε εἰς χεῖρας αὐτῶν, θανάτῳ δὲ οὐ θανατώσομέν σε· καὶ <u>ἔδησαν</u> αὐτὸν δύο καλωδίοις καινοῖς καὶ ἀνήγαγον αὐτὸν ἐκ τῆς πέτρας.

Verbal correspondence for both A and B: δέω; παραδίδωμι.

παραδίδωμι is very common, occurring roughly 250 times in the LXX. It occurs three times in these verses (twice more in Judg. 16.23-24). δέω is less common, but not rare, occurring about 60 times. It occurs five times in Judges 15 (and another nine times in chapter 16). In Judges 15–16, Samson is bound and handed over to the Philistines, in two separate incidents (once by the Israelites, once with the help of Delilah). Especially in Judges 15, there is a similarity of theme.

Derrett makes the suggestion, calling it a 'glancing allusion'. He was unable to find the parallel mentioned by any modern commentator, though he did find it in a seventeenth-century commentary by Cornelius à Lapide.[1]

---

1 Derrett, *The Making of Mark*, 2, p. 260.

The connection between the passages is certainly obscure, but obscurity alone is not proof against it. More telling is the dearth of any clear reference to Judges 15–16 in Second Temple literature. Josephus includes the account in *Ant.* 5.8.8. Samson and his bonds are mentioned in *L.A.B.* 43.4. Hebrews 11.32 and the *Hellenistic Synagogal Prayers* 6.7 include Samson in lists of the righteous. This rather meagre notice in the NT and other Second Temple literature tells against a reference in Mark. Verbal correspondence is moderate, but not sufficient on its own, and there is little other supporting evidence. A reference is unlikely.

Ps. 27(26).12
Mk: Καὶ εὐθὺς πρωῒ συμβούλιον ποιήσαντες οἱ ἀρχιερεῖς μετὰ τῶν πρεσβυτέρων καὶ γραμματέων καὶ ὅλον τὸ συνέδριον, δήσαντες τὸν Ἰησοῦν ἀπήνεγκαν καὶ <u>παρέδωκαν</u> Πιλάτῳ.
𝔊 : μὴ <u>παραδῷς</u> με εἰς ψυχὰς θλιβόντων με,
ὅτι ἐπανέστησάν μοι μάρτυρες ἄδικοι,
καὶ ἐψεύσατο ἡ ἀδικία ἑαυτῇ.

Corresponding word: παραδίδωμι.
παραδίδωμι is quite common. Verbal correspondence is too slight to indicate a reference.

Ps. 74(73).19
Mk: Καὶ εὐθὺς πρωῒ συμβούλιον ποιήσαντες οἱ ἀρχιερεῖς μετὰ τῶν πρεσβυτέρων καὶ γραμματέων καὶ ὅλον τὸ συνέδριον, δήσαντες τὸν Ἰησοῦν ἀπήνεγκαν καὶ <u>παρέδωκαν</u> Πιλάτῳ.
𝔊 : μὴ <u>παραδῷς</u> τοῖς θηρίοις ψυχὴν ἐξομολογουμένην σοι,
τῶν ψυχῶν τῶν πενήτων σου μὴ ἐπιλάθῃ εἰς τέλος.

Corresponding word: παραδίδωμι.
παραδίδωμι is quite common. Verbal correspondence is too slight to indicate a reference.

Ps. 119(118).121
Mk: Καὶ εὐθὺς πρωῒ συμβούλιον ποιήσαντες οἱ ἀρχιερεῖς μετὰ τῶν πρεσβυτέρων καὶ γραμματέων καὶ ὅλον τὸ συνέδριον, δήσαντες τὸν Ἰησοῦν ἀπήνεγκαν καὶ <u>παρέδωκαν</u> Πιλάτῳ.
𝔊 : Ἐποίησα κρίμα καὶ δικαιοσύνην·
μὴ <u>παραδῷς</u> με τοῖς ἀδικοῦσίν με.

Corresponding word: παραδίδωμι.
παραδίδωμι is quite common. Verbal correspondence is too slight to indicate a reference.

Isa. 53.6, 12
Mk: Καὶ εὐθὺς πρωῒ συμβούλιον ποιήσαντες οἱ ἀρχιερεῖς μετὰ τῶν πρεσβυτέρων καὶ γραμματέων καὶ ὅλον τὸ συνέδριον, δήσαντες τὸν Ἰησοῦν ἀπήνεγκαν καὶ <u>παρέδωκαν</u> Πιλάτῳ.
𝔊: ⁶ πάντες ὡς πρόβατα ἐπλανήθημεν, ἄνθρωπος τῇ ὁδῷ αὐτοῦ ἐπλανήθη· καὶ κύριος <u>παρέδωκεν</u> αὐτὸν ταῖς ἁμαρτίαις ἡμῶν. ¹² διὰ τοῦτο αὐτὸς κληρονομήσει πολλοὺς καὶ τῶν ἰσχυρῶν μεριεῖ σκῦλα, ἀνθ᾽ ὧν <u>παρεδόθη</u> εἰς θάνατον ἡ ψυχὴ αὐτοῦ, καὶ ἐν τοῖς ἀνόμοις ἐλογίσθη· καὶ αὐτὸς ἁμαρτίας πολλῶν ἀνήνεγκε καὶ διὰ τὰς ἁμαρτίας αὐτῶν <u>παρεδόθη</u>.

Corresponding word: παραδίδωμι

παραδίδωμι is quite common in the LXX, occurring about 250 times. Thus verbal correspondence is extremely weak. There are no clear references to Isaiah 53 in Mark to make up for that weakness. (See pp. 76–87 for further discussion.) The evidence is insufficient to support a reference.

Judg. 13.25
There are no significant words in common. This is not a reference.

Mark 15.2

Ps. 119(118).46
Mk: Καὶ ἐπηρώτησεν αὐτὸν ὁ Πιλᾶτος· σὺ εἶ ὁ <u>βασιλεὺς</u> τῶν Ἰουδαίων; ὁ δὲ ἀποκριθεὶς αὐτῷ λέγει· σὺ λέγεις.
𝔊: καὶ ἐλάλουν ἐν τοῖς μαρτυρίοις σου ἐναντίον <u>βασιλέων</u> καὶ οὐκ ᾐσχυνόμην.

Corresponding word: βασιλεύς.

βασιλεύς is common. Verbal correspondence is too slight to indicate a reference.

Zech. 9.9
Mk: Καὶ ἐπηρώτησεν αὐτὸν ὁ Πιλᾶτος· σὺ εἶ ὁ <u>βασιλεὺς</u> τῶν Ἰουδαίων; ὁ δὲ ἀποκριθεὶς αὐτῷ λέγει· σὺ λέγεις.
𝔊: χαῖρε σφόδρα, θύγατερ Σιων· κήρυσσε, θύγατερ Ιερουσαλημ· ἰδοὺ ὁ <u>βασιλεύς</u> σου ἔρχεταί σοι, δίκαιος καὶ σῴζων αὐτός, πραῢς καὶ ἐπιβεβηκὼς ἐπὶ ὑποζύγιον καὶ πῶλον νέον.

Corresponding word: βασιλεύς.
Verbal correspondence is too slight to indicate a reference.

Mark 15.2-5

Psalms 37(36).12; 109(108).3 with Mark 15.2-5 and Ps. 38(37).13-14; Isa. 53.7 with Mark 14.4-5: There are no significant words in common. There is no reference to these passages.

Mark 15.5

Isa. 52.15
Mk: ὁ δὲ Ἰησοῦς οὐκέτι οὐδὲν ἀπεκρίθη, ὥστε <u>θαυμάζειν</u> τὸν Πιλᾶτον.
𝔊: οὕτως <u>θαυμάσονται</u> ἔθνη πολλὰ ἐπ' αὐτῷ, καὶ συνέξουσι
βασιλεῖς τὸ στόμα αὐτῶν· ὅτι οἷς οὐκ ἀνηγγέλη περὶ αὐτοῦ,
ὄψονται, καὶ οἳ οὐκ ἀκηκόασι, συνήσουσι.

Corresponding word: θαυμάζω.

θαυμάζω is neither common nor rare in the LXX, occurring about 60 times. It is common in the New Testament, occurring over 40 times, including also Mark 5.20; 6.6; and 15.44. It is clearly not rare enough to direct a reader to this passage on its own. There are no clear references in Mark to Isaiah 52–53 to assist in drawing the reader's attention there. The evidence is insufficient to support a reference.

Others
Psalms 38(37).12-14; 109(108).4; Isa. 53.7, 9: There are no significant words in common. There is no reference to these passages.

Mark 15.6

Isaiah 53.12: There are no significant words in common. This is not a reference.

Mark 15.7

Isa. 53.9
Mk: ἦν δὲ ὁ λεγόμενος Βαραββᾶς μετὰ τῶν στασιαστῶν δεδεμένος
οἵτινες ἐν τῇ στάσει φόνον <u>πεποιήκεισαν</u>.
𝔊: καὶ δώσω τοὺς πονηροὺς ἀντὶ τῆς ταφῆς αὐτοῦ καὶ τοὺς
πλουσίους ἀντὶ τοῦ θανάτου αὐτοῦ· ὅτι ἀνομίαν οὐκ <u>ἐποίησεν</u>,
οὐδὲ εὑρέθη δόλος ἐν τῷ στόματι αὐτοῦ.

Corresponding word: ποιέω.

ποιέω is extremely common. Verbal correspondence is too slight to indicate a reference.

Lam. 3.58
There are no significant words in common. This is not a reference.

Mark 15.8-12

There are no suggested references.

Mark 15.13

Ps. 22(21).6
Mk: οἱ δὲ πάλιν <u>ἔκραξαν</u>· σταύρωσον αὐτόν.
𝔊: πρὸς σὲ <u>ἐκέκραξαν</u> καὶ ἐσώθησαν,
  ἐπὶ σοὶ ἤλπισαν καὶ οὐ κατῃσχύνθησαν.

Corresponding word: κράζω.

Mark clearly refers to Psalm 22 twice; so the reader's attention is drawn to the psalm. Nevertheless, κράζω occurs about 100 times in the LXX and is insufficiently distinct to indicate a reference. The evidence is insufficient to support a reference.

Isa. 53.3
There are no significant words in common. This is not a reference.

Mark 15.14

Ps. 38(37).20-21
Verbal correspondence exists only with v. 21:

Mk: ὁ δὲ Πιλᾶτος ἔλεγεν αὐτοῖς· τί γὰρ ἐποίησεν <u>κακόν</u>; οἱ δὲ
  περισσῶς ἔκραξαν· σταύρωσον αὐτόν.
𝔊: [21] οἱ ἀνταποδιδόντες <u>κακὰ</u> ἀντὶ ἀγαθῶν ἐνδιέβαλλόν με ...

Corresponding word: κακός.

κακός is very common, occurring roughly 400 times in the LXX. Verbal correspondence is too slight to indicate a reference.

Ps. 109(108).5
Mk: ὁ δὲ Πιλᾶτος ἔλεγεν αὐτοῖς· τί γὰρ ἐποίησεν <u>κακόν</u>; οἱ δὲ
  περισσῶς ἔκραξαν· σταύρωσον αὐτόν.
𝔊: καὶ ἔθεντο κατ' ἐμοῦ <u>κακὰ</u> ἀντὶ ἀγαθῶν
  καὶ μῖσος ἀντὶ τῆς ἀγαπήσεώς μου.

Corresponding word: κακός.
The verbal correspondence is too weak to indicate a reference.

Isa. 53.9
Mk: ὁ δὲ Πιλᾶτος ἔλεγεν αὐτοῖς· τί γὰρ <u>ἐποίησεν</u> κακόν; οἱ δὲ περισσῶς ἔκραξαν· σταύρωσον αὐτόν.
𝔊 : καὶ δώσω τοὺς πονηροὺς ἀντὶ τῆς ταφῆς αὐτοῦ καὶ τοὺς πλουσίους ἀντὶ τοῦ θανάτου αὐτοῦ· ὅτι ἀνομίαν οὐκ <u>ἐποίησεν</u>, οὐδὲ εὑρέθη δόλος ἐν τῷ στόματι αὐτοῦ.

Corresponding word: ποιέω.
The passage speaks of the servant who does not do lawless deeds; this is thematically parallel to Jesus, who has done nothing wrong. Nevertheless, ποιέω is very common, and there is no other corresponding word. Verbal correspondence is extremely weak and cannot support a reference.

Mark 15.15

Isa. 53.5-6, 12
Verbal correspondence exists only with vv. 6, 12:

Mk: ὁ δὲ Πιλᾶτος βουλόμενος τῷ ὄχλῳ τὸ ἱκανὸν ποιῆσαι ἀπέλυσεν αὐτοῖς τὸν Βαραββᾶν, καὶ <u>παρέδωκεν</u> τὸν Ἰησοῦν φραγελλώσας ἵνα σταυρωθῇ.
𝔊 : ⁶ πάντες ὡς πρόβατα ἐπλανήθημεν, ἄνθρωπος τῇ ὁδῷ αὐτοῦ ἐπλανήθη· καὶ κύριος <u>παρέδωκεν</u> αὐτὸν ταῖς ἁμαρτίαις ἡμῶν. ¹²διὰ τοῦτο αὐτὸς κληρονομήσει πολλοὺς καὶ τῶν ἰσχυρῶν μεριεῖ σκῦλα, ἀνθ᾿ ὧν <u>παρεδόθη</u> εἰς θάνατον ἡ ψυχὴ αὐτοῦ, καὶ ἐν τοῖς ἀνόμοις ἐλογίσθη· καὶ αὐτὸς ἁμαρτίας πολλῶν ἀνήνεγκε καὶ διὰ τὰς ἁμαρτίας αὐτῶν <u>παρεδόθη</u>.

Corresponding word: παραδίδωμι.
Though this provides a good thematic parallel, παραδίδωμι is too common to indicate a reference on its own. See pp. 76–87 for further discussion.

Others
Isaiah 58.6; 59.3; 63.3; Zech. 9.11-12: There are no words in common. Aquila has απολυε in Isa. 58.6, a relatively uncommon word, occurring about 40 times in the LXX, but not rare enough to draw a reader to the passage alone. There is no reference to these passages.

Mark 15.16

There are no suggested references.

Mark 15.17

Zech. 3.1-5
Verbal correspondence is only with Zech. 3.4:

Mk: <u>καὶ ἐνδιδύσκουσιν αὐτὸν</u> πορφύραν καὶ περιτιθέασιν αὐτῷ πλέξαντες ἀκάνθινον στέφανον·

𝔊: ⁴ καὶ ἀπεκρίθη καὶ εἶπε πρὸς τοὺς ἐστηκότας πρὸ προσώπου αὐτοῦ λέγων Ἀφέλετε τὰ ἱμάτια τὰ ῥυπαρὰ ἀπ' αὐτοῦ. καὶ εἶπε πρὸς αὐτόν Ἰδοὺ ἀφῄρηκα τὰς ἀνομίας σου, <u>καὶ ἐνδύσατε αὐτὸν</u> ποδήρη

Corresponding words: καὶ ἐνδιδύσκουσιν/ἐνδύσατε αὐτόν.

Verbal correspondence consists of three common words in sequence, with the action done to Ἰησοῦς (*Jesus/Joshua*) in both passages. The trouble is that the three words are not particularly distinct – *and [they] dressed him* – and the word for 'dressed' is not an exact match. How significant the correspondence is depends on how much volume Zech. 3.4 had in the period. While *2 Enoch* 22.8 uses it, there appears to be no other reference to it in Jewish literature of the Second Temple period or in the NT. This does not seem to be sufficient volume to direct the reader's attention to the verse without more verbal correspondence.

Zech. 6.11
Mk: καὶ ἐνδιδύσκουσιν αὐτὸν πορφύραν καὶ περιτιθέασιν αὐτῷ πλέξαντες ἀκάνθινον <u>στέφανον</u>·

𝔊: καὶ λήμψῃ ἀργύριον καὶ χρυσίον καὶ ποιήσεις <u>στεφάνους</u> καὶ ἐπιθήσεις ἐπὶ τὴν κεφαλὴν Ἰησοῦ τοῦ Ἰωσεδεκ τοῦ ἱερέως τοῦ μεγάλου

Corresponding word: στέφανος.

στέφανος is neither particularly common nor rare, occurring about 50 times in the LXX. Again, the action is performed on Ἰησοῦς in both, and περιτιθέασιν corresponds roughly with ἐπιθήσεις. Matthew 27.29 revises towards this passage:

καὶ πλέξαντες <u>στέφανον</u> ἐξ ἀκανθῶν <u>ἐπέθηκαν ἐπὶ τῆς κεφαλῆς αὐτοῦ</u> ...

Luke has no parallel. John does and uses language similar to that of Matt. 27.29, though not as close to the wording of Zech. 6.11:

καὶ οἱ στρατιῶται πλέξαντες <u>στέφανον</u> ἐξ ἀκανθῶν <u>ἐπέθηκαν αὐτοῦ τῇ κεφαλῇ</u> καὶ ἱμάτιον πορφυροῦν περιέβαλον αὐτόν. (John 19.2)

There are no clear references to Zech. 6.11 in the NT.[2] Because the language John and Matthew use for this event seems very natural, it is difficult to tell whether their common language is a coincidence. It is interesting to note that Matthew did not make two very easy changes that would have made a reference to Zech. 6.11 crystal clear: he could have changed αὐτόν to Ἰησοῦν and πλέξαντες to ποιήσαντες. Because he did not, it is difficult to tell if a reference to Zech. 6.11 is meant. It is still more difficult to recognize such a reference in Mark 15.17. That leads to the conclusion that a reference to Zech. 6.11 in Mark 15.17 is possible, but somewhat unlikely.

Lam. 5.16, 18
Verbal correspondence exists only with Lam. 5.16:

Mk: καὶ ἐνδιδύσκουσιν αὐτὸν πορφύραν καὶ περιτιθέασιν αὐτῷ πλέξαντες ἀκάνθινον <u>στέφανον</u>·
𝔊: ἔπεσεν ὁ <u>στέφανος</u> τῆς κεφαλῆς ἡμῶν· οὐαὶ δὴ ἡμῖν, ὅτι ἡμάρτομεν.

Corresponding word: στέφανος.

στέφανος is not rare enough to direct the reader to this particular passage on its own. The verbal correspondence is insufficient to indicate a reference.

Exod. 3.22
Mk: καὶ ἐνδιδύσκουσιν αὐτὸν πορφύραν καὶ <u>περιτιθέασιν</u> αὐτῷ πλέξαντες ἀκάνθινον στέφανον·
𝔊: ἀλλὰ αἰτήσει γυνὴ παρὰ γείτονος καὶ συσκήνου αὐτῆς σκεύη ἀργυρᾶ καὶ χρυσᾶ καὶ ἱματισμόν, καὶ ἐπιθήσετε ἐπὶ τοὺς υἱοὺς ὑμῶν καὶ ἐπὶ τὰς θυγατέρας ὑμῶν καὶ σκυλεύσετε τοὺς Αἰγυπτίους.
𝔐: וְשָׁאֲלָה אִשָּׁה מִשְּׁכֶנְתָּהּ וּמִגָּרַת בֵּיתָהּ כְּלֵי־כֶסֶף וּכְלֵי זָהָב וּשְׂמָלֹת וְשַׂמְתֶּם עַל־בְּנֵיכֶם וְעַל־בְּנֹתֵיכֶם וְנִצַּלְתֶּם אֶת־מִצְרָיִם:

Corresponding words: περιτιθέασιν/<u>שים</u>.

שים is a very common word. This is not a reference.

Tg. Isa. 55.13
There are no significant words in common. This is not a reference.

---

2   NA[27] suggests Rev. 4.4 and Heb. 10.21, but both are quite faint.

Mark 15.18

There are no suggested references.

Mark 15.19

Isa. 50.6
Mk: καὶ ἔτυπτον αὐτοῦ τὴν κεφαλὴν καλάμῳ καὶ ἐνέπτυον αὐτῷ καὶ τιθέντες τὰ γόνατα προσεκύνουν αὐτῷ.
𝔊 : τὸν νῶτόν μου δέδωκα εἰς μάστιγας, τὰς δὲ σιαγόνας μου εἰς ῥαπίσματα, τὸ δὲ πρόσωπόν μου οὐκ ἀπέστρεψα ἀπὸ αἰσχύνης ἐμπτυσμάτων·
𝔐: גֵּוִי נָתַתִּי לְמַכִּים וּלְחָיַי לְמֹרְטִים
פָּנַי לֹא הִסְתַּרְתִּי מִכְּלִמּוֹת וָרֹק׃

Corresponding words: ἔτυπτον/מכים; ἐνέπτυον/ἐμπτυσμάτων.

Verbal correspondence is not strong. However, Mark appears to refer to Isa. 50.6 at 14.65. Does that support the reference here? At 14.65, Mark uses two rare words, which occur together only at Isa. 50.6; this combination of words is the deciding factor in favour of a reference. Here only one of those words is retained. Is that because less was needed to call the passage to the reader's mind or because the parallel does not apply here? This is a matter of judgement. I take the latter position. The author dropped ῥάπισμα in this section, though it is equally applicable. In addition, at 15.20, he also uses the word ἐμπαίζω for *mockery*, rather than αἰσχύνης, as in Isa. 50.6. Thus the Markan passage comes closer to the passion prediction in 10.34 than to Isa. 50.6:

καὶ ἐμπαίξουσιν αὐτῷ καὶ ἐμπτύσουσιν αὐτῷ καὶ μαστιγώσουσιν αὐτὸν καὶ ἀποκτενοῦσιν, καὶ μετὰ τρεῖς ἡμέρας ἀναστήσεται. (Mark 10.34)

This is more likely an allusion to Mark 10.34 than to Isa. 50.6.

Isa. 53.4-5
Verbal correspondence is with Isa. 53.4:

Mk: καὶ ἔτυπτον αὐτοῦ τὴν κεφαλὴν καλάμῳ καὶ ἐνέπτυον αὐτῷ καὶ τιθέντες τὰ γόνατα προσεκύνουν αὐτῷ.
𝔊 : ⁴ οὗτος τὰς ἁμαρτίας ἡμῶν φέρει καὶ περὶ ἡμῶν ὀδυνᾶται, καὶ ἡμεῖς ἐλογισάμεθα αὐτὸν εἶναι ἐν πόνῳ καὶ ἐν πληγῇ καὶ ἐν κακώσει.
𝔐: ⁴ אָכֵן חֳלָיֵנוּ הוּא נָשָׂא וּמַכְאֹבֵינוּ סְבָלָם
וַאֲנַחְנוּ חֲשַׁבְנֻהוּ נָגוּעַ מֻכֵּה אֱלֹהִים וּמְעֻנֶּה׃

Corresponding words: ἔτυπτον/מכה.
נכה is too common to indicate a reference.

Mic. 4.14 (5.1)
Mk: καὶ ἔτυπτον αὐτοῦ τὴν κεφαλὴν καλάμῳ καὶ ἐνέπτυον αὐτῷ καὶ τιθέντες τὰ γόνατα προσεκύνουν αὐτῷ.
𝕲: νῦν ἐμφραχθήσεται θυγάτηρ ἐμφραγμῷ, συνοχὴν ἔταξεν ἐφ' ἡμᾶς, ἐν ῥάβδῳ πατάξουσιν ἐπὶ σιαγόνα τὰς φυλὰς τοῦ Ισραηλ.
𝔐: עַתָּה תִּתְגֹּדְדִי בַת־גְּדוּד מָצוֹר שָׂם עָלֵינוּ
בַּשֵּׁבֶט יַכּוּ עַל־הַלְּחִי אֵת שֹׁפֵט יִשְׂרָאֵל׃

Corresponding words: ἔτυπτον/יכו.
נכה is too common to indicate a reference.

Mark 15.20a

Psalm 22(21).6; Isa. 53.3: There are no significant words in common. There is no reference to these passages.

Mark 15.20b

Lev. 24.14
Mk: Καὶ ἐξάγουσιν αὐτὸν ἵνα σταυρώσωσιν αὐτόν.
𝕲: Ἐξάγαγε τὸν καταρασάμενον ἔξω τῆς παρεμβολῆς, καὶ ἐπιθήσουσιν πάντες οἱ ἀκούσαντες τὰς χεῖρας αὐτῶν ἐπὶ τὴν κεφαλὴν αὐτοῦ, καὶ λιθοβολήσουσιν αὐτὸν πᾶσα ἡ συναγωγή.

Corresponding word: ἐξάγω.
ἐξάγω occurs almost 200 times in the LXX and is too common to indicate a reference.

Num. 15.35-36
Verbal correspondence is only with v. 36:

Mk: Καὶ ἐξάγουσιν αὐτὸν ἵνα σταυρώσωσιν αὐτόν.
𝕲: ³⁶ καὶ ἐξήγαγον αὐτὸν πᾶσα ἡ συναγωγὴ ἔξω τῆς παρεμβολῆς, καὶ ἐλιθοβόλησαν αὐτὸν πᾶσα ἡ συναγωγὴ λίθοις ἔξω τῆς παρεμβολῆς, καθὰ συνέταξεν κύριος τῷ Μωυσῇ.

Corresponding word: ἐξάγω.
ἐξάγω is too common to indicate a reference.

Mark 15.21-22

There are no suggested references.

Mark 15.23

Prov. 31.6-7
Verbal correspondence is only with Prov. 31.6:

Mk: καὶ <u>ἐδίδουν</u> αὐτῷ ἐσμυρνισμένον <u>οἶνον</u>· ὃς δὲ οὐκ ἔλαβεν.
𝔊 : ⁶ <u>δίδοτε</u> μέθην τοῖς ἐν λύπαις
καὶ <u>οἶνον</u> πίνειν τοῖς ἐν ὀδύναις

Corresponding words: δίδωμι; οἶνον.
Some Markan MSS contain πιειν.

The words δίδωμι and οἶνος are very common: οἶνος occurs about 200 times in the LXX, δίδωμι over a thousand times. This proverb may present a thematic parallel or indicate a possible basis for Jewish practice. Even with the possible variant, however, correspondence is insufficient to indicate a reference.

Ps. 69(68).22
Mk: καὶ <u>ἐδίδουν</u> αὐτῷ ἐσμυρνισμένον οἶνον· ὃς δὲ οὐκ ἔλαβεν.
𝔊 : καὶ <u>ἔδωκαν</u> εἰς τὸ βρῶμά μου χολὴν
καὶ εἰς τὴν δίψαν μου ἐπότισάν με ὄξος.

Corresponding word: δίδωμι.

δίδωμι is very common; verbal correspondence is weak. This verse is suggested as a reference here because of the reference to it at 15.36. Matthew revised toward the psalm here. Rather than indicating that Matthew recognized that this parallel existed in Mark however, Matthew's revision represents an expansion, in line with his practice of increasing Scripture references in the passion narrative.

Mark 15.24

Ps. 22(21).19
Mk: Καὶ σταυροῦσιν αὐτὸν καὶ <u>διαμερίζονται τὰ ἱμάτια αὐτοῦ βάλλοντες κλῆρον</u> ἐπ' αὐτὰ τίς τί ἄρῃ.
𝔊 : <u>διεμερίσαντο τὰ ἱμάτιά μου</u> ἑαυτοῖς
καὶ ἐπὶ τὸν ἱματισμόν μου <u>ἔβαλον κλῆρον</u>.

Corresponding words: διαμερίζω τὰ ἱμάτια αὐτοῦ/μου; βάλλω κλῆρον.

There is significant verbal correspondence of words nearly in sequence. This is clearly a reference.

Others

Psalm 22(21).16; Lam. 1.14; 5.12-13: There are no significant words in common. There is no reference to these passages, though the sense of Ps. 22.16 is most likely incorporated into the meaning of the allusion to Ps. 22.19.

Mark 15.25-26

There are no suggested references.

Mark 15.27

Psalm 22(21).7; Isa. 53.12: There are no significant words in common. There is no reference here to these passages.

Mark 15.28

Mark 15.28 clearly contains a reference to Isa. 53.12, but it is considered by most scholars to be a later interpolation from Luke.[3]

Mark 15.29-30

Ps. 22(21).8-9
Mk: ²⁹ Καὶ οἱ παραπορευόμενοι ἐβλασφήμουν αὐτὸν <u>κινοῦντες τὰς κεφαλὰς</u> αὐτῶν καὶ λέγοντες· οὐὰ ὁ καταλύων τὸν ναὸν καὶ οἰκοδομῶν ἐν τρισὶν ἡμέραις, ³⁰<u>σῶσον σεαυτὸν</u> καταβὰς ἀπὸ τοῦ σταυροῦ.
𝔊 : ⁸ πάντες οἱ θεωροῦντές με ἐξεμυκτήρισάν με, ἐλάλησαν ἐν χείλεσιν, <u>ἐκίνησαν κεφαλήν</u>
⁹ Ἤλπισεν ἐπὶ κύριον, ῥυσάσθω αὐτόν·
<u>σωσάτω αὐτόν</u>, ὅτι θέλει αὐτόν.

---

3   Metzger, *Textual Commentary*, p. 99. Crossan, *Cross That Spoke*, p. 165; Lindars, *New Testament Apologetic*, p. 85; Pesch, *Markusevangelium*, 2, p. 485; Schnackenburg, *St Mark*, 1, p. 152; Schweizer, *Good News*, p. 347; Taylor, *St Mark*, p. 591. For a contrary view, see Rodgers, 'Mark 15.28', pp. 81–84.

Corresponding words: κινέω [τὰς] κεφαλάς(-ήν); σώζω (σε)αυτόν.

The phrase κινέω κεφαλήν occurs regularly in the LXX and cannot point to a single passage on its own. Mere coincidence is less likely, however, because the taunt of Mark 15.30 corresponds roughly to the taunt of Ps. 22.9. Verbal correspondence is bolstered by the two quotations of Psalm 22 in Mark 15, and the reference appears to have been seen by Matthew and Luke. For further discussion, see pp. 108–110. This is a reference.

Lam. 2.15
Mk: ²⁹Καὶ <u>οἱ παραπορευόμενοι</u> ἐβλασφήμουν αὐτὸν <u>κινοῦντες τὰς κεφαλὰς αὐτῶν</u> ...
𝔊 : Ἐκρότησαν ἐπὶ σὲ χεῖρας πάντες <u>οἱ παραπορευόμενοι</u> ὁδόν, ἐσύρισαν καὶ <u>ἐκίνησαν κεφαλὴν αὐτῶν</u> ἐπὶ τὴν θυγατέρα Ιερουσαλημ Εἰ αὕτη ἡ πόλις, ἣν ἐροῦσι Στέφανος δόξης, εὐφροσύνη πάσης τῆς γῆς;

Corresponding words: οἱ παραπορευόμενοι; κινέω [τὰς] κεφαλὰς(-ὴν) αὐτῶν.

There is significant verbal correspondence. While κινέω κεφαλήν is relatively common, in both passages here it is οἱ παραπορευόμενοι who do so. Gundry declares that οἱ παραπορευόμενοι is unexpected and thus proves that this is a combined allusion to Ps. 22.8 and Lam. 2.15.⁴ The degree of verbal correspondence to Lam. 2.15 is equal to that to Jer. 18.16, shown below. It is perhaps greater than that to Ps. 22.8-9. Nevertheless, Ps. 22.8-9 (see above) has the advantage of clear references to other verses in the psalm in nearby verses in Mark, as well as parallel references in Matthew and Luke.

Neither Matthew nor Luke revises their parallels towards either Lam. 2.15 or Jer. 18.16. There are no clear references to Lam. 2.15 in the NT; in fact, there are no quotations of any passage in Lamentations in the NT. Nor does it have a prominent place in Second Temple or early rabbinic literature. Jeremiah 18.16 suffers from the same obscurity; there are no quotations of this chapter and no apparent references to this verse in the NT.

A reference to either Lam. 2.15 or Jer. 18.16 is less likely than the reference to Ps. 22.8-9, and the case for a combined reference is not strong. There is no reference to either of these passages.

Jer. 18.16
Mk: ²⁹Καὶ οἱ παραπορευόμενοι ἐβλασφήμουν αὐτὸν <u>κινοῦντες τὰς κεφαλὰς αὐτῶν</u> ...
𝔊 : τοῦ τάξαι τὴν γῆν αὐτῶν εἰς ἀφανισμὸν καὶ σύριγμα αἰώνιον· πάντες οἱ διαπορευόμενοι δι' αὐτῆς ἐκστήσονται καὶ <u>κινήσουσι τὴν κεφαλὴν αὐτῶν</u>.

---
4   Gundry, *Use of the Old Testament*, pp. 62–63.

Corresponding words: κινέω ἡ κεφαλή αὐτῶν. Some LXX MSS have παραπορευόμενοι. This suggestion is discussed with that of Lam. 2.15 above.

Ps. 109(108).25
Mk: ²⁹ Καὶ οἱ παραπορευόμενοι ἐβλασφήμουν αὐτὸν <u>κινοῦντες τὰς κεφαλὰς αὐτῶν</u> ...
𝔊: καὶ ἐγὼ ἐγενήθην ὄνειδος αὐτοῖς·
εἴδοσάν με, ἐσάλευσαν <u>κεφαλὰς αὐτῶν</u>.
𝔐: וַאֲנִי הָיִיתִי חֶרְפָּה לָהֶם יִרְאוּנִי <u>יְנִיעוּן רֹאשָׁם</u>:

Corresponding words: κινοῦντες [τὰς] κεφαλὰς αὐτῶν/רֹאשָׁם יְנִיעוּן. The noun ὄνειδος/חֶרְפָּה used in Ps. 109.25 corresponds to the verb ὀνειδίζω in Mark 15.32.

The verbal correspondence between this verse and Mark is moderate. Though there is a difference in the verb between the LXX (σαλεύω) and Mark (κινέω), it is possible that the author of Mark or a previous source translated נוע with κινέω independently. However, neither Matthew nor Luke revises towards this passage; and the total evidence for a reference to Ps. 22.8-9 is stronger. A preference for simplicity favours the conclusion that Mark 15.29 is a reference to Ps. 22.8-9 alone and not to both Psalm 22 and Psalm 109.

Lam. 1.12
Mk: ²⁹Καὶ οἱ <u>παραπορευόμενοι</u> ἐβλασφήμουν αὐτὸν κινοῦντες τὰς κεφαλὰς αὐτῶν ...
𝔊: Οὐ πρὸς ὑμᾶς, πάντες <u>παραπορευόμενοι</u> ὁδόν· ἐπιστρέψατε καὶ ἴδετε εἰ ἔστιν ἄλγος κατὰ τὸ ἄλγος μου, ὃ ἐγενήθη· ἐταπείνωσέ με κύριος ἐν ἡμέρᾳ ὀργῆς θυμοῦ αὐτοῦ.

Corresponding word: παραπορευόμενοι.

παραπορεύομαι occurs about 40 times in the LXX and is not distinct enough on its own to indicate a reference.

Others
Isaiah 53.12; Wis. 2.17-18: There are no significant words in common. Several authors rightly argue against Wisdom 2 as a reference in Mark.[5] Matthew 27.43 is revised towards this passage; Luke 23.35-36 is not. Matthew's revision appears to be another expansion, not necessarily a recognition of the reference in Mark. There is no reference to these passages.

---

5   Gundry, *Mark*, p. 961; Schweizer, *Good News*, p. 347; Taylor, *St. Mark*, p. 592.

Mark 15.31

Isa. 46.1-2
Verbal correspondence exists only with v. 2:

Mk: ὁμοίως καὶ οἱ ἀρχιερεῖς ἐμπαίζοντες πρὸς ἀλλήλους μετὰ τῶν
γραμματέων ἔλεγον· ἄλλους <u>ἔσωσεν</u>, ἑαυτὸν <u>οὐ δύναται σῶσαι</u>·
𝔊 : ²καὶ πεινῶντι καὶ ἐκλελυμένῳ οὐκ ἰσχύοντι ἅμα, οἳ <u>οὐ δυνήσονται
σωθῆναι</u> ἀπὸ πολέμου, αὐτοὶ δὲ αἰχμάλωτοι ἤχθησαν.

Corresponding words: οὐ δύναμαι σῴζω.
Neither Matthew nor Luke revises toward this passage. This passage in Isaiah discusses the incapacity of idols and makes an unlikely thematic parallel. The σῴζω language probably echoes Ps. 22.9. The similarity in language appears accidental.

Ps. 22(21).9
Mk: ὁμοίως καὶ οἱ ἀρχιερεῖς ἐμπαίζοντες πρὸς ἀλλήλους μετὰ τῶν
γραμματέων ἔλεγον· ἄλλους <u>ἔσωσεν</u>, ἑαυτὸν οὐ δύναται <u>σῶσαι</u>·
𝔊 : Ἤλπισεν ἐπὶ κύριον, ῥυσάσθω αὐτόν·
<u>σωσάτω</u> αὐτόν, ὅτι θέλει αὐτόν.

Corresponding word: σῴζω.
The probable reference to Ps. 22.8-9 at Mark 15.29-30 makes continued influence by Ps. 22.9 at Mark 15.31 very likely. The sense of Ps. 22.9 is incorporated into the Markan passion narrative (cf. pp. 147–54), but this is not a reference.

Ps. 89(88).50-51
There are no significant words in common. This is a thematic parallel, not a reference.

Mark 15.32

Zeph. 3.15
Mk: ὁ χριστὸς ὁ <u>βασιλεὺς Ἰσραὴλ</u> καταβάτω νῦν ἀπὸ τοῦ σταυροῦ,
ἵνα ἴδωμεν καὶ πιστεύσωμεν. καὶ οἱ συνεσταυρωμένοι σὺν αὐτῷ
ὠνείδιζον αὐτόν.
𝔊 : περιεῖλε κύριος τὰ ἀδικήματά σου, λελύτρωταί σε ἐκ χειρὸς
ἐχθρῶν σου· <u>βασιλεὺς Ισραηλ</u> κύριος ἐν μέσῳ σου, οὐκ ὄψῃ κακὰ
οὐκέτι.

Corresponding words: βασιλεὺς Ἰσραηλ.

The phrase 'King of Israel' occurs over 100 times in the OT. Verbal correspondence is too slight to indicate a reference.

Ps. 42(41).11
Mk: ὁ χριστὸς ὁ βασιλεὺς Ἰσραὴλ καταβάτω νῦν ἀπὸ τοῦ σταυροῦ,
  ἵνα ἴδωμεν καὶ πιστεύσωμεν. καὶ οἱ συνεσταυρωμένοι σὺν αὐτῷ
  <u>ὠνείδιζον</u> αὐτόν.
𝕲: ἐν τῷ καταθλάσαι τὰ ὀστᾶ μου <u>ὠνείδισάν με</u> οἱ θλίβοντές με
  ἐν τῷ λέγειν αὐτούς μοι καθ' ἑκάστην ἡμέραν
    Ποῦ ἐστιν ὁ θεός σου;

Corresponding words: ὀνειδίζω αὐτόν/με.

Verbal correspondence is weak, but Mark 14.34 alludes to Ps. 42.12; so the requirement for verbal correspondence is lowered. Still, there are many places in Scripture that refer to mockery, and there is nothing in Mark here or in 14.34 to connect the mockery in Mark 15.32 to the mockery in this particular psalm. The evidence is insufficient to indicate a reference.

Ps. 69(68).10
Mk: ὁ χριστὸς ὁ βασιλεὺς Ἰσραὴλ καταβάτω νῦν ἀπὸ τοῦ σταυροῦ,
  ἵνα ἴδωμεν καὶ πιστεύσωμεν. καὶ οἱ συνεσταυρωμένοι σὺν αὐτῷ
  <u>ὠνείδιζον</u> αὐτόν.
𝕲: ὅτι ὁ ζῆλος τοῦ οἴκου σου κατέφαγέν με,
  καὶ οἱ ὀνειδισμοὶ τῶν <u>ὀνειδιζόντων σε</u> ἐπέπεσαν ἐπ' ἐμέ.

Corresponding words: ὀνειδίζω αὐτόν/σε.

Though Matthew and Luke do not use this verse, there are parallels in other parts of the NT: Rom. 15.3 uses the second half of this verse in this sense; John 2.17 uses the first half of the verse in a text related to the passion.

The significant word in common, ὀνειδίζω, is used roughly 50 times in the LXX and is not sufficient for a reference (and αὐτόν/σε adds too little to make up the difference). However, Mark alludes to Ps. 69.22 at 15.36; not only is that verse in the near vicinity of Mark 15.32, but it is also part of the same action: mockery at the cross. (Recognizing the similarity, Luke brings the two together.) So, while this is not an allusion here, Ps. 69.10 and Mark 15.32 are potentially incorporated into the meaning of the allusion at Mark 15.36. The meaning of Psalm 69 in Mark 15.36 is discussed on pp. 144–47.

Ps. 31(30).12
Mk: ὁ χριστὸς ὁ βασιλεὺς Ἰσραὴλ καταβάτω νῦν ἀπὸ τοῦ σταυροῦ,
  ἵνα ἴδωμεν καὶ πιστεύσωμεν. καὶ οἱ συνεσταυρωμένοι σὺν αὐτῷ
  <u>ὠνείδιζον</u> αὐτόν.
𝕲: παρὰ πάντας τοὺς ἐχθρούς μου ἐγενήθην <u>ὄνειδος</u>
  καὶ τοῖς γείτοσίν μου σφόδρα

Appendix C: Textual Analysis of Mark 15

καὶ φόβος τοῖς γνωστοῖς μου,
οἱ θεωροῦντές με ἔξω ἔφυγον ἀπ' ἐμοῦ.

Corresponding words: ὠνείδιζον/ὄνειδος.

Verbal correspondence is weak. Many places in Scripture refer to mockery, and there is nothing to connect the mockery in Mark to the mockery in this particular psalm. The evidence is insufficient to indicate a reference.

Wis. 2.17-18
Mk: ὁ χριστὸς ὁ βασιλεὺς Ἰσραὴλ καταβάτω νῦν ἀπὸ τοῦ σταυροῦ,
ἵνα ἴδωμεν καὶ πιστεύσωμεν. καὶ οἱ συνεσταυρωμένοι σὺν αὐτῷ
ὠνείδιζον αὐτόν.
𝔊 : ¹⁷ ἴδωμεν εἰ οἱ λόγοι αὐτοῦ ἀληθεῖς,
καὶ πειράσωμεν τὰ ἐν ἐκβάσει αὐτοῦ·
¹⁸ εἰ γάρ ἐστιν ὁ δίκαιος υἱὸς θεοῦ, ἀντιλήμψεται αὐτοῦ
καὶ ῥύσεται αὐτὸν ἐκ χειρὸς ἀνθεστηκότων.

Corresponding word: ἴδωμεν.

Verbal correspondence is extremely weak and cannot indicate a reference.

Ps. 22(21).13-14, 17
There are no significant words in common. This is not a reference. However, because the Markan passion narrative clearly alludes to this part of Psalm 22, its sense may be incorporated into the narrative. Psalm 22 is discussed on pp. 147–54.

Mark 15.33

Amos 8.9-10
Mk: Καὶ γενομένης ὥρας ἕκτης σκότος ἐγένετο ἐφ' ὅλην τὴν γῆν ἕως
ὥρας ἐνάτης.
𝔊 : ⁹ καὶ ἔσται ἐν ἐκείνῃ τῇ ἡμέρᾳ, λέγει κύριος, καὶ δύσεται ὁ ἥλιος
μεσημβρίας, καὶ συσκοτάσει ἐπὶ τῆς γῆς ἐν ἡμέρᾳ τὸ φῶς· ¹⁰ καὶ
μεταστρέψω τὰς ἑορτὰς ὑμῶν εἰς πένθος καὶ πάσας τὰς ᾠδὰς
ὑμῶν εἰς θρῆνον καὶ ἀναβιβῶ ἐπὶ πᾶσαν ὀσφὺν σάκκον καὶ ἐπὶ
πᾶσαν κεφαλὴν φαλάκρωμα καὶ θήσομαι αὐτὸν ὡς πένθος
ἀγαπητοῦ καὶ τοὺς μετ' αὐτοῦ ὡς ἡμέραν ὀδύνης.
𝔐: ⁹ וְהָיָה בַּיּוֹם הַהוּא נְאֻם אֲדֹנָי יְהוִה
וְהֵבֵאתִי הַשֶּׁמֶשׁ בַּצָּהֳרָיִם וְהַחֲשַׁכְתִּי לָאָרֶץ בְּיוֹם אוֹר׃
¹⁰ וְהָפַכְתִּי חַגֵּיכֶם לְאֵבֶל וְכָל־שִׁירֵיכֶם לְקִינָה
וְהַעֲלֵיתִי עַל־כָּל־מָתְנַיִם שָׂק וְעַל־כָּל־רֹאשׁ קָרְחָה
וְשַׂמְתִּיהָ כְּאֵבֶל יָחִיד וְאַחֲרִיתָהּ כְּיוֹם מָר׃

Corresponding words: σκότος ἐγένετο ἐφ᾽ [ὅλην τὴν] γῆν/והחשכתי לארץ; [ἑορτή; ἀγαπητός].

Luke does not revise toward Amos; Matthew does so in only a negligible way. There are no clear references to Amos 8.9-10 in the NT.

Verbal correspondence in Hebrew is somewhat greater than that in Greek, and in either case consists of a string of common words. That correspondence is supported by several additional connections: μεσημβρίας corresponds to ὥρας ἕκτης; ἑορτή occurs in Amos 8.10 and Mark 14.2 and 15.6; ἀγαπητός occurs in Amos 8.10 and is an epithet for Jesus in Mark (1.11; 9.7; 12.6; these connections remain with a Hebrew translation). For further discussion of the verbal correspondence, see pp. 110–111.

Though not certain, the total evidence makes this a probable reference.

Exod. 10.21-23
Verbal correspondence is with Exod. 10.21-22:

Mk: Καὶ γενομένης ὥρας ἕκτης <u>σκότος ἐγένετο ἐφ᾽</u> ὅλην τὴν <u>γῆν</u> ἕως ὥρας ἐνάτης.

𝔊: ²¹ Εἶπεν δὲ κύριος πρὸς Μωυσῆν Ἔκτεινον τὴν χεῖρά εἰς τὸν οὐρανόν, καὶ <u>γενηθήτω σκότος ἐπὶ γῆν</u> Αἰγύπτου, ψηλαφητὸν <u>σκότος</u>. ²² ἐξέτεινεν δὲ Μωυσῆς τὴν χεῖρα εἰς τὸν οὐρανόν, καὶ <u>ἐγένετο σκότος</u> γνόφος θύελλα ἐπὶ πᾶσαν γῆν Αἰγύπτου τρεῖς ἡμέρας

Corresponding words: σκότος γίνομαι ἐπί ... γῆν.

There is significant verbal correspondence between the two passages. However, neither Matthew nor Luke revises towards this passage. There is no clear reference to it in the NT. The reference to Amos 8.9-10 appears to be stronger because of the additional connections between it and Mark.

Isa. 60.2
Mk: Καὶ γενομένης ὥρας ἕκτης <u>σκότος</u> ἐγένετο ἐφ᾽ ὅλην τὴν <u>γῆν</u> ἕως ὥρας ἐνάτης.

𝔊: ἰδοὺ <u>σκότος</u> καὶ γνόφος καλύψει <u>γῆν</u> ἐπ᾽ ἔθνη· ἐπὶ δὲ σὲ φανήσεται κύριος, καὶ ἡ δόξα αὐτοῦ ἐπὶ σὲ ὀφθήσεται.

Corresponding words: σκότος; γῆν.

Verbal correspondence is less than that of Amos 8.9-10, which is to be preferred.

Isa. 13.9-10
Mk: Καὶ γενομένης ὥρας ἕκτης <u>σκότος</u> ἐγένετο ἐφ᾽ <u>ὅλην</u> τὴν γῆν ἕως ὥρας ἐνάτης.

𝔊: ⁹ ἰδοὺ γὰρ ἡμέρα κυρίου ἀνίατος ἔρχεται θυμοῦ καὶ ὀργῆς θεῖναι τὴν οἰκουμένην <u>ὅλην</u> ἔρημον καὶ τοὺς ἁμαρτωλοὺς ἀπολέσαι ἐξ

Appendix C: Textual Analysis of Mark 15

αὐτῆς. ¹⁰ οἱ γὰρ ἀστέρες τοῦ οὐρανοῦ καὶ ὁ Ὠρίων καὶ πᾶς ὁ κόσμος τοῦ οὐρανοῦ τὸ φῶς οὐ δώσουσι, καὶ <u>σκοτισθήσεται</u> τοῦ ἡλίου ἀνατέλλοντος, καὶ ἡ σελήνη οὐ δώσει τὸ φῶς αὐτῆς.

Corresponding words: σκότος/σκοτισθήσεται; ὅλην.

Verbal correspondence is not strong, though the reference is assisted by a quotation in Mark 13.24. Neither Matthew nor Luke revises towards this passage. The evidence for a reference to Amos 8.9-10 is stronger. This is probably not a reference.

Jer. 4.27-28
Mk: Καὶ γενομένης ὥρας ἕκτης <u>σκότος</u> ἐγένετο ἐφ' ὅλην <u>τὴν γῆν</u> ἕως ὥρας ἐνάτης.
𝔊 : ²⁷ τάδε λέγει κύριος Ἔρημος ἔσται πᾶσα <u>ἡ γῆ</u>, συντέλειαν δὲ οὐ μὴ ποιήσω. ²⁸ ἐπὶ τούτοις πενθείτω ἡ γῆ, καὶ <u>συσκοτασάτω</u> ὁ οὐρανὸς ἄνωθεν, διότι ἐλάλησα καὶ οὐ μετανοήσω, ὥρμησα καὶ οὐκ ἀποστρέψω ἀπ' αὐτῆς.

Corresponding words: σκότος/συσκοτασάτω; ἡ γῆ.

Verbal correspondence is not strong enough to indicate a reference.

Isa. 50.2-3
Verbal correspondence exists only with v. 3:

Mk: Καὶ γενομένης ὥρας ἕκτης <u>σκότος</u> ἐγένετο ἐφ' ὅλην τὴν γῆν ἕως ὥρας ἐνάτης.
𝔊 : ³καὶ ἐνδύσω τὸν οὐρανὸν <u>σκότος</u> καὶ θήσω ὡς σάκκον τὸ περιβόλαιον αὐτοῦ.

Corresponding word: σκότος.

Verbal correspondence is too slight to indicate a reference.

Others
Isaiah 34.4; Jer. 15.6-9: There are no significant words in common. There is no reference to these passages.

Mark 15.34

Ps. 22(21).2
Mk: ... <u>ὁ θεός μου ὁ θεός μου, εἰς τί ἐγκατέλιπές με</u>;
𝔊 : Ὁ θεὸς ὁ θεός μου, πρόσχες μοι· <u>ἵνα τί ἐγκατέλιπές με</u>; ...

Corresponding words: ὁ θεός [μου] ὁ θεός μου; εἰς/ἵνα τί ἐγκατέλιπές με;
This is an almost exact quotation. See pp. 213–14 for details regarding verbal correspondence.

Gen. 27.34
Mk: καὶ τῇ ἐνάτῃ ὥρᾳ ἐβόησεν ὁ Ἰησοῦς <u>φωνῇ μεγάλῃ</u>· ...
𝔊 : ἐγένετο δὲ ἡνίκα ἤκουσεν Ἠσαὺ τὰ ῥήματα Ἰσαὰκ τοῦ πατρὸς αὐτοῦ, καὶ ἀνεβόησεν <u>φωνὴν μεγάλην</u> καὶ πικρὰν σφόδρα, καὶ εἶπεν Εὐλόγησον δὴ κἀμέ, πάτερ.

Corresponding words: φωνή μεγάλη.
Some Markan MSS contain ανεβοησεν; one LXX MS has εβοησεν.
With the variants, correspondence of βοάω or ἀναβοάω is possible, and the verbal correspondence is moderate: a string of three common words. Luke edits away from the passage, but as Derrett argues, Matthew revises towards the LXX, by changing βοάω to ἀναβοάω (assuming that βοάω is original to Mark). Thematic correspondence is more problematic. In this passage, Esau cries out to his father to bless him also, after Jacob steals his blessing. Derrett points to the pathos of the cry and that both Esau and Jesus are crying out to their fathers.[6] Yet nothing else in the passages corresponds. Despite moderate verbal correspondence, this is probably not a reference.

Joel 4(3).16
Mk: καὶ τῇ ἐνάτῃ ὥρᾳ ἐβόησεν ὁ Ἰησοῦς <u>φωνῇ</u> μεγάλῃ· ...
𝔊 : ὁ δὲ κύριος ἐκ Σιων ἀνακεκράξεται καὶ ἐξ Ιερουσαλημ δώσει <u>φωνὴν</u> αὐτοῦ, καὶ σεισθήσεται ὁ οὐρανὸς καὶ ἡ γῆ· ὁ δὲ κύριος φείσεται τοῦ λαοῦ αὐτοῦ, καὶ ἐνισχύσει κύριος τοὺς υἱοὺς Ισραηλ.

Corresponding word: φωνή.
Verbal correspondence is too slight to indicate a reference.

Ps. 42(41).10-11
Verbal correspondence exists only with Ps. 42.10:

Mk: ...ὅ ἐστιν μεθερμηνευόμενον· ὁ θεός μου ὁ θεός μου, <u>εἰς τί</u> ἐγκατέλιπές με;
𝔊 : ¹⁰ἐρῶ τῷ θεῷ Ἀντιλήμπτωρ μου εἶ· <u>διὰ τί</u> μου ἐπελάθου; ἵνα τί σκυθρωπάζων πορεύομαι ἐν τῷ ἐκθλίβειν τὸν ἐχθρόν μου;

Corresponding words: εἰς/διὰ τί.
Some Markan MSS have ωνειδισας for ἐγκατέλιπες, corresponding to ὠνείδισαν in Ps. 42.11. Still, verbal correspondence is too slight to indicate a reference.

---

6 Derrett, *The Making of Mark*, 2, p. 273.

Mark 15.35

There are no suggested references.

Mark 15.36

Ps. 69(68).22
Mk: δραμὼν δέ τις [καὶ] γεμίσας σπόγγον <u>ὄξους</u> περιθεὶς καλάμῳ
<u>ἐπότιζεν αὐτόν</u> λέγων· ἄφετε ἴδωμεν εἰ ἔρχεται Ἠλίας καθελεῖν
αὐτόν.
𝔊 : καὶ ἔδωκαν εἰς τὸ βρῶμά μου χολὴν
καὶ εἰς τὴν δίψαν μου <u>ἐπότισάν με</u> <u>ὄξος</u>.

Corresponding words: ὄξος; ποτίζω αὐτόν/με.
Verbal correspondence is strong. ὄξος is rare, occurring four times in the LXX and in the NT six times, all of the latter with regard to this incident. This is a reference. For further discussion, see pp. 111–12.

Wis. 2.17
Mk: δραμὼν δέ τις [καὶ] γεμίσας σπόγγον ὄξους περιθεὶς καλάμῳ
ἐπότιζεν αὐτόν λέγων· ἄφετε <u>ἴδωμεν εἰ</u> ἔρχεται Ἠλίας καθελεῖν
αὐτόν.
𝔊 : <u>ἴδωμεν εἰ</u> οἱ λόγοι αὐτοῦ ἀληθεῖς,
καὶ πειράσωμεν τὰ ἐν ἐκβάσει αὐτοῦ·

Corresponding words: ἴδωμεν εἰ.
Thematic correspondence is strong, and this is the strongest suggestion for a reference to Wis. 2.10-20 in the Markan passion narrative. Nevertheless, verbal correspondence is still slight. Luke does not revise towards the passage. Matthew revises 27.40, 43 toward Wis. 2.17-18, perhaps, like modern day commentators, seeing the potential for a reference to Wis. 2.10-20 here. The parallel remains unexploited in Mark itself, however.

Others
Psalm 69(68).2; Lam. 3.15, 19: There are no significant words in common. There is no reference to these passages.

Mark 15.37

Ps. 31(30).23
Mk: ὁ δὲ Ἰησοῦς ἀφεὶς <u>φωνὴν</u> μεγάλην ἐξέπνευσεν.
𝔊 : ἐγὼ δὲ εἶπα ἐν τῇ ἐκστάσει μου
Ἀπέρριμμαι ἄρα ἀπὸ προσώπου τῶν ὀφθαλμῶν σου.

διὰ τοῦτο εἰσήκουσας τῆς φωνῆς τῆς δεήσεώς μου
ἐν τῷ κεκραγέναι με πρὸς σέ.

Corresponding word: φωνή.
Verbal correspondence is too slight to indicate a reference.

Others
Numbers 33.38; Ps. 68(67).20; Lam. 1.19; 5.13: There are no significant words in common. There is no reference to these passages.

Mark 15.38

Exod. 26.31-33
Verbal correspondence exists with Exod. 26.31, 33:

Mk: Καὶ τὸ καταπέτασμα τοῦ ναοῦ ἐσχίσθη εἰς δύο ἀπ᾽ ἄνωθεν ἕως κάτω.
𝔊: ³¹ καὶ ποιήσεις καταπέτασμα ἐξ ὑακίνθου καὶ πορφύρας καὶ κοκκίνου κεκλωσμένου καὶ βύσσου νενησμένης· ἔργον ὑφαντὸν ποιήσεις αὐτὸ χερουβίμ... ³³ καὶ θήσεις τὸ καταπέτασμα ἐπὶ τοὺς στύλους, καὶ εἰσοίσεις ἐκεῖ ἐσώτερον τοῦ καταπετάσματος τὴν κιβωτὸν τοῦ μαρτυρίου· καὶ διοριεῖ τὸ καταπέτασμα ὑμῖν ἀνὰ μέσον τοῦ ἁγίου καὶ ἀνὰ μέσον τοῦ ἁγίου τῶν ἁγίων.

Corresponding words: τὸ καταπέτασμα.
While καταπέτασμα is not common, there is no thematic connection between the passages. This is a verbal parallel, not a reference.

Lev. 21.23
Mk: Καὶ τὸ καταπέτασμα τοῦ ναοῦ ἐσχίσθη εἰς δύο ἀπ᾽ ἄνωθεν ἕως κάτω.
𝔊: πλὴν πρὸς τὸ καταπέτασμα οὐ προσελεύσεται καὶ πρὸς τὸ θυσιαστήριον οὐκ ἐγγιεῖ, ὅτι μῶμον ἔχει· καὶ οὐ βεβηλώσει τὸ ἅγιον τοῦ θεοῦ αὐτοῦ, ὅτι ἐγώ εἰμι κύριος ὁ ἁγιάζων αὐτούς.

Corresponding word: τὸ καταπέτασμα.
This is a verbal parallel, not a reference to the passage.

Others
Isaiah 25.7-8; Lam. 2.17: There are no significant words in common. There is no reference to these passages.

Mark 15.39

Isa. 52.13
Mk: Ἰδὼν δὲ ὁ κεντυρίων ὁ παρεστηκὼς ἐξ ἐναντίας αὐτοῦ ὅτι οὕτως ἐξέπνευσεν εἶπεν· ἀληθῶς οὗτος ὁ ἄνθρωπος υἱὸς θεοῦ ἦν.
𝔊 : Ἰδοὺ συνήσει ὁ παῖς μου καὶ ὑψωθήσεται καὶ δοξασθήσεται σφόδρα.

Corresponding words: ἰδών/ἰδού.
Verbal correspondence is too slight to indicate a reference.

Ps. 22(21).29
There are no significant words in common. This is not a reference.

Mark 15.40

Ps. 38(37).12
Mk: Ἦσαν δὲ καὶ γυναῖκες <u>ἀπὸ μακρόθεν</u> θεωροῦσαι, ἐν αἷς καὶ Μαρία ἡ Μαγδαληνὴ καὶ Μαρία ἡ Ἰακώβου τοῦ μικροῦ καὶ Ἰωσῆτος μήτηρ καὶ Σαλώμη
𝔊 : οἱ φίλοι μου καὶ οἱ πλησίον μου ἐξ ἐναντίας μου ἤγγισαν καὶ ἔστησαν, καὶ οἱ ἔγγιστά μου <u>ἀπὸ μακρόθεν</u> ἔστησαν·

Corresponding words: ἀπὸ μακρόθεν.
This verse was suggested as a reference to Mark 14.54. It fails here for the same reasons. See p. 250.

Mark 15.41-42

There are no suggested references.

Mark 15.43

1 Sam. 1.1
Mk: ἐλθὼν Ἰωσὴφ [ὁ] ἀπὸ <u>Ἁριμαθαίας</u> εὐσχήμων βουλευτής, ὃς καὶ αὐτὸς ἦν προσδεχόμενος τὴν βασιλείαν τοῦ θεοῦ, τολμήσας εἰσῆλθεν πρὸς τὸν Πιλᾶτον καὶ ᾐτήσατο τὸ σῶμα τοῦ Ἰησοῦ.
𝔊 : Ἄνθρωπος ἦν ἐξ <u>Αρμαθαιμ</u> Σιφα ἐξ ὄρους Εφραιμ, καὶ ὄνομα αὐτῷ Ελκανα υἱὸς Ιερεμεηλ υἱοῦ Ηλιου υἱοῦ Θοκε ἐν Νασιβ Εφραιμ.

Corresponding words: Ἁριμαθαίας/Αρμαθαιμ.

There is no thematic correspondence between the passages. This is a verbal parallel, not a reference.

Isa. 53.9, 12
There are no significant words in common. This is not a reference.

Mark 15.44-45

There are no suggested references.

Mark 15.46

1 Sam. 14.33
Mk: καὶ ἀγοράσας σινδόνα καθελὼν αὐτὸν ἐνείλησεν τῇ σινδόνι καὶ ἔθηκεν αὐτὸν ἐν μνημείῳ ὃ ἦν λελατομημένον ἐκ πέτρας καὶ <u>προσεκύλισεν</u> <u>λίθον</u> ἐπὶ τὴν θύραν τοῦ μνημείου.
𝔊 : καὶ ἀπηγγέλη τῷ Σαουλ λέγοντες Ἡμάρτηκεν ὁ λαὸς τῷ κυρίῳ φαγὼν σὺν τῷ αἵματι. καὶ εἶπεν Σαουλ ἐν Γεθθεμ <u>Κυλίσατέ</u> μοι <u>λίθον</u> ἐνταῦθα μέγαν.

Corresponding words: (προσ)κυλίω; λίθον.

λίθος is a common word, occurring about 250 times in the LXX. There is some correspondence between προσκυλίω and κυλίω, which are both rare (κυλίω occurs twelve times in the LXX), but that correspondence is not strong enough to indicate a reference.

Lam. 3.53
Mk: καὶ ἀγοράσας σινδόνα καθελὼν αὐτὸν ἐνείλησεν τῇ σινδόνι καὶ <u>ἔθηκεν</u> αὐτὸν ἐν μνημείῳ ὃ ἦν λελατομημένον ἐκ πέτρας καὶ προσεκύλισεν <u>λίθον ἐπὶ</u> τὴν θύραν τοῦ μνημείου.
𝔊 : ἐθανάτωσαν ἐν λάκκῳ ζωήν μου καὶ <u>ἐπέθηκαν</u> <u>λίθον ἐπ'</u> ἐμοί

Corresponding words: (ἐπι)τίθημι; λίθον ἐπί.
These words are too common to indicate a reference.

1 Sam. 7.12
Mk: καὶ ἀγοράσας σινδόνα καθελὼν αὐτὸν ἐνείλησεν τῇ σινδόνι καὶ ἔθηκεν αὐτὸν ἐν μνημείῳ ὃ ἦν λελατομημένον ἐκ πέτρας καὶ προσεκύλισεν <u>λίθον</u> ἐπὶ τὴν θύραν τοῦ μνημείου.
𝔊 : καὶ ἔλαβεν Σαμουηλ <u>λίθον</u> ἕνα καὶ ἔστησεν αὐτὸν ἀνὰ μέσον Μασσηφαθ καὶ ἀνὰ μέσον τῆς παλαιᾶς καὶ ἐκάλεσεν τὸ ὄνομα αὐτοῦ Αβενεζερ, <u>Λίθος</u> τοῦ βοηθοῦ, καὶ εἶπεν Ἕως ἐνταῦθα ἐβοήθησεν ἡμῖν κύριος.

Appendix C: Textual Analysis of Mark 15

Corresponding word: λίθον.
λίθος is too common to indicate a reference.

Isa. 53.9
There are no significant words in common. This is not a reference.

Mark 15.47

There are no suggested references.

Bibliography

Achtemeier, Paul J., 'Gospel of Mark', in vol. 4 of *The Anchor Bible Dictionary*, ed. David Noel Freedman, 6 vols, New York: Doubleday, 1992, pp. 541–57.

Aland, Barbara et al. (eds), *Novum Testamentum Graece*, 27th edition, Stuttgart: Deutsche Bibelgesellschaft, 1993.

Albl, Martin, *'And Scripture Cannot Be Broken': The Form and Function of the Early Christian Testimonia Collections*, Supplements to Novum Testamentum 96, Leiden: Brill, 1999.

Albrecht, Evelin, 'The Silence of Jesus in the Passion', in *Good News in History: Essays in Honor of Bo Reicke*, ed. L. Miller, Atlanta: Scholars Press, 1993, pp. 35–43.

Allegro, J. M., 'A Newly Discovered Fragment of a Commentary on Psalm XXXVII', *Palestine Exploration Quarterly* 86 (1954), pp. 69–75.

Allison, Dale C., Jr, *The End of the Ages Has Come: An Early Interpretation of the Passion and Resurrection of Jesus*, Philadelphia: Fortress, 1985.

Alter, Robert, *The Pleasures of Reading in an Ideological Age*, New York: Simon and Schuster, 1989.

Attridge, Harold W., *The Epistle to the Hebrews*, ed. Helmut Koester, Hermeneia, Philadelphia: Fortress, 1989.

Auerbach, E., *Mimesis: The Representation of Reality in Western Literature*, trans. Willard Trask, Garden City, NY: Doubleday, 1957.

Aune, David E., *Revelation*, Word Biblical Commentary, vol. 52, 3 vols, Dallas: Word Books, 1997.

Aus, Rodger David, *Samuel, Saul, and Jesus: Three Early Palestinian Jewish Christian Gospel Haggadoth*, Atlanta: Scholars Press, 1994.

Bailey, Kenneth E., 'The Fall of Jerusalem and Mark's Account of the Cross', *Expository Times* 102 (1991), pp. 102–5.

Barrett, C. K., 'The Background of Mark 10:45', in *New Testament Essays: Studies in Memory of Thomas Walter Manson*, ed. A. J. B. Higgins, Manchester: Manchester University Press, 1959, pp. 1–18.

Barthélemy, D. and J. T. Milik, *Qumran Cave 1*, Discoveries in the Judaean Desert I, Oxford: Clarendon Press, 1955.

Bellinger, William H., Jr and William R. Farmer (eds), *Jesus and the Suffering Servant: Isaiah 53 and Christian Origins*, Harrisburg, Penn.: Trinity Press International, 1998.

Best, Ernest, *Mark: The Gospel as Story*, Edinburgh: T&T Clark, 1983.
——, *The Temptation and the Passion: The Markan Soteriology*, 2nd edn, Cambridge: Cambridge University Press, 1990.
Beutler, Johannes, 'Psalm 42/43 im Johannesevangelium', *New Testament Studies* 25 (1978), pp. 33–57.
Black, Matthew, 'The Theological Appropriation of the Old Testament by the New Testament', *Scottish Journal of Theology* 39 (1986), pp. 1–17.
Bloom, Harold, *The Anxiety of Influence: A Theory of Poetry*, New York: Oxford University Press, 1973.
Bornkamm, Günther, *Early Christian Experience*, New York: Harper & Row, 1969.
Booth, Wayne C., *A Rhetoric of Irony*, Chicago: University of Chicago Press, 1974.
Bousset, Wilhelm, *Kyrios Christos*, trans. John E. Steely, Nashville: Abingdon, 1970.
Boyarin, Daniel, *Intertextuality and the Reading of Midrash*, Bloomington: Indiana University Press, 1990.
Braude, William (trans.), *The Midrash on Psalms*, New Haven: Yale University Press, 1959.
Brawley, Robert L., *Text to Text Pours Forth Speech: Voices of Scripture in Luke–Acts*, Bloomington: Indiana University Press, 1995.
Broadhead, Edwin K., *Prophet, Son, Messiah: Narrative Form and Function in Mark 14-16*, Journal for the Study of the New Testament Supplement Series 97, Sheffield: JSOT Press, 1994.
——, *Mark*, Sheffield: Sheffield Academic Press, 2001.
Brooke, George J., *Exegesis at Qumran: 4Q Florilegium in its Jewish Context*, Sheffield: JSOT Press, 1985.
——, '4Q500 and the Use of Scripture in the Parable of the Vineyard', *Dead Sea Discoveries* 2 (1995), pp. 268–294.
Brooks, James A., *Mark*, The New American Commentary 23, Nashville: Broadman, 1991.
Brower, Kent, 'Elijah and the Markan Passion Narrative', *Journal for the Study of the New Testament* 18 (1983), pp. 85–101.
Brown, Raymond E., *The Death of the Messiah*, New York: Doubleday, 1994.
——, D. W. Johnson and Kevin G. O'Connell, 'Texts and Versions', *The New Jerome Biblical Commentary*, ed. Raymond E. Brown et al. Englewood Cliffs, NJ: Prentice Hall, 1990, pp. 1091–96.
Bryan, Christopher, 'As It Is Written: Notes on the Essentially Oral Characteristics of Mark's Appeal to Scripture', *Sewanee Theological Review* 36 (1992), pp. 78–90.
Bultmann, Rudolf, *History of the Synoptic Tradition*, trans. John Marsh, New York: Harper & Row, 1963.
Burkill, T. A., 'St Mark's Philosophy of the Passion', *Novum Testamentum* 2 (1958), pp. 245–71.
Caragounis, Chrys C., *The Son of Man: Vision and Interpretation*, Wissenschaftliche Untersuchungen zum Neuen Testament 38, Tübingen: J. C. B. Mohr (Siebeck), 1986.

Carlston, C. E., 'Transfiguration and Resurrection', *Journal of Biblical Literature* 80 (1961), pp. 233–40.

Carson, D. A. and H. G. M. Williamson (eds), *It Is Written: Scripture Citing Scripture: Essays in Honour of Barnabas Lindars, SSF*, Cambridge: Cambridge University Press, 1988.

Casey, Maurice, 'The Use of the Term "Son of Man" in the Similitudes of Enoch', *Journal for the Study of Judaism* 7 (1976), pp. 11–29.

———, *Son of Man: The Interpretation and Influence of Daniel 7*, London: SPCK, 1979.

———, *The Solution to the 'Son of Man' Problem*, ed. Mark Goodacre, Library of New Testament Studies 343, London: T&T Clark, 2007.

Charles, R. H. (ed.), *The Apocrypha and Pseudepigrapha of the Old Testament*, 2 vols, Oxford: Clarendon Press, 1913.

Charlesworth, J. H. (ed.), *The Old Testament Pseudepigrapha*, 2 vols, New York: Doubleday, 1983.

——— et al. (eds), *The Messiah: Developments in Earliest Judaism and Christianity*, Minneapolis: Fortress, 1992.

Chilton, Bruce, 'The Transfiguration: Dominical Assurance and Apostolic Vision', *New Testament Studies* 27 (1980), pp. 115–24.

Clayton, Jay and Eric Rothstein, 'Figures in the Corpus: Theories of Influence and Intertextuality', in *Influence and Intertextuality*, ed. Jay Clayton and Eric Rothstein, Madison: University of Wisconsin Press, 1991, pp. 11–29.

Collins, Adela Yarbro, '"Remove This Cup": Suffering and Healing in the Gospel of Mark', in *Suffering and Healing in Our Day*, ed. Francis A. Eigo, OSA, Proceedings of the Theology Institute of Villanova University, Villanova, Penn.: Villanova University Press, 1990, pp. 29–61.

———, *Mark: A Commentary*, ed. Harold Attridge, Hermeneia, Minneapolis: Fortress, 2007.

Collins, John J., 'The Son of Man in First-Century Judaism', *New Testament Studies* 38 (1992), pp. 448–66.

———, *Daniel: A Commentary on the Book of Daniel*, with an essay by Adela Yarbro Collins, 'The Influence of Daniel on the New Testament', Hermeneia, Minneapolis: Fortress, 1993.

———, 'The Son of God Text from Qumran', in *From Jesus to John: Essays on Jesus and New Testament Christology in Honour of Marinus de Jonge*, ed. M. C. de Boer, Sheffield: Sheffield Academic Press, 1993, pp. 65–82.

———, *The Scepter and the Star: The Messiahs of the Dead Sea Scrolls and Other Ancient Literature*, New York: Doubleday, 1995.

Cook, Stephen L., 'The Metamorphosis of a Shepherd: The Tradition History of Zechariah 11:17 + 13:7-9', *Catholic Biblical Quarterly* 55 (1993), pp. 453–66.

Cranfield, C. E. B., *The Gospel According to Saint Mark: An Introduction and Commentary*, Cambridge Greek Testament Commentary, Cambridge: Cambridge University Press, 1959.

Crossan, John Dominic, *The Cross That Spoke*, San Francisco: Harper & Row, 1988.

———, *Jesus: A Revolutionary Biography*, San Francisco: HarperSanFrancisco, 1994.

Dahl, N. A., *The Crucified Messiah and Other Essays*, Minneapolis: Augsburg, 1974.

Danker, Frederick W., 'The Literary Unity of Mark 14:1-25', *Journal of Biblical Literature* 85 (1966), pp. 467–72.

Delamarter, Steve and James H. Charlesworth, *A Scripture Index to Charlesworth's The Old Testament Pseudepigrapha*, London: Sheffield Academic Press, 2002.

Derrett, J. Duncan M., *The Making of Mark: The Scriptural Bases of the Earliest Gospel*, 2 vols, Shipston-on-Stour, Engl.: Drinkwater, 1985.

Dibelius, Martin, *Botschaft und Geschichte: Erster Band, Zur Evangelienforschung*, Tübingen: Mohr Siebeck, 1953.

———, *From Tradition to Gospel*, trans. Bertram Lee Woolf, New York: Scribner, 1965.

Dodd, Charles H., *According to the Scriptures*, London: Nisbet, 1952.

———, *Historical Tradition in the Fourth Gospel*, Cambridge: Cambridge University Press, 1963.

———, *The Apostolic Preaching and Its Developments*, New York: Harper & Row, 1964.

———, *The Old Testament in the New*, Philadelphia: Fortress, 1965.

Donahue, John R., SJ, *Are You the Christ? The Trial Narrative in the Gospel of Mark*, Society for Biblical Literature Dissertation Series 10, Missoula, Mont.: Scholars Press, 1973.

———, 'Recent Studies on the Origin of "Son of Man" in the Gospels', *Catholic Biblical Quarterly* 48 (1986), pp. 484–98.

———, *The Gospel of Mark*, Sacra Pagina 2, Collegeville, Minn.: Liturgical Press, 2002.

Dormeyer, Detlev, *Die Passion Jesu als Verhaltensmodell: Literarische und theologische Analyse der Traditions- und Redaktionsgeschichte der Markuspassion*, Munster: Aschendorff, 1974.

Dowd, Sharyn E., 'Reading Mark Reading Isaiah', *Lexington Theological Quarterly* 30 (1995), pp. 133–43.

———, *Reading Mark: A Literary and Theological Commentary on the Second Gospel*, Macon, Ga.: Smyth & Helwys, 2000.

Draisma, Sipke (ed.), *Intertextuality in Biblical Writings: Essays in Honor of Bas van Iersel*, Kampen: Kok, 1989.

Duff, Paul Brooks, 'The March of the Divine Warrior and the Advent of the Greco-Roman King: Mark's Account of Jesus' Entry into Jerusalem', *Journal of Biblical Literature* 111 (1992), pp. 55–71.

Duling, Dennis C., 'Promises to David', *New Testament Studies* 20 (1973), pp. 55–77.
Duncan-Jones, Katherine (ed.), *Shakespeare's Sonnets*, Thomas Nelson, 1997.
Dunn, James D. G., *The Theology of Paul the Apostle*, Grand Rapids: Eerdmans, 1998.
Durling, Robert M. (trans.), *Petrarch's Lyric Poems: The Rime sparse and Other Lyrics*, Cambridge, Mass.: Harvard University Press, 1976.
Elliger, K. and W. Rudolph (eds), *Biblia Hebraica Stuttgartensia*, 15th edition, Stuttgart: Deutsche Bibelgesellschaft, 1997.
Ellis, E. Earle, *Paul's Use of the Old Testament*, Edinburgh: Oliver and Boyd, 1957.
———, *The Old Testament in Early Christianity: Canon and Interpretation in the Light of Modern Research*, Wissenschaftliche Untersuchungen zum Neuen Testament 54, Tübingen: J. C. B. Mohr (Paul Siebeck), 1991.
Emerton, J. A., 'Mark XIV. 24 and the Targum to the Psalter', *Journal of Theological Studies* n.s. 15 (1964), pp. 58–59.
Epstein, I. (ed.), *The Babylonian Talmud*, London: Soncino, 1961.
Epstein, J. N. and Ezra Zion Melamed (eds), *Mekhilta de Rabi Shim'on ben Yohai*, Jerusalem: 1979.
Eslinger, L., 'The Wooing of the Woman at the Well', in *The Gospel of John as Literature: An Anthology of Twentieth-Century Perspectives*, ed. Mark W. G. Stibbe, Leiden: Brill, 1993.
Evans, Christopher, 'I Will Go Before You Into Galilee', *Journal of Theological Studies* n.s. 5 (1954), pp. 3–18.
Evans, Craig A., 'On the Vineyard Parables of Isaiah 5 and Mark 12', *Biblische Zeitschrift* 28 (1984), pp. 82–86.
———, 'On the Isaianic Background of the Sower Parable', *Catholic Biblical Quarterly* 47 (1985), pp. 464–468.
———, 'In What Sense "Blasphemy"?', in *Society of Biblical Literature Seminar Papers, 1991*, ed. Eugene H. Lovering, Jr, Society of Biblical Literature Seminar Papers 30, Atlanta: Scholars Press, 1991, pp. 215–34.
——— and W. Richard Stegner (eds), *The Gospels and the Scriptures of Israel*, Journal for the Study of the New Testament Supplement Series 104, Sheffield: Sheffield Academic Press, 1994.
———, *Jesus and His Contemporaries: Comparative Studies*, Leiden: Brill, 1995.
——— and Peter Flint (eds), *Eschatology, Messianism, and the Dead Sea Scrolls*, Grand Rapids, Mich.: Eerdmans, 1997.
——— and James A. Sanders (eds), *Early Christian Interpretation of the Scriptures of Israel: Investigations and Proposals*, Journal for the Study of the New Testament Supplement Series 148, Sheffield: Sheffield Academic Press, 1997.
———, *Mark 8:27-16:20*, Word Biblical Commentary, vol. 34B, Nashville: Thomas Nelson, 2001.

Fabry, Heinz-Josef, 'Die Wirkungsgeschichte des Psalms 22', in *Beiträge zur Psalmenforschung: Psalm 2 und 22*, ed. J. Schreiner, Forschung zur Bibel 60, Würzburg: Echter, 1988, pp. 279–317.

Fishbane, Michael, *Biblical Interpretation in Ancient Israel*, Oxford: Clarendon Press, 1985.

——, 'Inner Biblical Exegesis: Types and Strategies of Interpretation in Ancient Israel', in *Midrash and Literature*, ed. S. Budick and G. Hartmann, New Haven: Yale University Press, 1986, pp. 19–37.

Fitzmyer, Joseph A., SJ, 'Judaic Studies and the Gospels: The Seminar', in *The Relationships Among the Gospels: An Interdisciplinary Dialogue*, ed. William O. Walker, Jr, San Antonio: Trinity University Press, 1978, pp. 237–58.

——, *The Semitic Background of the New Testament: Combined Edition of Essays on the Semitic Background of the New Testament, and A Wandering Aramean: Collected Aramaic Essays*, Grand Rapids: Eerdmans, 1997.

——, *The Dead Sea Scrolls and Christian Origins*, Studies in the Dead Sea Scrolls and Related Literature, Grand Rapids: Eerdmans, 2000.

Flint, Peter W. and James C. VanderKam (eds), *The Dead Sea Scrolls After Fifty Years: A Comprehensive Assessment*, 2 vols, Leiden: Brill, 1998–99.

Fowler, Robert M., 'Irony and the Messianic Secret in the Gospel of Mark', *Proceedings: Eastern Great Lakes Biblical Society* 1 (1981), pp. 26–36.

Freed, Edwin D., 'Psalm 42/43 in John's Gospel', *New Testament Studies* 29 (1983), pp. 52–73.

Gamble, Harry Y., *Books and Readers in the Early Church: A History of Early Christian Texts*, New Haven: Yale University Press, 1995.

García Martínez, Florentino and Eibert J. C. Tigchelaar, *The Dead Sea Scrolls Study Edition*, 2 vols, Leiden: Brill, 1997.

Garland, David E., *Mark*, The NIV Application Commentary, Grand Rapids: Zondervan, 1996.

Garner, Richard, *From Homer to Tragedy: The Art of Allusion in Greek Poetry*, London: Routledge, 1990.

Gnilka, Joachim, *Das Evangelium nach Markus*, 2 vols, Evangelisch-Katholischer Kommentar zum Neuen Testament, Zürich: Benziger, 1978–79.

Gordis, Robert, 'The "Begotten" Messiah in the Qumran Scrolls', *Vetus Testamentum* 7 (1957), pp. 191–94.

Gould, Ezra P., *Critical and Exegetical Commentary on the Gospel According to St Mark*, The International Critical Commentary, Edinburgh: T&T Clark, 1982.

Gray, Martin, *A Dictionary of Literary Terms*, 2nd rev. edn, Harlow: Longman, 1992.

Greenspoon, L., 'The Use and Abuse of the Term "LXX" and Related Terminology in Recent Scholarship', *Bulletin of the International*

Organization for Septuagint and Cognate Studies 20 (1987), pp. 21–29.

Grundmann, Walter, *Das Evangelium nach Markus*, 7th rev. edn, Theologischer Handkommentar zum Neuen Testament 2, Berlin: Evangelische Verlagsanstalt, 1977.

Guelich, Robert A., '"The Beginning of the Gospel": Mark 1:1-15', *Biblical Research* 27 (1982), pp. 5–15.

——, *Mark 1-8:26*, Word Biblical Commentary, vol. 34A, Dallas: Word Books, 1989.

Guichard, Daniel, 'La reprise du Psaume 22 dans le récit de la mort de Jésus (Marc 15, 21-41)', *Foi et Vie* 87 (Sept. 1988), pp. 59–65.

Gundry, Robert Horton, *The Use of the Old Testament in St Matthew's Gospel: With Special Reference to the Messianic Hope*, Leiden: Brill, 1967.

——, *Mark: A Commentary on His Apology for the Cross*, Grand Rapids: Eerdmans, 1993.

Haenchen, Ernst, *Der Weg Jesu: Eine Erklärung des Markus-Evangeliums und der kanonischen Parallelen*, Berlin: Alfred Töpelmann, 1966.

Hare, D., *The Son of Man Tradition*, Minneapolis: Fortress, 1990.

Harmon, William and C. Hugh Holman, *A Handbook to Literature*, 7th edn, Upper Saddle River, NJ: Prentice Hall, 1996.

Harnack, A. von, *Bible Reading in the Early Church*, New York: G. P. Putnam's Sons, 1912.

Hartman, Lars, *Prophecy Interpreted: The Formation of Some Jewish Apocalyptic Texts and of the Eschatological Discourse Mark 13 par.*, Lund: Gleerup, 1966.

Hatch, Edwin and Henry A. Redpath et al., *A Concordance to the Septuagint: And the Other Greek Versions of the Old Testament (Including the Apocryphal Books)*, 2nd edn, Grand Rapids: Baker, 1998.

Hawthorne, Gerald F. and Otto Betz (eds), *Tradition and Interpretation in the New Testament: Essays in Honor of E. Earle Ellis for His 60th Birthday*, Grand Rapids: Eerdmans, 1987.

Hay, David M., *Glory at the Right Hand: Psalm 110 in Early Christianity*, Nashville: Abingdon, 1973.

Hays, R., *Echoes of Scripture in the Letters of Paul*, New Haven: Yale University Press, 1989.

——, '"Who Has Believed Our Message?" Paul's Reading of Isaiah', in vol. 1 of *SBL Seminar Papers, 1998*, 2 vols, Society of Biblical Literature Seminar Papers 37, Atlanta: Scholars Press, 1998, pp. 205–225.

Hengel, Martin, *Studies in the Gospel of Mark*, trans. John Bowden, London: SCM Press, 1985.

Hilber, John W., 'Theology of Worship in Exodus 24', *Journal of the Evangelical Theological Society* 39 (1996), pp. 177–89.

Hollander, J., *The Figure of Echo: A Mode of Allusion in Milton and After*, Berkeley: University of California Press, 1981.

Hooker, Morna D., *Jesus and the Servant: The Influence of the Servant Concept of Deutero-Isaiah in the New Testament*, London: SPCK, 1959.

———, *The Son of Man in Mark: A Study of the Background of the Term 'Son of Man' and Its Use in St Mark's Gospel*, Montreal: McGill University Press, 1967.

———, 'Is the Son of Man Problem Really Insoluble?' in *Text and Interpretation: Studies in the New Testament Presented to Matthew Black*, ed. Ernest Best and R. McL. Wilson, Cambridge: Cambridge University Press, 1979, pp. 155–68.

———, *The Message of Mark*, London: Epworth, 1983.

———, *Not Ashamed of the Gospel: New Testament Interpretations of the Death of Christ*, Grand Rapids: Eerdmans, 1994.

Horbury, William, 'The Messianic Associations of the "Son of Man"', *Journal of Theological Studies* n.s. 36 (1985), pp. 34–55.

Horton, Fred, *The Melchizedek Tradition: A Critical Examination of the Sources, to the Fifth Century A.D. and in the Epistle to the Hebrews*, Cambridge: Cambridge University Press, 1976.

Hurtado, Larry W., *Mark*, New International Biblical Commentary 2, Peabody, Mass.: Hendrickson, 1989.

———, *Lord Jesus Christ: Devotion to Jesus in Earliest Christianity*, Grand Rapids: Eerdmans, 2003.

Iersel, Bas van, '"Son of God" in the New Testament', in *Jesus, Son of God?*, ed. Edward Schillebeeckx and Johannes-Baptist Metz, New York: Seabury, 1982, pp. 37–48.

———, *Mark: A Reader Response Commentary*, trans. W. H. Bisscheroux, Journal for the Study of New Testament Supplement Series 164, Sheffield: Sheffield Academic Press, 1998.

Jellicoe, S., *The Septuagint and Modern Study*, Oxford: Clarendon Press, 1968.

Jinkins, Michael and Stephen Breck Reid, 'God's Forsakenness: The Cry of Dereliction as an Utterance Within the Trinity', *Horizons in Biblical Theology* 19 (1997), pp. 33–57.

Jonge, Marinus de and A. S. van der Woude, '11Q Melchizedek and the New Testament', *New Testament Studies* 12 (1966), pp. 301–26.

———, 'Jesus' Death for Others and the Death of the Maccabean Martyrs', in *Text and Testimony: Essays on New Testament and Apocryphal Literature in Honour of A. F. J. Klijn*, ed. T. Baarda et al., Kampen: Kok, 1988, pp. 142–51.

Juel, Donald H., *Messiah and Temple*, Society of Biblical Literature Dissertation Series 31, Missoula: Scholars Press, 1977.

———, *Messianic Exegesis: Christological Interpretation of the Old Testament in Early Christianity*, Philadelphia: Fortress, 1988.

———, *Mark*, Augsburg Commentary on the New Testament, Minneapolis: Augsburg, 1990.

———, *The Gospel of Mark*, Interpreting Biblical Texts, Nashville: Abingdon, 1999.
Kee, Howard Clark, 'The Function of Scriptural Quotations and Allusions in Mark 11-16', in *Jesus und Paulus: Festschrift für Werner Georg Kümmel zum 70. Geburtstag*, ed. E. Earle Ellis and Erich Grässer, Göttingen: Vandenhoeck & Ruprecht, 1975, pp. 165–88.
———, *Community of the New Age: Studies in Mark's Gospel*, Philadelphia: Westminster, 1977.
Kelber, Werner H. (ed.), *The Passion in Mark: Studies on Mark 14–16*, Philadelphia: Fortress, 1976.
Kempthorne, Renatus, 'The Marcan Text of Jesus' Answer to the High Priest (Mark XIV 62)', *Novum Testamentum* 19 (1977), pp. 197–208.
Kennedy, George A., *Classical Rhetoric and Its Christian and Secular Tradition from Ancient to Modern Times*, Chapel Hill: University of North Carolina Press, 1980.
Kermode, F., *The Genesis of Secrecy: On the Interpretation of Narrative*, Cambridge, Mass.: Harvard University Press, 1979.
Kiley, Mark, '"Lord, Save My Life" (Ps 116:4) as Generative Text for Jesus' Gethsemane Prayer (Mark 14:36a)', *Catholic Biblical Quarterly* 48 (1986), pp. 655–59.
Kittel, G. and G. Friedrich (eds), *Theological Dictionary of the New Testament*, trans. G. W. Bromiley, 10 vols, Grand Rapids: Eerdmans, 1964–76.
Knibb, Michael A., with Edward Ullendorff, *The Ethiopic Book of Enoch: A New Edition in the Light of the Aramaic Dead Sea Fragments*, 2 vols, Oxford: Clarendon, 1978.
———, 'The Date of the Parables of Enoch: A Critical Review', *New Testament Studies* 25 (1979), pp. 345–359.
Kobelski, Paul J., *Melchizedek and Melchireša*, Washington, DC: Catholic Biblical Association of America, 1981.
Koester, Helmut, *Ancient Christian Gospels*, Philadelphia: Trinity, 1990.
Kort, Wesley A., *'Take, Read'*, University Park, Penn.: Penn State Press, 1996.
Kugel, James L., *In Potiphar's House*, San Francisco: HarperSanFrancisco, 1990.
———, *Traditions of the Bible: A Guide to the Bible As It Was at the Start of the Common Era*, Cambridge, Mass.: Harvard University Press, 1998.
Lake, Kirsopp (trans.), *Apostolic Fathers*, Loeb Classical Library, 2 vols, Cambridge: Harvard University Press, 1912–13.
Lampe, G. W. H., *A Patristic Greek Lexicon*, Oxford: Clarendon Press, 1961.
Landes, George M., 'The "Three Days and Three Nights" Motif in Jonah 2:1', *Journal of Biblical Literature* 86 (1967), pp. 446–50.
Lauterbach, Jacob Z. (trans.), *Mekilta de-Rabbi Ishmael*, 2 vols, Philadelphia: Jewish Publication Society of America, 1933, 2004.

Lee, Aquila H. I., *From Messiah to Preexistent Son: Jesus' Self-Consciousness and Early Christian Exegesis of Messianic Psalms*, Tübingen: Mohr Siebeck, 2005.

Legg, S. C. E., *Nouum Testamentum Graece: Secundum Textum Westcotto-Hortianum: Euangelium Secundum Markum*, Oxford: Clarendon Press, 1935.

Leivestad, R., 'Exit the Apocalyptic Son of Man', *New Testament Studies* 18 (1972), pp. 243–67.

Liddell, Henry George and Robert Scott, *A Greek-English Lexicon*, 9th edn, Oxford: Clarendon Press, 1996.

Lindars, Barnabas, SSF, *New Testament Apologetic*, Philadelphia: Westminster, 1961.

———, 'The Place of the Old Testament in the Formation of New Testament Theology', with response by Peder Borgan, *New Testament Studies* 23 (1977), pp. 59–75.

———, *Jesus, Son of Man: A Fresh Examination of the Son of Man Sayings in the Gospels in the Light of Recent Research*, Grand Rapids: Eerdmans, 1983.

Linnemann, Eta, *Studien zur Passionsgeschichte*, Göttingen: Vandenhoeck & Ruprecht, 1970.

Lohse, E., *History of the Suffering and Death of Jesus Christ*, trans. Martin O. Dietrich, Philadelphia: Fortress, 1967.

Lührmann, Dieter, *Das Markusevangelium*, Handbuch zum Neuen Testament 3, Tübingen: J. C. B. Mohr (Paul Siebeck), 1987.

Mack, Burton, *A Myth of Innocence*, Philadelphia: Fortress, 1988.

Manson, T. W., *The Teaching of Jesus: Studies of its Form and Content*, Cambridge: Cambridge University Press, 1967.

Marcus, Joel, 'Mark 9,11-13: "As It Has Been Written"', *Zeitschrift für die neutestamentliche Wissenschaft* 80 (1989), pp. 42–63.

———, 'The Jewish War and the Sitz im Leben of Mark', *Journal of Biblical Literature* 111 (1992), pp. 441–62.

———, *The Way of the Lord: Christological Exegesis of the Old Testament in the Gospel of Mark*, Louisville: Westminster/John Knox, 1992.

———, 'Mark and Isaiah', in *Fortunate the Eyes That See: Essays in Honor of David Noel Freedman in Celebration of His Seventieth Birthday*, ed. Astrid B. Beck et al., Grand Rapids: Eerdmans, 1995, pp. 449–66.

———, *Mark 1-8: A New Translation with Introduction and Commentary*, Anchor Bible 27, New York: Doubleday, 2000.

Matera, Frank J., *The Kingship of Jesus: Composition and Theology in Mark 15*, Society of Biblical Literature Dissertation Series 66, Chico: Scholars Press, 1982.

Maurer, Christian, 'Knecht Gottes und Sohn Gottes im Passionsbericht des Markusevangeliums', *Zeitschrift für Theologie und Kirche* 50 (1953), pp. 1–38.

Mays, James L., 'Prayer and Christology: Psalm 22 as Perspective on the Passion', *Theology Today* 42 (1985), pp. 322–31.

McArthur, Harvey K., '"On the Third Day"', *New Testament Studies* 18 (1971), pp. 81–86.

McNamara, Martin, *The New Testament and the Palestinian Targum to the Pentateuch*, Rome: Pontifical Biblical Institute, 1966.

—— et al. (eds), *The Aramaic Bible: The Targums*, 21 vols, Collegeville: Liturgical Press, 1987–.

Metzger, Bruce M., *A Textual Commentary on the Greek New Testament: A Companion Volume to the United Bible Societies' Greek New Testament (fourth revised edition)*, 2nd edn, Stuttgart: Deutsche Bibelgesellschaft, 1994.

Milik, J. T., 'Problèmes de la littérature Hénochique à la lumière des fragments Araméens de Qumrân', *Harvard Theological Review* 64 (1971), pp. 333–78.

Miller, Patrick, *Interpreting the Psalms*, Philadelphia: Fortress, 1986.

Mitchell, Alan C., *Hebrews*, Sacra Pagina 13, Collegeville: Liturgical Press, 2007.

Moo, Douglas J., *The Old Testament in the Gospel Passion Narratives*, Sheffield: Almond, 1983.

Morner, Kathleen, *NTC's Dictionary of Literary Terms*, Lincolnwood, Ill.: National Textbook, 1991.

Moule, C. F. D., *The Gospel According to Mark*, Cambridge: Cambridge University Press, 1965.

Moyise, Steve (ed.), *The Old Testament in the New Testament: Essays in Honour of J. L. North*, Journal for the Study of the New Testament: Supplement Series 189, Sheffield: Sheffield Academic Press, 2000.

Neirynck, Frans, *Duality in Mark: Contributions to the Study of the Markan Redaction*, Bibliotheca Ephemeridum Theologicarum Lovaniensium 31, rev. edn with supplementary notes, Louvain: Leuven University Press, 1988.

Neusner, Jacob, *The Talmud of the Land of Israel*, 35 vols, Chicago: University of Chicago Press, 1982–94.

Nickelsburg, George W. E., 'The Genre and Function of the Markan Passion Narrative', *Harvard Theological Review* 73 (1980), pp. 153–84.

Nineham, D. E., *The Gospel of St Mark*, Middlesex: Penguin, 1963.

Nogalski, James D., 'Zechariah 13.7-9 as a Transition Text: An Appreciation and Re-evaluation of the Work of Rex Mason', in *Bringing Out the Treasure: Inner Biblical Allusion in Zechariah 9-14*, ed. Mark Boda and Michael Floyd, London: Sheffield Academic Press, 2003, pp. 292–304.

O'Brien, Kelli S., 'Innocence and Guilt: Apologetic, Martyr Stories, and Allusion in the Markan Trial Narrative', in *The Trial and Death of Jesus: Essays on the Passion Narrative in Mark*, ed. G. C. M. van Oyen and Tom Shepherd, Contributions in Biblical Exegesis and Theology 45, Louvain: Peeters, 2006, pp. 205–28.

Oegema, Gerbern S., *The Anointed and His People: Messianic Expectations from the Maccabees to Bar Kochba*, trans. and revised by the author, Journal for the Study of the Pseudepigrapha Supplement Series 27, Sheffield: Sheffield Academic Press, 1998.

Owen, Paul and David Shepherd, 'Speaking Up for Qumran, Dalman and the Son of Man: Was *Bar Enasha* a Common Term for "Man" in the Time of Jesus?', *Journal for the Study of the New Testament* 81 (2001), pp. 81–122.

Pace, Sharon, 'The Stratigraphy of the Text of Daniel', *Bulletin of the International Organization for Septuagint and Cognate Studies* 17 (1984), pp. 15–35.

Paulien, Jon, *Decoding Revelation's Trumpets: Literary Allusions and Interpretation of Revelation 8:7-12*, Berrien Springs, Mich.: Andrews University Press, 1987.

Perri, Carmela, 'On Alluding', *Poetics* 7 (1978), pp. 289–307.

Perrin, Norman, 'Mark XIV. 62: The End Product of a Christian Pesher Tradition?', *New Testament Studies* 12 (1966), pp. 150–55.

———, *Rediscovering the Teaching of Jesus*, New York: Harper & Row, 1967.

———, 'The Use of (παρα)διδόναι in Connection with the Passion of Jesus in the New Testament', in *Der Ruf Jesu und die Antwort der Gemeinde: Festschrift für Joachim Jeremias*, ed. E. Lohse et al., Göttingen: Vandenhoeck & Ruprecht, 1970, pp. 204–12.

———, *A Modern Pilgrimage in New Testament Christology*, Philadelphia: Fortress, 1974.

Pesch, Rudolf, *Das Markusevangelium*, 2 vols, Herders theologischer Kommentar zum Neuen Testament, Freiburg: Herder, 1976–77.

Piper, Otto, 'God's Good News: The Passion Story According to Mark', *Interpretation* 9 (1955), pp. 165–82.

Puech, Émile, 'Un hymne essénien en partie retrouvé et les Béatitudes: 1QH V 12-VI 18 (=col. XIII-XIV 7) et 4Q Béat.', *Revue de Qumran* 13 (1988), pp. 59–88, pl. III.

Rahlfs, Alfred (ed.), *Septuaginta: Id est Vetus Testamentum graece iuxta LXX interpretes*, 2 vols in 1, Stuttgart: Deutsche Bibelgesellschaft, 1979.

Reumann, John H., 'Psalm 22 at the Cross: Lament and Thanksgiving for Jesus Christ', *Interpretation* 28 (1974), pp. 39–58.

Rhodes, D., J. Dewey and D. Michie, *Mark as Story: An Introduction to the Narrative of a Gospel*, 2nd edn, Philadelphia: Fortress, 1999.

Robbins, V. K., *Jesus the Teacher: A Socio-Rhetorical Interpretation of Mark*, Philadelphia: Fortress, 1984.

———, 'The Reversed Contextualization of Psalm 22 in the Markan Crucifixion: A Socio-Rhetorical Analysis', in *The Four Gospels*, ed. R. van Segbroeck et al., Louvain: Leuven University Press, 1992, pp. 1161–83.

Rodgers, Peter Robert, 'Mark 15:28', *Evangelical Quarterly* 61 (1989), pp. 81–84.
Rossé, Gérard, *The Cry of Jesus on the Cross: A Biblical and Theological Study*, trans. Stephen Wentworth Arndt, New York: Paulist, 1987.
Roth, Wolfgang, 'Mark, John and Their Old Testament Codes', in *John and the Synoptics*, ed. Adelbert Denaux, Louvain: Leuven University Press, 1992, pp. 458–65.
Ruppert, Lothar, *Jesus als der leidende Gerechte?: Der Weg Jesu im Lichte eines alt- und zwischentestamentlichen Motivs*, Bibelstudien 59, Stüttgart: KBW, 1972.
Russell, D. A. and M. Winterbottom (eds), *Ancient Literary Criticism: The Principal Texts in New Translations*, Oxford: Clarendon Press, 1972.
Sanders, E. P., *Jesus and Judaism*, Philadelphia: Fortress, 1985.
Sänger, Dieter (ed.), *Gottessohn und Menschensohn: exegetische Studien zu zwei Paradigmen biblischer Intertextualität*, Neukirchen-Vluyn: Neukirchener Verlag, 2004.
Schaberg, Jane, 'Daniel 7, 12 and the New Testament Passion-Resurrection Predictions', *New Testament Studies* 31 (1985), pp. 208–222.
Schiffman, Lawrence, *The Eschatological Community of the Dead Sea Scrolls*, Society of Biblical Literature Monograph Series 38, Atlanta: Scholars Press, 1989.
Schmithals, Walter, *Das Evangelium nach Markus*, Ökumenischer Taschenbuchkommentar zum Neuen Testament, 2 vols, rev. edn, Gütersloh: Gütersloher Verlagshaus Mohn, 1986.
Schnackenburg, Rudolf, *The Gospel According to St Mark*, 2 vols, trans. Werner Kruppa and W. J. O'Hara, New York: Herder & Herder, 1971.
Schweizer, Eduard, *The Good News According to Mark*, Richmond: John Knox, 1970.
Senior, Donald, *The Passion of Jesus in the Gospel of Mark*, Wilmington: Michael Glazier, 1984.
Septuaginta: Vetus Testamentum graece auctoritate Societatis Göttingensis editum, Göttingen: Vandenhoeck & Ruprecht, 1931–.
Seters, John van, *Abraham in History and Tradition*, New Haven: Yale University Press, 1975.
Shiner, Whitney T., 'The Ambiguous Pronouncement of the Centurion and the Shrouding of Meaning in Mark', *Journal for the Study of the New Testament* 78 (2000), pp. 3–22.
Signer, Michael, 'King/Messiah: Rashi's Exegesis of Psalm 2', *Prooftexts* 3 (1983), pp. 273–78.
Slater, Thomas, 'One Like a Son of Man in First-Century CE Judaism', *New Testament Studies* 41 (1995), pp. 183–98.
Smith, Robert H., 'Darkness at Noon: Mark's Passion Narrative', *Concordia Theological Monthly* 44 (1973), pp. 325–38.

Sommer, Benjamin, *A Prophet Reads Scripture: Allusion in Isaiah 40–66*, Stanford: Stanford University Press, 1998.
Stegner, William Richard, *Narrative Theology in Early Jewish Christianity*, Louisville: Westminster/John Knox, 1989.
Stendahl, Krister, *The School of St Matthew, and Its Use of the Old Testament*, Ramsey, NJ: Sigler, 1991.
Stevens, Bruce A., 'Why *Must* the Son of Man Suffer: The Divine Warrior in the Gospel of Mark', *Biblische Zeitschrift* n.s. 31 (1987), pp. 101–10.
Steyn, Gert J., 'Psalm 2 in Hebrews', *Neotestamentica* 37 (2003), pp. 262–82.
Stone, Michael, *Fourth Ezra*, ed. Frank Moore Cross, Hermeneia, Minneapolis: Fortress, 1990.
Strack, H. L. and G. Stemberger, *Introduction to the Talmud and Midrash*, trans. Markus Bockmuel, Edinburgh: T&T Clark, 1991.
Suhl, Alfred, *Die Funktion der alttestamentlichen Zitate und Anspielungen im Markusevangelium*, Gütersloh: Mohn, 1965.
Sukenik, E. L., *The Dead Sea Scrolls of the Hebrew University*, Jerusalem: Magnes Press, Hebrew University, 1955.
Sundberg, Albert C., 'On Testimonies', *Novum Testamentum* 3 (1959), pp. 268–81.
———, *The Old Testament of the Early Church*, Harvard Theological Studies 20, Cambridge, Mass.: Harvard University Press, 1964.
Swartley, Willard M., *Israel's Scripture Traditions and the Synoptic Gospels: Story Shaping Story*, Peabody, Mass.: Hendrickson, 1994.
Swete, Henry B., *An Introduction to the Old Testament in Greek*, revised by R. R. Ottley, New York: Ktav, 1968.
Talmon, S., 'The "Desert Motif" in the Bible and in Qumran Literature', *Biblical Motifs: Origins and Transformations*, ed. A. Altmann, Cambridge, Mass.: Harvard University Press, 1966, pp. 31–63.
Tannehill, Robert C., 'The Gospel of Mark as Narrative Christology', *Semeia* 16 (1979), pp. 57–95.
Taylor, Vincent, *Jesus and His Sacrifice*, London: MacMillan & Co, 1959.
———, *The Gospel According to St Mark*, London: Macmillan, 1966.
Theissen, Gerd, *The Gospels in Context: Social and Political History in the Synoptic Tradition*, trans. Linda Maloney, Minneapolis: Fortress, 1991.
Thompson, Michael, *Clothed with Christ: The Example and Teaching of Jesus in Romans 12.1–15.13*, Journal for the Study of the New Testament Supplement Series 59, Sheffield: JSOT Press, 1991.
Tödt, H. E., *The Son of Man in the Synoptic Tradition*, trans. Dorothea M. Barton, Philadelphia: Westminster, 1965.
Tolbert, Mary Ann, *Sowing the Gospel*, Minneapolis: Fortress, 1989.
Tov, Emmanuel, *The Text-Critical Use of the Septuagint in Biblical Research*, Jerusalem Biblical Studies 3, 2nd edn, revised and enlarged, Jerusalem: Simor, 1997.
Trochmé, Etienne, *The Passion as Liturgy: A Study in the Origin of the Passion Narratives in the Four Gospels*, London: SCM Press, 1983.

Tuckett, C. M. (ed.), *The Scriptures in the Gospels*, Louvain: Leuven University Press, 1997.
Ulrich, Eugene, *The Dead Sea Scrolls and the Origins of the Bible*, Grand Rapids: Eerdmans, 1999.
—— et al. (eds), *Qumran Cave 4: XI Psalms to Chronicles*, Discoveries in the Judaean Desert XVI, Oxford: Clarendon, 2000.
Utzschneider, Helmut, 'Situation und Szene: Überlegungen zum Verhältnis historischer und literarischer Deutung prophetischer Texte am Beispiel von Hos. 5,8-6,6', *Zeitschrift für die alttestamentliche Wissenschaft* 114 (2002), pp. 80–105.
VanderKam, James C., *From Revelation to Canon: Studies in the Hebrew Bible and Second Temple Literature*, Supplements to the Journal for the Study of Judaism 62, Leiden: Brill, 2000.
Vermès, Géza, 'Appendix E: The Use of בר נשא/בר נש in Jewish Aramaic', in Matthew Black, *An Aramaic Approach to the Gospels and Acts*, Oxford: Clarendon Press, 1967, pp. 310–30.
——, *Scripture and Tradition in Judaism*, Leiden: Brill 1973.
——, *The Complete Dead Sea Scrolls in English*, New York: Penguin Books, 2004.
Vieweger, Dieter and Annette Böckler, '"Ich gebe Ägypten als Lösegeld für dich": Mk 10,45 und die jüdische Tradition zu Jes 43,3b.4', *Zeitschrift für die alttestamentliche Wissenschaft* 108 (1996), pp. 594–607.
Watts, James W., 'Psalm 2 in the Context of Biblical Theology', *Horizons in Biblical Theology* 12 (1990), pp. 73–91.
Watts, Rikki E., *Isaiah's New Exodus and Mark*, Wissenschaftliche Untersuchungen zum Neuen Testament 2. Reihe 88, Tübingen: Mohr Siebeck, 1997.
Weeden, Theodore J., *Mark – Traditions in Conflict*, Philadelphia: Fortress, 1971.
Wentling, Judith L., 'A Comparison of the Elijan Motifs in the Gospels of Matthew and Mark', *Proceedings: Eastern Great Lakes Biblical Society* 2 (1982), pp. 104–25.
Westermann, Claus, *Praise and Lament in the Psalms*, Atlanta: John Knox, 1981.
Willey, Patricia Tull, *Remember the Former Things: The Recollection of Texts in Second Isaiah*, Society for Biblical Literature Dissertation Series 161, Atlanta: Scholars, 1997.
Wimsatt, W. K., Jr and Monroe C. Beardsley, 'The Intentional Fallacy', in *The Verbal Icon*, Lexington, Ky.: University of Kentucky Press, 1954, pp. 3–18.
Witherington, Ben, III, *Gospel of Mark: A Socio-Rhetorical Commentary*, Grand Rapids: Eerdmans, 2001.
Wrede, William, *The Messianic Secret*, trans. J. C. G. Greig, Cambridge: J. Clarke, 1971.

Index of Ancient Sources

Old Testament

Genesis
1.27	205
2.24	205
4	93
12.10-20	30
14.17-24	167
15.5-6	54
15.10, 17-18	228
17.5	54
18.14	239
20.1-18	30
21.1-10	54
21.10	33
22.2	107, 111, 158
22.12	111
22.16	111
26.1-16	30
27.34	284
38.8	38, 211
39.12	248
41.29	33
44.16	242
49.5-7	246
49.11	8

Exodus
3.6	211
3.7-9	53
3.14	259
3.22	272
4.22	42, 107, 158–59
4.23	107
8.16-24	53
10.21-23	282
12.1-6, 14-20	222
14	31, 53
15	53
16.18	65
16.29	100
19.16-19	117
20.12-16	38, 206
20.16	99, 105, 133–35, 192, 252
21.17	37, 205
23.20	2, 40, 206, 209
24	117–21
24.8	103, 117–21, 195, 198, 227
26.31-33	286
30.25, 34	219
31.18	54
32.15–33.3	119
32.32	86
34.7	51, 53
34.34	33

Leviticus
4.12	83
19.18	37, 205, 208, 213
21.5-6	52
21.23	24, 286
24.14	274
24.16	261
25.13	168

Numbers
6.23-27	54
9.22	100
11.19	100
12.10	219
12.13	149
15.35-36	274
27.17	210, 231
33.38	286

Deuteronomy
1.6	243
2.3	243
4.35	205
5.6	253
5.16	205
5.16-20	208
5.20	see 'Exod. 20.16'
6.4	205, 213
6.5	37, 205, 211, 213
8.11-20	65
14.1-2	52
15.2	168
15.11	219
16.2	222
16.3	223
21.22-23	145
25.5	211
30.12-14	33
32	61

Joshua
3–4	53

Judges
11.34	111
13.25	267
15.9-13	79, 265

Ruth
2.14	225

1 Samuel
1.1	75, 287
7.12	288
10.1-10	223
14.33	288
17.45	246
17.51	247

2 Samuel
1.1	100
7	157, 161, 163–64
7.10-14	155
7.12-13	33
7.12-16	23
7.14	41, 257
12.10	246

19.5	264			127, 154, 213–14, 283	38.15-16	88
1 Kings		22.3		89	38.20-21	269
18.28	83	22.5		153	39.10	88, 257
19.8-12	119	22.6		153, 269, 274	39.12	263
22.17	231–32				39.13	235
22.24-25	263	22.7		148, 276	41.2, 6, 8	220
22.49-50	33	22.8		6, 108–10, 148, 276	41.10	82, 91, 220–21, 225, 244
2 Kings		22.9		108–10, 148, 276, 279	42–43	104, 125–28, 193, 235
1.8	3					
20.8	114					
		22.13-14		281		
1 Chronicles		22.15		235, 240	42.6	104, 125–28, 208
28.6	33	22.16		237, 240, 258, 276	42.10	284
					42.11	280, 284
2 Chronicles		22.17		281	42.12	104, 125–28, 195, 235
18.16	231	22.19		1, 37–38, 109, 150, 154, 209, 214, 275		
20.35-37	33				43.1-5	241
35.17	42–44, 216				43.5	104, 125–28
		22.20		238	51.13-14	241
Esther	89	22.23		150	52.4	217–18
2.1	98	22.29		287	54.5	252
5.2	148	23.5		239	55.13-16	221
9.27	100	27.12		253, 258, 266	62.3	235
					63.10	258
Job		27.13		258	68.20	286
9.8	194	31.6		127, 150	69	6, 87, 144–47, 151
13.16	50, 56, 65	31.10		234, 236		
16.19	210	31.11		236	69.1-5	237
42.2	238	31.12		264, 280	69.2	285
		31.13		241	69.4	89
Psalms		31.14		250, 253	69.10	280
1	155	31.23		236, 241, 285	69.11	241
2	155–66, 188–89, 192				69.22	111, 144–47, 193, 195, 275, 285
2.1	50, 54	32.1-21		54		
2.2	107, 256	35.11-12		253, 258		
2.7	41, 106–7, 152, 155–66, 194, 196–97, 256	35.20		218		
		37		75, 128–33, 137, 151	70.2-4	258
					74.19	266
		37.12		268	75.9	226, 240
		37.12-14		258	83.2	89
2.9	171	37.32		104, 128–33, 193, 195, 216–17, 252, 258	86.14-17	258
6.4	236				88.9, 19	264
6.4-9	127				89	14, 151
8.6	206				89.26-27	258
10.7-9	217–18				89.50-51	279
16.5	239	37.33		258	104.12	39, 209
22	6, 55, 57, 75, 87, 147–54, 193, 195	38.11-18		256	109.1	89
		38.12		250, 268, 287	109.2	253, 258
					109.3	253, 258, 268
		38.13		268		
22.2	89, 109,	38.14		88, 268	109.4	221, 253,

Index of Ancient Sources

	258, 268	13.10	143, 181, 208		135, 223, 247, 257, 268
109.5	221, 253, 269	19.19-25	53		
109.8	221	24.23	117	53.9	220, 268, 270, 288–89
109.16	258	25.6	230		
109.25	278	25.6-10	117, 120	53.10	84–87
110	8, 160–61, 166–72, 188–89, 192, 194–95	25.7-8	286	53.10-12	183
		29.13	205	53.11	85, 228
		31.7	233	53.12	78–86, 220, 226, 228, 235–36, 242, 247, 258, 267–68, 270, 276, 278, 288
		31.8-9	249		
110.1	37–38, 97–98, 132, 152, 159, 163, 166–72, 187, 198, 205–6, 213, 259	34.4	181, 212, 283		
		36–37	135–38		
		36.21	89, 105–6, 135–38, 193, 256		
		40.3	3–4, 14, 34, 62, 86, 206	56.7	205
		42.1	107, 164	58.6	270
113–118	8	43.5-9	53	59.3	270
116.3	237	43.16-21	49, 53	59.10	142
116.6-10	243	44.10-20	250	60.2	282
116.11	235	45.21	205	61.1	168
116.13	226, 239–40	46.1-2	279	61.1-11	52
118.22-23	36–37, 192, 205	49.7-8	85	62.9	230
		50	138–41	63.3	270
118.25	39-40, 210	50.2-3	283	63.19 (64.1)	125, 164, 165
118.26	40, 210	50.4	81		
118.27	149	50.6	6, 86–87, 99, 108, 138–41, 193, 262, 273	65.13	229
119.46	267			65.17	53
119.121	266			66.24	205
119.145-50	234				
119.165	232			**Jeremiah**	
132.9-18	52			4.27-28	283
148.1	210	50.10	263	5.21	210
		50.11	251, 264	6.26	111
Proverbs		51.17, 22	240	7.11	208
4.3	111	52.1-8	52	14.8	224
12.6-7	218	52.13	287	15.6-9	283
27.6	244	52.13–53.12	75-6, see also 'Isa. 53'	16.14-15	49, 53
31.6-7	275			18.16	277
		52.15	268	23.5	163
Canticles		53	7, 13, 75–87, 94, 112, 120, 182–83, 196, 198	25.11	51
1.12-13	44-46, 218			25.15, 17, 28	239
4.13-14	45			26.11	261
				31.1-8	53
Isaiah				31.29-30	51, 53
3.4	249, 263	53.3	269, 274	31.31	229
5.1-7	192	53.3-5	263	31.33	54
6.9-10	206	53.4	273	49.12	240
11	157–58, 163	53.5	270, 273	51.7	240
11.1	155	53.6	78–80, 220, 242, 267, 270		
11.1-4	263			**Lamentations**	
11.4	161			1.12	278
13.9-10	282	53.7	80–81, 88,	1.14	243, 276

1.15	252	10.15	89		267
1.18	246	10.16, 18	174	9.11	103, 227,
1.19	243, 246,	11.31	208		228, 270
	250, 286	12.10	208, 242	9.12	270
2.15	6, 8, 277	12.11	62, 208	11	121
2.16	8			11.7	122
2.17	286	**Hosea**		11.12-13	6, 123, 221
2.21	223, 249	2.16-17	53	12–14	122
3.15, 19	285	6.1	115–16	12.6	260
3.53	288	6.2	100–3,	12.10	32, 96-98,
3.58	269		113–17,		111, 123,
4.21	227		193,		180, 187,
5.8	263		196–97,		260
5.9	229		216, 254	12.10-14	97, 123
5.12	276	6.3	114, 116	12.10–13.6	121
5.13	276, 286	11.1	42, 57	12.12	96
5.16, 18	272			13	121–25
		Joel		13.7	82, 115–16,
Ezekiel		4.16	284		121–25,
17.23	209				196, 198,
18	51	**Amos**			206,
21.8-10	245	2.16	248		230–31,
23.24-31	244	8.9	117, 195		247–48
23.31-34	240	8.9-10	110–11,	13.8	232
34.5	231–32		141–44,	13.9	116, 232
36.26	54		193, 197,	14.5	122, 123
45.21	43–44, 222		281	14.7	122, 142
Daniel		**Jonah**		**Malachi**	
2.34	254	4.8-9	235	1.6–2.9	54
2.45	254			3	4
3	89, 93	**Micah**		3.1	2–3, 40, 62,
4.9, 18	209	4.14	262, 274		165, 206,
6	221	7.15	49, 53		209
7	158–59,			3.2	3
	166–67,	**Nahum**		3.23 (4.5)	2, 3, 62, 210
	172–89, 196	2.1-3	52		
7.9	165				
7.13	14, 37,	**Habakkuk**		**Apocryphal/Deuterocanoni**	
	96–98, 132,	1.13	56	**cal Books**	
	139, 152,	2.4	56		
	159,	2.18	89	**Tobit**	
	170–89,			2.6	142
	193–94,	**Zephaniah**		5.6	100
	197, 198,	3.15	279		
	208,			**Judith**	
	212–13, 259	**Zechariah**		6.2-3	136
7.14	139, 159,	3.1-5	271	11.19	231
	212	3.8-9	23		
7.27	174	4.7-10	23	**Wisdom of Solomon**	
8.15	174	6.11	109, 271	2.10-20	8, 87,
9.24-27	51	6.12-13	23		89–91, 94,
9.27	208	8.6	238		257
10.5-7	180	9.9	123, 177,	2.13, 16	241

Index of Ancient Sources

2.17	278, 281, 285	17.23	101–2		143, 164, 194, 256, 282		
2.18	41, 241, 278, 281	19.18	134				
		19.18-19	207				
2.20	262	20.19	101–2	1.15	186, 198		
4.16	98	21.5-7	98	1.22	193		
5.1-7	87	21.9	210	1.23-27	198		
		22.44	169	1.24-25	184		
		23.35	84	1.27	193		
Sirach		24.15	62	1.29-34	198		
4.1	38, 206	24.30	97–98, 123, 139, 180	1.44	124, 184		
20.6	106			1.45	184		
27.15	83	24.31	123	2.5	198		
30.9	234	24.36	122	2.5-12	121, 193		
37.2	236	25.31	180	2.7	185–86		
48.17-25	136	25.31-34	139	2.10	184		
		25.31-46	182	2.15-17	121		
Susanna	89	26.2	100	2.17	186		
22–23	93	26.6-7	46	2.20	131		
42–43	93	26.15	123, 221	2.24-26	124		
53	98–99, 260	26.17	43	2.25	185		
61	98–99, 105, 252	26.23	91	2.28	184–85, 194		
		26.28	84, 118–19, 198, 227–29	3.4	81, 106, 124, 199		
1 Maccabees		26.31	122	3.5	199		
1.39	142	26.38	104, 127	3.6	185		
1.54	208	26.59-60	134	3.11, 27	193		
7.34-43	136	26.64	169, 180, 213	3.28-29	137		
				3.29	98		
2 Maccabees	93	26.67	108, 139	4.12	124, 206		
6–7	89	27.9	6, 98, 123	4.16-17	131		
7	195	27.24	261	4.29	79		
8.19	136	27.29	109, 271	4.32	39, 209		
15.22-24	136	27.30	108	4.39	81, 106		
		27.34	145	5.7	106, 193		
4 Maccabees	89, 93, 195	27.35	149	5.23, 28	199		
6.29-30	78	27.39-43	109	6.11	131		
17.21-22	78	27.43	137, 278	6.18	124		
		27.46	150	6.26	104		
1 Esdras		27.48	111, 145	6.34	210, 231		
1.17	42–44	27.63-64	101–2	6.45-52	31		
				6.48	194		
		Mark		7.6	124, 205		
New Testament		1.1	106, 193	7.7	205		
		1.2	2–3, 16, 40, 62, 124, 164–65, 209	7.9-13	199		
Matthew				7.10	37, 124, 205		
2.15	57, 103			7.13	79		
5.39	108, 139	1.3	14, 16, 34, 62, 86, 124, 164–65, 194, 206	7.22	217		
8.17	76			8.18	210		
9.13	103			8.27	199		
11.14	2			8.29-31	120, 184–85		
12.7	103	1.4	198	8.31	101, 115, 165, 189, 193		
12.40	101	1.6	3				
16.21	101–2	1.10	125				
16.27-28	182	1.11	106–7, 111,	8.34-38	131, 199		

8.35	133, 199		192–93		216–18
8.38	181–83	12.2-6	186	14.1-9	116
9.1	181, 183	12.6	111, 282	14.2	42–44, 111,
9.1-8	119–20, 165	12.6-9	165		218, 282
9.4-7	194	12.10	36–37, 124,	14.3	44–45,
9.7	106, 111,		205		218–19
	143, 282	12.11	36–37, 205	14.4-6	219
9.9	120, 165	12.14	124	14.7	219–20
9.10	120	12.19	38, 124,	14.8	45, 220
9.11	3, 11, 120,		211, 213	14.9	220
	210	12.24	124	14.10	220–21
9.12	3, 11, 120,	12.26	124, 211	14.11	6, 221
	124, 186	12.28-31	124	14.12	43–44,
9.13	120, 124,	12.29	205		222–23
	186	12.30	37, 134,	14.12-16	223–24
9.19	119		205, 211,	14.14-17	224
9.31	101, 189,		212	14.17-25	120
	193	12.31	37, 134,	14.18	82, 91, 225
9.34	81, 106		205, 208	14.19	225
9.48	205	12.32	205	14.20	91, 225
10.2-4	124	12.33	37, 208, 211	14.21	11, 124, 226
10.6-8	205	12.36	37–38, 124,	14.22	226
10.17-22	135		170, 172,	14.23	226–27
10.19	38, 99, 105,		205, 213	14.24	75, 83–84,
	124, 134,	13	116, 123,		103,
	206		132, 143–44		117–21,
10.27	238	13.2	143		196, 198,
10.28-30	131	13.9-13	199		200, 227–29
10.33-34	101, 139,	13.9-23	131	14.25	193, 229–30
	189, 193	13.13	199	14.26	230
10.34	102, 108,	13.14	62, 122, 208	14.27	11, 82, 115,
	273	13.24	117, 143,		121–25,
10.38	239		181, 197,		200, 206,
10.39	131		208		231–32
10.45	80, 84–87,	13.25	117, 124,	14.28	123, 193,
	182–83,		181, 212		232–33
	186, 196	13.26	37, 96–98,	14.29	233
10.47-52	170		117, 124,	14.30	199, 233
10.48	81, 106		180–81,	14.31-42	234
11	192		183,	14.33	234–35
11.1	18		188–89,	14.34	104,
11.1-11	128		208, 212–13		125–28,
11.2-7	123	13.27	117, 122,		200, 208,
11.3	116, 194,		181, 189		235–38
	223	13.32	122	14.35	238
11.9	39–40, 124,	14–15	1, 17–18,	14.36	140, 238–41
	210		68, 113,	14.37	241
11.10	124, 210		116, 191,	14.38	241–42
11.15-18	3		215	14.39-40	242
11.17	124, 205,	14.1	42–44,	14.41	242–43
	208		100–3,	14.42-43	243
11.27–12.12	3		113–17,	14.44	243–44
12	192		127–28,	14.45-46	244
12.1-12	3, 23,		166, 200,	14.47	244–46

Index of Ancient Sources

14.48	81–82, 246–47	15.16	271	15.47	289
14.49	11, 81–82, 124, 247	15.17	127, 271–72	16.6-7	193
		15.18	127, 151, 273	**Luke**	
14.50	247–48	15.19	108, 127, 140, 273–74	1.17	2, 62
14.51-52	248–50			1.76	62
14.53	166, 250	15.20	127, 274	5.37	84
14.54	250–51	15.21-22	275	7.36-38	46
14.55	75, 104, 128–33, 166, 193, 217, 252	15.23	145, 275	9.22	101–2
		15.24	1, 37, 109, 147, 151, 209, 214, 275–76	11.50	84
				18.20	134, 207
				18.23	104
14.55-65	200			18.32	108
14.56	98–99, 105, 131, 133–35, 192, 252–54	15.24-36	200	18.33	101–2, 115
		15.25	276	19.38	210
		15.26	151, 276	20.42-43	169
		15.27	276	21.27	180
14.57	3, 105, 131, 133–35, 192, 253–54	15.28	83, 276	22.1	43, 100
		15.29	3, 6, 108–10, 127, 131, 143, 147, 151, 276–78	22.7	43
				22.20	84, 118, 228–29
14.58	3, 131, 253–55			22.21	91
14.59	131, 253–55			22.37	76
14.60	255	15.30	3, 6, 108–10, 127, 143, 147, 276–78	22.40, 45	127
14.61	41–42, 75, 80, 88, 90, 105–7, 135–38, 155–66, 184–86, 193, 256–58			22.54	250
				22.63-65	139
				22.69	169, 180, 213
		15.31	6, 127, 137, 143, 279	23.30	103
		15.32	6, 127, 137, 143, 146, 151, 279–81	23.34	149
				23.35	109, 278
14.62	37–38, 96–98, 124, 166–89, 193, 208, 213, 259–60	15.33	110–11, 117, 132, 141–44, 193, 197, 281–83	23.36	111, 145–46, 278
				23.44-45	142
				23.46	127, 150
				23.48	142
14.63	260			23.49	250
14.64	90, 98–99, 260–62	15.34	109, 124, 127, 129, 133, 147, 151, 213–14, 283–84	24.7	101–2
				24.46	101–2, 115
14.65	86–87, 99, 108, 138–41, 262–63, 273			26.67	139
				27.30	139
				John	
14.66-72	263–64	15.35	285	2.17	145
15.1	78–80, 265–67	15.36	90, 111, 144–47, 193, 285	2.19-22	101–2, 115, 131
15.2	267			4.40-43	100
15.2-5	268	15.37	285–86	9.2	95
15.6	111, 268, 282	15.38	24, 286	10.18	133
		15.39	106, 287	11.6	100
15.7	268–69	15.40-42	287	12.2-3	45
15.8-13	269	15.43	75, 287–88	12.7	220
15.14	269–70	15.44-45	288	12.13	40, 210
15.15	140, 270	15.46	288–89	12.15	123

12.27	126	10.4	61	7.21	169
12.38	76	10.20-21	120	8.6-13	118
13.18	91	10.22	61	8.8-12	229
18.22	108	11.25	84, 118, 228–29	9.13-22	118
19.2	272			10.9	118
19.3	108	15.3-5	1, 9	10.12-13	169
19.23-24	53, 149	15.4	101–2, 115	10.19	119
19.29	145	15.25	169–71	10.21	272
19.29-30	111	15.26	169	10.26-31	118
19.37	32, 96, 123	15.55	103	11.32	266
				12.18-24	119
Acts		**2 Corinthians**		13.20-21	118
1.18	84	3.1-3	54		
1.20	145	3.13	53	**James**	
2.34-35	169	3.16	33	2.11	207
4.25	50, 54, 161	6.2	51		
4.25-31	161	6.18	161	**1 Peter**	
4.27	50	8.14-15	65	1.18-19	85
6.13	134			2.10	103
7.32	211	**Galatians**		2.22-25	76
7.47-50	169	4.21-31	54		
7.54	130	4.25	53	**Jude**	
7.56	187	4.30	33	11	84
8.27-35	64				
8.32-33	76	**Ephesians**		**Revelation**	
10.40	101–2	1.7	85	1.5-7	180
10.45	84			1.7	96–97, 123
13.22-37	161–62	**Philippians**		1.13	169, 180
13.33	156, 163–64	1.19	50, 56, 65	1.14-15, 17	180
20.26	261	2.5-11	194	2.26-27	161
22.20	84	2.28	64	4.4	272
28.4	95			6.12-13	143
		1 Thessalonians		6.16	103
Romans		3.13	122–23	8.12	143
1.3-4	164	5.27	64	11.15	161
1.17	56			12.5	161
3.14	217	**Titus**		14.14-20	180
3.24	85	2.14	85	17.18	161
4	54			19.15	161, 163
4.23-24	51	**Hebrews**		19.19	161
4.25	76, 80	1	163, 165	20.11	165
5.5	84	1.1-4	161	21.25	122
9.25-27	103	1.2	161		
10.6-8	33	1.2-5	164		
11.9-10	145	1.5	156	**Pseudepigrapha**	
13.9	207	1.13	169		
15.3	145–46	2.5-13	197	*Apocalypse of Moses*	
15.4	51, 63	2.12	150	36	143
16.1	64	5.5	160–61		
		5.6	160, 169	*1 Enoch*	
1 Corinthians		5.6-10	167	14.20-21	165
3	54	5.7-8	126–27	14.21	120
8.6	194	6.19–7.28	167	45.3-4	175
9.10	51	7.17	169	45.4-5	175, 176

Index of Ancient Sources

46.1	173	*Martyrdom and Ascension of Isaiah*		ii	120, 156, 161
46.1-5	158				
46.5	158	10.7-16	169		
47.3	158, 173			4Q158	
48.5	176	*Odes of Solomon*		frg. 4	117
48.6	175	5.5	145		
48.8-10	158	31.9	150	4Q171	137
48.10	175	31.10	81	ii–iv	129–32
49.2	175			i–ii	155, 161
49.4	175	*Psalms of Solomon*			
50.3	175	2	157–58, 161–62	4Q356	
51.1-5	175			frg. 15	117
51.3	175, 176	8	157		
55.4	175	17	156–58, 163, 165	4Q369	156, 157
61.8	175				
62.7	175	18	157–58	4QPs^f	149
70.1	175				
71.1	120	*Sibylline Oracles*		11QMelch	4, 167–68, 171–72, 194
71.14	175	1.367	145		
80.4	141, 143	3.605	233		
		3.663-700	158	*Damascus Document*	
2 Enoch		6.24-25	145	CD^B xix	122
22.8	271	8.248	158		
67	143	8.290	139		
		8.290-94	81	**RABBINIC LITERATURE**	
3 Enoch		8.303	145		
28.10	114			*Avot of Rabbi Nathan*	
		Syr. Men.		38	122
4 Ezra		144	134	41	122
5.4	141				
7.28	176	*T. Adam*		*Leviticus Rabbah*	
9.29-31	117	4.6	136	Emor 27.11	159
11	176				
12.11-12, 31-32	176			*Mekilta*	
13	163	**DEAD SEA SCROLLS**		*Pis.* 10.4	222
13.1-3	159, 173			*Besh.*	
13.1-4, 10, 26	177	1QapGen^{ar}		1.142	134
13.31-39	158–59	xxii	167	4.63	248
13.37-52	176			*Shir.*	
13.52	177	Hodayot (1QH)		6.38-50	168, 169
		x	149	7.64-65	159, 161
Joseph and Aseneth		xii	144–47	*Bah.*	
12.11	148	xiii	91	3.102	46
13.9	148	xvi–xvii	126–27	3.24-32	118
Jubilees		1QIsa^a	212	*Midrash Psalms*	
1.28	117			2	157, 159, 161–62
13.25	167	1QpHab			
		xi	51	42.5	126
Life of Adam and Eve				118	159
46	143	1QS			
		ix 3-6	78	*Mishnah*	
				*Mak.*1.3	134
		1QSa			

Sifre
Haazinu 329   114
Re'eh 134   222

Song of Songs Rabbah
1.12   46

Talmud, Babylonian
Ber.
7a, b   159
9b-10a   155
10a   159
16b   142
Šab 88b   46
Pesaḥ.
4b   222
119a   177
Yoma 29a   149
Sukk.
25b   142
52   129, 159, 161
Roš Haš. 31a   114
Meg. 15b   149
Mo'ed Qat. 15b, 20a, 21a, 25b   142
Ḥag. 14a   177
Yebam. 46b   118
Ned. 32b   168
Soṭah 36b   248
Git. 36b   46
Qidd. 30b   129
Sanh.
10a   134
38b   177
97a   114
98a   177
107a, b   91
108b   168
Avod. Zar. 3a, b   159
Zebaḥ. 100b   142
Ḥul. 87a   144
Ker. 9a   118

Talmud, Jerusalem
Ber. 5.2   114
Ta'an. 1.1   114
Mo'ed Qat. 3.5   142
Ketub. 3.1   134
Ned. 3.9   118
Sanh. 11.6   114, 134
Mak. 1.1   134

Tanḥuma
2.25   159
3.12   159
5.9   159

Targums
Gen. 39.12   248
Exod. 20.16   134
Exod. 24   117–18
Ps. 2   160
Isa. 53   79, 255, 272
Hos. 6.2   114
Zech. 13.7   122

Tosefta
Šeb. 3.6   134
Ned. 2.5   118
B. Qam. 9.31   138
Mak. 1.5   134

EARLY CHRISTIAN LITERATURE

Acts of Peter
24.5   181

Barnabas
4.1-2   76
4.4-5   180
5.11–6.7   139
5.2   76
5.12   122
6.6   150
7.3   145
12.10-11   169

1 Clement
14.3-5   130
16   76
16.15-17   150
34.5-7   180
36.5   169
53.1   63

2 Clement
14.2   63

Clement of Alexandria
Instr.
1.6   164
3.12   134
Prot. 10   134
Strom. 5.14   137

Didache
1.2   134
2.3   134

Diognetus
11.5   164

Eusebius
Hist. eccl., 3.39.15.   1

Gospel of the Ebionites
   107, 164

Gospel of Peter   6–8
3.9   139
4.12   150
5.15   142
5.16-17   145
5.19   150

Ignatius
Phld. 8.2   63

Irenaeus
Dem.
48   169
49   160
68   139
76   122
80   150
82   145
85   170
90   229
Haer.
2.28   169
3.6   169
3.10   170
3.16   169
3.19   145, 180, 181
4.20   181
4.33   139, 142, 150, 170, 181

Justin Martyr
1 Apol.
38   139, 150
44   63
45   170
51   181, 208
Dial.
7–8   63
11.3   229

Index of Ancient Sources

31	180, 208	4.16.17	134	10.1.2-4	136
32, 36	170	4.39	181	10.4.5	43
53.5-6	122	4.41	170, 181		
56	169	4.42	142, 150	*Liber antiquitatum bibli-*	
76, 79	181	4.43.1	115		*carum*
88.8	107, 164	5.17.6	170	11.12	134
97–106	150	*Prax.*		43.4	266
102	81	4.2	170		
111	76	7.2	164	Pseudo-Phocylides	
122.6	160	11.3	164	12-13	134
127	169	11.7	170		
		13.3	169	Philo	
Polycarp, *Phil.*		30.5	170	*Conf.* 96	117
12.1	63	*Res.*		*Congr.* 99	167
		20.5	139, 145,	*Decal.*	
Shepherd of Hermas			150	10	207
2.4	64	22	142	138-41	134
		22.9	170	*Dreams*	
Tertullian				62	117
Apol. 21.19	142	Theophilus, *Autol.*		222	117
Carn. 15	181	1.14	63	*Leg. All.* 3.79-82	167
Fuga 11.2	122			*Legat.* 18-20	195
Jud.				*Migr.* 168	117
10.4	145, 150	OTHER LITERATURE		*Spec.* 2.150-161	222
10.13	150				
10.17	142	*Aristobulus*		Plutarch, *Romulus*	
12.1	160	frg. 2.13	117	27.6	143
13.10	145				
13.23	115	Demetrius, *On Style*		Tatian, *Orat.*	
14.4	181	103	65	29	63
14.5	170	222	64		
14.12	160			Virgil, *Georgics*	
Marc.		*Hellenistic Synagogal Prayers*		1.466-67	143
3.7	181	6.7	266		
3.19.5	150				
3.20.3	160	Josephus, *Jewish Antiquities*			
4.1.6	229	1.10.2	167		
4.10	180–81	3.5	117		
4.12.10	222	5.8.8	266		

GENERAL INDEX

4 *Ezra*, date   174

Aaron, messiah of   *see 'messiah, priestly'*
abandonment   129, 133, 152
Abel   93, 119
Abraham   54, 76, 93, 168
abuse   6, 13, 138–41, 145–46, 152, 195, 200
according to the Scriptures   9, 102
Acts of Peter   181, *see also specific passages in the Index of Ancient Sources*
actualizing exegesis   131
Adam   130, 139, 194
Ahiqar   93
Akedah   15
Akiba   177
Albl, Martin   36
Albrecht, Evelin   15, 88
Allegro, J. M.   129
Allison, Dale C.   78, 142–43, 197–98
alludere   27
allusio   27–28
allusions
   accepted   99
   context and   55–57
   defining   22–28
   demonstrating accepted   99–112
   explicit citation   124–25
   function   4, 9–16, 48, 125, 133
   interpretation   47–66, 113–99
   locating   16–18, 28–34, 67–112
   treating the original context   47–59
   verbal changes and techniques   32–34
Alter, Robert   58–59, 63
analogy   53, 55
angels   4, 89, 120, 136, 149, 164, 168–69, 174, 176, 180–81, 187
anointed   *see 'Christ' and 'messiah'*
   priest   *see 'messiah, priestly'*
anointing scene   46

answer to the high priest   90, 132–33, 155–90
Antiochus IV   93
apocrypha   58
apologetic   4, 6, 10–11, 22, 48–50, 56, 80, 95, 122, 125, 169–70, 181, 191
Aramaic   31, 39, 79, 213
arrest   81, 116, 127–28, 201
as it is written   124
ascension   97, 163, 169–71, 187
Aseneth   148, 153
Assyria   52, 135–38
atonement   78, 84, 95, 118–21, 144, 168, 171–72, 196, 198, 202, *see also 'salvation'*
Attridge, Harold W.   118
audience
   authorial   24–28, 46, 64–65, 77, 88–91, 130–33
   of Isaiah   60–61
   of Paul   61
   recognition   30–31
Aune, D. E.   169, 180
Aus, Rodger David   142
author of Mark   36, 39, 130, 200–1
authorial
   audience   *see 'audience, authorial'*
   intention   22–27, 30, 48, 56, 59, 62
authorities   *see 'Jewish authorities', 'Roman authorities', and 'temple leadership'*
Avot of Rabbi Nathan   122

Babylon   52, 143
Bailey, Kenneth   8
Balaam's error   84
bandit   81–82, 85
baptismal scene   107, 143, 164–65, 198
Barnabas   8, 150, 169, *see also specific passages in the Index of Ancient Sources*
Barrett, C. K.   85, 182–83

Barthélemy, D. 156
Bartimaeus 170
Beardsley, Monroe C. 26
Bellinger, William, Jr 76–78
Ben-Porat, Ziva 59
Best, Ernest 12, 15–16, 60, 131, 144, 152, 182, 192, 198–99, 201
Bethany 44, 116–17
Betz, Otto 13, 76
Beutler, Johannes 126
Bible numbers used 2
Black, Matthew 57, 178–79, 182, 189, 196
blasphemy 135–38, 185–86
blood
    Abel 119
    covenant, of the *see 'covenant, blood of the'*
    martyrs 78
    woman with flow of 199
Bloom, Harold 48, 52
Booth, Wayne C. 54
booths 119
Borsch, F. H. 178
Bousset, Wilhelm 6–7
Boyarin, Daniel 23, 49
Branch of David 155
Braude, William 159
Brawley, Robert L. 23, 50
Broadhead, Edwin 198
Brooke, George 192
Brooks, James A. 67
Brower, K. 146, 195
Brown, Raymond E. 5, 8, 13, 15, 36, 39, 60, 130, 142–43, 146, 151–52, 188, 195, 208, 214
Bultmann, Rudolf 5, 6, 178
Burkill, T. A. 143, 152, 194–95

Calvin, John 21
canon 20–21, 42
canonical gospels 7, 150
Caragounis, Chrys 177, 179
Casey, Maurice 4, 97, 171, 173, 175–76, 178, 184, 187, 189
catchword association 14, 109
centurion 106, 146
Chilton, Bruce 119
Christ 87, 94, 96, 107, 139, 166, *see also 'messiah'*
    covenant in 118, 121
    epiphany 120, 198
    suffering 139, 145, 150
    using Scripture to interpret 10, 12, 75, 155–90
Christian community *see 'community'*
christology 4, 12–16, 138, 164, 193–95, *see also 'Christ'*
church *see also 'community'*
    early 13–14, 29, 48, 125, 163
    fathers 11, 45, 57, 62–63, 81, *see also specific entries in the Index of Ancient Sources*
citation
    explicit 124–25
    use of term 28
Clayton, Jay 22
Clement of Alexandria 134, 137
Clement of Rome 76, 150, 169, 180
clothes
    division of garments 1, 6, 147, 150, 152, 154
    transfiguration 119, 120, 165
Collins, Adela Yarbro 14–15, 57, 67, 78, 95, 151–52, 184, 188, 197, 199
Collins, John J. 156, 158–59, 166, 173–76, 178–79, 189, 196
community 14, *see also 'Israel' and 'Jewish'*
    canon and 21
    Christian 9, 11, 13, 16, 26, 95, 120–21, 131, 141, 161–62, 180, 188, 190, 202
    exegesis 51, 54, 57–58, 113
    Markan 16, 46, 81, 153
    new 129, 131–32, 195, 198
    Qumran 58, 78, 129–30, 132, 157, 161
    reading in 64
    righteous 123–24, 176
    salvation of 130, 195–98
    Scripture interpretation in 75
context incorporated into allusions 55–57
Cook, Stephen L. 121
court *see also 'trial'*
    heavenly 133, 167–69, 175, 186, 188
    tale 197
covenant 46, 117–21
    blood of the 83, 103, 196, 198
    initiation 118
    new 54, 118–21, 229
    Sinai 54, 103

General Index

Cranfield, C. E. B.   67
cross
    abandonment   133, 152
    cry of dereliction   144–54
    description through allusion   195
    discipleship   197, 199
    divine warrior   15
    eschatological signs   132, 142–44, 197
    human suffering   199
    mockery   *see* 'mockery'
Cross Gospel   7–8
Crossan, J. D.   5, 7–8, 17, 81, 139, 142, 145, 150, 197, 276
crucifixion
    cry of dereliction   6, 109, 127, 144–54, 195
    narrative, interpreting   141–54
cultural concerns   22, 31, 63, 174
cup   239
    word   83–84, 103, 117–21, 193, 198

Daniel   89, 93
Danker, F.   152
darkness   110, 117, 132, 141–44, 195, 197, 201
David   14, 33, 52, 124, 151, 155, 157, 159, 161–63, 165, 168–70, 177, 185
Dead Sea Scrolls   *see* 'Qumran'
Decalogue   38, 99, 105, 133–35, 207
definition of terms   20–28, 34
Delling, Gerhard   101
Demetrius   64
Derrett, J. Duncan M.   67, 79, 265, 284
Dewey, J.   12
diapsalma   160
Dibelius, Martin   5–6, 9, 11, 16–17, 64
Didache   134
disciples   7, 76–77, 95, 119–20, 122, 127, 166, 197, *see also* 'James and John' and 'Peter'
    flight   123, 125, 193, 200–1
    ideal   170
divine status   3–4, 120, 143, 164–65, 169, 177, 181, 185–86, 193, 194, *see also* 'exalted status'
divine warrior   14, 15, 195
division of garments   1, 6, 147, 150, 152, 154
Dodd, C. H.   3, 5–6, 12–13, 30, 49, 55–56, 77, 151–52, 195, 197, 198
Donahue, John   7–8, 13, 67, 90, 131, 171–72, 178, 182, 184, 188, 199
Dormeyer, Detlev   93
Dowd, Sharyn E.   14, 35, 82
Draisma, Sipke   23
Duff, P.   15
Duling, Dennis C.   155, 161, 163

Easter-faith   11
echo, use of term   28
Elijah   2–4, 15–16, 62, 78, 111, 119–20, 124, 146, 165, 186, 194
Elisha   15
Ellis, E. Earle   21, 49
Enoch   143, 174–76, 186
entry into Jerusalem   8, 123, 128, 200
epiphany   120, 198
Esau   159–60
eschatology   117, 120, 123, 130, 132, 158, 165
    banquet   117, 120
    cross   78, 143–44, 197
    darkness   132, 141–44, 197, 201
    judgement   131–32, 143, 157–59, 164, 166, 168, 175–76, 179–81, 189, 194, 196, 198, 201
    Mark 13   116, 122, 143–44
    Reign of God   165, 194, 196–97, 201
    resurrection   117
    reward   131–32, 168, 175, 181, 189, 196, 198
    scripture interpretation   43–44, 117, 122, 125, 129, 132, 157, 161–62, 169, 171, 180, 197
    temple veil   201
    trials   116, 131, 132, 197
    war   159, 161–62
Eslinger, L.   45
Esther   89, 148–49, 153
Ethiopian eunuch   64
Evans, Craig A.   57, 156–57, 171, 186, 192
exaltation   13, 55, 95–96, 129, 133, 151, 164, 166, 189–90, 193, 195–97, 200
exalted status   14, 116, 157, 164–66, 169, 175–76, 178,

180–81, 186, 193–94, 196, 198, 200, *see also* 'divine status'
exegetical traditions 57–58, 113
Exodus, the 15, 49, 53, 78, 117–21, 209
Ezra 176

Fabry, Heinz-Josef 149
false witness 80, 105, 131, 133–35, 137, 192
Farmer, William 76–78
Fishbane, Michael 25, 30, 33, 48–54, 61–62, 65
Fitzmyer, Joseph 63, 167, 185
Flint, Peter 149
Florilegium 155, 157, 161, 163
focus and goals of the study 18
for it is written 124
forgiveness of sin 84, 118–19, 121, 185–86, 193, 198–99, 202
fourscore 30–31
Freed, Edwin D. 127
fulfilment citations 124
Fuller, R. H. 178
function of allusion 4, 9–16, 48, 125, 133

Gamble, Harry Y. 63, 64
Garland, David 82
Garner, Richard 50, 55, 59
gathering of the elect 123, 143, 180, 188, 196
Genesis Apocryphon 167
Gentiles 50, 53–54, 126, 129, 135, 137, 139–40, 155, 157–61, 164, 166–68, 171, 176, 181, 183
Gethsemane 8, 104, 125, 140, 195, 200
Gettysburg Address 31
Glasson, T. F. 187
Gnilka, Joachim 67, 78, 88, 97
goals of the study 18
Gog and Magog 159, 161
Gospel of Peter 7–8, 139, 142, 145, 150, see also specific passages in the Index of Ancient Sources
Göttingen edition of the Septuagint *see* 'Septuagint, Göttingen edition'
Greek and verbal correspondence 31–34, 39–41, 203–15

Grundmann, Walter 67
Guelich, R. 39, 194
Guichard, Daniel 152
guilt-offering 85
Gundry, Robert 17, 36–37, 49, 67, 80, 188, 207–9, 211, 213, 214, 259, 277–78

Haenchen, Ernst 67, 188
Hagar 53
Hallel psalms 8
Hamlet 31
handed over 78
Handel, George Frideric 23
Hare, D. 173–74, 176–78, 180, 183–84
Harman, Lars 49
Hay, David 167, 169
Hays, Richard 20, 23, 25, 29, 33–34, 47–61, 65
Hebrew and verbal correspondence 31–31, 203–14, 215
Hengel, M. 39, 78, 198
Herod 104
Hezekiah 114, 136–37
hidden messiah 175–78, 186
high priest 107, 137, 155, 186
   Jesus as 161, 169
   question and Jesus' answer 90, 132–33, 155–90
Hilber, John W. 117
historical concerns 2, 4–10, 12, 17–19, 22, 27, 60–65, 78, 125, 151, 173, 200–1
Hodayot 126–27, 144, *see also* specific passages in the Index of Ancient Sources
Hollander, John 24–25, 27, 33, 47, 48, 52
Holy Spirit 52, 84, 124, 131, 137, 164, 170
Hooker, Morna 2–4, 13–17, 32, 57, 75–77, 85, 87, 108, 171, 182–83, 186, 189, 194–95, 197, 199
Horbury, W. 179, 184
Horeb *see 'Sinai'*
Horton, Fred 167, 168
hosanna 39
Huie-Jolly, Mary J. 15
humiliation 13, 140–41, 146, 148, 150, 152, 195, 200

Iersel, Bas M. F. van 12, 67, 82, 154,

General Index

188, 194
Ignatius 63
Iliad, the 23
influence, use of term 23
intended audience *see 'audience, authorial'*
intentional fallacy, the 26
interplay in allusion 47–59
interpreting allusions 47–66, 113–99
intertextuality, use of term 22–3
irony 50, 54, 153
Isaac 15, 33–34, 54, 76
Isaac, E. 174
Ishmael 54
Israel 45, 52, 86, 126, 135, 143, 155, 158–62, 165
   in *Barnabas* 122
   covenant 118
   God's will for 56, 76
   restoration 43, 116, 121, 123, 130, 158, 176, 196
   resurrection 114
   Scripture in ancient 51, 61
   son of God 157–59, 165

Jacob 76
James and John 119–20, 127, 166
Jellicoe, S. 35
Jewish
   authorities 98, 128, 133, 137–38, 140, 143, 161, 166, 192–93, *see also 'temple leadership'*
   canon 21, 42
   exegesis 49, 51, 57–58, 113–14, 117, 121, 126, 129, 134, 136, 138, 141, 144, 148, 155, 167, 173, 200
   intermediaries 4, 120, 194
   liturgy 19
   people 50, 54, *see also 'community' and 'Israel'*
   Revolt 193
   rhetoric 10
   trial *see 'trial'*
Job 50, 56, 89, 93, 95
John the Baptist 2–4, 15–16, 62, 104, 198
Jonge, M. de 168, 172, 188, 196
Joseph 33, 93, 134
Joseph of Arimathea 146
Josephus 38, 43, 58, 167, *see also specific passages in the Index of Ancient Sources*
Joshua 119

Judas 6, 84, 123, 145, 201
Judas Maccabeus 136
judge, Son of man figure as 175–76, 179–80, 182, 184, 188, 200–1
judgement 121–23, 129–30, 132, 157–58
   of the Assyrians 136
   of enemies 89, 147, 154, 157–58, 162, 167, 172, 188–89, 192–93
   final 3, 114, 117, 123, 130–32, 143–44, 159–60, 164, 166, 168–69, 171, 176, 180–82, 187, 189
   of Jesus 128–9, 133, 140
   of the nations 157, 159, 165, 167–68, 171
   of the righteous 126, 129, 131, 133–34, 140, 192
   of Stephen 130
Juel, Donald 3, 5–6, 10–11, 13–14, 18, 36, 49, 57, 67, 78, 131–32, 150–51, 185, 192, 194

Kahl, Werner 160
Kee, Howard Clark 4, 16–17, 39, 67, 77, 182, 189, 194, 197, 199, 201
Kelber, Werner 5, 185
Kennedy, George A. 10, 11
kerygma 5, 10, 19, 198
Kiley, Mark 8
Kim, Seyoon 23
king *see 'messiah' and 'royal'*
king-beasts 167, 179, 182, 185, 188–89, 196
Kingdom of God *see 'reign, God's'*
Knibb, Michael 158, 169, 173
Koester, Helmut 5, 8
Kort, Wesley A. 21
Krause, Deborah 8
Kristeva, Julia 22
Kugel, James 49, 55, 167–68

lamb 43, 80
lamentation psalms 87, 126, 144–54, 195
Landes, George M. 255
Last Supper 117–21, 193, 195, 200
Laura, the lady of Petrarch 92
Law *see 'Torah'*
lawful 124
Lazarus 45, 100

leaders　　　　see 'Jewish authorities',
　　　　　　　'Roman authorities', and
　　　　　　　'temple leadership'
Lee, Aquila H. I.　158, 162–64
Leivestad, Regnar　173, 184
let the Scriptures be fulfilled　124
Lincoln, Abraham　31
Lindars, Barnabas　10–1, 13, 49, 55–57,
　　　　　　　67, 75, 77, 97, 173,
　　　　　　　178–79, 181–82, 184,
　　　　　　　186, 197–98, 213, 276
Linnemann, Eta　5–6, 9, 12, 80, 109, 131
literary figure　91–94, 163
literary method　2, 19
　　defining terms　22–28
　　interpretation　47–66
　　locating allusions　28–34
literacy rates　64
liturgy　　　36
　　Christian　19
　　Jewish　19
locating allusions　16–18, 28–34, 67–112
Logos　　　4, 194
ludere　　27
Lührmann, Dieter　39, 67, 80, 88
LXX　　　see 'Septuagint'

Mack, Burton　7, 17, 35
Mailberger, Paul　156, 162
Manson, T. W.　175, 197
Marcus, Joel　13–5, 18, 27, 39, 49, 55,
　　　　　　57, 107, 149, 151–52,
　　　　　　164–65, 167, 181, 197,
　　　　　　209
Markan priority　27, 62
Martha　　　45
martyrs　　78, 89, 93, 192
Mary, sister of Martha and Lazarus　45
Masoretic Text　2, 34–41, 203–14, 215
Matera, Frank J.　42, 95, 151–54, 172,
　　　　　　　182, 185, 197
Matriarch of Israel in Danger　30
Maurer, Christian　8, 82, 89–90
McArthur, Harvey K.　101
Mekilta　　58, 118, 134, 149, 153,
　　　　　　168, 172, *see also specific
　　　　　　passages in the Index of
　　　　　　Ancient Sources*
Melchizedek　4, 167–68, 171, 194
messiah　　15, 101, 160, 166, 172,
　　　　　　174, *see also 'Christ'*
　　apologetic　48
　　designations for　155, 184
　　exaltation　195

　　expectation of　185
　　hidden　175–78, 186
　　of Israel　156
　　judgement　122
　　messianic age　*see 'eschatology'*
　　new temple　255
　　priestly　156–57, 159, 161–62,
　　　　　　169, 171
　　royal　45
　　suffering　10, 14, 120, 151–52,
　　　　　　195
　　using Scripture to interpret　9, 14,
　　　　　　124, 151–52, 161, 165,
　　　　　　176–77, 179, 182, 184,
　　　　　　155–90
messianic secret　184
metalepsis　　47, 58–59
Metzger, Bruce M.　159, 174, 228–29,
　　　　　　276
Michie, D.　　12
midrash　　8, 179
Milik, J. T.　156, 173
Miller, Patrick　152–54
Milton, John　*see 'Paradise Lost'*
Miriam　　　149
Mishnah　　58, 186
Mitchell, Alan C.　118
mockery　　6–7, 90, 108, 127,
　　　　　　136–40, 145–47, 150,
　　　　　　152, 154, 195, 200–1
Moo, Douglas J.　13, 17, 52, 57, 67,
　　　　　　75–77, 79–80, 83, 85
Moses　　　33, 53, 78, 86, 103,
　　　　　　117–21, 124, 165, 194
Moule, C. F. D.　82
mourning　　142, 144
MT　　　　*see 'Masoretic Text'*

nations　　　*see 'Gentiles'*
Neirynck, F.　106, 199
Nickelsburg, George W. E.　5, 93
Nineham, D. E.　95, 191
Nogalski, James D.　122
numbering used for Scripture references　2

obedience　　88, 93, 96, 138–41, 154,
　　　　　　164
Odes of Solomon　145
Oegema, G.　174
Old Greek, use of term　34
Old Testament, use of term　21
oral tradition　5, 30
original audience　*see 'audience, authorial'*

General Index

Pace, Sharon 208
Palestine 39
Palestinian lectionary 54
Papias 1, 62
Parable of the Vineyard 23, 87, 111, 165–66, 186, 192, 193
Paradise Lost 23, 26, 29–30, 34, 48, 52
Parousia 12, 97, 116, 131–32, 144, 169–72, 177, 180–81, 187–88, 190, 200–1
passion narrative, extent of 18
passion predictions 101–3, 108, 115–16, 139–40, 193
Passover 42–44, 100, 113, 116, 142–43
Paul 15, 29, 33–34, 48–51, 53–54, 56–57, 59–61, 64–65, 76–78, 102, 111, 118, 120, 146, 161–62, 194, 196–97, *see also specific passages in the Index of Ancient Sources*
Paulien, Jon 49
people of God *see 'community', 'Israel', and 'Jewish'*
Perrin, Norman 80, 96–97, 175, 178–79, 185, 187–88, 206, 260
Pesch, Rudolf 67, 75, 80, 88, 97, 276
Peter 119–20, 127, 166, 184, 198, 201
Petrarchan Lady, the 92
Pharaoh 10, 33, 159–61, 168
Philip 64
Philo 4, 50, 58, 134–35, 167, *see also specific passages in the Index of Ancient Sources*
Pilate 146, 186, 201
Piper, Otto 152, 182, 194
plot and use of Scripture 13, 55, 147, 151–53
Polycarp 63
Pompey 157–61
pour out 83–4
prayer
    Aseneth 148, 153
    cry of dereliction 152
    Esther 148, 153
    Gethsemane 8, 140, 200
    innocent suffering 93–94, 145
    Judas Maccabeus 136
    Lord's 35
    rain and resurrection 114
pre-existence 175, 177, 186, 194

pre-Markan passion narrative *see 'historical concerns' and 'sources, Markan'*
priestly
    blessing 54
    messiah *see 'messiah, priestly'*
priority of Mark 27, 62
prophetic proofs *see 'apologetic'*
promise and fulfillment 7, *see also 'prophecy-fulfilment'*
promises to David 33, 52, 155, 161, 163
proof-texts *see 'apologetic'*
prophecy-fulfilment 11, 12, 139
propitiation *see 'atonement' and 'salvation'*
Protestant canon 20, 42
psalter at Qumran 149
pseudepigrapha 58, 158

Qumran 157, 161
    community 155
    psalter 149
    Scripture interpretation 51, 58, 129, 131–33, 156–57
    similarity to Markan community 130–31
quotation, use of term 28

Rahlfs edition of the Septuagint *see 'Septuagint, Rahlfs edition'*
ransom 84–85, 182–83, 196–97, 201
reader recognition 24–27, 30–31, 60–65
rebels, political 82
redaction 18
redemption *see 'salvation'*
reference, use of term 22
reign
    God's 120, 135, 181–82, 186–93, 197–201
    messiah 133, 158, 165, 167, 169, 171–72, 180, 185, 189, 194–96, 199
remnant *see 'community', 'Israel', and 'Jewish'*
representative head 14, 165, 189, 196–97, 200
restoration 116
    disciples 124
    Israel 43, 121, 123, 130, 158, 176, 196
resurrection 100–3, 114–17, 120, 131, 133, 153, 162–65, 170,

193, 196, 202
  appearance 8
  passion and, plot 152
Reumann, John 67, 153, 154
reward, eschatological 123, 131–32, 157, 164–65, 168, 172, 178–80, 188–89, 196, 200
rhetoric 10, 27, 30, 64
Rhodes, D. 12
rich man 104, 134–35
Robbins, V. K. 199
Robinson, J. A. T. 187
Rodgers, Peter Robert 83, 276
Roman 15
  abuse 139–40, 201
  authorities 7, 139–40, 192
  divine warrior image 15
  origin of Mark 39
  reader recognition 64
  rule, condemnation of 137, 157
  rule, rebels against 82
  trial 7, 80, 90, 137, 139–40, 201
Rossé, Gérard 95, 151, 154
Roth, Wolfgang 15
Rothstein, Eric 22
royal 161, 185
  attribution 14, 151
  messiah 14, 45, 151, 156–58, 161, 177, 182, 185–86, 195
  portrayal of Jesus 13, 46, 152, 165, 172, 185, 189
  psalm 161, 163, 165
Rule of the Congregation 156
Ruppert, Lothar 8, 13, 55, 89–90, 93–95, 151

sacrifice 85, 196
salvation 7, 11, 14, 56, 77–78, 95–96, 126, 128, 130, 134, 147, 183–84, 195–200, 202, *see also* '*atonement*' *and* '*suffering, salvation*'
salvation history 7
Sanders, E. P. 192
Schiffman, Lawrence 156
Schmithals, Walter 67
Schnackenburg, Rudolf 4, 67, 276
Schweizer, Eduard 67, 80, 82, 94, 276, 278
Scripture
  use of term 20

explicit citation 124–25
number system 2
proof-texts *see 'apologetic'*
Second Temple period 21, 51, 58, 78, 95, 136, 138, 167–68, 173, 188, 192, 196
Senior, Donald 13, 75, 80, 131, 188
Sennacherib 135, 159, 168
Septuagint 34–41, 203–14, 215
  use of term 34
  Göttingen edition 34–35, 203, 215, 235
  Rahlfs edition 34–35, 203, 215
Sermon on the Mount 139
Servant of the Lord *see 'Suffering Servant'*
Servant Songs 17, 83, 86–87
Seters, John van 30
Shadrach, Meshach, and Abednego 93
Shakespeare, William 31, 92
shepherd 121–23, 160
Shiner, Whitney 153
Sibylline Oracles 139, 158, *see also specific passages in the Index of Ancient Sources*
silence 80–81, 88–89, 93–94, 105–6, 112, 135–38, 184
Similitudes, date 173
Simon 198, *see also 'Peter'*
Simon of Cyrene 16
Simon the leper 44
sin 9, 51, 53, 77, 79, 81–83, 85–86, 88, 98, 119, 134–35, 137, 150, 152, 157, *see also 'forgiveness of sin'*
Sinai 45, 53, 103, 117, 119, 120–21
Sisera 168
Slater, Thomas 174, 179
Smith, Robert H. 88, 144, 197
Soards, Marion 5, 18, 90
Solomon 33
Sommer, Benjamin 25, 31, 48, 52–53, 59–61
son of David 33, 155, 157, 159, 161–63, 165, 168–70, 177, 185
Son of God 4, 14, 16, 41–42, 75, 87, 89, 94, 96, 106–7, 146, 155, 157, 159, 164–66, 169, 176, 184–86, 193
son of man 15, 57, 84, 96, 101, 115, 117, 121, 124, 132, 139,

General Index

148, 158, 166, 169, 171–89, 194, 196, 212
coming with the clouds 132, 144, 177, 187
concept 177–79
Enoch as 174–76
meaning of the phrase 173, 178
sources, Markan 5, 18–19, 36, 39–40, 58, 90, 95, 97, 169
suffering 14, 184, 189, 197
Stegner, W. Richard 15, 31
Stemberger, G. 58, 114, 118, 122
Stendahl, Krister 49
Stephen's death 84, 130, 134, 169, 187
Steudel, Annette 156
Stevens, Bruce A. 15, 196, 197
Steyn, Gert J. 157
Strack, H. L. 58, 114, 118, 122
suffering 140, 146, 150, 152, 154, 195, 200
atonement 95, 150
discipleship 197
divine aid 131, 139–41, 153–54, 200
divine plan 115–16, 123, 128, 139, 150
divine punishment 13, 95–96, 126, 157
divine warrior 15
eschatological 143, 195, 197
exaltation 13, 195, 200
Hodayot 127
innocent 87, 93, 95–96, 131, 145, 192, 201, *see also* 'suffering righteous'
Jesus' interpretation of 78
messiah *see 'messiah, suffering'*
obedience 141
prayer 125, 148, 153–54
salvation 116, 126, 128, 153–54, 195, 197–202
Son of Man *see 'son of man, suffering'*
vindication 13, 55, 95–96, 154, 179, 188
suffering rigteous one 7, 13–15, 55, 87–96, 112, 145, 151, 163, 192, 197
Suffering Servant 13–15, 17, 76–87, 90, 94, 135, 183
suggested allusions, testing 67–112
Suhl, Alfred 9, 11–12, 17, 30, 55, 90, 108, 112, 135, 139, 141,
154, 201
Sundberg, Albert C. 14, 21, 55–56
Susanna 93, 98–99, 105
Swete, Henry B. 208
Syria 39

table
suggested allusions 68
textual analysis of Markan quotations 204
Talmon, S. 53
Tanak 20, 21, 42
Tatian 63
Taylor, Vincent 67, 85, 276, 278
Teacher of Righteousness 51, 129, 131
temple 3, 81, 101, 114, 128, 132, 136–38, 142, 145–46, 158, 161, 165, 169–70, 192
built without hands 131
charge 3, 90, 131
condemnation 3, 16, 130–31, 169
leadership 3, 129–32, 137, 161, 192, *see also* 'Jewish authorities'
rebuilding the 102, 108, 115, 131, 148, 255
veil 142–43, 197, 201
temptation in the wilderness 165
Ten Commandments 38, 99, 105, 133–35, 207
testimony books 19, 36
testing suggested allusions 67–112
Text critical issues 34–41, 203–14
thanksgiving portion of Psalm 22 55, 150, 152–53
Theissen, Gerd 39
thematic coherence 29, 47–59
theophany 117, 119, 177, 180
Theophilus 63
third day 101, 114–15
thirty pieces of silver 6, 123
Thomas Aquinas 21
Thompson, Michael 29, 30
three days 101, 115
Tödt, H. E. 173, 178
Tolbert, Mary Ann 12, 17
Torah 33, 53–54, 118, 134, 144, 159, 176–7
Tov, Emmanuel 34–35
transfiguration 119–20, 143, 165–66
translation and verbal correspondence 31
trial 3, 7–8, 50, 88–90,

        131–33, 139–40, 184,
        192, 200
    abuse   108, 138
    eschatology   116, 131–32
    false witnesses   128, 133, 135
    judges   128
    martyr stories   93–94
    narrative, interpreting   128–41
    Roman   80, 89–90, 137, 139–40, 201
    silence   80, 105, 112
    of Stephen   130, 134
    of Susanna   99
    theme in allusions   127, 129, 140
Trochmé, Etienne   5
two days   100–2, 113
type
    Jesus, not one of a   13–14
    scene   30
    suffering rigteous figure types   93
typology   53

Ulrich, Eugene   21, 34, 38, 208
Unleavened Bread, festival of   42–44, 100, 116

VanderKam, James C.   21, 174–75
variants   34–42, 83, 156, 203–15
veil, temple   142–43, 197, 201
verbal correspondence   8, 30–41
    for well-known allusions   77
    testing suggested allusions 67–112
Verheyden, Jozef   212
Vermès, Géza   15, 126, 156, 178
vindication   13, 55, 93, 95–96, 126–29, 133, 138, 140, 145, 152, 154, 168, 172, 188–89, 191, 193

vinegar   6, 111, 144–47
Vineyard, Parable of   23, 87, 111, 165–66, 186, 192–93
voice, divine   51, 106–7, 111, 119–20, 143, 164–65, 194

Watts, James W.   107
Watts, Rikki E.   4, 13, 15, 30, 49, 75, 78, 137, 183, 209
Weeden, T. J.   201
Wentling, Judith   2
Westermann, Claus   152–53
Wicked Priest   51, 129
wilderness   2–4, 53, 61, 118–19, 165
will of God   4, 9–12, 76, 115, 118, 123, 130, 133, 140–41, 144, 152, 186
Willey, Patricia Tull   50–51, 62
Wimsatt, W. K., Jr.   26
Wisdom   194
Witherington, Ben, III   82
women
    Samaritan woman   100
    standing far away   146
    woman who anoints Jesus   44, 116–17
    woman with flow of blood   199
Wordsworth, William   29–30, 48, 50
Woude, A. S. van der   168
wrath of God   144, 159, 181
Wrede, William   2

Zion   119, 136, 158–59, 161, 163, 166, 171–72